HYMNS FROM THE ṚGVEDA

HYMNS FROM THE ṚGVEDA

[SAṀHITĀ TEXT]

(English Translation, Notes with Pada Text and Sāyaṇa's Commentary)

PETER PETERSON

Edited By

R. ZIMMERMANN, S.J.

BHARATIYA KALA PRAKASHAN

DELHI (INDIA)

First Revised Edition : 2004

Published by **C.P. Gautam**
BHARATIYA KALA PRAKASHAN
3421-A, IInd Floor, Narang Colony, Tri Nagar,
Delhi-110035. Phone : (O) 27393083, 30967505, (R) 27522129

ISBN : 81-8090-061-4

Laser Type Setting by
A-ONE GRAPHICS
JD-18C, IInd Floor, Pitampura, Delhi
Phone : 55640278, Mob.: 9811167357

Printed By
BDH Printer at Salasar Imaging Systems, Delhi.
Phone : 31045804

PREFACE

The Hymns from the Ṛgveda in this selection were prescribed by the University of Bombay as an alternative course for candidates for its B. A. degree. Two of the Hymns (Nos. 1 and 22 here) are repeated from the previous volume as, perhaps by inadvertence, they figure in other selections. I am not responsible for the choice of the Hymns in the present selection. In editing Sāyaṇa's commentary I have made constant reference to two manuscripts, one of the first five ashtakas belonging to the Bhao Daji collection, and one of the last seven ashtakas which was kindly lent to me by my friend, Professor Apte, of Kolhapore. The manuscript in the collection at Elphinstone college was also occasionally consulted, but not to much purpose. It is really a greatly abbreviated edition of Sayana of little or no value for critical purposes. It need not, I hope, be said that wherever I have differed from Max Müller it has only been after careful consideration and from what seemed to me to be strong reasons. It is matter of gratification to me that the introduction of the Veda into the B. A. course of the University at Bombay, orginally made at my instance, has proved so successful an experiment, and has wiped away the reproach of the exclusion from the ordinary curriculum in Sanskrit here of the most important books in the Sanskrit language. I cannot hope that have not made mistakes in my two volumes. But do hope that I have done something in them the student's way.

—Peter Peterson

EDITORIAL

With the exception of the Saṁhitāpāṭha, the Padapāṭha, and Sāyaṇa's Commentary, the first edition is changed. The lexicographical and exegetical notes have been substituted by new ones; a translation, appendices on Grammar, Metre, Accent, and Vedic Mythology, as well as some remarks on the age of the Ṛgveda have been added. Strictly speaking only the Padapātha has been left as it was in the first edition. That in the Saṁhitāpāṭha a minor technical detail of little consequence is that Sāyaṇa's Bhāṣya of the first edition (प्रथमावृत्तिः) has been compared with that of Max Müller's large Ṛgveda edition (the आदर्शपुस्तकम्). The difference of reading, if any, has been registered at the foot of the Bhāṣya. The reading of the प्रथमावृत्तिः has been kept against the आदर्शपुस्तकम् where it seemed preferable; where the आदर्शपुस्तकम् was better, it has been adopted and marked so that Peterson's original reading has not been altogether thrown out. The ms. from the Bhau Daji Collection and the Kolhapur ms. on which the first edition was based, deserve that their readings should be preserved. The quotations in Sāyaṇa have been traced, compared, and the figures given where possible and practical.

The purpose of the book and the progress of Vedic studies have made the other more radical changes necessary. The notes after the Padapāṭha and Sāyaṇa's commentary on each mantra are of a lexicographical and exegetical nature.

The lexicographical notes are intended to substitute the complete Vedic dictionary, which for more than one reason, in the majority of cases the beginner is unable to use. Sāyaṇa's commentary will help only a śāstric वैयाकरण, not a beginner, as far as grammatical forms are concerned. The exegetical notes try to give views advanced by ancient and modern Veda interpreters. The views of authors used does not claim to be complete, but it least prove useful. Where their views were practically to acceptable the editor had as little reason as right to put them in proper order. When their opinions were divided, the most likely where none of them could claim preference on account of greater probability, the question was left open, or (in rare cases) the editor ventured upon an idea of his own.

The appendices are meant to serve mainly a utilitarian purpose. This is also the reason why the notes on Grammar, Metre, and Accent follow so closely greater models. If a thing has been done well once, there is no ground why it should be done only as well, or worse, once more. And there is, after all, no higher tribute paid to an author than that others utilize his labours. Whatever has been taken over in a body has been acknowledged , the longer passages by giving the source explicity; wordings borrowed have been put into inverted commas. The editor trusts that no omission has been made on this side. He has refrained गौरवभयात् from putting too much ballast at the foot of the pages, either in the shape of references to works used or of matter concerning side issues. The beginner who peruses the mythological notes, for instance, will be interested more to know what views have been put forward, than on what page of a particular work, in most cases inaccessible to him, they are to be found. The advanced student will easily find his way by means of the Bibliography given at the end. The editor has, in particular, thought it his plain duty to avoid quoting stray etymologies, wild guesses in matters mythological, and the like. It would be a comparatively easy task to make a book like this bristle with learned looking scraps of etymology and comparative mythology. But a little knoweldge of this kind serves neither an educational nor a scientific purpose; it may even, as the proverb wisely puts it, become dangerous.

The translation, with the exceptions explicity mentioned, has to be taken as the work of the editor. He consulted other translations only after having made his own, to learn from others he could, to differ from them there where he thought that he would be able in doing so. The suppositions for clearing up of Vedic mythology and giving a final, all-round translation of Vedic hymns are not yet given. For reasons the editor has not mentioned views such which quite lately saw Agni in Vṛtrahan.

Vedic scholars will recognise without difficulty that in writing the remarks on the age of the ṚV. the editor has mainly followed Professor M. Winterniz, the best Vedic literary historian. Some reflections and conclusions have been added by the editor. He has frankly to own apostasy from Max Müller's view in this matter.

In the question on the literary merit and the underlying tendency of the Vedic sūktas the editor cannot bring himself to believe that Viśvāmitra and his fellow-ṛṣis considered religion and poetry mainly as a कामधेनु which could and should be milked whenever a यजमान invited them to officiate. Those who are so eloquent and sarcastic in this matter seem to forget that some four or five thousand years back the Āryas had founded and well endowed University chairs with a certain and regular income for people who devoted themselves to matters above the sword and the plough.

To publish a book of this kind, even if it were done well, is nothing to be proud of. For originaly there is little room, for mistakes plenty of scope, and the editor cannot flatter himself to have committed mistakes freely. His chief motive throughout been to be of some help to the B. A. and M.A. students in way as not to preclude the beginner from thinking, and out to him the road for work in the same line.

The editor has utilized the best literature on the subject but in the beginning especially he too was hampered by difficulty of communication with certain sources and centres of Vedic learning. He hopes, however, not to have been careless in this matter either. Finally due thanks must be given to Prof. Dr. S.K. Belvalkar, M.A., Ph.D., Superintendent of the Publica-tion Department, Bhandarkar Oriental Research Institute, Poona, to whose technical experience and advice this edition owes much of its improved looks. Bhavānīśaṁkar Sukthankar, Śāstri of this College, has rendered loyal help throughout. His śāstric learning and memory tracked more than one elusive grammatical or exegetical sūtra.

C.P. Gautama the propietor of Bharatiya Kala Prakashan has done a commendable job in bringing out this book in an appropriate form.

—R. Zimmermann, S.J.

CONTENTS

SAṀHITĀ TEXT

म० १ No. 1 सू० २५

यच्चिद्धि ते विशो यथा प्र देव वरुण व्रतम्।

मिनीमसि द्यविद्यवि॥१॥

Though indeed we may, as people (transgress the king's law, so) violate the command, O god Varuṇa, day by day:

मा नो वधाय हत्नवे जिहीळानस्य रीरधः।

मा हृणानस्य मन्यवे॥२॥

(yet) hand us not over to the deadly weapon of (thee,) the angry one, not to the wrath of (thee,) the furious one.

वि मृळीकाय ते मनो रथीरश्वं न संदितम्।

गीर्भिर्वरुण सीमहि॥३॥

For mercy we make accessible, O Varuṇa, the mind by songs, as a charioteer (satisfies) the tied up horse.

परा हि मे विमन्यवः पतन्ति वस्यइष्टये।

वयो न वसतीरुप॥४॥

Away fly my calming prayers to seek (my) salvation, as birds (fly) up to their nests.

कदा क्षत्रश्रियं नरमा वरुणं करामहे।

मृळीकायोरुचक्षसम्॥५॥

When shall we bring hither Varuṇa, the Man, the

ornament of princes, for (exercising) mercy, the far-seeing one?

तदित्स॑मा॒नमा॑शाते॒ वेन॑न्ता॒ न प्र यु॑च्छतः।
धृ॒तव्र॑ताय दा॒शुषे॑॥६॥

That (क्षत्रम्) they two possess in common, heeding they are not forgetting him who keeps the law, the pious one.

वेदा॒ यो वी॒नां प॒दम॒न्तरि॑क्षेण॒ पत॑ताम्।
वेद॑ ना॒वः स॑मु॒द्रियः॑॥७॥

He who knows the track of the birds flying through the air, knows, residing in the water, (the track) of the ship.

वेद॑ मा॒सो धृ॒तव्र॑तो॒ द्वाद॑श प्र॒जाव॑तः।
वेदा॒ य उ॑प॒जाय॑ते॥८॥

The upholder of the law knows the twelve months with their offspring, knows him that is born after (the intercalary month).

वेद॒ वात॑स्य वर्त॒निमु॒रोर्ऋ॒ष्वस्य॑ बृह॒तः।
वेदा॒ ये अ॒ध्यास॑ते॥९॥

He knows the path of the wind, the wide, the high, the strong; knows those that dwell above.

नि ष॑साद धृ॒तव्र॑तो॒ वरु॑णः प॒स्त्या॒३॑स्वा।
साम्रा॑ज्याय सु॒क्रतुः॑॥१०॥

Varuṇa, the upholder of the law, has taken residence in the waters to exercise his overlordship, he, the wise one.

अतो॒ विश्वा॒न्यद्भु॑ता चिकि॒त्वाँ अ॒भि प॑श्यति।
कृ॒तानि॒ या च॒ कर्त्वा॑॥११॥

From there, knowing all the secrets, he watches all that has been done and is to be done.

स नो॑ वि॒श्वाहा॑ सु॒क्रतु॑रादि॒त्यः सु॒पथा॑ करत्।

प्र ण॒ आयूं॑षि तारिषत्॥१२॥

May the kind Āditya make our paths always smooth; may he prolong our lives.

बिभ्र॑द्द्रा॒पिं हि॑र॒ण्ययं॒ वरु॑णो वस्त नि॒र्णिज॑म्।

परि॒ स्पशो॒ नि षे॑दिरे॥१३॥

Varuṇa, wearing a golden harness, clothes himself in splendour; his spies sit all around.

न यं दिप्स॑न्ति दि॒प्सवो॒ न द्रुह्वा॑णो॒ जना॑नाम्।

न दे॒वम॒भिमा॑तयः॥ १४॥

The god whom the cheats do not try to cheat, nor those who lay snares for men, nor (any other) enemies;

उ॒त यो मानु॑षे॒ष्वा यश॑श्च॒क्रे असा॒म्या।

अ॒स्माक॑मु॒दरे॒ष्वा॥१५॥

(Varuṇa) who moreover has fully established (his) glory among men, in our bellies.

परा॑ मे यन्ति धी॒तयो॒ गावो॒ न गव्यू॑ती॒रनु॑।

इ॒च्छन्ती॑रुरु॒चक्ष॑सम्॥१६॥

Off go my thoughts, as cattle along their track, longing for the far-seeing.

सं नु वो॑चावहै॒ पुन॒र्यतो॑ मे॒ मध्वाभृ॑तम्।

होते॑व॒ क्षद॑से प्रियम्॥१७॥

Now let us talk together once more, since the sweet drink haas been brought to me, to taste of thedear (juice) like a होतृ.

दर्शं नु विश्वदर्शतं दर्शं रथमधि क्षमि।

एता जुषत मे गिरः।।१८।।

May I see the all-visible, see (his) car on earth, may he be pleased with these my songs.

इमं मे वरुण श्रुधी हवमद्या च मृळय।

त्वामवस्युरा चके।।१९।

Hear, O Varuṇa this may call, and be merciful to-day in need of help I wish to have thee here.

त्वं विश्वस्य मेधिर दिवश्च ग्मश्च राजसि।

स यामनि प्रति श्रुधि।।२०।।

Thou, O wise one, rulest over the universe, heaven and earth; thou then listen in the hour of need.

उदुत्तमं मुमुग्धि नो वि पाशं मध्यमं चृत।

अवाधमानि जीवसे।। २१।।

Our topmost fetter loose, the middle one untie, off, down the lowest ones that we may live.

म० १ **No. 2** सू० ३२

इन्द्रस्य नु वीर्याणि प्र वोचं

यानि चकार प्रथमानि वज्री।

अहन्नहिमन्वपस्ततर्द

प्र वक्षणा अभिनत्पर्वतानाम्।।१।।

Now I will proclaim Indra's great deeds which first he perfomed, with his thunderbolt; he killed the serpent, let afterwards loose the waters, split open the womb of the mountains.

अहन्नहिं पर्वते शिश्रियाणं
त्वष्टास्मै वज्रं स्वर्यं ततक्ष।
वाश्रा इव धेनवः स्यन्दमाना
अञ्जः समुद्रमव जग्मुरापः।।२।।

He killed the serpent that lay hidden in the mountain, Tvaṣṭṛ had fashioned him the whizzing thunderbolt; like lowing cows, the flowing waters rushed straight to the sea.

वृषायमाणोऽवृणीत सोमं
त्रिकद्रुकेष्वपिबत्सुतस्य।
आ सायकं मघवादत्त वज्र-
महन्नेनं प्रथमजामहीनाम्।।३।।

Strong like a bull he chose the soma, at the त्रिकद्रुक (or, from the त्रिकद्रुक vats) he drank of the pressed juice; the liberal one took up the missile, the thunderbolt, he struck that first-born of serpents.

यदिन्द्राहन्प्रथमजामहीना-
मान्मायिनाममिनाः प्रोत मायाः।
आत्सूर्यं जनयन्द्यामुषासं
तादीत्ना शत्रुं न किला विवित्से।।४।।

When thou, O Indra, didst kill the first-born of the serpents, and also thoroughly didst thwart the deceit of the deceivers, bringing forth anon heaven (and) dawn then already forsooth thou disdst not find an opponent.

अहन्वृत्रं वृत्रतरं व्यंस-
मिन्द्रो वज्रेण महता वधेन।
स्कन्धांसीव कुलिशेना विवृक्णा-
हिः शयत उपपृक्पृथिव्याः॥५॥

With the thunderbolt, the great weapon, Indra killed Vṛtra, the Arch-vṛtra, without shoulders; like trunks of trees cut down with the axe, the serpent lies flat on the earth.

अयोद्धेव दुर्मद आ हि जुह्वे
महावीरं तुविबाधमृजीषम्।
नातारीदस्य समृतिं वधानां
सं रुजानाः पिपिष इन्द्रशत्रुः॥६॥

Like one without a fighting (opponent), the mad one challenged the mighty hero, the hard pressing, the drinker of the dregs; (Vṛtra) could not overcome the onslaught of his weapons; by crushing the noseless one was smashed, he whose enemy was Indra.

अपादहस्तो अपृतन्यदिन्द्र-
मास्य वज्रमधि सानौ जघान।
वृष्णो वध्रिः प्रतिमानं बुभूष-
न्पुरुत्रा वृत्रो अशयद्व्यस्तः॥७॥

Footless, handless he fought Indra; (Indra) threw the thunderbolt on (Vṛtra's) back: a castrated ox, trying to be equal to the bull, Vṛtra lay cut to pieces in many places.

नदं न भिन्नममुया शयानं
मनो रुहाणा अति यन्त्यापः।
याश्चिद्वृत्रो महिना पर्यतिष्ठ-
त्तासामहिः पत्सुतःशीर्बभूव।।८।।

Past him who was lying thus there like a broken reed, the waters rushed flowing for (the benefit of) man; just at the feet of those which Vṛtra had hemmed in with his might the serpent was lying.

नीचावया अभवद्वृत्रपुत्रे-
न्द्रो अस्या अव वधर्जभार।
उत्तरा सूरधरः पुत्र आसी-
द्दानुः शये सहवत्सा न धेनुः।।९।।

The strength of Vṛtr's mother was (dwindling) away; Indra flung the thunderbolt on her; on top was the mother, below the son, Dānu lies there like a cow with the calf.

अतिष्ठन्तीनामविवशनानां
काष्ठानां मध्ये निहितं शरीरम्।
वृत्रस्य निण्यं वि चरन्त्यापो
दीर्घं तम आशयदिन्द्रशत्रुः।।१०।।

In the midst of the never standing, never resting rivers lies hidden the corpse; over Vṛtra's shame flow the waters, he, whose enemy Indra, has entered eternal darkness.

दासपत्नीरहिगोपा अतिष्ठ-
न्निरुद्धा आपः पणिनेव गावः।

अपां बिलमपिहितं यदासीं
वृत्रं जघन्वाँ अप तद्ववार॥११॥

The waters, whose matters the Dāsas, were locked up watched by the serpent, as the cows by a Paṇi; the killer of Vṛtra opened the cave of the waters that had been blocked up.

अश्व्यो वारो अभवस्तदिन्द्र
सृके यत्त्वा प्रत्यहन्देव एकः।
अजयो गा अजयः शूर सोम-
मवासृजः सर्तवे सप्त सिन्धून्॥१२॥

A horse's hair thou wast when he hit back against thee at the thunderbolt; alone as god thou didst conquer the cows; conquer, o hero, the soma, let loose the seven rivers to flow.

नास्मै विद्युन्न तन्यतुः सिषेध
न यां मिहमकिरद्ध्रादुनिं च।
इन्द्रश्च यद्युयुधाते अहिं
श्चोतापरीभ्यो मघवा वि जिग्ये॥१३॥

Nor was the lighting or the thunder of any avail to him, nor the mist and hail-stone which he spread (round about); when Indra and the serpent fought then the generous one conquered for days to come.

अहेर्यातारं कमपश्य इन्द्र
हृदि यत्ते जघ्नुषो भीरगच्छत्।
नव च यन्नवतिं च स्रवन्तीः
श्येनो न भीतो अतरो रजांसि॥१४॥

Whom didst thou see as the serpent's avenger when fear in thy, the killer's heart came, and thou didst cross, like a frightened eagle, the 99 rivers, the spaces ?

इन्द्रो यातोऽवसितस्य राजा

शमस्य च शृङ्गिणो वज्रबाहुः।

सेदु राजा क्षयति चर्षणीना-

मरान्न नेमिः परि ता बभूव।।१५।।

Indra is lord of that which moves and which rests, of the tame and the horned (animals), he in whose arm there is the thunderbolt; as such a one, forsooth, he rules over the people, he encompasses them as the fully the spokes.

म० १ **No. 3** सू० ४८

सह वामेन न उषो

व्युच्छा दुहितर्दिवः।

सह द्युम्नेन बृहता विभावरि

राया देवि दास्वती।।१।।

O Dawn, together with prospertiy, become quite bright for us, O daughter of heaven, with great glory, O brilliant one, with wealth, O goddess, being a bountiful one.

अश्वावतीर्गोमतीर्विश्वसुविदो

भूरि च्यवन्त वस्तवे।

उदीरय प्रति मा सूनृता उष-

श्चोद राधो मघोनाम्।।२।।

Rich in horses, cows, easily finding everything, they often move to shine; send out to me rich gifts, O Dawn, further the offering of the generous.

उवासोषा उच्छाच्च नु
देवी जीरा रथानाम्।
ये अस्या आचरणेषु दध्रिरे
समुद्रे न श्रवस्यवः ॥३॥

Dawn (always) flamed up now, the goddess, stirring on the chariots, which at her arrivals are steadied as the ambitious (sailors) in the sea.

उषो ये ते प्र यामेषु युञ्जते
मनो दानाय सूरयः।
अत्राह तत्कण्व एषां कण्वतमो
नाम गृणाति नृणाम्॥४॥

O Dawn, the lords of the sacrifice, who set their mind on giving at thy approaches: Kaṇva, the truest of Kaṇvas, indeed here praises the (great) name of those very men.

आ घा योषेव सून–
र्युषा याति प्रभुञ्जती।
जरयन्ती वृजनं पद्वदीयत
उत्पातयति पक्षिणः॥५॥

Truly, like a noble young woman Dawn comes, creating happiness; she causes to age every creature, whatever has feet bestirs itself, she makes the birds fly up.

वि या सृजति समनं व्यर्थिनः
पदं न वेत्योदती।
वयो नकिष्टे पप्तिवांस आसते
व्युष्टौ वाजिनीवति॥६॥

She opens the feast (sets going the bazar ?), sends out the busy (Tradesmen), anxioualy Odati follows the trace, as it were; not a single one of the birds which flew up at the rise sits quietly, O rich in gifts.

एषायुक्त परावतः
सूर्यस्योदयनादधि।
शतं रथेभिः सुभगोषा इयं
वि यात्यभि मानुषान्।।७।।

She yoked (the horses coming) from the far distance, from the rising of the sun; with a hundred chariots this blisssful Dawn spreads herself out towards men.

विश्वमस्या नानाम चक्षसे जग-
ज्ज्योतिष्कृणोति सूनरी।
अप द्वेषो मघोनी दुहिता दिव
उषा उच्छदप स्रिधः।।८।।

Every living creature bent to her splendour, the nobel one creates light; may the generous daughter of heaven remove by her rays hatred, may Dawn remove annoyance.

उष आ भाहि भानुना
चन्द्रेण दुहितर्दिवः।
आवहन्ती भूर्यस्मभ्यं सौभगं
व्युच्छन्ती दिविष्टिषु।।९।।

Dawn, shine hither with the pleasing light, O daughter of heaven, bringing us overflowing fortune, flaming up at the sacrificial feasts.

विश्व॑स्य॒ हि प्राण॑नं॒ जीव॑नं॒ त्वे
वि यदु॒च्छसि॑ सूनरि।
सा नो॒ रथे॑न बृह॒ता वि॑भावरि
श्रु॒धि चि॑त्रामघे॒ हव॑म्॥१०॥

The breath (and) life of everything depends on thee, when thou flamest up, O noble one; as such (come) towards us with your big car, brilliant one, hear thou, of glorious gifts, our call.

उषो॒ वाजं॒ हि वंस्व॒
यश्चि॒त्रो मानु॑षे॒ जने॑।
तेना॑ वह सु॒कृतो॑ अध्व॒राँ उप॒
ये त्वा॑ गृ॒णन्ति॒ वह्न॑यः॥११॥

For thou, O Dawn, art to acquire for us strength that is famous among mankind; with that come to the sacrifices of the pious one, to the priests that praise thee.

विश्वा॑न्दे॒वाँ आ व॑ह॒ सोम॑पीतये॒-
ऽन्तरि॑क्षादुष॒स्त्वम्।
सास्मासु॑ धा॒ गोम॒दश्वा॑वदु॒क्थ्य१॒॑-
मुषो॒ वाजं॑ सु॒वीर्य॑म्॥१२॥

All the gods from the firmament bring here to drink the soma; thou, O Dawn, being such, bestow on us possession of cows, of horses, O Dawn, praise worthy strength, heroic progeny.

यस्या॒ रूश॑न्तो अ॒र्चयः॒
प्रति॑ भ॒द्रा अदृ॑क्षत।

सा नो॑ र॒यिं वि॒श्ववा॑रं सु॒पेश॑स-

मु॒षा द॑दातु सु॒ग्म्य॑म्॥१३॥

She whose lucky rays were beheld, the Dawn, grant us wealth of every boon, well adorned, prosperous.

ये चि॒द्धि त्वामृष॑यः पूर्व॑ ऊ॒तये॑

जु॒हूरेऽव॑से महि।

सा नः॒ स्तोमाँ॑ अ॒भि गृ॑णीहि॒ राध॒-

सोषः॑ शु॒क्रेण॑ शो॒चिषा॑॥१४॥

Thou upon whom the seers of old called for help and assistance, O great one, answer our praises with the (grant of) grace, O Dawn, with pure flame.

उषो॒ यद॒द्य भा॒नुना॒

वि द्वारा॑वृ॒णवो॑ दि॒वः।

प्र नो॑ यच्छतादवृ॒कं पृ॒थु च्छर्दिः

प्र दे॑वि॒ गोम॑ती॒रिषः॑॥१५॥

Dawn, if to-day thou openest the two doors of heaven with they splendour, then grant us peaceful, spacious protection, give us, O goddess, food and drink from the cow.

सं नो॑ रा॒या बृ॑ह॒ता वि॒श्वपे॑शसा

मिमि॒क्ष्वा समिळा॑भि॒रा।

सं द्यु॒म्नेन॑ विश्व॒तुरो॑षो महि॒

सं वाजै॑र्वाजिनीवति॥१६॥

Endow (us) here with great, well adorned wealth, with blessings, with all-surpassing splendour, O Dawn, O great one, with victorious strength, O strong one.

म० १ **No. 4** सू० ४९

उषो भद्रेभिरा गहि
दिवश्चिद्रोचनादधि।
वहन्त्वरुणप्सव
उप त्वा सोमिनो गृहम्॥१॥

O Dawn, come with good things, far from heaven's sphere of light; may they of red appearance bring you to the soma offerer's home.

सुपेशसं सुखं रथं
यमध्यस्था उषस्त्वम्।
तेना सुश्रवसं जनं
प्रावाद्य दुहितर्दिवः॥२॥

With the well adorned, light car which thou didst mount, O Dawn, with that, O daughter of heaven, help to-day the people of good reputation.

वयश्चित्ते पतत्रिणो
द्विपच्चतुष्पदर्जुनि।
उषः प्रारन्नृतूँरनु
दिवो अन्तेभ्यस्परि॥३॥

The winged birds, the two and four-footed (animals), O brilliant one, have at every one of the fixed times quickely come from the ends of heaven, O Dawn.

व्युच्छन्ती हि रश्मिभि-
र्विश्वमाभासि रोचनम्।

तां त्वामुषर्वसूयवो

गीर्भिः कण्वा अहूषत ।।४।।

For, flaming up with rays thou enlightnest the whole sphere of light; on such a one, on thee, O Dawn, the Kaṇvas, desirous of wealth, have called with their songs.

म० १ **No. 1** सू० ११६

नासत्याभ्यां बर्हिरिव प्र वृञ्जे

स्तोमाँ इयर्म्यभ्रियेव वातः।

यावर्भगाय विमदाय जायां

सेनाजुवा न्यूहतू रथेन ।।१।।

To the two Nāsatyā I brun बर्हिस् as it were (viz.) the songs of praise; I send them upwards as wind the clouds, to them who adduced to the young Vimada a wife together with a car as swift as a (storming) army.

वीळुपत्मभिराशुहेमभिर्वा

देवानां वा जूतिभिः शाशदाना।

तद्रासभो नासत्या सहस्र-

माजा यमस्य प्रधने जिगाय ।।२।।

May be you distinguished yourselves by the strong flights, by the quick drives, may be by the inciting shouts of the gods: (but) the donkey won that thousand in the fray at Yama's tournament, O Nāsatyā.

तुग्रो ह भुज्युमश्विनोदमेघे

रयिं न कश्चिन्ममृवाँ अवाहाः।

तमूहथुर्नौभिरात्मन्वतीभि-

रन्तरिक्षप्रुद्भिरपोदकाभिः ।।३।।

Tugra had left, O Aśvinā, Bhujyu in the vast sea, as any dying man (leaves his) wealth (behind); you carried him on your animated, the air-crossing, watertight ships.

ति॒स्रः क्ष॒प॒स्त्रिरहा॑ति॒व्रज॑द्भि-

नास॑त्या भु॒जयुमूहथुः पत॒ङ्गैः।

स॒मु॒द्रस्य॒ धन्व॑न्ना॒दस्य॑ पा॒रे

त्रि॒भी रथैः॑ श॒तप॑द्भिः षळ॑श्वैः॥४॥

With winged (horses) that gallop over three nights and three days, O Nāsatyā, you rescued Bhujyu on the shore of the sea, on the bank of the water, by means of three cars with hundred feet and six horses.

अ॒ना॒र॒म्भ॒णे तद॑वीरयेथा-

मनास्था॒ने अ॑ग्रभ॒णे स॑मु॒द्रे।

यद॑श्विना ऊ॒हथु॑र्भु॒जयुमस्तं॑

श॒तारि॑त्रां॒ नाव॑मातस्थि॒वांस॑म्॥५॥

On the sea, where there is nothing to lean upon, nothing to stand on, nothing to catch hold of, you did the heroic deed when you, Aśvinā, brought home Bhujyu who was standing in the hundred-oared ship.

यम॑श्विना द॒दथुः॑ श्वे॒तमश्व॑-

म॒घाश्वा॑य॒ शश्व॒दित्स्व॒स्ति।

तद्वां॑ दा॒त्रं महि॑ की॒र्तेन्यं॑ भू-

त्पै॒द्वो वा॒जी सद॒मिद्धव्यो॑ अर्थः॥६॥

The white horse that you, O Aśvinā, gave to him who had bad horses, (to be his) sheer good luck : this your great gift had to be extolled; Pedu's horse is to be made known for ever, even more than the mighty one.

युवं नरा स्तुवते पज्रियाय

कक्षीवते अरदतं पुरंधिम्।

कारोतराच्छफादश्वस्य वृष्णः

शतं कुम्भाँ असिञ्चतं सुरायाः॥७॥

You, O Men, opened up abundance to the singing Pajriya Kakṣivat; out of the hoof, the strainer of the stallion, you let flow hundred pots of liquor.

हिमेनाग्निं घ्रंसमवारयेथां

पितुमतीमूर्जमस्मा अधत्तम्।

ऋबीसे अत्रिमश्विनावनीत-

मुन्निन्यथुः सर्वगणं स्वस्ति॥८॥

With cold (snow?) you warded off flames and heat, noorishing food you gave him; you, Aśvinā, safely led up with his whole kin Atri buried in the subterranean fire.

परावतं नासत्यानुदेथा-

मुच्चाबुध्नं चक्रथुर्जिह्मबारम्।

क्षरन्नापो न पायनाय राये

सहस्राय तृष्यते गोतमस्य॥९॥

A well you upset, Nāsatyā, you made it with the bottom on top and with the brim starting; the waters did not flow for drinking (on behalf) of thirsty Gotama (but) for thousandfold wealth.

Or : the waters did not flow (so much) for drinking

on behalf of the thirsty, (as) for Gotama's thousand fold wealth.

Or : Gotama's well you upset…

जुजुरूषो नासत्योत वव्रिं
प्रामुञ्चतं द्रापिमिव च्यवानात्।
प्रातिरतं जहितस्यायुर्दस्रा-
दित्पतिमकृणुतं कनीनाम्।।१०।।

Moreover, Nāsatyā, you took the bodily shape from the ageing Cyavāna like a cloak; you, wonder-workers, prolonged the life of the forsaken one and then still made him the husband of maidens.

तद्वां नरा शंस्यं राध्यं
चाभिष्टिमन्नासत्य वरूथम्।
यद्विद्वांसा निधिमिवापगूळ्ह-
मुद्दर्शतादूपथुर्वन्दनाय।।११।।

That, O heroes, was your praiseworthy, safeguarding protection, worthy to be gained, Nāsatyā, when, as it were, knowing about a hidden treasure you dug out from the visible (well Vandana) for (your) praise.

तद्वां नरा सनये दंस उग्र-
माविष्कृणोमि तन्यतुर्न वृष्टिम्।
दध्यङ् ह यन्मध्वाथर्वणो वा-
मश्वस्य शीर्ष्णा प्र यदीमुवाच।।१२।।

That awe-inspiring, wonderful deed of yours, O Men,

I with a view to reward make known as thunder the rain: That Dadhyañc, the Ātharvan, indeed proclaimed it to you by means of a horse's head what the मधु is.

अजोहवीन्नासत्या करा वां
महे यामन्पुरुभुजा पुरंधिः।
श्रुतं तच्छासुरिव वध्रिमत्या
हिरण्यहस्तमश्विनावदत्तम्।।१३।।

Upon your hands, Nāsatyā, helping many, entreatingly called at the decisive hour Puraṁdhi; this was heard like an order of Vadhrimatī, the Aśvinā granted Hiraṇyahasta.

आस्नो वृकस्य वर्तिकामभीके
युवं नरा नासत्यामुमुक्तम्।
उतो कविं पुरूभुजा युवं ह
कृपमाणमकृणुतं विचक्षे।।१४।।

Right (अभीके) from the mouth of the wolf you heroes, Nāsatyā, rescued the quail; moreover, you, helper of many, made indeed the imploring कवि (fit) to see.

चरित्रं हि वेरिवाच्छेदि पर्ण-
माजा खेलस्य परितक्म्यायाम्।
सद्यो जङ्घामायसीं विश्पलायै
धने हिते सर्तवे प्रत्यधत्तम्।।१५।।

The leg was cut off (to Viśpalā), as the wing to a bird, in the fray at the tournament (in honour) of Khela; at once you put Viśpalā an iron leg on, instead, to run (the race), the prize being at stake.

शतं मेषान्वृक्यै चक्षदान-
मृज्राश्वं तं पितान्धं चकार।
तस्मां अक्षी नासत्या विचक्ष
आधत्तं दस्रा भिषजावनर्वन्।।१६।।

The father had blinded his (own son) Ṛjrāśvs, who gave hundred he-goats to the she-wolf to eat; to him; you restored the eyes to see, o wonder-workers, unrivalled physicians.

आ वां रथं दुहिता सूर्यस्य
कार्ष्मेवातिष्ठदर्वता जयन्ती।
विश्वे देवा अन्वमन्यन्त हृद्भिः
समु श्रिया नासत्या सचेथे।।१७।।

Sūrya's daughter mounted your car, winning the goal as it were on horseback; all the gods approved of it in their hearts; you, Nāsatyā, are indeed united with fortune.

यदयातं दिवोदासाय वर्ति-
र्भरद्वाजायाश्विना हयन्ता।
रेवदुवाह सचनो रथो वां
वृषभश्च शिंशुमारश्च युक्ता।।१८।।

When you drove round to Divodāsa, to Bharadvāja, Aśvinā, urging on (the horses), your accompanying car carried rich gifts, and the bull and the dolphin (were) harnassed together to the car.

रयिं सुक्षत्रं स्वपत्यमायुः
सुवीर्यं नासत्या वहन्ता।

आ जह्नावीं समनसोप वाजै
स्त्रिरह्नो भागं दधतीमयातम्।।१९।।

Carrying wealth with good rule, (long) life with excellent progency, heroic sons, you , Nāsatyā, of one mind come with booty to Jahnu's sons who offered (you) the portion thrice a day.

परिविष्टं जाहुषं विश्वतः सीं
सुगेभिर्नक्तमूहथू रजोभिः।
विभिन्दुना नासत्या रथेन
वि पर्वताँ अजरयू अयातम्।।२०।।

Jahuṣa's son, besieged all round, him you rescued through passable regions at night; with a car cutting a way you came through the mountains unharmed, O Nāsatyā, being always young.

एकस्या वस्तोरावतं रणाय
वशमश्विना सनये सहस्रा।
निरहतं दुच्छुना इन्द्रवन्ता
पृथुश्रवसो वृषणावरातीः।।२१।।

One morning you helped Vaśa to joy, Aśvinā, to gain thousandfold wealth; accompanied by Indra you warded off the demons, the enemy of Pṛthuśravas, O bulls.

शरस्य चिदार्चत्कस्यावतादा
नीचादुच्चा चक्रथुः पातवे वाः।
शयवे चिन्नासत्या शचीभि
र्जसुरये स्तर्यं पिप्यथुर्गाम्।।२२।।

From Śara Ārcatka's well you brought water up from below to drink; for Śayu who was dying of thirst you, Nāsatyā, by your powers made the dry cow swell.

अवस्यते स्तुवते कृष्णियाय
ऋजूयते नासतया शचीभिः।
पशुं न नष्टमिव दर्शनाय
विष्णाप्वं ददथुर्विश्वकाय ॥२३॥

To the help-seeking, praising, straight-acting Viśvaka, son of Kṛṣṇa you, O Nāsatyā, did restore Viṣṇāpu, lost as it were like cattle, to see him again.

दश रात्रीरशिवेना नव द्यू-
नवनद्धं श्नथितमप्स्व१न्तः।
बिप्रुतं रेभमुदनि प्रवृक्त-
मुन्निन्यथुः सोममिव स्रुवेण ॥२४॥

Rebha, who was ten nights and nine days fettered, mangled by the enemy, falling to pieces in the floods, tied down in the water, him you brought up, like soma with a ladle.

प्र वां दंसांस्यश्विनाववोच-
मस्य पतिः स्यां सुगवः सुवीरः।
उत पश्यन्नश्नुवन्दीर्घमायु-
रस्तमिवेज्जरिमाणं जगम्याम् ॥२५॥

I have, OA'svinā, made known your wondrous deeds, may I, with good cattle, good sons, be the lord of this; may I seeing (well), attaining a long life, come to old age, just as to my home.

म० १ **No. 1** सू० १८४

ता वा॒मद्य ताव॑प॒रं हु॑वे

मो॒च्छन्त्या॑मु॒षसि॒ वह्नि॑रु॒क्थैः।

नास॑त्य कुह॑ चि॒त्सन्ता॑व॒र्यो

दि॒वो नपा॑ता सु॒दास्त॑राय॥१॥

You let us invite today, *you* tomorrow; when the dawn begins to shine the priest with his songs (invites you), the Nāsatyā (and) the Soma of heaven, wherever you may be, for the (यजमान) more liberal than (any other)rich man.

अ॒स्मे ऊ॒ षु वृ॑षणा मादयेथा-

मुत्प॒णीँर्ह॑तमू॒र्म्या मद॑न्ता।

श्रु॒तं मे॒ अच्छो॑क्तिभिर्मती॒ना-

मेष्टा॑ नरा॒ निचे॑तारा च॒ कर्णैः॑॥२॥

With us, O bulls, you must enjoy yourselves, drunk with the wave strike the misers, listen to the invocation of my prayers; called here by sacrifice, O heroes, be listeners with your ears.

श्रि॒ये पू॑षन्निषु॒कृते॑व दे॒वा

नास॑त्या वह॒तुं सू॒र्या॑याः।

व॒च्यन्ते॑ वां ककु॒हा अ॒प्सु जा॒ता

युगा जू॒र्णेव॒ वरु॑णस्य॒ भूरेः॑॥३॥

For good luck you, O Pūṣan (and) you, O Nāsatyā, as gods (came) like archers to the marriage of Sūryā; your bulls born in the water move on like the passing (?) yokes of the mighty Varuṇa.

अस्मे सा वां माध्वी रातिरस्तु

स्तोमं हिनोतं मान्यस्य कारोः।

अनु यद्वां श्रवस्या सुदानू

सुवीर्याय चर्षणयो मदन्ति।।४।।

Let your gift, O lovers of sweetness, be with us; inspire the hymn of Māna's son, the singer, when the people rejoice over your glorious deeds, O givers, (to get) heroic progeny.

एष वां स्तोमो अश्विनावकारि–

मानेभिर्मघवाना सुवृक्ति।

यातं वर्तिस्तनयाय त्मने

चागस्त्ये नासत्या मदन्ता।।५।।

This song was made in a well-finished manner by Māna's sons for you, O Aśvinā, liberal ones; being delighted with Agastya, O Nāsatyā, make your round to his sons and to himself.

अतारिष्म तमसस्पारमस्य

प्रति वां स्तोमो अश्विनावधायि।

एह यातं पथिभिर्देवयानै

र्विद्यामेषं वृजनं जीरदानुम्।।६।।

We have crossed the bank of this darkness, a song has been placed before you, Aśvinā; come hither on paths trodden by gods, may we find food and drink , strength with quick gifts.

म० १ **No. 7** सू० २३

गणानां त्वा गणपतिं हवामहे

कविं कवीनामुपमश्रवस्तमम्।

ज्येष्ठराजं ब्रह्मणां ब्रह्मणस्पत

आ नः शृण्वन्नूतिभिः सीद सादनम्।।१।।

We call upon thee, lord of hosts, of (all) the hosts, the wise one of the wise ones, the first and foremost in fame, the overlord of prayers, O Brahmaṇaspati, hearing us here with your helps take the seat.

देवाश्चित्ते असुर्य प्रचेतसो

बृहस्पते यज्ञियं भागमानशुः।

उस्रा इव सूर्यो ज्योतिषा महो

विश्वेषामिज्जनिता ब्रह्मणामसि।।२।।

O divine one, Bṛhaspati, the gods have indeed from thee, the wise one, obtained the share of the sacrifce; as through light the glorious sun (is the parent) of the dawn, so thou truly art the parent of all the prayers.

आ विबाध्या परिरापस्तमांसि च

ज्योतिष्मन्तं रथमृतस्य तिष्ठसि।

बृहस्पते भीमममित्रदम्भनं

रक्षोहणं गोत्रभिदं स्वर्विदम्।।३।।

Having chased away those who whisper all round as well as darknesses, thou as endest the luminous car of righteousness, O Bṛhaspati, the terrible, enemy-thwarting, demon-killing, cowpen-cleaving, light-finding (car).

सुनीतिभिर्नयसि त्रायसे जनं
यस्तुभ्यं दाशान्न तमंहो अश्नवत्।
ब्रह्मद्विषस्तपनो मन्युमीरसि
बृहस्पते महि तत्ते महित्वनम्।।४।।

By good guidance thou leadest, protectest the people, him who makes offering to thee no anxiety will approach; thou art the tormentor of the brahma-hater, the destroyer of (his) wrath, Bṛhaspati: that is thy great glory.

न तमंहो न दुरितं कुतश्चन
नारातयस्तितिरुर्न द्वयाविनः।
विश्वा इदस्माद्ध्वरसो वि बाधसे
यं सुगोपा रक्षसि ब्रह्मणस्पते।।५।।

No anxiety, no harm from anywhere, no enemies will overcome (him), no double-dealers; thou indeed banishest far from him all the cheats over whom thou, Brahmaṇaspati, as a good shepherd watchest.

त्वं नो गोपाः पथिकृद्विचक्षण-
स्तव व्रताय मतिभिर्जरामहे।
बृहस्पते यो नो अभि ह्वरो दधे
स्वा तं मर्मर्तु दुच्छुना हरस्वती।।६।।

Thou art our shepherd, preparing the way, looking all-round, we offer up praise with songs in honour of thy law; Bṛhaspati, may his own impetous mischief crush him whosoever lays us a trap.

उत वा यो नो मर्चयादनागसो
ऽरातीवा मर्तः सानुको वृकः।

बृहस्पते अप तं वर्तया पथः
सुगं नो अस्यै देववीतये कृधि॥७॥

And him too who damages us innocent ones, the hostile man, the wolf greedy of prey, Bṛhaspati, revome him from the way, make our road easy to this beast of the gods.

त्रातारं त्वा तनूनां हवामहे-
ऽवस्पर्तरधिवक्तारमस्मयुम्।
बृहस्पते देवनिदो नि बर्हय
मा दुरेवा उत्तरं सुम्नमुन्नशन्॥८॥

We call upon thee, the protector of our persons, O saviour, the advocate who loves us; Bṛhaspati, put down the revilers, of the gods, may not the wicked ones attain higher fortune.

त्वया वयं सुवृधा ब्रह्मणस्पते
स्पार्हा वसु मनुष्या ददीमहि।
या नो दूरे तळितो या अरातयो-
ऽभि सन्ति जम्भया ता अनप्नसः॥९॥

May we men, helped by thee, Brahmaṇaspati, the increaser, gain desirable good; our enemies, those far and those near, that (try to) good; our enemies, those far and those near, that (try to) overpower us; crush them (that they may become) penniless.

त्वया वयमुत्तमं धीमहे वयो
बृहस्पते पप्रिणा सस्निना युजा।

मा नो दुःशंसो अभिदिप्सुरीशत
प्र सुशंसा मतिभिस्तारिषीमहि।।१०।।

May we attain, through thee, the amply bestowing, winning companion, O Bṛhaspati, the happiest life; may not the evil-tongued, the cheat rule over us; may we, well speaking, get on by our songs.

अनानुदो वृषभो जग्मिराहव
निष्टप्ता शत्रुं पृतनासु सासहिः।
असि सत्य ऋणया ब्रह्मणस्पत
उग्रस्य चिद्दमिता वीलुहर्षिणः।।११।।

Strong, not giving way, hurrying to the challenge, a burner of foes, holding out in battles, thou art a true exactor of debt (sin), Brahmaṇaspati, coercing the fierce, him who rejoices in strength.

अदेवेन मनसा यो रिषण्यति
शासामुग्रो मन्यमानो जिघांसति।
बृहस्पते मा प्रणक्तस्य नो वधो
नि कर्म मन्युं दुरेवस्य शर्धतः।।१२।।

He who damages with a godless mind, who thinking to be strong in commands, tries to hurt, O Bṛhaspati, may not his weapon get at us; may we put down the wrath of the ill-disposed, defiant one.

भरेषु हव्यो नमसोपसद्यो
गन्ता वाजेषु सनिता धनंधनम्।
विश्वा इदर्यो अभिदिप्स्वोऽमृधो
बृहस्पतिर्वि ववर्हा रथाँ इव।।१३।।

To be invoked in fights, to be approached in worship, thou marchest in battles, winning prize upon prize; all the stingy, deceiving enemies Bṛhaspati overthrew like cars. (Or :—) all the onslaughts (malice, harm) of the deceiving rival Bṛhaspati overthrew like cars.

तेजिष्ठया तपनी रक्षसस्तप
ये त्वा निदे दधिरे दृष्टवीर्यम्।
आविस्तत्कृष्व यदसत्त उक्थ्यं१
बृहस्पते वि परिरापो अर्दय।।१४।।

With the hottest glow burn the demons who exposed to scorn thee whose volour is proved; make known that which is (to be found) praiseworthy in thee, Bṛhaspati, destroy those that whisper about.

बृहस्पते अति यदर्यो अर्हा-
द्द्युमद्विभाति क्रतुमज्जनेषु।
यद्दीदयच्छवस ऋतप्रजात
तदस्मासु द्रविणं धेहि चित्रम्।।१५।।

O Bṛhaspati, that whose worth is beyond the (deserts of) the rivals, that which, splendid, strong, is renowned among the people, that which shines by its strength, O offspring of the law, that marvellous property bestown on us.

मा नः स्तेनेभ्यो ये अभि द्रुहस्पदे
निरामिणो रिपवोऽन्नेषु जागृधुः।
आ देवानामोहते वि व्रयो हृदि
बृहस्पते न परः साम्नो विदुः।।१६।।

Hand us not over to the thieves who, lying in ambush, are greedy after our food; the rogues, they despise in their heart the overpowering might of the gods, (yet) they know nothing beyond the सामन्, O Bṛhaspati.

विश्वेभ्यो हि त्वा भुवनेभ्यस्परि
त्वष्टाजनत्साम्नः साम्नः कविः।
स ऋणचिदृणया ब्रह्मणस्पति
र्द्रुहो हन्ता मह ऋतस्य धर्तरि।।१७।।

For (the good of) all the beings Tvaṣṭṛ, the knower of every सामन्, has created thee; such then is the gatherer and the exactor of debts, Brahmaṇaspati, the slayer of witches the supporter of the great order.

तव श्रिये व्यजिहीत पर्वतो
गवां गोत्रमुदसृजो यदङ्गिरः।
इन्द्रेण युजा तमसा परीवृतं
बृहस्पते निरपामौब्जो अर्णवम्।।१८।।

To thy majesty the mountain opened up, when thou, Aṅgiras, emptiest the cow-pen; with Indra as companion thou, Bṛhaspati, lettest loose the flood of the waters wrapped up in darkness.

ब्रह्मणस्पते त्वमस्य यन्ता
सूक्तस्य बोधि तनयं च जिन्व।
विश्वं तद्भद्रं यदवन्ति देवा
बृहद्वदेम विदथे सुवीराः।।१९।।

Brahmaṇaspati, be the guide of this hymn and quicken

posterity; all that is good which the gods support; may we with doughty heroes speak loud in the assembly.

म० २ No. 2 (II. 28.) सू० २८

इ॒दं क॒वेरा॑दि॒त्यस्य॑ स्व॒राजो॒

विश्वा॑नि॒ सान्त्य॒भ्यस्तु म॒ह्ना।

अति॒ यो म॒न्द्रो य॒जथा॑य दे॒वः

सु॑की॒र्तिं भि॑क्षे॒ वरु॑णस्य॒ भूरेः॑॥१॥

This (hymn is) for the wise Āditya, the self-ruler: let it (him ?) surpass in greatness all that there is; from the god who is so well disposed towards the sacrifice, I beg fame, from Varuṇa, the opulent one.

तव॑ व्र॒ते सु॒भगा॑सः स्याम

स्वा॒ध्यो॑ वरुण तुष्टु॒वांसः॑।

उ॒पाय॑न उ॒षसां॒ गोम॑तीना-

म॒ग्नायो॒ न जर॑माणा॒ अनु॒ द्यून्॥२॥

May we who devoutly praise (thee) be prosperous under thy law, O Varuṇa, lauding like the fires day after day at the approach of the dawns rich in cattle.

तव॑ स्याम पुरु॒वीर॑स्य॒ शर्म॑-

न्नुरु॒शंस॑स्य वरुण प्रणेतः।

यू॒यं नः॑ पुत्रा अदितेरदब्धा

अ॒भि क्ष॑मध्वं॒ युज्या॑य देवाः॥३॥

Let us be in the protection of thee who art rich in heroes, far-famed, O leader, Varuṇa; you, O undeceivable sons of Aditi, be favourable to an alliance with us, O gods.

प्र सीमादित्यो असृजद्विधर्ता
ऋतं सिन्धवो वरुणस्य यन्ति।
न श्राम्यन्ति न वि मुचन्त्येते
वयो न पप्तू रघुया परिज्मन्॥४॥

The protector, the Āditya let them flow; according to Varuṇa's law the rivers move: they do not get tired, nor do they make a halt, like birds they quickly rush on everywhere.

वि मच्छ्रथाय रशनामिवाग
ऋध्याम ते वरुण खामृतस्य।
मा तन्तुश्छेदि वयतो धियं मे
मा मात्रा शार्यपसः पुर ऋतोः॥५॥

Take away from me like a rope the sin, let us, Varuṇa, increase the fount of Right; let not the thread be cut short whilst I am weaving the prayer, may not the measure of the work be shortened before the (proper) season.

अपो सु म्यक्ष वरुण भियसं म-
त्सम्राळृतावोऽनु मा गृभाय।
दामेव वत्साद्वि मुमुग्ध्यंहो
नहि त्वदारे निमिषश्चनेशे॥६॥

Remove nicely fear from me, O Varuṇa, holy lord, favour me; like the halter from the calf, loose anguish from me, for apart from thee I have not the power over a single twinkle (closing) of the eye.

मा नो वधैर्वरुण ये त इष्टा-
वेनः कृण्वन्तमसुर भ्रीणन्ति।

मा ज्योतिषः प्रवसथानि गन्म

वि षू मृधः शिश्रथो जीवसे नः॥७॥

Strike us not, Varuṇa, with weapons that burn at thy word the evil-doer, O Asura; may we not go into banishment from light; disperse wie the enemies that we may live.

नमः पुरा ते वरुणोत नून-

मुतापरं तुविजात ब्रवाम।

त्वे हि कं पर्वते न श्रिता-

न्यप्रच्युतानि दूळभ व्रतानि॥८॥

Worship to thee, O Varuṇa, (as) before, so now let us pronounce, O mighty one; in thee forsooth, just as in a mountain, the immoveable laws are fixed, O undeceivabale one.

परं ऋणा सावीरध मत्कृतानि

माहं राजन्नन्यकृतेन भोजम्।

अव्युष्टा इन्नु भूयसीरुषास

आ नो जीवान्वरुण तासु शाधि॥९॥

Remove far the debts made by me, O Varuṇa, may I not live on the (Wealth) made by others, O king; yes, surely a good many dawn have not (yet) shone; ordain us to live at those, O Varuṇa.

यो मे राजन्युज्यो वा सखा वा

स्वप्ने भयं भीरवे मह्यमाह।

स्तेनो वा यो दिप्सति नो वृको वा

त्वं तस्माद्वरुण पाह्यस्मान्॥१०॥

From him who speaks to me, timid one, something frightful (seen) in sleep, be he one of my own people or a friend, from the thief who tries to deceive, and the wolf: from him thou, O Varuṇa, protect us.

माहं मघोनों वरुण प्रियस्यं
भूरिदान्न आ विदं शूनमापेः।
मा रायो राजन्सुयमादवं स्थां
बृहद्वदेम विदथें सुवीराः॥११॥

May I not meet, Varuṇa, with the want of the potent dear, richly giving, good friend; may I not lose the well-controlled possession, O king, may we with doughty heroes speak loud in the assembly.

म० २ **No. 9** सू० ३८

उदु ष्य देवः संविता सवायं
शश्वत्तमं तदंपा वह्निरस्थात्।
नूनं देवेभ्यो वि हि धाति रत्न-
मथाभंजद्वीतिहोत्रं स्वस्तौ॥१॥

There has risen (stands on high in his car) anew god Savitṛ to give the command, he, the priest whose work this is; for surely he is to distribute wealth to the gods: now he (will) let share in happiness him whose libatin is agreeable.

विश्वंस्य हि श्रुष्टये देव ऊर्ध्वः
प्र बाहवां पृथुपाणिः सिसंर्ति।
आपंश्चिदस्य व्रत आ निमृंग्रा
अयं चिद्वातों रमते परिंज्मन्॥२॥

That the world should listen, on high the god with large hands extends his arms; both the waters indeed are obeying his behest and the wind here stops in its course.

आ॒शुभि॑श्चि॒द्यान्वि मु॑चाति नू॒न-

मरी॑रम॒दत॑मानं चि॒देतो॑ः।

अ॒ह्यर्षू॑णां चिन्न्य॑याँ अवि॒ष्य॑-

मनु॑ व्र॒तं स॑वि॒तुर्मोक्यागा॑त्॥३॥

He who travels with fleet (horses) has to unyoke them now, and (savitṛ) stops the wanderer from going as will; and even the greed of the birds of prey he checked: according to Savitṛ's order the night has come.

पुनः सम॑व्य॒द्वित॑तं॒ वय॑न्ती

म॒ध्या कर्तो॒र्न्य॑धा॒च्छक्म॒ धीर॑ः।

उत्संहाया॑स्था॒द्व्यृ१॑तूँर॑दर्ध-

र॒रम॑तिः सवि॒ता दे॒व आगा॑त्॥४॥

The weaving woman again rolls up the spread out (cloth); in the middle of doing the clever (craftsman) puts down his work: god Savitṛ having arisen has stood high up, has arranged the seasons, has appered punctually.

नानौकां॑सि॒ दुर्यो॒ विश्व॒मायु॒-

र्वि ति॑ष्ठते प्रभ॒वः शोको॑ अ॒ग्नेः

ज्येष्ठं॑ मा॒ता सू॒नवे॑ भा॒गमाधा॒

दन्व॑स्य॒ केत॑मिषि॒तं स॑वि॒त्रा॥५॥

All life-time (always) the mighty glow of the home fire is spread over all the various houses; the mother puts before the son the best piece, according to the desire after it, awakened by Savitṛ.

समावव॑र्ति॒ विष्ठि॑तो जिगी॒षु-
विश्वे॑षां॒ काम॒श्चर॑ताम॒माभू॑त्।
शश्वाँ॒ अपो॒ विकृ॑तं हि॒त्व्यागा॒-
दनु॑ व्र॒तं स॑वि॒तुर्दैव्य॑स्य॥६॥

The fortune-hunter abroad returns, the desire of all the wanderers goes homewards; one after the other, leaving off the half-done work, comes back according to the divine Savitṛ's behest.

त्वया॑ हि॒तमप्य॑म॒प्सु भा॒गं
धन्वान्वा मृ॑ग॒यसो॒ वि त॑स्थुः।
वना॑नि॒ विभ्यो॒ नकि॑रस्य॒ तानि॑
व्र॒ता दे॒वस्य॑ सवि॒तुर्मि॑नन्ति॥७॥

The beasts (look for) their share put by thee into the waters, (and they) spread over the dry land; the woods are for the birds: not one violates these orders of god Savitṛ.

या॒द्रा॒ध्यं॑ वरु॑णो॒ योनि॒मप्य॒-
मनि॑शितं नि॒मिषि॒ जर्भु॑राणः।
विश्वो॑ मार्ता॒ण्डो व्र॒जमा प॒शुर्गा॑-
त्स्थ॒शो जन्मा॑नि सवि॒ता व्याकः॑॥८॥

Varuṇa occupies as long as he likes the watery abode, incessantly moving about every moment; every bird, the cattle go to their pen, Savitṛ has arranged the (different) creatures according to their places.

न यस्येन्द्रो वरुणो न मित्रो
व्रतमर्यमा न मिनन्ति रुद्रः।
नारातयस्तमिदं स्वस्ति
हुवे देवं सवितारं नमोभिः॥९॥

Whose law neither Indra, nor Varuṇa, nor Mitra, nor Aryaman, nor Rudra transgress, nor the fiends: upon (that) god Savitṛ with worship I call for welfare here.

भगं धियं वाजयन्तः पुरंधिं
नराशंसो ग्नास्पतिर्नो अव्याः।
आये वामस्य संगथे रयीणां
प्रिया देवस्य सवितुः स्याम॥१०॥

May we, furthering the fortune, the hymn, the opulence—that it may please Narāśaṁsa, the lord of goddesses, to help us —, be dear to god Savitṛ in the arrival of good things, in the collecting of wealth.

अस्मभ्यं तद्दिवो अद्भ्यः पृथिव्या-
स्त्वया दत्तं काम्यं राध आ गात्।
शं यत्स्तोतृभ्य आपये भवा-
त्युरुशंसाय सवितर्जरित्रे॥११॥

May from heaven, from the waters, the earth, that desirable grace granted by thee come to us that is to be a blessing for the singers, for the friend, for the poet who is loud in his praise, O Savitṛ.

मं० ३ **No. 10** सू० ९

सखायस्त्वा ववृमहे
देवं मर्तास ऊतये।
अपां नपातं सुभगं सुदीदितिं
सुप्रतूर्तिमनेहसम्॥१॥

We, as friends, have chosen thee for our protection, (we) the mortals (thee) the god, the offspring of the Waters, the blessed one, with fine splendour, advancing unchecked, unmolested.

कायमानो वना त्वं
यन्मातृरजगन्नपः।
न तत्ते अग्ने प्रमृषे निवर्तनं
यद्दूरे सन्निहाभवः॥२॥

If seeing the woods thou didst go into the waters, the mothers, (may) thy return from there not (be) a matter of slight, since (though now) being far, (yet formerly) thou wert here.

अति तृष्टं ववक्षिथ-
थैव सुमना असि।
प्रप्रान्ये यन्ति पर्यन्य आसते
येषां सख्ये असि श्रितः॥३॥

Thou hast overcome the obnoxious (रक्षस्), and now thou art so kind-hearted. Some go forward here and there, others sit round, in whose friendship thou art established.

ईयिवांसमति स्रिधः
शश्वतीरति सश्चतः
अन्वीमविन्दन्निचिरासो अद्रु-
होऽप्सु सिंहमिव श्रितम्।।४।।

Him who has passed beyond obstacles, beyond all dangers, the watchful, guileless ones found in the waters like a lion gone (to his den).

ससृवांसमिव त्म-
नाग्निमित्था तिरोहितम्।
ऐनं नयन्मातरिश्वा परावतो
देवेभ्यो मथितं परि।।५।।

Agni who had run away, as it were, at his own will (and) was hidden thus, him Mātariśvan brought back from afar, from the gods, when produced by friction.

तं त्वा मर्ता अगृभ्णत
देवेभ्यो हव्यवाहन।
विश्वान्यद्यज्ञाँ अभिपासि मानुष
तव क्रत्वा यविष्ठ्य।।६।।

Thus the mortals have got thee, O carrier of oblations to the gods, since thou, O belonging to Man, by the mind's power protectest all the sacrifices, O youngest one.

तद्भद्रं तव दंसना
पाकाय चिच्छदयति।
त्वां यदग्ने पशवः समासते
समिद्धमपिशर्वरे।।७।।

This kindness, thy wonderful power, is manifest even to the simple, as at the beginning of the night the beasts lie round about thee when thou art kindled, O Agni.

आ जुहोता स्वध्वरं

शीरं पावकशोचिषम्।

आशुं दूतमजिरं प्रत्नमीड्यं

श्रुष्टी देवं सपर्यत॥८॥

Offer in him, fit for fine oblations, the glowing one, whose flames are purifying, serve obediently the god, the quick messenger, the nimble, the ancient, the adorable one.

त्रीणि शता त्री सहस्राण्यग्निं

त्रिंशच्च देवा नव चासपर्यन्।

औक्षन्घृतैरस्तृणन्बर्हिरस्मा

आदिद्धोतारं न्यसादयन्त॥९॥

Three hundred three thousand thirty and nine gods have done homage to Agni; they sprinkled (him with) ghee, strew the sacred grass for him, then they made him sit down as होतृ.

म० ३ **No. 11** सू० ३३

इन्द्र सोमं सोमपते पिबेमं

माध्यंदिनं सवनं चारु यत्ते।

प्रप्रुथ्या शिप्रे मघवन्नृजीषि-

न्विमुच्या हरी इह मादयस्व॥१॥

O Indra, lord of soma, drink this soma here, the midday libation which is agreeable to thee; blow the moustache, O liberal one, who drinkest down to the rest, unyoke the horses, get drunk here.

गवाशिरं मन्थिनमिन्द्र शुक्रं
पिबा सोमं ररिमा ते मदाय।
ब्रह्मकृता मारुतेना गणेन
सजोषा रुद्रैस्तृपदा वृषस्व।।२।।

Drink, Indra, the soma mixed with milk, mixed with flour, the white one; we have offered it (for) thy intoxication; revelling together with the brahma-inspiring host of Maruts, with the Rudras, pour down to full satisfaction;—

ये ते शुष्मं ये तविषीमवर्ध-
न्नर्चन्त इन्द्र मरुतस्त ओजः।
माध्यंदिने सवने वज्रहस्त
पिबा रुद्रेभिः सगणः सुशिप्र।।३।।

The Maruts who increased thy energy (and) strength, O Indra, praising thy power; thou with thunderbolt in hand, drink at the mid-day libation, accompanied by the Rudras, thus with a fine moustache.

त इन्न्वस्य मधुमद्विविप्र
इन्द्रस्य शर्धो मरुतो य आसन्।
येभिर्वृत्रस्यैषितो विवे-
दामर्मणो मन्यमानस्य मर्म।।४।।

Those same indeed encouraged him with sweet speech, the Maruts, who were Indra's guard; by whom impelled he found out the vulnerable parts of Vṛtra who deemed himself invulnerable.

मनुष्यदिन्द्र सवनं जुषाणः

पिबा सोमं शश्वते वीर्याय।

स आ ववृत्स्व हर्यश्व यज्ञैः

सरण्युभिरपो अर्णा सिसर्षि।।५।।

Like a man enjoying the libation (Enjoying the libations s Manu's), drink the soma for ever-renewed heroic strength; turn in, thou with tawny horses, (attracted) by the sacrifices. Together with the quick moving ones thou lettest flow the waters, the streams.

त्वमपो यद्ध वृत्रं जघन्वाँ

अत्याँ इव प्रासृजः सर्तवाजौ।

शयानमिन्द्र चरता वधेन

वव्रिवांसं परि देवीरदेवम्।।६।।

When thou indeed didst send off the waters like race horses to run at the tournament, having with the whirling weapon killed Vṛtra who (then) was lying there, him the demon who had shut up the goddesses.

यजाम इन्नमसा वृद्धमिन्द्रं

बृहन्तमृष्वमजरं युवानम्।

यस्य प्रिये ममतुर्यज्ञियस्य

न रोदसी महिमानं ममाते।।७।।

With adoration let us worship the full-grown, big exalted, never-ageing, ever-young Indra, whose—the adorable one's—greatness, the two dear worlds did measure, but not encompass.

इन्द्रस्य कर्म सुकृता पुरूणि
व्रतानि देवा न मिनन्ति विश्वे।
दाधार यः पृथिवीं द्यामुतेमां
जजान सूर्यमुषसं सुदंसाः॥८॥

Many are Indra's well-done deeds, none of the gods does infringe (his) laws; he steaded the earth and also the heaven there, he, the graet wonder-worker, brought forth the sun nd dawn.

अद्रोघ सत्यं तव तन्महित्वं
सद्यो यज्जातो अपिबो ह सोमम्।
न द्याव इन्द्र तवसस्त ओजो
नाहा न मासाः शरदो वरन्त॥९॥

O thou without guile, true is this the greatness that thou, hardly born, didst drink soma indeed; neither the days, nor the days and the nights, nor months, nor years may check the power of thee, O Indra, the strong one.

त्वं सद्यो अपिबो जात इन्द्र
मदाय सोमं परमे व्योमन्।
यद्ध द्यावापृथिवी आविवेशी-
रथाभवः पूर्व्यः कारुधायाः॥१०॥

Thou, Indra, when born didst partake at once of the soma unto intoxication in the highest heaven; when thou hadst indeed penetrated heaven and earth, then thou becamest the first feeder of the singer.

अहन्नहिं परिशयानमर्ण
ओजायमर्यानं तुविजात तव्यान्।
न तें महित्वमनु भूदध द्यौ-
र्यदन्यया स्फिग्याइक्षामवस्थाः।।११।।

Thou didst kill the dragon that did lie round the streams (and) was showing his strength, O strong born, O very strong one; heaven indeed did not equal thy greatness, whilst with one hip thou didst cover the earth.

यज्ञो हि तं इन्द्र वर्धनो भू-
दुत प्रियः सुतसोमो मियेधः।
यज्ञेन यज्ञमव यज्ञियः स-
न्यज्ञस्ते वज्रमहिहत्य आवत्।।१२।।

The sacrifice made thee wax strong, O Indra, and dear is to thee the sacrificial meal with the pressed soma juice; on account of the (former) sacrifice thy thunderbolt in the slaugher of Vṛtra.

यज्ञेनेन्द्रमवसा चक्रे अर्वा-
गैनं सुम्नाय नव्यसे ववृत्याम्।
यः स्तोमेभिर्वावृधे पूर्वेभि-
र्यो मध्यमेभिरुत नूतनेभिः।।१३।।

Through the sacrifice I brought here Indra with help: may I make him turn in for a new fortune, he who has grown strong by the old hymns, who did so by the middle and by the new ones.

विवेष यन्मा धिषणा जजान
स्तवै पुरा पार्यादिन्द्रमह्नः।

अंहसो यत्र पीपरद्यथा नो
नावेव यान्तमुभये हवन्ते।।१४।।

Since the divine inspiration has filled me, (the hymn) has come forth; I will praise Indra before the day of decision so that he may get us out of difficulty (there) where they on both sides call on him going in a ship,as it were.

आपूर्णो अस्य कलशः स्वाहा
सेक्तेव कोशं सिसिचे पिबध्यै।
समु प्रिया आववृत्रन्मदाय
प्रदक्षिणिदभि सोमास इन्द्रम्।।१५।।

Full to the brim is his cup, health ! Like a man pouring into a skin I have poured in for drinking; and indeed the dear soma-drinks turned to the right towards Indra for (his) intoxication.

न त्वा गभीरः पुरुहूत सिन्धु-
र्नाद्रयः परि षन्तो वरन्त।
इत्था सखिभ्य इषितो यदिन्द्रा
दृळ्हं चिदरुजो गव्यमूर्वम्।।१६।।

Not thee, O thou often called upon, did keep away the deep water, nor the surrounding mountains when thou, Indra, truly urged on didst for the friends break open the very firm mountain-cave of the cows.

शुनं हुवेम मघवानमिन्द्र-
मस्मिन्भरे नृतमं वाजसातौ।
शृण्वन्तमुग्रमूतये समत्सु
घ्नन्तं वृत्राणि संजितं धनानाम्।।१७।।

Hail! We call for help, in this battle, on the generous Indra, the gretest of man in winning booty, on him who listens, the fierce one in frays, the killer of enemies, the conqueror of riches.

म० ३ **No. 12** सू० ३३

प्र पर्वतानामुशती उपस्था-

दश्वे इव विषिते हासमाने।

गावेव शुभ्रे मातरा रिहाणे

विपाट्छुतुद्री पयसा जवेते।।१।।

[Viśvāmitra speaks:-] Forth from the womb of the mountains, eager like two untied racing steeds, like two fine cows, licking mothers, Vipāṭ and Śutudrī with their milky fluid are hurrying on.

इन्द्रेषिते प्रसवं भिक्षमाणे

अच्छा समुद्रं रथ्येव याथः।

समाराणे ऊर्मिभिः पिन्वमाने

अन्या वामन्यामप्येति शुभ्रे।।२।।

Sent on by Indra, praying for a strong current, you tend towards the sea like two charioteers, going together, swelling in waves; one of you, bright ones, follows the other.

अच्छा सिन्धुं मातृतमामयासं

विपाशमुर्वीं सुभगामगन्म।

वत्समिव मातरा संरिहाणे

समानं योनिमनु संचरन्ती।।३।।

I have come to the river, the most motherly, we have reached the broad and rich Vipāṭ; the two mothers are, as it were, licking the calf, moving together along the same (womb=) bed.

एना वयं पयसा पिन्वमाना
अनु योनिं देवकृतं चरन्तीः।
न वर्तवे प्रसवः सर्गतक्तः
किंयुर्विप्रो नद्यो जोहवीति॥४॥

[The rivers speak : —] We are swelling with this fluid, moving along the bed made by the god; the hurriedly galloping current is not to be checked; what is the desire of the priest tht he calls our entreatingly to the rivers?

रमध्वं मे वचसे सोम्याय
ऋतावरीरुप मुहूर्तमेवैः।
प्र सिन्धुमच्छा बृहती मनी-
षावस्युरह्वे कुशिकस्य सूनुः॥५॥

[Viśvāmitra :—] Stop a while in your hurry, you everflowing ones, for (the sake of) my kindly speech; the mighty hymn goes towards the river; desirous of help Kuśika's son has called out.

इन्द्रो अस्माँ अरदद्वज्रबाहु-
रपाहन्वृत्रं परिधिं नदीनाम्।
देवोऽनयत्सविता सुपाणि-
स्तस्य वयं प्रसवे याम उर्वीः॥६॥

[The rivers :—] Indra with the thunderbolt in his arms has unearthed us, he put out of the way Vṛtra, the enclosure of the rivers; the impelling god (Savitṛ?) with fine hands led us: at his behest we broad ones flow.

प्रवाच्यं शश्वधा वीर्यं१त-
दिन्द्रस्य कर्म यदहिं विवृश्चत्।
वि वज्रेण परिषदो जघा-
नायन्नापोऽयनमिच्छमानाः ॥७॥

[Viśvāmitra :—] To be praised for ever is this heroic feat, the deed of Indra, that he cut up the serpent; with the thunderbolt he smote away the besiegers, the waters flowed forth, eager for the course.

एतद्वचो जरितर्मापि मृष्ठा
आ यत्ते घोषानुत्तरा युगानि।
उक्थेषु कारो प्रति नो जुषस्व
मा नो नि कः पुरुषत्रा नमस्ते ॥८॥

[The rivers :—] This word of thine, to which the coming generations shall listen, do not forget; in the hymns praise us, O poet, do not run us down among men: honour to thee!

ओ षु स्वसारः कारवे शृणोत
ययौ वो दूरादनसा रथेन।
नि षू नमध्वं भवता सुपारा
अधोअक्षाः सिन्धवः स्रोत्याभिः ॥९॥

[Viśvāmitra :—] Listen, O Sisters, to the singer, he came from afar to you with cart and chariot; bent low down, be of easy banes (fordable) (be) blow the axle, O rivers, with your currents.

आ ते कारो शृणवामा वचांसि
ययाथ दूरादनसा रथेन।
नि ते नंसै पीप्यानेव योषा
मर्यायेव कन्या शश्वचै ते।।१०।।

[Viśvāmitra :—] We will listen to thy words, O singer, thou hast come from a far with cart and chariot; [one of the two rivers :] like a sucking woman I will bend down to thee; [the other river:]like a girl to a young man I will give way to thee (for an embrace, Sāy.).

यदङ्ग त्वा भरताः संतरेयु-
र्गव्यन्ग्राम इषित इन्द्रजूतः।
अर्षादह प्रसवः सर्गतक्त
आ वो वृणे सुमतिं यज्ञियानाम्।।११।।

If indeed the Bharatas, the band eager for booty, sent, impelled by Indra, have crossed thee, then may rush the hurriedly galloping current. (May the hurriedly galloping current flow off, when indeed the Bahratas....cross thee. (Hillebrandt, Lieder des Ṛgveda, p. 138). I request good grace of you who are worthy of worship.

अतारिषुर्भरता गव्यवः स-
मभक्त विप्रः सुमतिं नदीनाम्।
प्र पिन्वध्वमिषयन्तीः सुराधा
आ वक्षणाः पृणध्वं यात शीभम्।।१२।।

The conquering Bhratas have crossed, the singer has shared in the favour of the rivers; now swell, giving food (being) full of good gifts, fill the beds, go quickly !

उद्व ऊर्मिः शम्या हु-

न्त्वापो योक्त्राणि मुञ्चत।

मादुष्कृतौ व्येन-

साघ्न्यो शूनमारंताम्।।१३।।

May your wave lift up the pin, may the waters let go the thongs, may the two harmless, sinless bulls not come to grief.

म० ३ **No. 13** सू० ४२

उप नः सुतमा गहि सोममिन्द्र गवाशिरम्।

हरिभ्यां यस्ते अस्मयुः।।१।।

O Indra, with the two bay (horses) come to what we have pressed, to the soma mixed with milk; he who is our friend is thine.

तमिन्द्र मदमा गहि बर्हिःष्ठां ग्रावभिः सुतम्।

कुविन्न्वस्य तृष्णवः।।२।।

Approach, Indra, this drink standing on the बर्हिस्, pressed by the stones; with thou enjoy it? I wonder.

इन्द्रमित्था गिरो ममाच्छागुरिषिता इतः।

आवृते सोमपीतये।।३।।

Rightly my songs have gone towards Indra, sent from here, to turn him to the soma draught.

इन्द्रं सोमस्य पीतये स्तोमैरिह हवामहे।

उक्थेभिः कुविदागमत्।।४।।

With hymns we call Indra here for a drught of the soma I trust he may come (attracted) by the praises.

इन्द्र सोमाः सुता इमे तान्दधिष्व शतक्रतो।
जठरे वाजिनीवसो।।५।।

Indra, the somas are pressed here, you, of hundred powers, put them inside, into the belly, you rich in gifts (horses).

विद्या हि त्वा धनंजयं वाजेषु दधृषं कवे।
अधा ते सुम्नमीमहे।।६।।

We know thee as the conqueror of wealth, intrepid in battles, O wise one; hence we beg of thee good luck.

इममिन्द्र गवाशिरं यवाशिरं च नः पिब।
आगत्या वृषभिः सुतम्।।७।।

Indra, having come with the stallions, drink this our juice mixed with milk and mixed with barley.

तुभ्येदिन्द्र स्व ओक्ये३सोमं चोदामि पीतये।
एष रारन्तु ते हृदि।।८।।

In the own home I force the soma on thee for a draught; may it be well in the heart.

त्वां सुतस्य पीतये प्रत्नमिन्द्र हवामहे।
कुशिकासो अवस्यवः।।९।।

We call thee, Indra, the ancient one, to the drinking of the juice, we Kuśikas, needy of help.

म० ४ **No. 14** सू० ३०

नकिरिन्द्र त्वदुत्तरो न ज्यायाँ अस्ति वृत्रहन्।
नकिरेवा यथा त्वम्।।१।।

None, O Indra, is superior to thee, none is mightier, O killer of Vṛtra; no one even like unto thee.

सत्रा ते अनु कृष्टयो विश्वा चक्रेव वावृतुः।
सत्रा महाँ असि श्रुतः॥२॥

The people all together turn after thee like cart wheels, everywhere thou art heard of as great.

विश्वे चनेदना त्वा देवास इन्द्र युयुधुः।
यदहा नक्तमातिरः॥३॥

For, not even all the gods have then fought (vanquished) thee, when thou didst prolong the days into the night;

यत्रोत बाधितेभ्यश्चक्रं कुत्साय युध्यते।
मुषाय इन्द्र सूर्यम्॥४॥

And (on the occasion) where thou didst rob the wheel the sun, on behalf of the harassed ones, on behalf of Kutsa;

यत्र देवाँ ऋघायतो विश्वाँ अयुध्य एक इत्।
त्वमिन्द्र वनूँरहन्॥५॥

(On the occasion) where thou single-handed didst fight all the furious gods (and)didst slay the enemies, O Indra;—

यत्रोत मर्त्याय कमरिणा इन्द्र सूर्यम्।
प्रावः शचीभिरेतशम्॥६॥

When, moreover, thou didst, free the sun for a mere mortal, O Indra, thou didst help Etaśa with the powers.

किमादुतासि वृत्रहन्मघवन्मन्युमत्तमः।
अत्राह दानुमातिरः॥ ७॥

What ? Vṛtra-killer, liberal one, art thou not finally, full of the mightiest wrath? So in that (wrath) thou didst prevail over Dānu.

एतद्घेदुत वीर्यमिन्द्र चकर्थ पौंस्यम्।
स्त्रियं यद्दुर्हणायुवं वधीर्दुहितरं दिवः॥८॥

Besides, forsooth, Indra, thou didst perform this manly, heroic deed that thou didst kill the hard-hearted woman, the daughter of Dyaus.

दिवश्चिद्घा दुहितरं महान्महीयमानाम्।
उषासमिन्द्र सं पिणक्॥९॥

Thou Indra, great one, didst crush even Dyauś's daughter Uṣas, who behaved haughtily.

अपोषा अनसः सरत्संपिष्टादह बिभ्युषी।
नि यत्सीं शिश्नथद्वृषा॥१०॥

Uṣas, frightened, then jumped from the wrecked car when the strong one hasd smashed it to pieces.

एतदस्या अनः शये सुसंपिष्टं विपाश्या।
ससार सीं परावतः॥११॥

This her vehicle, smashed to bits, lies in the Vipāṭ; she had made it to run from afar.

उत सिन्धुं विबाल्यं वितस्थानामधि क्षमि।
परिष्ठा इन्द्र मायया॥१२॥

By divine art thou, Indra, didst hem in as well the river Vibālī which spread over the earth.

उत शुष्णस्य धृष्णुया प्र मृक्षो अभि वेदनम्।
पुरो यदस्य सं पिणक्॥१३॥

Boldly thou didst seize Śuṣṇa's property when thou didst break his strongholds.

उत दासं कौलितरं बृहतः पर्वतादधि।
अवाहन्निन्द्र शम्बरम्।।१४।।

Also the Dāsa Śambara, Kulitara's son, thou, Indra, didst throw down from the mighty mountain.

उत दासस्य वर्चिनः सहस्राणि शतावधीः।
अधि पञ्च प्रधीँरिव।।१५।।

Again, a hundred thousand and five (thousand), besides, of the Dāsa Varcin's men thou didst cut up like fellies.

उत त्यं पुत्रमग्रुवः परावृक्तं शतक्रतुः।
उक्थेष्विन्द्र आभजत्।।१६।।

The Śatakratu made the son of the unmarried, the castaway, also share in the songs.

उत त्या तुर्वशायदू अस्नातारा शचीपतिः।
इन्द्रो विद्वाँ अपारयत्।।१७।।

And wise Indra, the lord of strength, brought over (the water) the two , Yadu and Turvaśa, without their getting wet.

उत त्या सद्य आर्या सरयोरिन्द्र पारतः।
अर्णाचित्ररथावधीः।। १८।।

Again thou, Indra, didst all of sudden kill the two Āryas, Aruṇa and Citraratha, from the other bank of the Sarayu.

अनु द्वा जहिता नयोऽन्धं श्रोणं च वृत्रहन्।
न तत्ते सुम्नमष्टवे।।१९।।

Thou, Vṛtra-killer, didst lead a long the two forsaken ones, the blind and the lame: such a blessing of thine is not to be attained (by others).

शतमश्मन्मयीनां पुरामिन्द्रो व्यास्यत्।
दिवोदासाय दाशुषे।।२०।।

For Divodāsa, liberal in offering, Indra broke one hundred strongholds of solid rock.

अस्वापयद्दभीतये सहस्रा त्रिंशतं हथैः।
दासानामिन्द्रो मायया।।२१।।

On behalf of Dabhīti Indra by his divine power sent asleep 30,000 Dāsas with deadly blows.

स घेदुतासि वृत्रहन्समान इन्द्र गोपतिः।
यस्ता विश्वानि चिच्युषे।।२२।।

Being such of a truth, thou, O Vṛtra-killer, art the universal lord of cattle, Indra, who hast shaken everything.

उत नूनं यदिन्द्रियं करिष्या इन्द्र पौंस्यम्।
अद्या नकिष्टदा मिनत्।।२३।।

And whatever manly Indra-deed thou shouldst perform to-day, O Indra, none could prevent it.

वामंवामं त आदुरे
देवो ददात्वर्यमा।
वामं पूषा वामं भगो
वामं देवः करूळती।।२४।।

May, O attentive one, god Aryaman grant thee merely

nice things, nice things Bhaga, nice things Pūṣan, nice things the god with decaying teeth.

म० ५ **No. 15** सू० १

अबो॑ध्य॒ग्निः स॒मिधा॒ जना॑नां॒

प्रति॑ धे॒नुमि॑वाय॒तीमु॒षास॑म्।

य॒हा इ॑व॒ प्र व॒यामु॒ज्जिहा॑ना॒ः

प्र भा॒नवः॑ सिस्रते॒ नाक॒मच्छ॑।।१।।

Agni has been awakened by the fuel of the people towards (the time when) Uṣas was approaching like milch cow; as birds fly up to the branch, (his) rays stream towards the sky.

अबो॑धि॒ होता॑ य॒जथा॑य दे॒वा-

नू॒र्ध्वो॑ अ॒ग्निः सु॒मना॑ः प्रा॒तर॑स्थात्।

समि॑द्धस्य॒ रूश॑ददर्शि॒ पाजो॑

म॒होन्द्रेवस्तम॑सो॒ निर॑मोचि।।२।।

The हो has been awakened to worship the gods, the kind Agni a rose high in the morning; the glow of the kindled one was seen, the great god was released from darkness.

यदीं॑ ग॒णस्य॑ रश॒नामजी॑ग॒ः

शुचि॑रङ्क्ते॒ शुचि॑भि॒र्गोभि॑र॒ग्निः।

आद्दक्षि॑णा युज्यते वाज॒य-

न्त्यु॑त्ता॒नामू॒र्ध्वो अ॑ध्यज्जु॒हूभिः॑।।३।।

When he has roused the row (rope) of the host (of followers), the pure Agni is anointed with pure ghee; then the strength-giving sacrificial gift is prepared; he, erect, drinks with (his) tongues (that which is raised and) sprayed (into the fire).

अग्निमच्छा देवयतां मनांसि
चक्षूंषीव सूर्ये सं चरन्ति।
यदीं सुवाते उषसा विरूपे
श्वेतो वाजी जायते अग्रे अह्नाम्।।४।।

The hearts of the pious (turn) towrads Agni, as the eyes meet in the sun; when the two of different colour, Uṣas (and the night) bring him forth, then he is born as a white horse at daybreak.

जनिष्ट ही जेन्यो अग्रे अह्नां
हितो हितेष्वरुषो वनेषु।
दमेदमे सप्त रत्ना दधानो-
ऽग्निर्होता नि षसादा यजीयान्।।५।।

The noble one was born at the beginning of the days, the red one, laid well in the well laid fuel; distributing seven treasures in every house, Agni is seated as the होतृ, very skilled in sacrifice.

अग्निर्होता न्यसीदद्यजीया-
नुपस्थे मातुः सुरभा उ लोके।
युवा कविः पुरूनिःष्ठ ऋतावा
धर्ता कृष्टीनामुत मध्य इद्धः।।६।।

A होतृ, very skilled in sacrifice, Agni sat down at the mother's bosom, a sweet smelling, wide place; the youth, the wise one, residing in many places, the holy, the upholder, being kindled in the midst of the people.

प्र णु त्यं विप्रमध्वरेषु साधु-
मग्निं होतारमीळते नमोभिः।
आ यस्ततान रोदसी ऋतेन
नित्यं मृजन्ति वाजिनं घृतेन॥७॥

Now this priest, good at sacrifices, Agni, the होतृ, they praise with worship, him who according to law spread out afar heaven and earth; with ghee they make him shine, the never-failing charger.

मार्जाल्यो मृज्यते स्वे दमूनाः
कविप्रशस्तो अतिथिः शिवो नः।
सहस्रसृङ्गो वृषभस्तदोजा
विश्वाँ अग्ने सहसा प्रास्यन्यान्॥८॥

He who likes to be cleaned is cleansed in the his own proper palce, the house-friend, the guest, praised by singers, kind to us; the bull with thousand horns with the strength of that; in power, Agni, thou surpassest all the tohers.

प्र सद्यो अग्ने अत्येष्यन्या-
नाविर्यस्मै चारुतमो बभूथ।
ईळेन्यो वपुष्यो विभावा
प्रियो विशामतिथिर्मानुषीणाम्॥९॥

O Agni, at once thou surpssest the others for him to whom thou hast appeared as the most lovely, praiseworthy, of andsome form, shining, the dear guest of the human clans.

तुभ्यं भरन्ति क्षितयो यविष्ठ
बलिमग्ने अन्तित ओत दूरात्।
आ भन्दिष्ठस्य सुमतिं चिकिद्धि
बृहत्ते अग्ने महि शर्म भद्रम्।।१०।।

O Agni, most youthful one, to thee the people bring (their) offering from near and afar; notice the good will of the best worshipper; mighty, great, auspicious is the protection,Agni.

आद्य रथं भानुमो भानुमन्त-
मग्ने तिष्ठ यजतेभिः समन्तम्।
विद्वान्पथीनामुर्व१न्तरिक्ष-
मेह देवान्हविरद्याय वक्षि।।११।।

Ascend to-day, brilliant one, the brilliant car, Agni, together with the gods; knowing the large midspace (distance) between (of) the ways, bring the gods here to this हविस्-feast. (Or and better:—) knowing the ways, bring the gods along the large mid-space here to this हविस् -feast.

अवोचाम कवये मेध्याय-
वचो वन्दारु वृषभाय वृष्णे।
गविष्ठिरो नमसा स्तोममग्नौ
दिवीव रुक्ममुरुव्यञ्चमश्रेत्।।१२।।

To the wise one, worthy of worship, we have promounced. This praising speech, to the strong bull; Gaviṣ ṭaira has, worshipping, made this song to before Agni, the Love spreading gold in the sky, as it were.

मं० ५ **No. 16** सू० ६३

ऋतस्य गोपावधि तिष्ठथो रथं
सत्यधर्माणा परमे व्योममनि।
यमत्र मित्रावरुणावथे युवं
तस्मै वृष्टिर्मधुमत्पिन्वते दिवः॥१॥

O keepers of the (world's) order, whose law prevails in the highest heaven, you ascend the car; whom you, mitrā-Varuṇā, help here, to him the rain with sweetness streams from heaven.

सम्राजावस्य भुवनस्य राजथो
मित्रावरुणा विदथे स्वर्दृशा।
वृष्टिं वां राधो अमृतत्वमीमहे
द्यावापृथिवी वि चरन्ति तन्यवः॥२॥

As overlords over this world you, Mitrā_Varuṇā, rule in wisdom, you, looking like the sun, we beg for rain, your grace, (and) immortality; the thunders hurry right through heaven and earth.

सम्राजा उग्रा वृषभा दिवस्पती
पृथिव्या मित्रावरुणा विचर्षणी।
चित्रेभिरभ्रैरुप तिष्ठथो रवं
द्यां वर्षयथो असुरस्य मायया॥३॥

Fierce overlords, bills, masters of heaven (and) earth, Mitrā-Varuṇā, the ever-active ones, you appraoch in manycoloured clouds to (at) the crash (of the thunder). By Asura power you make heaven rain.

माया वां मित्रावरुणा दिवि श्रिता
सूर्यो ज्योतिश्चरति चित्रमायुधम्।
तमभ्रेण वृष्ट्या गूहथो दिवि
पर्जन्य द्रप्सा मधुमन्त ईरते।।४।।

Your power, Mitrā-Varuṇā, is set in heaven; the sun, a light and a marvellous weapon, moves on; with cloud (and) rain you hide him in the sky; the sweet drops, Parjanya, come (down).

रथं युञ्जते मरुतः शुभे सुखं
शूरो न मित्रावरुणा गविष्टिषु।
रजांसि चित्रा वि चरन्ति तन्यवो
दिवः सम्राजा पयसा न उक्षतम्।।५।।

Like a hero in battles the Maruts yoke the easy-moving car for a pageant, O Mitrā-Varuṇā; the thunderers rush through the paces of various hues; sprinkle us, O overlords, with heaven's milk.

वाचं सु मित्रावरुणाविरावतीं
पर्जन्यश्चित्रां वदति त्विषीमतीम्।
अभ्रा वसत मरुतः सु मायया
द्यां वर्षयतमरुणामरेपसम्।।६।।

O Mitrā-Varuṇā, a very refreshing, wondrous, flashing speech Parjanya speaks, the Maruts by their power shall clad themselves wholly in clouds; you make heaven, the red, bright one, rain.

धर्मणा मित्रावरुणा विपश्चिता
व्रता रक्षेथे असुरस्य मायया।

ऋतेन विश्वं भुवनं वि राजथः
सूर्यमा धत्थो दिवि चित्र्यं रथम्।।७।।

Following the law you, wise Mitrā-Varuṇā, guard with Asura power the ordinances; rightly you govern all the world, you fix the sun, the luminous car, in heaven.

म० ५ **No. 17** सू० ७३

यदद्य स्थः परावति
यदर्वावत्यश्विना।
यद्वा पुरू पुरुभुजा
यदन्तरिक्ष आ गतम्।।१।।

Whether you stay now far or near, O Aśvinā, whether in many places (here on earth) on in the mid-space, come here, you who are helping many.

इह त्या पुरुभूतमा
पुरू दंसांसि बिभ्रता।
वरस्या याम्यध्रिगू
हुवे तुविष्टमा भुजे।।२।।

These very same here, present in most places, carrying many wonderful things, them who proceed unchecked I approach; the strongest oncs from a desire after fortune I call here for enjoyment.

ईर्मान्यद्वपुषे वपु-
श्चक्रं रथस्य येमथुः।
पर्यन्या नाहुषा युगा
मह्ना रजांसि दीयथः।।३।।

The one beautiful wheel of the car you stopped here (on earth) for your glory; with the other you hurry quick through the spaces to the clans of Nahus.

तदू षु वामेना कृतं
विश्वा यद्वामनु ष्टवे।
नाना जातावरेपसा
समस्मे बन्धुमेयथुः।।४।।

Acomplished through that (wheel) was this your deed which I praise as yours (especially), O Viśvās; born otherwise, without taint, you have entered kinship with us.

आ यद्वां सूर्या रथं
तिष्ठद्रघुष्यदं सदा।
परि वामरुषा वयो
घृणा वरन्त आतपः।।५।।

When Sūryā got on your ever-swiftly moving car, the red birds kept the glowing heat away from you.

युवोरत्रिश्चिकेतति
नरा सुम्नेन चेतसा।
धर्मं यद्वामरेपसं
नासत्यास्ना भुरण्यति।।६।।

May Atri think of you with a friendly mind, O Men, when with (his) mouth he fans the spotless glow for you, O Nāsatyā.

उग्रो वां ककुहो ययिः शृण्वे यामेषु संतनिः।
यद्वां दंसोभिरश्विनात्रिर्नराववर्तति।।७।।

Huge is your excellent animal, used to going; the sound during his marches is heard, when on account of (your) wondrous deeds, O Aśvins, O Men, Atri makes you turn in.

मध्व ऊ षु मधूयुवा
रुद्रा सिषक्ति पिप्युषी।
यत्समुद्राति पर्षथः
पक्वाः पृक्षो भरन्त वाम्।।८।।

You lovers of sweetness, Rudras, she, swelling with sweetness, accompanies you; when you have crossed the airy oceans, cooked food is brought to you.

सत्यमिद्वा उ अश्विना
युवामाहुर्मयोभुवा।
ता यामन्यामहूतमा
यामन्ना मृळयत्तमा।।९।।

Truly indeed they call you Aśvins, bringers of good cheer, you two who are called upon most at the sacrifice and in need, most gracious at the sacrifice here.

इमा ब्रह्माणि वर्ध-
नाश्विभ्यां सन्तु शंतमा।
या तक्षाम रथाँ इ-
वावोचाम बृहन्नमः।।१०।।

May these furthering prayers be most pleasing to the Aśvins, (Prayers) which we fashion like cars; we have pronounced a mighty (hymn of) worship.

म० ५ **No. 18** सू० ८०

द्युतद्यामानं बृहतीमृतेन
ऋतावरीमरुणप्सुं विभातीम्।
देवीमुषसं स्वरावहन्तीं
प्रति विप्रासो मतिभिर्जरन्ते॥१॥

Her on the brilliant road, the sublime, who moves on ccording to eternal order her of red appearance the shining a one, the goddess Uṣas, who brings the realm of light: (her) the priests welcome with their songs.

एषा जनं दर्शता बोधयन्ती
सुगान्पथः कृण्वती यात्यग्रे॥
बृहद्रथा बृहती विश्वमि-
न्वोषा ज्योतिर्यच्छत्यग्रे अह्नाम्॥२॥

She, the beautiful, rousing the people (from sleep), making easily passable the paths, marches ahead (of the sun); she with lofty car, the sublime, all-impelling one, yields the light in the beginning of the days.

एषा गोभिररुणेभिर्युजा-
नास्रेधन्ती रयिमप्रायु चक्रे।
पथो रदन्ती सुविताय देवी
पुरुष्टुता विश्ववारा वि भाति॥३॥

She, driving with the red oxen, not going wrong, never failing, has granted wealth; the goddess, digging paths of a safe progress, praised by all, in whom every boon, she shines around.

एषाव्यैनी भवति द्विबर्हा

आविष्कृण्वाना तन्वं पुरस्तात्।

ऋतस्य पन्थामन्वेति साधु

प्रजानतीव न दिशो मिनाति।।४।।

She of changing clours there becomes of duble greatness, displaying her appearance (body) in the East; she follows closely the path of the eternal order, as one well aware she does not miss the quarters.

एषा शुभ्रा न तन्वो विदा-

नोर्ध्वेव स्नाती दृशये नो अस्थात्।

अप द्वेषो बाधमाना तमां-

स्युषा दिवो दुहिता ज्योतिषागात्।।५।।

She there like a beautiful (woman) finding her limbs (to be well-formed), stands when bathing erect, as it were, before our sight; banishing hatred (and)darkness Uṣas, the daughter of heaven, has come with light.

एषा प्रतीची दुहिता दिवो नॄ-

न्योषेव भद्रा नि रिणीते अप्सः।

व्यूर्ण्वती दाशुषे वार्याणि

पुनर्ज्योतिर्युवतिः पूर्वथाकः।।६।।

She, the daughter of heaven, bends like a gentlewoman in the presence of men her form; she unfolds boons to the liberal sacrificer; again as before the maid has created light.

म० ७ **No. 19** सू० ६१

उद्वां चक्षुर्वरुण सुप्रतीकं

देवयोरेति सूर्यस्ततन्वान्।

अभि यो विश्वा भुवनानि चष्टे

स मन्युं मर्त्येष्वा चिकेत॥१॥

The lovely eye of you two gods, O (Mitra and) Varuṇa, rises, the sun, spreading (light); he who looks after all (creatures), he notices, the zealous mind in mortals here.

प्र वां स मित्रावरुणावृतावा

विप्रो मन्मानि दीर्घश्रुदियर्ति।

यस्य ब्रह्माणि सुक्रतू अवाथ

आ यत्क्रत्वा न शरदः पृणैथे॥२॥

For you, O Mitrā-Varuṇā, this pious priest renowned after, sends forth his songs of devotion that you, wise, ones, may his prayers, that you may make full his years according, as it were, to (his) wish.

प्रोरोर्मित्रावरुणा पृथिव्याः

प्र दिव ऋष्वाद्बृहतः सुदानू।

स्पशो दधाथे ओषधीषु वि-

क्ष्वृधग्यतो अनिमिषं रक्षमाणा॥३॥

Further than the wide earth and the lofty, huge sky you, O bounteous ones, extend; you have placed into the plants and the human abodes the spies, you, watching without a winking of the eye those that go glone. (Or :—)...placed your spies that go separately, in plants and abodes, ye that protect with unwinking eye. (Macdonell, Reader, p. 121).

शंसा मित्रस्य वरुणस्य धाम
शुष्मो रोदसी बद्बधे महित्वा।
अयन्मासा अयज्वनामवीराः
प्र यज्ञमन्मा वृजनं तिराते।।४।।

I will praise the ordinance of Mitra (and) Varuṇa; their force presses apart the two worlds with might. May the months of non-sacrificers pass without sons; may he whose heart is set on sacrifice further his party.

अमूरा विश्वा वृषणाविमा वां
न यासु चित्रं ददृशे न यक्षम्।
द्रुहः सचन्ते अनृता जनानां
न वां निण्यान्यचिते अभूवन्।।५।।

Clever bulls that both of you are, yours are these (songs) in which there is neither marvel nor magic. Misfortune follows dishonesty of men, no secrets were (ever) unknown to you.

समु वां यज्ञं महयं नमोभि-
र्हुवे वां मित्रावरुणा सवाधः।
प्र वां मन्मान्यृचसे नवानि
कृतानि ब्रह्म जुजुषन्निमानि।।६।।

For you I will solemnis the sacrifice with worship, I call on you, Mitrā-Varuṇā, with zeal; for your praise are the new hymns, may these prayers offered you be pleasing.

इ॒यं दे॑व पु॒रोहि॑तिर्यु॒वभ्यां॑

य॒ज्ञेषु॑ मित्रावरुणावकारि।

विश्वा॑नि दु॒र्गा पि॑पृतं ति॒रो नो॑

यू॒यं पा॑त स्व॒स्तिभि॒ः सदा॑ नः।।७।।

This priestly service, O gods, has been rendered to you two at sacrifices, O Mitrā-Varuṇā. Take us across all hardships. Do you protect us with blessings evermore.

म० ७ **No. 20** सू० ७१

अप॒ स्वसु॑रु॒षसो॒ नग्जि॑हीते

रि॒णाक्ति॑ कृ॒ष्णवीर॑रु॒षाय॒ पन्था॑म्।

अश्वा॑मघा॒ गोम॑घा वां हुवेम॒

दिवा॒ नक्तं॒ शरु॑म॒स्मद्यु॑योतम्।।१।।

Night departs from her sister Dawn. The black one yields a path to the ruddy (sun). O you that are rich in horses, rich in cows, on you two we would call: by day (and) night ward of the arrow from us.

उ॒पाया॑तं दा॒शुषे॒ मर्त्या॑य॒

रथे॑न वा॒मम॑श्विना॒ वह॑न्ता।

यु॒यु॒तम॒स्मदनि॑रा॒ममी॑वां॒

दिवा॒ नक्तं॑ माध्वी॒ त्रासी॑थां नः।।२।।

Come here to (the aid of) the pious mortal, carrying wealth on (your) car, O Aśvinā, keep away from us drought (and) disease; may you, lovers fo honey, protect us day (and) night.

आ वां रथमवमस्यां व्युष्टौ
सुम्नायवो वृषणो वर्तयन्तु।
स्यूमगभस्तिमृतयुग्भि-
रश्वैराश्विना वसुमन्तं वहेथाम्।।३।।

Let your kindly stallions whirl hither our car at (this) latest day-break. Do you, O Aśvinā bring (the car), whose shafts are thongs, with your horses yoked in due time hither, laden with wealth.

यो वां रथो नृपती अस्ति वोळ्हा
त्रिवन्धुरो वसुमाँ उस्रयामा।
आ न एना नासत्योप यात-
मभि यद्वां विश्वप्स्न्यो जिगाति।।४।।

The car, O lords of men, that is your vehicle, three-seated, filled with riches, faring at day-break, with that come hither to us Nāsatyā, in order that, laden with all food, for you it may approach us.

युवं च्यवानं जरसोऽमुमुक्तं
नि पेदव ऊहथुराशुमश्वम्।
निरंहसस्तमसः स्पर्तमत्रिं
नि जाहुषं शिथिरे धातमन्तः।।५।।

You two released Cyavāna from old age, you brought a swift horse to pedu; you rescued Atri from distress and darkness; you placed Jāhuṣa right into the open.

इयं मनीषा इयमश्विना गी-
रिमां सुवृक्तिं वृषणा जुषेथाम्।

इमा ब्रह्माणि युवयून्यग्म-

न्यूयं पात स्वस्तिभिः सदा नः ॥६॥

This is my thought, this, O Aśvins, my song, Accept gladly this song of prise, you mighty ones. These prayers have gone, addressed to you. Do you protect us with blessings evermore.

मं० ७ **No. 21** सू० ७७

उपो रुरुचे युवतिर्न योषा

विश्वं जीवं प्रसुवन्ती चरायै।

अभूदग्निः समिधे मानुषाणा-

मकर्ज्योतिर्बाधमाना तमांसि ॥१॥

Hither she has shone like a youthful woman, stirring every living creature to motion, Agni was ready to be lit (by) men, forcing away darkness (Uṣas) made light.

विश्वं प्रतीची सप्रथा उदस्था-

द्रुशद्वासो बिभ्रती शुक्रमश्वैत्।

हिरण्यवर्णा सुदृशीकसंदृ-

ग्गवां माता नेत्र्यह्नामरोचि ॥२॥

In the face of the universe she rose, spread far and wide; wearing a glowing robe she shone (all) white; of golden colour, beautiful countenance, the mother of kine, the leader of days, she beamed forth.

देवानां चक्षुः सुभगा वहन्ती

श्वेतं नयन्ती सुदृशीकमश्वम्।

उषा अदर्शि रश्मिभिर्व्यक्ता
चित्रामघा विश्वमनु प्रभूता ॥३॥

The blessed one, carrying the gods' eye, leading the white, beautiful horse, Uṣas has been seen adorned with (her) rays, with wondrous gifts, spreading all over the world.

अन्तिवामा दूरे अमित्रमुच्छो-
र्वीं गव्यूतिमभयं कृधी नः।
यावय द्वेष आ भरा वसूनि
चोदय राधो गृणते मघोनि ॥४॥

With riches at hand shine far off the foe, grant wide pasture (and) safety to us, ward off foes, bring wealth, speed bounty for the singer, O generous one.

अस्मे श्रेष्ठेभिर्भानुभिर्वि भा-
ह्युषो देवि प्रतिरन्ती न आयुः।
इषं च नो दधती विश्ववारे
गोमदश्वावद्रथवच्च राधः ॥५॥

Among us flame up with most brilliant rays, O Dawn, O goddess, lengthening our life, granting us food and bounty in kine, horses and chariots, O you with every gift.

यां त्वा दिवो दुहितर्वर्धय-
न्त्युषः सुजाते मतिभिर्वसिष्ठाः।
सास्मासु धा रयिमृष्वं बृहन्तं
यूयं पात स्वस्तिभिः सदा नः ॥६॥

Thou, O daughter of heaven, Dawn, nobly born, whom

the Vasiṣṭhas make great by their songs, do thou bestow on us vast, increasing riches; do you protect us with blessings evermore.

म० ७ **No. 22** सू० ८६

धीरा त्वस्य महिना जनूंषि
वि यस्तस्तम्भ रोदसी चिदुर्वी।
प्र नाकमृष्वं नुनुदे बृहन्तं
द्विता नक्षत्रं पप्रथच्च भूम।।१।।

Firm (stand) the generations (creatures) through the might of him who has propped asunder even the two wide worlds; he has set in motion the lofty expanded firmament, and the day-star in both directions, and he spread out the earth.

उत स्वया तन्वा३ सं वदे त-
त्कदा न्वं१ तर्वरुणे भुवानि।
किं मे हव्यमहृणानो जुषेत
कदा मृळीकं सुमना अभि ख्यम्।।२।।

And I converse thus with myself: "When, pray, shall I be in (the favour of) Varuṇa? Will he enjoy free from wrath, an oblation of mine ? when shall I, of good cheer, perceive his mercy ?

पृच्छे तदेनो वरुण दिदृ-
क्षूपो एमि चिकितुषो विपृचछम्।
समानमिन्मे कवयश्चिदाहु-
रयं ह तुभ्यं वरुणो हृणीते।।३।।

I ask about that sin, O Varuṇa, with a desire to find out; I approach the wise in order to ask; the sages say one and the same thing to me: "This Varuṇa is wroth with thee".

किमाग॑ आस वरुण॒ ज्येष्ठं॒
यत्स्तो॒तारं॒ जिघां॑ससि॒ सखा॑यम्।
प्र तन्मे॑ वोचो दूळभ स्वधा॒मो-
ऽव॑ त्वाने॒ना नम॑सा तु॒र इ॑याम्॥४॥

What has been that chief sin, O Varuṇa, that thou desirest to slay thy praiser, a friend ? Proclaim that to me, thou that art hard to deceive, self-dependent one: thee would I, free from sin, eagerly appease with adoration.

अव॑ द्रु॒गधानि॒ पित्र्या॑ सृजा॒ नो-
ऽव॒ या व॒यं च॑कृ॒मा त॒नूभिः॑।
अव॑ राजन्पशु॒तृपं॒ न ता॒युं
सृ॒जा व॒त्सं न दाम्नो॒ वसि॑ष्ठम्॥५॥

Set us free from the misdeeds of our fathers from those that we have committed by ourselves, Release Vasiṣṭha, O King, like a cattle-steling thief, like a calf from a rope.

न स स्वो दक्षो॑ वरुण॒ ध्रुति॒ः सा
सुरा॑ म॒न्युर्वि॑भीद॑को॒ अचि॑त्तिः।
अस्ति॒ ज्याया॒न्कनी॑यस उपा॒रे
स्वप्न॑श्च॒नेदनृ॑तस्य प्रयो॒ता॥६॥

It was not my own intent, O, Varuṇa, it was a trap: liquor, anger, dice, thoughtlessness, the elder is in (fault of) the offence of the younger; not even sleep is the warder off of wrong.

अरं दासो न मीळ्हुषे करा-
ण्यहं देवाय भूर्णयेऽनागाः।
अचेतयदचितो देवो अर्यो
गृत्सं राये कवितरो जुनाति॥७॥

I will, like a slave, sinless do service to the gracious, zealous god. The lord, the god made the thoughtless think; he, the wiser, speeds the experienced man to wealth.

अयं सु तुभ्यं वरुण स्वधावो
हृदि स्तोम उपश्रितश्चिदस्तु।
शं नः क्षेमे शमु योगे नो अस्तु
यूयं पात स्वस्तिभिः सदा नः॥८॥

Let this praise be well impressed on thy heart, O self-dependent Varuṇa. Let us have prosperity in possession, prosperity also in acquisition. Do you protect us with blessings evermore.

मं० ७ **No. 23** सू० ९५

प्र क्षोदसा धायसा सस्र एषा
सरस्वती धरुणमायसी पूः।
प्रबाबधाना रथ्येव याति
विश्वा अपो महिना सिन्धुरन्याः॥१॥

With her refreshing flood Sarasvatī here flows on, a stronghold, an iron fort, the river moves on a road, as it were, pressing on by its might all other waters.

एकाचेतत्सरस्वती नदीनां
शुचिर्यती गिरिभ्य आ समुद्रात्।
रायश्चेतन्ती भुवनस्य भूरे-
र्घृतं पयो दुदुहे नाहुषाय।।२।।

Sarasvatī alone of the rivers is famous, the pure, moving from the mountains to the sea, watching over wealth and the many beings; for Nīhuṣa she let flow ghee and milk.

स वावृधे नर्यो योषणासु
वृषा शिशुर्वृषभो यज्ञियासु।
स वाजिनं मघवभ्द्यो दधाति
वि सातये तन्वं मामृजीत।।३।।

He (Sarasvat) friendly to men, prospered among females, the strong young bull among (the) sacred women; he bestows a conquering horse on the liberl ones, may he stroke the (horse's) body for gain.

उत स्या न सरस्वती जुषा-
णोप श्रवत्सुभगा यज्ञे अस्मिन्।
मितज्ञुभिर्नमस्यैरियाना
राया युजा चिदुत्तरा सखिभ्यः।।४।।

May now the blessed Sarasvatī here, pleased, give ear to us at this sacrifice; she is approached by worshipping (people) with knees bent, she through her lasting wealth better than her friends.

इमा जुह्वाना युष्मदा नमोभिः
प्रति स्तोमं सरस्वति जुषस्व।

तव शर्मन्प्रियतमे दधाना

उप स्थेयाम शरणं न वृक्षम्॥५॥

We are scrificing these (oblations) with worship in your name, accept, O Sarasvatī, our hymn of praise. May we placing ourselves under the most appreciated protection, get near thy shelter as to a tree.

अयमु ते सरवति वसिष्ठो

द्वारावृतस्य सुभगे व्यावः।

वर्ध शुभ्रे स्तुवते रासि वाजा-

न्यूयं पात स्वस्तिभिः सदा नः॥६॥

For thee, Sarasvatī, Vasiṣṭha here has unlocked the two doors fo the rite, O blessed one; grow, beautiful one, give strength to him who praises thee. Do you protect us with blessings evermore.

मं० ८ **No. 24** सू० २९

बभ्रुरेको विषुणः सूनरो

युवाञ्ज्यङ्क्ते हिरण्ययम्॥१॥

One is brown, varied in form, bountiful, young. He derns himself with a golden ornament.

योनिमेक आ ससाद द्योतनो

ऽन्तर्देवेषु मेधिरः॥२॥

One has, shining, occupied his receptacle, the wise among the gods.

वाशीमेको बिभर्ति हस्त आयसी-

मन्तर्देवेषु निध्रुविः॥३॥

One bears in his hand an iron axe, strenuous among the gods.

व॒ज्रमेको॑ बिभर्ति॒ हस्त॒ आहि॑तं॒

तेन॑ वृ॒त्राणि॑ जिघ्नते ॥४॥

One bears a bolt placed in this hand: with it he slays the foes.

ति॒ग्ममेको॑ बिभर्ति॒ हस्त॒ आयु॑धं॒

शुचि॑रु॒ग्रो जला॑षभेषजः ॥५॥

One, bright, fierce, with cooling remedies, bears in his hand a sharp weapon.

प॒थ एकः॑ पीपाय॒ तस्क॑रो यथाँ

एष वे॑द निधी॒नाम् ॥६॥

One makes the paths prosperous; like a thief he knows of treasures.

त्रीण्येक॑ उरुगा॒यो वि च॑क्रमे॒

यत्र॑ दे॒वासो॒ मद॑न्ति ॥७॥

One, wide-spacing, makes three strides to where the gods are exhilarated.

विभि॒र्द्वा च॑रत॒ एक॑या स॒ह

प्र प्र॑वा॒सेव॑ वसतः ॥८॥

With birds two fare, together with one woman: like two travellers they go on journeys.

सदो॒ द्वा च॑क्राते उप॒मा दिवि

स॒म्राजा॑ स॒र्पिरा॑सुती ॥९॥

Two, as highest, have made for themselves a seat in heaven: two sovereign kings who receive melted butter as their draught.

अर्च॑न्त॒ एके॒ महि॒ साम॑ मन्वत॒

तेन॒ सूर्य॑मरोचयन्॥१०॥

Singing, some thought of a great chant: by it they caused the sun to shine.

(Translation taken over from Macdonell, Reader, pp. 147-52).

म० १० **No. 25** सू० ७२

दे॒वानां॒ न व॒यं जाना॒

प्र वो॑चाम विप॒न्यया॑।

उ॒क्थेषु॑ श॒स्यमा॑नेषु

यः पश्या॒दुत्त॑रे यु॒गे॥१॥

Let us now in admiration announce the births of the gods (on behalf of him) who is to see them in the hymns to be chanted at a coming age.

ब्रह्म॑ण॒स्पति॑रे॒ता सं

क॒र्मार॑ इवाधमत्।

दे॒वानां॑ पू॒र्व्ये॑ यु॒गे-

ऽस॑त॒ सद॑जायत॥२॥

Brahmaṇaspati like a smith forged together these (births), in a former age of the gods existence sprang from nonexistence.

देवानां पूर्व्ये युगे-

ऽसतः सदजायत।

तदाशा अन्वजायन्त

तदुत्तानपदस्परि ॥३॥

In the mist age of the gods existence sprang from non-existence, after that the quarters were produced, from that Uttānapad.

भूर्जज्ञ उत्तानपदो

भुव आशा अजायन्त।

अदितेर्दक्षो अजायत

दक्षाद्वदितिः परि ॥४॥

The earth was produced from Uttānpad, the quarters from the earth; from Aditi Dakṣa was born, from Dakṣa in her turn Aditi.

अदितिर्ह्यजनिष्ट

दक्ष या दुहिता तव।

तां देवा अन्वजायन्त

भद्रा अमृतबन्धवः ॥५॥

Aditi, who is thy daughter, O Dakṣa, was brought forth; after her the blessed gods were born, the immortal relation.

यद्देवा अदः सलिले

सुसंरब्धा अतिष्ठत।

अत्रा वो नृत्यतामिव

तीव्रो रेणुरपायत॥ ६॥

When you, gods, were in that place in the ocean, supporting one another, there a rose from you who danced, as it were, an excessive dust.

यद्देवा यतयो यथा
भुवनान्यपिन्वत।
अत्रा समुद्र आ गूळ्ह-
मा सूर्यमजभर्तन।।७।।

When you, O gods, like the Yatis (or like workmen) made the beings grow, then you brought here the sun hidden away in the ocean.

अष्टौ पुत्रासो अदिते-
र्ये जातास्तन्व१स्परि
देवाँ उप प्रैत्सप्ताभिः
परा मार्ताण्डमास्यत्।।८।।

There are eight sons of Aditi that are born from her body, with seven she met the gods, Mārtāṇḍa she cast off.

सप्तभिः पुत्रैरदिति-
रुप प्रैत्पूर्व्यं युगम्।
प्रजायै मृत्यवे त्व-
त्पुनर्मार्ताण्डमाभरत्।।९।।

With seven sons Aditi met the generation of old, for birth and death alternately she brought Mārtāṇḍa back.

म० १० **No. 26** सू० १०८

किमिच्छन्ती सरमा प्रेदमानड्
दूरे ह्यध्वा जगुरिः पराचैः।
कास्मेहितिः का परितकम्यासी-
त्कथं रसाया अतरः पयांसि।।१।।

[The Paṇis speak :—] With what wish has Saramā come here? Far is the path, losing itself in the distance; what was the mission to us, what (is) the racket ? How didst thou cross the waters of the Rasā?

इन्द्रस्य दूतीरिषिता चरामि
मह इच्छन्ती पणयो निधीन्वः।
अतिष्कदो भियसा तन्न आव-
त्तथा रसाया अतरं पयांसि।।२।।

[Saramā speaks :—] Indra's appointed messenger I come, seeking your large treasures, O Paṇis; in this Rasā has helped me through fear of (my) jumping over: that's how I got over Rasā's waters.

कीदृङ्ङिन्द्रः सरमे का दृशीका
यस्येदं दूतीरसरः पराकात्।
आ च गच्छान्मित्रमेना दधा-
माथा गवां गोपतिर्नो भवाति।।३।

[The Paṇis:—] Whom is this Indra like, O Saramā ? What (is the) appearance (of him) whose messenger thou camest here from afar? Let him come here, we shall make friendship with him; moreover he shall be the lord of our king.

नाहं तं वेद दभ्यं दभत्स
यस्येदं दूतीरसरं पराकात्।
न तं गूहन्ति स्रवतो गभीरा
हता इन्द्रेण पणयः शयध्वे।।४।।

[Saramā:—] I do not know that he can be brought to grief, (but) he whose messenger I have some here from afar shall bring (you) to grief, deep rivers do not hide him, slain by Indra you, Paṇis, will lie.

इमा गावः सरमे या ऐच्छः
परि दिवो अन्तान्सुभगे पतन्ती।
कस्त एना अव सृजादयु-
ध्व्युतास्माकमायुधा सन्ति तिग्मा।।५।।

[The Paṇis:—] There are the kine, Saramā, which thou seekest running up to the ends of heaven, O blessed one; we shall loosen them without fighting, and ours are sharp weapons.

असेन्या वः पणयो वचां-
स्यनिषव्यास्तन्वः सन्तु पापीः।
अधृष्टो व एतवा अस्तु पन्था
बृहस्पतिर्व उभया न मृळात्।।६।।

[Saramā :—] Your words may be no target for a weapon; let your wicked persons (bodies) be arrow-proof, let the road to you be unsurmountable for going: yet Bṛhaspati will in no way spare you.

अयं निधिः सरमे अद्रिबुध्नो
गोभिरश्वेभिर्वसुभिर्न्यृष्टः।

रक्षन्ति त पणयो ये सुगोपा
रेकु पदमलकमा जगन्थ॥७॥

[The Paṇis:—] Saramā, this our treasure-chamber has a pavement of rock, it is filled with kine, horses and valuables; the Paṇis who are good guards watch it, in vain hast thou come (here) where there is nothing to be had.

एह गमन्नृषयः सोमशिता
अयास्यो अङ्गिरसो नवग्वाः।
त एतमूर्वं वि भजन्त गोना-
मथैतद्वचः पणयो वमन्नित्॥८॥

[Saramā :—] There shall come here ṛṣis inspired by soma, Ayāsya, Aṅgiras, Navagvas; they will divide (among themselves) this stable of cattle; then would the Paṇis fain give back this (vain) word.

एवा च त्वं सरम आजगन्थ
प्रबाधिता सहसा दैव्येन।
स्वसारं त्वा कृणवै मा पुनर्गा
अप ते गवां सुभगे भजाम॥९॥

[The Paṇi chief:—] Even so Saramā, thou hast come here urged on by divine force; I will make thee sister do not turn back, we will let thee have of the cattle, blessed one.

नाहं वेद भ्रातृत्वं नो स्वसृत्व-
मिन्द्रो विदुरङ्गिरसश्च घोराः।
गोकामा मे अच्छदयन्रूदाय-
मपात इत पणयो वरीयः॥१०॥

[Saramā :—] I know of no brotherhood, no sisterhood; Indra and the dread Aṅgiras know (this); they appeared to be desirous of kine when I left; hence off now, you Paṇis, as far as possible.

दूरमित पणयो वरीय
उग्दावो यन्तु मिनतीर्ऋतेन।
बृहस्पतिर्या अविन्दन्निगूळ्हाः
सोमो ग्रावाण विप्राः।।११।।

Away, hence, Paṇis, as far as possible, may the cows escape, lawfully, breaking out, (the cows) which hidden away Bṛhaspatī, Soma, the press-stones, the sages, the priests have found.

म० १० **No. 27** सू० १३९

सूर्यरश्मिर्हरिकेशः पुरस्ता-
त्सविता ज्योतिरुदयाँ अजस्रम्।
तस्य पूषा प्रसवे याति विद्वा-
न्संपश्यन्विश्वा भुवनानि गोपाः।।१।।

Savitṛ with rays of the sun, yellow-haired, his raised in the East the unfailin light; at his order Pūṣan, the wise, marches (as) a shepherd, surveying all beings.

नृचक्षा एष दिवो मध्य आस्त
आपप्रिवान्रोदसी अन्तरिक्षम्।
स विश्वाचीरभि चष्टे घृताची-
रन्तरा पूर्वमपरं च केतुम्।।२।।

Overseeing all men, there he sits in the centre of heaven, filling heaven and earth and the mid-space; he observes the far-extending (quarters) yielding ghee, between the Eastern and Western, light.

रायो बुध्नः संगमनो वसूनां
विश्वा रूपाभि चष्टे शचीभिः।
देव इव सविता सत्यध-
र्मेन्द्रो न तस्थौ समरे धनानाम्॥३॥

The foundation of wealth, the gatherer of treasures, by his powers beholds all shaped things; as god, whose law holds good, Savitṛ stands like Indra in the fight for riches.

विश्वावसुं सोम गन्धर्वमापो
ददृशुषीस्तदृतेना व्यायन्।
तदन्ववैदिन्द्रो रारहाण आसां
परि सूर्यस्य परिधीँरपश्यत्॥४॥

When,O Soma, the waters had seen the Gandharva Viśvāvasu, they ran away with the sacrifice (Soma); then Indra in haste followed them, he saw round the sun's enclosures.

विश्वावसुरभि तन्नो गृणातु
दिव्यो गन्धर्वो रजसो विमानः।
यद्वा घा सत्यमुत यन्न विद्म धियो
हिन्वानो धिय इन्नो अव्याः॥५॥

Viśvāvasu, the celestial Gandharva, the measurer of space, may announce us that which we know for certain as well as that which we do not; may he, inciting thoughts, help indeed our thoughts.

सस्निं मविन्दच्चरणे नदीना-
मपावृणोद्दुरो अश्मव्रजानाम्।
प्रासां गन्धर्वो अमृतानि वोच-
दिन्द्रो दक्षं परि जानादहीनाम्।।६।।

He found the immerged one in the course of the rivers, he opened the doors of (the waters) whose stabel is the rock; the Gandharva indicated their nectar, Indra, learnt the cleverness (intent?) of the women.

NOTES

NO. 1

Maṇḍala I **Sūkta 25**

यच्चिदित्येकविंशत्यृचं द्वितीयं सूक्तम्। तथा चानुक्रान्तम्। यच्चित्सैकेति। ऋषिश्चान्यस्मादिति परिभाषया शुनः शेप एव ऋषिः। आदौ गायत्रमिति परिभाषितत्वाग्द्गायत्री छन्दः। वारुणं त्विति पूर्वोक्तत्वात्तुह्यादिपरिभाषया (अनु० १२-३) वरुणो देवता। विनियोग उक्तः शौनः शेपाख्याने। विशेषविनियोगस्तु आभिप्लवषडह इदं सूक्तं होत्रकशस्त्रे स्तोमनिमित्तमावापार्थम्। अभिप्लव-पृष्ठ्याहानीति खण्डे तथैव सूत्रितम्। यच्चिद्धि ते विश इति वारुणमेतस्य तृचमावपेत मैत्रावरुणः। (आ० ७-५) इति।।

The Anukramṇīs give Śunaḥśepa as the seer of the hymn. Their tradition, however, seems to rest mainly on the fact that the sūkta occurs between those which Aitareya Brāhmaṇa VII. 17 ascribes to Śunaḥśepa. For, with the possible execption of the second ṛc : —मा नो॑ व॒धाय॑० and the last उदु॑त्त॒मं मु॑मुग्धि०, the whole hymn is in a rather loose connection with the Śunaḥśepa legend. It is indeed more likely that this sūkta was originally the prayer of a penitent sinner addressed to Varuṇa, the guardian of the moral order.

Both contents and form (the similar beginning of ṛcas 7-9, for instance) suggest that the hymn consists of tṛcs, groups of three ṛcas. Perhaps the first four tṛcas, ṛcas 1-12, and the last three, ṛcas 13-21, originally formed independent sūktas (Oldbg. Textkr.)

Verse 1

यत्। चित्। हि । ते विशः। यथा। प्र । देव । वरुण। व्रतम्।
मिनीमसि द्यविऽद्यवि।१ ।।

हे वरुण यथा लोके विशः प्रजाः कदाचित्प्रमादं कुर्वन्ति तथा वयमपि ते तव संबन्धि यच्चिद्धि यदेव किंचिद्व्रतं कर्म द्यविद्यवि प्रतिदिनं [१]प्रमिनीमसि प्रमादेन हिंसितवन्तः। तदपि व्रतं प्रमादपरिहारेण साङ्गं कुर्विति शेषः। यथा लित्स्वेरेणाद्युदात्तत्वे प्राप्ते यथेति पादान्त (फि० ४-१७) इति सर्वानुदात्तत्वम्। मिनीमसि। मीञ् हिंसायाम्। इदन्तो मसिः। क्र्यादिभ्यः श्न (पा० ३-१-८१) मीनातेर्निगमे (पा० ७-३-८१) इति ह्रस्वत्वम्। ई हल्यघोः (पा० ६-४-११३) इतीकारः। सति शिष्टस्वरबलीयस्त्वमन्यत्र विकरणेभ्य इति वचनात्तिङ एव स्वरः शिष्यते। यद्वृत्तयोगान्निघाताभावः।।

मिनीमसि, 1. pl. pres. par.; rt. मी 9., to mix up, miss, transgress, disturb; प्र मी, the same meaning.

यच् चिद्, though, यच् चिद् धि, though indeed.

द्यविद्यवि, āmreḍita (iterative) compound, day by day.

Ṛcas 1 and 2 form (against Sāyaṇa's interpretation) one sentence.

यथा introduces an abbreviated comparison: though indeed we, as people (transgress the king's law so) violate…

Verse 2

मा। नः। वधाय। हत्नवे। जिहीळानस्य। रीरधः। मा हृणानस्य।
मन्यवे।।२।।

हे वरुण जिहीळानस्यानादरं कृतवतो हत्नवे हन्तुः[२] पापिहननशीलस्य तव संबन्धिने त्वत्कर्तृकाय वधाय नः अस्मान्। मा रीरधः संसिद्धान्विषयभूतान्मा कुरु। हृणानस्य हृणीयमानस्य क्रुद्धस्य तव मन्यवे क्रोधाय मा अस्मान्रीरधः।

---

१. आदर्शपुस्तके 'प्र मिनीमसि' इत्यादयः सोपसर्गाः क्रियापदपाठाः सान्तरा निर्दिष्टाः।

२. प्रथमावृत्तौ 'पापहननशीलस्य' इति पाठः।

वधाय। हनश्च वधः (पा० ३-३-७६) इत्यबन्तो वधशब्दः। उञ्छादिषु पाठादन्तोदात्तः। हत्नवे। हन हिंसागत्योः। कृहनिभ्यां क्नुः (उ० ३-३०) इति क्नुप्रत्ययः। धातोर्नकारस्य तकारः। जिहीळानस्य। हेडृ अनादरे। अस्माल्लिटः कानच्। (पा० ३-२-१०६) द्विर्भावहलादिशेषह्रस्वचुत्वजश्त्वानि। एकारस्य ईकारादेशश्छान्दसः। चितः (पा० ६-१-१६३) इत्यन्तोदात्तत्वम्। रीरधः। राध साध संसिद्धौ। चङि णिलोप उपधाह्रस्वत्वम्। द्विर्वचनहलादिशेषः। ह्रस्वत्व-सन्वद्भावत्वाभ्यासदीर्घाः। न माङ्योगे (पा० ६-४-७४) इत्यडभावः। हृणानस्य। हृणीङ् लज्जायाम्। अस्माच्छानचि पृषोदरादित्वादभिमतरूपसिद्धिः।।

जि॒ही॒ळा॒न, pt. pf. ātm.; rt. हीड्, (par). to make angry, (ātm.) to be angry.

हृ॒णा॒न, Pt. pf, ātm.; rt. हृ, to be furious.

री॒र॒धः, 2. sg. inj. aor. par. caus.; rt. रध्, or रन्ध्, to succumb, to surrender; caus.to hand over.

व॒ध m., murderer, (deadly) weapon, murder.

ह॒त्नु, deadly.

जि॒ही॒ळा॒नस्य॑ and हृ॒णा॒नस्य॑ refer to Varuṇa, hence तव॑ has to be understood. The ह॒त्नु व॒ध, dropsy, is at the service of his म॒न्यु or indignation at the moral infringement.

Verse 3

वि। मृ॒ळी॒काय॑। ते॒। मनः॑। र॒थीः। अश्व॑म्। न। सम्ऽदि॑तम्।
गी॒ःऽभिः। व॒रु॒ण। सी॒म॒हि॒।।३।।

हे वरुण मृळीकायास्मत्सुखाय ते तव मनो गीर्भिः स्तुतिभिः वि सीमहि विशेषेण बध्नीमः प्रसादयाम इत्यर्थः। तत्र दृष्टान्तः। रथीः रथस्वामी संदितं सम्यक्खण्डितं दूरगमनेन श्रान्तमश्वं न अश्वमिव। यथा स्वामी श्रान्तमश्वं घासप्रदानादिना प्रसादयति तद्वत्। रथीः मत्वर्थीय ईकारः। सदितम्। दो अवखण्डने। निष्ठा (पा० ३-२-१०२) इति क्तः। द्यतिस्यति-मास्थामित्ति* किति (पा० ७-४-४०) इतीकारन्तादेशः गतिरनन्तरः (पा०

* 'मित्ति किति' इश्यानंश आदर्शपुस्तके नोपन्यस्तः।

६-२-४९) इति गतेः प्रकृतिस्वरत्वम्। गीर्भिः। सावेकाचः० (पा० ६-१-१६८) इति भिस उदात्तत्वम्। सीमहिषिवु तन्तुसंताने। व्यत्यये- नात्मनेपदम्। बहुलं छन्दसि (पा० २-४-७३) इतिविकरणस्य लुक् वलि लोपः। यद्वा षिञ् बन्धन इत्यस्याद्विकरणस्य लुक्। दीर्घश्छान्दसः।।

वि सी॒म॒हि॒, 1. pl. opt. (?), aor.ātm.; rt. वि सो 4., t untie, open, make ccessible (मन॑स्), stisfy (Sāy. प्रसादयति).

सं॑दि॑त, pt. pf,; rt. सम् दो, 4., to tie up.

मृ॒ळी॒क n., forgiveness, remittance of sin, mercy, grace.

र॒थीः m. nom. sg., chrioteer. न, not, like.

Sāyaṇa's interpretation, though grammatically free, lhits off well the meaning of the ṛc.

Verse 4.

परा॑। हि। मे॒। विऽम॑न्यवः। पत॑न्ति वस्य॑ःऽइष्टये। वय॑ः। न। व॒स॒तीः। उप॑।।४।।

हे वरुण मे मम शुनःशेपस्य विमन्यवः क्रोधरहिता बुद्धयो वस्यइष्टये वसीयसोऽतिशेयन वसुमतो जीवनस्य प्राप्तये परा पतन्ति पराङ्मुखाः पुनरावृत्ति- रहिताःप्रसरन्ति। हिशब्दोऽस्मिन्नर्थे सर्वजनप्रसिद्धिमाह। परापतने दृष्टान्तः। वयो न पक्षिणो यथा बसतीर्निवासस्थानान्युप सामीप्येन प्राप्नुवन्ति तद्वत्। पतन्ति पादादित्वान्निघाताभावः। वस्यइष्टये। वसुमच्छब्दाद्विन्मतोर्लुक् (पा० ५-३-६५) इति मतुपो लुकि टिलोप ईयसुनो यकारलोपश्छान्दसः। वसतीः। शतुरनुमः० (पा० ६-१-१७३) इति ङीप उदात्तत्वम्।।

विम॑न्यवः m. pl., Sāy.: free from anger, viz. the feelings of Śunaḥśepa.

Roth, Grassmann: Desires longings.

Geldner: Cares, Sorrows (?).

Bergaigne, v. Schroeder, Oldbg.: prayers the clam (Varuṇa's) wrath.

वस्यइष्टि (वस्यस्+इष्टि) f., the seeking, trying of one's luck, salvation.

वसति f., nest.

Verse 5.

कदा। क्षत्रऽश्रियम्। नरम्। आ। वरुणम्। करामहे। मृळीकाय। उरुऽचक्षसम्।।५।।

मृळीकायास्मत्सुखाय कदा कस्मिन्काले आ करामहे अस्मिन्कर्मण्यागतं करवाम। कीदृशम्। क्षत्रश्रियं बलसेविनं नरं नेतारं उरुचक्षसं बहूनां द्रष्टारम्। क्षत्रश्रियम्। क्षत्राणि श्रयतीति क्षत्रश्रीः। क्विप्। क्विब्वचीत्यादिना (पा० ३-२-१७८-२) क्विप् दीर्घश्च। कृदुत्तरपदकृतिस्वरत्वम्। नरम्। ऋदोरप् (पा० ३-३-५७) इत्यबन्त आद्युदात्तः। करामहे करोतेर्व्यत्ययेन शप्। उरुचक्षसम् चक्षेर्बहुलं शिच्च (उ० ४-२३२) इत्यसुन्। शिद्वद्भा-वात्ख्याञादेशाभावः।।

आ करामहे, 1. pl. Subj. aor, ātm.; rt. आ कृ, to move to come, to bring hither.

Verse 6.

तत्। इत्।। समानम्। आशाते इति। वेनन्ता। न। प्र। युच्छतः। धृतऽव्रताय। दाशुषे।।६।।

धृतव्रतपायानुष्ठितकर्मणे दाशुषे हविर्दत्तवते यजमानाय वेनन्तो कामयमानौ। मित्रावरुणाविति शेषः। तावुभौ समानं साधारणं तदिदस्माभिर्दत्तं तदेव हविराशते अश्नुवाते। न प्रयुच्छतः कदाचिदपि प्रमादं न कुरुतः। आशाते। अश्नोतेर्लिटि द्विर्भावहलादिशेषौ। अत आदेः (पा० ७-४-७०) इत्यात्वम्। अनित्यमागमशासनमिति वचनादश्नोतेश्च (पा० ७-४-७२) इति नुडभावः। वेनन्ता वेनतिः कान्तिकर्मा। सुपां सुलुग् (पा० ७-१-३९) इत्याकारः। प्र युच्छतः। युच्छ प्रमादे। दाशुषे। दाशृ दान इत्यास्माद्दाश्वान्साह्वान्० (पा० ६-१-१२) इति क्वसुप्रत्ययो निपातितः। वसोः संप्रसारणम् (पा० ६-४-१३१) इति संप्रसारणम्। शासिवसिघसीनां च (पा० ८-३-६०) इति षत्वम्।।

आ॒शा॒ते॒, 3. du. pf. ātm.; rt. अश् 5., to reach; they two have reached, they possess. The subject is Mitrā-Varuṇā.

वेन॑न्ता, du. pt. pr.: rt. वेन् १., to look out, to heed.

प्र यु॒च्छ॒तः, 3. du. pr. pr. present stem युच्छ्; rt. यु 3., to be inattentive, careless.

दा॒श्वस्, pt. pf.; rt. दाश्, worshipping, pious.

तत् refers to क्ष॒त्र in क्ष॒त्रश्रि॑यम् ṛc 5; तद् इत्, that very.

verse 7.

वेद॑। यः। वी॒नाम्। प॒दम्। अ॒न्तरि॑क्षेण। पत॑ताम्। वेद॑। ना॒वः। स॒मु॒द्रियः॑॥७॥

अन्तरिक्षेण पतताम् आकाशमार्गेण गच्छतां वीनां पक्षिणां पदं यो वरुणो वेद। तथा समुद्रियः समुद्रेऽवस्थितो वरुणो नावो जले गच्छन्त्याः पदं वेद जानाति। सोऽस्मान्बन्धनान्मोचयत्विति शेषः। वेद। विद ज्ञाने। विदो लटो वा (वा० ३-४-८३) इति तिपो णल्। लित्स्वरेणाद्युदात्तत्वम्। द्व्यचोऽतस्तिङः (पा० ६-३-१३५) इति संहितायां दीर्घः। वीनाम्। नामन्यतरस्याम् (पा० ६-१-१६८) इति षष्ठ्या उदात्तत्वम्। समुद्रियः। भवार्थे। समुद्राभ्राद्धः (पा० ४-४-११८) इति घप्रत्ययः॥

Read वी॒न+अम्. स॒मु॒द्रियः॑, m. nom. sg., residing in the ocean.

स॒मु॒द्रियः॑ ना॒वः taken by Roth, Delbrück, Grassmann and Oldbg. to be acc. pl. f.; Sāy. (m. Müller), Geldner understand स॒मु॒द्रिय॑ to be nom, sg. masc., ना॒वः gen, sg. fem. Contents and accent rather suggest this interpretation, in spite of the apparent parallelism between अ॒न्तरि॑क्षेण पत॑ताम् and स॒मु॒द्रियः॑. The prevalent idea is that Varuṇa sees things whitch are hidden to other eyes, among others the track of birds and ships. Cp. ṛc 10.

Verse 8.

वेद। मासः। धृतऽव्रतः। द्वादश। प्रजाऽवतः। वेद। यः। उपऽजायते।।८।।

धृतव्रतः स्वीकृतकर्मविशेषो यथोक्तमहिमोपेतो वरुणः। प्रजावतस्तदा तदोत्वद्यमानप्रजायुक्तान्द्वादश मासश्चैत्रादीन्फाल्गुनान्तान्वेद जानाति। यस्त्रयोदशोऽधिकमास उपजायते संवत्सरसमीपे स्वयमेवोत्पद्यते तमपि वेद। वाक्यशेषः पूर्ववत्। मासः। पद्दन्नितयादिना (पा०६-१-६३) मासशब्दस्य मासित्यादेशः। ऊडिदमित्यादिना (पा० ६-१-१७१) शस उदात्तत्वम्। द्वादश। द्वौ च दश चेति द्वन्द्वः। द्व्यष्टनः संसख्यायाम् (पा० ६-३-१७१) इत्यात्वम्। संख्या (पा० ६-२-३५) इति सूत्रेण पूर्वपदप्रकृतिस्वरत्वम्। प्रजावतः। जनी प्रादुर्भावे। प्रपूर्वाज्जनसनखनक्रमगमोविट् (पा० ३-२-६७) इतिवट् प्रत्ययः विड्वो- रित्यात्वम् (पा० ६-४-४१) कुदुत्तरपदप्रकृतिस्वरत्वम्। प्रजा एषां सन्तीति पदस्यास्त्यस्मिन्निति मतुप् (पा० ५-४-९४) मादुपधाया (पा० ८-२-९) इति मतुपो वत्त्वम्। उपजायते। जनेः कर्मकर्तरि लट्। कर्मवद्भावा-दात्मनेपदम् यक् (पा० ३-१-८७) जनादीनामुपदेश एवात्वं वक्तव्यम् (पा० ६-१-१९५-३) इति वचनादचः कर्तृयकि (पा० ६-१-१९५) इत्याद्युदात्तत्वम्। तिङि चोदात्तवत (पा० ८-१-७१) इत्युपसर्गस्य निघातः। न च तिङ्ङःतिङ (पा० ८-१-२८) इति निघातः। यद्वृत्तान्नित्यम् (पा० ८-१-६६) इति प्रतिषेघात्।।

मास् m., month. Read दुआदश. Cp. Lat. duodecim.

मासः प्रजावतः, there is no reason to reject Sāyaṇa's interpretation. मासः (as well as other measures of time) stand in the ṚV. for the abstract notion of time; and time as well as all that takes origin in it is an object of Varuṇa's omniscienee. This ṛc proves the intercalary month in the Vedic calendar.

Verse 9.

वेद। वातस्य। वर्तनिम्। उरोः। ऋष्वस्य बृहतः। वेद। ये। अधिऽआसते।।९।।

उरोर्विस्तीर्णस्य ऋष्वस्य दर्शनीयस्य बृहतो गुणैरधिकस्य वातस्य वायोर्वर्तनिं मार्गं वेद । वरुणो जानाति। ये देवा अध्यासते उपरि तिष्ठन्ति तानपि वेद जानाति। वातस्य। असिहसीत्यादिना (उ० ३-८६) तन्प्रत्ययान्तो वातशब्दोनित्त्वादाद्युदात्तः। वर्तनिम्। वर्ततेऽनेनेति वर्तनिः स्तोत्र इति स्तोत्र-वाचकस्य वर्तनिशब्दस्यान्तोदात्तत्वसिद्ध्यर्थमुच्छादिषु पाठादस्य प्रत्ययस्वरेण मध्योदात्तत्वे प्राप्ते व्यत्ययेनान्तोदात्तत्वम्। बृहतः। बृहन्महतोरुपसंख्यानमिति ङस उदात्तत्वम्। अध्यासते। लसार्वधातुकानुदात्तत्वे सति धातुस्वरः।।

Read अ॒धि॒ आस॑ते. व॒र्त॒नि f., way, track.

ऋ॒ष्व, (Naigh. 3.3) महत्, (frequently together with बृ॒हत्) high.

बृहत्, strong.

ये अ॒धि॒ आस॑ते (दे॒वाः) is to be taken in a concrete sense: those who dwell above, no high.

Verse 10.

नि स॒सा॒द॒। धृ॒तऽव्र॑तः।। वरु॑णः। प॒स्त्या॑सु। आ। सां॒ऽरा॒ज्याय। सु॒ऽक्रतुः॑।।१०।।

धृतव्रतः पूर्वोक्तो वरुणः पस्त्यासु दैवीषु प्रजासु आ नि षसाद आगत्य निषण्णवान्। किमर्थम्। प्रजानां साम्राज्यसिद्ध्यर्थम्। सुक्रतुः शोभनकर्मा। निषसाद। * सदिरप्रतेः। (पा० ८-३-६६) इति षत्वम्। साम्राज्याय। सम्राजो भावः साम्राज्यम्। गुणवचनब्राह्मणादिभ्यः (पा० ५-१-१२४) इति ष्यञ्। ञ्नित्यादिर्नित्यम् (पा० ६-१-१७९) इत्याद्युदात्तत्वम्। सुक्रतुः। क्रत्वादयश्च (पा० ६-२-११८) इत्युत्तरपदाद्युदात्तत्वम्।।

Read प॒स्तिआ॑सु आ, साम्रा॑जिआय.

Sāyaṇa in the commentary (unnecessarily?) corrects Pāṇini VIII. 3.66: सदिरप्रतेः into सदेरप्रतेः.

---

* आदर्शपुस्तके 'सदेरप्रतेः' इति पाठः।

पु॒स्त्यां f., river, water, See Ved. Stud. II. 212. आ, after loc., in.

Verse 11.

अतः॑। विश्वा॑नि। अद्भु॑ता। चि॒कि॒त्वान्। अ॒भि। प॒श्य॒ति॒। कृ॒तानि॑। या। च॒। कर्त्वा॑॥ ११॥

अतोऽस्माद्वरुणाद्विश्वान्युद्भुता सर्वाण्याश्चर्याणि चिकित्वान्प्रज्ञावानभिपश्यति सर्वतोऽवलोकयति। या कृतानि यान्याश्चर्याणि पूर्वं वरुणेन संपादितानि। चकारादन्यानि यान्याश्चर्याणि कर्त्वा इतः परं कर्तव्यानि। तानि सर्वाण्यभि-पश्यतीति पूर्वत्रान्वयः। अद्भुता। शेश्छन्दसि बहुलम् (पा० ६-१-७०) इति शेर्लोपः। प्रत्ययलक्षणेन नपुंसकस्य झलचः (पा० ६-७१-७२) इति नुम्। नलोपः। चिकित्वान्। कित ज्ञाने। लिटः। कूसुः। अभ्यासहलादिशेष-चुत्वानि। वस्वेकाजाद्धसाम् (पा० ७-२-६७) इति नियमादिडभावः। रुत्वानुनासिकावुक्तौ संहितायाम्। पश्यति। पाघ्रेत्यादिना (पा० ७-३-७८) दृशेः पश्यादेशः। कर्त्वा। कृत्यार्थे तवैकेन्केन्यत्वनः। (पा० ३-४-१४) इति करोतेस्त्वन्। नित्त्वादाद्युदात्तत्वम्। पूर्ववच्छेर्लोपः॥

सु॒क्रतु॑, being of good intellect, wise; of good will, kind. Read क्र॒तुआ॑.

चि॒कि॒त्वस्, pt. pf.; rt. चित् 3., knowing, wise.

अतः॑, viz. from the place of residence.

अद्भु॑त, wonderful, secret.

Verse 12.

सः। नः॒। वि॒श्वाहा॑। सु॒ऽक्रतुः॑। आ॒दि॒त्यः। सु॒ऽपथा॑। क॒र॒त्। प्र। न॒ः। आयूं॑षि। ता॒रि॒ष॒त्॥१२॥

सुक्रतुः शोभानप्रज्ञः स आदित्यो वरुणो विश्वाहा सर्वेष्वहः सु नोऽस्मान् सुपथा शोभनमार्गेण सहितान्करत्करोतु। किंच नोऽस्माकमायूंषि प्र तारिषत्प्रवर्धयतु। सुपथा स्वती पूजायाम् (पा २-२-१८-२) इति समासे न

पूजनात् (पा० ५-४-६९) इति समासान्तप्रतिषेधः। अव्ययपूर्वपदप्रकृतिस्वरे प्राप्ते परादिश्छन्दसि बहुलम् (पा० ६-२-१९९) इत्युत्तरपदाद्युदात्तत्वम्। क्रत्वादयश्चेत्येतन्न भवति। अबव्रीहित्वात्। बहुव्रीहौ हि तद्विधीयते। आद्युदात्तं द्च्छन्दसि (पा०६-२-११९) इत्येतदपि न भवति। पथिन्शब्दस्यान्तोदात्तत्वात्। करत्। करोतेर्लेटिव्यत्ययेन शप्। शपो *लुकि लेटोऽडाटौ (पा० ३-४-९४) इत्यडागमः। इतश्च लोपः (पा० ३-४-९७) इतीकारलोपः। यद्वा छान्दसे लुङि कृमृदृरुहिभ्यः (पा० ३-१-५९) इति च्लेरङ्। ऋदृशोऽङि गुणः (पा० ७-४-१६) इति गुणः। बहुलं छन्दस्यमाङ्योगेऽपि (पा० ६-४-७५) इत्यडभावः। प्र णः। उपसर्गाद्बहुलम्। (पा० ८-४-२८) इति नसो णत्वम्। तारिषत्। तारयतेर्लेट्यडागमः। सिब् बहुलं लेटि (पा० ३-१-३४) इति सिप्। आदेशप्रत्यययोः (पा० ८-३-५९) इति षत्वम्।।

क॒र॒त्, 3. sg. subj. aor. par.; rt. कृ.

ता॒रि॒ष॒त्, the same grammatical form as करत्; rt. तॄ, to cross, used in a causal sense.

वि॒श्वाहा॑, (not separated in the Padapāṭha, the same meaning as वि॒श्वहा॑, or °ह॑), always, every day (Sāy.). सु॒पथ॑ n., easy way, well-being.

Verse 13.

बिभ्र॑त्। द्रा॒पिम्। हि॒र॒ण्यय॑म्। वरु॑णः। व॒स्त॒। नि॒ःऽनिजं॑म्। परि॑। स्पशः॑। नि। से॒दि॒रे॒।।१३।।

हिरण्ययं सुवर्णमयं द्रापिं कवचं बिभ्रद्धारयन्वरुणो निर्णिजं पुष्टं स्वशरीरं वस्त आच्छादयति। स्पशो हिरण्यस्पर्शिनो रश्मयः परिनिषेदिरे सर्वतो निषण्णाः। बिभ्रत्। बिभर्तेः शतरि नाभ्यस्ताच्छतुः (पा० ७-१-७८) इति नुमभावः। अभ्यस्तानामादिः (पा० ६-१-१८९) इत्याद्युदात्तत्वम्। द्रापिम्। द्रा कुत्सायां गतौ। द्रापयतीषून्कुत्सितां गतिं प्रापयतीति द्रापिः कवचम्। अर्तिह्रीत्यादिना '(पा० ७-३-३६) पुगागमः। औणादिक इप्रत्यये णिलोपः। हिरण्ययम्। ऋत्व्यवास्त्व्यवास्त्वमाध्वीहिरण्ययानि च्छन्दसि (पा०

---

* प्रथमावृत्तौ 'वा लुकि' इति पाठः।

६-४-१७५) इति हिरण्यशब्दाद्विकारार्थे विहितस्य मयटो मशब्दलोपो निपातितः। वस्त। वस आच्छादने। लङ्यदादित्वाच्छपो लुक्। पूर्ववदडभावः। निर्णिजम्। णिजिर् शौचपोषणयोः। स्पशः। स्पश बाधनस्पर्शनयोः। क्विप्च (पा० ३-२-७६) इति क्विप्। निषेदिरे षदलृ विशरणगत्यवसादनेषु। अस्मात्यद्गत्यर्थात्कर्मणि लिय्येत्वाभ्यासलोपौ सदिरप्रतेरिति षत्वम्।।

(अ) वस्त, 3. sg. impf. ātm.; rt. वस् 2., to wear.

द्रापि m. harness, armour.

निर्णिज् f., glowing colour, splendour.

Verse 14.

न। यम्। दिप्सन्ति। दिप्सवः । न। द्रुह्वाणः। जनानाम्। न। देवम्। अभिऽमातयः।।१४।।

दिप्सवो हिंसितुमिच्छन्तो वैरिणो यं वरुणं न दिप्सन्ति भीताः सन्तो हिंसितुमिच्छां परित्यजन्नि जनानां प्राणिनां द्रुह्वाणो द्रोग्धारोऽपि यं वरुणं प्रति नद्रुह्यन्ति। अभिमातयः पाप्मानः। पाप्मा वा अभिमातिः (तै० सं. २-१-३-५) इति श्रुत्यन्तरात्। तं वरुणं न स्पृशन्ति। दिप्सन्ति। दम्भु दम्भे। अस्मात्सनि सनीवन्तर्धेत्यादिना (पा० ७-२-४९)इडभावः। हलन्ताच्च (पा० १-२-१०) इत्यत्र हलग्रहणस्य जातिवाचित्वात्सनः कित्त्वाद्दम्भ इच्च (पा० ७-४-५६) इतिदकारात्परस्याकारस्येकारः। अनिदिताम्० (पा० 6-4-28) इति नलोपः।। भष्भावाभावश्छान्दसः (पा० ८-२-३७) अत्र लोपोऽभ्यासस्य (पा० ७-४-५८) इत्यभ्यासलोपः। शपः पित्त्वादनुदात्तत्वम्। तिङश्च लसार्वध ातुकस्वरेण सनो नित्वान्नित्स्वरेणाद्युदात्तत्वम् यद्वृत्तयोगादनिघातः। दिप्सवः सन्नन्ताद्दम्भेः सनाशंसभिक्ष उः (पा० ३-२-१६८) इत्युप्रत्ययः। प्रत्ययस्वरः। द्रुह्वाणः। द्रुह जिघांसायाम्। अन्येभ्योऽपि दृश्यन्ते (पा० ३-२-७५) इति क्वनिप्। प्रत्ययस्य पित्त्वादनुदात्तत्वे धातुस्वरेणाद्युदात्तत्वम्।।

दिप्सन्ति, des. rt. दभ् 1., to cheat.

द्रुह्वन्, hostile, insidious, waylaying, laying snares.

अभिमाति (अभि मन्) f., enmity, enemy.

जनानाम्, gen. of the object; read जनान+अम्

Verse 15.

उत। यः। मानुषेषु। आ। यशः। चक्रे। असामि। आ। अस्माकम्। उदरेषु। आ।। १५।।

उत अपि च यो वरुणो मानुषेषु यशोऽन्नम् आ चक्रे सर्वतः कृतवान्। स वरुणः कुर्वन्नपि आ सर्वतः असामि। संपूर्णं चक्रे नतु न्यूनं कृतवान्। विशेषतोऽस्माकमुदरेषु आ सर्वतश्चक्रे। मानुषेषु। मनोर्जातावञ्यतौ षुक् च। (पा० ४-१-१६१) इत्यञ्। ञ्नित्यादिर्नित्यमित्याद्युदात्तत्वम्। चक्रे। प्रत्ययस्वरः। असामि। अव्यये नञ्कुनिपातानामिति वक्तव्यम् (पा० ६-२-२-२) *'यशः'। अशेर्युट् च (उ० ४-१९०) इत्यसुन्। उदरेषु। उदि दृणातेरजलौ पूर्वपदान्त्यलोपश्च (उ० ५-१९) इत्यल्। लित्स्वरः। गतिकारकोपपदा० (पा० ६-२-१३९) इत्युत्तरपदप्रकृतिस्वरत्वम्।।

असामि, not half, complete.

आ (after असामि) particle of emphasis, indeed.

उत indecl., and, and also.

मानुष adj., human; subst. m., man, n., mankind, human life.

Read मानुषेषु आ, असामि आ, उदरेषु आ.

Sāyaṇa, with Naigh. 2.7, takes यशस् to mean अन्न. उदरेषु he does not seem to take in the literal sense. The tendency of the whole hymn as well as grammar suggest that we have to consider Varuṇa also in ṛc 15 as the revenger of sin. For, उत links up this ṛc more closely with the preceding one. Ṛc 14 says that even professional cheats, those who freely entrap men, in fact, enemies of any kind dare not to cheat Varuṇa,

* 'यशः' इत्यादि 'स्वरत्वम्' इत्यन्तः पाठः प्रथमावृत्तौ नास्ति।

the god. Now ṛc 15 continues: And even among those men who may, like ourselves, foolishly have attempted to deceive him, he has fully established his glory, viz., by putting dropsy into our bellies. अ॒स्माक॑मु॒दरे॑षु may be ironical (Geldner, Komm.) or may not.

Verse 16.

परा॑। मे॒। य॒न्ति॒। धी॒तय॑:। गाव॑:। न। गव्यू॑तीः। अनु॑। इ॒च्छन्ती॑:। उ॒रु॒ऽचक्ष॑सम्॥१६॥

उरुचक्षसं बहुभिर्द्रष्टव्यं वरुणमिच्छन्तीर्मे धीतयः शुनःशेपस्य बुद्धयः परा यन्ति पराङ्मुखा निवृत्तिरहिता गच्छन्ति। तत्र दृष्टान्तः। गावो न यथा गावो गव्यूतीरनु गोष्ठान्यनुलक्ष्य गच्छन्ति तद्वत्। गव्यूतीः। गावोऽत्र यूयन्त इत्यधिकरणे क्तिन्। गोर्यूतौ छन्दसि (पा० ६-१-७९-२) इत्यवादेशः। दासीभारादित्वात्पूर्वपदप्रकृतिस्वरत्वम्। यद्वा यूतिर्यवनं गवां यवनमत्रेति बहुव्रीहौ पूर्वपदप्रकृतिस्वरत्वम्। इच्छन्तीः। इषु इच्छायाम्। ततः शतृ० (पा० २-२-१२४) तुदादिभ्यः शः (पा० ३-१-७७) इषुगमियमां छः (पा० ७-३-७७) इति च्छत्वम्। अदुपदेशाल्लसार्वधातुकानुदात्तत्वे विकरणस्वरः शिष्यते॥

परा॑ इ, to go out, off, into a distance.

गव्यू॑ति f, cattle track, cattle herd; see Ved. Stud. II. 287.

In form and contents this ṛc bears a likeness to ṛc 4.

Verse 17.

सम्। नु। वो॒चा॒व॒है॒। पुन॑:। यत॑:। मे॒। मधु॑। आऽभृ॑तम्। होता॑ऽइव। क्षद॑से। प्रि॒यम्॥१७॥

यतो यस्मात्कारणात् मे मज्जीवनार्थं मधुरं हविराभृतम् अञ्जःसवाख्ये कर्मणि संपादितम्। अतः कारणाद्धोतेव होमकर्तेव त्वमपि प्रियं हविः क्षदसे अश्नासि। पुनर्हविःस्वीकारादूर्ध्वं तृप्तस्त्वं जीवन्नहं च नु अवश्यं संवोचावहै। संभूय प्रियवार्तां करवावहै। वोचावहै। लोडर्थे छान्दसे लुङि

ब्रुवो वचिः। (पा० २-४-५३) अस्यतिवक्ति० (पा० ३-१-५२) इति च्लेरङादेशः। वच उम् (पा० ७-४-२०) इत्युमागमे गुणः। व्यत्ययेन टेरैत्वम्। यद्वा लोट एव लुङादेशः। स्थानिवद्भावादैत्वम्। आभृतम्। हृग्रहोर्भः (पा० ३-१-८४-२) गतिरनन्तर इति गतेः प्रकृतिस्वरत्वम्।।

वो॒चा॒व॒है, १. du. aor, subj. ātm.; rt. वच् ३.

क्षद॑से, inf. dat.; rt. क्षद्, to taste, partake (first). Sāyaṇa takes it to be 2. sg. pr. ātm. = अश्नासि.

Verse 18.

दर्श॑म्। नु। वि॒श्वऽद॑र्शतम्। दर्श॑म् । दर्श॑म्। रथ॑म्। अधि॑। क्षमि॑। ए॒ताः। जु॒ष॒त। मे॒ । गिर॑ः।।१८।।

विश्वदर्शतं सर्वैर्दशनीयमस्मदनुग्रहार्थमत्राविर्भूतं वरुणं दर्शं नु। अहं दृष्टवान्खलु। क्षमि क्षमायां भूमौ रथं वरुणसबन्धिनमधिदर्शम् आधिक्येन दृष्टवानस्मि एता उच्यमाना मे गिरो मदीयाः स्तुतीर्जुषत वरुणः सेवितवान्। दर्शम्। दृशेः इरितो वा (पा० ३-१-५७) इति च्लेरङादेशः। ऋदृशोऽङि गुणः। (पा० ७-४-१६) इति गुणः। विश्वदर्शतम्। दृशेर्भृमृदृशीत्यादिना (उ० ३-१०९) अतच्प्रत्ययान्तो दर्शतशब्दः। मरुद्वृधादित्वात्पूर्वपदान्तोदात्तत्वम् (पा० ६-२-१०६-२) यद्वा विश्वं दर्शनीयमस्येति बहुव्रीहिः। बहुव्रीहौ विश्वं संज्ञायाम् (पा० ६-२-१०६) इति पूर्वपदान्तोदात्तत्वम्। क्षमि आतो धातोः (पा० ६-४-१४०) इत्यत्रात इति योगविभागादाकारलोपः।।

दर्श॑म्, 1. sg. ar. inj. par.; rt. दृश्.

जु॒ष॒त, 3. sg. inj. ātm.; rt. जुष्.

विश्वद॑र्शत, all-visible.

क्षम् f., loc. क्षमि॑, earth. अधि॑ with loc., upon.

Verse 19.

वरुणप्रघासेषु इमं मे वरुणेति वारुणस्य हविषोऽनुवाक्या पञ्चम्यां पौर्णमास्यामिति खण्डे सूत्रितम्। इमं मे वरुण श्रुधि तत्त्वा यामि ब्रह्मणा वन्दमानः (आ० २-१७) इति।।

इमम्। मे। वरुण। श्रुधि। हवं। अद्य। च मृळय। त्वाम्। अवस्युः। आ। चके। १९।।

हे वरुण मे मदीयमिमं हवमाह्वानं श्रुधि शृणु। किंच अद्य अस्मिन्दिने मूळय अस्मान्सुखय। अवस्युः रक्षणेच्छुरहं त्वां वरुणमाभिमुख्येन चके शब्दयामि स्तौमीत्यर्थः। श्रुधि। श्रु श्रवणे। लोटो हिः (पा० ३-४-८७) श्रुशृणुपृ कृवृभ्यश्छन्दसीति (पा० ६-४-१०२) हेर्धिरादेशः। बहुलं छन्दसीति कविकरणस्य लुक्। अन्येष। मपि दृश्यत। (पा० ६-३-१३७) इति संहितायां दीर्घः। अवस्युः। अवस्शब्दात् सुप आत्मनः क्यच् (पा० ३-१-८) क्याच्छन्दसीत्युप्रत्ययः। (पा० ३-२-१७०) आ चके। कै गै शब्दे। अस्माल्लिट्यादेशः (पा० ६-१-४५) इत्यात्वम्। द्विर्भावचुत्वे। आतो लोप इटि च (पा० ६-४-६४) इत्याकारलोपः। तिङ्ङतिङ इति निघातः।।

चके, 1. sg. pf. ātm.; rt. का, कन्, to desire, enjoy, आ का, to call, ask here.

हवं m. n. (rt. ह्वे), call, invitation.

मृड् 6., मृळय, to spare, to be merciful.

अवस्यु, in need of help, imploring help.

Verse 20.

त्वम्। विश्वस्य। मेधिर। दिवः। च। ग्मः। च। राजसि। सः। यामनि। प्रति। श्रुधि।।२०।।

हे मेधिर मेधाविन्वरुण त्वं दिवश्च द्युलोकस्यापि ग्मश्च भूलोकस्यापि एवमात्मकस्य विश्वस्य सर्वस्य जगतो मध्ये राजसि दीप्यसे। स तादृशस्त्वं यामनि क्षेमप्रापणेऽस्मदीये प्रतिश्रुधि प्रतिश्रवणमाज्ञापनं कुरु रक्षिष्यामीति प्रत्युत्तरं देहीत्यर्थः। दिवः। ऊडिदमित्यादिना षष्ठ्या उदात्तत्वम् (पा० ६-१-१७१) ग्मः। ग्मेत्येतद्भूनामसु पठितम्। आतो धातोः (पा० ६-४-१४०) इत्यत्रात इति योगविभागादातो लोप इति प्रतिषेधेऽपि व्यत्ययेनाकारलोपः। उदात्तनिवृत्तिस्वरेण विभक्तेरुदात्तत्वम्। यामनि। या प्रापणे। आतो मनिन्क्वनिब्वनिपश्चेति मनिन् (पा० ३-२-७४) नित्त्वादाद्युदात्तत्वम्। श्रुधि। उक्तम्।।

ग्मस्, gen, sg. of ग्म् f., earth.

यार्मन् n., march, arrival, hour of arrival, proper time, hour of need.

सः, thou being such a one, thou then.

दिवश्च ग्मश्च is in apposition to विश्वस्य.

Verse 21.

उत्। उत्ऽतमम्। मुमुग्धि। नः। वि। पाशम्। मध्यमम्। चृत। अव। अधमानि। जीवसे।।२१।।

नोऽस्माकमुत्तमं शिरोगतं पाशमुन्मुमुग्धि उत्कृष्य मोचय। मध्यममुदरगतं पाशं विचृत वियुज्य नाशय। जीवसे जीवितुमधमानि मदीयान्पादगतान्पाशानवचृत अवकृष्य नाशय उत्तमम्। उञ्छादिषु पाठादन्तोदात्तत्वम्। मुमुग्धि। मुच्लमोक्षणे। बहुलं छन्दसीति विकरणस्य श्लुः। द्विर्भावः। हलादिशेषः। हुझल्भ्यो हेर्धिः (पा० ६-४-१०१) इति हेर्धिरादेशः। तिङ्ङतिङ इति निघातः। चृत। चृती हिंसाग्रन्थनयोः। लोटो हिः। तुदादिभ्यः शः। अतो हेरिति हेर्लुक्। जीवसे। जीव प्राणधारणे। तुमर्थे सेसेनित्यसेप्रत्ययः (प्रा० ३-४-९) प्रत्ययस्वरः।।

उद् मुच्, to loose, to take away from above,

वि चृत्, to untie.

In the third pāda the expression is elliptical: Down the lowest :- चृत or मुमुग्धि बन्धनानि are to be understood from the two preceding pādas.

NO. 2

MAṆḌALA I. **SŪKTA 32.**

इन्द्रस्य नु वीर्याणीति पञ्चदशर्चं द्वितीयं सूक्तम्। आङ्गिरसो हिरण्यस्तूप ऋषिस्त्रिष्टुप् छन्दः। इन्द्रो देवता। इन्द्रस्य पञ्चोनेत्यनुक्रमणिका। अग्निष्टोमे मध्यंदिने सवने निष्केवल्यशस्त्र इन्द्रस्य नु वीर्याणीति निविद्धानीयं सूक्तं निष्केवल्यस्येति खण्डे इन्द्रस्य नु वीर्याणीत्येतस्मिन्नैन्द्रीं निविदं दध्यात्

(आ० ५-१५) विषुवत्यपि तस्मिन् शस्त्रे एतद्विनियुक्तं विषुवान् दिवा कीर्त्य इति खण्डे सूत्रितम्। इन्द्रस्य नु वीर्याणीत्येतस्मिन्नैन्द्रीं निविदं शस्त्वा (आ ८-६) इति। महाव्रते निष्केवल्येऽपि एतदेव विनियुक्तम् राथन्तरो दक्षिणः पक्ष इति खण्डे चतस्रः सतीः षड्बृहतीः करोति। इन्द्रस्य नु वीर्याणि प्रवोच (ऐ० आ० ५-२-२) इति।।

Verse 1.

इन्द्रस्य। नु। वीर्याणि। प्र। वोचम्। यानि। चकार। प्रथमानि। वज्री। अहन्। अहिम्। अनु। अपः। ततर्द। प्र। वक्षणाः। अभिनत्। पर्वतानाम्।।१।।

वज्री वज्रयुक्त इन्द्रः प्रथमानि पूर्वसिद्धानि मुख्यानि वा* यानि वीर्याणि पराक्रमयुक्तानि कर्माणि चकार। तस्येन्द्रस्य तानि वीर्याणि नु क्षिप्रं प्रब्रवीमि। कानि वीर्याणि इति तदुच्यते। अहिं मेघम् अहन्। हतवान्। तदेतदेकं वीर्यम्। अनु पश्चादपो जलानि ततर्द। हिंसितवान्। भूमौ पातितवानित्यर्थः। इदं द्वितीयं वीर्यम्। पर्वतानां संबन्धिनीर्वक्षणाः। प्रवहणशीला नदीः प्राभिनत्। भिन्नवान्। कूलद्वयकर्षणेन प्रवाहितवानित्यर्थः। इदं तृतीयं वीर्यम्। एवमुत्तरत्रापि द्रष्टव्यम्। वीर्याणि। शूर वीर विक्रान्तौ। ण्यन्तादचो यदिति यत्। (पा० ३-१-९७) णेरनिटीति (पा० ६-४-५१) णिलोपः। तित्स्वरितमिति (पा० ६-१-१८५) स्वरितत्वम्। यतोऽनावः (पा० ६-१-२१३) इत्याद्युदात्तत्वं न भवति। आद्युदात्तत्वे हि सुशब्देन बहुव्रीहौ आद्युदात्तं द्व्यचछंन्दसि (पा० ६-२-११९) इत्यनेनैवोत्तरपदाद्युदात्तत्वस्य सिद्धत्वाद्वीरवीर्यौ च (पा० ६-२-१२०) इति पुनस्तद्विधानमनर्थकं स्यात्। अतोऽवगम्यते यतोऽनाव (पा० ६-२-२१३) इत्याद्युदात्तत्वं वीर्यशब्दे न प्रवर्तत इति। अतः परिशेषात्तित्स्वरितम् (पा० ६-१-१८५) इति प्रत्ययस्य स्वरितत्वमेव। वोचम्। अस्यतिवक्तिख्यातिभ्योऽङ् (पा० ३-१-५२) इति च्लेरङादेशः। बहुलं छन्दस्यमाङ्योगेऽपि (पा० ६-४-७५) इत्यडभावः। चकार। णलि लित्स्वरेण प्रत्ययात्पूर्वस्योदात्तत्वम्। यद्वृत्तयोगादनिघातः। अहन्। लङि

* प्रथमावृत्तौ वा इति नास्ति।

इतश्चेतीकारलोपे हल्ङ्याब्भ्यः० (पा० ६-१-६८) इति तकारलोपः। अहिम्। आङ्पूर्वाद्धन्तेः आङि श्रिहनिभ्यां ह्रस्वश्च (उ० ४-१३७) इतीण्प्रत्ययः। आङो ह्रस्वत्वं च। चशब्देन वेञो डित् (उ० ४७२) सामने ख्यश्चोदात्त (उव ४.१३६) इति डित्त्वं पूर्वपदान्तोदात्तत्वं* चानुकृष्यते। ततष्टिलोपे पूर्वपदस्योदात्तत्वम्। ततर्द। उतृदिर् हिंसानादरयोः। तिङ्ङतिङ इति निघातः। वक्षणाः+। वक्ष रोषे क्रुधमण्डार्थेभ्यश्च (पा० ३-२-१५१) इति युच् चित्स्वरं बाधित्वा व्यत्ययेन प्रत्ययस्वरः।।

तृद् 7., to split open, to let loose, let out; अनु तृद्, to let out after.

प्र वोचम्, 1. sg. aor, inj. par.;rt. वच् 3., to pronounce, proclaim, praise, sing.

वक्षणा f., lower part of the body, belly, womb.

प्र भिद्, to split, smash open.

Read विरिआणि, अनु अपस्.

Verse 2.

अहन् अहिम्। पर्वते। शिश्रियाणम्। त्वष्टा। अस्मै। वज्रम् स्वर्यम्। ततक्ष। वाश्राःऽइव। धेनवः। स्यन्दमानाः। अञ्जः। समुद्रम्। अव। जग्मुः। आपः।।२।।

पर्वते शिश्रियाणमाश्रितम्। अहिं मेघम्। अहन् हतवान्। अस्मा इन्द्राय स्वर्यं सुष्ठु प्रेरणीयं यद्वा शब्दनीयं स्तुत्यं त्वष्टा विश्वकर्मा वज्रं ततक्ष। तनूकृतवान्। तेन वज्रेण मेघे भिन्ने सति स्यन्दमानाः प्रस्रवणयुक्ता आपः समुद्रमञ्जः सम्यगवजग्मुः प्राप्ताः। तत्र दृष्टान्तः। वाश्रा वत्सान् प्रति हम्भारवोपेता धेनव इव। यथा धेनवः सहसा वत्सगृहे गच्छन्ति तद्वत्। शिश्रियाणम्। श्रिञ् सेवायाम्। लिटः कानच्। द्विर्भावहलादिशेषेयङादेशाः। चित्त इत्यातोदात्वम्। स्वर्यम्। ऋ गतौ अस्मात् सुपूर्वात् ऋहलोर्ण्यदिति ण्यत्। संज्ञापूर्वको विधिरनित्य इति वृद्ध्यभावः। यद्वा स्वृ शब्दोपतायोरित्यस्मात्

---

* पदोदात्तत्वमित्यादर्शपाठः।

\+ वक्षणाः इत्यादिपाठः प्रथमावृत्तौ नास्ति।

ण्यति पूर्ववद्वृद्ध्यभावः। तित्स्वरितमिति स्वरितत्वम्। वाश्यन्त इति वाश्राः। वाशृ शब्दे। स्फायितञ्चीत्यदिना रक् (उ० २-१३) जग्मुः। उसि गमहनेत्युपधा-लोपः।।

शिश्रियाण, pt. pf. ātm.; rt. श्रि.

स्वर्य adj., with a good voice, loud, shrill, whizzing.

वाश्र adj., lowing, bleating.

अञ्जः =अञ्जसा, adv., at once, straight.

Ṛcas 1 and 2 are closely interlinked with each other.

Verse 3.

वृषऽयमाणः। अवृणीत। सोमम्। त्रिऽकद्रुकेषु। अपिबत्। सुतस्य। आ। सायकम्। मघऽवा। अदत्त। वज्रम्। अहन्। एनम्। प्रथमऽजाम्। अहीनाम्।।३।।

*वृषायमाणः वृष इवाचरन्निन्द्रः सोममवृणीत वृतवान्। त्रिकद्रुकेषु ज्योतिगौरायुरित्येतन्नामकास्त्रयो यागास्त्रिकद्रुका उच्यन्ते। तेषु सुतस्य अभिषुतस्य सोमस्यांशमपिबत् पीतवान्। मघवा धनवानिन्द्रः सायकं बन्धकं वज्रमादत्त स्वीकृतवान्। तेन च वज्रेण अहीनां मेघानां मध्ये प्रथमजां प्रथमोत्पन्नं मेघम् अहन् हतवान्। वृषायमाणः वृष इवाचरन्। कर्तुः क्यङ्सलोपश्च (पा० ३-१-११) इति क्यङ्। अकृत्वर्वधातुकयोरिति दीर्घः। अदुपदेशाद्धातोरन्तो-दात्तत्वे क्यङन्ताद्धातोरन्तोदात्तत्वम्। सायकम्। षिञ् वन्धने। सिनोति इति सायकः। ण्वुल्। लित्स्वरेणाद्युदात्तत्वम्। प्रथमजां प्रथम जायते इति प्रथमजाः। जनसनखनक्रमगमो विट् (पा० ३-२-६७) विड्वनोरित्यात्वम्।।

वृषायमाण, tyak-formation, meaning see Sāy., comm.

त्रिकद्रुक, name of a soma feast or celebration which foṛmed in the later ritual the first half of the abhiplava. Before the Vṛta fight it was celebrated by the gods in honour

---

* वृषऽयमाणः इत्यादर्शपाठः।।

of Indra. Less brahmnically, but probably more correctly, त्रिकद्रुकाः might be interpeted as the three vessels of soma (कुद्रू, f., soma Vessel).

मघवन् (मघ, plenty, Present), adj., rich, noble, bountiful, generous.

सायक n., missile, arrow.

एनम्, unaccented, defective demonstrative pron. of the 3. person, acc. sg. m.

प्रथमजा adj., m. f., first-born, firstling.

Verse 4.

यत्। इन्द्र। अहन्। प्रथमऽजाम्। अहीनाम्। आत्। मायिनाम्। अमिनाः। प्र। उत। मायाः। आत्। सूर्यम्। जनयन्। द्याम्। उषसम्। तादीत्ना। शत्रुम्। न। किल। विवित्से।।४।।

उत अपि च हे इन्द्र यत् यदा अहीनां मेघानां मध्ये प्रथमजा प्रथमोत्पन्नं मेघं अहन् हतवानसि*। तदनन्तरं मायिनां +माययोपेतानामसुराणां संवन्धिनीर्मायाः प्रामिनाः प्रकर्षेण नाशितवानसि। अनन्तरं सूर्यमुषसम् उषःकालं द्यामाकाशं च जनयन्नुत्पादयन्नावरकमेघनिवारणेन प्रकाशयन् वर्तसे। तादीत्रा तदानीम्। आवरकान्धकाराभावाच्छत्रुं घातकं वैरिणं न विवित्से किल। त्वं न लब्धवान् खलु अहन् हन्तेर्लङि हल्ङ्याब्भ्य इति सिलोपः। अडागम उदात्तः। यद्वृत्तयोगादनिघातः। मायिनां। मायाशब्दस्य ब्रीह्यादिषु पाठात् ब्रीह्यादिभ्यश्च (पा० ५-२-११६) मत्वर्थीय हनिः। अमिनाः। मीञ् हिंसायाम् कैयादिकः। मीनातेर्निगमे। (पा० ७-३-८१) इति ह्रस्वत्वम्। तादीत्रा। तदानीमित्यस्य पृषौदरादित्वाद्वर्णविपर्ययः। किल। निपातस्य ++च (पा० ६-३-१३६) इति दीर्घत्वम्। विवित्से। विद्लृ लाभे क्रादिनियमात् प्राप्त इट् व्यत्ययेन न भवति।।

---

* आदर्शे इतवानसि इल्यत्र न चरणचिह्नं दृश्यते।

\+ आदर्शे मायोपेतानामिति पाठः।

++ आदर्शे स्येति।

आत् conj., therefore, then; आत् उत, and, and also.

ता॒दीत्ना॑, adv.=तदानीम् (Sāy.), then already, ever since.

वि॒वित्से॒, 2. sg. pf. ātm.; rt. विद्द 6.

जन् १. U. causat., to produce, manifest, Sāy. प्रकाशय. Note the (natural) attempt at the anuprāsa in the second triṣṭubh.

Verse 5.

अह॑न्। वृ॒त्रम्। वृ॒त्र॒ऽत॑रम्। वि॒ऽअं॑सम्। इन्द्रः॑ वज्रे॑ण। म॒ह॒ता। व॒धेन॑। स्कन्धां॑सिऽइव। कु॒लिश॑न। विऽवृ॑क्णा। अहिः॑। श॒य॒ते॒। उ॒प॒ऽपृक्। पृ॒थि॒व्याः।।५।।

अयमिन्द्रो वज्रेण संपादिता यो महान् वधः तेन वज्रेण वृत्रतरम् अतिशयेन लोकानामावरकमन्धकाररूपम्। यद्वा। वृत्रैरावरणैः सर्वान् शत्रूंस्तरति तम्। वृत्रमेतन्नामकमसुरं व्यंसं विगतासं छिन्नबाहुर्यथा भवति तथा अहन् हतवान्। अंसच्छेदे दृष्टान्तः। कुलिशेन कुठारेण विवृक्णा विशेषतः छिन्नानि स्कन्धांसीव। यथा वृक्षस्कन्धाश्छिन्ना भवन्ति तद्वत्। तथा सति अहिर्वृत्रः। पृथिव्या उपरि उपपृक् सामीप्येन संपृक्तः शयने शयनं करोति। छिन्नकाष्ठवद्भूमौ पततीत्यर्थः। वृत्रतरम्। वृतु वर्तने। स्फायितञ्चि (उ० १३-२) इत्यादिना भावे रक्प्रत्ययान्तो वृत्रशब्दः। वृत्रेणावरणेन सर्व तरतीति वृत्रतरः। तरतेः पच्चाद्यच् (पा० ३-१-१३४) पारादिश्छन्दसि बहुलम्। (पा० ६-२-१९९) इत्युत्तरपदाद्युदात्तत्वम्। तरपि तु व्यत्ययेन। व्यंसम्। बहुव्रीहौ पूर्वपदप्रकृतिस्वरितत्वे उदात्तस्वरितयोर्यणः (पा० ८-२-४) इति स्वरितत्वम्। वधेन हनश्च वध इति भावे अप्। तत्सन्नियोगेन धातोर्वधादेशः। स चान्तोदात्तः। अन्त्यस्याकारस्य अतो लोपः (पा० ६-४-४८) इति लोप उदात्तनिवृत्तिस्वरेण प्रत्ययस्योदात्तत्वम्। विवृक्णा। ओव्रश्चू छेदने। कर्मणि निष्ठा। यस्य विभाषा (पा० ७-२-१५) इतीट्प्रतिषेधः। ओदितश्च (पा० ८-२-४५) इति परत्वान्निष्ठानत्वम्। ततो व्रश्च भ्रस्जेति० (पा० ८-२-३६) षत्वे प्राप्ते निष्ठादेशः षत्वस्वरप्रत्ययेड्विधिषु सिद्धो वक्तव्यः (पा० ८-२-६२) इति नत्वस्य सिद्धत्वेन झल्परत्वाभावात् षत्वं न भवति। कुत्वे तु कर्तव्ये

तदसिद्धमेव (पा० ८-२-२१) इति चोः कुः (पा० ८-२-३०) इति कुत्वम्। शेश्छन्दसि बहुलमिति शेर्लोपः। गतिरनन्तर इति गतेः प्रकृतिस्वरत्वम्। शयते। बहुलं छन्दसीति शपो लुगभावः। पृथिव्याः। उदात्तयणो हल्पूर्वात् (पा० ६-१-१७४) इति विभक्तेरुदात्तत्वम्।।

व्यंस adj., without shoulder; name or epithet of Vṛtra. It is better to take with Sāy. व्यंस as a mere epithet of Vṛtra than as an independent proper name of another demon besides Vṛtra.

स्कन्धंस् n. = स्कन्ध, trunk of a tree.

विवृक्ण, pt. pres, ātm; rt. (वि) व्रश्च्, to cut to pieces.

उप पृक् adv., covering, flat on, with genit.

Verse 6.

अयोद्धाऽइव। दुःऽमदः। आ। हि। जुह्वे। महावीरम्। तुविऽबाधम्। ऋजीषम्। न। अतारीत्। अस्य। संऽऋतिम्। वधानाम्। सम्। रुजानाः। पिपिषे। इन्द्रऽशत्रुः।।६।।

दुर्मदो *दुष्टमदोपेतो दर्पयुक्तो वृत्रः अयोद्धेव योद्धृरहित इव इन्द्रमा जुह्वे हि आहूतवान् खलु। कीदृशमिन्द्रम् महावीरं गुणैर्महान् भूत्वा शैर्योपेतं तुविबाधं बहूनां बाधकमृजीषं शत्रूणामपार्जकम्। अस्येदृशस्येन्द्रस्य संबन्धिनो ये शत्रुबधाः सन्ति तेषां वधानां समृतिं संगमं नातारीत्। पूर्वोक्तो दुर्मदः तरीतुं नाशक्नोत्। इन्द्रशत्रुः इन्द्रः शत्रुर्घातको यस्य वृत्रस्य तादृशो वृत्रः इन्द्रेण हतो नदीषु पतितः सन् रुजाना नदीः संपिपिषे सम्यक् पिष्टवान्। सर्वान् लोकानावृण्वतो वृत्रदेहस्य पातेन नदीनां कूलानि तत्रत्यपाषाणादिकं च चूर्णीभूतमित्यर्थः अयोद्धाऽइव। न विद्यते योद्धास्येति बहुव्रीहौ नञ्सुभ्यामित्युत्तरपदान्तोदात्तत्वं समासान्तविधेरनित्यत्वात्। (परि० ८४) नद्यृतश्च (पा० ५-४-१५३) इति कबभावः। जुह्वे। ह्वेञ स्पर्धायां शब्दे च। अभ्यस्तस्य

* हर्षयुक्तो इति प्रथमावृत्तौ।

च (पा० ६-१-३३) इति सप्रसारणम्। उवङादेशाभावश्छान्दसः। यद्वा छन्दस्युभयथेति सार्वधातुकसज्ञायां हुश्नुवोः सार्वधातुके (पा० ६-४-८७) इति यणादेशः। अत्र लक्षणप्रतिपदोक्तपरिभाषा (पा० १०५) लक्ष्यारोनुधान्नाश्रीयते। इतरथा हि आजुह्वान इत्यादिषु यणादेशो न स्यात्। च चैवं साति सातये हुवे वाम्। (ऋ० ६-७-१३) इत्यादावपि तथा स्यादिति वाच्यम्। अनेकाच्त्वाभावात्। अनेकाच इति हि तत्रानुवर्तते। प्रत्यस्वरेणान्तोदात्तत्वम्। हिचेति निघातप्रतिषेधः। महावीरं महांश्चासौ वीरश्च महावीरः। आन्महतः० (पा० ६-३-४६) इति आत्त्वम् तुविबाधम्। बाधृ विलोडने। तुवीन् प्रभूतान् बाधते इति तुविबाधः। पचाद्यच्। कृदुत्तरपदप्रकृतिस्वरत्वम्। समृतिम्। तादौ चेति गतेः प्रकृतिस्वरत्वम्। रुजानाः रुजो भङ्गे। रुजन्ति कूलानीति रुजानाः नद्यः रुजाना नद्यो भवन्ति रुजन्ति कूलानि (नि० ६-४) इति यास्कः। व्यत्ययेन शानच्। तुदादिभ्यः शः। नुमभावश्छान्दसः। अदुपदेशाल्लसार्वधातुकानुदात्तत्वे विकरणस्वरः। पिपिषे। पिष्लृ संचूर्णने। व्यत्ययेन लिट्। इन्द्रशत्रुः। बहुब्रीहौ पूर्वपदप्रकृतिस्वरत्वम्।।

अ॒योधृ is by Sāy. here according to the bahuvrīhi accent interpreted by योधृरहित, This is correct, and his interpretation योद्धुमशक्त whic he suggests in Taitt. Brāhm., and which is accepted by Geldner, Glossar, is wrong.

तु॒वि॒वा॒ध adj., many or hard pressing, cornering.

ऋ॒जी॒ष n., remains of the soma plant after it has once been squeezed for the libation.

ऋ॒जी॒ष=ऋजीषिन् (see Nirukta 5.12, Durga), drinking the remains of the soma, drinking the soma to the dregs or less.

अ॒ता॒री॒त्, 3. sg. aor. par.; rt. तॄ, to cross, stand, withstand, escpe.

सम॑ृति f., clash, onslaught.

रुजाना f., river (Naigh. 1.13). Sāy. interprets the fourth pāda as follows :—Through the fall of Vṛtra's body, which covered everything around, the river banks and all that was there, stones, etc., were crushed to atoms. —Geldner, commentar i. 1., accepts this view, adding :—Even when dying Vṛtra would not let go the rivers.—According to Sāy. (and Durga) the rivers are रुजानाः, becuse they break and tear away the binks. Hence the translation :—He pulverised the rigers. (Ṛiksangraha, ed. V.G. Bijāpūrkr, M.A., note i.I.). Everybody will agree that the "image is no doubt a little too strained", but not everybody may find that it is "none the less admirable."

On the contrary, the mention of the effect of the waters flowing does not fit in well here. More over, thee etymological authority on which the interpretation of रुजाना by river rests, is not very strong. Another conjecture, referring रुजानाः to Vṛtra, is opposed by the change of gender and accent it would require.

Oldenberg (Ṛgveda, Textkritische und Exegetische Noten. i.1) suggests that रुजानाः is a sandhi compound of रुजा (instr. sg. of the root-noun रुज्, f., the breaking smashing) and अनास्, (bahuvr. cpd., without nose). Cp. व्यंस (5), अपाद्, अहस्त (7). The original accent of the sandhi cpd. रुजानाः may have been changed into the present one रुजानाः as the compound was considered to be one word. The context and the grammatical form seem to favour this interpretation. Other explanations see 1.c.

Verse 7.

अपात्। अहस्तः। अपृतन्यत्। इन्द्रम्। आ। अस्य। वज्रम्। अधि। सानौ। जघान । वृष्णः। वध्रि। प्रतिऽमानम्। बुभूषन्। पुरुऽत्रा वृत्रः। अशयत्। विऽअस्तः।।७।।

अपात् वज्रेण *च्छिन्नत्वात्पादरहितः अहस्तः हस्तरहितो वृत्रः इन्द्र-मुद्दिश्य अपृतन्यत्। पृतनां युद्धमैच्छत्। द्वेषाधिक्येन बहुधा विद्धोऽपि युद्धं न परित्यक्तवानित्यर्थः। अस्य हस्तपादहीनस्य वृत्रस्य सानौ पर्वतसानुसदृशे प्रौढस्कन्धे +अधि उपरि वज्रं जघान इन्द्र आभिमुख्येन प्रक्षिप्तवान्। अशक्तस्यापि युद्धेच्छायां दृष्टान्तः। वध्रिः छिन्नमुष्कः पुरुषः वृष्णो रेतः सेचनसमर्थस्य पुरुषान्तरस्य प्रतिमानं सादृश्यं बुभूषन् प्राप्तुमिच्छन् यथा न शक्नोति तद्वदयमिति शेषः। स वृत्रः पुरुत्रा बहुष्ववयवेषु व्यस्तः विविधं क्षिप्तः ताडितः सन् अशयत् भूमो पतितवान्। अपात्। बहुव्रीहौ पादशब्दस्यान्त्यलोपश्छान्दसः। अहस्तः। बहुब्रीहौ नञसुभ्यामित्युत्तरपदान्तो दात्तत्वम्। अपृतन्यत्। सुप आत्मनः क्यच्। कव्यध्वरपृतनस्येत्यन्त्यलोपः बुभूषन्। सनिग्रहगुहोश्च (पा० ७-२-१२) इतीट्प्रतिषेधः। पुरुत्रा। देवमनुष्यपुरुषपुरुमर्त्येभ्यो द्वितीयासप्तम्योर्बहुलम् (पा० ५-४-५६) इति सप्तम्यर्थे। त्राप्रत्ययः अशयत्। व्यत्ययेन परस्मैपदम्। बहुलं छन्दसीति शपो लुगभावः। व्यस्तः। असु क्षेपणे इत्यस्मात् कर्मणि क्तः। यस्य विभा-षेतीट्प्रतिषेधः। गतिरनन्तर इति गतेः प्रकृतिस्वरत्वम्। संहितायामुदात्तस्वरित-योर्यण इति परस्यानुदात्तस्य स्वरितत्वम्।।

पृतन्य, denom. vb. from पृतना, to attack, pick a quarrel, fight.

आ हन्, to hit, drive into, fix into (अधि with locat.)

वध्रि m., castrated bull.

बुभूषन्, pt. pres. desid.; rt. भू.

प्रतिमान n., counterbalance, mtch for; ep. अयोधृ in 6.

Vṛtra according to Sāy. is अपाद्, अहस्त, because he has lost hands and feet in the fight. It is not likely that these epithets refer to his serpentine shape.

---

* 'छित्वा पाद' इति प्रथमावृत्तौ।

+ न्धेऽध्युपरि आदर्शपाठः।

Verse 8.

नदम्। न। भिन्नम्। अमुया। शयानम्। मनः। रुहाणाः। अति। यन्ति। आपः। याः। चित्। वृत्रः। महिना। परिऽअतिष्ठत्। तासाम्। अहिः। पत्सुतःऽशीः। बभूव।।८।।

*अमुयामुष्यां पृथिव्यां शयानं पतितं मृतं वृत्रमापो जलानि अति यन्ति अतिक्रम्य गच्छन्ति। तत्र दृष्टान्तः। भिन्नं बहुधा भिन्नकूलं नदं न सिंधुमिवां यथा वृष्टिकाले प्रभूता आपो नद्याः कूलं भित्त्वातिक्रम्य गच्छन्ति तद्वत्। कीदृश्य आपः। +मनो रुहाणाः। नृणां चित्तमारोहन्त्यः। पुरा वृत्रे जीवति सति तेन निरुद्धा मेघस्थिता आपो भूमौ वृष्टा न भवन्ति तदानीं नृणां मनः खिद्यते। मृते तु वृत्रे निरोधरहिता आपो वृत्रशरीरमुल्लङ्घ्य प्रवहन्ति तदा वृष्टिलाभेन तु मनुष्यस्तुष्यन्तीत्यर्थः। तदेतदुत्तरार्धेन स्पष्टीक्रियते। वृत्रो जीवनदशायां महिना स्वकीयेन महिम्ना याश्चित् या एव मेघगता अपः पर्यतिष्ठत् परिवृत्य स्थितवान्। अहिर्वृत्रो मेघः तासामपां पत्सुतःशीः पादस्याधः शयानो बभूव। यद्यप्यपा पादो नास्ति तथा प्यद्भिर्वृत्रस्याभिलङ्घितत्वात् पादस्याधः शयनमुपपद्यते। भिन्नम्। रदाभ्यां निष्ठातो न (पा० ८-२-४२) इति नत्वम्। अमुया। सुपां सुलुगिति सप्तम्या याजादेशः। शयानम्। शीङः सार्वधातुके गुणः (पा० ७-४-२१)। धातोर्ङित्त्वाल्लसर्वधातुकानुदात्तत्वे धातुस्वरः। रुहाणाः। रुह बीजजन्मनि प्रादुर्भावे। व्यत्ययेन शानच्। कर्तरि शपि प्राप्ते व्यत्ययेन शः। अनित्यमागमशासनमिति वचनान्मुमभावः। अदुप-देशाल्लसार्वधातुकानुदात्तत्वे विकरणस्वरे प्राप्ते धातुस्वरः। महिना। मह पूजायाम् सर्वधातुभ्य इन् (उ० ४-११७) इतीन्प्रत्ययः। व्यत्ययेन विभक्तेरुदात्तत्वम्। यद्वा महिना महिम्ना। महच्छब्दस्य पृथ्वादिषु पाठात्तस्य भाव इत्येतस्मिन्नर्थे पृथ्वादिभ्य इमनिज्वा (पा० ५-१-१२२) इति इमनिच् प्रत्ययः। टेरिति टिलोपः। चित इत्यन्तोदात्तत्वम्। तृतीयैकवचने अल्लोपे सति उदात्तनिवृत्तिस्वरेण तस्योदात्तत्वम्। मकारलोपश्छान्दसः। पत्सुतःशीः। पादस्याधःशेत इति

---

* प्रथमावृत्तौ अमुया अमुष्यां इति पाठः।

+ प्रथमावृत्तौ मनोरूहाणाः इति संयुक्तः पाठः।

पत्सुतःशीः। क्विप् चेति क्विप्। तसि पद्दन्नित्यादिना पादशब्दस्य पदादेशः। शस्प्रभृतिष्विति प्रभृतिशब्दः प्रकारवचन इति शलादोषणीत्यत्रापि दोषन्नादेशो भवति (का० ६-१-६३) इत्युक्तत्वात्। मध्ये सु इति शब्दोपजनश्छान्दसः यद्वा पादशब्दस्य सप्तमीबहुवचने पदादेशे कृते इतराभ्योऽपि दृश्यन्ते (पा० ५-३-१४) इति सप्तम्यर्थे तसिल् लुगभावश्छान्दसः।

न॒द m., river (Sāy.), roarer, bull (Roth, Grassmann, Oldenberg); नद =नळ, नल, reed (Pischel, Ved, Stud. I. 183 f.; ZDMG. 35, 717).

अ॒मु॒या adv. from अ॒दस्, in this way, in vain, without much ado.

प॒त्सु॒तःशी adj., lying at one's feet.

The first two pādas have been variously interpreted :—

Sāy :— Past him who was lying on the earth the waters passed, raising the spirits of the men, as (during the rainy season) the waters of a river overflow the banks which have been broken.

Geldner, Glossar,takes मनो॑ रुहा॑णाः, like the later मनोनिरुध्, to mean to be without sympathy, hard hearted; in the Glossar, Nachträge and verbesserungen, he seems inclined to translate मनों रुह् by to resolve, take heart, pluck up courage.

Pischel, Ved. Stud. I.c., taking न॒द to be नल, a reed, instead of मनो॑ रुहा॑णाः reads मनो॑र् उहा॑णाः flowing for (the benefit of) man.

Verse 9.

नी॒चाऽव॑याः। अ॒भ॒व॒त्। वृ॒त्रऽपु॑त्रा। इन्द्रः॑। अ॒स्याः। अव॑। वधः॑। ज॒भा॒र। उत्ऽत॑रा सूः। अध॑रः। पु॒त्रः। आ॒सी॒त्। दानुः॑। श॒ये॒। स॒हऽव॑त्सा। न। धे॒नुः।। ९।।

वृत्रपुत्रा वृत्रः पुत्रो यस्या मातुः सेयं माता वृत्रपुत्रा नीचावया न्यग्भावं प्राप्त इताभवत्। पुत्रं प्रहारादक्षितुं पुत्रदेहस्योपरि तिरश्री पतितवतीत्यर्थः।

तदानीमयमिन्द्रोऽस्या मातुरवाऽधोभागे वृत्रस्योपरि वधो हननसाधनमायुधं जभार प्रहृतवान्। तदानीं सूर्मातोत्तरोपरिस्थितासीत्। पुत्रस्त्वधोभागस्थित आसीत्। सा च दानुर्दानवी वृत्रमाता शये। मृता शयनं कृतवती। तत्र दृष्टान्तः। धेनुर्लोकप्रसिद्धा गौः सहवत्सा न यथा वत्ससहिता शयनं करोति तद्वत्। नीचावयाः। वेति खादतीति वयो बाहुः। औणादिकोऽसिप्रत्ययः। न्यञ्चौ वयसौ यस्याः सा नीचावयाः। *न्यचशब्दादुत्तरस्या विभक्तेः सुपा सुपो भवन्तीति तृतीयैकवचनादेशः। अच इत्यकारलोपे चाविति दीर्घत्वम्। अञ्चेश्छन्दस्यसर्वनामस्थानम् (पा० ६-१-१७०) इति तस्योदात्तत्वम् सामसे लुगभावश्छान्दसः। बहुव्रीहौ पूर्वपदप्रकृतिस्वरत्वम्। यद्वा नीचौ निकृष्टौ वयसौ यस्याः सा। पूर्वपदस्य दीर्घश्छान्दसः। वधः। हन्यतेऽनेनेति वधः। असुनि। हन्तेर्वधादेशः। नित्त्वादाद्युदात्तत्वम्। जभार। हृग्रहोर्भ इति भत्वम्।। सूः। षूङ् प्राणिगर्भविमोचने। सूते गर्भं विमुञ्चतीति सूर्माता। क्विप् चेति क्विप्। दानुः। दो अवखण्डने। दाभाभ्यां नुः। (उ० ३-३२) शये। लटि लोपस्त आत्मनेपदेषु (पा० ७-१-४१) इति तलोपः। शीङः सार्वधातुक इति गुणेऽयादेशः।।

नी॒चाव॑यस्, one whose strength, life, is going down, coming to an end.

जभार, 3.sg. pf. par.; rt. भृः; अव भृ, throw, fling on; for Sāy.'s explanation see comm.

वध॑र् n. = वध m., weapon.

सू f., mother.

न, as; usually after the upamāna; before the upamāna especially as the last but one word to the pāda.

शये, 3. sg. pres. ātm.; शी २, to lie.

दानु॑, f., proper name of the mother of the demons, in particular of Vṛtra's mother.

---

* प्रथमावृतौ न्यञ्च इति पाठः।

Verse 10.

अति॑ष्ठन्तीनाम्। अ॒नि॒ऽवे॒श॒नाना॑म्। काष्ठा॑नाम्। मध्ये॑। निऽहि॑तम्। शरी॑रम्। वृ॒त्रस्य॑। नि॒ण्यम्। वि। च॒र॒न्ति॒। आप॑:। दी॒र्घम्। तम॑:। आ अ॒श॒य॒त्॥ इन्द्र॑ऽशत्रुः॥१०॥

वृत्रस्य शरीरमापो विचरन्ति *विशेषेणपर्याक्रम्य प्रवहन्ति। कीदृशं शरीरम् निण्यम्। निर्नामधेयम् अप्सु मग्नत्वेन गूढत्वात्तदीयं नाम न केनापि ज्ञायते। एतदेव स्पष्टीक्रियते। काष्टानामपां मध्ये निहितं निक्षिप्तम्। कीदृशानां काष्ठानाम् अतिष्ठन्तीनां स्थितिरहितानाम्। अनिवेशनानामुपवेशनरहितानाम्। प्रवहणस्वभावत्वादेतासां मनुष्यवन्न क्वापि स्थितिः संभवति। इन्द्रशत्रुः वृत्रो जलमध्ये शरीरे प्रक्षिप्ते सति दीर्घं तमो +दीर्घनिद्रात्मकं मरणं यथा भवति तथा आशयत्। सर्वतः पतितवान्। अतिष्ठन्तीनाम्। अव्ययपूर्वपदप्रकृतिस्वर-त्वम्। अनिवेशनानाम्। ++निविशन्तेऽस्मिन्निति निवेशनं स्थानम्। करणाधि-करणयोश्च (पा० ३-३-११७) इत्यधिकरणे ल्युट्। तद्रहितानां बहुव्रीहौ नञ्सुभ्यामित्युत्तरपदान्तोपदात्तत्वम्। क्रान्त्व स्थिताः काष्ठाः पृषोदरादि। निहितम्। गतिरनन्तर इति गतेः प्रकृतिस्वरत्वम्। अत्र यास्कः। अतिष्ठन्ती-नामनिवशमानानामित्यस्थावराणां काष्ठानां मध्ये निहितं शरीरं मेघः। शरीरम्। शृणातेः शम्नातेर्वा वृत्रस्य निण्यं निर्णामं विचरन्ति विजानन्ति आप इति। दीर्घं द्राघतेस्तमस्तनोतेराशयदाशेतेरिन्द्रशत्रुरिन्द्रोऽस्य शमयिता वा शातयिता वा तस्मादिन्द्रशत्रुः। तत्को वृत्रो मेघ इति नैरुक्तास्त्वाष्ट्रोऽसुरः इत्यैतिहासिकाः (नि० २-१६) इति॥

अ॒नि॒वे॒श॒न adj., restless.

काष्ठा॑ f., goal (of the race); battlefield, river bed, river.

नि॒ण्य adj., hidden; subst. n., secret (गुह्यम्), shame; Sāy: nameless.

आ शी, sink (down) into.

---

* आदर्शे णोपर्या इति पाठः।

\+ दीर्घ इत्यादर्शपाठः।

++ शन्त्य इति प्रथमावृत्तौ।

Verse 11.

दासऽपत्नीः। अहिऽगोपाः। अतिष्ठन्। निऽरुद्धाः। आपः। पणिनाऽइव। गावः। अपाम्। बिलम्। अपिऽहितम्। यत्। आसीत्। वृत्रम्। जघन्वान्। अप। तत्। ववार ।११ ।।

दासपत्नीः। दासो *विश्वोपक्षयहेतुर्वृत्रः पतिः स्वामी यासामपां ता दासपत्नीः। अतएवाहिगोपाः। अहिर्वृत्रो गोपा रक्षको यासां ताः। गोपनं नाम स्वच्छन्देन यथा न प्रवहन्ति तथा निरोधनम्। एतदेव स्पष्टीक्रियते। आपो निरुद्धा अतिष्ठन्निति। तत्र दृष्टान्तः। पणिनेव गावः। पणिनामकोऽसुरो गा अपहृत्य बिले स्थापयित्वा बिलद्वारमाच्छाद्य यथा निरुद्धवांस्तथेत्यर्थः। अपां यद्बिलं प्रवहणद्वारमपिहितं वृत्रेण निरुद्धमासीत् तद्बिलं प्रवहणद्वारं वृत्रं जघन्वान् हतवानिन्द्रोऽपववार अपवृत्तमकरोत्। वृत्रकृतमपां निरोधं परिहृतवान्। हतवानिन्द्रोऽपववार अपवृत्तमकरोत्। वृत्रकृतमपां निरोधं परिहृतवान्। हतवान्। अत्र यास्कः। दासवृत्तमकरोत्। वृत्रकृतमपां निरोधं परिहृतवान्। हतवान्। अत्र यास्कः। दासपतेर्दासाधिपत्नयो दासो दस्यतेरूपदासयति कर्माण्यहिगोपा अतिष्ठन्नहिना गुप्ताः। अहिरयनादेत्यन्तरिक्षेऽयमपीतरोऽहिरेतस्मादेव निर्ह्रसितोपसर्ग आहन्तीति। निरुद्धा आपः पणिनेव गावः। पणिर्वणिग् भवति पणिः पणाद्वणिक् पण्यं नेनेक्ति। अपां बिलमपिहितं यदासीत्। बिलं भरं भवति बिभर्तेर्वृत्रं जघ्निवानप ववार तद्वृत्रो वृणोतेर्वा वर्ततेर्वा वर्धतेर्वा यदावृणोत्तद्वृत्रस्य वृत्रत्वमिति विज्ञायते। यदवर्तत तद्वृत्रस्य वृत्रत्वमिति विज्ञायते। (नि० २-१७) इति। दासपत्नीः। दसु उपक्षये। दासयतीति दासो वृत्रः। पचाद्यच्। चित इत्यन्तोदात्तत्वम्। दासः पतिर्यासां विभाषासपूर्वस्य (पा० ४-१-३४) इति ङीप्। तत्सन्नियोगेनेकारस्य नकारः बहुव्रीहौ पूर्वपदप्रकृति-स्वरत्वम्। अहिगोपाः। गुपू रक्षणे। गोपायीति गोपाः। आयादय आर्धधातुके वा (पा० ३-१-३१) इत्यायप्रत्ययः। ततः क्विप्। अतो लोपः। वेरपृक्तलोपाद्वलि लोपोबलीयानिति पूर्वं यकारलोपः। (पा० ६-१-६६-६७) नचाचः परस्मिन्नित्यतो लोपस्य स्थानिवत्त्वम्। न पदान्तद्विर्वचनेति प्रतिषेधात्। अहिर्गोपा यासां। पूर्ववत्स्वरः। निरूद्धाः। रूधिर आवरणे। झपस्तथोर्धोऽधः (पा० ८-८२-४०) इति निष्ठातकारस्य धकारः। गतिरनन्तर इति गतेः प्रकृतिस्वर-

---

* क्षपण इत्यादर्शः।

त्वम्। जघन्वान् हन्तेर्लिटः क्वसुः। अभ्यासाच्च (पा० ७-३-५५) इत्याभ्या-7 सादुत्तरस्य हकारस्य कुत्वम्। क्रादिनियमप्राप्तस्येटो विभाषा गमहनेत्यादिना (पा० ७-२-६८) विकल्पविधानादभावः। संहितायां नकारस्य रुत्वानुनासिका-वुक्तौ।।

बिल n., hole, cave, opening; प्रवाहनद्वारम्.

Verse 12.

अश्व्यः। वारः। अभवः। तत्। इन्द्र। सृके। यत्। त्वा। प्रतिऽअहन्। देवः। एकः। अजयः। गाः। अजयः। शूर। सोमम्। अव। असृजः। सर्तवे। सप्त। सिन्धून्।।१२।।

सृके वज्रे। सृको वृक इति वज्रामसु पठितत्वात्। *युद्धे देवो दीप्य-मानः सर्वायुधकुशल एकोऽद्वितीयो वृत्रो यद्यदा त्वा त्वां प्रत्यहन्तप्रतिकूलत्वेन प्रहृतवान् तत्तदानीं त्वमश्वयो वारोऽश्वसंबन्धी वालोऽभवः। यथाश्वस्य बालोऽनायासेन +मक्षिकादीन्निवारयति तद्वत्रमगणयित्वा निराकृतवानित्यर्थः। किं च गाः पणिनापहृतास्त्वमजयः। जितवान्। हे शूर शौर्ययुक्तेन्द्र सोममजयः। जितवान्। तथाच तैत्तिरीयाः त्वष्टा हतपुत्र इत्यस्मिन्नुपाख्यो समामनन्ति। स यज्ञवेशसं कृत्वाप्रासहा सोममपिबत् (तै० सं० २-४-१२) इति। सप्त सिन्धून्—इमं मे गङ्गे (ऋ० १०-७५-५) इत्यस्यामृच्याम्नाता गङ्गाद्याः सप्तसंख्याका नदीः। सर्तवे सर्तुप्रवाहरूपेण गन्तुम् अवासृजः। स त्यक्तवान्। वृत्रकृतं प्रवाहनिरोधं निराकृतवानित्यर्थः। अश्व्यः अश्वे भवः। भवे छन्दसीति यत्। यतोनाव इत्याद्युदात्तत्वम्। वारयति दंशमशकानिति वारः। पचाद्यच्। कपिलकादित्वाल्लत्वविकल्पः। (म० ८-२-१८) वृषादित्वादाद्युदात्तत्वम्। प्रत्यहन्। यद्वृत्तान्नित्यमिति निधातप्रतिषेधः। तिङि चोदात्तवतीति गतेरनुदात्तत्वम्।
प्रत्यहन्। यद्वृत्तान्नित्यमिति निधातप्रतिषेधः। तिङि चोदात्तवतीति गतेरनुदात्तत्वम्।
अजयः। गा इत्यस्य वाक्यान्तरगतत्वात्तदपेक्षयास्य तिङ्ङतिङ इति निघातो न भवति। समानवाक्ये निघातयुष्मस्मदादेशा वक्तव्याः (पा० १-१-१८-५) इति वचनात्। सर्तवे। तुमर्थे सेसेनिति तवेन् प्रत्ययः। नित्त्वादाद्युदात्ततवम्।।

वार m. = वाल, hair of a horse's tail.

* आदर्शे युद्धे इति नास्ति।

+ प्रथमावृत्तौ दीनि इति पाठः।

सृ॒क m., pointed object, sharp edge, spear, वज्र (Naigh. 2.20).

सर्त॑वे, dat.inf. rt. सृ.

स॒प्त सिंध॑वः occur only once in the Ṛgveda as the designation of a definite country (VIII. 2427), while elsewhere (in the Ṛgveda, Atharvaveda, the Vājasaneyisaṁhitā, Taittirīyasaṁhitā) the seven rivers themselves are meant. Max Müller thinks that the five streams of the Panjab, with the Indus and the Sarasvatī, are intended; others (Ludwig, Lassen, Whitney) hold that the Kubhā should be substituted for the Sarasvatī, or (as Thomaṣ suggests) that perhaps the Ozus must orginally have been one of the seven. Zimmer is probably right in laying no stress at all on any identifications; "seven" being one of the favourite numbers in the Ṛgveda and later. (Macdonell and keith, Vedic Index of Names and Subjects, s.v.)

दे॒व एक॑ः may be taken as belonging to the principal clause, being in apposition to अ॒भ॒व॒स्... इन्द्र; सृके अ॑हन्... अह॑न् in that case would appear as an insertion into the principal clause. Or, दे॒व एक॑ः may be taken to start the sentence अज॑यो॒ गाः in the third pāda. In any case it would mean: being alone as god (in the fight) or unique as god. Sāy. Connects it with Vṛtra. Cp. No. 14 5: (इ॒न्द्र॒) एक॒ इत्, and No. 11. 6: (वृ॒त्रम्) अदे॑वम्.

Verse 13.

न। अ॒स्मै॒। वि॒ऽद्युत्। न। त॒न्य॒तुः। सि॒षे॒ध। न। याम्। मिह॑म्। अकि॑रत्। ह्रा॒दुनि॑म्। च॒। इन्द्र॑। च॒। यत्। यु॒यु॒धाते॑ इति॑। अहिः॑। च॒। उ॒त। अ॒त॒रीभ्यः॑। म॒घऽवा॑। वि। जि॒ग्ये॥ १३॥

इन्द्रं निषेद्धुं वृत्रो यान्विद्युदादीन् मायया निर्मितवान् ते सर्वेऽप्येनं निषेद्धुमशक्ताः। सोऽयमर्थोऽनेन मन्त्रेणोच्यते। अस्मै इन्द्रार्थं निर्मिता विद्युन्न

सिषेधइन्द्रं न प्राप्नोत्। तथा तन्यतुः गर्जनं यां मिहं सेचनं यां वृष्टिमकिरत् वृत्रो विक्षिप्तवान् साऽपि वृष्टिर्न सिषेधं ह्रादुनिं चाशनिमपि यां वृत्रः प्रयुक्तवान् सापि न सिषेधं इन्द्रश्चाहिश्च इन्द्रवृत्रावुभावपि यद्यदा युयुधाते युद्धं कृतवन्तौ। तदानीं विद्युदादयो न प्राप्ता इति पूर्वत्रान्वयः। उतापि च मघवा धनवानिन्द्रः अपरीभ्यः अपराभ्यः अन्यासामपि वृत्रनिर्मितानां मायानां सकाशाद्विजिग्ये विशेषेण जितवान्। सिषेघ। षिधु गत्याम्। मिहम्। मिह सेचने। मेहति सिञ्चतीति मिट्वृष्टिः। क्विप् चेति क्विप्। अकिरत्। कॄ विक्षेपे। तुदादिभ्यः शः। ऋत इद्धातोरितीत्वम्। अडागम उदात्तः। यद्वृत्तयोगादनिघातः। युयुधाते। युध संप्रहारे। लिटि प्रत्ययस्वरः। जिग्ये। सन्लिटोर्जेः। (पा० ७-३-५७) इत्यभ्यासादुत्तरस्य जकारस्य कुत्वम्।।

सिध् 4, Succeed , be of any avail to.

मिह् f., clouds, mist, shower.

ह्रादुनि॑ f., haistone.

अ॒प॒री viz. रात्री॑ f., plur., coming nights, coming "days", future.

verse 14.

अहे॑ः। या॒तार॑म्। कम्। अ॒प॒श्यः। इ॒न्द्र॒। हृदि। यत्। ते॒। ज॒घ्नुषे॑ः। भीः। अग॑च्छत्। नव॑। च॑। यत्। न॒व॒तिम्। च॒। स्रव॑न्तीः। श्ये॒नः। न। भी॒तः। अत॑रः। रजां॑सि।।१४।।

हे इन्द्र जघ्नुषो वृत्रं हतवतस्तव हृदि चित्ते यद्यदि भीरगाच्छत् न हतवानस्मीति बुद्ध्या भयं प्राप्नुयात् तर्ह्यहेर्वृत्रस्य यातारं हन्तारं कमपश्यः। त्वत्तोऽन्यं कं पुरुषं दृष्टवानसि तादृशस्य पुरुषान्तरस्याभावान्माभूत्तव लयमित्यर्थः। यद्यस्मात्कारणात्त्वं नव च नवतिं च स्त्रवन्तीः एकोनशत-संख्याकाः प्रवहन्तीर्नदीः प्राप्य रजांसि तत्रत्यान्युदकान्यतरः। तीर्णवानसि। तत्र दृष्टान्तः। श्येनो न। श्येननामको बलवान् पक्षीव। दूरगमनात्तव भयमासीदिति गम्यते। तद्भयं माभूदित्यभिप्रायः। तच्च दूरगमनं ब्राह्मणे समाम्नातम्। इन्द्रो वै वृत्रं हत्वा नास्तृषीति मन्यमानः पराः परावतोऽगच्छत् (ऐ० ब्रा०३-१५) इति। तैत्तिरीयाश्चमनन्ति-इन्द्रो वृत्रं हत्वा परां

परावतमगच्छदराधमिति मन्यमानः (तै० ब्रा० १-६-७-४) इति। हार्द। पद्दन्नित्यादिना हृदयशब्दस्य हृदादेशः। ऊडिदमित्यादिना विभक्तेरुदात्तत्वम्। जघ्नुषः। हन्तेर्लिटः क्वसुः। षष्ठ्येकवचने वसोः। संप्रसारणपरपूर्वत्वे। शासिवसिघसीनां चेति षत्वम्। न च षत्वतुकोनसिद्धः (पा० ६-१-८६) इति एकादेशस्यासिद्धत्वात् षत्वं न प्राप्नुयादिति वाच्यम्। संप्रसारणङीट्सु प्रतिषेधो वक्तव्यः (का० ६-१-८६-१) इति असिद्धवद्भत्वात्। गमहनेत्यादिना (पा० ६-४-९८) उपधालोपः। नचासिद्धवदत्राभावात् (पा० ६-४-२२) इति संप्रसारनणस्यासिद्धवद्भावः। भिन्नाश्रयत्वम्। स्त्रवन्तीः। स्त्रु गतौ। शपृश्यनोर्नित्यम् (पा० ७-१-८१) इतिनुमागमः। शपः पित्त्वाद- नुदात्तत्वम्। शतुश्च लसार्वधातुस्वरेणाद्युदात्तत्वम्। अतरः। यद्वृत्तयोगादनिघातः।।

या॒तृ m., exactor of punishment for the murder of someone, one who avenges a crime.

The Itihāsa alluded to here is repeatedly mentioned in the Sruti: Satap. Br. 4,1,3,1; Ait, Br. 3. 15; *etc.,* and in Mbh. 5, 10, 45.

Verse 15.

इन्द्र॑ः। या॒तः। अव॑ऽसितस्य। राजा॑। शम॑स्य। च॒। शृ॒ङ्गिण॑ः। वज्र॑ऽबाहुः। सः। इत्। ऊँ॒ इति॑। राजा॑। क्ष॒य॒ति॒। च॒र्ष॒णी॒नाम्। अ॒रान्। न। ने॒मिः। परि॑। ता। ब॒भू॒व॒।।१५।।

वज्रबाहुरिन्द्रः शत्रौ हते सति निःसपत्रो भूत्वा यातो गच्छतो जङ्गमस्यावसितस्य एकत्रैव स्थितस्य स्थावरस्य शमस्य शान्तस्य श्रृङ्गोपेतस्योग्रस्य महिषबलीवर्दादेश्च राजाभूत्। सेदु स एवेन्द्रङ्गार्षणीनां मनुष्याणां राजा भूत्वा क्षयति निवसति। ता तानि पूर्वोक्तानि जङ्गमादीनि सर्वाणि परिबभूव व्यातवान्। तत्र हष्टान्तः। अरान्न नेमिः। यथा रथचक्रस्य परितो वर्तमाना नेमिररान्नाभौ कीलितान्काष्ठविशेषान्व्याप्नोति तद्वत्। यातः। या प्रापणे। याति गच्छतीति यात्। लट् शतृ सावेकाच इति विभक्तेरुदात्तत्वम्। सः। सोऽचि लोपे चेदिति (पा० ६-१-१३४) संहितायां सोर्लोपः। ता। शेश्छन्दसि बहुलमिति शेर्लोपः। बभूव। भवतेर्लिटोणलि भवतेरः (पा० ७-४-७३)

इत्यभासस्यात्वम्। कृताकृतप्रसङ्गितया वुगामस्य नित्यत्वाद्वृद्धेः पूर्वं वुगागमः। यद्वा। इन्धिभवतिभ्यां च (पा० १-२-६) इति नित्यकित्त्वाद्वृद्ध्यभावः। न चासिद्धवदत्राभावादिति (पा० ६-४-२२) तस्यासिद्धत्वादु वडादेशः शङ्कनीयः। वुग्युटावुवङ्यणो सिद्धो भवतः (पा० ६-४-२२-१४) इति तस्य सिद्धत्वात्। तिङ्ङतिङ इति निघातः।।

अव॑ सा 6., to let go, unyoke, make a halt, rest.

इद् उ॒, and, and also.

च॒र्ष॒णि f., plur., men, people, clans, nations.

परि॑ भू, embrace, encircle, having in one's power.

NO. 3.

MAṆḌALA I. **SŪKTA 48.**

सह वामेनेति षोडशर्च पञ्चमं सूक्तम्। प्रस्कण्व ऋषिः। बार्हतत्वादयुजो बृहत्यो युजः सतोबृहत्यः उषा देवता। सह षोळशोषस्यं त्वित्यनुक्रमणिका। प्रातरनुवाक उषस्ये क्रतौ बार्हते छन्दसीदं सूक्तम्। अथोषस्य इति खण्डे सूत्रितम्। प्रत्यु अदर्शि सह वामनेति बार्हतमिति। तथाश्विनशस्त्रेऽप्येतत्सूक्तम् (आ० ४-१४) प्रातरनुवाकन्यायेन (आ० ६-५) इत्यतिदिष्टत्वात्।।

Verse 1.

स॒ह। वा॒मेन॑ न॒ः। उ॒ष॒ः। वि। उ॒च्छ॒। दु॒हि॒त॒ः। दि॒व॒ः। स॒ह। द्यु॒म्नेन॑। बृ॒ह॒ता। वि॒भा॒ऽव॒रि॒। रा॒या। दे॒वि॒। दास्व॑ती।।१।।

हे दुहितर्दिवो द्युदेवतायाः पुत्रि उष उषः कालदेवते नोऽस्मदर्थ वामेन धनेन सह व्युच्छ प्रभातं कुरु। हे विभावर्युषोदेवते बृहता प्रभूतेन द्युम्नेनान्नेन सह व्युच्छ। हे देवि त्वं दास्वती दानयुक्ता सती राया पशुलक्षणेन धनेन सह व्युच्छ। उच्छ उच्छी विवासे। दुहितर्दिवः। सुबामन्त्रिते पराँवत्स्वर इत्यत्र परमपि छन्दसि (पा० २-१-२-६) इति वचनाद्दिव इत्यस्य पूर्वाङ्गवद्भावे सत्यामन्त्रितस्य चेति षष्ठ्यामन्त्रितसमुदायस्याष्टमिकं सर्वानुदात्तत्वम्। बृहता। बृहन्महतोरूपसंख्यानमिति विभक्तेरुदात्तत्वम्। विभावरि। भा दीप्तौ। आतो मनिन्नित्यादिना वनिप् वनोरचेति ङीप्। तत्संनियोगेन

नकारस्य रेफादेशः। संबुद्धौ ह्रस्वत्वम्। दास्वती। डुदाञ् दाने। भावे असुन् प्रत्ययः। [1]दाः दानमस्या अस्तीति दास्वती। मादुपधाया इति मतुपो वत्वम्। उगितश्चेति ङीप्।।

व्य् उच्छा, 2. sg. impv. par.; rt. वस् 6., to shine; वि वस्, to become quite bright.

द्युम्न n., glory, fame, dignity.

वि॒भाव॑न्, f. व्व॒री, adj., brilliant, subst., illuminator.

दास्व॑न्, rich in gifts, bountiful.

Read दअस्व॑ती, वि॑उच्छ. The vowel distentions and the resolutions of saṁdhi, required by the metre, are unusually frequent in this hymn.

Verse 2.

अश्व॑ऽवतीः। गोम॑तीः। वि॒श्व॑ऽसु॒विद॑ः। भूरि॑। च्य॒व॒न्त॒। वस्त॑वे। उत्। ई॒र॒य॒। प्रति॑। मा॒। सू॒नृता॒ः। उ॒ष॒ः। चोद॑। राध॑ः। म॒घोना॑म्।।२।।

अश्वावतीर्बह्वश्वोपेता गोमतीर्बहुभिर्गोभिर्युक्ता विश्वसुविदः कृत्स्नस्य धनस्य सुष्ठु लम्भयित्र्य उषो देवता वस्तवे प्रजानां निवासाय भूरि प्रभूतं यथा भवति तथा च्यवन्त प्राप्ताः। हे उषोदेवते मा प्रति मासुद्दिश्य सूनृताः प्रियहितवाच उदीरय ब्रूहि। मघोनां धनवतां संबन्धि राधो धनं चोद। अस्मदर्थं प्रेरथ। अश्वावतीः। मन्त्रे सोमाश्वेन्द्रियविश्वदेव्यस्य मतौ। (पा० ६-३-१३१) इति पूर्वपदस्य दीर्घत्वम्। वा छन्दसीति पूर्वसवर्णदीर्घनिषेधस्य पाक्षिकस्योक्तेः पूर्वसवर्णदीर्घत्वम्। च्यवन्त। च्युङ् गतौ। लङि बहुलं छन्दस्यमाङ्योगेऽपीत्यडभावः। वस्तवे। वस निवासे। तुमर्थे। सयेसेनिति तवेन्प्रत्ययः। नित्वारदाद्युदात्तत्वम्। ईरय। ईर गतौ। कम्पने च। हेतुमति णिच्। चोद्। चुद संचोदने। चौरादिकः। लोटि छन्दस्युभयथेति शप आर्धधातुकत्वात् णेरनिटीति णिलोपः। शपः पित्त्वादनुदात्तत्वे धातुस्वरः। पादादित्वान्निघाताभावः। मघोनाम्। षष्ठीबहुवचने श्वयुवमघोनामतद्धिते (पा० ६-४-१३३) इति संप्रसारणम्।।

1. तदस्यास्ति। पा० ५-२-९४ इत्यादर्शः

उद् ईर् 2., caus., to drive out, send out, stir up.

भूरि॑ adv., often,

च्यु 1., to move, to be about to.

वस्त॑वे, inf. dat. rt. वस्.

सू॒नृता॑ f. sg., *noblesse,* generosity, happiness;

f. pl., rich gifts, prosperity.

The plur. in the first two pādas refers to the dawns in former days. Cp. the following ṛc.

Verse 3.

उ॒वास॑। उ॒षाः। उ॒च्छात्। च॒। नु। दे॒वी। जी॒रा। रथा॑नाम्। ये।
अ॒स्या॒ः। आ॒ऽचर॑णेषु। द॒ध्रि॒रे। स॒मु॒द्रे। न। श्र॒व॒स्यव॑ः।।३।।

उषा देव्युवास। पुरा निवासमकरोत्। प्रभातं कृतवतीत्यर्थः। च नु अद्याप्युच्छात् व्युच्छति। प्रभातं करोति। कीदृशी देवी। रथानां जीरा प्रेरयित्री। उषः काले हि रथाः प्रेर्यन्ते। अस्या उषस आचरणेष्वागमनेषु यचे रथा दध्रिरे धृताः सज्जीकृता भवन्ति। तेषां रथानामिति पूर्वत्रान्वयः। रथप्रेरणे दृष्टान्तः। श्रवस्यवो धनकामाः समुद्रे न। यथा समुद्रमध्ये नावः सज्जीकृत्य प्रेरयन्ति तद्वत्। उवास। वस निवासे। णलि लिट्यभ्यासस्योभयचेषाम् (पा० ६-१-१७) इत्यभ्यासस्य संप्रसारणम्। लित्स्वरेण प्रत्ययात्पूर्वस्सयोदात्तत्वम्। उच्छात्। लेट्याडागमः। इतश्च लोप इतीकारलोपः। तुदादित्वाच्छप्रत्ययः। आगमानुदात्तत्वे प्रत्ययस्वरः। उशा इत्यस्य वाक्यान्तरगतत्वात्तदपेक्षयास्य निधातो न भवति। समानवाक्ये निर्धातयुष्मदस्मदादेशा वक्तव्याः (पा० ८-१-१८-५) इति वचनात्। जीरा। जु इति गत्यर्थः सौत्रौ धातुः। जोरी च (उ० २-२३) इति रक् प्रत्ययः। अस्याः। इदमोऽन्वादेश इत्यशादेशोऽनुदात्तः। विभक्तिरपि सुस्वादनुदात्तेति सर्वानुदात्तत्वम्। आचरणेषु। चर गत्यर्थः। ल्युट् च (पा० ३-३-११५) इति भावे ल्युट् लित्स्वरेण प्रत्ययात्पूर्वस्योदात्तत्वम्। कृदुत्तरपदप्रकृतिस्वरत्वम्। दध्रिरे। धृङ् अवस्थाने। लिटः कित्त्वादुणाभावे यणादेशः। चित्त्वादन्तोदात्तत्वम्।

यच्छब्दयोगादनिघातः। श्रवस्यवः। श्रूयत इति श्रवो धनम्। असुन्। तदात्मन इच्छन्तीति श्रवस्यवः। सुप आत्मनः क्यच्। क्याच्छन्दसीत्युप्रत्ययः।।

उ॒च्छात्, 3. sg. sbj. par.; rt. वस्.

जी॒र adj., quick, quickening, stirring.

आ॒चर॑ण n., coming, arrival.

श्र॒व॒स्यु adj., desirous of fame, ambitious.

Resolve either ये असिआः, or इए अस्याः.

The simile in pāda 4 betrays a good insight into life at Vedic (and all) times. The (mercentile) sailors are said to be as ambitious as the chariots, *i.e.* the occupants of them, the charioteers and soldiers. Stylistically, too, the simile is complete as it stands.

Verse 4.

उष॑ः। ये। ते॒। प्र। यामे॑षु। यु॒ञ्जते॑। मन॑ः। दा॒नाय॑। सू॒रय॑ः। अत्र॑। अह॑। तत्। कण्व॑ः। ए॒षाम्। कण्व॑ऽतमः। नाम॑। गृ॒णा॒ति॒। नृ॒णाम्।।४।।

हे उषस्ते तव यामेषु गमनेषु सत्सु ये सूरयो विद्वांसो दानाभिज्ञा दानाय धनादिदानार्थं मनः स्वकीयं प्रयुञ्जते प्रेरयन्ति दानशीला उदाराः प्रभवः प्रातःकाले दातुमिच्छन्तीत्यर्थः। एषां दातुमिच्छतां नृणां तन्नाम दानविषये लोकप्रसिद्धं नाम। कण्वतमोऽतिशयेन मेधावी कण्वो महर्षिरत्राह। अत्रैवोषःकाले गृणाति। उच्चरयति। यो दातुमिच्छति यश्च नामग्रहणेन दातारं प्रशंसति तावुभाप्युषःकाल एव तथाकुरुत इत्युषसः स्तुतिः। गृणाति। गृ शब्दे। क्रैयादिकः। प्वादीनां ह्रस्व इति ह्रस्वत्वम्। नणाम्। नामि नृच (पा० ६-४-६) इति दीर्घप्रतिषेधः। नृ चान्यतरस्याम् (पा० ६-१-१४८) इति विभक्तेरुदात्तत्वम्।।

सू॒रि m., great lord, master, authority, patron (of the sacrifice).

अह॑ indecl., indeed, forsooth, this very.

नाम॑न् n., name, character, nature, in a laudatory sense.

गृ 9., to praise.

Read either पर for प्र, or यअमेषु for यामेषु.

Verse 5.

आ। घ। योषाऽइव। सूनरी। उषाः। याति। प्रऽभुञ्जती। जरयन्ती। वृजनम्। पत्ऽवत्। ईयते। उत्। पातयति। पक्षिणः।।५।।

उषा देवी प्रभुञ्जती प्रकर्षेण सर्वं पालयन्त्यायाति। घ प्रतिदिनमागच्छति खलु। तत्र दृष्टान्तः। सूनरी सुष्ठु गृहकृत्यस्य नेत्री योषेव गृहिणीव। कीदृश्युषाः। वृजनं गमनशीलं जङ्गमं प्राणिजातं जरयन्ती जरां प्रापयन्ती। असकृदुषस्यावृत्तायां वयोहान्या प्राणिनो जीर्णा भवन्ति। किं च उषःकाले पद्वत् पादयुक्तं प्राणिजातमीयते। निद्रां परित्यज्य स्वस्वकृत्यर्थं गच्छति। किं च इयमुषाः पक्षिण उत्पातयति पक्षिणो ह्युषःकाले समुत्थाय तत्र तत्र व्रजन्ति। व। ऋचितुनु घेत्यादिना संहितायां दीर्घः। सुष्ठु नयतीति सूनरी। नृ नये। अच इरितीप्रत्ययः। गतिसमासे कृद्ग्रहणे गतिकारकपूर्वस्यापि ग्रहणम् (परि० २८) इति वचनात्कृदिकारादक्तिनः (पा० ४-१-४५) इति ङीप्। परादिश्छन्दसि बहुलमित्युत्तरपदाद्युदात्तत्वम् निपातस्य चेति पूर्वपदस्य दीर्घः। प्रभुञ्जती। भुज पालनाभ्य- वहारयोः। लटः शतृ। रूधादित्वाच्छम्। रसोरल्लोप इत्यकारलोपः। उगितश्चेति ङीप्। शतुरनुम इति नद्या उदात्तत्वम्। वृजनम्। वृजी वर्जने। वर्ज्यत इति वृजनं प्राणिजातम्। कृ पॄ वृजिमन्दिनिधाञ्भ्यः क्युः (उ० २-८१) इति क्युप्रत्ययः। कित्त्वाल्लघूपधगुणाभावः। योरनादेशे प्रत्ययस्वरः पद्वत्। पत् पादः तदस्यास्तीति पद्वत्। झय इति मतुपो वत्वम्। व्यत्ययेन मतुप उदात्तत्वम्। न च स०वरविधौ व्यञ्जनमविद्यमानवत् (प० ६९) इति व्यञ्जनस्याविद्यमानवत्त्वे सति ह्रस्वनुड्ग्रहणसामर्थ्यादेषा परिभाषा नाश्रीयत इति वृत्तावुक्तम् (का० ६-१-१७६)। इतरथा हि मरुत्वानित्यत्रापि मतुप उदात्तत्वं स्यात्।।

घ, घा indecl., particle of emphasis, =एव, खलु.

योषा f., maid, young Woman.

सूनर adj., gentle, noble, auspicious.

प्र भुज् 7., to give enjoyment, create happiness.

जृ 1., to become, to make old; causat. जरय, to make old; जरयन्ती seems to be used here in the way of a pun on the causative forms of rt. जृ, जृ (= गृ and जागृ), to wake up, and rt. जृ, to age.

वृजनं n., =वर्ग, flock, totality, all creatures. The usual form of this word is वृजन, the meaning of both is probably the same.

As Uṣas return again and again, rousing the creatures, their life is wasting away. Uṣas thus makes them grow old. (Sāy.).

Verse 6.

वि। या। सृजति। समनम्। वि। अर्थिनः। पदम्। न। वेति। ओदती। वयः। नकिः। ते। पप्तिऽवांसः। आसते। विऽउष्टौ। वाजिनीऽवति ॥६॥

या देवता समनं समीचीनचेष्टावन्तं पुरूषं विसृजति प्रेरयति। गृहारामादिचेष्टाकुशलान्पुरूषानुषःकालः शयनादुत्थाप्य स्वस्वव्यापारे प्रेरयतीति प्रसिद्धम्। किं च। उषा अर्थिनो याचकान् विसृजति। तेऽप्युषःकाले समुत्थाय स्वकीयदातृगृहे गच्छन्ति। ओदत्युषोदेवता पदं स्थानं न वेति। न कामयते। उषःकालः शीघ्रं गच्छतीत्यर्थः। हे वाजिनीवत्युषोदेवते ते व्युष्टौ स्वदीये प्रभातकाले पप्तिवांसः पतनयुक्ता वयः पक्षिणः न किरासते। न तिष्ठन्ति। किन्तु स्वस्वनीडाद्विनिर्गत्य गच्छन्तीत्यर्थः। सृजति। सृज विसर्गे। तुदादित्वाच्छः। तस्य ङित्त्वाल्लघूपधगुणाभावः। प्रत्ययस्य पित्त्वादनुदात्तत्वे विकरणस्वरः। यद्वृत्तयोगादनिधातः। ओदती। उन्दी क्लेदने। उनत्ति सर्वं नीहारेणेत्योदत्युषाः। शतरि व्यत्ययेन शप्। व्यत्ययेनानुनासिकलोपे लघूपधगुणः। उगितश्च (पा० ४-१-६) इति ङीप्। आगमानुशासनस्यानित्यत्वान्नुमभावः। शपः पित्त्वादनुदात्तत्वम्। शतुरुदुपदेशाल्लसार्वधातुकानुदात्तत्वे धातुस्वरेणाद्युदात्तत्वम्। नच शतुरनुम इति नद्या उदात्तत्वम्। अन्तोदात्ताच्छतुः परस्यास्तद्विधानात्। नकिष्टे। युष्मत्तत्तक्षुष्वन्तःपादम् (पा० ८-३-१०३) इति षत्वम्। पप्तिवांसः

पत गतौ। लिटः क्वसुः। क्रादिनियमात् प्राप्त इट् वस्वेकाजाद्घसामिति नियमान्न प्राप्नोति तत्क्रियते। सर्वविधीनां छन्दसि विकल्पितत्वात्। तनिपत्योश्छन्दसि (पा० ६-४-९९) इत्युपधालोपः। द्विर्वचनेचीति स्थानिवद्भावाद् द्विर्भावः। प्रत्यययस्वरः। वाजिनीवति। वाजोऽन्नमस्या अस्तीति वाजिनी क्रिया। मत्वर्थीय इनिः। ऋन्नेभ्यः (पा० ४-१-५) इति ङीप् तादृशी क्रिया यस्याः सा। तदस्यास्तीति मतुप्। संज्ञायामिति मतुपो वत्त्वम्।।

स॒मन n., company, feast, battle, bazaar (?).

वी 2., to guide; undertake, take care of; desire; enjoy; प॒दं वी, follow a track or trace, = प॒दं नी; cp. प॒द॒वी (VII. 36. 2) the guide.

ओद॑ती f., Uṣas, (proper noun).

वा॒जिनी॑वत् adj., with good steeds, possessing, granting good gifts.

नकि॑ः, none, not even one.

व्यु॑ष्टि f., the flaming up, the rise.

In the first line we have to understand another सृजति॑ with the second वि.

In Ved. Stud. I 195f. Pischel tries to prove that ओद॑ती means the lecherous courtezan, and he translates the second pāda;- She, the lewd (harlot), shows, as it were, the track.-In GGA. 1890, 540 he connects न with ओदु॒ती. Neither of the suggestions is too convincing, though the former especially is based on a good deal of material and put forth with decision. In the interpretation of ओद॑ती we have not got much beyond Sāyaṇa and have to be satisfied with the comfortable translation:—Anxiously she, ओद॑ती, follows the trace, as it were.—Sāy.'s interpretation of प॒दं न वे॑ति, however, is hardly correct.

Verse 7.

एषा। अयुक्त। पराऽवतः। सूर्यस्य। उत्ऽअयनात्। अधि। शतम्। रथेभिः। सुऽभगा। उषाः। इयम्। वि। याति। अभि। मानुषान्।।७।।

एषोषादेवी शतमयुक्त। स्वकीयानां रथानां शतं योजितवती। सुभगा सौभाग्ययुक्तेयमुषाः परावतो दूरस्थात् सूर्यस्योदयनादधि सूर्योदयस्थानादधिकाद्द्युलोकाच्मानुषानभि मनुष्यानुद्दिश्य रथेभिः शतसंख्याकैर्युक्तै रथैर्वियाति विशेषेण गच्छति। अयुक्त। लुङि झलो झलि (पा० ८-२-२६) इति सिचो लोपः। उदयनात्। उदेत्यत्रेत्युदयनम्। इण् गतौ। अधिकरणे ल्युट्। कृदुत्तरपदप्रकृति स्वरत्वम्। सुभगा। शोभनो भगो यस्याः सा। आद्युदात्तं द्व्यच्छन्दसीत्युत्तरपदाद्युदात्तत्वम्। मानुषान्। मनोः पुत्रा मानुषाः मनोर्जातावञ्यतौ षुक् चेत्यञ् षुगागमश्च। ञित्त्वादाद्युदात्तत्वम्।।

पुरावत् f., distance.

अधि adv., with abl., from.

अभि वि या, to penetrate to.

Verse 8.

विश्वम्। अस्याः। ननाम। चक्षसे। जगत्। ज्योतिः। कृणोति। सूनरी। अप। द्वेषः। मघोनी। दुहिता। दिवः। उषाः। उच्छत्। अपः। स्रिधः।।८।।

विश्वं सर्वं जगत् जङ्गमं प्राणिजातमस्या उषसश्चक्षसे प्रकाशाय ननाम। प्रह्वीभवति। रात्रौ तमसि निमग्नाः सर्वे जनास्तन्निवारयित्रीमुषसमुपलभ्य नमस्कुर्वन्तीत्यर्थः। कुतः। यस्मादेषा सूनरी सूष्ठुनेत्री अभिमतफलस्य प्रापयित्र्युषाः ज्योतिष्कृणोति सर्वं प्रकाशयति। किंच मघोनी मघवती धनवती दिवो दुहिता द्युलोकसकाशादुत्पन्नोषा द्वेषो द्वेष्टनपोच्छत् अपवर्जयति। तथा स्रिधः शोषयितृ नपोच्छत्। अपवर्जयति। तस्मादिष्टप्राप्त्यनिष्टपरिहारहेतुभूतामुषोदेवतां विश्वं जगन्नमस्करोतीत्यर्थः। अस्याः। इदमोऽन्वादेश० (पा० २-४-३२) इत्यशादेशोनुदात्तः। विभक्तिश्च सुस्वादनुदात्तेति सर्वानुदात्तत्वम्। ननाम संहिता-

यामन्येषामपि दृश्यते इत्यभ्यासस्य दीर्घत्वम्। तुजादित्वे हि तूतुजान इत्यादाविव पदकालेऽपि दीर्घः श्रूयते। ज्योतिः। इणः ष इत्यनुवृत्ताविसुसोः सामर्थ्ये (पा० ८-३-४४) इति विसर्जनीयस्य षत्वम्। द्वेषः। द्विष् अप्रीतौ। अन्येभ्योऽपि दृश्यन्ते (पा० ३-२-७६) इति विच्। लघूपधगुणः। मधोनी। मधं वनति संभूजत इति मधोनी। श्वन्नुक्षन्नित्यादिना (उ० १-१५७) मधवञ्शबदः कनिन्- प्रत्ययान्तो निपातितः। स्त्रियामृन्नोभ्यो ङीबिति ङीप्। भसंज्ञायां श्वयुवमधोनामतद्धत (पा० ६-४-१३३) इति संप्रसारणम्। उच्छत्। उच्छी विवासे विवासो वर्जनम्। छन्दसि लुङ्लङ्लिटः (पा० ३-४-६) इति वर्तमाने लङ्। बहुलं छन्दस्यमाङयोगेऽपीत्यडागमाभावः। स्त्रिधः। स्त्रिधु शोषणे। क्विप् चेति क्विप्।।

चक्ष॑स् n., light, splendour.

जग॑त् n., (living) world, living creature.

उ॒च्छ॒त्, 3. sg. inj. par.; rt. वस्; अप॑ वस्, to shine away, drive away by the light.

स्त्रिध् f., collision, attack, annoyance.

Verse 9.

उष॑ः। आ। भ॒हि॒ं भा॒नुना॑ च॒न्द्रेण॑। दु॒हि॒त॒ः। दि॒व॒ः। आ॒ऽवह॑न्ती। भूरि॑। अ॒स्मभ्य॑म्। सौभ॑गम्। वि॒ऽउ॒च्छन्ती॑। दिवि॑ष्टिषु।।९।।

हे दिवो दुहितर्द्युलोकस्य पुत्रि उषा उषोदेवते चन्द्रेण सर्वेषामाह्लादकेन भानुना प्रकाशेन आ समन्तात् भाहि। प्रकाशस्वं किं कुर्वती। दिविष्टिषु दिवसेषु भूरि प्रभूतं सौभगं सौभाग्यमस्मभ्यमावहनत संपादयन्ती। तथा व्युच्छन्ती तमांसि वर्जयन्ती। उषः। षाष्ठिकमामन्त्रिताद्युदात्तत्वम्। दुहितर्दिवः। परमपि छन्दसीलति दिव इत्यस्य परस्य षष्ठ्यन्तस्य पूर्वामत्रिताङ्गवद्भावे सति षष्ठ्यामन्त्रितसमुदायस्याष्टमिकं सर्वानुदात्तत्वम्। आवहन्ती। ङीप्शपौ पित्त्वादनुदात्तौ। शतुश्चादुपदेशाल्लसार्वधातुकस्वरेणानुदात्तत्वम्। अतो धातुस्वरः शिष्यते। समासे कृदुत्तरपदप्रकृतिस्वरत्वम्। भूरि। भवति न विनश्यतीति भूरि अदिशदिभूशु मिभ्यः किन् (उ० ४-६५) इति क्रिन्। नित्त्वादाद्युदात्तत्वम्। सुभगस्य भावः सौभगम्। सुभगान्मत्रे (पा० ५-१-१२९) इत्युद्गात्रादिषु पाठादञ्-

प्रत्ययः। हृद्भगसिन्ध्वन्ते पूर्वपदस्य च (पा० ७-३-१९) इत्युभयपदवृद्धौ प्राप्तायां सर्वे विधयश्छन्दसि विकल्प्यन्त इति वचनादत्रोत्तरपदवृद्धिर्न भवति इति वृत्तावुक्तम्। (का० ७-३-१९) व्यच्छन्ती। उच्छी विवासे। विवासो वर्जनं तौदादिकः। अदुपदेशाल्लसार्वधातुकानुदात्तत्वे विकरणस्वरः। दिविष्टिषु। दिव्शब्देन दिविष्ठ आदित्यो लक्ष्यते। तस्येष्टय एषणानि गमनानि येषु दिवसेषु ते दिविष्टयः। बहुव्रीहौ पूर्वपदप्रकृतिस्वरत्वम्।।

भानु m., splendour, light, ray.

चन्द्र adj., dear, brilliant, pleasing.

दिविष्टि f., heavenly wish, sacrificial feast.

Verse 10.

विश्वस्य। हि। प्राणनम्। जीवनम्। त्वे इति। वि। यत्। उच्छसि। सूनरि। सा। नः। रथेन। बृहता। विभाऽवरि। श्रुधि। चित्रऽमघे। हवम्।।१०।।

हे सूनरि उषोदेवि विश्वस्य सर्वस्य प्राणिजातस्य प्राणनं चेष्टनं जीवनं प्राणधारणं च त्वे हि त्वय्येव वर्तते। यद्यस्मात्त्वं व्युच्छसि तामे वर्जयसि। हे विभावरि विशिष्टप्रकाशयुक्ते सा तादृशीर्त्वं नोऽस्मान्प्रति बृहता प्रौढेन रथेनायाहीति शेषः। तथा हे चित्रामधे विचित्रधनयुक्ते *उषोदेवते नोऽस्मदीयं हवमाह्वानं श्रुधि। श्रृणु। प्राणनम्। अन चेष्टायाम्। ल्युट् च (पा० ३-३-११५) इति भावे ल्युट्। योरनादेशः। समासेऽनिते। (पा० ८-४-१९) इत्युपसर्गस्था †न्निमित्तादुत्तरस्य नकारस्य णत्वम्। नन्वनितेरितीटा निर्देशात्कथमनचेष्टाया-मित्यस्य णत्वम्। तर्हि जीवनस्य पृथगुपादानात्तेनैव धातुना चेष्टा लक्ष्यते। समासे कृदुत्तरपदप्रकृतिस्वरत्वम्। संहितायामेकादेशस्वरेणैकादेशस्योदात्तत्वम्। त्वे। सुपां सुलुगिति सप्तम्याःशे आदेशः। उच्छसि। उच्छी विवासे। तौदादिकः। सिपः पित्त्वादनु दात्तत्वे विकरणस्वरः। निपातैर्यद्यदि हन्त० (पा० ८-१-३०) इति निघातप्रतिषेधः। सूनरी। सुष्ठु नयतीति सूनरी। नृ

*उषो देवि इत्यादर्शः।

†इकारान्नि इत्यादर्शः।

नय इत्यस्मादच इः (उ० ४-१३८) इत्यौणादिक इप्रत्ययः। गतिसमासे कृद्ग्रहणे गतिकारकपूर्वस्यापि ग्रहणात्कृदिकारादक्तिन इति ङीप्। निपातस्यच च (पा० ६-३-१३६) इति पूर्वपदस्य दीर्घत्वम्। परादिश्छन्दसि बहुल-मित्युत्तरपदाद्युत्तत्वे प्राप्त आमन्त्रितस्य च (पा० ८-१-१९) इत्याष्टमिको निघातः। विभावरि विशिष्टा भा यस्याः सा। छन्छसीवनपो (पा० ५-२-१०९-२) इति मत्वर्थीयो वनिप्। वनोरचेति ङीप्। तत्संनियोगेन नकारस्य रेफादेशश्च। श्रुधि। श्रुशृणुपृ कृवृभ्यश्छन्दसि इति हेर्धिरादेशः। बहुलं छन्दसीति विकरणस्य लुक्। हेरपित्त्वेन प्रत्यस्वरे- णान्तोदात्तत्वम् पादादित्वान्निघाताभावः। मघमिति धननाम। चित्रं मधं यस्याः सा चित्रमधा। अन्येषामपि दृश्यत इति संहितायां पूर्वपदस्य दीर्घत्वम्। हवम्। ह्वेञ् स्पर्द्धायां शब्दे च। भावेऽनुपसर्गस्य (पा० ३-३-७५) 'इत्यप्प्रत्ययः। तत्संनियोगेन संप्रसारणं च।।

प्रार्णन n, breathing, breath; जीवन n., life.

चित्रामंध adj., with brilliant, glorious gifts.

The elevated lyric tone of this ṛc accounts for the use of प्राणंनम्, जीवंनम् in the first pāda, and the omission of the verb in the third.

Verse 11.

उषः। वाजम्। हि। वंस्व। यः। चित्रः। मानुषे। जने। तेन। आ। वह। सुऽकृतः। अध्वरान्। उप। ये। त्वा। गृणन्ति। वह्नयः।।११।।

हे उषः वाजं हविर्लक्षणमन्नं हि श्रुतिषु प्रसिद्धं वंस्व। याचस्व। स्वीकुर्वित्यर्थः। यो वाजश्चिन्नश्चायनीयो मानुषे मनुष्ये जने जाते यजमाने वर्तते। तं वाजमिति पूर्वत्रान्वयः। तेन कारणेन सुकृतः सुष्ठुकृतवतो यजमानान-ध्वरान् हिंसारहितान् यागानुपावह प्रापय। ये यजमाना वह्नयो यज्ञनिर्वाहकास्त्वा त्वां गृणन्ति स्तुवन्ति। तान् सुकृत इति पूर्वेण संबन्धः। एतदुक्तं भवति। यजमानैः प्रत्तं हविः स्वीकृत्य इति पूर्वेण संबन्धः। एतदुक्तं भवति। यजमानैः प्रत्तं हविः स्वीकृत्य पुनरपि तेषां यज्ञं संपादयेति। वाजम्। व्रज गतौ। कर्मणि धञ्। अजिव्रज्योश्च (पा० ७-३-६०) इत्यत्र चशब्दस्यानुक्त-समुश्चयार्थत्वाद्वाजोवाज्यमित्यत्रापि कुत्वाभाव इति वृत्तावुक्तत्वाकत्वाभावः।

कर्षात्वत (पा० ६-१-१५९) इत्यन्तोदात्तत्वे प्राप्ते वृषादित्वादाद्युदात्तत्वम्। वंस्व। वनु याचने। अत्र याचनवाचिना धातुना तदुत्तरभावी स्वीकारो लक्ष्यते। बहुलं छन्दसीति विकरणस्य लुक्। अनुदात्तत्वाल्लसार्वधातुकानुदात्तत्वे धातुस्वरः। हि च (पा० ८-१-३४) इति निघातप्रतिषेधः। सुकृतः। सुकर्मपापेत्यादिना (पा० ३-२-१७२) करोते र्भूतार्थे क्विप्। तुगागमः। कृदुत्तरपदप्रकृतिस्वरत्वम्। अध्वरान्। ध्वरो हिंसा नास्त्यस्मिन्निति बहुव्रीहौ नञ्सुभ्याम् (पा० ६-२-१७२) इत्युत्तरनपदान्तोदात्तत्वम्। अध्वरानित्यस्येप्सिततमत्वात्कर्तुरीप्सिततमम् (पा० १-४-४९) इति कर्मसंज्ञा। सुकृत इत्यस्य त्वकथितं च (पा० १-४-५१) इति नीवह्योर्हरतेश्च (पा० १-४-५१) इति द्विकर्मकेषु वहतेः परिगणितत्वात्। अध्वरानित्यत्र नकारस्य संहितायां दीर्घादटीति रुत्वम्। आतोऽटि नित्यमिति पूर्वस्याकारस्य सानुनासिकता। गृणनित। गृ शब्दे। क्रयादिभ्यः श्रा। प्वादीनां हस्व इति हस्वत्वम्। श्राभ्यस्तयोरात इत्याकारलोपः। प्रत्ययस्वरः। यद्वृत्तयोगादनिघातः।।

वाजं m., victory, conquest, booty, donation out of the booty prize.

वंस्वं, 2. sg. impv. aor. ātm.; rt. वन्, to win, to get.

उपं वह्, to drive to.

वह्निं m., charioteer, priest (either as हुव्युवह् or as charioteer of the hymns conceived as horses).

तेनं, sociative instr. sg., referring to वाजं.

सुकृतंः, gen. sg., (better than) acc. plur. (Sāy.).

Verse 12.

विश्वांन्। देवान्। आ। वह। सोमंऽपीतये। अन्तरिंक्षात्। उषः। त्वम्। सा। अस्मासुं। धाः। गोऽमंत्। अश्वंऽवत्। उक्थ्यंम्। उषंः। वाजंम्। सुऽवीर्यंम्।। १२ ।।

हे उषस्त्वं सोमपीतये सोमपानायान्तरिक्षदन्तरिक्षलोकाद्विश्वान्सर्वान्देवान्

आवह अस्मदीयदेशं प्रापय। हे उषः सा तादृशी त्वं गोमत् गोमन्तं बहुभिर्गोभिर्युक्तमश्वावदश्वैरूपेतमुक्थ्यं प्रशस्यं सुवीर्यं शोभनवीर्योपेतं वाजमन्नमस्मासु धाः। निधेहि। स्थापयेत्यर्थः। धाः। दधातेश्छन्दसि लुङ्लङ्लिट इति प्रार्थनायां लुङ्। गातिस्थेति सिचो लुक्। बहुलं छन्दस्यचमाङ्योगेऽपीत्यडभावः। गोमत्। अश्ववत्। मन्त्रे सोमाश्वेन्द्रियेति मतुपि दीर्घत्वम्। उभयतत्र सुपां सुलुगिति विभक्तेर्लुक्। उक्थ्यम् उक्थं स्तोत्रं तत्र भवमुक्थ्यम्। भवे छन्दसीति यत्। सर्वे विधयश्छन्दसि विकल्प्यन्त इति। यतोऽनाव इत्याद्युदात्तत्वाभावे तित्स्वरित- गिति स्वरितत्वम्। उषः। आमन्त्रिताद्युदात्तत्वम्। पादादित्वान्निधाताभावः। सुवीर्यम्। शोभनं वीर्यं यस्य। वीरवीर्यौ चेत्युत्तरपदाद्युदात्तत्वम्।।

धा॒ः, 2. sg., sbj. aor. par,; rt. धा, with loc., to bestow on.

गोम॑त्, अश्वा॑वत् adj., consisting of cows, horses; subst. n., riches in cows, horses.

उ॒क्थ्य॑ adj., praiseworthy.

सु॒वीर्य॑ n., heroic strength; a (great) number of good fighters, horses.

Verse 13.

यस्या॑ः। रु॒शन्त॑ः। अ॒र्चय॑ः। प्रति॑। भ॑द्राः। अ॑क्षत। सा। न॒ः। र॒यिम्। वि॒श्वऽवा॑रम्। सु॒ऽपेश॑सम्। उ॒षः। द॒दा॒तु॒। सु॒ग्म्य॑म्।।१३।।

यचस्या उवसापेऽर्चयः प्रकाशा रुशन्तः शत्रून्हिंसन्तो भद्राः कल्याणाः प्रत्यदृक्षत प्रतिदृश्यन्ते सा तथाभूतोषा नोऽस्मभ्यं रयिं ददातु। कीदृशं रयिम्। विश्ववारं विश्वस्य वारकम्। यद्वा। विश्वैर्वरणीयम्। सुपेशसम्। पेश इति रूपनाम। शोभनरूपोपेतं सग्म्यं सुष्ठु गन्तव्यम्। यद्वा। सुग्म्यमिति सुखनाम। तद्धेतुत्वात्ताच्छब्द्यम्। रुशन्तः। रूश रिश हिंसायाम्। शतरि तुदादित्वाच्छः। अदुपदेशाल्लसार्वधातुकानुदात्तत्वे सति शिष्टत्वाद्विकरणस्वरे प्राप्ते व्यत्ययेनाद्युदात्तत्वम्। अदृक्षत। दृशेः कर्मणि लुङि झस्यादादेशः। च्लेः सिच्। न दृशः (पा० ३-१-४७) इति क्सप्रतिषेधः। एकाच इतीट्प्रतिषेधः।

लिङ्सिचावात्मनेपदेषु (पा० १-२-११) इति सिचः कित्त्वाल्लघूपधगुणाभावः। सृजिदृशोर्झल्यमकिति (पा० ६-१-५८) इत्यमागमाभावश्च। कित्त्वादेव षसत्व-कत्वषत्वानि। अडागम उदात्तः। यद्वृत्तयऐगादनिधातः। विश्ववारम्। विश्वं वृणातीति विश्ववारः। वृञ् वरणे। कर्मण्यण्। यद्वा विश्वैर्व्रियत इति विश्ववारः। कर्मणि धञ्। मरूद्वृधादित्वात्पूर्वपदान्तोदात्तत्वम्। सुग्म्यम्। सुष्ठु गन्तव्यः सुग्मः। गमेर्धञर्थे कविधानमिति कप्रत्ययः। गमहनेत्यादिनोपधालोपः। तत्र भवं सुग्म्यम्। भवे छन्दसीति यत्। यतोऽनाव इत्याद्युदात्तत्वम्।।

अ॒र्चि m., ray.

अदृ॑क्षत, 3. plur. aor. ātm.; rt. दृश्, प्रति॑ दृश्, to re-appears, to shine.

सुपेश॑स् adj., well adorned, magnificent.

र॑यि m., riches in the Widest sense, fortune, treasure.

रूश्, only pt. = रूच्, brilliant, light, clear.

सुग्म्य॑ adj., auspicious, prosperous.

Verse 14.

ये। चि॒त्। हि। त्वाम्। ऋष॑यः। पूर्वे॑। ऊ॒तये॑। जु॒हूरे। अव॑से। म॒हि॒। सा। नः। स्तोमा॑न्। अ॒भि। गृ॒णी॒हि॒। राध॑सा। उष॑ः। शु॒क्रेण॑। शो॒चिषा।।१४।।

हे महि महिते पूजनीये वर उषोदेवते त्वां ये चिद्धि ये खलु प्रसिद्धाः पूर्वे चिरंतना ऋषयो मन्त्रद्रष्टार ऊतये रक्षणाय। अव इत्यन्ननाम। अवसे। अन्नाय च जुहूरे जुह्विरे आहूतवन्तः। सूक्तरूपैर्मन्त्रैः स्तुतवन्त इत्यर्थः। हे उषः सा तादृशी त्वं राधसास्माभिर्दत्तेन हविर्लक्षणेन धनेन शुक्रेण शोचिषा दीप्तेन तमो निवारयितुं समर्थेन तेजसा चोपलक्षिता सती तेषामृषीलणामिव नोऽस्माकं स्तोमानभि सतुतीरल्लिक्ष्य गृणीहि। सम्यक् स्तुतमिति शब्दय। अस्मदीयाभिः स्तुतिभिः संतुष्टा भवेत्यर्थः। त्य ऊतये। अवतेः क्तिनि ज्वरत्वर (पा० ६-४-२०) इत्यादिना वकारस्योपधायाश्चाट्। ऊतियूति (पा० ३-३-९७) इत्यादिना क्तिन्नुदात्तो निपातितः जुहूरे। ह्वेञ् स्पर्द्धायां शब्दे च।

लिट्यभ्यस्तस्य च (पा० ६-१-३३) इति द्विर्वचनात्पूर्वमेवाभ्यस्तकारणभूतस्य ह्वयतेः संप्रसारणम्। अभ्यस्तस्य यो ह्वयतिः कश्चाभ्यस्तस्य ह्वयतिः यस्तस्य कारणम् (का० ६-१-३३) इति व्याख्यातत्वात्। परपूर्वत्वे हल (पा० ६-४-२) इति दीर्घत्वम्। द्विर्वचनादीनि इरयो रे (पा० ६-४-७६) इतीरेचो रेआदेशः। चित इत्यन्तोदात्तत्वम्। यद्वृत्तयोगादनिघातः। तत्र हि पञ्चमीनिर्देशेऽपि व्यवहितेऽपि कार्यं भवतीत्युक्तम् (का० ८-१-६६)। महि। मह पूजायाम्। औणादिक इप्रत्ययः। कृदिकारादक्तिन इति ङीप्। संबुद्धावम्बार्थेति हसवत्वम्। (पा० ७-३-१०७) स्तोमान्। संहितायां नकारस्य रूत्वाद्युक्तम्। (पा० ८-३-९) नित्त्वादाद्युदात्तत्वम्। गृणीहि। गॄ शब्दे क्रैयादिकः। शिति प्वादीनां ह्रस्व इति ह्रस्वत्वम्। राधसा। राध्नोत्यनेनेति राधः। असुनो नित्त्वादाद्युदात्तत्वम्। उषः। पाददित्वादाष्टमिकनिघाताभावे षाष्टिकमामन्त्रिताद्युदात्तत्वम्।।

ऊ॒ति (rt. अव्) f., = अव॑स् n., help, assistance, grace.

जु॒हू॒रे, 3. plur. pf. ātm.; rt. ह्व 1., to call.

महि f., vicat. of मह्, great.

अ॒भि गृ, to recognise, answer.

रा॒धस् n., = धानम्, grace, donation.

One would expect यं चि॒द्. It looks as if the author had had in his mind to say:— Whatever former ṛṣis have called upon thee, those thou didst hear: thus hear us now.— The demonstrative clause answering to the relative one is omitted and another less accurate one is substituted.

Verse 15.

उष॑ः। यत्। अ॒द्य। भा॒नुना॑। वि। द्वारौ॑। ऋ॒णव॑ः। दि॒वः। प्र। न॒ः। य॒च्छ॒तात्। अ॒वृ॒कम्। पृ॒थु। छ॒र्दिः। प्र। दे॒वि॒। गोऽम॑तीः। इष॑ः।।१५।।

हे उषः त्वमद्यास्मिन्प्रभातसमये यद्यस्माद्भानुना प्रकाशेन दिवोऽन्तरिक्षस्य द्वारौ द्वारभूतौ पूर्वापरदिग्भागावन्णकारेणाच्छादितौ व्पृणवः विश्लष्य प्राप्नोषि तस्मात्त्वं नोऽस्मभ्यं छर्दिस्तेजस्वि गृहं प्रयच्छतात्। देहि। कीदृशं छर्दिः।

अवृकं हिंसकरहितम्। पृथु विस्तीर्णम्। अपि च हे देवि देवनीले गोमती-र्बहुभिर्गोभिर्युक्ता इषोऽन्नानि प्रेत्युपसर्गस्यावृत्तेर्यच्छतादित्यनुषःयते। प्रयच्छतात् देहि। त्वदागमनस्यास्मद्रक्षणार्थत्वादस्मदभीष्टं गृहादिकं प्रयच्छेत्यर्थः। छर्दिरिति गृहनाम। छर्दिश्छदिरिति तन्नामसु पाठात्। ऋणवः। ऋण गतौ। छान्दसे लङि सिपि तादित्वादुप्रत्ययः। ततो व्यत्ययेन शपि गुणावादेशौ। शपः पित्त्वादनुदात्तत्व उप्रत्ययस्वरः शिष्यते। यद्वृत्तयोगादनिधतः। दिवः। ऊडिदमित्यादिना विभक्तेरुदात्तस्वम्। प्र नः। उपसर्गाद्बहुलमिति बहुवचनान्नासो णत्वाभावः। यच्छतात्। दाण् दाने। शपि पाघ्रेत्यादिना यच्छादेशः। अवृकं नास्ति वृकोऽस्मिन्निति बहुव्रीहौ नञ्सुभ्यामित्युत्तरपदान्तोदात्तत्वम्। पृथु प्रथ प्रख्याने। प्रथिम्रदिभ्रसं संप्रसारणं सलोपश्च (उ० २-१०९) इतीसिप्रत्ययः। लघूपधगुणः। प्रत्ययस्वरः॥

ऋ 5., to move, incite; वि ऋ, to open.

यच्छतात्, 3. sg. impv. par.; rt. यम् प्र यम्, to offer, give.

अवृक adj., harmless, peaceful, friendly.

छर्दिः n. (metrically correct छदिः), protection, cover, defence.

इष् f., drink, refreshment, hourishment, food and drink.

Verse 16.

सम्। नः। राया। बृहता। विश्वऽपेशसा। मिमिक्ष्व। सम्। इळाभिः। आ। सम्। द्युम्नेन। विश्वऽतुरा। उषः। महि। सम्। वाजैः। वाजिनीऽवति॥१६॥

हे उषो नोऽस्मान्राया धनेन संमिमिक्ष्व। संसिञ्च। संयोजयेत्यर्थः। कीदृशेन धनेने। बृहता प्रभूतेन विश्वपोसा। पेश इति रूपनाम। बहुविध-रूपयुक्तेन। तथेळाभिरा गोभिश्चास्मान्संमिमिक्ष्व। इळेति गोनाम। इळा जगतीति (नि० १-१) तन्नामसु पाठात्। आकारः समुच्चये पदान्ते वर्तमानत्वात्। उक्तं च। एतस्मिन्नोवार्थे देवेभ्यश्च पितृभ्य एत्याकारः (नि० १-४) इति। किंच हे महि महनीये उषोदेवते द्युम्नेन यशसा संमिमिक्ष्व। द्युम्नं द्योततेर्यशो वान्नं

वेति यास्कः। (नि० ५-५) कीदृशेन द्युम्नेन। विश्वतुरा। सर्वेषां शत्रूणां हिंसकेन। तथा हे वाजिनीवति अन्नासाधनभूतक्रियायुक्ते वाजैरन्नौरस्मान् संमिमिक्ष्व। अन्नां वै वाजः (श. ब्रा. ९-३-४-१) इति श्रुत्यन्तरात। राया। ऊडिदमित्यादिना विभक्तेरुदात्तत्वम्। बृहता। बृहन्महतोरूपसंख्यानमिति विभक्तिरुदात्ता। विश्वपेशसा। विश्वानि पेशांसि यस्यासौ विश्वपेशाः। बहुव्रीहौ विश्वं संज्ञायाम् (पा० ६-२-१०६) इति व्यत्ययेनासंज्ञायामपि पूर्वपदान्तोदात्तत्वम्। यद्वा। मरुद्वृधादिर्द्रष्टव्यः। मिमिक्ष्व मिह सेचने। व्यत्ययेनात्मनेपदम्। लोटि बहुलं छन्दसीति शपः श्लुः। द्विर्भावहलादिशेषौ ढत्वकत्वपत्वानि। प्रत्ययस्वरस्य *सविशिष्टत्वात्स एव शिष्यते। पूर्वपदस्यासमानवाक्यस्थत्वात्तिङ्ङतिङ इति निघातो न भवति। समानवाक्ये निघातयुष्मदस्मदादेशा वक्तव्या इति वचनात्। विश्वतुरा। तूर्वतीति तूः। तुर्वी हिंसार्थः। क्विप् चेति क्विप्। राल्लोप इति वलोपः। विश्वेषां तूर्विश्वः। समासस्येत्यन्तोदात्तत्वम्। वाजिनीवति। वाजोऽन्नातूमस्या अस्तीति वाजिनी क्रियाा तादृशी क्रिया यस्याः सा तथोक्ताः॥

मि॒मि॒क्ष्वा, 2. sg. impv. ātm.; stem मिमिह्, rt. मिह् सम् मिह्, to pour out (over), spice, richly eudow with.

इळा॑ f., affluence, sacrificial donation.

आ conj., and, and also.

NO. 4.

MAṆḌALA I. **SŪKTA 49.**

उषो भद्रेभिरिति चतुर्ऋचं षष्ठं सूक्तम्। अन्नानुक्रम्यते। उपश्चतुष्कमानुष्टुभं त्विति। कण्वपुत्रः प्रस्कण्वऋषिः। तुह्यादिपरिभाषयेदमुत्तरं चानुष्टुभम्। पूर्वत्रोषस्यं त्वित्युक्तत्वादिदमपि सूक्तमुषस्यम्। प्रातरनुवाकस्योषस्ये क्रतावानुष्टुभे छन्दस्येतत्सूक्तम्। सूत्र्यते हि उषो भद्रेारित्यानुष्टुभम् (आ० ४-१४) इति। आश्विनशस्त्रेऽप्येतत्सूक्तम्। प्रातरनुवाकन्यायेन (आ० ४-१४) इत्यतिदेशात्।

Verse 1.

हे उष उषोदेवते भद्रेभिर्भन्दनीयैः शोभनैर्मार्गैर्दिवोऽन्तरिक्षलोकात्।

* प्रथमावृत्तौ सतिवशिष्टत्वात् च सति शिष्टवात् इति पाठः।

रोच नाद्रोचमानाद्दीप्यमानात्। अधिरूपर्यर्थः। उपरिवर्तमानात्। चिदिति पूजितार्थः। पूजितादेवविधान्तरिक्षलोकात्। आगहि। आगच्छ। हे उषः अरुणप्सवोऽरुवर्णाः गावः सोमिनः सोमयुक्तस्य यजमानस्य गृहं देवयजनरूपं यज्ञगृहं त्वा त्वामु पवहन्तु प्रापयन्तु। गहि। गमेर्लोटि बहुलं छन्दसीति शपो लुक्। हेरपित्त्वेन ङित्त्वेऽनुदात्तोपदेशेत्यादिनाऽनुनासिकलोपः। अतो हेरिति लुग्र भवतिं असिद्ध वदत्राभादित्यनुनासिकलोपस्यासिद्धत्वात्। रोचनात्। रूच दीप्तौ। अनुदात्तेतश्च हलादेरिति युच्। योरनादेशे चित इत्यन्तोदात्तत्वम्। अरूणप्सवः। प्सा भक्षणे। प्सान्ति भक्षयन्ति स्तनं पिबन्ति इति प्सवो वत्साः। औणादिकः कुप्रत्ययः। आतो लोप इटि चेत्याकारलोपः। अरूणाः प्सवो यासां तास्तथोक्ताः। अत्र वत्सानामारूण्यप्रतिपादनान्मातृणामपि तथात्वं गम्यते। पैतृकमश्वा अनुहरन्ते मातृकं गावोऽनुहरन्ते। (म० १३-२१-५) इति गोनर्दीयः। तासां चोषो वाहनत्वं निघण्टावुक्तम्। अरुण्यासे गाव उषसामिति। अरुणशब्दोऽर्तेश्च (उ० ३-७) इति उनन्प्रत्ययान्तः। तृणाख्यायां चित् (उ० ३-५९) इत्यतश्चिदित्य-नुवृत्तेरन्तोदात्तः। स एव बहुव्रीहौ पूर्वपदकृतिस्वरत्वेन शिष्यते।।

गहि, 2. sg. aor. impv. par.; rt. गम्.

भद्र n., a good thing, favour, happiness.

चित्, even, from as far as.

रोचन n., splendour, light, sphere of light, heaven.

अरूणप्सु (rt. भास्? or from अरूणः पशु?) adj., of red appearance, Sāy.: अरूणवर्ण.

Verse 2.

सुऽपेशसम्। सुऽखम्। रथम्। यम्। अधिऽअस्थाः। उषः। त्वम्। तेन। सुऽश्रवसम्। जनम्। प्र। अव। अद्य। दुहितः। दिवः।।२।।

हे उषस्त्वं यं रथमध्यस्था अधितिष्ठसि। कीदृशं रथम्। सुपेशसं शोभनावयवं शोभनरूपयुक्तं वा। पेश इति रूपनामेति यास्कः। (नि० ८-११) यद्वा शोभनहिरण्ययुक्तम्। पेशः कृशनम् (नि० १-२) इति तन्नामसु पाठात्। सुखं शोभनेन खेनाकाशेन युक्तं विस्तृतमित्यर्थः। यद्वा। सुखहेतुभूतम्। अथवा सुखमिति। क्रियाविशेषणम्। सुखं यथा भवति तथेत्यर्थः। हे दिवोदुहित-

र्द्युलोकसकाशादुत्पन्ने उषोदेवते तेन रथेनाद्यास्मिन्काले सुश्रवसं शोभनहविर्युक्तं जनं यजमानं प्राव। प्रकर्षेण गच्छ। सुपेशसम्। पिश अवयवे। अस्माद-सुन्प्रत्ययः। नित्त्वादाद्युदात्तः पेशस्शब्दः। शोभनं पेशो यस्यासौ सुपेशाः। आद्युदात्तं व्द्यच्छन्दसीत्युत्तरपदाद्युदात्तत्वम्। अध्यस्थाः तिष्ठतेश्छन्दसि लुङ्लङ्लिट इति वर्तमाने लुङि गातिस्थेति सिचो लुक्। अडागम उदात्तः यद्वृत्तयोगादनिघातः। तिङि चोदात्तवतीति गतेरनुदात्तत्वम्। तेन अन्येषामपि दृश्यत इति संहितायां दीर्घः। सुश्रवसम्। श्रव इत्यन्ननाम। श्रूयत इति सतः (नि० १०-३) इति यास्कः। सुपेशसमिति वदुत्तरपदाद्युदात्तत्वम्। अव। अवरक्षणगतिप्रीतितृप्तीत्युक्तत्वादत्रावतिर्गत्यर्थः। दुहितर्दिवः। परमपि छन्दसीति षष्ठ्यन्तस्य पूर्वामन्त्रिताङ्गवद्भावे सति पदद्वयसमुदायस्याष्टमिकं सर्वानुदात्तत्वम्।।

अधि॑ स्था With acc., to mount (a car, horse).

सुख adj., of a car, with good wheels (?), easy moving, light.

सुश्रव॑स् adj., glorious, of good reputation.

प्र अव् 1., to come to rescue, help.

Verse 3.

वयः॑। चि॒त्। ते॒। प॒त॒त्रिणः॑। द्वि॒ऽपत्। चतु॑ःऽपत्। अ॒र्जु॒नि॒। उषः॑। प्र। आ॒र॒न्। ऋ॒तून्। अनु॑। दि॒वः। अन्ते॑भ्यः। परि॑।।३।।

हे अर्जुनि शुभ्रवर्ण उष उषोदेवते ते तव ऋतूँरनु गमनान्यनुलक्ष्य द्विपत् द्विपात् मनुष्यादिकं चतुष्पत् गवादिकं तथा पतत्रिणः पतत्रवन्तः पक्षोपेता वयश्चित् पक्षिणश्च दिवोऽन्तेभ्य आकाशप्रान्तेभ्यः पर्युपरिप्रारन्। प्रकर्षेण प्रारन्। प्रकर्षेण गच्छन्ति। रात्रावन्धकारेणाभिभूताः सर्वे प्राणिनस्त्वदागमनानन्तरं चेष्टावन्तो भवन्तीत्यर्थः। पतत्रिणः। पत्लृ गतौ। पतत्यनेनेति। एतत्रम्। अभिनक्षीत्यादिना। (उ० ३-१०५) अत्रन् प्रत्ययः। ततो मत्वर्थीय इति। द्विपत्। द्वौ पादावस्येति संख्यासुपूर्वस्य (पा० ५-४-१४०) इति पादशब्द-स्यान्त्यलोपः समासान्तः। अयस्मयादित्वेन भत्वात् पादः पत् (पा०

६-४-१३०) इति पद्भावः। द्वित्रिभ्यां पाद्दन्मूर्द्धसु बहुव्रीहौ (पा० ६-२-१९७) इति उत्तरपदान्तोदात्तत्वम्। चतुष्पत्। चत्वारः पादा अस्य। स्वरव्यतिरिक्तं पूर्ववत्। बहुव्रीहौ पूर्वपद- प्रकृतिस्वरत्वम्। इणः ष इत्यनुवृत्तौ इदुदुपधस्य चाप्रत्यय (पा० ८-३-४१) इति विसर्जनीयस्य षत्वम्। *नच परत्वेनास्या-सिद्धत्वात् कुप्वो क पौ च (पा० ८-३-३७) इति उपध्मानीयादेशः शङ्कनीयः। येन नाप्राप्तिन्यायेन (प० ५८) तस्यापवादत्वात्। अपवादस्तु परमपि पूर्वं बाधत एवेति वृत्तावुक्तम्। आरन्। ऋ गतौ। छन्दसि लुङ्लङ्लिट इति वर्तमाने लुङि सर्तिशास्त्यर्तिभ्यश्चेति चेरङादेशः। ऋ दृशोऽङि गुण इति गुणः। आडागमः। ऋतून्। ऋ गतौ। असमादौणादिको भावे कुप्रत्ययः। अनु२। अनुर्लक्षणे (पा० २-३-८) इति द्वितीया। संहितायां दीर्घादटि समानपादे इति नकारस्य रूत्वम्। अत्रानुनासिकः पूर्वस्य तु वेति रोः पूर्वस्य वर्णस्य सानुनासिकत्वम्। दिवः। ऊडिदमिति विभक्तिरुदात्ता। अन्तेभ्यः। पञ्चम्याः परावध्यर्थ इति विसर्जनीयस्य सत्वम्।।

आरन्, 3., plur. aor. par.; rt. ऋ प्र ऋ, to advance, turn up.

ऋतु m., time, proper time.

Verse 4.

विऽउच्छन्ती। हि। रश्मिऽभिः। विश्वम्। आऽभासि। रोचनम्। ताम्। त्वाम्। उषः। वसुऽयवः। गीःऽभिः। कण्वाः। अहूषत।।४।।

हे उषो ब्युच्छन्ती तामे वर्जयन्ती त्वं रश्मिभिः स्वकीयैस्तेजोभिर्विश्वं सर्वं भूतजातं रोचनं रोचमानं प्रकाशयुक्तं यथा भवति तथाभासि। आ †समन्तात्प्रकाशयसि। हि यस्मादेवं तस्मात्तां तादृशीं त्वां वसूयवः वसुकामाः कण्वा मेधाविन ऋत्विजः कण्वगोत्रोत्पन्ना वा महर्षयो गीर्भिः स्तुतिलक्षणैर्व-चोभिरहूषत। स्तुतवन्त इत्यर्थः। कण्व इति मेधाविनाम। कण्व ऋभुरिति तन्नामसु पाठात्। आभासि। भा दीप्तौ। अदादित्वाच्छपो लुक्। सिपः पित्त्वा-

* नास्यविद्धत्वात् इत्यादर्शः।

† प्रकाशसे इत्यादर्शः।

दनुदात्तत्वे धातुस्वरः। हि चेति निधातप्रतिषेधः। तिङि चोदात्तवतीतिगतेर-नुदात्तत्वम्। वसूयवः। वसु धनमात्मन इच्छन्तः। सुप आत्मनः क्यच्। अकृत्सार्वधातुकयोर्दीर्घः। क्याच्छन्दसीत्युप्रत्ययः। गीर्भिः। सावेकाच इति विभक्तेरुदात्तत्वम्। कण्वाः। कण शब्दार्थः। अशिप्रुषिलटिकणीत्यादिना क्वन्प्रत्ययः। नित्वादाद्युदात्तत्वम्। अहूषत। ह्वेञो लुङि ह्वः सम्प्रसारणमित्यनुवृत्तौ बहुलं च्छन्दसीति संप्रसारणम्। परपूर्वत्वे हल इति दीर्घत्वम्। च्लेः सिच्। एकाच इतीट्प्रतिषेधः। संज्ञापूर्वकस्य विधेरनित्यत्वादुणाभावः।।

व॒सू॒यु adj., desirous of riches, fortune, wealth.

अ॒हू॒ष॒त, 3. plur. aor. ātm.; rt. हू, to call.

रो॒च॒नम् is used proleptically.

NO. 5.

MAṆḌALA I. **SŪKTA 116.**

सप्तदशेऽनुवाके पञ्च सूक्तानि। तत्र नासत्याभ्यामितिपञ्चविंशत्यृचं प्रथमं सूक्तम्। उशिक्संज्ञायामङ्गराजस्य महिष्या दास्यां दीर्घतमसोत्पादितः कक्षीवानस्य सूक्तस्य ऋषिः। त्रिष्टुप् छन्दः। अश्विनौ देवता। तथाचानुक्रान्तम्। नासत्याभ्यां पञ्चाधिका कक्षीवान्दैर्धतमस उशिक्प्रसूत आश्विनं वा इति। तुह्यादिपरिभाषयेदमादीनि पञ्च सूक्तान्यश्विदेवत्यानि। प्रापरनुवाकस्याश्विने क्रतौ त्रैष्टुभे छन्दसि इदमादीनि त्रीणि सूक्तानि। अथाश्विन इति खण्डे सूत्रितम्। ग्रावाणेव नासत्याभ्यामिति त्रीणि (आ० ४-१५) इति। आश्विनशस्त्रे चैतानि शस्यानि प्रातरनुवाकन्यायेन। (आ० ६-५) इत्यतिदिष्टत्वात्।।

Verse 1.

नास॑त्याभ्याम्। ब॒र्हिःऽइ॑व। प्र। वृ॒ञ्जे॒। स्तोमा॑न्। इ॒य॒र्मि॒। अ॒भ्रिया॒ऽइव। वात॑ः। यौ। अर्भ॑गाय। वि॒ऽम॒दाय॑। जा॒याम्। सेना॒ऽजुवा॑। नि॒ऽऊ॒हतुः॑। रथे॑न।।१।।

बर्हिरिव यथा कश्चिद्यजमानो यागार्थं बर्हिः प्रवृञ्जे प्रकर्षेणान्यूनानतिरिक्तं यागाय पर्याप्तं दर्भं वृङ्क्ते छिनत्ति। संपादयतीति यावत्। एवमहं नासत्या-भ्यामश्विभ्यां स्तोमान्स्तुतीरियर्मि। संपादयामि। एतदेव विशदीक्रियते। अभ्रियेव।

यथाभ्रियाण्यभ्रेषु मेघेऽवस्थितान्युदकानि वातो वायुर्वर्षणार्थं बहुशः प्रेरयति एवमहमश्विभ्यां स्तोत्राणीयर्मि। बहुशः प्रेरयामि। कीदृशावश्विनै। अर्भगाय बालाय स्वयंवरलब्धभार्याय विमदायैतत्संज्ञाय राजर्षये मध्येमार्ग स्वयंवरार्थमागतैस्तामलभमानैरन्यैर्नृपैः सह योद्धुमशक्नुवतेऽपि तस्मै सेनाजुवा शत्रुसेनायाः प्रेरकेण शत्रुभिर्दुष्प्रापेण रथेन यावश्विनौ जायां भार्यां *परैरनाक्रान्तां न्यूहतः शत्रून्निहत्य तदीयं गृं प्रापयामासतुः। ताभ्यामित्यर्थः। नासत्याभ्याम्। सत्सु भवौ सत्यौ। न सत्या वसत्यौ। न असत्यौ नासत्यौ। नभ्राण् नपादित्यादिना नञः प्रकृतिभावः। अव्ययपूर्वपदप्रकृतिस्वरत्वम्। वृङ्क्ते वृजी वर्जने। आदिदिकः। इदित्त्वान्नुम्। लोपस्त आत्मनेपदेष्विति तलोपः। इयर्मि। ऋ गतो।। जौहोत्यादिकः। अर्तिपिपर्त्योश्चेत्यभ्यासस्येत्वम् अभ्यासस्यासवर्ण इतीयङ्। अभ्रियेव। समुद्राभ्राद्ध इति भवार्थे घः। घस्येयादेशः। शेच्छन्दसि बहुलमिति शेर्लोपः। अर्भगाय। अर्तिगृभ्यां भन् (उ० ३-१५२) इत्यर्तेर्भन्। अर्भ एवार्भ्भकः। संज्ञायां कन्। (पा० ५-३-८७)। छान्दसो गकारः। अपर आह। अर्भमल्पं गायति शब्दयतीत्यर्भगः। कै गै शब्दे। गापोष्टक् (पा० ३-२-८) आतो लोप इटि चेत्याकारलोपः तदेतत्पदकृतः शाकल्यस्याभिमतम्। सेनाजुवा। जु इति सौत्रो धातुर्गत्यर्थः। अस्मादन्तर्भावितण्यथ्रत् क्विब्वचिप्रच्छीत्यादिना क्विब्दीर्घौ। तन्वादित्वादुवङ्। (पा० ६-४-७७) न्यूहतुः। वह प्रापणे। लिठ्यतुसि यजादित्वात्संप्रसारणम्। यद्वृत्तान्नित्यमिति निघातप्रतिषेधः।।

नासत्य, name of the two Aśvinā.

वृज् 7., (of बुर्हिस्) to cut, fetch, (possibly better) to put round; प्र वृज्, to put near the fire, heat, burn.

अभ्रिय n., mass of clouds.

अर्भग adj., young.

The first pāda contains a luptopamā in which the upameya

* रनुक्रान्ताम् इत्यादर्शः।

is omitted. Sāyaṇa does not give the authority for his statement that Vimada had won the जाया, Purumitra's योषणा, at a स्वयंवर. The passages in the Ṛgveda: I. 112. 19; 117. 20; X. 39. 7; 65. 12, alluding to the event, give to understand that the As'vinā helped Vimada to get a wife or wives; that this (future) wife of Vimada had been Purumitra's consort seems to be the unbiassed interpretation of all these passages.

Verse 2.

वीळुपत्मऽभिः। आशुहेमऽभिः। वा। देवानाम्। वा। जूतिऽभिः। शाशदाना। तत्। रासभः। नासत्या। सहस्रम्। आजा। यमस्य। प्रऽधने। जिगाय॥२॥

वीळुपत्मभिः। वीळु इति बलनाम। बलवदुत्पतनैः आशुहेमभिः शीघ्रगमनैः। वाशब्दः समुच्चये। हे नासत्याश्विनौ एवं भूतैरश्वैश्च देवानामिन्द्रादीनां जूतिभिः प्रेरणैश्च शाशदाना शाशद्यमानयोरत्यर्थ प्रेर्यमाणयोर्युवयोर्वाहनभूतोयो रासभः प्रजापत्तिना दत्तः स यमस्य वैवस्वतस्य प्रीतिकरे प्रधने प्रकीर्णधनोपेत आजा आजौ संग्रामे तच्छत्रूणां सहस्रं जिगाय जितवान्। वैवस्वतो हि बहूनां मररणहेतुना संग्रामेण तुष्टो भवति। यद्वा। जेतव्यत्वेन प्रजापतिना निहितमृक्सहस्रं शीघ्रगमनयुक्तो रासभो जिगाय जयेनालभत। अन्येभ्यो देवेभ्यः पूर्वमेवाजिं प्राप्य युवां जयं प्रापयामास। तथा चास्मिन्नर्थे प्रजापतिर्वै सोमाय राज्ञे दुहितरं प्रायच्छत् (ऐ० ब्रा० ४-७) इत्यादिकं ब्राह्मणमनुसन्धेयम्। वीळुपत्मभिः। वीळु बलवत्प तन्तीति वीळुपत्मानः। आशुहेमभिः। आश्रु शीघ्रं हिन्वन्ति गच्छन्तीत्याशुहेमानः। तै हि गतौ वृद्धौ च। अन्येभ्योऽपि दृश्यन्त इति मनिन्। कृदुत्तरपदप्रकृतिस्वरत्वम्। जूतिभिः। ऊतियुतिजूतीत्यादिना क्तिन उदात्तत्वम्। शाशदाना। शद्लृ शातने। अत्र गत्यर्थो धातूनामनेकार्थत्वात्। अस्माद्यङ्लुन्ताल्लटः शानच्। तस्य च्छन्दस्युभयथेत्यार्धधातुकत्वात् श्यन्भावः। अतोलोपयलोपौ। अभ्यस्तानामादिरित्याद्युदात्तत्वम्। सुपां सुलुगिति षष्ठ्याः पूर्वसवर्णदीर्घः। आजा। तेनैव सूत्रेण डादेशः। जिगाय। जि जये। सँल्लिटोर्जेरित्यभ्यासादुत्तरस्य कुत्वं गकारः॥

वी॒ळुप॒त्मन् n., (Karmadh. cpd.), the strong, persevering flight, the strong wing (?).

आ॒शु॒हेमन् adj., quickly driving; subst. n., quick start, quick driving.

जू॒ति f., swiftness, impetus, encouraging shout.

शाशदान, pt. pf. rt. शद्, to conquer, be the first, distinguish oneself. The pt. stands for the finite vb. Pāṇ. III.2. 106.

प्र॒धने n., fight, tournament.

वा॒-वा॒, either-or; may be that-or that.

तद्, the well known.

Read either: नअसत्य, or ना॒सतिआ. The former is preferable.

The ṛc treats of the winning of the prize by the Aśvinā with the donkey at Yama's tournament. Sāy. is of opinion that the race of the gods run at Sūryā's marriage is meant. The Kauṣīt. Brāhmn. XVIII. 1, and the Ait. Brāhm. IV. 7-8 mention the race. Though both the Brāhmaṇas give the स॒हस्रम्, the prize, it should not be over looked that our ṛc does not mention Sūryā.— It seems more likely that वी॒ळुप॒त्मभिः, आ॒शु॒हेमभिः, जू॒तिभिः are three co-ordinated nouns than that वी॒ळुप॒त्मभिः and आ॒शु॒हेमभिः should be attributes of जू॒तिभिः (Sāy.). य॒मस्य प्र॒धने, arranged by Yama or in honour of Yama, better than Sāy.'s version in his comm. Cp. Ved. Stud. I. 172.

Verse 3.

तुग्रः। ह॒। भु॒ज्युम्। अ॒श्वि॒ना॒। उ॒द॒ऽमे॒घे। र॒यिम्। न। कः। चि॒त्। म॒मृ॒ऽवान्। अव। अ॒हाः। तम्। ऊ॒ह॒थुः। नौ॒भिः। आ॒त्म॒न्ऽवतीभिः। अ॒न्त॒रि॒क्ष॒प्रुत्ऽभिः। अप॒ऽउदकाभिः॥३॥

अत्रेयमाख्यायिका। तुग्रो नामाश्विनोः प्रियः कश्चिद्राजर्षिः स च द्वीपान्तरवर्तिभिः शत्रुभिरत्यन्तमुपद्रुतः सन् तेषां जयाय स्वपुत्रं भुज्युं सेनया सह नावा प्राहौषीत् सा च नौर्मध्येसमुद्रमतिदूरं गता वायुवशेन भिन्नासीत्। तदानीं स भुज्युः शीघ्रमश्विनौ तुष्टाव। *स्तुतौ च तौ सेनया सहितमात्मीयासु नौष्वारोप्य पितुस्तुग्रस्य समीपं त्रिभिरहोरात्रैः प्रापयामासतुरिति। अयमर्थ इदमादिकेन तृचेन प्रतिपाद्यते। हशब्दः प्रसिद्धौ। तुग्रः खलु पूर्वं शत्रुभिः पीडितः सन् तज्जयार्थमुदमेघे। उदकैर्मिह्यते सिच्यत †इत्युदमेघः समुद्रः। तस्मिन् भुज्युमेतत्संज्ञं प्रियं पुत्रमवाहाः। नावा गन्तुं पर्यत्याक्षीत्। तत्र दृष्टान्तः। ममृवान् म्रियमाणः सन्धनलोभी कश्चिन्मनुष्यो रयिं न यचथा धनं परित्यजति तद्वत्। हे आश्विनौ तं च भुज्युं मध्येसमुद्रं निमग्नं नौभिः पितृसमीपमूहथुः। युवां प्रापितवन्तौ। कीदृशीभिः आत्मन्वतीभिरात्मीयाभिः। यचुवयोः स्वभूता- भिरित्यर्थः। यद्वा। ††धृतिरात्मावधारणवतीभिरित्यर्थः। अन्तरिक्षप्रुद्भिः। अति- स्वच्छत्वादन्तरिक्षे जलस्योपरिष्टादेव गन्त्रीभिः। अपोदकाभिः सुश्लिष्टत्वाद- पगतोदकाभिः। अप्रविष्टोदकाभिरित्यर्थः। उदमेघे। मिह सेचने। कर्मणि घञ्। न्यँक्वादीनां च (पा० ७-३-५३) इति कुत्वम्। उदकस्योदः संज्ञायाम्। (पा० ६-७-५७) थाथादिनोत्तरपदान्तोदात्तत्वम्। ममृवान्। मृङ् प्राणत्यागे। लिटः क्वसुः। क्रादिनियमात्प्राप्तस्येटो वस्वेकाजाद्धसामिति नियमादभावः। अहाः। ओहाक् त्यागे। लुङि तिपि च्लेः सिच्। आगमानुशासनस्यानित्यत्वात्सगिटौ न क्रियेते। बहुलं छन्दसीतीडभावः हल्ङ्याब्भ्य इति तिलोपः। रुत्वविसर्गौ। यद्वा। मन्त्रे घसेति च्लेर्लुक्। च्लेर्लुप्तत्वादिण् न क्रियते। नौभिः। सावेकाच इति विभक्तेरुदात्तत्वम्। आत्मन्वतीभिः। आत्मनो मतुप्। मादुपधाया इति वत्वम्। अनो नुट्। नलोपः। ह्रस्वनुड्भ्यां मतुबिति मतुप उदात्तत्वम्। अन्तरिक्षप्रुद्भिः। प्रुङ् गतौ। क्विप् चेति क्विप्।।

उ॒द॒मे॒घ m., = समुद्र (Sāy.).

अव॑ अ॒हाः, 3. sg. par. aor.; rt. हा 3., to leave behind, leave in the lurch.

---

* तौच स्तुतौ इत्यादर्शः।

† त्युदकमेघ इत्यादर्शः।

†† धृतिरात्मा। धारणवतीभिः इत्यादर्शः।

अन्तरिक्षप्रुत् adj. (rt. प्रु, प्लु), sailing in the air.

अपोदक adj., watertight.

Ṛcas 3-5 speak of the Bhujyu legend. Sāy.'s interpretation seems to be forced and against the syntactical setting.

Verse 4.

तिस्रः। क्षपः। त्रिः। अहा। अतिव्रजत्ऽभिः। नासत्या। भुज्युम्। ऊहथुः। पतङ्गैः। समुद्रस्य। धन्वन्। आर्द्रस्य। पारे। त्रिऽभिः। रथैः। शतपत्ऽभिः। षट्ऽअश्वैः।।४।।

हे नासत्यो सेनया सहोदके निमग्नं भुज्युं तिस्रः क्षपस्त्रिसंख्याका रात्रीस्त्रिरहा त्रिवारमावृत्तान्यहानि च। अतिव्रजद्भिरतिक्रम्य गच्छद्भिरेतावन्तं कालमतिव्याप्य वर्तमानैः पतङ्गैः पतद्भिस्त्रिभिस्त्रिसंख्याकै रथै/हथुः। युवामूढवन्तौ। क्वेति चेदुच्यते। समुद्रस्याम्बुराशेर्मध्ये धन्वन् धन्वनि जलवर्जितप्रदेशे आर्द्रस्योदकेनार्द्रीभूतस्य समुद्रस्य पारे तीरदेशे च। कथंभूतै रथैः। शतपद्भिः शतसंख्याकैश्चक्रलक्षणैज्पादरुपेतैः। षळश्वैः षड्भिरश्वैर्युक्तैः। तिस्रः। त्रिचतुरोः स्त्रियामिति त्रिशब्दस्य तिस्रादेशः। स चान्तोदात्तः। अचि र ऋत इति रेफादेश उदात्तयणो हल्पूर्वादिति विभक्तेरुदात्तत्वम्। क्षपः। विभक्त्यन्तस्य छान्दसं ह्रस्व त्वम्। यद्वा। शास्यात इति योगविभागादधातोरप्याकारलोपः। अहा। शेश्छन्दसि बहलमिति शेर्लोपः। पतङ्गैः। पत्लृ गतौ। पतेरङ्गच्। (उ० १-११८) धन्वन्। धविर्गत्यर्थः। इदित्वान्नुम्। कनिन्युवृषीत्यादिना कनन्। सुपां सुलुगिति सप्तम्या लुक्। शतपद्भिः। शतं पादा येषाम्। सुख्यासुपूर्वस्येति पदशब्दस्यान्त्यलोपः समासान्तः। अयस्मयादित्वेन भत्वात् पादः पदिति पद्भावः। यद्वा। पादसमानार्थः पच्छब्दः प्रकृत्यन्तरं द्रष्टव्यम्।।

क्षप् f., night.

अति व्रज् 1., to exceed a certain time, last longer than, march over a certain time.

पतङ्ग adj., winged (bird, horse).

धन्वन् n., desert, dry land, bank.

धन्वन् पारे are locatives of the goal, dependent on ऊहथुः.

The number three is peculiar to the Aśvinā.— Sāy, thinks that the "feet" of the cars mentioned here are the wheels. But the रथाः of ṛc 4 are the same as the नावः in ṛc 3. Considering that the latter are आत्मन्वत्, it will be better to take them as preternatural, celestial vehicles which, like an animated being, move on their legs.

Verse 5.

अनारम्भणे। तत्। अवीरयेथाम्। अनास्थाने। अग्रभणे। समुद्रे। यत्। अश्विनौ। ऊहथुः। भुज्युम्। अस्तम्। शतऽअरित्राम्। नावम्। आतस्थिऽवांसम्।।५।।

*अश्विनौ अनारम्भण आलम्बनरहिते समुद्रे तत्कर्मावीरयेथाम् विक्रान्तं कृतवन्तौ युवाम्। अनारम्भणत्वमेव स्पष्टीकरोति। अनास्थाने। आस्थीयतेऽस्मिन्नित्यास्थानो भूप्रदेशः। तद्रहिते। स्थानतुमशक्ये जल इत्यर्थः। अग्रभणेऽग्रहणे। हस्तेन ग्राह्यं शाखादिकमपि यत्र नास्ति तस्मिन्नित्यर्थः। किं पुनस्तत्कर्म। भुज्यं समुद्रे मग्नं शतारित्रां वह्वरित्राम्। यैः काष्ठैः पार्श्वतोबद्धैर्जलालोडने सति नौः शीघ्रं गच्छति तान्यरित्राणि। ईदृशीं नावमातस्थिवांसमास्थितवन्तमारूढवन्तं कृत्वा अस्तं गृहनामैतत्। पितुस्तुग्रस्य गृहं प्रति यदूहथुः तत्प्रापणमन्यैर्दुःशकं युवां समुद्रमध्ये कृतवन्तावित्यर्थः। अनारम्भणे। आरभ्यत इत्यारम्भणम्। कृत्यल्युटो बहुलमिति कर्मणि ल्युट्। नञ्सुभ्यामित्युत्तरपदान्तो दात्तत्वम्। अवीरयेथाम्। शूरवीर विक्रान्तौ। चुरादिरात्मनेपदी। अनास्थाना ग्रभणयोः पूर्ववल्ल्युट्स्वरौ। अयं तु विशेषः हृग्रहोर्भ इति भत्वम्। अस्तम्। अस्यतेऽस्मिन्सर्वमित्यस्तं गृहम्। असिहसीत्यादिना तन्प्रत्ययः। शतारित्राम्। ऋ गतौ। अर्तिलूधूसू (पा० ३-२-१८४) इति करण इत्रप्रत्ययः। बहुव्रीहौ। पूर्वपदप्रकृति स्वरत्वम्।।

अग्रभण, With nothing to grasp, catch hold of.

---

* आदर्शे हे अश्वनौ इति पाठः।

वीरय, denom. ātm., to act as a hero, do some heroic deed.

शतारित्र With hundred oars.

अस्तं n., house, home; वह् अस्तम् to bring home.

Verse 6.

यम्। अश्विना। ददथुः। श्वेतम्। अश्वम्। अघऽअश्वाय। शश्वत्। इत्। स्वस्ति। तत्। वाम्। दात्रम्। महि। कीर्तेन्यम्। भूत्। पैद्वः। वाजी। सदम्। इत्। हव्यः। अर्यः।।६।।

अत्रेदमाख्यायते। पेदुर्नाम कश्चित्। स चाश्विनौ तुष्टाव। तस्मै प्रीतौ कंचित् श्वेतवर्णमश्वं दत्तवन्तौ। सचाश्वस्तस्य प्रौढं जयं चकारेति। एतदत्र प्रतिपाद्यते। अश्विनौ युवामघाश्वायाहन्तव्याश्वाय पेदुनाम्ने राजर्षये यं श्वेतवर्णमश्वं ददथुः दत्तवन्तौ सोऽश्वस्तस्मै स्वस्ति जयलक्षणं मङ्गलं शश्वदित् नित्यमेव चकार। वां युवयोस्तद्दात्रं दानं महि महदति गम्भीरम् अत एव कीर्तेन्यं सर्वैः कीर्तनीयं प्रशस्यं भूत् अभूत्। तस्मात् पैद्वः पेदोः संबन्धी पतनशीलः शीध्रगामी वार्यः शत्रूणां प्रेरयिता युद्धेषु प्रेरयितव्यो वा वाजी वेजनवान् सोऽश्वः सदमित् सदैव हव्यो ऽस्माभिरप्याह्वातव्यः। दात्रम्। ददातेर्भाव औणादिकस्त्रप्रत्ययः। महि। मह पूजायाम्। इन् सर्वधातुभ्य इतीन्। कीर्तेन्यम्। कृत इद्धातोरितीत्वम्। भूत्। बहुलं छन्दस्यमाङ्योगेऽपीत्यडभावः। पैद्वः पेदरोः संबन्धी। तस्येदमित्यण्। छान्दसो वर्णलोपः। हव्यः। ह्वयतेरचो यदिति यत्। बहुलं छन्दसीति संप्रसारणम्। १११) इत्यौणादिको यत् व्यत्ययेनान्तोदात्तत्वम्।।

अघ अश्व (proper noun?) with bad horses, badly horsed.

शश्वत् adv., complete, many, great, sheer (luck).

अरि adj. and subst., mighty, rich.

वाजिन् m., horse, charger, racer.

हव्य (ह्वे), to be invoked, praised.

कीर्तेन्य, to be praised, extolled.

सदम् indecl., always, at any time; सदम् इत्, for ever.

Read अधाशुआय, सुअस्ति.

The ṛc refers to the white, serpent-killing horse of Pedu. The Aśvinā gave it to him, as he on account of his bad horses continually had been defeated. शश्वदित्स्वस्ति is in apposition to अश्वम्.—अर्यः is dependent on हव्यः according to Geldner, Ved. Stud. III. 76-77 and Kommentar, it is abl. sg.: to be praised higher even than a potent man.

Verse 7.

युवम्। नरा। स्तुवते। पज्रियाय। कक्षीवते। अरदतम्। पुरम्ऽधिम्। कारोतरात्। शफात्। अश्वस्य। वृष्णः। शतम्। कुम्भान्। असिञ्चतम्। सुरायाः ।।७।।

अत्रेयमाख्यायिका। कक्षीवानृषिः पुरा तमसा तिरोहितज्ञानः सन् ज्ञानार्थ-मश्विनौ तुष्टाव। तस्मा अश्विनौ प्रभूतां धियं दत्तवन्ताविति। तदाह। हे नरा नेतारावश्विनो युवं युवां पज्रियाय। पज्रा इत्यङ्गिरसामाख्या। पज्रा वा अङ्गिरस इत्याम्नाततत्वात्। तेषां कुले जाताय कक्षीवते। कच्या रज्जुरश्वस्य तद्वते तत्संज्ञाय। स्तुवते युवयोः स्तुतिं कुर्वते मह्यं पुरंधिं प्रभूतां धियं बुद्धिमरदतम् व्यलिखतम् यथा सर्वार्थगोचरा भवति तथा कृतवन्तावित्यर्थः। अपि च कारोतरात्। कारोतरो नाम वैदलश्चर्मवेष्टितो भाजनविशेषः। यस्मिन्सुरायाः स्रावणं क्रियते। लुप्तोपममेतत्। कारोतरा यथा सुरायाः संपादकास्तां स्रावयन्ति एवमेव युवां वृष्णः सेचनसमर्थस्य युष्मदीयस्याश्वस्य शफात् खुरात् सुरायाः शतं कुम्भान् असंख्यातान्सुराघटानसिञ्चतम्। अक्षारयतम्। यद्वा। सिञ्चतिः पूरणार्थः। कारोतरस्थानीयाद्युष्मदीयाश्वखुरात् या सुरा प्रवहति तयासंख्यातान् घटानसिञ्चतम्। अपूरयतम्। ये जनाः सौत्रामण्यादिकर्मणि युष्मद्यागाय सुरां याचन्ते तेषामित्यर्थः। स्तुवते। स्तौतेर्लटः शतृ। अदादित्वाच्छपो लुक्। शतुरनुम इति विभक्तेरूदात्तत्वम्। पज्रियाय। पज्रशब्दातच्छैषिको घच्। कक्षीवते। आसन्दीवदष्ठीवच्चक्रीवत्कक्षीवदिति निपातनात्कक्ष्यशब्दस्य संप्रसारणं वत्वं च। अरदतम्। दर विलेखने। पुरंधिम्। पुरंधिर्बहुधीरिति यास्कः (नि०

६-१३)। पृषोदरादित्वात्पुरंधिभावः। यद्वा। पुरं पूरयितव्यं सर्वविषयजातमस्यां धीयतेऽवस्थाप्यत इति पुरंधिर्बुद्धिः। कर्मण्यधिकरणे चेति दधातेः किः प्रत्ययः। तत्पुरुषे कृति बहुलमिति बहुलवचनादलुक्। इदं तु व्युत्पत्तिमात्रम्। वस्तुतः पृषोदरादिरेव। असिञ्चतम्। षिचिर् क्षरणे। तौदादिकः। शेमुचादीनामिति नुम्।।

रद् 1., to make furrows, dig, open up.

पुरंधि f., fortune, generosity, favour; Sāy., प्रभूता धीः.

कारोतर m., filter, strainer (of a distiller).

The same legend about Kakṣīvat, a member of the Pajra branch of the Aṅgiras is touched upon in ṚV. I. 117.6. I.51. 13 says that Indra gave a young wife to the ageing Kakṣīvat; and according to X. 143. 1 he himself was by the Aśvinā given back his former youth.—On कारोतर see Sāy., comm.—The third pāda contains a *luptopamā*.—The mention of सुरा in this connection is apt to throw some light on the attitude of the Vedic antiquity towards this beverage, so much abhorred by the later Sruti. Cp. also Vājasan. Saṁh. IX, where सुरा is permitted at the sacrifice, and the same Saṁh. XIX-XXI, where it is prescribed instead of Soma.

Verse 8.

हिमेन। अग्निम्। घ्रंसम्। अवारयेथाम्। पितुऽमतीम्। ऊर्जम्। अस्मै। अधत्तम्। ऋबीसे। अत्रिम्। अश्विना। अवऽनीतम्। उत्। निन्यथुः। सर्वऽगणम्। स्वस्ति।।८।।

अत्रेदमाख्यानम्। अत्रिमृषिमसुराः शतद्वारे पीडायन्त्रगृहे प्रवेश्य तुषाग्निना बाधिषत। तदानीं तेन ऋषिणा स्तुतावश्विनावग्निमुदकेनोपशमय्य तस्मात्पीडा-गृहादविकलेन्द्रियवर्गं सन्तं निरगमयतामिति। तदेतत्प्रतिपाद्यते। हे अश्विनौ हिमेन हिमवच्छीतेनोदकेन घ्रंसं दीप्यमानमत्रेर्बाधनार्थमसुरैः प्रक्षिप्तं तुषाग्नि-मवारयेथाम्। युवां निवारितवन्तौ। शीतीकृतवन्तावित्यर्थः। अपि चास्मा असुरपीडया कार्श्यं प्राप्तायात्रये पितुमतीम्। पितुरित्यन्ननाम्। अन्नयुक्तमूर्जं

बलप्रदं रसात्मकं क्षीरादिकमधत्तम्। पुष्ट्यर्थं प्रायच्छतम्। ऋबीसेऽपगतप्रकाशे पीडायन्नगृहेऽवनीतमवाङ्मुखतयासुरैः प्रापितमत्रिं सर्वगणम्। गणः समूहः। सर्वेषामिन्द्रियाणां पुत्रादीनां वा गणेनोपेतं स्वस्ति अविनाशो यथा भवति तथोन्निन्यथुः। तस्मादृहादुद्रमय्य युवां स्वगृहं प्रापितवन्तौ। यद्वा। हिमेन शीतेन वृष्ट्युदकेनाग्निमाग्निवत्तीक्ष्णं घ्रंसम् अहर्नामैतत्। सामर्थ्यान्निादाघकालीनमहरवारयेथाम्। तस्याह्नस्तैक्ष्ण्यं निवारितवन्तौ। अपि चास्मा अग्नये पितुमतीं चरुपुराडाशादिलक्षणान्नोपेतमूर्जं बलकरं रसात्मकमुपस्तरणाभिधारणात्मकं घृतमाधत्तम्। वृष्ट्युत्पादनेनाग्नेर्यागार्थं हवींषि निष्पादितवन्तावित्यर्थः। ऋबीसेऽपगततेजस्के पृथिवीद्रव्येऽवनीतमोषधीनामुत्पादनायाधस्तान्नीतम्। पार्थिवाग्निा परिपक्वा उदकेन क्लिन्ना ह्योषधिवनस्पतयो विरोहन्ति। अत्रिं हविषामत्तारमौषधिवनस्पत्यादीनां वा। एवंविधमग्निं सर्वगणं व्रीह्याद्योषधिगणोपेतं हे अश्विनौ युवां स्वस्ति अविनाशो यथा भवति तथोन्निन्यथुः। व्रीह्याद्योषधि वनस्पतिरूपेण भूमेरूपरिष्टान्नीतवन्तौ। कारणात्मना पार्थिवाग्नौ वर्तमानं सर्वमोषधिवनस्पत्यादिकमश्विनौ प्रवर्षणेन व्यक्तीकृतवन्तावित्यर्थः। अयं पक्षो यास्केन हिमेनोदकेनेत्यादिनोक्तः (नि०६-३६)। पितुमतीम्। ह्रस्व- नुड्भ्यां मतुबिति मतुप्। उदात्तत्वम्। ऋबीसे। अत्र यास्कः ऋबीसमपगतभासमपचितभासमपहृतभासं* वेति (नि० ६-३५)। पृषोदरादित्वादभिमतरूपस्वरसिद्धिः। अन्निम्। अद भक्षणे। अदेस्त्रिनिचेति चशब्दान्निः। अवनीतम्। गतिनन्तर इति गतेः प्रकृतिस्वरत्वम्। स्वस्ति। अस भुवि। भावे क्तिन्। छन्दस्युभयथेति सार्वधातुकत्वादस्तेर्भूभावाभावः।।

घ्रंस m., heat, glow.

पितुमत् adj., nourishing.

ऊर्ज् f., nourishment, food.

ऋबीस m., fire glowing under the earth or under embers.

स्वस्ति adv. (स्वस्तिभिः), hail, unharmed, safely.

अग्निम् acc., may be attraction to घ्रंसम् acc., or we may take both acc. as co-ordinated:—flames and heat.

---

* आदर्शे गतभासं वा इत्यधिकम्।

ṚV. X. 80.3 speaks of the saving of Atri by Agni; VI.50. 10 and VIII. 71.5 show him rescued out of तमस् by the Aśvinā. According to Sāy. Atri was thrown by the Asuras into a torture-chamber and covered with burning straw.

Verse 9.

परा। अवतम्। नासत्या। अनुदेथाम्। उच्चऽबुंधन्म्। चक्रथुः। जिह्मऽबारम्। क्षरन्। आपः। न। पायनाय। राये। सहस्राय। तृष्यते। गोतमस्य।।९।।

अत्रोदमाख्यानम्। कदाचिन्मरुभूमौ वर्तमानस्य स्तोतुर्गोतमस्य ऋषेः समीपं देशान्तरे वर्तमानं कूपमुत्खायाश्विनौ प्रापयेताम्। प्रापय्य च तं कूपं स्नानपानादिसौकर्यायोपरिमूलमधोबिलमवास्थापयतामिति। तदेतदाह हे नासत्यासत्यस्वभावौ सत्यस्य नेतारौ नासिकाप्रभवौ वा एतत्संज्ञावश्विनौ युवामवतम्। कूपनामैतत्। अवस्तात्ततं कूपं परानुदेथां गोतमस्य ऋषेः समीपं प्रेरिषाथाम्। तदनन्तरं तं कूपमुच्चाबुघनम्। उच्चैरुपरिष्टाद्बुधनो मूलं यस्य स तथोक्तः। जिह्मवारम्। जिह्ममधस्ताद्वर्त्तमानतया वक्रं बारं द्वारं यस्य स तथोक्तः। एवंगुणविशिष्टं चक्रथुः। युवामकृषाथाम्। तस्मात्कूपात्तृष्यते पिपासतो गोतमस्य पायनाय पानार्थमापो न आपश्च। अयं नशब्दश्चार्थे। क्षरन्। प्रवाहरूपेण निरगमन्। कीदृशस्य। राये हवींषि दत्तवते*। सहस्राय सहनशीलाय। यद्वा। सहस्रसंख्याकाय राये धनाय एतत्संख्यधनलाभार्थं चाक्षरन्। अनुदेथाम्। णुद प्रेरणे। तौदादिकः। जिह्मबारम् द्वारशब्दस्य पृषोदरादित्वात् बारादेशः। क्षरन्। क्षर संचलने। बहुलं छन्दस्यमाङ्योगेऽपीत्यडभावः। शपः पित्त्वादनुदात्तत्वम्। तिङो लसार्वधातुकस्वरेण धातुस्वरः। पायनाय। हेतुमति णिच्। शाच्छापसाह्वेति युक्। भावे ल्युट्। राये। रा दाने। राति ददातीति राः। रातेर्डैः (उ० २-६६)। ऊडिदमिति विभक्तेरुदात्तत्वम्। तृष्यते। ञितृषा पिपासायाम्। श्यन्। लटः शतृ। श्यनो नित्वादाद्युदात्तत्वम्। षष्ठ्यर्थे चतुर्थी वक्तव्या (पा० २-३-६२-१) इति चतुर्थी।।

परा नुद् 6., to upset, turn over.

---

* दत्तवतः इत्यादर्शः।

अवत m., well.

उच्चाबुंधन, with bottom, base on top, upside down.

जिह्मबांर, with brim slanting (?).

तृष्यंते either has to be taken together with क्षरन्नापो न पायनाय and राये together with गोतमस्य, or तृष्यंते has been attracted by राये and stands for तृष्यंतः (Sāy. पिपासतः). Or does गोतमस्य depend on अवतम्?—In this ṛc again an extraordinary feat, otherwise belonging to the Maruts, has been transferred to the Aśvinā.—On सहस्राय see Sāy., comm. It would not be out of place to think that Gotama, the author of the ṚV. hymns I. 74-93, on a professional journey to perform a great sacrifice, got into distress, the salvation from which our ṛc relates.—Pādas 3 and 4 seem to contain a comparison: आपः is to be understood to be comprised in the simile.

Verse 10.

जुजुरुषः। नासत्या। उत। वव्रिम्। प्र। अमुञ्चतम्। द्रापिम्ऽइव। च्यवानात्। प्र। अतिरतम्। जहितस्य। आयुः। दस्रा। आत्। इत्। पतिम्। अकृणुतम्। कनीनाम्॥१०॥

अत्रेदमाख्यानम्। वलीपलितादिभिरुपेतो जीर्णाङ्गः पुत्रादिभिः परित्यक्तश्च्यवनाख्य ऋषिरश्विनौ तुष्टाव। स्तुतावश्विनौ तस्मा ऋषये जरामपगमय्य पुनर्यौवनमकुरुतामिति। तदेतदाह। हे नासत्यावश्विनौ जुजुरुषो जीर्णाच्च्यवानाच्च्यवनाख्यान्महर्षेः सकाशाद्वव्रिं कृत्स्नं शरीरमावृत्यावस्थितां जरां प्रामुञ्चतं प्रकर्षेणामोचयतम्। तत्र दृष्टान्तः। द्रापिमिव। द्रापिरिति कवचस्याख्या। यथा कश्चित्कवचं कृत्स्नशरीरव्यापकं धृत्वा पश्चात् शरीरात्पृथक् करोति तद्वत्। उतापि च हे दस्रा एतत्संज्ञौ दर्शनीयौ वाश्विनौ जहितस्य पुत्रादिभिः परित्यक्तस्य ऋषेरायुर्जीवनं प्रातिरतम्। प्रावर्धयताम्। प्रपूर्वस्तिरतिर्वर्धनार्थः। आदित्। अनन्तरमेनं युवानं सन्तं कनीनां कन्यानां पतिं भर्तारमकृणुतमकुरुतम्। जुजुरुषः। जॄष् वयोहानौ। लिटः क्वसुः। बहुलं छन्दसीत्युत्वम्। द्विर्भावः।

पञ्चम्येकवचने वसोः संप्रसारणमिति संप्रसारणम्। शासिवसिघसीनां चेति षत्वम्। वव्रिम्। वृञ् वरणे। आदृगमहन इति किप्रत्ययः। जहितस्य। ओहाक् त्यागे। कर्मणि निष्ठा। तस्य छन्दस्युभयथेति सार्वधातुकत्वाद्यक्। तस्य बहुलं छन्दसीति श्लुः जहातेश्च (पा० ६-४-११६) इतीत्वम्। कनीनाम्। रयेर्मतौ बहुलमिति बहुलवचनात्कन्याशब्दस्यात्र संप्रसारणम्।।

जुजुर्वान्, pt. pf. rt. जुर् जृ, to get old.

वव्रि m., shape, body (Naigh. III. 7).

अतिरतम्, 2. du. impf. par.; rt. तृ 6., to corss; प्र तृ, to prolong, renew; प्र तृ आयुः, to prolong the life, rejuvenate. दस्र m. (दंस्), a vafourite attribute of the Aśvinā: past-master, wonder-worder.

आद् इत्, and then still.

प्र मुच्, to take away (from).

कनी, कनीन् (only gen. plur.)=कन्या.

Cyavāna in the ṚV. is called Cyavana in the Satap. Br., IV. 1.5. 1; Mbh. III. 122. if.; the legend of the rejuvenated Cyavana is mentioned in not less than six ṚV. passages.—Note the plural कनीनाम्.

Verse 11.

तत्। वाम्। नरा। शंस्यम्। राध्यम्। च। अभिष्टिऽमत्। नासत्या। वरूथम्। यत्। विद्वांसा। निधिम्ऽइव। अपऽगूळ्हम्। उत्। दर्शतात्। ऊपथुः। वन्दनाय।।११।।

अत्रेदमाख्यानम्। वन्दनो नाम कश्चिदृषिः। स चासुरैः कूपे निखात उत्तरीतुमशक्नुवन्नाश्विनावस्तौत्। तमश्विनौ कूपादुत्रिन्यतुरिति। तदाह। नरा आरोग्यस्य नेतारौ हे नासत्यावश्विनौ वां युवयोः संबन्ध्यभिष्टिमदभ्येषण-युक्तमाभिमुख्येन प्राप्तव्यं तथा वरूथं वरणीयं कामयितव्यं तत्कर्म शंस्यम्। अस्माभिः प्रशंसनीयम्। राध्यम्। आराधनीयं च। किं पुनस्तत्कर्म। विद्वांसा

जानन्तौ युवां निधिमिव निक्षिप्तं धनविवापगूळहमरण्ये निर्जने देशे कूपमध्येऽ-सुरैर्निगूढं विन्दनाथ वन्दनमृषिं दर्शतादध्वगैः पिपासुभिर्द्रष्टव्यात्कूपाददूपथुः। उदाहार्ष्टम्। एवं यदेत्कूपादुद्धरणं तदित्यर्थः। शंस्यम्। शंसु स्तुतौ। अस्माण्यन्तादचो यदिति यत्। यतोऽनाव इत्याद्युदात्तत्वम्। अभिष्टिमत्। अभिपूर्वादिष गतावित्य-स्माद्भावे क्तिन्। मन्त्रे वृषेति क्तिन उदात्तत्वम्। कृदुत्तरपदप्रकृतिस्वरत्वेन स एव शिष्यते। शकन्ध्वादित्वात्पररूपत्वम्। तादौ चेति तु गतिस्वरस्य सर्वविधीनां छन्दसि विकल्पितत्वाादप्रवृत्तिः। ततो मतुप्। अन्तोदात्तादुत्तरस्य तस्य ह्रस्वनु-ड्भ्यामि त्युदात्तत्वम्। वरूथम्। जृवृञ्भ्यामूथन्। विद्वांसा। सुषांसुलुगिति विभक्तेराकारः। अपगूळहम्। गुहू संवरणे। कर्मणि निष्ठा। यस्य विभाषेतीट्-प्रतिषेधः। ढत्वधत्वष्टुत्वढलोपदीर्घाः। गतिरनन्तर इति गतेः प्रकृतिस्वरीत्वम्। दर्शनात्। भृमृदृशीत्यादिनातच्। ऊपथुः। टुवप् बीजतन्तुसंताने। लिट्यथुसि यजादित्वात्संप्रसारणम्। द्विर्वचनादि। वन्दनाय। क्रियाग्रहणं कर्तव्यमिति कर्मणः संप्रदानत्वाच्चतुर्थी।।

राध् 1., to be successful; राध्यं, to be gained.

अभिष्टिमत् adj., protecting, safe.

उद् वप्, to dig out, fetch out.

वरूथ (वृ) n., protection, shield.

Both the legend about Vandana and this ṛc are obscure. Ṛv. I. 119. 6,7 says that the Aśvinā prolonged Vandana's life, put him who had fallen to pieces again together and made a ऋषि rise from the groung (?). Sāy. has it that Vandana had been dropped by Asuras into a cistern, and according to ṚV. X. 39.8 the Aśvinā rescued him out of a ऋष्यद. ऋष्यद is interpreted by the commentators as कूप and our दर्शतात् is in Ludwig's view a corruption of ऋष्यदात्. Sāy. anyhow understands कूपात् along with दर्शतात् —from a well that could easily be seen by thirsty travellers. वन्दनाय is interpreted by Sāyaṇa as acc.; the best solution seems to be offered by

Ludwig who sees in वन्दनाय a play on the name of Vandana, the fourth pāda then meaning:— you dug out from the well Vandana for (your) praise. The acc. वन्दनम् has to be understood as object to उदूपथुः— it droped out on account of the neighbouring datives. Whether it was the deliberate intention of the poet to veil his thoughts, or whether corruption of tradition or text have made the legend so obscure, the fact remains that the meaning of the ṛc itself is for the time being not clear. Nor does the parallel ṚV. I. 119. 7 throw sufficient light on our passage.—क्षेत्रादा विप्रं जनथः— may mean the unearthing of a corpse or of someone buried alive.

Verse 12.

तत्। वाम्। नरा। सनये दंसः। उग्रम्। आविः। कृणोमि। तन्यतुः। न। वृष्टिम्। दुध्यङ्। ह। यत्। मधु। आथर्वणः। वाम्। अश्वस्य। शीर्ष्णा। प्र। यत्। ईम्। उवाच॥१२॥

अत्रेयमाख्यायिका। इन्द्रो दधीचे प्रवर्ग्यविद्यां चोपदिश्य यदि इमामन्यस्मै वक्ष्यसि शिरस्ते छेत्स्यामीत्युवाच। ततोऽश्विनावश्वस्य शिरश्छित्वा दधीचः शिरः प्रच्छिद्यान्यत्र निधाय तत्राशब्यं शिरः प्रत्यधत्ताम्। तेन च दध्यङ्ङृचः सामानि यजूंषि च पवर्ग्यविषयाणि मधुविद्याप्रतिपादकं ब्राह्मणं चाश्विनावध्यापयामास। तदिन्द्रो ज्ञात्वा वज्रेण तच्छिरोऽच्छिनत्। अथाश्विनौ तस्य स्वकीयं मानुषं शिरः प्रत्यधत्तामिति शट्यायनवाजसनेययोः प्रपञ्चेनोक्तम्। तदेतत्प्रतिपाद्यते। नरा हे नरौ अश्विनौ वां युवयोः संबनिधन्युग्रमुद्गूर्णमन्यैर्दुः-शकंदंसः। कर्मनामैतत्। युवाभ्यां पुरा कृतं तत्कर्म सनये धनलाभार्थमाविष्कृणोमि। प्रकटीकरोमि। तत्र दृष्टान्तः। तन्यतुर्न। यथरा मेघस्थः शब्दो वृष्टिं मेघान्तर्वर्त मानमुदकं प्रवर्षणेन सर्वत्र प्रकटयति तद्वत्। किं तत्कर्म। अथर्वणः पुत्रो दध्यङ् एतत्संज्ञ ऋषिरश्वस्य शीर्ष्णा युष्मत्सामर्थ्येन प्रतिहितेन शिरसा वां युवाभ्यामीमिमां *मधु मधुविद्यां यद्ध यदा खलु प्रोवाच प्रोक्तवान्। तदानीमश्वस्य शिरसः संघानलक्षणं पुनर्मानुषस्य शिरसः प्रतिसंधान-

* आदर्शे मधु इति नास्ति।

लक्षणं च यद्धवदीयं कर्म तदाविष्कृणोमीत्यर्थः। सनये। षणु दाने। खनिकषिकस्यज्ज्यसिवसिधनिस्तनिवनिसनि ग्रन्थिचरिभ्यश्चेतीप्रत्ययः। तन्यतुः। तनु विस्तारे। ऋतन्यञ्जीत्यादिना यतुच्। यद्वा। स्तन शब्दे। बाहुलकाद्यतुच्। छान्दसः सलोपः। वृष्टिम्। वृष्यते सिच्यतेऽनेनेति वृष्टिः। मन्त्रे वृषेत्यादिना क्तिन् उदात्तत्वम्। आथर्वणः। अपत्यार्थेऽण्यन् (पा० ६-४-१६७) इति प्रकृतिभावाट्टिलोपाभावः। शीर्ष्णा। शीर्ष छन्दसि (पा० ६-१-६०) इति शिरःशब्दपर्यायः शीर्षञ्शब्दोऽन्तोदात्तो निपात्यते। अल्लोपे सत्युदात्तनिवृत्तिस्वरेण विभक्तेउदात्तत्वम्।।

स॒नि (सन्) m., the gaining, being rewarded.

ई॒म्, isolated enclit. acc. of a personal pron. for all numbers and genders; here n., it.

यन्मधु॑, यद् in pāda 3 is relat. pron.; यद्, conj. in pāda 4, corresponds to तद् in pāda 1.

On this and the following legends see Sāy., comm.

Verse 13.

अजोह॑वीत्। ना॒स॒त्या॒। क॒रा। वा॒म्। म॒हे। याम॑न्। पु॒रू॒ऽभु॒जा॒। पुर॑म्ऽधिः। श्रु॒तम्। तत्। शासुः॑ऽइव। व॒ध्रि॒ऽम॒त्याः। हिर॑ण्यऽहसतम्। अ॒श्वि॒नौ॒।।१३।।

वध्रिमती नाम कस्यचिद्राजर्षेः पुत्री नपुंसकभर्तृका। सा पुत्रलाभार्थ-मश्विनावाजुहाव। तदाह्वानं श्रुत्वाश्विनावागत्य तस्यै हिरण्यहस्ताख्यं पुत्रं ददतुः। तदेतदाह। पुरूभुजा बहूनां पालकौ प्रभूतहस्तौ वा। हे नासत्यावश्विनौ महे महनीये पूजनीये यामन्यामनि। याति गच्छतीति यामः स्तोत्रम्। तस्मिन्सति करा अभिमतफलस्य कर्तारौ वां युवां पुरांधिर्बहुधीः वध्रिमती। वध्रिः पुत्रोत्पादनाशक्तः पण्डकः। तद्वती एतत्संज्ञा राजपुत्री अजोहवीत्। पुनः पुनः स्तुत्या पुत्रलाभार्थमाहूतवती। युवां च वध्रिमत्यास्तदाह्वानं श्रुतम्। अशृणुतम्। तत्र दृष्टान्तः। शासुरिव यथा शासुराचार्यस्य वचनं शिष्योऽवहितः सन्नैकाग्र्येण शृणोति तद्वत्। श्रुत्वा च हे अश्विनौ तस्यै हिरण्यहस्तं सुवर्णमयपाणिं

हितरमणीयपाणिं वा एतत्संज्ञं पुत्रमदत्तं प्रायच्छतम्। अजोहवीत्। ह्वयतेर्यङ्लुगन्ताल्लङ्। यङो वेति तिप ईडागमः। करा। करोतेः पचाद्यच्। सुपां सुलुगिति विभक्तेराकारः। यारमन्। आतो मनिन् क्वनिब्वनिपश्चेति मनिन्। सुपां सुलुगिति सप्तम्या लुक्। श्रुतम्। लङिबहुलं छन्दसीति विकरणस्य लुक्। बहुलं छन्दस्यमाङ्योगेऽपीत्यडभावः। शासुः। शास्तुः शासु अनुशिष्टौ। शंसिशसिशासीत्यादिना (उ० २-९४) संज्ञायां तृन्। इडभावः। छान्दसस्तलोपः॥

क॒र m., hand, (not कर्तृ, Sāy.). Or, क॒रा nom. fem. sg. from क॒ळ, (कल) horse, mute.

पुरं॑धि f., prop. n. of a woman, or epithet?

पुरूभुज् adj., helping many; having many or large arms.

शासुः॑ n. = शासन, order, command. Sāy. takes it as gen. sg. of शासृ, शास्तृ.

अजो॑हवीत्, 3. sg. impf. intens. par.; rt. हू१., to call.

म॒हे यार्म॑न्, at the great decision, at the critical moment, hour.

Verse 14.

आ॒स्नः। वृक॑स्य। वर्ति॑काम्। अ॒भीके॑। यु॒वम्। न॒रा। ना॒स॒त्या॒। अ॒मु॒मु॒क्त॒म्। उ॒तोऽइति॑। क॒विम्। पु॒रू॒ऽभु॒जा॒। यु॒वम्। ह॒। कृप॑माणम्। अ॒कृ॒णु॒त॒म्। वि॒ऽचक्षे॑॥१४॥

वर्तिका चटकासदृशस्य पक्षिणः स्त्री। तामरण्ये वर्तमानेन शुना ग्रस्तां पुरा किलाश्विनावमोचयताम्। तदेतदाह। हे नरा नेतारौ नासत्यावश्विनौ युवं युवामभीकेऽभिगते वृकवर्तिकयोः संग्रामे वृकस्य विकर्तकस्य शुन आस्न आस्याद्वर्तिकां चटकसदृशीममुमुक्तम्। अमोचयतम्। यास्कस्त्वाह। पुनःपुनर्वर्तते प्रतिदिवसमावर्तत इति वर्तिकोषाः। तां वृकेणावरकेण सर्वजगत्प्रकाशेनाच्छादयित्रा सूर्येण ग्रस्तां तदीयमुखादश्विनावमुञ्चतामिति। उतोपि च पुरूभुजा महाबाहू प्रभूतहस्तौ वा युवं ह युवां खलु कृपमाणं स्तुवन्तं कविमेतत्संज्ञमन्धमृषिं विचक्षे विशेषेण द्रष्टुं समर्थमकृणुतम्। अकुरुतम्। आस्नः। पद्दन्नित्यादिना आस्यस्यासन्नादेशः। अल्लोपो न इत्यकारलोप उदात्तनिवृत्तिस्वरेणोडिदमिति

विभक्तेरुदात्तत्वम्। अमुमुक्तम्। मुचेरन्तर्भावितण्यर्थाल्लङि बहुलं छन्दसीति विकरणस्य श्लुः। कृपमाणम्। कृपिः स्तुतिकर्मा तुदादिषु द्रष्टव्यः। विकरणस्वरे प्राप्ते वृषादीनां चेत्याद्युदात्तत्वम्। विचक्षे। तुमर्थे सेसेनिति सेन्प्रत्ययः। स्कोः संयोगाद्योरिति सलोपः।।

वर्तिका f., quail.

आसन् n., mouth.

अभीके n., the getting at one, the fight; immediate neighbourhood; only in loc., quite close by.

कृप् 1., to lament, implore.

अमुमुक्तम्, 2. du. plup.; rt. मुच् 6.

वि चक्षे dat. inf. चक्ष्.

The legend of the quail is again alluded to in the ṚV. hymns I. 117. 16; 118.8. Who the कवि cured in our ṛc may be is not known. Sāy. takes कवि to be a proper noun. Another cure of blindness is mentioned in ṛc 16, below.

Verse 15.

चरित्रम्। हि। वेःऽइव। अच्छेदि। पर्णम्। आजा। खेलस्य। परिऽतक्म्यायाम्। सद्यः। जङ्घाम्। आयसीम्। विश्पलायै। धने। हिते। सर्तवे। प्रति। अधत्तम्।।१५।।

अगस्त्यपुरोहितः खेलो नाम राजा। तस्य संबन्धिनी विश्पला नाम स्त्री संग्रामे शत्रुभिश्छिन्नापादासीत्। पुरोहितेनागस्त्येन स्तुतावश्विनौ रात्रावागत्यायोमयं पादं समधत्ताम्। तदेदाह। आजा आजौ संग्रामेऽगस्त्यपुरोहितस्य खेलस्य संबन्धिन्या विश्पलाख्यायाश्चरित्रं चरणं वेरिव वेः पक्षिणः पर्णं पतत्रमिवाच्छेदि हि। पुरा छिन्नमभूत्खलु। हे अश्विनौ युवामगस्त्येन स्तुतौ सन्तौ परितक्त्यायाम्। परितक्म्या रात्रिः परित एनां तकतीति यास्कः। (नि० ११-२५) एनामुभयतः सूर्यो गच्छतीति तस्यार्थः। रात्रावगत्य सद्यस्तदानीमेव हिते शत्रुषु निहिते

धने जेतव्ये विषयभूते सति सर्तवे सर्तुं गन्तुं विश्पलाया आयसीमयोमयीं जङ्घोपलक्षितं पादं प्रत्यधत्तम्। संधानमेकीलकरणं कृतवन्तावित्यर्थः। चरित्रम्। अर्तिलूधूसूखनसहचर इत्र इति करण इत्रः। आजा। सुपां सुलुगिति विभक्तेर्डादेशः। आयसीम्। अयःशब्दाद्विकारार्थे प्राणिरजतादिभ्योऽञ्। (पा० ४-३-१५४) टिड्ढाणञिति ङीप्।।

च॒रित्रं॑ n., leg.

प॒र्णं n., wing, feather.

आ॒जि m., battle, tournament.

प॒रि॒त॒क्म्या f., running about, turmoil, racket, row, fray.

धनं॑ n., conquered treasure, prize in battle or in sport, esp. at a race

For the legendary background to this ṛc, which Sāy, assumes see comm.—Pischel, Ved. Stud. I. 171 ff., supposes the following version:—Agastya's son or patron had a steed, called Viśpalā, which at a race in honour of Vivasvant (Khela) had a leg torn off. Agastya implored the Aśvinā, his favourite deities, to help him. They substituted an iron leg, which enabled the steed to win the prize.—Considering both language and contents, Pischel's view seems to be preferable to that of Sāy. Whether it is to be called "no more than an improbable conjecture" (Macdonell and Keith, Vedic Index, s. Viśpalā) future Veda exegesis may decide.

Verse 16.

श॒तम्। मे॒षान्। वृ॒क्ये॑। च॒क्ष॒दा॒नम्। ऋ॒ज्रऽअ॑श्वम्। तम्। पि॒ता। अ॒न्धम्। च॒का॒र। तस्मै॑। अ॒क्षी इति॑। ना॒स॒त्या॒। वि॒ऽचक्षे॑। आ। अ॒ध॒त्तम्। द॒स्रा॒। भि॒ष॒जौ॒। अ॒न॒र्वन्।।१६।।

वृषागिरः पुत्र ऋज्राश्वो नाम राजर्षिः। तस्य समीपेऽश्विनोर्वानभूतो रासभो वृकी भूत्वाऽवतस्थे। स च तस्या आहारार्थमेकोत्तरशतसंख्यान्पौर-

जनानांस्वभूतान्मेषान् शकलीकृत्य प्रददौ। ऋज्राश्वः शतमेकं च मेषानिति *मन्त्रान्तरे दर्शनात्। एवं पौराणामहिते प्रवृत्तं पिता शापेन नेत्रहीनमकरोत्। तेन स्तूयमानावश्विनावस्मद्वाहननिमित्त †मस्यान्ध्यं जातमिति जानन्तौ तस्मा अक्षिणी प्रायच्छतामिति। तदेतदाह। अत्र तच्छब्दश्रुतेर्यच्छब्दाध्याहारः। य ऋज्राश्वः शतं शतसंख्याकान्मेषान्वृक्य आत्मना पोषितायै बृकस्त्रियै शकलीकृत्य प्रादात्तं चक्षुदानम्। क्षदतिरत्तिकर्मात्र शकलीकरणार्थः। शकलीकृत्य दत्तवन्त-मृज्राश्वं पिता शापेनान्धं दृष्टिहीनं चकार। कृतवान्।। हे नासत्या सत्यस्वभावौ सत्यस्य नेतारौ वा भिषजौ देवानां वैद्यभूतौ। अश्विनौ वै देवानां भिषजौ (ऐ० ब्रा० १-१८) इति श्रुतेः। दस्रा दर्शनीरयावेतत्संज्ञौ वा। हे अश्विनावन-र्वन्ननर्वणी। द्रष्टव्यं प्रति पितृशापाद्रमनरहिते अक्षी चक्षुषी। विचक्षे विविधं द्रष्टुं समर्थे तस्मै ऋज्राश्वाय आ अधत्तं व्यधत्तम्। अकुरुतम्। वृक्ये। वृकोऽरण्यश्वा तस्य स्त्री वृकी। जातेर स्त्रीविषया (पा० ४-१-६३) इति ङीप्। जसादिषु छन्दसि वा वचनमिति चतुर्थ्येकवचनस्याडभावे यणादेश उदात्तस्वरितयोर्यण इति परस्यानुदात्तस्य स्वरितत्वम्। चक्षुदानम्। क्षदेर्लिटः कानच्। चित्स्वरः। अक्षी। ईच द्विवचने (पा० ७-१-७७) इति परत्वादक्षशब्दस्येकारान्तादेशः स चोदात्तः। तस्मिन्कृते सकृद्गतौ विप्रतिषेधे (प० ४०) इति परिभाषया पुनर्नुम्न भवति। विचक्षे। चक्षेः संपदादिलक्षणो भावे क्विप्। अनर्वन्। ऋ गतौ। अस्मादन्येभ्योऽपि दृश्यन्त इति दृशिग्रहणस्य विध्यन्तरोपसंग्रहार्थत्वाद्भावे वनिप्। अर्व गमनं विषयं प्रत्येनयोर्नास्तीति बहुव्रीहौ नञ्सुभ्यामित्युत्तरपदान्तोदात्तत्वम्। सुपां सुलुगिति द्विवचनस्य लुक्। छान्दसो नलोपाभावः।।

चक्षुदान, pt. pf. ātm. rt. क्षद्, to taste, to offer, to divide.

अनर्वन् (here du., ending आ or ई dropped), without enemy, without rival; to be taken either with भिषजौ or अक्षी. —Probably to be read as ऋज्राशुअम्.

Here the titles Nāsatyā and Dasrā are applied to both the Aśvinā together; later on one of them is called Nāsatya and the other Dasra.

* क्र. सं. १-८-१६.

† निमित्तमन्धं जातमिति प्रथमावृत्तौ।

Verse 17.

आ। वाम्। रथम्। दुहिता। सूर्यस्य। कार्ष्मऽइव। अतिष्ठत्। अर्वता। जयन्ती। विश्वे। देवाः। अनु। अमन्यन्त। हृत्ऽभिः। सम्। ऊम् इति। श्रिया। नासत्या। सचेथे इति।।१७।।

सविता दुहितरं सूर्याख्यां सोमाय राज्ञे प्रदातुमैच्छत्। तां सूर्यां सर्वे देवा वरयामासुः। तेऽन्योन्यमूचुः। आदित्यमवधिं कृत्वाजिं धावाम्। योऽस्माकं मध्य उज्जेष्यति तस्येयं भविष्यतीति। तत्राश्विनाबुदजयताम्। सा च सूर्या जितवतो स्तयोरथमारूरोह। अत्र प्रजापतिर्वै सोमाय राज्ञे दुहितरं प्रायच्छत् (ऐ० ब्रा० ४-७) इत्यादिकं ब्राह्मणमनुसंधेयम्। इदं चाख्यानं सूर्याविवाहस्य स्तावकेन *सत्येनोत्तभिता भूमिरिति सूक्तेन विस्पष्टयिष्यते। हे अश्विनौ वां युवयो रथं कार्ष्मेव। कार्ष्मशब्दः काष्ठवाची। यथा काष्ठमाजिधावनस्यावधितया निर्दिष्टं लक्ष्यमाशुगामी कश्चित्सर्वेभ्यो धावद्भ्यः पूर्वं प्राप्नोति एवमेव सर्वेभ्यो देवेभ्यः पूर्वमर्वता शीघ्रमवधिं प्राप्नुवता युष्मदीयेनाश्वेन करणभूतेन युवाभ्यां जयन्ती जीयमाना सूर्यस्य सवितुर्दुहिता अतिष्ठत्। आरूढवती। विश्वे सर्व इतरे देवा एतदारोहणस्थानं हृद्भिर्हृदयैरन्वमन्यन्त। अन्वजानन्। तदानीं हे नासत्यावश्विनौ श्रिया ऋक्सहस्रलाभरूपया संपदा कान्त्या वा युवां संसचेथे। संगच्छेथे। जयन्ती। व्यत्ययेन कर्मणि शतृप्रत्ययः। हृद्भिः। पद्दन्नित्यादिना हृदयशब्दस्य हृद्भावः। सचेथे। पच समवाये। स्वरितेत्त्वादात्मनेपदम्।।

सम् सच्, ātm., to be together, united, linked together.

कर्ष्मन् n., (कृष्), the goal at the race.

अर्वत् m., horse, charger, racer; अर्वता, with a horse, on horseback.

Verse 18.

यत्। अयातम्। दिवःऽदासाय। वर्तिः। भरत्ऽवाजाय। अश्विना। हयन्ता। रेवत्। उवाह। सचनः। रथः। वाम्। वृषभः। च शिंशुमारः। च। युक्ता।।१८।।

---

* ऋ. सं. ८-३-२०.

हे अश्विनौ हयन्ता स्तुतिभिराहूयमानौ युवां भरद्वाजाय संभ्रियमाणहविर्लक्षणान्नाय यजमानाय दिवोदासायैतत्संज्ञाय राजर्षयेऽभीष्टं फलं दातुं वर्तिस्तदीयं गृहं यद्यदायातम् अगच्छतं तदानीं रेवद्धनयुक्तमन्नं वां युवयोः सचनः सेवनो रथ उवाह तस्मै दिवोदासाय प्रापयामास। अपि च तस्मिन्नथे वृषभोऽनडान् शिंशुमारो गाहश्च परस्परविरुद्धावपि स्वसामर्थ्यप्रकटनाय युक्ता। वाहनतया संयुक्तावास्ताम्। दिवोदासार्य। दिवश्च दासे षष्ठ्या अलुक् वक्तव्यः। (का० ६-३-२१-५) इत्यलुक्। दिवोदासादीनां छन्दस्युपसंख्यानमिति पूर्वपदाद्युदात्तत्वम्। भरद्वाजाय। भृञ् भरणे। अस्माद्यत्ययेन कर्मणि शतृप्रत्ययः। शतुश्छन्दस्युभयथेत्यार्धधातुकत्वेन लसार्वधातुकानुदात्तत्वम्। बहुव्रीहौ पूर्वपदप्रकृतिस्वरत्वम्। हयन्ता। ह्वेञः कर्मणि लटो व्यत्ययेन शतृ। बहुलं छन्दसीति संप्रसारणम्। शपि गुणे छान्दसोऽयादेशः। रेवत्। रयिशब्दान्मतुप्। रयेर्मतौ बहुलमिति संप्रसारणम्। छन्दसीर इति मतुपो वत्वम्। रयिशब्दाच्च (का० ६-१-१७६) इति मतुप उदात्तत्वम्। सचनः। षच सेवने। अनुदात्तेतश्च हलादेरिति युच्। युक्ता। सुपां सुलुगिति विभक्तेराकारः।।

व॒र्तिः n., a drive round (in a carriage), with या.

हय॑न्ता, pt. pres. rt. हि 5., to urge on (horse).

रे॒वत् adj., rich; subst. n., riches, rich gifts.

स॒च॒न (rt. सच्), accompanying, or (rt. चन्), of the same wish, sympathetic. Sāt. सेवन obedient.

शिंशु॒मार॑ (शिशुमार), m., dolphin.

Verse 19.

र॒यिम्। सु॒ऽअ॒प॒त्यम्। आयु॑ः। सु॒ऽवीर्य॑म्। ना॒स॒त्या॒। वह॑न्ता। आ। ज॒ह्नावी॑म्। सऽम॑नसा। उप॑। वाजैः॑। त्रिः। अह्नः॑। भा॒गम्। दध॑तीम्। अ॒या॒त॒म्।।१९।।

हे नासत्यावश्विनौ सुक्षत्रं शोभनबलं रयिं धनं स्वपत्यं शोभनैः पुत्रादिभिरुपेतं सुवीर्यं शोभनवीर्योपेतमायुः। अन्ननामैतत्। एवंगुणविशिष्टमन्नं च वहन्ता धारयन्तौ युवां समनसा समानमनस्कौ सन्तौ जह्नावीं जह्नोर्महर्षेः

संबन्धिनीं प्रजामायातम्। आभिमुख्येनागच्छतम्। कीदृशीं वाजैर्हविर्लक्षणैर-न्नैष्वेतसम्। अह्नः। अत्राहःशब्देन तत्रानुष्ठेयः सोमयागो लक्ष्यते। तस्य प्रातःसवना दिरूपेण त्रिस्त्रिधा विभक्तं भागमंशं दधतीं बिभ्रतीम्। अनुसवनं हविर्भिर्यजमानामित्यर्थः। सुक्षत्रम्। बहुव्रीहौ नञ्सुभ्यामित्युत्तरपदान्तोदात्तत्वम्। सुवीर्यम्। वीरवीयो। चेति बहुव्रीहावुत्तरपदाद्युदात्तत्वम्। जह्नावीं जह्नुशब्दात्त-स्येदमित्यर्थेऽण्। टिड्ढाणञ् इति ङीप्। जाह्नवीं ह्रस्वदीर्घयोर्विनिमयः पृषोदरादित्वात्। उक्तं च वर्णागमो वर्णविपयर्यश्च (का० ६-३-१०९) इति। अत एव मध्योदात्तत्वम्।।

सुक्षत्र, exercising a good rule, consisting in a good rule.

स्वपत्य, consisting in, producing, excellent progeny.

जह्नावी, descendants of Jahnu (Sāy.).

The ṛc probably alludes to a fight for the supermacy between the Jahnuites and the Vṛcīvats, in which the former conquered. Cp. Tāṇḍ. Br. XXI. 12.2.

Verse 20.

परिऽविष्टम्। जाहुषम्। विश्वतः। सीम्। सुऽगेभिः। नक्तम्। ऊहथुः। रजःऽभिः। विऽभिन्दुना। नासत्या। रथेन। वि। पर्वतान्। अजरयू इति। अयातम्।।२०।।

जाहुषो नाम कश्चिद्राजा। विश्वतः सर्वतः परिविष्टं शत्रुभिः परिवृतं तं राजानं हे नासत्यावश्विनावजरयू जरारहितौ नित्यतरुणौ युवां विभिन्दुना विशेषेण सर्वस्य भेदकेनात्मीयेन रथेन नक्तं रात्रौ सुगेभिः सुष्ठु गन्तुं शक्यै रजोभी रञ्जकैर्मार्गैरुहथुः। तस्माच्छत्रुसमूहान्निरगमयतम्। सीमित्येतत्पादपूरणम्। निर्गतेन तेन सह पर्वतान् शत्रुभिरारोढुमशक्यान् शिलोच्चयान् व्ययातम्। विशेषेणागच्छतम्। परिविष्टम्। विश प्रवेशने। कर्मणि निष्ठा। गतिरनन्तर इति गतेः प्रकृतिस्वरत्वम्। सुगेभिः। सुदुरोरधिकरण इति गमेर्डः। विभिन्दुना। भिदिर् विदारणे। औणादिक उप्रत्ययो नुमागमश्च। अजरयू। न जरा अजरा। तामात्मन इच्छतः। सुप आत्मनः क्यच्। न च्छन्दस्यपुत्रस्येति ईतवदीर्घयोर्नि-षेधः। क्याच्छन्दसीत्युप्रत्ययः।।

सीम्, acc. of a defective pron. 3. pers. m. f. n.; sg. plur.: him, she, it, they.

अजरयु adj., indestructible, always young, unharmed. वि या, to go through, across, to cut a way through. Sāy. takes पर्वतान् to mean the place where the Aśvinā safely deposited Jāhuṣa; this is hardly correct.

Verse 21.

एकस्याः। वस्तोः। आवतम्। रणाय। वशम्। अश्विना। सनये। सहस्रा। निः। अहतम्। दुच्छुनाः। इन्द्रऽवन्ता। पृथुऽश्रवसः। वृषणौ। अरातीः।।२१।।

हे अश्विनौ वशमेतत्संज्ञमृषिमेकस्या वस्तोरेकस्याह्नो रणाय रमणीयाय सहस्रा सहस्रसंख्याकाय सनये धनलाभायावतम्। अरक्षतम्। स ऋषिः प्रत्यहं यथां सहस्रसंख्यं धनं लभते तथा रक्षितवन्तावित्यर्थः। अपि च हे वृषणौ कामानां वर्षितारावश्विनौ इन्द्रवन्ता इन्द्रेण संयुक्तौ युवां दुच्छुना दुष्टसुखान् दुःखस्य कर्तॄन्पृथुश्रवसो विस्तीर्णयशसोऽरातीः शत्रून्निरहतं निःशेषेणावधिष्टम्। यद्वा। कानीनस्य पृथुश्रवःसंज्ञस्य राज्ञः शत्रूनिति योज्यम्। सहस्रा। सुपां सुलुगिति चतुर्थ्या डादेशः। अहतम्। लङि थसस्तम्। अनुदात्तोपदेशेत्यादि- नानुनासिकलोपः। दुच्छुनाः। शुनमिति सुखनाम। दुष्टं सुखं यासां तास्तथोक्ताः। परादिश्छन्दसि बहुलमित्युत्तरपदाद्युदात्तत्वम्।।

निर् हन्, to ward off

वस्तु f., morning.

रण m., pleasure; fight.

दुच्छुना f., misfortune, harmful magic, mischief, राक्षस.

अराति f., jealousy, enmity, enemy.

The acc. सहस्रा depends on सनये.

Verse 22.

शरस्य। चित्। आर्चत्ऽकस्य। अवतात्। आ। नीचात्। उच्चा।

चक्रथुः। पातवे। वारिति वाः। शयवे। चित्। नासत्या। शचीभिः। जसुरये। स्तर्यम्। पिप्यथुः। गाम्।।२२।।

आर्चत्कस्य ऋचत्कपुत्रस्य शरस्य* चित्। एतत्संज्ञस्यापि स्तोतुः पिपासितस्य पातवे पानार्थं नीचान्नीचीनादावतात्कूपात् उच्चा उच्चैरुपरिष्टा- द्वारुदकं हे अश्विनौ युवाम्। आ चक्रथुः। आभिमुख्येन कृतवन्तौ। तथा हे नासत्यावश्विनौ शचीभिर्युष्मदीयैः कर्मभिः परिचरणैर्जसुरये श्रान्ताय शयवेचित् शयुनाम्ने ऋषये स्तर्यं निवृत्तप्रसवां गामग्निहोत्रार्थस्य पयसो दोग्ध्रीं पिप्यथुः। पयसा युवामापूरितवन्तौ। पातवे। पा पाने। तुमर्थे सेसेनिति तवेन् प्रत्ययः। जसुरये। जसु हिंसायाम्। जसिसहोरुरिन्। (उ० २-७३) स्तर्यम्। स्तीर्यते आच्छाद्यते प्रसवसामर्थ्यालावेनेति स्तरीः। अवितृस्तुतन्त्रिभ्य ईः (उ० ३-१५७) इतीकारप्रत्ययः। वा छन्दसीत्यमिपूर्वत्वस्य विकल्पितत्वादभावे यणादेशः। उदात्तस्वरितयोर्यण इति परस्यानुदात्तस्य स्वरितत्वम्। पिप्यथुः। प्यायी वृद्धौ। लिटि व्यत्ययेन परस्मैपदम्। लिड्यङोश्च (पा० ६-१-२९) इति पीभावः।।

अवस्य demon., to seek help, protection.

ऋजूय denom., acting straight, living a just life.

According to Sāy. comm. I. 8. 86 and to judge from the simile पशुं न नष्टमिव, Viśvaka's son was abroad and the father felt anxious about his return.

Verse 23.

अवस्यते। स्तुवते। कृष्णियाय। ऋजुऽयते। नासत्या। शचीभिः। पशुम्। न। नष्टम्ऽइव। दर्शनाय। विष्णाप्वम्। ददथुः। विश्वकाय।।२३।।

अवस्यते अवनं रक्षणमात्मन इच्छते स्तुवते स्तुतिं कुर्वते कृष्णियाय। कृष्णो नाम कश्चित्। तस्य पुत्राय ऋजूयत आर्जवमिच्छते विश्वकायैतत्संज्ञाय। ऋषये हे नासत्यौ युवां शचीभिरात्मीयैः कर्मभिर्विष्णाप्वं नाम विनष्टं पुत्रं दर्शनाय दर्शनार्थं ददथुः। दत्तवन्तौ। तत्र दृष्टान्तः। पशुं न नष्टमिव। एक उपमार्थीयः पूरकः। यथा कश्चिद्विनष्टं पशुं स्वामिनो दृष्टि पथं प्रापयति

* आदर्शे चित् इति न दृश्यते।

तद्वत्। अवस्यते। अवस् शब्दात् सुप आत्मनः क्यच्। शतुरनुम इति विभक्तेरुदात्तत्वम्। कृष्णियाय। कृष्णशब्दादपत्यार्थे छान्दसो घच्।।

जसु॑रि adj., dying of hunger, thirst.

स्त॒रि f., barren, dry (cow).

The ṛṣi Śara occurs only here, the Sūri Sara in VIII. 70.13 necessarily being another person.

Verse 24.

दश॑। रात्री॑ः। अशि॑वेन। नव॑। द्यून्। अव॑ऽनद्धम्। श्र॒थि॒तम्। अ॒प्ऽसु। अ॒न्तरिति॑। रे॒भम्। उ॒दनि॑। प्रऽवृ॑क्तम्। उत्। नि॒न्य॒थु॒ः। सोम॑म्ऽइव। स्रु॒वेण॑।।२४।।

पुरा खलु रेभमृषिं पाशैर्बद्वा सुराः कूपे कस्यचिद्दिवसस्य सायंकाले प्रचिक्षिपुः। स चाश्विनौ स्तुवन् दशरात्रीर्नवाहानि च कूपमध्ये तथैवावतस्थे दशमेऽहनि प्रातरश्विनौ तं कूपादुदतारयतामिति। तदाह। अप्सु कूपान्तर्वर्तमाना-स्वन्तर्मध्येऽसुरैः पातितमशिवेन दुःखहेतुना दाम्नावनद्धं बद्धं श्रथितं शत्रुभिर्हिंसितं दशरात्रीर्दशसंख्याका निशाः नव द्यून् नवसंख्याकान्यहानि च। अत्यन्तसंयोगे द्वितीया। एतावन्तं कालं तत्रैव कूपेऽवस्थितमत एव उदन्युदके विप्रुतं विन्लुतं व्याक्षिप्तसर्वाङ्गं प्रवृक्तम्। लुप्तोपममेतत्। प्रवृञ्जनेन संतप्तं धर्ममिव व्यथयासन्तप्यमानमेवंभूतं रेभं हे अश्विनौ युवां उन्निन्यथुः। तस्मात्कूपादुन्नीतमुत्तीर्णं कृतवन्तौ। तत्र दृष्टान्तः। सोममिव यथाग्निहोत्रहोमार्थमभिषुतं सोमरसं कूपसदृशेऽग्निहोत्रस्थालीमध्ये वर्तमानं स्रुवेणाध्वर्युरुन्नयति ऊर्ध्वं नयति तद्वत्। अवनद्धम्। णह बन्धने। कर्मणि निष्ठा। नहो धः। (पा० ८-२-३४) झष-स्तथोर्धोऽध इति निष्ठातकारस्य धत्वम्। गतिरनन्तर इति गतेः प्रकृतिस्वरत्वम्। श्रथितम्। श्रथ हिंसार्थः। निष्ठा। विप्रुतम्। प्रुङ् गतौ। अवनद्धवत्प्रत्ययस्वरौ। कपिलकादित्वाल्लत्वविकल्पः। उदनि। पद्दन्नित्यादिना उदकशब्दस्योदन्भावः।।

वि प्रु (प्लु), to decay, fall to pieces.

प्र वृज् (cp. ṛc 1) to tie down.

अशि॑व adj., bad, malign; subst., enemy.

Verse 25.

प्र। वाम्। दंसांसि। अश्विनौ। अवरेचम्। अस्य। पतिः। स्याम्। सुऽगवः। सुऽवीरः। उत। पश्यन्। अश्नुवन्। दीर्घम्। आयुः। अस्तम्ऽइव। इत्। जरिमाणम्। जगम्याम्।।२५।।

एवमनेन सूक्तेनाश्विनोर्महिमानं प्रशस्याधुना मन्त्रद्रष्टस स्वाभीष्टं प्रार्थयते। हे अश्विनौ वां युवयोर्दसांसि पुरा कृतानि कर्माणि प्रावोचम्। इत्थमुक्तवानस्मि। सोऽहं सुगवः शोभनगोयुक्तः सुवीरः शोभनवीरश्च भूत्वास्य राष्ट्रस्य पतिर-धिपतिः स्यां भवेयम्। उतापि च पश्यन्। अक्षिभ्यां पश्यन् उपलक्षणमेतत्। सर्वैरिन्द्रियैः स्वस्वविषयदर्शनसमर्थैर्दीर्घं वर्षशतरूपेणायतमायुर्जीवितं चाश्नुवन् प्राप्नुवन्नाहमस्तमिव यथा गृहं स्वामी निष्कण्टकं प्रविशति एवं जरिमाणं जरां जगम्याम्। कण्टकराहित्येन प्राप्तुयाम्। वृद्धः संश्चिरकालं निवसेयमित्यर्थः। स्याम्। अस्तेः प्रार्थनायां लिङ्। यासुट्। श्नसोरल्लोप इत्यकारलोपः। अश्नुवन्। अशू व्याप्तौ। व्यत्ययेन शतृ। जरिमाणम्। जृ ष् वयोहानौ। अस्मादौणादिक इमनिच्। जगम्याम्। गमेः प्रार्थनायां लिङि बहुलं छन्दसीति विकरणस्य श्लुः।।

जगम्याम् 1. sg. pf. opt. par.; rt. गम्.

जरिमन् (जृ) m., old age.

अस्य, Sāy.: राष्ट्रस्य; better: the possession of the यजमान.

NO. 6.

MAṆḌALA I. **SŪKTA 184.**

यस्य निःश्वसितं वेदा यो वेदेभ्योऽखिलं जगत्। निर्ममे तमहं वन्दे विद्यातीर्थमहेश्वरम्।।१।। द्वितीयाष्टकमध्यस्थश्चतुर्थोऽध्याय आदरात्। व्याख्यातः सायणा (चा)र्येण पञ्चमो व्याकरिष्यते।।२।। तत्र ता वामितीदं प्रथममण्डलस्य चतुर्विंशेऽनुवाके पञ्चमं सूक्तम्। पूर्वसूक्ते षळित्युक्तत्वात्सूक्तसंख्यानुवर्तत इति परिभाषितत्वात् षळृचम्। ऋषिश्चान्यस्मादिति परिभाषयागस्त्यं तथाश्विनं वा इत्युक्तत्वात्तुह्यादिपरिभाषयेदमप्याश्विनम्। अनादेशपरिभाषया त्रैष्टुभम्।

तावामत्यनुक्रान्तम्। युवोरजांसीत्यादीनां पञ्चसूक्तानां तृतीयवर्जितानां प्रातरनुवाकाश्विनशस्त्रयोर्विनियोग उक्तः। तत्रेदं पञ्चमम्।।

Verse 1.

ता। वाम्। अद्य। तौ। अपरम्। हुवेम। उच्छन्त्याप्। उषसि। वह्निः। उक्थैः। नासत्या। कुह। चित्। सन्तौ। अर्यः। दिवः। नपाता। सुदाःऽतराय।।१।।

ता तौ रक्षकत्वेन प्रसिद्धौ वां युवामद्यास्मिन्यागदिने हुवेम आह्वयाम् इत्याशीः। तथापरमपरस्मिन्नपि दिने तौ युवां हुवेम। अपरमित्येतदपरस्मिन्नित्यर्थे समभिव्याहारात्। अद्या च नो मृळयतापरं च (ऋ० २-२९-२) इत्यादि मन्त्रान्तरे तथा दर्शनाच्च। अपरयागं प्रत्यपीति वा। कस्मिन्काले। उषस्युषोदेवताया-मुच्छन्त्यां तमो विवासयन्त्यां सत्याम्। उषःकाले हि प्रातरनुवाकाश्विनशस्त्रे प्रयुज्येते। उक्ते काले हे नासत्या असत्यरहितौ दिवो नपाता द्युलोकस्य न पातयितारौ नप्तृस्थानीयौ वा कुहचित्सन्तौ कुत्रचिद्देशे वर्त्तमानौ युवां वह्निः स्तुतेर्वोढार्य ईरयिता स्तुतेरीश्वरो वा ईदृशोऽहं होता सुदास्तरायात्यर्थं शोभनंहविर्दात्रे यजमानाय तदर्थं तौ युवामुक्थैः शस्त्रैर्हुवेममेति संबन्धः। अत्राख्यातं पदमेकवचनतया नेतव्यम्। वह्निरर्यशब्दौ वा बहुवचनत्वेन नेतव्यौ। अथवा वाक्यद्वयम्। यस्माद्वह्निरर्यो होतोक्तगुणकौ युवां शंसति तस्माद्वयं यजमानास्तौ युवामाह्वयाम इति।।

उच्छन्त्, pt. pres. rt. वस् 6.

अर्यो, abl. sg. (against Sāy.).

सुदास् (सु दा), liberal; pr. n. of the Tṛtsu king whose related in the Sāṅkhāyana Srauta Sūtra. सुदास्तर is hardly to be taken as an abstract noun meaning liberality.

The ṛc is important for the personality of the Aśvinā. नासत्या-दिवो नपाता appear to be a dissolved cpd., corresponding to the नासत्या-दस्रा, the names of the Aśvinā in the epos. See Ved. Stud. III. 72; Wackernagel Gr. II. 152.

Verse 2.

अस्मे इति। ऊँ इति। सु। वृषणा। मादयेथाम्। उत्। पणीन्। हतम्। ऊर्म्या। मदन्ता। श्रुतम् मे। अच्छोक्तिऽभिः। मतीनाम्। एष्टा। नरा। निऽचेतारा। चं कर्णैः।।२।।

हे वृषणा कामानां वर्षकावश्विनौ युवामस्मे उ अस्मास्वेव सुमादयेथाम्। सुष्ठु तृप्यतम्। अस्मभ्यं तर्पयतमभिमतम्। तथा पणीन्वणिजो लुब्धकान-यष्टॄन् उत् उन्मूल्य हतम्। नाशयतम्। कीदृशौ युवाम्। ऊर्म्याम् रात्रिनामैतत्। रात्रौ मदन्ता माद्यन्तौ यद्वा ऊर्मिर्यस्ते पवित्र आ (ऋ० ९-६४-११) इत्यादिषु तथसा प्रयोगात् अस्मदीयेन सोभेन मदन्ता। तादृशौ युवां मे ममाच्छोक्तिभिराभिमुख्यकरैर्निर्मलवेदवाक्यै रचिता मतीनाम्। कर्मणि षष्ठी। मननसाधनाः स्तुतीः कर्णैराकर्णनसधनैः श्रोत्रैः श्रुतम्। शृणुतम्। हे नरा नेतारौ युवां खल्वेष्टान्वेष्टारावस्मत्स्तुतीनां तथा निचेतारा लब्धानां तासां संचयकर्तारौ निरित्येष समित्येतस्य स्थाने। यस्मादेवंविधौ तस्माच्छृणुतमिति।।

पणि m., the trader, miser.   अच्छोक्ति f., benediction.

निचेत् (rt. चि) m., listener.

एष्टा, m. du. एष्ट, pf. pass आ यज्, to bring near by sacrifice.

Verse 3.

श्रिये। पूषन्। इषुकृताऽइव। देवा। नासत्या। वहतुम्। सूर्यायाः। वच्यन्ते। वाम्। ककुहाः। अप्ऽसु। जाताः। युगा। जूर्णाऽइव। वरुणस्य। भूरेः।।३।।

सविता सूर्यो दुहितरं सूर्याख्यां प्रदातुमना देवानाहूय सामर्थ्यसमीक्षणायाजिं परिकल्प्य य इमं जेष्यति स एषां कन्यकामृक्सहस्त्रक्लृप्तं स्तोत्रं च लभत इत्यकल्पयत्। तमग्निः प्रथममजयत्तमन्वश्विनावपि जित्वाग्निं प्रधृष्य ऋक्सहस्त्रं कन्यकां चालभताम्। तत इन्द्र उषाश्चजयताम्। तौ च तैरग्न्यादिभिः प्रार्थितौ

---

* आदर्शे उत् इति नास्ति।

स्वशस्त्रस्य कंचित्कंचिद्भागं तेभ्यः परिकल्प्य सूर्या स्वरथे धारयतामिति। अयमितिहासो ब्राह्मणे प्रजापतिर्वै सोमाय राज्ञे (ऐ० ब्रा० ४-७) इत्यत्राम्नातोऽस्माभिः प्रथमाष्टमे आवां पतित्वं सख्याय (ऋ० १-११९-५) इत्यत्र प्रपञ्चितः। अत्राहं हे पूषन् पोषक सूर्य एतञ्चन्द्रस्याप्युपलक्षणं सूर्याचन्द्रमसोरेवाश्वित्वात्। सूर्याचन्द्रमसावितत्येके (नि० १२-१) इति यास्केनोक्तत्वात्। अतः पूषन्नित्युक्ते हे पोषकावश्विनावित्युक्तं भवति। हे पोषकौ हे नासत्या असत्यरहितौ देवा देवौ युवां श्रिये श्रेयसे। शस्त्रस्य कन्यायाश्च लाभायेत्यर्थः। इषुकृतेव। इवशब्द एवार्थे। आजिधावनायेषुवच्छीघ्रमृजुगामिनौ कृतावेव सन्तौ सूर्याया एतन्नामिकायाः सवितुः पुत्र्याः। कर्मणि षष्ठी। सूर्या वहतुं रथे धारयितुमाजिमुदजयतामित्यर्थः। यस्मादेवं तस्मादप्सु जाताः कर्मसु संपादिताः ककुहाः शस्त्ररूपाः स्तुतयो भूरेरविच्छिन्नप्रवाहस्य वरुणस्य फलप्रतिबन्धकपापनिवारकस्य यागस्य विद्ध्यर्थं तत्संबन्धिन्यो वां प्रति वच्यन्ते होत्रादिभिः। युवामेव शस्त्रगतमन्त्रैर्यागकाले च स्तुवन्तीत्यर्थः। युगा जूर्णेव जीर्णानि युगानीव। इवशब्दः संप्रत्यर्थः। पुरातना यागकाला यथा तद्वदद्यतना अपीत्यर्थः। पूर्वकाले यथा युवामेव स्तुवन्ति तद्वदिदानीमपीति तात्पर्यम्।।

इ॒षु॒कृत् m., one who makes arrows, an archer.

व॒ह॒तु m., marriage, bridal feast, bridal procession.

वञ्च्, to move crookedly.

क॒कु॒ह m., buffalo, yoked to the car of the Aśvinā, जू॒र्ण (जॄ), wasted, decaying, ancient, passing (?), भू॒रि, great, mighty.

Pūṣan is fifty mentioned here with the Aśvinā,k as he was present at the marriage.—The first two pādas have been interpreted by pischel (Ved. Stud. I. 18):—For good luck you, O Pūṣan, (and) you, O Nāsatyā, as gods (came) like archers to the marriage of Sūryā, viz., to gain the prize like archers at a shooting match. Oldenberg (Textkrit. i. 1.) interprets:—For good fortune, O Pūṣan, as two who make arrows (prepare the arrows for the lucky shot, so) you two

Nāsatyā (prepare) the bridal procession of Sūryā.—In any case the first two pādas form an independent sentence the verb of which has to be understood.

The युगा जूर्णा of the mighty Varuṇa are probably the waves of the ocean.

Verse 4.

अस्मे इति। सा। वाम्। माध्वी इति। रातिः। अस्तु। स्तोमम्। हिनोतम्। मापन्यस्य। कारोः। अनु। यत्। वाम्। श्रवस्या। सुदानू इति सुऽदानू। सुऽवीर्याय। चर्षणयः। मदन्ति।।४।।

हे माध्वी मधुपूर्णपात्रयुक्तावश्विनौ वां युवयोः संबन्धिनी सा प्रसिद्धा रातिर्दानमस्मे अस्माकमस्तु। भवतु। तदर्थं मान्यस्य मननीयस्य कारोः स्तोतुर- गस्त्यस्य स्तोमं स्तुतिं हिनोतम्। प्रीणयतम्। हे सुदानू सशोभनफलदानौ वां युवां श्रवस्या कीर्तेरन्नस्य वेच्छया यद्यस्मात्सुवीर्याय यजमानाय शोभनबलाय वा चर्षणयो मनुष्या ऋत्विग्रूपा अनुमदन्ति। अनुक्रमेण माद्यन्ति युवाभ्यां सह स्वयं वा।।

माध्वि adj., containing or loving sweetness.

राति f., gift, grace.

सुदानु adj., nicely trickling, richly giving; subst. m., giver.

मान्य, मान, son of Māna, Agastya.

श्रवस्य, praiseworthy; subst. n., glorious deed.

Verse 5.

एषः। वाम्। स्तोमः। अश्विनौ। अकारि। मानेभिः। मघऽवाना। सुऽवृक्तिः। यातम्। वर्तिः। तनयाय। त्मने। च। अगस्त्ये। नासत्या। मदन्ता।।५।।

हे अश्विनौ हे मघवाना हविर्लक्षणान्नवन्तौ वां युवाभ्यामेष स्तोमः स्तोत्रं सुवृक्ति सुष्ठु पापवर्जनं यथा भवति तथा यद्वा सुसमाप्तयकारि कृतः।

कीदृशोऽयम्। मानेभिर्मानैर्हविष्प्रदानरूपैः *सहितः। हे नासत्यासत्यरहितौ युवामगस्त्य एतन्नाम्नि महर्षौ मयि मदन्ता माद्यन्तौ सन्तौ वर्त्तिर्गृहं यज्ञसंबन्धि यातम्। प्राप्नुतम्। किमर्थम्। तनयाय पुत्रादिलाभायात्मन आत्मने च हिताय।।

सुवृक्ति adj., well prepared, well finished; subst. f., the well prepared offering of a song or sacrifice.

On the grammatical form see Sāy., comm.

Unless we read म+अनैभिः, the beginning of the second half of the first line is anomalous.

Verse 6.

अतारिष्म। तमसः। पारम्। अस्य। प्रति। वाम्। स्तोमः। अशनौ। अधायि। आ। इह। यातम्। पथिऽभिः। देवऽयानैः। विद्याम। इषम्। वृजनम्। जीरऽदानुम्।।६।।

हे अश्विनौ युवयोः प्रसादादस्य तमसस्तमनहेतोः श्रेयःप्रतिबन्धरूपस्य दुःखस्य पारं पर्यन्तभूमिमतारिष्म। उत्तीर्णाः स्म। हे अश्विनौ वां प्रति स्तोमः स्तोत्रमधायि। अकारीत्यर्थः। युवां देवयानैर्देवगन्तव्यैर्मार्गैरिहास्मद्यज्ञ आ यातम्। आगच्छतम्। शिष्टो व्याख्यातः।। इषमन्नं वृजनं बलं जीरदानुं चिरकालजीवनं च विद्याम। *लभेमहि।।

वृजन m., strength (Sāy.).

जीरदानु, with quick gifts.

NO.7.

MAṆḌALA II. **SŪKTA 23.**

तृतीयेऽनुवाके दश सूक्तानि। तत्रेदमेकोनविंशस्यृचं गार्त्समदं प्रथमं सूक्तम्। अत्रेयमनुक्रमणिका। गणानामेकोना ब्राह्मणस्पत्यं ह बार्हस्पत्यास्तु

---

* प्रथमावृत्तौ हविष्प्रदानरूपाभिः इति पाठः।

* अयं चारणो बहुशः समायातः। परं भाष्यकृता १-१६६-१५ किंच १-१६५-१५ इत्यात्रैव व्याख्यातः। तत्र च केवलं जीरदानुं जयशीलदानम् इति व्याख्यातम्। एतावानेव भेदः

दृष्टलिङ्गाः। बृहस्पतिशब्दः श्रूयते ता बार्हस्पत्याः शिष्टा ब्राह्मणस्पत्याः। प्रवर्ग्येऽभिष्टव एतत्सूक्तम्। स्पृष्टोदकमिति खण्डे सूत्रितम्। गणानां त्वा प्रेशिश्च यस्य (आ० ४-६) इति।

Verse 1.

गणानाम्। त्वा। गणऽपतिम्। हवामहे। कविम्। कवीनाम्। उपमश्रवःऽतमम्। ज्येष्ठऽराजम्। ब्रह्मणाम्। ब्रह्मणः। पते। आ। नः। शृण्वन्। ऊतिऽभिः। सीद। सदनम्।।१।।

हे ब्रह्मणस्पते ब्रह्मणोऽन्नस्य परिवृढस्य कर्मणो वा पते पालयितः गणानां देवादिगणानां संबन्धिनं गणपतिं स्वीयानां पतिम्। कवीनां क्रान्तदर्शिनां कविम्। उपमश्रवस्तमम्। उपमीयतेऽनयेत्युपमा। सर्वेषामन्नानामुपमानं श्रवोऽन्नं यस्य स तथोक्तः। अतिशयेनोपमश्रवा उपमश्रवस्तमः। उपमः। माङ् माने। आतश्चोपसर्गे करणेऽङ्प्रत्ययः। ङ्यापोः संज्ञाछन्दसोरिति ह्रस्वत्वम्। ज्येष्ठराजम्। ज्येष्ठाः प्रशस्यतमाः। तेषां मध्ये राजन्तं ब्रह्मणं मन्त्राणां स्वामिनं त्वा त्वां हवामहे। अस्मिन्कर्मणि आह्वयामः। किं च नोऽस्माकं स्तुतीः श्रृण्वन् त्वमूतिभिः पालनैर्हेतुभूतैः सादनम्। सीदन्त्यस्मिन्निति सदनम्। यज्ञगृहमासीलद। उपविश।।

आ श्रु, to lend an ear, to hear.

Verse 2.

देवाः। चित्। ते। असुर्य। बृहस्पते। यज्ञियम्। भागम्। आनशुः। उस्राःऽइव। सूर्यः। ज्योतिषा। महः। विश्वेषाम्। इत्। जनिता। ब्रह्मणाम्। असि।।२।।

असुर्य असुराणां हनतः हे बृहस्पते प्रचेतसः प्रकृष्टज्ञानास्ते त्वदीया देवाश्चित् देवा यज्ञियं यज्ञार्हं भागमानशुः। प्राप्नुवन्। यद्वा प्रचेतस इति बृहस्पतेर्विशेषणम्। प्रकृष्टज्ञानवतस्ते तव संबन्धिनो देवा इति योजनीयम्। यद्वा प्रचेतसः। विभक्तिविपरिणामः। प्रचेतसि त्वयि सति देवा यज्ञियं भागमानशिरे। कर्मविघ्नकारिणामसुराणां रक्षोघ्नमन्त्रैरपाकरणात्। न वै ब्रह्मण्वद्रिष्यति (ऐ० ब्रा० १-१३) इति श्रवणात्। ज्योतिषा तेजसा महो महनीयः सूर्य उस्रा इव। उस्राः किरणाः। स्फायितञ्चीत्यादिना रक्प्रत्ययः।

यथा किरणान् जनयति तथा विश्वसेषां सर्वेषां ब्रह्मणां मन्त्राणां जनिता जनयितैवासि। जनिता मन्त्र इति निपातनाणि लोपः।।

असुर्य adj., celestial, divine; subst., god. Note the application of this epithet to Bṛhaspati.

उस्रा f., dawn; उस्राः, better gen. sg. than acc. pl.

महस् adj., great, glorious.

Verse 3.

आ। विऽबाध्य। परिऽरपः। तमांसि। च। ज्योतिंऽष्मन्तम्। रथम्। ऋतस्य। तिष्ठसि। बृहस्पते। भीमम्। अमित्रऽदम्भनम्। रक्षः़ऽहनम्। गोत्रऽभिदम्। स्वःऽविदम्।।३।।

हे बृहस्पते परिरपः। परितो रपः पापरूपं रक्षः। यद्वा रप लप व्यक्तायां वाचि। क्विप्। परिवदतो निन्दकान् तमांसिच विबाध्य तेजसा निराकृत्य ज्योतिष्मन्तं ज्योतिषा तद्वन्तमृतस्य यज्ञस्य प्रापकं भीमं शत्रूणां भयंकरममित्रदम्भनं शत्रूणां हिंसकम्। तदेवाह रक्षोहणं रक्षसां हन्तारं गोत्रभिदं मेघानां भेत्तारं सवर्विदं स्वर्गस्य लम्भकं रथमातिष्ठसि। अधितिष्ठसि।।

वि बाध्, to chase away, discomfit.

परि रप्, to whisper about; परिराप् (metrically lengthened, see Padap.) m., reviler.

दम्भ् (दभ्), to injure by tricks, to cheat; thwart.

स्वर् विद्, finding light, giving light.

Verse 4.

सुनीतिऽभिः। नयसि। त्रायसे। जनम्। यः। तुभ्यम्। दाशात्। न। तम्। अंहः। अश्नवत्। ब्रह्मऽद्विषः। तपनः। मन्युऽमीः। असि। बृहस्पते। महि। तत्। ते। महिऽत्वनम्।।४।।

हे बृहस्पते सुनीतिभिः। *शोभना नीतयो येषु ते सुनतयः सन्मार्गाः।

---

* शोभनं नीतयो इत्यादर्शः।

तैर्जनं नयसि। अपेक्षितफलं प्रापयसि। त्रायसे। जनमापद्भ्यो रक्षसि च। यो यजमानस्तुभ्यं हविर्लक्षणमन्नं दाशात् प्रयच्छेत्। दाशृ दाने। लेट्यडागमः। तमंहः पापं पापरूपं दारिद्र्यं वा नाश्नवत्। न प्राप्नुयात्। अश्नोतेर्लेटि व्यत्ययेन परस्मैपदम्। अडागमः। ब्रह्मद्विषो। ब्राह्मणानां मन्त्राणां वा द्वेष्टुस्तपन-स्तापकोऽसि। किं च मन्युमीर्मन्योः क्रोधस्य परेषां ज्ञानस्य वा हिंसकोऽसि। किं च मन्युमीर्मन्योः क्रोधस्य परेषां ज्ञानस्य वा हिंसकोऽसि। मीङ् हिंसायाम्। क्विप्। ते तव तत्तद्दशं महि महत्प्रभूतं महित्वनं माहात्म्यमस्ति।।

दाश् 1., to make an offering; दाशात्, subj.

अंश् 5., to attain; अश्नवत्, subj.

मन्युमी adj., obstructing the wrath (of the enemy).

महि=मह् adj., great.

महित्वन n.= महित्व.

Verse 5.

न। तम्। अंहः। न। दुःऽइतम्। कुतः। चन। न। अरातयः। तितिरुः। न। द्वयाविनः। रक्षसि। ब्रह्मणः। पते।।५।।

हे ब्रह्मणस्पते सुगोपाः सुष्ठु पालयिता त्वं यं जनं रक्षसि पालयसि तं जनमहं आहन्तव्यं दुःखं न वाधते। दुरितं तत्कारणं पापं च न बाधते। अरातयो हिंसकास्तं वजनं कुतश्चन सर्वासु दिक्षु न तितिरुः। तिरतिर्हिंसाकर्मा। लिट्। न हिंसन्ति। तथा द्वयाविनः। मनस्यन्यत्क्रियायासं चानयदित्यसेतद्द्वयं येषामस्ति ते द्वयाविनो वञ्चकाः। तेऽपि तं जनं न बाधन्ते। किंच †अस्मात् ध्वरसो हिंसिका विश्वाः सर्वाः सेनास्तदर्थं विबाधसे। विशेषेण बाधस एव।।

तितिरुः, 3. plur. pf. par.; rt. तॄ, to cross, overcome.

ध्वरस् (ध्वृ), m., deceiver, cheat.

Verse 6.

त्वम्। नः। गोपाः। पथिऽकृत्। विऽचक्षणः। तव। व्रताय। मतिऽभिः।

† आदर्शे अस्मात् इति नास्ति।

जरामहे। बृहस्पते। यः। नः। अभि। ह्वरः। ह्वृ कौटिल्ये। भावेऽसुन्। कौटिल्यं दधे विदधाति तं स्वा स्वीया दुच्छुना दुर्बुद्धिर्हरस्वती वेगवती सती मर्मर्तु। मोचयतु। मृङ् प्राणत्यागे। अन्तर्भावितण्यर्थस्य यङ्लुकि लोटि रूपम्।।

मृ 9; to crush; मर्मर्तु intens. impv.

ह्वरस् (ह्वृ) n., network, deceipt.

हरस्वत् adj., full of energy, strength, wrathy; impetuous.

Verse 7.

उत। वा। यः। नः। मर्चयात्। अनागसः। अरातिऽवा। मर्तः। सानुकः। वृकः। बृहस्पते। अप। तम्। वर्तय। पथः। सुऽगम्। नः। अस्यै। देवऽवीतये। कृधि।।७।।

उत वा अपि च हे बृहस्पते आतीवाभिमुखमागमनवान् सानुकः समुच्छ्रितः। सानु समुच्छ्रितमिति यास्कः (नि० २-२४)। वृकः। वृक आदाने। धनादीनामादाता यो मर्तो मनुष्योऽनागसोऽपराधहीनान्नोऽस्मान् मर्चयात्। मर्चयतिर्हिंसाकर्मा। हिंस्यात्। तं मर्तं पथो वैदिकान्मार्गादपवर्तय। निवर्तय। नोऽस्माकमस्यै देववीतये। देवानां वीतिं सोमभक्षणमर्चयतीति देववीतिर्यज्ञः। अस्यै देववीतयेऽस्मै यज्ञाय नोऽस्माकं सुगं सुष्ठु गन्तव्यं मार्गं कृधि। कुरु। यज्ञानुष्ठानाय सुमतिं देहीत्यर्थः।।

मर्चयात्, sbj. मृच्, to injure.

अरातीवन् (Padap. अरातिवन्), adj., hostile.

सानुक adj., has been interpreted in the following ways:—

(1) स अनुक, with his following;

(2) सारनुक, derived from सानुः

(a) elevated, Sāy., referring to Yāska, Nir. 2. 24;

(b) from the back, Ludwig;

(c) at the back=अनुचर, Hillebrandt.

(३) सानुक connected with सनुतर्, सनुत्य, near, Oldenberg;

(4) सानुक derived from सन्, to win, to get (by fight and violence), greedy of prey, Roth, Grassmann.

The interpretation of Roth and Grassmann seems to be preferable.

देवताति f., feast of the gods.—

Probably to be read मर्तिअः for मर्तः.

Verse 8.

त्रातारम्। त्वा। तनूनाम्। हवामहे। अवऽस्पर्तः। अधिऽवक्तारम्। अस्मऽयुम्। बृहस्पते। देवऽनिदः। नि। बर्हय। मा। दुःऽएवाः। उत्ऽतरम्। सुम्नम्। उत्। नशन्।।८।।

अवस्पर्तः उपद्रवेभ्यः पारयितः। यद्वा अवसा रक्षणेनापद्भ्यः। पारयितः हे बृहस्पते तनूनामङ्गानां पुत्रादीनां वा त्रातारं पालयितारमधिवक्तारमस्मासु पक्षपातेनाधिकं वक्तारमस्मयुं हविष्प्रदानस्मान् कामयमानं त्वां हवामहे। अस्मिन्कर्मण्याह्वयामः। किं च देवनिदो देवनिन्दकानसुरान्निबर्हय। विनाशय। दुरेवा दुष्टगमना दर्बुद्धयः शत्रव उत्तरमुत्कृष्टतरं सुम्नं सुखं मा उन्नशन्। मा व्याप्नुवन्तु।।

नि बर्ह् (वृह्) 6., to fling down, put down.

उत् नशन्, sbj. rt. नश् 1., to attain.

अवस्पर्तृ (स्पृ) m., saviour.

अस्मयु adj., loving us.

दुरेव adj., mischievous, wicked.

सुम्न n., grace, object of grace, prosperity.

Read तनून+अम्.

Verse 9.

त्वया। वयम्। सुऽवृधा। ब्रह्मणः। पते। स्पार्हा। वसु। मनुष्या। याः। नः। दूरे। तळितः। याः। अरातयः। अभि। अन्ति। जम्भय। ताः। अनप्रसः।।९।।

हे ब्रह्मणस्पते सुवृधा सुष्ठु वर्धयित्रा त्वया हेतुना वयं स्पार्हा स्पृहणीयानि वसु धनानि। मनुष्या। सुपां सुलुगिति चतुर्थीबहुवचनस्याकरः। मनुष्येभ्यो दातृभ्य आददीमहि। गृह्णीमहि। आङो दोऽनास्यविहरण इत्यात्मनेपदम्। दूरे दूरदेशे या अरातयः याश्च तळितोऽन्तिकेऽरातयो नोऽस्मानभिसन्ति। अभिभवन्ति। अनप्रसः कर्महीनान् ता अरातीस्तान् शत्रून् जम्भय। नाशय। जभि नाशने चुरादिः। अत्र निरुक्तम्। त्वया वयं सुवर्धयित्रा ब्रह्मणस्पते स्पृहणीयानि वसूनि मनुष्येभ्य आददीमहि याश्च नो दूरे तळितो याश्चान्तिकेऽ-रातयोऽदानकर्माणो वा दानप्रज्ञा वा जम्भय ता अनप्रसोऽप्न इति रूपनाम (नि० ३-११) इति।

अ॒भि अस्, to overpower.

जम्भ् 1., to chew; causal: to crush.

त॒ळित्, त॒ळित॑ः (तङ्, to push, touch?), neighbouring, near (Sāy.).

अ॒न॒प्रस्, without possession, penniless.

Read म॒नु॒षिआ॑. वसु॑, acc. plur.

Verse 10.

त्वया॑। व॒यम्। उ॒त्ऽत॒मम्। धी॒म॒हे॒। वयः॑। बृह॑स्पते। पप्रि॑णा। सस्नि॑ना। यु॒जा। मा। न॒ः। दु॒ःऽशंसः॑। अ॒भि॒ऽदि॒प्सुः। ई॒श॒त॒। प्र। सु॒ऽशंसाः॑। म॒तिऽभिः॑। ता॒रि॒षी॒म॒हि॒॥१०॥

हे बृहस्पते पप्रिणा। पॄ पालनपूरणयोः। आदृगमहनेति किन्प्रत्ययः। छान्दसो यणादेशः। कामानां पूरकेण सस्निना शुद्धेन युजा सहायेन त्वयाहेतुनोत्तमं वयो हविर्लक्षणमन्नं वयं धीमहे। धारयामः। धि धारणे। दैवादिकः। दुःशंसो दुःशंसनीयोऽभिदिप्सुरभिदम्भितुमभिभवितुमिच्छुः पुरूषो नोऽस्माकं मा ईशत। मा ईशिष्ट। ईश्वरो मा भवतु। ईश ऐश्वर्ये। लेट्यडागमः। वयं मतिभिः स्तोत्रैः सुशंसा शोभनशंसनोपेताः सन्तः प्रतारिषीमहि। प्रकर्षेण वर्धेमहि॥

ता॒रि॒षी॒म॒हि॒, aor. opt. ātm.; प्र तॄ, to get on, prosper.

पप्रि (पॄ to fill) adj., bestowing amply.

सस्निन् (सन्) adj., winning.

Verse 11.

अनानुऽदः। वृषभः। जग्मिः। आऽहवम्। निःतप्ता। शत्रुम्। पृतनासु। ससहिः। असि। सत्यः। ऋणऽयाः। ब्रह्मणः। पते। उग्रस्य। चित्। दमिता। वीळुऽहर्षिणः॥११॥

हे ब्रह्मणस्पते अनानुदः। अनु पश्चाद्ददातीत्यनुदः। स यस्य नास्तीत्यननुदः। दात्रन्तरशून्य इत्यर्थः। अत एव वृषभः कामानां वर्षिता। आहवम्। आहूयतेऽत्रेत्याहवो युद्धम्। आङि युद्धे (पा० ३-३-७३) इत्यप्प्रत्ययः संप्रसारणं च। तद्युद्धं जग्मिर्गन्ता। आदृगमहनेति किन्प्रत्ययः। लिङ्द्भावादाहवमित्यत्र षष्ठीप्रतिषेधः। शत्रुं शातयितारम्। निष्टप्ता नितरां तस्य तापकः। तृन्नन्तत्वात्षष्ठीप्रतिषेधः। निसस्तपतावनासेवने (पा० ८-३-१०२) इत षत्वम्। तादौ च नितीति गतेः स्वरः। पृतनासु संग्रामेषु सासहिः शत्रूणामभिभविता। एतादृशस्त्वं सत्यः सत्यपराक्रमः सत्यप्रज्ञो वासि। ऋणया ऋणस्य यावयिता। यु मिश्रणामिश्रणोः। ण्यन्तस्य क्विपि णिलोपे लोपो व्योर्वलीति वलोपः। किंच उग्रस्य चित् ओजस्विनोऽपि दमितोपशमयिता वीळुहर्षिणो दृढहर्षस्य कामुकस्य नास्तिकस्य चिद्दमितासि॥

अन् अनु (आनु) द (दा) adj., not yielding, not giving way.

जग्मि (intens. rt. गम्), hurrying.

सासहि (सह्) adj., holding out, victorious.

ऋण या adj., going after the debt, exacting the debt

वीळु हर्षिन् adj., rejoicing, confiding in one's strength.

Verse 12.

अदेवेन। मनसा। यः। रिषण्यति। शासाम्। उग्रः। मन्यमानः। जिघांसति। बृहस्पते। मा। प्रणक्। तस्य। नः। वधः। नि। कर्म। मन्युम्। दुःऽएवस्य। शर्धतः॥१२॥

य: पुमान् अदेवेन देवानमन्यमानेन यद्वा आसुरवृत्तिविशिष्टेन मनसास्मान् रिषण्यति। हिनस्ति। दुरस्युर्द्रविणस्युर्वृषण्यतिरिषण्यतीति निपातित:। यश्चोग्र: पापचित्तो मन्यमान आत्मानं बहुमन्यमान: पुमान् शासामुक्थस्य शंसितारम्। यद्वा अस्माकमाशंसाम्। शसितॄणामुग्र इति वा योजनीयम्। अस्मान् जिघांसति। हन्तुमिच्छति। हन्तेः सनि अज्झनगमां सनीति दीर्घ:। हे बृहस्पते तस्य वध:। वध्यतेऽनेनेति वध आयुधम्। नोऽस्मान्मा पृणक्। *मा संपर्कयतु। पृची संपर्के रम्विकरणी। व्यत्ययेनामागम:। चादिलोप इति न निधात:। व्यत्ययेना- द्युदात्त:। किंच दुरेवस्य दुष्टगमनस्य शर्धतो बलवत:। यद्वा दुष्टाभिसन्धेर्वेगं कुर्वतस्तस्य मन्युं क्रोधं ज्ञानं वा निकर्म। त्वत्प्रसादान्निराकुर्मश्च।।

रि॒ष॒ण्यति॑, rt. रिष् 4., to try to do harm, to act wrongly.

शा॒साम् gen. plur. शास् m., the mighty, powerful one; f., command; शा॒साम् उ॒ग्र, fierce, strong in commands. प्र णं॑क् and नि क॑र्म, injj., rts. नश् and कृ.

शृध् 1., to be defiant.

Verse 13.

भरे॑षु। हव्यः॑। नम॑सा। उ॒प॒ऽसद्यः॑। गन्ता॑। वाजे॑षु। सनि॑ता। धनं॑ऽधनम्। विश्वाः॑। इत्। अ॒र्यः। अ॒भि॒ऽदि॒प्स्वः॑। मृधः॑। बृ॒ह॒स्पतिः॑। वि। व॒व॒र्ह॒। रथा॑न्ऽइव।।१३।।

स बृहस्पतिर्भरेषु संग्रामेषु हव्यो योद्धृभि: स्वरक्षणार्थमाह्वातव्यो नमसोपसद्य: सर्वैर्नमसोपसदनीय:। किंच वाजेषु गन्ता। संग्रामेषु रक्षार्थं गमनशील:। तथा धनं धनं सनिता संभक्ता दाता †वा। तृन्नन्तत्वात्षष्ठीप्रतिषेध:। तथार्य: स्वामी बृहस्पतिरभिदिप्स्वोऽभिभवनेच्छावतीर्विश्वा इत् सर्वा एव मृधो हिंसिका: सेना रथानिव युद्धे वेगेन परकीयात्रथानिव विववर्ह। विशेषेण शिथिलीचकार। यद्वा इवशब्दश्चार्थे। विववर्ह। लडर्थे लिट्।।

वि वृह् 6., to overthrow.

---

* आदर्शे 'मा संपर्कयतु' इति नास्ति।

† आदर्शे वा नास्ति।

भरं m., the gain by conquest, the fight.

मृध् f., battle; enemy.

अ॒र्यस् acc. plur. f., अ॒रि (Sāy.: nom. sg. m.).

Possibly to be read उ॒प॒सदिंओ.

Verse 14.

तेजिंष्ठया। त॒प॒नी। र॒क्षसंः। त॒प॒। ये। त्वा॒। नि॒दे। द॒धि॒रे। दृ॒ष्टऽवीर्यम्। आ॒विः। तत्। कृ॒ष्व॒। यत्। असंत्। ते॒। उ॒क्थ्यंम्। बृहंस्पते। वि। प॒रि॒ऽरपंः। अ॒र्द॒य॒।।१४।।

हे बृहस्पते तेजिष्ठयातिशयेन तिग्मया तपनी तापकारिण्या हेत्या रक्षसो राक्षसांस्तप। तापय। ये राक्षसा दृष्टपराक्रमं त्वा त्वां निदे निन्दाया विषयं दधिरे। कृतवन्तः। तान् तापयेति समन्वयः। ते तव उक्थ्यं सर्वैः प्रशंसनीयं यद्वीर्यमसत् पूर्वमासीत् तदधुना आविष्कृष्व। प्रकटीकुरु। तेन च वीर्येण परिरपः परिवदतो निन्दकानसुरान् व्यर्दय। विशेषेण बाधस्व।।

ऋद् 6., to give way: वि अर्दय, to hit, wound mortally.

बार्हस्पत्ये पशावेषा हविषोऽनुवाक्या। प्रदानानामिति खण्डे सूत्रितम्। बृहस्पते अति यदर्यो अर्हात्तमृत्विाक्या उपवाचः सचन्ते (आ० ३-७) इति। एषैवाश्विनशस्त्रे परिधानीया। सूत्रितम्। बृहस्पते अति यदर्यो अर्हादिति परिधानीया (आ ६-५) इति।।

Verse 15.

बृहंस्पते। अतिं। यत्। अ॒र्यः। अर्हात्। द्यु॒ऽमत्। वि॒ऽभाति। क्रतुंऽमत्। जनेषु। यत्। दी॒दयंत्। शवंसा। ऋ॒त॒ऽप्र॒जा॒त॒। तत्। अ॒स्मासुं। द्रविंणम्। धे॒हि॒। चि॒त्रम्।।१५।।

ऋतप्रजात सत्येनोत्पन्न हे बृहस्पते अर्यः श्रेष्ठो ब्राह्मणः सर्वान् कामानतीत्य यद्ब्रह्मवर्चसं विभाति। विशेषेण दीप्यते। यच्च शवसा बलेन स्वाश्रयं जनं दीदयत्। दीदयतिर्दीप्तिकर्मा। दीपयति। चित्रं चायनीयं तद्ब्रह्मवर्चसरूपं द्रविणमस्मासु धेहि। निधेहि। यद्वा अर्य उदारोऽपि त्वया

दत्तं धनमतीव अर्हात् श्रद्दधीत। यच्च त्वद्दत्तं धनं जनेषु तव स्तोत्रं कुर्वाणेषुदीप्तियुक्तं कर्मसाधनं च विभाति यच्च धनं शवसा अन्नादिसमृद्ध्या दीदयत् स्वाश्रयं दीपयति तादृशं धनमस्मासु धेहि। तथा च ब्राह्मणम्। बृहस्पते अतियदर्यो अर्हादित्येतया परिदध्यात्तेजस्कामो ब्रह्मवर्चसकामोऽतीवान्यान्ब्रह्मवर्चसमर्हति द्युमदिति द्युमदिव वै ब्रह्मवर्चसं विभातीति वीव वै ब्रह्मवर्चसं भाति यद्दीदयच्छवस ऋतप्रजातेति दीदायेच वै ब्रह्मवर्चसं तदस्मासु द्रविणं धेहि चित्रमिति चित्रमिव वै ब्रह्मवर्चसं ब्रह्मवर्चसी ब्रह्मयशसी भवति (ऐ० ब्रा० ४-११) इति।

We may interpret either:— यद् अति॒ अर्हा॑द् अ॒र्यो, (gen. sg.) a possession worth more than that of the rival.—Or:—यद् अर्हा॒द् अति॑ अ॒र्यो (acc. plur.), that whose worth is beyond (that of the deserts of) the rivals.

वि॒भाति॑ may be sbj., like अर्हात्, दु॒दय॑त्.

क्रतु॑मत् adj., strong.

दु॒दय॑त्, sbj., stem दीदी, rt. दीए to shine.

शव॑स् n., strength.

Verse 16.

मा। न॒ः। स्ते॒नेभ्य॑ः। ये। अ॒भि। द्रु॒हः। प॒दे। नि॒रा॒मिण॑ः। रि॒पव॑ः। अन्ने॑षु। ज॒गृ॒धुः। आ। दे॒वाना॑म्। ओह॑ते। वि। व्रय॑ः। हृ॒दि। बृह॑स्पते। न। प॒रः। साम्न॑ः। वि॒दुः॥१६॥

हे बृहस्पते नोऽस्मान् स्तेनेभ्यः स्त्यानमस्ति येषु इति स्तेनाश्चौराः। तेभ्यो मा दाः। तान् दर्शयति। ये चौरा द्रुहः प्राणद्रोहस्य पदे स्थाने निरामिणो नितरां रमणशीला रिपवो हिंसकाः सन्तोऽन्नेषु परकीयेष्वभिजागृधुः। अभिकाङ्क्षन्ति। गृधु अभिकाङ्क्षायाम्। लिटि रूपम्। ये च देवानां विव्रयो विशेषेण वर्जनम्। व्री व्ली इति धातू वर्जने वर्तेते। य एवं विद्वान् दक्षिणां प्रतिगृह्णाति नैनं दक्षिणा व्लीनाति (तै० ब्रा० २-२-५-३) इत्येकस्य

वर्जनार्थे *दृष्टत्वादपरस्यापि वर्जनार्थत्वम्। तत् हृदि स्वकीये हृदय आ ओहते। आवहन्ति। देवानां यागान् स्तुतीश्च न करवाम इति मन्यन्त इति यावत्। तेभ्योऽस्मान् मा दा इति समन्वयः। ये पुमांसः साम्नः साममयात्त्वत्तः परः परस्तादन्यदुत्कृष्टं साम यद्रक्षोध्नम्। साम वै रक्षोहेति। न विदुः। न जानन्ति। किन्तु सर्वसाधकं साम त्वामेव विदुषोऽस्मान् स्तेनेभ्यो मा दाः।।

अभि गृध् 4., to be greedy.

ओहते, 3., plur.; rt. ऊह् 2., to consider, to be selfesteeming; वि आ ऊह्, to despise.

व्रयस् (व्री, व्ली) n., overpowering might.

In the first pāda the verb (दाः) is to be understood.—The सामन् in the last pāda is most likely the liturgical song. Brahmaṇaspati knows the सामन् better than anyone; the godless, consequently, will never be a match for him.

Verse 17.

विश्वेभ्यः। हि। त्वा। भुवनेभ्यः। परि। त्वष्टा। अजनत्। साम्नःऽसाम्नः। कविः। सः। ऋणऽचित्। ऋणऽयाः। ब्रह्मणः। पतिः। द्रुहः। हनता। महः। ऋतस्य। धर्तरि।।१७।।

हे ब्रह्मणस्पते त्वष्टा प्रजापतिर्विश्वेभ्यो भुवनेभ्यः परि सर्वेभ्यो भूतजातेभ्य उत्कृष्टं त्वामजनद्धि। अजीजनत्। खलु। ततस्त्वं साम्नः साम्नः कविः। कु शब्दे। अच इरिति इप्रत्ययः। उच्चारयिता कर्तासि। यद्वा कविः क्रान्तदर्शी त्वष्टा साम्नः सर्वस्यापि साम्नः सारेण त्वामजीजनत्। किंच स ब्रह्मणस्पतिर्महो महत ऋतस्य यज्ञस्य धर्तरि धारके यजमाने ऋणचित् स्तोतृकाममृणमिव चिनोतीति ऋणचित्। किंच ऋणयाः पापरूपस्य ऋणस्य यावयिता पृथक्कर्ता च। द्रुहः कर्मणो द्रोग्धुरसुरस्य हनता भवेति।।

परि with abl.;, from, out of, on account of (Grassmann); superior to (Sāy.).

---

* आदर्शे दृष्टस्यापि इति पाठः।

Since in the previous ṛc Brahmaṇaspati is said to know the सामन्, साम्नः साम्नः might be taken parallel to भुवनेभ्यः,out of all beings and the सामन्. From the mythological point it does not seem advisable to consider Bṛhaspati as made out of all things or beings, but rather superior to, or for the sake of, all the beings, remembering the role he played in the slaying of Vala and the liberation of the cows.

धर्तरि seems to be nom. sg. Cp. ZDMG 55. 302.

Verse 18.

तव। श्रिये। वि। अजिहुरत। पर्वतः। गवाम्। गोत्रम्। उत्ऽअसृजः। यत् अङ्गिरः। इन्द्रेण। युजा। तमसा। परिऽवृतम्। बृहस्पते। निः। अपाम्। औब्जः। अर्णवम्।।१८।।

अङ्गिर आङ्गिरस हे बृहस्पते गवामावारको बलेनाधिष्ठितः र्वतस्तव श्रिय आश्रयणार्थं व्यजिहीत। विवृतद्वारतामगच्छत्। ततस्त्वं यद्यदा गोत्रम्। इनित्रकट्यचश्चेति समूहार्थे त्रप्रत्ययः। गवां समूहमुदसृजः। निरगमयः। तदेन्द्रेण युजा सहायेन युक्तस्त्वं तमसा वृत्रासुरेण परीवृतं परित आक्रान्त-मपामर्णवं स्थानभूतं मेघं निरौब्जः। नितरामधोमुखमकार्षीः।।

वि अजिहीत, impf. ātm.; rt. वि हा 3., to open.

उब्ज् 6., to force, निर् उब्ज्, to let loose.

Verse 19.

ब्रह्मणः। पते। त्वम्। अस्य। यन्ता। सुऽउक्तस्य। बोधि। तनयम्। च। जिन्व। विश्वम्। तत्। भद्रम्। यत्। अवन्ति। देवाः बृहत्। वदेम। विदथे। सुवीराः।।१९।।

हे ब्रह्मणस्पते ब्रह्मणां स्तोत्राणामधिपते अस्य जगतो यन्ता नियामकस्त्वं सूक्तस्यास्मदीयमिदं ब्राह्मणस्पत्यं सूक्तं बोधि। बुध्यस्व। त्वं तनयं पुत्रपौत्रादि-लक्षणं सन्तानं जिन्व। जिविः प्रीणनार्थः। लोटि रूपम्। प्रीणय। भवादृशा देवा यदवन्ति रक्षन्ति तत्तादृशं विश्वं सर्वं भद्रं कल्याणं भवति। अतो वयं

विदथेऽस्मिन्यज्ञे सुवीराः शोभनपुत्रपौत्राः सन्तो बृहत्प्रभूतमिदं स्तोत्रं वदेम ब्रूयाम।।

बो॒धि॒, 2. sg. aor. impv.; rt. भू॒.

वि॒दथे॑ (विद्) n., assembly; worship,. cult (rt. विध्) See Oldenberg, Vedaforschung, p. 28, note 1.

The last pāda:—बृ॒हद्व॑देम वि॒दथे॑ सु॒वीराः॑ shows the author ship of Gr̥tsamada or his family.

NO. 8.

MAṆḌALA II. **SŪKATA 28.**

इदमित्येकादशर्चं षष्ठं सूक्तम्। अत्रानुक्रम्यते। इदमेकादश वारूणमिति। पूर्वसूक्ते कूर्मो गार्त्समदो हिवेत्युक्तत्वादस्योत्तरस्य च कूर्मो गृत्समदो वा ऋषिः। त्रिष्टुप् छन्दः। वरुणो देवता। विनियोगो लैङ्गिकः। अत्र केचिदाहुः। इदमेकादशर्चं तु वारूणं भयपापनुत्। ऋणदारिद्यदुःस्वप्ननाशनं चेति शुश्रुम (ऋग्विधा० १-२५-१) इति।

Verse 1.

इ॒दम्। क॒वेः। आ॒दि॒त्यस्य॑। स्व॒ऽराजः॑। विश्वा॑नि। सन्ति॑। अ॒भि। अ॒स्तु॒। म॒ह्ना। अति॑ यः। म॒न्द्रः। य॒जथा॑य। दे॒वः। सु॒ऽकी॒र्तिम्। भि॒क्षे॒। वरु॑णस्य। भूरेः॑।।१।।

कवेः क्रान्तदर्शिन आदित्यस्यादितेः पुत्रस्य स्वराजः स्वयमेव राजमानस्येश्वरस्य वा वरुणस्येदं हविः स्तात्रं वा यजमानः करोतिति शेषः। स च विश्वानि सर्वाणि सान्ति द्वितीयभावविकारभाञ्जि भूतजातानि मह्ना महिम्ना वरुणप्रसादाल्लब्धेनाभ्यस्तु। अभिभवतु। यो देवो द्योतमानो वरुणो यजथाय यष्ट्रे पुरुषाय अति अतिशयेन मन्द्रः स्तुत्यो हर्षयिता वा भवति तस्य भूरेर्भर्तुर्वरुणस्य सुकीर्तिं शोभनां स्तुतिं भिक्षे। प्रार्थये। यद्वा वरुणस्येति तृतीयार्थे षष्ठी। तेन वरुणेन दातव्यां शोभनां कीर्तिमहं याचे।।

इ॒दम्, viz., स्तोत्रम् (Sāy.).

स्वराज् adj., self-rulling, self-luminous

महान् n., instr. sg. मह्ना, greatness, glory, power.

मन्द्र adj., agreeable, charming, well disposed towards.

यजथ=यज्ञ, dative used like an infinitive.

Verse 2.

तव। व्रते। सुऽभगासः। स्याम। सुऽआध्यः। वरुण। तुस्तुऽवांसः। उपऽअयने। उषसाम्। गोऽमतीनाम्। अग्नयः। न। जरमाणाः। अनु। द्यून्।।२।।

हे वरुण स्वाध्यः। शोभनाध्यानास्तुष्टुवांसः स्तुतवन्तो वयं तव व्रते त्वदीये परिचरणाख्ये कर्मणि वर्तमानाः सुभगासः स्याम। शोभनधना भवेम। अपि च गोमतीनां रश्मिभिर्युक्तानामुपायन उपागमने सत्यग्नयो न यथाग्नयोऽग्नि-होत्रादिकर्मार्थं समिध्यन्ते एवमनुद्यून् अनुदिनं जरमाणास्त्वां स्तुवन्तो वयं दीप्यमाना भवेम।।

स्वाधी (सु आधी), attentive (of gods), devout (of men).

Verse 3.

तव। स्याम। पुरुऽवीरस्य। शर्मन्। उरुऽशंसस्य। वरुण। प्रनेतरिति प्रऽनेतः। यूयम्। नः। पुत्राः। अदितेः। अदब्धाः। अभि। क्षमध्वम्। युज्याय। देवाः।।३।।

हे प्रणेतः सर्वस्य जगतः प्रकर्षेण नेतर्वरुण पुरुवीरस्य पुरुभिर्बहुभि-र्वीरैरूपेतस्य यद्वा पुरूणां बहूनां शत्रूणां विशेषेण प्रेरकस्योरुशंसस्योरुभिर्बहुभिः स्तूयमानस्य तव शर्मन् शर्मणि सुखे गृहे वा स्याम। अदितेः पुत्रा मित्रादयः। परमपि च्छन्दसीति परस्य षष्ठ्यन्तस्य पूर्वामन्त्रिताङ्गवद्भावेनानुप्रवेशात् पदद्वय-समुदायस्याष्टमिकं सर्वानुदात्तत्वम्। अदब्धाः शत्रुभिरहिंसिताः। एवंभूता हे देवा यूयं नोऽस्मान् कृतापराधान् युज्याय सख्यायाभिक्षमध्वम्। अस्माभिः कृतमपराधं सहध्वम्।।

शर्मन् (श्रि) n., home, refuge, protection.

उरू शंस, crying far, praising loud, ruling far.

युज्यं n., alliance.

अभि क्षम्, with dat., to be favourable to.

The plural in यूयं नः पुत्राः... includes Mitra besides Varuṇa.

Verse 4.

प्र। सीम्। आदित्यः। असृजत्। विऽधर्ता। ऋतम्। सिन्धवः। वरुणस्य। यन्ति। न। श्रम्यन्ति। न। वि। मुचन्ति। एते। वयः। न। पप्तुः। रघुऽया। परिऽज्मन्।।४।।

विधर्ता सेतुरिव जलस्य विधारयितादित्योऽदितेः पुत्रो वरुण ऋतं विधारणहेतुभूतं सत्यम् यद्वा नदीनामुपादानभूतमुदकं सीं सर्वतः प्रासृजत्। प्रकर्षेण सृष्टवान्। अणोऽप्रगृह्यस्यानुनासिक इत्याकारः सानुनासिकः। तेन वरुणस्य ऋतेन सिन्धवः स्यन्दनशीला नद्यो यन्ति। गच्छन्ति प्रवहन्ति। एते सिन्धवो न श्राम्यन्ति श्रान्तिं न प्राप्नुवन्ति न विमुचन्ति उपरता न भवन्ति। अनलसाः सर्वदैकरूपेण प्रवहन्तीत्यर्थः। एतदेवोच्यते। वयो न वयः पक्षिण इव रघुया रघवः शीघ्रगामिनः परिज्मनि भूम्यां। पप्तुः। पतन्ति। पतॢ गतौ। लिट्युसि तनिपत्योश्छन्दसीत्युपधालोपः। स्थानिवद्भावाद्द्विर्वचनादि। रघुया इत्यत्र सुपां सुलुगिति जसो याजादेशः।।

वि मुच्, to loose (horse, ropes), to rest.

ऋतम्, acc. = instrum., according to the law, in the right manner.

रघुया adv. from instrum., f., रघु.

परिज्मन् adj. subst., the walking about, course, drive; locative: everywhere, all round.

Verse 5.

वि। मत्। श्रथय। रशनांऽइव। आगः। ऋध्याम। ते। वरुण।

खाम्। ऋतस्य॑। मा। तन्तुः। छेदि। वय॑तः। धियम्। मे। मा। मात्रा। शारि। अपसः। पुरा। ऋतोः।।५।।

हे वरुण मत् मत्सकाशात् रशनामव रज्जुमिव आगो विहिताननुष्ठानजनितं पापं विश्रथय शिथिलीकुरु। विमोचयेत्यर्थः। ते त्वत्संबन्धिन ऋतस्योदकस्य पूर्णां खां नदीम्। खा इति नदीनाम। तामृध्याम लभेमहि। अपि च धियं कर्मं वयतः संतन्वतो मे मम तन्तुः कर्मसंततिः मा छेदि छिन्नो मा भूत्। नैरन्तर्येणेत्यर्थः। तथा ऋतोः समाप्तिकालात्पुरा पूर्वमपसः कर्मणो मात्रा शरीरं प्राच्योदीच्याङ्गलक्षणं मा शारि शीर्णं विकलं मा भूत्। शृ हिसायाम्। कर्मणि लुङ्। पुर ऋतोरित्यत्र ऋत्यक इति प्रकृतिभावः।।

वि श्रथ् 9., to loose. ऋध् 4., to thrive, increase.

खा f., fount, well.

छेदि, शारि, injj. pass. rts. छिद्, to cut, शृ, to separate, destroy, shorten.

अपस् n., work, duty, business.

मत्, मद्, abl. of अहम्, from me.

Note *asahe khāo,* the Avestan parallel to ऋतसय खा.

Verse 6.

अपो। इति। सु। म्यक्ष। वरुण। भियसम्। मत्। सम्ऽराट्। ऋतऽवः। अनु। मा। गृभाय। दामऽइव। वत्सात्। वि। मुमुग्धि। अंहः। नहि। त्वत्। आरे। निऽमिषः। चन। ईशे।।६।।

हे वरुण भियसं भयं मत् मत्तः सु सुष्ठु अपो म्यक्ष। अपगमय। हे सम्राट् सम्यग्राजमान हे ऋतावः सत्यवन् यज्ञवन्वा वरुण मामनुगृभाय। अनुगृहाण। छन्दसि शायजपीति श्रः शायजादेशः। हृग्रहोर्भ इति भत्वम्। अपि च दामेव वत्सात् यथा दोग्धा वत्ससकाशाद्बन्धनीं रज्जुं विमुञ्चति तथांहः पापं मत्सकाशाद्विमुमुग्धि। विमुञ्च। छान्दसः शपः श्लुः। पृथक्कुरु। त्वदारे त्वत्तो दूरदेशे वर्तमानः त्वदन्य इत्यर्थः। त्वत्तोऽन्यः कश्चित् निमिषश्चन

निमेषस्यापि अक्षिपक्ष्मचलनस्यापि नहीशे। नेष्टे। त्वमेवेश्वर इत्यर्थः। लोपस्त आत्मनेपदेष्विति तलोपः।।

म्यक्ष् 1., to apply, अप म्यक्ष्, to remove.

भि॒यस् (भी) m., fear; read भ्यसं॑म्.

गृ॒भा॒य॒, impv. pres. (denom?): rt. ग्रभ् 9., to get hold of:

अनु॑ ग्री॒ to be favourable to.

दाम॒न् n., halter.

मु॒मु॒ग्धि॒, pf. impv.

नि मिष् (मिष॑स् gen. inf.) to close the eyes.

आ॒र m.n., distance.

Note the voc. accent of ऋता॑वो, and अपो॑ (for अप॑ उ) in the Padapāṭha.

Verse 7.

मा। न॒ः। व॒धैः। व॒रु॒ण॒। ये। ते॒। इ॒ष्टौ। एनः॑। कृ॒ण्वन्त॑म्। अ॒सु॒र॒। भ्री॒णन्ति॑। मा। ज्योति॑षः। प्र॒ऽव॒स॒थानि॑। ग॒न्म॒। वि। सु। मृधः॑। शि॒श्र॒थ॒ः। जी॒वसे॑। न॒ः।।७।।

हे वरुण नोऽस्मान् वधैर्हननसाधनैरायुधैर्मा हिंसीरिति शेषः। हे असुर पापकृतां निरसितः ते त्वदीय इष्टौ यज्ञ एनो विहिताननुष्ठानेन जनितं पापं कृण्वन्तं कुर्वन्तं पुरूषं ये वधा भ्रीणन्ति हिंसन्ति तैरिति पूर्वत्र संबन्धः। भ्रीष् हिंसायां क्रैयादिकः। अपि च ज्योतिषो गृहे वर्तमानादग्नेः सौरप्रकाशाद्वा प्रवसथानि प्रवासान्मा गन्म। मा गच्छाम। सर्वदा गृहे वर्तमानः सूर्यं पश्यंश्चिरकालं जीवेयमित्यर्थः। गमेर्लुङि मन्त्रे घसेति च्लेर्लुक्। तथा नोऽस्माकं जीवसे जीवनाय मृधो हिंसकान् सु सुष्टु विशिश्रथः। विश्लेषय। बाधस्वेत्यर्थः।।

भ्री 9., to hit. शिश्रथः, subj. aor.

इ॒ष्टि (इष्, to set in motion) f., command, word. In the first pāda the verb (व॒धी॒ः strike) has to be understood.

Verse 8.

नम॑ः। पु॒रा। ते॒। व॒रु॒ण॒। उ॒त। नू॒नम्। उ॒त। अ॒प॒रम्। तु॒वि॒ऽज॒ा॒त॒। ब्र॒वा॒म॒। त्वे इति॑। हि। कु॒म्। पर्व॑ते। न। श्रि॒तानि॑। अप्र॑ऽच्युतानि। दु॒ःऽद॒भ॒। व्र॒तानि॑॥८॥

हे वरुण पुरा पूर्वस्मिन्काले ते तुभ्यं नमो नमस्कारप्रतिपादकं नम इति शब्दमवादिष्म। उत अपि च नूनमद्यापि ब्रवाम। उत अपि च हे तुविजात बहुषु प्रदेशेषु प्रादुर्भूत वरुणापरमागामिन्यपि काले नमःशब्दं ब्रवाम। उच्चारयाम। कस्मादिति चेदुच्यते। दूळभ दुर्दभ दम्भितुं हिंसितुमशक्य। दुरो दशनाशदभध्येषु (पा० ६-३-१०९-५) इति रेफस्योत्वमुत्तरपदादेः। ष्टुत्वें च। कमित्येतत्पादपूरणम्। हि यस्मात्त्वे त्वयि पर्वते न शिलोच्चय इवाप्रच्युतान्यन्यैः प्रच्यावयितुमशक्यानि व्रतानि कर्माणि विधरणानि श्रितानि। आश्रितानि। तस्मादित्यर्थः॥

तु॒वि॒ज॒ात adj., of a strong nature, mighty.

ब्र॒वा॒म॒, subj. कम् (without accent), truly, indeed.

Verse 9.

परा॑। ऋ॒णा। अध॑। मत्ऽकृ॑तानि। मा। अ॒हम्। रा॒ज॒न्। अ॒न्यऽकृ॑तेन। भो॒ज॒म्। अवि॑ऽउष्टाः। इत्। नु। भूय॑सीः। उ॒षस॑ः। आ। न॒ः। जी॒वान्। व॒रु॒ण॒। तासु॑। शा॒धि॒॥९॥

हे वरुण ऋणा ऋणानि पित्रादिभिः कृतान्यस्माभिर्देयानि परा साबीः। परासुव। पराचीलनं प्रेरय। षू प्रेरणे। छान्दसो लङ्। अध अधुना मत्कृतानि मया निष्पादितानि ऋणानि परासुव। अपि च हे राजन् स्वामिन् वरुण अहमन्यकृतेनान्यैरर्जितेन धनेन मा भोजम्। भोगं मा लभेयम्। किं कारणमिति चेदुच्यते। भूयसीर्भूयस्यो बहुतरा उषसोऽव्युष्टा इन्नु सत्यमव्युष्टा एव। अपररात्रेषूत्थाय ऋणानि चिन्तयतो जाग्रतो मम व्युष्टकलपा आसन्। हे वरुण तासूषःसु नोऽस्मान् जीवान् जीवनवत आशधि। आ समन्तादनुशिष्टान् कुरु। ऋणान्यपहत्य भोगपर्याप्तं धनं प्रयच्छेत्यर्थः॥

* न्यपकृत्य इत्यादर्शः।

परा सू 6., aor. सावीः, to push off, remove.

(अ) व्युंष्ट, pt. pf. pass.; rt. वि वस्, to shine.

आ शास् 2., to order, ordain. भोजम्, inj.

भुज् with instrum. does not imply anything bad; Sāy. is correct in understanding with अन्यकृतेन rather धनेन than एनसा. Nor are the ऋणा in the first pāda so much moral guilts as financial debts.

Verse 10.

यः। मे। राजन्। युज्यः। वा। स्वप्ने। भयम्। भीरवे। मह्यम्। आह स्तेनः। वा। यः। दिप्सति। नः। वृकः। वा। त्वम्। तस्मात्। वरुण। पाहि। अस्मान्।।१०।।

हे राजन् वरुण मे मदीयो युज्यो योजनसमर्थः पित्रादिर्वा सखा समान ख्यानोऽन्यो बान्धवो वा स्वप्ने दृष्टं त्वद्विषयं भयं भीरवे भयशीलाय मह्यं य आह ब्रूते। तथा स्तेनश्चौरो वा वृकोऽरण्यश्वा वा यो नोऽस्मान् दिप्सति जिघांसति। सनीवन्तर्धेति विकलपनादिडभावः। दम्भ इश्चेतीत्वम्। हे वरुण त्वं तस्मात्सर्वस्मादस्मान्पाहि रक्ष।।

Sāy. seems to be right in supplying दृष्टम् after स्पप्ने.

Verse 11.

मा। अहम्। मघोनः। वरुण। प्रियस्य। भूरिऽदाव्नः। आ। विदम्। शूनम्। आपेः। मा। रायः। राजन्। सुऽयमात्। अव। स्थाम्। बृहत्। वदेम। विदथे। सुऽवीराः।।११।।

हे वरुण *मघोनः धनवतः प्रियस्यानुकूलस्य भूरिदावनो भूरेर्बहुलस्य

* आदर्शे भाष्यक्रमः हे वरुण प्रियस्य भूरिदाव्नो भूरेर्धनस्य दातुर्धनवत आढ्यस्य पुरतः पुत्रादेर्दारिद्र्यमहं मा आविदम्। आवेदयानि ज्ञापयानि। हे राजन् सुष्ठु नियाम-काद्धनादवयुत्य स्थितो माभूवम्। शोभनपुत्रा यज्ञे गृहे वा वर्तमानाः प्रौढं स्तोत्रमुच्चारयाम। इति दृश्यते।

दातुराढ्यस्याहं मा आविदं मावेदयानि आवेदनं विज्ञापनं मा करवाणि। किं तदनावेद्यम्। आपेर्ज्ञातिः शूनं शून्यं दारिद्यम्। वर्णलोपश्छान्दसः। यद्वा शूनं गतं प्राप्तं दारिद्यम्। टुओश्वि गतिवृद्ध्योः। श्वीदितो निष्ठायामितीट्प्रतिषेधः। यजादित्वात्संप्रसारणम्। आदितश्चेति नकारः। वृषादित्वादाद्युदात्तत्वम्। एतदुक्तं भवति। अस्मदीयाः पुत्रादयः क्षुधिता इति प्रभुप्रभुसमीपेऽभिधाय याचमानो मा भूवमिति। हे राजन् सुयमात्। सुष्ठु नियम्यतेऽनेन पुरूषो गृह इति सुयमः। माईषद्दुःसुष्विति खल्। तादृशद्रायो धनान्मावस्थां अवयुत्य स्थितो मा भूवम्। वयं सुवीराः शोभनपुत्रा विदथे यज्ञे गृहे वर्तमानाः। सन्तो वृहत् प्रौढं स्तोत्रं वदेम। उच्चारयामः।।

शूनं n., the void, ant.

आपि m., intimate friend, companion.

अव स्था with abl., to lose.

NO. 9.

MAṆḌALA II. **SŪKTA 38.**

उदु ष्य इत्येकादशच षष्ठं सूक्तं गार्त्समदं त्रैष्टुभं सवितृदेवताकम्। अत्रानुक्रमणिका। उदु ष्य एकादश सवित्रिनिबिद्धानीयम्। व्यूह्लश्चेदिति खण्डे सूत्रितम्। षष्ठस्योदु ष्यदे व इति गार्त्समदम् (आ० ८-८) इति।

The Sūkta is "an evening hymn to Savitṛ. This god has the double function of ushering in both the day and the night (ṚV. V. 82. 8) and betrays in that an essential relationship with the Greek Hermes. He is invoked to keep bad dreams off. The preset hymn has reference to that side of his activity only in virtue of which Savitṛ, coming at evening time, leads in the night; in the morning and in the evening he is the impeller or inciter, who sometimes calls men to their work, sometimes as here, to rest, verse 1. When he stretches out his arm in command over the world, all obey, even the water and the wind share the stillness of the approaching night, verse 2. The traveller halts, the bird of prey rests, verse 3.

Man's work comes to a sudden stop, when the god divides the day from the nigh, verse 4. Now the evening fires are seen to blaze everywhere, the son of the house returning from labour receives his evening meal, verse 5. Everything seeks its home, verse 6. Even the restless fish and the birds do that, and the cattle make for their stalls, verse 8. No other power, of gods or demons, can disturb this ordained order of day and night, verse 9. The closing verses are a prayer for the good things which Savitṛ can bring to his worshippers from all quarters." (First edition, from Roth, Siebenzig Lieder.)

Verse 1.

उत्। ऊं इति॑। स्यः। दे॒वः। स॒वि॒ता। स॒वाय॑। श॒श्व॒त्ऽत॒मम्। तत्ऽअ॑पाः। वह्नि॑ः। अ॑स्थात्। नू॒नम्। दे॒वेभ्य॑ः। वि। हि। धाति॑। र॒त्नम्। अथ॑। आ। अ॒भ॒ज॒त्। वी॒तिऽहो॑त्रम्। स्व॒स्तौ।।१।।

स्यः स देवो द्योतमानः सविता सवाय लोकानां प्रसवायानुज्ञायै शश्वत्तमं प्रतिदिनमुदस्थात्। उत्तिष्ठति। कीदृशः सविता। तदपाः तत्प्रसवकर्मा। अपः अग्र (नि० २-१) इति कर्मनामसु पाठात्। वह्निर्वोढा जगताम्। किंच नूनं संप्रति देवेभ्यः स्तोतृभ्यो रत्नं धनं वि हि धाति। प्रयच्छति। हीति पूरणे। अथ अपि च वीतिहोत्रं कान्तयज्ञं यजमानं स्वस्तावविनाशे क्षेमेऽभजत्। भागिनं करोतु। यद्यपि स्वस्तिशब्दो विभक्त्यन्तनिर्दिष्टशब्दपरस्तथाप्य-पर्यवसानादर्थपरो भवति।।

स्यः, nom. sg. for त्यः, demonstr. pron.

वह्नि॑ m., leader, priest.

स॒व (सू) m., the setting in motion, the command.

शश्व॑त् adj., complete, one after the other; adv, repeatedly, श॒ (T) श्वत्तमम्, a new.

वीतिहो॑त्र, (babuvr, cpd.)one whose sacrifice is a pleasure or gives pleasure.

वि धाति॑, subj. rt. धा, in a future sense.

Verse 2.

विश्वस्य। हि। श्रुष्टये। देवः। ऊर्ध्वः। प्र। बाहवा। पृथुऽपाणिः। सिसर्ति। आपः। चित्। अस्य। व्रते। आ। निऽमृग्राः। अयम्। चित्। वातः। रमते। परिऽज्मन्।।२।।

देवो द्योतमानः सविता पृथुपाणिर्महत्करो विश्वस्य श्रुष्टये जगतः सुखाय ऊर्ध्वमुद्गतः सन् बाहवा बाहू प्रसिसर्ति। प्रसारयति। आपश्चित् आपोऽप्यस्य व्रते प्रसवाख्ये कर्मणि सति। व्रतं कर्वरम्। (नि० २-१) इति तन्नामसु पाठात्। आ स्यन्दन्त इति शेषः। ताश्च निमृग्रा नितरां शोधयित्र्यो गङ्गादिरूपेण जगत्पावयन्तीत्यर्थः। अयं चिद्वातोऽयमपि वायुः परिज्मन् परितो गते व्याप्तेऽन्तरिक्षे रमते।।

प्र सृ 3., to stretch out.

श्रुष्टि f., hearing, obediene.

निमृग्र (नि मृज्) adj. with loc., clasping round, leaning on, inclined to, obeying; Sāy.: नितरां शोधयित्र्यः (आपः).

चिद्-चिद्, both, this as well as that.

Verse 3.

आशुऽभिः। चित्। यान्। वि। मुचाति। नूनम्। अरीरमत्। अतमानम्। चित्। एतोः। अह्यर्षूणाम्। चित्। नि। अयान्। अविष्याम्। अनु। व्रतम्। सवितुः। मोकी। आ। अगात्।।३।।

यान् गच्छन् सविताशुभिश्चिच्छीघ्रगामिभिरपि रश्मिभिर्विमुचाति। विमुच्यते। नूनमिति पूरणः। अतमानं चित्सततं गच्छन्तमपि जनमेतोर्गमनादरीरमत्। उपरमयति। किंच अह्यर्षूणामहिमाहन्तारं शत्रुमर्षन्त्यभिगच्छन्तीत्यह्यर्षवः। तेषामप्यविष्यां गमनेच्छां न्ययान्। नियच्छति। सवितुः प्रेरकस्य सूर्यस्य व्रतं कर्मानु पश्चान्मोकी रात्रिः। मोकी शोकीति (नि० १-७) रात्रिनामसु पाठात्। आगात्। आगच्छति। सवितुश्चेष्टोपरतौ रात्रिरागच्छतीति यावत्।।

अयान्, 3. sg. aor. par.; rt. यम् 1.

अह्य् अर्षु (rt. ऋष), rushing, moving like a serpent; or, rushing on the serpent, bird of prey.

अविष्या f., greed.

मोकी f., night.

मुचाति, 3. sg. aor. sbj. par.; rt. मुच्,

Verse 4.

पुनरिति। सम्। अव्यत्। विऽततम्। वयन्ती। मध्या। कर्तोः। नि। अधात्। शक्म। धीरः। उत्। संऽहाय। अस्थात्। वि। ऋतून्। अदर्धः। अरमतिः। सविता। देवः। आ। अगात्।।४।।

वयन्ती वस्त्रं वयन्ती नारीव रात्रिर्विततमालोकं पुनः समव्यत्। संवेष्टयते। पुनःशब्दः पूर्वेद्युरप्येवमकार्षीदिति द्योतयति। धीरः प्रज्ञोऽपि सर्वो लोकः कर्तोः क्रियमाणं कर्म। कर्तोः कर्तवै (नि० २-१) इति तन्नामसु पाठात्। शक्म कर्तुं शक्यमपि मध्या मध्य उपक्रान्तं कर्मापरिसमाप्येत्यर्थः। न्यधात् निहितवान्। सवितर्युपरत इति शेषः। सर्वो लोकः संहाय शय्यां विहायोदस्थात्। अवशिष्टं कर्म कर्तुं पुररुत्तिष्ठति। संपूर्वो जहातिः शय्यापरित्यागे वर्तते। तथा च श्रूयते। कलिः शयानो भवति संजिहानस्तु द्वापरः (ऐ० ब्रा० ७-१५) इति। सविता सर्वस्य प्रसविता सूर्योऽरमतिरनुपरतिर्देवो द्योतमान आगात्। आगच्छति। उदेतीति यावत्। ऋतून् कालविशेषांश्च व्यदर्धः। विदारयति।।

वा 4., to weave. व्या 4., aor. अव्यत्, to cover, envelop; सम् व्या, to roll up.

सम् हा 3., to rise. अदर्धः, 3. sg. impf. intens.; rt. धृ मध्या in the middle of. अर(म्)मति adj., punctually. Sāy's interpretation may be seen in his commentary. Durga in his Bhāṣya on Nirukta (IV. 11) does not agree with Sāy. He interprets:—As a woman, weaving a cloth, rolls it up at sunset and stretches it out again at sunrise, so—in this passage—the night rolls up darkness.—The best Indian commentators not being agreed on one explanation, we may just as well, with Roth and Geldner, go our own way. The context suggests that this ṛc too refers to the evening. The first line depicts the stopping of human activity, singling out in the first pāda the work of the weaving woman, in the second that of the artisan or craftsman. The second line treats again of Savitṛ's own activity.

Verse 5.

नाना। ओकांसि। दुर्यः। विश्वम्। आयुः। वि। तिष्ठते। प्रऽभवः। शोकः। अश्नेः। ज्येष्ठम्। माता। सूनवे। भागम्। आ। अधात्। अनु। अस्य। केतम्। इषितम्। सवित्रा।।५।।

प्रभवः प्रभूतोऽवनेः शोकस्तेजो दुर्यो गृहे भवो नानौकांसि यजमानानां पृथग्भूतान्गृहान्वितिष्ठते। अधितिष्ठति। विश्वमायुः। सर्वमन्नं चाधितिष्ठति। आयुः सूनृत (नि० २-७) इत्यन्ननामसु पाठात्। मातोषाः सवित्रान्विषितं प्रेषितमस्य केतं प्रज्ञापकमग्रेर्ज्येष्ठं प्रथममग्निहोत्राख्यं भागं सूनवेऽग्नय आधात् आदधाति।।

दुर्य, belonging to the house; subst., dweller in houses.

प्रभव adj., great. केत m., desire.

इषित, pt. pf. caus.; rt. इष् 4., to send.

Sāy. is certainly right in taking the first and second pādas as one sentence.

Verse 6.

संऽआववर्ति। विऽस्थितः। जिगीषुः। विश्वेषाम्। कामः। चरताम्। अमा। अभूत्। शश्वान्। अपः। विऽकृतम्। हित्वी। आ। अगात्। अनु। व्रतम्। सवितुः। दैव्यस्य।।६।।

जिगीषुर्विजयेच्छुर्योद्धा प्रस्थितः समाववर्ति। समावर्तयति। विश्वेषां सर्वेषां चरतां जङ्गमानाममा। अमा दम (नि० ३-४) इति गृहनामसु पाठात्। गृहं प्रति कामोऽभूत्। भवति। शश्वान् नित्यं कर्मरतोऽपः कर्म विकृतमर्द्धकृतं

हित्वी हित्वागात्। गृहमागच्छति। एतत्सर्वं दैव्यस्य दिवि भवस्य सवितुः प्रेरकस्य सूर्यस्य व्रतमस्तमयाख्यं कर्मानुजायत इत्यर्थः।। return.

समा वृत् 3., to

जिगीषु, desider. rt. जि 1., fortune-hunter.

अमा, home, homewards.

Verse 7.

त्वया। हितम्। अप्यम्। अप्ऽसु। भागम्। धन्व। अनु। आ। मृगयसः। वि। तस्थुः। वनानि। विऽभ्यः। नकिः। अस्य। तानि। व्रता। देवस्य। सवितुः। मिनन्ति।।७।।

हे सवितस्त्वया अप्स्वन्तरिक्षे। आपः पृथिवी (नि० १-३) इत्यन्तरिक्षनामसु पाठात्। जलाधारे वा हितं निहितमप्यमपां संबन्धिनं भागु धन्वानु निर्जलप्रदेशेऽरण्येषु *यथा मृगयसो मृगयमाणा मृगा आ समन्ताद्वितस्थुः अधितिष्ठन्ति। किंच वनानि वृक्षा विभ्यः पक्षिभ्य आवासादिरूपेण त्वया भागो दत्तः। अस्य देवस्य सवितुस्तानि तादृशानि व्रता व्रतानि कर्माणि नकिर्मिनन्ति। केऽपि न हिंसन्ति।।

आ (in the second pāda), and, too.

मृगयस्, hunter, or equivalent to मृगयमाण, acting like a मृग, animal. धन्व n., plain, desert.

The interpretation hinges on the word मृगयसः. If we take it to mean hunter (from the denom. मृगय्), the translation would be:—(The fishermen search for their) share in the waters, put there by thee, the hunters too spread on the desert land (the fowlers go) into the woods for the birds: never do they transgress these orders of god Savitṛ.—But it seems better to take with Sāy. मृगयसः as animals, beasts, both of the water and the desert (dry) land. For, firstly, the

* आदर्शे यथा इति नास्ति।

syntactical construction becomes thus smoother; secondly, the last pāda says that none of those mentioned in the previous three pādas ever violate Savitṛ's law: this, even in Vedic times, fits better the brute world than hunters, fishers, and fowlers. Finally, ṛc 8 seems to take up the thought expressed in ṛc 7, and there the animal world also is in question. And as in ṛc 6 mankind is said to be retiring to their resting places, so in ṛc 7 the beasts resort to their respective haunts. The fourth Pādas of ṛcas 6 and 7 apparently suggest the parallelism between the two ṛcas.

Verse 8.

यात्ऽराध्यम्। वरुणः। योनिम्। अप्यम्। अनिऽशितम्। निऽमिषि। जर्भुराणः। विश्वः। मार्ताण्डः। व्रजम्। आ। पशुः। गात्। स्थऽशः। जनमसपि। सविता। वि। आ। अकरित्यकः।।८।।

वरुणो याद्राध्यं यातां गच्छतां राध्यं राधनीयमप्यमाप्तुं योग्यमनिशितमतीक्ष्णम्। सुखकरमिति यावत्। योनिं स्थानं निमिषि निमेषे सवितुरस्तमये सति विश्रमार्थं प्राणिभ्यः प्रयच्छति। वरुणस्य रात्रेर्निर्वाहकत्वात्। जर्भुराणो भृशं गच्छन् विश्वः सर्वो मार्ताण्डो मृताद्भिन्नादण्डादुत्पद्यमानः पक्ष्यागात्। आगच्छति। विश्वः पशुरपि व्रजं गोष्ठमागात्। सविता प्रेरकः स्थशः स्थाने स्थाने जन्मानि जातानि भूतानि व्याकः। पृथगकार्षीत्।।

याद्राध्यम् (avyayībhāva cpd. with irregular accent), in so far as attainable,. as long as it suits, as long as it is granted. Sāy.'s explanation is hardly correct.

भुर् 6., to move, quiver; intens. जर्भुर्, to flutter. The pt. stands for the fin. vb.

मार्ताण्ड m., bird. Cp. below 25. 8,9.

योनि m., womb, place, home, resting place.

अनिशितम्=अनिशम्, without a pause. निमिष् f., moment.

स्थशः indecl., according to the place.

From the point of grammar, metre, and contents it is preferable to take—with Sāy. and Oldenberg, against Geldner—the second pāda with the first instead of with विश्वे॑ मा॒र्ताण्डो in the third. The idea of निमिष् is decidedly connected with Varuṇa, and Mitrā-Varuṇā, the Ādityas. नि॒मिषि॒ in the second pāda does not refer to Varuṇa's own twinkling, but to the twinkling of men, cp. II. 28.6. Or, नि॒मिषि॒ might perhaps be taken in the āmreḍita sense, नि॒मिषि॑निमिषि, every moment.

Verse 9.

न। यस्य॑। इन्द्रः॑। वरु॑णः। न। मि॒त्रः। व्र॒तम्। अ॒र्य॒मा। न। मि॒नन्ति॑। रु॒द्रः। न। अरा॑तयः। तम्। इ॒दम्। स्व॒स्ति। हु॒वे। दे॒वम्। स॒वि॒तार॑म्। नम॑ःऽभिः॥९॥

यस्य सवितुर्देवस्य व्रतं प्रसवाख्यं कर्मेन्द्रो न मिनाति। न हिनस्ति। वरुणश्च न मिनाति मित्रश्चार्यमा च न मिनाति रुद्रश्च न मिनाति। अरातयोऽसुराश्च न मिनन्ति। मिनातीति श्रुतमाख्यातं यथायोगं विपरिणामेन प्रत्येकमभि-संबध्यते। तं सवितारं सर्वस्य प्रेरकं देवं द्योतमानमिदमिदानीं नमोभिरन्न-रूपैर्हविर्भिः सह। नम आयुः (नि० २-८) इत्यत्रनामसु पाठात्। स्वस्ति क्षेमाय हुवे। स्तौमि॥

स्व॒स्ति acc. n., with a dative sense and a concrete meaning, welfare.

Read यस्य॑ इन्द्रो॑ and न अरा॑तयस्.

Verse 10.

भग॑म्। धिय॑म्। वा॒जय॑न्तः। पुर॑ऽधिम्। नरा॒शंस॑ः। ग्राःपति॑ः। नः। अ॒व्याः। आ॒ऽअ॒ये। वा॒मस्य॑। सं॒ऽग॒थे। र॒यी॒णाम्। प्रि॒याः। दे॒वस्य॑। स॒वि॒तुः। स्या॒म॒॥१०॥

भगं भजनीयं धियं ध्यातव्यं पुरंधिं पुरस्य धारयितारं बहुप्रज्ञं वा सवितारम्। पुरंधिर्बहुधिः (नि० ४-३) इति यास्कः। वाजयन्तः वाजिनं

बलिनं *कुर्वन्तः। विभक्तिव्यत्ययः। नः स्तुवतोऽस्मान् नराशंसो नरैः शंसनीयो †ग्नाःपतिर्देवपत्नीनां पतिश्छन्दसां पतिर्वा। तथा च श्रुयते। छन्दांसि वै ग्ना इति उत ग्ना व्यन्तु देवपत्नी (ऋ. ५-४६-८) इति च। सविताव्याः। अव्यात्। किंच वामस्य धनस्य रयीणां पशूनां च। तथा च श्रूयते। पशवो वै रयिरिति। आय आगमने संगथे संगमने च निमित्ते देवस्य द्योतमानस्य सवितुः प्रेरकस्य वयं प्रियाः स्याम। भवेम।।

पुरंधि f., favour, good fortune, opulence, reward (दक्षिणा).

नराशंस m., genius of sacred speech.

ग्नास्पति m., see Sāy. comm. Read ग्न अस्पति.

The second pāda of the first line is a parenthesis between the first pāda and the second line, which belong together.

Verse 11.

अस्मभ्यम्। तत्। दिवः। अत्ऽभ्यः। पृथिव्याः। त्वया। दत्तम्। काम्यम्। राधः। आ। गात्। शम्। यत्। स्तोतृऽभ्यः। आपये। भवाति। उरुऽशंसाय। सवितः। जरित्रे।।११।।

हे सवितः अस्मभ्यं त्वया दत्तं तत् प्रसिद्धं काम्यं कमनीयं राधो धनं दिवो द्युलोकात् अद्भ्योऽन्तरिक्षलोकात् पृथिव्या भूमेश्चागात्। आगच्छतु। किंच स्तोतृभ्यः स्तोतृणामापये बन्धवे तद्वंशजाय यद्धनं शं सुखकरं भवति भवेत् उरुशंसाय बहुस्तुतये जरित्रे स्तोत्रे मह्यम्। जरिता कारुः (नि० ३-१७) इति स्तोतृनामसु पाठात्। हे सवितः तत्प्रयच्छ।।

NO. 10.

MAṆḌALA III. **SŪKTA 9.**

सखायस्त्वेति नवर्चं नवं सूक्तं वैश्वामित्रम्। अत्रेयमनुक्रमणिका। सखायो नव बार्हतं त्रिष्टुबन्तमिति। अन्त्या त्रिष्टुप्। शिष्टा अष्टौ बृहत्यः। प्रातरनुवाका

* आदर्शे कुर्वत इति पाठः।

† आदर्शे ग्रास्पतिः इति पाठः।

श्विनशस्त्रयोर्बार्हते छन्दस्यस्य सूक्तस्य विनियोगः। अथैतस्या इति खण्डे सूत्रितम्। सखायस्त्वायमग्निरग्र आ याहि (आ० ४-१३) इति।।

Verse 1.

सखायः। त्वा। ववृमहे। देवम्। मर्तासः। ऊतये। अपाम्। नपातम्। सुऽभगम्। सुऽदीदितिम्। सुऽप्रतूर्तिम्। अनेहसम्।।१।।

विश्वमित्रः स्तौति। हे अग्ने सखायः सोमाज्यादिहविष्प्रदानेनोपकारकत्वान्मित्राणि मर्तासो मनुष्या ऋत्विजो वयमपां नपातमपां नप्तारं सुभगं शोभनधनयुक्तं सुदीधितिं शोभनदीप्तिं सुप्रतूर्तिं शोभनप्रतरणं कर्मानुष्ठातृभिः सुखेन गन्तव्यमनेहसमुपद्रवरहितमेतादृशं देपं त्वामूतये रक्षणाय ववृमहे। वृणीमहे। सखायः। ख्या प्रकथने। समाने ख्यश्चोदात्त इति समान उपपदे डिदित्यनुवृत्तौ ख्यातेरिण्। तस्य डित्त्वाट्टिलोपः। तत्संनियोगेन यलोपः। समानस्य छन्दस्यमूर्द्धेति सभावः। उपपदस्योदात्तत्वम्। णिदित्यनुवृत्तौ सख्युरसंबुद्धौ (पा० ७-१-९२) इति णिद्वद्भावः। वृद्ध्यादेशौ। आद्युदात्तः। ववृमहे। वृङ् संभक्तौ। छन्दसि लुङ्लङ्लिट इति वर्तमाने लिट्। क्रादित्वादिडभावः। निघातः। ऊतये। अव रक्षण इत्यस्य उदात्त इत्यनुवृत्तावूतियूतीत्यादिना क्तिन्नन्तत्वेन निपातनादन्तोदात्तः। अपाम्। ऊडिदमिति विभक्तेरुदात्तत्वम्। सुभगम्। आद्युदात्तं द्व्यच्छन्दसीत्युत्तरपदाद्युदात्तत्वम्। सुप्रतूर्तिम्। क्रत्वादयश्चेत्युत्तरपदाद्युदात्तत्वम्।।

नपात् m., grandson, child, अपां नपात्, a form of Agni.

ववृमहे, pf. ātm.; rt. वृ 9.

अनेहस्, उपद्रवरहित, Sāy. एहस्=क्रोध, Nigh. II. 13.

Verse 2.

कायमानः। वना। त्वम्। यत्। मातृः। अजगन्। अपः। न। तत्। ते। अग्ने। प्रऽमृषे। निऽवर्तनम्। यत्। दूरे। सन्। इह। अभवः।।२।।

हे अग्ने वाना काननानि *रक्षितुं कायमानः कामयमानस्त्वं यद्यस्मात्कारणात्तानि विहाय मातृरपो मातृभूता अपोऽजगत् अगमः। गतवानसि।

* आदर्शे रक्षितुं इति नास्ति।

अप्सु प्रविष्टत्वाच्छान्तो वर्तसे। तत्तस्मात्ते तव निवर्तनम्। नितरां तत्रैव वर्तनम्। तेन च विनाशो लक्ष्यते। स विनाशो न प्रमृषे। न सह्यते। कुत इत्यत आह। यद्यस्मात्कारणाद्दूरे सन् अदृश्यतया वर्तमानस्त्वमिहास्मत्संबन्धिष्वरणिरूपेषु काष्ठेष्वभवः मन्थनात् क्षणमात्रेणास्माकं समीपे भवसि। तस्मात्तव दूरतो वर्तनमस्मभ्यं न रोचते। अस्मिन्नर्थे यास्कः। कायमानश्चायमानः कामयमान (नि० ४-१) इति वा। वनानि त्वं यन्तामृरपोऽगम उपशम्यन्। न तत्ते अग्ने प्रमृष्यते निवर्तनं दूरे यत्सन्निह भवसि जायमानः (नि० ४-१४) इति। कायमानः। कमु कान्तौ। कमेर्णिङ्। लटः शानच्। मकारलोपश्छान्दसः। अजगन्। गम्लृ गतावित्यस्य लङि बहुलं छन्दसीति शपः श्लुः। हल्ङ्यादिना सिलोपः। मो नो धातोरिति नकारः। यच्छब्दयोगादनिघातः। अडागमस्वरः। प्रमृषे। मृष तितिक्षायाम्। व्यत्ययेन कर्मणि तप्रत्ययः। लोपस्त आत्मनेपदेष्विति तलोपः। धातुस्वरः। अभवः। छन्दसि लुङ्लङ्लिट इति लडर्थे लङ् यद्योगादनिघातः।।

अजगन्, 2.3. sg. aor.; rt. गम्.

काय् ātm. = चाय्, to descry, see Nir. IV. 14.

मृष् 6., to touch, प्र मृष्, to forget, slight, मृषे, inf. dat.

The situation in which the hymn seems to have been composed may give a clue for the understanding of this ṛc. The person entrusted with the kindling of the sacrificial wood finds the process laborious. An explanation why the fire comes so slowly is given by the old, well-known myth that Agni had taken refuge, and stops, in the water—according to ṚV. X. 51 out of fear of the great exertion awaiting him at the sacrifice. Now he is besought not to act as he did that time and is reminded that he has been इह, in the wood and at the sacrifice, before.

Verse 3.

अति। तृष्टम्। ववक्षिथ। अथ। एव। सुऽमनाः। असि। प्रऽप्र। अन्ये। यन्ति। परि। अन्ये। आसते। येषाम्। सख्ये। असि। श्रितः।।३।।

हे अग्ने तृष्टं स्तोतुस्तृष्णाभिलाषं तदुचितफलप्रदानेन सफलं कर्तुमतिववक्षिथ। अतिशयेन वोढुमिच्छसि। अथैव अथापि त्वं सुमना असि। संतुष्टमनस्को वर्तसे। किंच। त्वं येषां षोडशानामृत्विजां सख्ये मैत्रे श्रितोऽसि वर्तसे तेषां मध्येऽन्येऽध्वर्युप्रभृतयो द्वादशर्त्विजः प्रयन्ति। प्रकर्षेण होतुं गच्छन्ति। अन्ये उद्गदातृप्रभृतयश्चत्वारः। पर्यासते। परित आसीना वर्तन्ते। ववक्षिथ। वह प्रापण इत्यस्य सनि रूपम्। अभ्यासस्य सन्यन इतीत्वाभावश्छान्दसः। तदन्ताद्वर्तमाने लिट्। थल आर्द्धधातुकस्येड्वलादेरितीट्। कास्प्रत्ययादामित्याम् न भवति मन्त्रत्वात्। निघातः। प्रप्र। प्रसमुपोद इति द्विर्वचनम्। यन्ति। इण् गतावित्यस्य लटि रूपम्। एकान्याभ्यां समर्थाभ्यामित्यन्यशब्दयोगात्पूर्वस्य निघाताभावः। आसते। आस उपवेशने। उत्तरत्वान्निघातः। असि। अस् भुवि। तासस्त्योर्लोप इति तकारलोपः। यद्वृत्तयोगान्न निहन्यते।।

व॒व॒क्षि॒थ॒, pf. par. rt. वक्ष्, उक्ष्, to increase; अति वक्ष्, to overcome.

तृष्ट, poisonous, obnoxious (Sāy. comm. AV.; here he explains it with तृष्णा), a rakṣasa preventing the flaming up of Agni.

Verse 4.

ई॒यि॒ऽवांस॑म्। अति॑। स्रिधः॑। शश्व॑तीः। अति॑। स॒श्चतः॑। अनु॑। ई॒म्। अ॒वि॒न्द॒न्। नि॒ऽचि॒रासः॑। अ॒द्रुहः॑। अ॒प्ऽसु। सिं॒हम्ऽइ॑व। श्रि॒तम्।।४।।

हे अग्ने अद्रुहोऽद्रोग्धारो निचिरासो नितरां चिरासश्चिरतना विश्वेदेवाः स्रिधः शोषकाञ्छत्रून्बलेनातिक्रम्येयिवांसं गच्छन्तं शश्वतीर्बह्वीः सश्चतः संगतिकारिणिः सेनाश्चात्यतिक्रम्य गच्छन्तं अप्सु श्रितं तिरोहितमत एव सिंहमिव गुहाप्रविष्टं सिंहमिव भीममीमेनं त्वामन्वविन्दन्। अनुगम्यालभन्त। ईयिवांसम्। इण् गतावित्यस्य क्वसावुपेयिवाननाश्वाननूचानश्च (पा० ३-२-१०९) इति निपातितः। प्रत्ययस्वरः। स्रिधः। स्रिधेः क्षयार्थस्य शोषणार्थस्य वा क्विप् चेति क्विप्। धातुस्वरः। सश्चतः। षस्ज गतौ। जकारस्य व्यत्ययेन चकारः। लटः शत्रादेशः प्रत्ययस्वरः। अविन्दन् विद्लृ लाभ इत्यस्य लङि रूपम्। निचिरासः। नितरां चिराः। आज्जसेरसुगित्यसुक्। समासस्वरः। अद्रुहः। द्रुह

जिघांसायाम्। संपदादित्वाद्भावे क्विप्। बहुव्रीहौ नञ्सुभ्यामित्युत्तरपदान्तोदात्तत्वम्। श्रितम्। श्रिञ् सेवायामित्यस्य श्रयुकः कितीतीट्प्रतिषेधः। प्रत्ययस्वरः।।

स्रिध् f., obstacle, failure.

निचिर (rt.चि) adj., attentive, watchful.

सश्चत् (सश्च्, to obstruct) f., danger, difficulty.

Ṛcas 4-6 treat once more of Agni's flight into the waters.

Verse 5.

ससृवांसंऽइव। त्मना। अग्निम्। इत्था। तिरःऽहितम्। आ। एनम्। नयत्। मातरिश्वा। पराऽवतः। देवेभ्यः। मथितम्। परि।।५।।

मातरिश्वा वायुरित्थेत्थं त्मना स्वेच्छयाप्सु प्रवेशेन तिरोहितं निलीनं परि परितो मथितं मन्थनेन निष्पादितमेनमग्निं देवेभ्यः। तादर्थ्ये चतुर्थी। देवार्थं परावतो दूरदेशादानयत्। आनीतवान्। तत्र दृष्टान्तः ससृवांसमिव। यथा स्वाच्छन्द्येन ससृवांसं सरन्तं गच्छन्तं पुत्रं पिता बलादानयति तद्वत्। ससृवांसमिव। सृ गत वित्यस्माल्लिट्। तस्य क्वसुः। इवेन विभक्त्यलोप इत्युक्तत्वात्प्रत्ययस्वरः। त्मना। आत्मन्शब्दस्य मन्त्रेष्वाङ्यादेरात्मन इत्याकारलोपः। इत्था। था हेतौ च छन्दसीति व्यत्ययेन थाप्रत्ययः। प्रत्ययस्वरः। एनम्। अन्वादेशे द्वितीयाटौस्वेन इत्येनादेशः। अनुदात्तश्च। नयत्। णीञ् प्रापण इत्यस्य लङि रूपम्। अडभावश्छान्दसः। मातरिश्वा मातर्यन्तरिक्षे श्वन्नुक्षन्नित्यादिना निपातितः।।

इत्था, thus. (आ)त्मना, own his on initiative, at his will.

परि देवेभ्यो, away from the gods, corresponding to परावतो.

Verse 6.

तम्। त्वा। मर्ताः। अगृभ्णत। देवेभ्यः। हव्यऽवाहन। विश्वान्। यत्। यज्ञान्। अभिऽपासि। मानुष। तव। क्रत्वा। यविष्ठ्य।।६।।

हे हव्यवाहन हव्यानां वोढर्हे अग्ने मर्ता मनुष्या अध्वर्युप्रभृतयस्तं तादृशमप्सु तिरोहितं त्वा त्वां देवेभ्यो यष्टव्यदेवतार्थमगृभ्णत्। अगृह्णत। मानुष मनुष्याणां हितकारिन्यविष्ठ्य युवतम हे अग्ने तव कत्वा *कर्मणा

* तव कर्मणा इत्यादर्शः।

माहात्म्येन विश्वान्सर्वानस्माभिः क्रियमाणान् यज्ञान् यद् यस्मात्कारणादभिपासि सर्वतः पालयसि तस्मात्त्वामगृह्णतेति† पूर्वत्रान्वयः। अगृम्णत। ग्रह उपादाने। क्र्यादित्वाच्छ्ना। ग्रहिज्यावयीति संप्रसारणम्। हृग्रहोर्भश्छन्दसीति हकारस्य भकारः। तिङ्ङतिङ इति निघातः। हव्यवाहन। वह प्रापण इति धातो-र्ञ्युडित्यनुवृत्तौ हव्येऽनन्तः पादमिति ञ्युट्। उपधावृद्धिः। योरनादेशः। अपादादित्वादाष्टमिकमनुदात्तत्वम्। विश्वान्। विश प्रवेशन इत्यस्मादशि-प्रुषिलटिरणिकणिखटिबिशिभ्यः क्वन्निति क्वन्। कित्त्वाद्गुणाभावः। नित्त्वादा-द्युदात्तत्वम्। अभिपासि। पा रक्षणे। अस्य धातो रक्षणार्थत्वान्न पिबादेशः। यच्छब्दयोगान्न निघातः धातुस्वरः। ऋत्वा। टा। जसादयश्छन्दसि विकल्प्यन्त इत्यत्र नादेशाभावः। यणादेशः। प्रत्ययस्वरः। यविष्ठ्य युवशब्दादतिशायने तमबिष्ठनावितीष्ठन्। स्थूलदूरयुवेति यणदिपरं लुप्यते पूर्वस्य च गुणः। वस्वादित्वात्स्वार्थिको यप्रत्ययः।।

दे॒वेभ्यो॑, to judge from parallel passages, better dat., depending on ह॒व्य॒वा॒ह॒न॒, than abl., dependent on अ॒गृ॒भ्ण॒त॒.

Verse 7.

तत्। भ॒द्रम्। तव॑। दं॒सना॑। पाका॑य। चि॒त्। छ॒द॒य॒ति॒। त्वाम्। यत्। अ॒ग्ने॒। प॒शव॑ः। संऽआस॑ते। संऽइ॑द्धम्। अ॒पि॒ऽश॒र्व॒रे।।७।।

हे अग्ने तव संबन्धित तदिदं भद्रं शोभनं दंसना अग्निहोत्रादिकं कर्म पाकाय चित्। चिच्छब्दोऽप्यर्थे। पाकायेति कर्मणि चतुर्थी। पाकोऽर्भकः। तद्वदज्ञमपि यजमानं छदयति। स्वफलप्रदानेन पूजयति। पशुपुत्रादिभिः परिवृतं करोतीत्यर्थः छदयतिशब्दोऽर्चतिकर्मा। छन्दयति छदयति (नि० ३-१४) इति तन्नामसु पाठात्। यद्वा। पाकशब्दः प्रशस्यं वक्ति। पाको वाम (नि० ३-८) इति प्रशस्यनामसु पठितत्वात्। तद्भद्रं प्रशस्यं यजमानमभि-मतफलप्रदानेन पूजयतीत्यर्थः। यद्यस्मात्कारणादपिशर्वरे शर्वरीमुखेऽग्नि-विहरणकाल एव *यत् यं समिद्धं दीप्यमानं त्वां पशवो द्विपदाश्चतुष्पदाश्चोभये पशवः समासते। सम्यगासते। पर्युपासन इत्यर्थः। तदिदं पश्वादिलक्षणं फलं

† मगृभ्णत इत्यादर्शः।

* आदर्शे यत् यं इति नास्ति।

यजमानाय प्रयच्छतीत्यर्थः'। भद्रम्। भदि कल्याण इत्यस्माद्धातोरुपरि रक्प्रत्ययेन निपातनादन्तोदात्तत्वम्। पाकाय। पा रक्षण इत्यस्मादिण्भी-कापाशलेत्यादिना कन्। पायते रक्ष्यते राजादिनेति पाकः। नित्त्वादाद्युदात्तः। छदयति। छद अपवारणे। स्वार्थे णिच् अदन्तत्वाद्वृद्ध्यभावः। निघातः। समासते। आस उपवेशने। अदादित्वाच्छपो लुक्। अनकारान्तत्वाज्झस्यादादेशः। यद्योगादनिघातः तिङि चोदात्तवतीति गतेर्निघातः। धातुस्वरः।।

छद् 2. 10. (छदय U.), be clear, to appear to be.

भद्र n., kindness.

दंसना f., art. wonderful power, wonder.

पाक=अर्भक, "baby", simple, simpleton.

अपिशर्वरी, beginning of night, night-time.

Verse 8.

आ। जुहोत। सुऽअध्वरम्। शीरम्। पावकऽशोचिषम्। आशुम्। दूतम्। अजिरम्। त्नम्। ईड्यम्। श्रुष्टी। देवम्। सपर्यत।।८।।

ऋत्विजो यजमानः प्रेरयति। हे ऋत्विजः पावकशोचिषं शोधकदीप्तिं शरीरं काष्ठेष्वोषधीषु चानुशायिनं स्वध्वरं शोभनयज्ञोपेतमिमग्निमाजुहोत। आहुतिभिरासमन्तात्तर्पय। अपि च। आशुं कर्मणि व्याप्तं दूतमाह्वनकारित्वेन देवानां दूतमजिरं क्षिप्रं गन्तारं प्रत्नं पुरातनमीड्यं स्तोतव्यं देवं द्योतमानमिमग्निं श्रुष्टी सपर्यत। श्रुष्टीति क्षिप्रनाम (नि० ४-३) इति यास्कः। क्षिप्रं पूजयत। जुहोत। हु दानादनयोः। अस्माद्धातोर्लोट्। जुहोत्यादिभ्यः श्लुरिति शपः श्लुः। श्लाविति द्विर्वचनम्। लोटो लङ्वदिति लङ्वद्भावे तस्थस्थमिपामिति थस्य तादेशः। छन्दसीत्यनुवृत्तौ तस्य तप्तनप्तनथनाश्चेति तबादेशः पित्त्वादुद्गणः निघातः। स्वध्वरम्। बहुव्रीहौ नञ्सुभ्यामित्युत्तरपदान्तोदात्तत्वम्। शीरम्। शीङ् स्वप्ने। अस्माद्धातोः स्फायितञ्चिवञ्चीत्यादिना रक्प्रत्ययः। कित्त्वाद्गुणाभावः। प्रत्ययस्वरः। पावकशोचिषमित्यत्र पवनं पावः शुद्धिः। तं काहतीति पावकः। आतोऽनुपसर्गे कः। प्रत्ययस्वरः। बहुव्रीहौ प्रकृत्या पूर्वपदमिति पूर्वपदप्रकृतिस्वरत्वम्। आशुम्। अशू व्याप्तौ। अस्माद्धातोः

कृवापाजिमीत्यादिना उण्। उपधावृद्धिः। प्रत्ययस्वरः। अजिरम्। अज् गतिक्षेपणयोरित्यस्माद्धातोरजिरशिशिरशिथिलेति किरच्। प्रत्ययान्तत्वेन निपातनादन्तोदात्तत्वम्। प्रत्नम्। प्रगस्य छन्दसि गलोपश्च (पा० ४-३-२३-२) इति। गलोपः। चकारात् त्नप्रत्ययः। प्रत्ययस्वरः। ईड्यम्। ईड स्तुतौ। अस्माण्ण्यत्। ईड वन्देत्यादिनाद्युदात्तत्वम्। सपर्यत। सपरशब्दात्कण्ड्वादिभ्यो यक् पूजायां वर्तते। लोण्मध्यमपुरुषबहुवचनम्। शप्। अतो गुण इति पूर्वरूपत्वम्। निघातः।।

शीर (शीर्, to boil), adj., hot, glowing.

सपर्य denom., to worship, do homage, serve.

श्रुष्टी instr. sg., readily, obediently.

Verse 9.

त्रीणि। शता। त्री। सहस्राणि। अग्निम्। त्रिंशत्। च। देवाः। नव। च। असपर्यन्। औक्षन्। घृतैः। अस्तृणन्। बर्हिः। अस्मै। आत्। इत्। होतारम्। नि। असादयन्त।।९।।

त्रीणि शता त्रीणि शतानि त्री सहस्राणि त्रीणि सहस्राणि त्रिंशच्च नव चैकोनचत्वारिंशदधिकशतत्रयोपेतत्रिसहस्रसंख्याका देवा इममग्निमसपर्यन्। अपूजयन् किंच ते देवा घृतैरिममग्निमौक्षन्। असिंचन्। तथास्मा अग्नये तदर्थं बर्हिरस्तृणन्। बर्हिषास्तरणं वेद्याच्छादनमकुर्वन्। आदिदनन्तरमेव ते देवास्तस्मिन्बर्हिष्येनमग्निं होतारं कृत्वा न्यसादयन्त। उपावेशयन्। देवैः पूज्यमिममग्निं सपर्यतेति पूर्वेणान्वयः। देवसंख्या च बृहदारण्यकेऽभिहिता। महिमान एवैषामेते त्रयस्त्रिंशत्त्वेव देवा इति। कतमे ते त्रयस्त्रिंशदष्टौ वसव एकादश रुद्रा द्वादशादित्यास्त एकत्रिंशदिन्द्रश्चैव प्रजापतिश्च त्रयस्त्रिंशे (बृ० आ० ३-९) इति। शता। दशानां दशतां शभावस्तश्च प्रत्ययः। दश दशतः परिमाणमेषां शतानि। सुपां सुलुगित्यादिना सुपो डादेशः। प्रत्ययस्वरः। त्री। सुपां सुलुगिति पूर्वसवर्णदीर्घः। फिट्स्वरः। सहस्राणि। कर्दमादित्वान्मध्योदात्तः। त्रिंशत्। त्रयाणां दशतां त्रिन्भावः शच्च प्रत्ययः। त्रयोदशतः परिमाणमस्य त्रिंशत्। प्रत्ययस्वरः। नव। कनिन्नित्यनुवृत्तौ णु स्तुतावित्यस्माद्धातोर्णुदंशोर्नुदश्चेति कनिन्। गुणश्च। नित्वादाद्युदात्तः। असपर्यन्। लङ्

रूपम्। निघातः। औक्षन्। उक्ष सेचने। *लङि आडजादीनामित्याडागमः। वृद्धिः। पादादित्वान्न निहन्यते। आगमस्वरः। अस्तृणन्। स्तृञ् आच्छादने। लङ् बहुवचने त्र्यादित्वाच्श्न। झोरन्तादेशः नित्यं ङित इतीकारलोपः। संयोगान्तलोपः। श्नाभ्यस्तयोरात इत्याकारलोपः। लुङ्लङ्लृङ्क्ष्वित्यडागमः। स चोदात्तः। आगमस्वरः। वाक्येत्यनुवृत्तौ चादित्वान्निघाताभावः। बर्हिः। इसिरित्यनुवृत्तौ बृंहेर्नलोपश्चेतीसिः। तत्संनियोगेन नलोपः। प्रत्ययस्वरः। असादयन्त। षद्लृ विशरणगत्यवसादनेषु। अस्माद्धेतुमति चेति णिच्। उपधा-वृद्धिः। णिचश्चेत्यात्मनेपदम्। लङि बहुवचने रूपम्। निघातः॥

NO.11.

MAṆḌALA III. **SŪKTA 32.**

इन्द्र सोमं सोमपत इति सप्तदशर्चं तृतीयं सूक्तं वैश्वामित्रं त्रैष्टुभमैन्द्रम्। अनुक्रान्तं च। इन्द्र सोमं त्र्यूनेति। पृष्ठ्यभिप्लवषडहयोर्द्वितीयेऽहनि मरुत्वतीय इन्द्र सोममितीदं सूक्तं निविद्धानीयम्। द्वितीयस्येति खण्डे सूचितम्। इन्द्र सोमं या त ऊतिरवमेति मध्यंदिनः (आ० ७-६) इति। गोसवविवधयोरपि मरुत्वतीयशस्त्र एतत्सूक्तम्। सूत्रितं च। इन्द्र सोममेतायामेति मध्यंदिनः (आ० ९-८) इति। उद्भिद्बलभिदोरपि मरुत्वतीय एतत्सूक्तम्। सूत्रितं च। इन्द्र सोममिन्द्रः पूर्भिदिति मध्यंदिनः (आ० ९-८) इति॥

Verse 1.

इन्द्र॑। सोम॑म्। सो॒म॒ऽप॒ते॒। पिब॑ इ॒म्। माध्यं॑दिनम्। सव॑नम्। चारु॑। यत्। ते॒। प्र॒ऽप्रुथ्य॑। शिप्रे॒ इति॑। म॒घ॒ऽव॒न्। ऋ॒जी॒षि॒न्। वि॒ऽमुच्य॑। हरी॒ इति॑। इ॒ह। मा॒द॒य॒स्व॒॥१॥

विश्वामित्रो ब्रूते। सोमपते सोमस्याधिपते हे इन्द्र इममस्माभिर्माध्यंदिने सवने क्रियमाणं सोमं सोमरसं पिब। यद्यस्मात्ते त्वदर्थं क्रियमाणं माध्यंदिनं मध्यदिनसंबन्धि सवनं निष्केवल्याख्यं शस्त्रं चापरू रमणीयं वर्तते। मघवन् धनवन् ऋजीषिन्। ऋजीषशब्देन गतसारं सोमद्रव्यमुच्यते। तद्वन् हे इन्द्र हरी रथे योजितावश्वौ रथाद्विमुच्य शिप्रे हनू प्रप्रुथ्यात्रत्येन ग्रासेन पूरयित्वेह देवयजनदेशे मादयस्व। ता अश्वौ हर्षय। प्रप्रुथ्य। प्रोथृ पर्याप्तावित्यस्यल्यपि

* आदर्शे लङि इति नास्ति।

रूपम्। ह्रस्वश्छान्दसः। लित्स्वरः। ऋजीषिन्। अर्ज षर्ज अर्जन इत्यस्मादर्जेश्च ऋजि च (उ० ४-२८) इतीषन्प्रत्यय ऋजि इत्यादेशश्च धातोः। अर्ज्यत इत्यृजीषम्। तदस्यास्तीतीनिप्रत्ययः। आमन्त्रितत्वान्निघातः। मादयस्व। मदि स्तुत्यादिषु हेतुमण्णिच्। निघातः।।

प्रु 1., to breath; प पु, to breath heavily, to blow.

शिप्र n., lip, moustache.

ऋजीषिन् adj., drinking the soma down to the rest; he whose are the sprouts (Hillebrandt, Lieder des Ṛ.V., p. 41.

पिब may, against the rule, be accented to emphasize the request.—The Ṛ.V. does not tell enough about Indra's personal habits to enable us to say whether शिप्रे here is to mean lips or moustache, and to decide whether our ṛc speaks of Indra's blowing the soma out of his moustache or of smacking his lips either in anticipation of, or after, the draught.

Verse 2.

गोऽआशिरम्। मन्थिनम्। इन्द्र। शुक्रम्। पिब। सोमम्। ररिम। ते। मदाय। ब्रह्मऽकृता। मारुतेन। गणेन। सऽजोषाः। रुद्रैः। तृपत्। आ। वृषस्व।।२।।

हे इन्द्र गवाशिरं गव्यस्य पयस आशीर्मिश्रणं यस्मिन् तं सोमम्। अपि च मन्थिनं मन्थसंयुक्तं शुक्रमभिनवं यद्वा शुक्रामन्थिग्रहे वर्तमानम्। एवं त्रिषु सवनेषु वर्तमानमिमं सोमं पिब। ते तव मदाय हर्षाय ररिम्। तं सोमं वयं प्रयच्छामः। मारुतेन। मरुतां गणो मारुतः। स च ब्रह्मकृत्। ब्रह्म स्तोत्रं करोतीति ब्रह्मकृत्। इन्द्रस्तोत्रं कुर्वाणेन मारुतेन गणेन रुद्रैरेकादशसंख्याकै रुद्रैश्च सजोषाः संगतस्त्वं तृपत सोमपानेन तृप्यन् आ वृषस्व। तमिमं सर्वतो जठरे सिञ्च। धारय। गवाशिरम्। श्रीणातेराङ्पूर्वात्क्विप्यपस्पृधेथामानृचुरित्यादिना निपवातनादशिरादेशः। बहुव्रीहौ पूर्वपदप्रकृतिस्वरः। पिबा। ब्यचोऽतस्तिङ इति संहितायां दीर्घः। ररिम्। रातेश्छान्दसे वर्तमाने लिटि रूपम्। असमान-वाक्यत्वान्निघाताभावः। आगमा अनुदात्ता इतीटोऽनुदात्तत्वात्प्रत्ययस्वरः। तृपत।

तृप प्रीणने। तुदादिः। आगमानुशासनस्यानित्यत्वान्नुमभावः। वृषस्व। वृषु सेचने। व्यत्ययेन शः।

रा 3., pf. ररिम, to give, to offer (up) as a sacrifice.

आ वृष् 1., par., to rain on; ātm., to rain on, or into, oneself, to drink heavily.

सजोषस् (nom. sg. सजोषाः), united, together with.

गवाशीर्, mixed with milk. मन्थिन्, soma mixed with flour.

तृपत् adv., satisfied.

Verse 3.

ये। ते। शुष्मम्। ये। तविषीम्। अवर्धन्। अर्चन्तः। इन्द्र। मरुतः। ते। ओजः। माध्यन्दिने। सवने। वज्रऽहस्त। पिब। रुद्रेभिः। सऽगणः। सुऽशिप्र।।३।।

हे इन्द्र ये मरुस्ते तव शुष्मं शत्रूणां शोषकं तेजो ये च मरुतस्तविषीं बलं चावर्धन् युद्धसहकारितयावर्धयन् ते मरुतोऽर्चन्तस्त्वां स्तुवन्तः सन्तः ते तवौजो युद्धसामर्थ्यमवर्धयन्। वज्रहस्त वज्रयुक्तौ हस्तौ यस्येति तादृश। सुशिप्रशोभनहनो। शिप्रे हनू नासिके वा (नि० ४-१) इति यास्कः। हे इन्द्र रुद्रेभिः। रोदयन्ति शत्रूनिति रुद्रा मरुतः। तैः सगणस्त्वं माध्यंदिने सवने सोमं पिब। अवर्धन्। वृधु वर्धने। अन्तर्भावितण्यर्थः। यद्वृत्तयोगादनिघातः। माध्यन्दिने। उत्सादित्वादञ्। ञित्वादाद्युदात्तः।

The Rudras in pāda 4 are the Maruts.

Verse 4.

ते। इत्। नु। अस्य। मधुऽमत्। विविप्रे। इन्द्रस्य। शर्धः। मरुतः। ये। आसन्। येभिः। वृत्रस्य इषितः। विवेद। अमर्मणः। मन्यमानस्य। मर्म।।४।।

ये मरुत इन्द्रस्य शर्धे बलभूता आसन् त इत् त एव मरुतोऽस्य। द्वितीयार्थे षष्ठी। इममिन्द्रं मधुमत्। तव सहाया वयमास्महे त्वं युद्धमभिगच्छेति

माधुर्योपेतं वाक्यं यथा भवति तथा विविप्रे नु। क्षिप्रं प्रैरयन्। येमिर्यैर्युद्ध-सहायैर्मरुद्भिरिषितः प्रेरित इन्द्रोऽमर्मणः परैरविदितमर्मस्थानस्यात एव मन्य-मानस्य न कोऽपि ममहन्तेत्यमिमन्यमानस्य वृत्रस्यासुरस्य मर्म यस्मिन् स्थाने प्रहृतौ सत्यां स मरिष्यति तादृशं स्थानं विवेद। अज्ञासीत्। विविप्रे। विप क्षेपण इत्यस्य लिटि व्यत्ययेनात्मनेपदम्। इरेच इरयो र इति रे इत्यादेशः। निघातः। आसन्। अस भुवीत्यस्य लङि रूपम्। यद्वृत्तयोगान्निघाताभावः। विवेद। विद ज्ञान इत्यस्य लिटि रूपम्। लित्स्वरः। मर्म। मृङ् प्राणत्याग इत्यस्मादौणादिको मनिन्। नित्स्वरः।।

विप् ātm., to incite, encourage, to get inspired.

विवेद, rt. विद् 6. U., to find out.

मधुमत् n., the honey-drink, here acc. sg. depending on विप्.

शर्ध॑ः n., troup, guard.

मर्म॑न् n., vulnerable or weak spot, weak part.

Verse 5.

म॒नु॒ष्वत्। इ॒न्द्र॒। सव॑नम्। जु॒षा॒णः। पिब॒। सोम॑म्। शश्व॑ते। वी॒र्या॑य। सः। आ। व॒वृ॒त्स्व॒। ह॒रि॒ऽअ॒श्व। य॒ज्ञैः। स॒र॒ण्युऽभि॑ः। अ॒पः। अर्णा॑। सि॒स॒र्षि॒।।५।।

हे इन्द्र मनुष्वत्। मनोर्यज्ञमिव ममेदं सवनं यज्ञं जुषाणः सेवमानस्त्वं शश्वते शाश्वताय वीर्याय परपरिभवलक्षणाय सामर्थ्यायेमं सोमं पिब। हे हर्यश्व स तादृशस्त्वं यज्ञैर्यजनीयैर्मरुद्भिः साकमाववृत्स्व। आगच्छ। किंच सरण्युभिरेकश्रुतिमन्मन्त्रानात्मन इच्छद्भिः यद्वा सरण्युभिः सरणशीलैर्मरुद्भिः सहितस्त्वमपोऽन्तरिक्षस्थितान्युदकानि अर्णा पार्थिवान्युदकानि सिसर्षि। प्रापय यद्वा अपः। पञ्चम्यन्तमेतत्पदम्। अपो व्याप्तादन्तरिक्षात्सकशादर्णांसि प्रापय। ववृत्स्व। वृतु वर्तने। व्यत्ययेन शपः श्लुः। लोटि रूपम्। सरण्युभिः। रण शब्दार्थः। क्विप्। समानो रणो ध्वनिर्येषां ते सरणा मन्त्राः। तानिच्छन्तः। सुपः क्यच्। क्यादित्युप्रत्ययः। यद्वा सृ गतौ। सृयुवचिभ्योन्युजागूजक्नुचः

(उ० ३-८१) इत्यन्युच्प्रत्ययः। रषाभ्याम्० (पा० ८-४-४) इति णत्वम्। चित्त्वादन्तोदात्तः। अपः। आप्लृ व्याप्तौ। आप्नोतेः क्विप् ह्रस्वश्चेति क्विप् धातोर्ह्रस्वश्च। सावेकाच इति विभक्तेरुदात्तत्वम्। सिसर्षि। सृ गतौ। छान्दसो जुहोत्यादिः। बहुलं छन्दसीत्यभ्यासस्येत्वम्।।

सरण्यु adj., quick, hurried. अर्ण n., stream.

Verse 6.

त्वम्। अपः। यत्। ह। वृत्रम्। जघन्वान्। अत्यान्ऽइव। प्र। असृजः। सर्तवै। आजौ। शयानम्। इन्द्र। चरता। वधेन। वव्रिऽवांसम्। परि। देवीः। अदेवम्।।६।।

हे इन्द्र त्वं देवीर्देवनशीला अपः परि वव्रिवांसं परित आवृत्य वर्तमानमत एव अदेवं बहूदकतया स्वच्छत्वेनाप्रतिभासमानं शयानमेकत्र निश्चलतया वर्तमानं वृत्रं मेघं यद्यदा चरतातमुद्दिश्य वर्तमानेन वधेन युद्धेन जघन्वान् हतवानसि तदा त्वमाजौ युद्ध सर्तवै अतिवेगगमनायात्यानिव यथाश्वान् प्रेरयसि तथा त्वमप उदकान्यन्तरिक्षादाकाशात् प्रासृजो ह। प्रकर्षेण मेघभेदनं कृत्वा असृजः खलु। तं यजाम इत्युत्तरेणान्वयः। जघन्वान्। हन हिंसा-गत्योरित्यस्य क्वसौ विभाषा गमहनविदविशामितीटो विकल्पितत्वादत्रेडभावः। अभ्यासाच्चेति हकारस्य घत्वम्। प्रत्ययस्वरः। असृजः। सृज विसर्गे। शविकरणी। यद्योगादनिघातः। सर्तवै। सृ गतौ। तुमर्थे तवैप्रत्ययः। अन्तश्च तवै युगपदिति धातोः प्रत्ययस्य चोदात्तत्वम्। आजौ। अज गतिक्षेपणयोः। अज्यतिभ्यां च (उ० ४-१३०) इति इण्प्रत्ययः। णित्त्वादुपधावृद्धिः। अजन्ति गच्छन्त्यस्मिन्नित्याजिर्युद्धम्। प्रत्ययस्वरः। सर्तवाजावित्यत्र संहितायामायादेशे कृते तस्य लोपः शाकल्यस्येति यकारलोपः। सर्वविधीनां छन्दसि विकल्पितत्वात्सवर्णदीर्घत्वे कर्तव्ये यलोपो नासिद्धो भवति। सवर्णदीर्घः। शयानम् शीङ् स्वप्ने। शानच्। अदादित्वाच्छपो लुक्। ङित्त्वाल्लसार्वधातुकस्वरेण शानचोऽनुदात्तत्वे धातुस्वरः। वधेन। हन्तेर्भावे हनश्च वध इत्यप्प्रत्ययो वधादेशश्च धातोरन्तोदात्तश्च। वव्रिवांसम्। वृञ् वरण इत्यस्य क्वसाविडागमश्छान्दसः। प्रत्ययस्वरः।

The Padapāṭha puts the accent on असृजः, considers therefore प्र असृजः to be the verb of the subordinate clause, the principal clause being either यजामः in ṛc 7 (Sāy.), or the last pāda in ṛc 5. Or we may take यद् to belong to जघन्वान्, which would stand for जगन्थ. Note the saṁdhi and accent of सर्तवाजौ.

Verse 7.

यजामः। इत्। नमसा। वृद्धम्। इन्द्रम्। बृहन्तम्। ऋष्वम्। अजरम्। युवानम्। यस्य। प्रिये इति। ममतुः। यज्ञियस्य। न। रोदसी इति। महिमानम्। ममाते इति॥७॥

नमसा हविर्लक्षणेनान्नेन वृद्धं प्रवृद्धमत एव बृहन्तम् महान्तमृष्वम्। ऋष्यते गम्यते स्तुतिलक्षणैर्मन्त्रैरिति ऋष्वं स्तोतव्यम्। अजरं जरारहितमत एव युवानं नित्यतरुणमेवंविधमिन्द्रं यजाम इत्। कुशिका वयं यज्ञसिद्ध्यर्थं स्तुति वाक्यैः पूजयाम एव*। प्रिये प्रियतमे अपरिमिते रोदसी द्यावापृथिव्यौ यज्ञियस्य यज्ञार्हस्य यस्येन्द्रस्य त व महिमानं वैभवं न ममतुः। न परिच्छेत्तुं शक्नुतः। न ममाते इति द्वितीयं क्रियापदमादरार्थम्। यजामः। यजेर्लटि रूपम्। ऋष्वम्। ऋषि गतौ। सर्वनिघृष्वऋष्वेत्यादिना वप्रत्ययान्तो निपातितः। प्रत्ययस्वरः। प्रिये। ईदूदेदिति प्रगृह्यसंज्ञा। ममतुः। मा मान इत्यस्य लिट्यतुसि रूपम्। यद्वृत्तयोगादनिघातः। प्रत्ययस्वरः। महिमानम्। महिशब्दात्तस्य भाव इत्यर्थे पृथ्वादित्वादिमनिच्। चित्स्वरः। ममाते। माङ् माने शब्दे चेत्यस्य लिट्याताभि रूपम्॥

मा 3., ātm., to measure fully, to encompass, to equal; par., to measure, to examine, to put a measure on.

ऋष्व adj., lofty, erect, exalted.

Verse 8.

इन्द्रस्य। कर्म। सुऽकृता। पुरूणि। व्रतानि। देवाः। न। मिनन्ति।

---

* आदर्शे एव इति नास्ति।

विश्वे॑। दा॒धार॑। यः। पृ॒थि॒वीम्। द्याम्। उ॒त। इ॒माम्। ज॒जान॑। सूर्य॑म्। उ॒षस॑म्। सु॒ऽदंसाः॑॥८॥

विश्वे सर्वे देवा इन्द्रस्य तव कर्म कर्माणि सुकृता सुकृतानि सुष्ठु निर्मितानि पृथिव्यादीनि पुरूणि बहूनि व्रतानि यज्ञादीनि च न मिनन्ति। एतानि सर्वाणि तव कर्माणि न हिंसन्ति। किंत्वाद्रियन्ते। किंच योऽयमिन्द्रः पृथिवीं भूलोकं द्यां द्युलोकमुत अपि चेमामिममन्तरिक्षलोकं च एतांस्त्रीन् लोकान् दाधार। *किंच सुदंसाः सुकर्मा शोभनकर्मा सन्निन्द्रः सूर्यं लोकप्रकाश-कमादित्यम् उषसमग्निहोत्रादिकर्मनिर्वाहकमुषःकालं जजान। उत्पादयामास। इन्द्रस्य कर्म सुकृता पुरूणीत्येतत्पदकदम्बकमेको द्वे वसुमतीत्यस्मिन्वर्गे (ऋ० ३-२-३) पठितम्। अत्रापि तदेव पठ्यते। पदकाले नोत्सृज्यत इति चेन्न। वाक्यभेदात्। तत्रेन्द्रस्य कर्म सुकृता पुरूणीत्येकं वाक्यम्। अत्र तु कर्म सुकृतेत्येकं वाक्यम्। पुरूणि व्रतानीत्यपरम्। किंच तत्रत्यं पदकदम्बकं ग्रथमान्तमत्रत्यं द्वितीयान्तम्। अतो वाक्यभेदाद्विभक्तिभेदाच्च पदकाले नोत्सृज्यते। मिनन्ति। मीञ् हिंसायामित्यस्य लटि रूपम्। निघातः। दाधार। धृञ् धारण इत्यस्य लिटि रूपम्। तुजादित्वादभ्यासस्य दीर्घः। लित्स्वरः। जजान। जन जनन इत्यस्यान्तर्भावितण्यर्थस्य लिटि रूपम्। लित्स्वरः। सुदंसाः। सोर्मनसी इत्युत्तरपदाद्युदात्तत्वम्॥

कर्म॑=कर्माणि.

Verse 9.

अद्रो॑घ। स॒त्यम्। तव॑। तत्। म॒हि॒ऽत्वम्। स॒द्यः। यत्। जा॒तः। अपि॑बः। ह॒। सोम॑म्। न। द्याव॑ः। इ॒न्द्र। त॒वस॒ः। ते॒। ओज॑ः। न। अहा॑। न। मासाः॑। श॒रद॑ः। व॒र॒न्त॒॥९॥

अद्रोघ द्रोहवर्जित हे इन्द्र तव तन्महित्वं तादृशं माहात्म्यं सत्यं यथार्थम्। यद्यस्माज्जात उत्पन्नः सद्यस्तदानीमेव सोममस्माभिर्दीयमानं सोमरसमपिबः। ह प्रसिद्धौ। किंच तवसो बलवतस्ते तवौजः सामर्थ्यं द्यावो दिवोपलक्षिताः सर्वे लोका न वरन्त। न वारयन्ति। किंच। अहा प्रतिपदा-

* आदर्शे किंच इति नास्ति।

दीन्यहानि न वारयन्ति। तथा मासाश्चैत्राद्याः शरदः संवत्सराश्च तव सामर्थ्यं न वारयन्ति। किंतु तव सामर्थ्यमनुसृत्य सर्वे वर्तन्त इति भावः। अद्रोघ। आमन्त्रितस्य चेति षाष्ठिकमाद्युदात्तत्वम्। अपिबः। यद्योगादनिघातः। मासाः। मसी परिमाणे। मस्यते परिमीयते त्रिंशता दिनैरिति मासः। कर्मणि घञ्। ञित्त्वादाद्युदात्तः। शरदः। शॄ हिंसायामित्यस्मात् शॄदॄ सोऽदिरित्यधिकरणेऽदिप्रत्ययः। शीर्यन्तेऽस्यां तृणगुल्मवनस्पतीनां तेजांसीति शरत्। प्रत्ययस्वरः। वरन्त। वृञ् वरणे। अन्तर्भावितण्यर्थोऽत्रातिवारणे वर्तते। भौवादिकः। छान्दसे लङि रूपम्। निघातः॥

तवस् adj., strong; subst. n., strength.

वरन्त, subj. rt. वृ, to check.

दिव्, द्यावः, day (from morning till night).

अहन्, astronomical day from one sunrise to the other, day and night together.

Verse 10.

त्वम्। सद्यः। अपिबः। जातः। इन्द्र। मदाय। सोमम्। परमे। विऽओमन्। यत्। ह। द्यावापृथिवी इति। आ। अविवेशीः। अथ। अभवः। पूर्व्यः। कारुऽधायाः॥१०॥

हे इन्द्र सद्यस्तदानीमेव जातः परमे व्योमन् उत्तमे स्थाने स्थितस्त्वं मदाय हर्षाय सोममपिबः। यत् यदा त्वं द्यावापृथिवी द्यावापृथिव्यौ आविवेशीर्ह। आसमन्ताद्भृशं प्रविष्टोऽसि खलु। अथानन्तरं पूर्व्यः पुरातनः सन् कारुधायाः कर्मणां विधाताभवः खलु। व्योमन्। अव रक्षणगत्यादिषु। विपूर्वस्यावतेर्नामन्सीमन्नित्यादिना मनिन्। ज्वरत्वरेत्यादिना ऊठ्। विशेषेणौम व्याप्तिर्यस्य तत्। सुपां सुलुगित्यादिना सुपो लुक्। बहुव्रीहौ पूर्वपदप्रकृतिस्वरः। आविवेशीः। विश प्रवेशन इत्यस्य यङ्लुकि लङि सिपि यङो वेतीडागमः। इतश्चेति

---

* 'सद्यस्क्रीनाम्न्येकाहे निष्केवल्यशस्त्रे त्वं सद्यो अपिब इति सूक्तमुखीया। सूत्रितं च। त्वं सद्यो अपिबो जात इन्द्रानु त्वा हि घ्ने अध देव देवाः (आ० ९-५) इति।' अयमंश आदर्शे विशेषः।

सिप इकारलोपः। यद्योगादनिघातः। कारुधायाः। कारुः। करोतेः कृवापाजिमिस्वदिसाध्यशूभ्य उणप्रत्ययः। णित्त्वाद्वृद्धिः। दधातेतेर्वहिहाधाञ्भ्यश्छन्दसीत्यसुन्। णिदित्यनुवृत्तेरातो युक् चिण्कृतोरिति युगागमः। समासे गतिकारकयोरपि पूर्वपदप्रकृतिस्वरत्वं चेति सूत्रात्पूर्वपदप्रकृतिस्वरः।।

अविवेशीः, plupf. par. rt. विश् 6.

कारुधायस् (rt. ध्यै), feeding, supporting the poet.

Verse 11.

अहन्। अहिम्। परिऽशयानम्। अर्णः। ओजायमानम्। तुविऽजात। तव्यान्। न। ते। महिऽत्वम्। अनु। भूत्। अध। द्यौः। यत्। अन्यया। स्फिग्या। क्षाम्। अवऽस्थाः।।११।।

तुविजात। बहूनि जातानि पृथिव्यादीनि यस्मात्सोऽयं तुविजातः हे तुविजात इन्द्र तव्यानतिशयेन प्रवृद्धस्त्वमर्णः परिशयानमुदकं परितः शयानमुदकमन्तः कृत्वा परितो वर्तमानमत एवौजायमानं बलमाचरन्तमहिम्। आ समन्ताद्धन्त्यपहरत्युदकमित्यहिर्मेघः। तमिमं मेघमहन्। उदकप्रेरणाय हतवानसि। अध अथ ते महित्वं महिमानं द्यौर्नानुभूत्। नानुभवति। न जानाति। यद्यस्मात्त्वमन्यया एकतरया स्फिग्या कट्या क्षां भूमिमवस्थाः। अवच्छाद्य तिष्ठसि। अहन्। हन्तेर्लङि सिब्लोपे रूपम्। अहिम्। हन हिंसागत्योः। आङि श्रिहनिभ्यां ह्रस्वश्चेति इणप्रत्ययः। डिश्च पूर्वपदस्य ह्रस्वश्च। वृषादित्वादाद्युदात्तत्वम्। ओजायमानम्। ओजःशब्दादाचारार्थे कर्तुः क्यङ् सलोपश्चेति क्यङ्प्रत्ययः सलोपश्च। ङित्त्वादात्मनेपदम्। प्रत्ययस्वरः। तव्यान्। तु इति सौत्रो धातुः। अस्मात्तुजन्तात्तुश्छन्दसीतीयसुन्। तुरिष्ठेमेयःस्विति तृचो लोपः। भसंज्ञायामोर्गुणः। इकारलोपश्छान्दसः। नित्स्वरः। भूत्। भवतेर्लुङि रूपम्। स्फिग्या। यचि भमिति भसंज्ञां बाधित्वा स्वादिष्वसर्वनामस्थान इति पदसंज्ञायां जश्त्वम्। तृतीयायाः पूर्वसवर्णः क्षाम्। क्षि निवासगत्योः। अन्येभ्योऽपि दृश्यत इति निरूपपदादपि डप्रत्ययः। ततष्टाप्। क्षियन्ति निवसन्त्यस्यां प्राणिन इति भूमिः। उदात्तनिवृत्तिस्वरेणान्तोदात्तः। अवस्थाः। वस आच्छादन इत्यस्य लङ्यनुदात्तत्वादात्मनेपदम्। थास्यदादित्वाच्छपो लुक्। यद्योगादनिघातः। अडागमस्वरः।।

स्फिगी f., hip, side. क्षा f., earth.

अवस्थाः 2. sg. impf. ātm; rt. वस् 2., to wear (used in a causative sense).

Verse 12.

यज्ञः। हि। ते। इन्द्र। वर्धनः। भूत्। उत। प्रियः। सुतऽसोमः। मियेधः। यज्ञेन। यज्ञम्। अव। यज्ञियः। सन्। यज्ञः। ते। वज्रम्। अहिऽहत्ये। आवत्।।१२।।

हे इन्द्र अस्मदीयो यज्ञस्ते तव वर्धनो हविष्प्रदानेन वर्धयिता भूद्धि। भवति खलु। उत अपि च सुतसोमः अभिषुतसोमवान्मियेधो यज्ञस्तव प्रियः। स त्वं यज्ञियो यज्ञार्हः सन् यज्ञं यज्ञस्य कर्तारं यजमानं यज्ञेनानुष्ठीयमानेनानेनाव। फलप्रदानेन रक्ष। किंचायं यज्ञस्ते तव वज्रमहिहत्ये वृत्रहनने कर्मणि आवत्। रक्षतु। वर्धनः। वृधु वर्धन इत्यस्य ण्यन्तस्य नन्द्यादित्वात् ल्युप्रत्ययः। लित्स्वरः। भूत्। हियोगादनिघातः। अव। अवतेर्लोटि रूपम्। निघातः। सन्। असेः शतरि रूपम्। प्रत्ययस्वरः। अहिहत्ये। हन हिंसा गत्योरित्यस्य भावे हनस्त चेति क्यप् तकारश्चान्तादेशः। कृदुत्तरपदस्वरः। आवत्। अवतेश्छान्दसे लङि रूपम्। निघातः।।

मियेध (Avesta: *myazda*) m., libation, sacrificial meal; compare मेघ.

Verse 13.

यज्ञेन। इन्द्रम्। अवसा। आ। चक्रे। अर्वाक्। आ। एनम्। सुम्नाय। ववृत्याम्। यः। स्तोमेभिः। ववृधे। पूर्व्येभिः। यः। मध्यमेभिः। उत। नूतनेभिः।।१३।।

हे इन्द्र सर्वो यजमानोऽवसा स्वरक्षकेण यज्ञेनेन्द्रं त्वामर्वागा चक्रे। हविष्प्रदानेनाभिमुखं करोति। तथाहं नव्यसे नवतराय सुम्नाय धनायैनं त्वामा ववृत्याम्। यज्ञेनावृतं मदभिमुखं कुर्याम्। कीदृशस्त्वम्। यः पूर्वेभिः पुरातनैः स्तोमेभिः स्तोत्रैर्ववृधे। तथा य इन्द्रो मध्यमेभिर्मध्ये भवैः स्तोत्रैरुतापि च नूतनेभिरस्माभिः क्रियमाणैरधुनातनैः स्तोत्रैर्वर्धते। चक्रे। करोतेर्लिटि रूपम्।

नव्यसे। नवशब्दादीयसुनि भसंज्ञायामकारलोप ईकारलोपश्छान्दसः। नित्त्वादाद्युदात्तः। ववृत्याम्। वृतु वर्तने। लिङि बहुलं छन्दसीति शपः श्लुः। व्यत्ययेन परस्मैपदम्। निघातः। ववृधे। वृधु वर्धन इत्यस्य लिटि रूपम्। प्रत्ययस्वरः। मध्यमेभिः। मध्यशब्दात् शैषिकार्थे मध्यान्मः (पा० ४-३-८) इति मप्रत्ययः। प्रत्ययस्वरः। नूतनेभिः। नवशब्दस्य त्नप्तनप्खाश्च प्रत्यया वक्तव्या नू इत्यादेशश्चेति तनप्प्रत्ययो नू इत्यादेशश्च।।

ववृत्याम्।, opt. pres. rt. वृत् 3., used with causal meaning.

सुम्न n.=सुखम्.

Verse 14.

विवेष। यत्। मा। धिषणा। जजान। स्तवै। पुरा। पार्यात्। इन्द्रम्। अह्नः। अंहसः। यत्र। पीपरत्। यथा। नः। नावाऽइव। यान्तम्। उभये। हवन्ते।।१४।।

यद्यदा धिषणा इन्द्रं स्तवानीति मदीया बुद्धिर्मां विवेष व्याप्रोत् तदाहं स्तोत्रं जजान। करोमि। बुद्धेः स्वरूपं दर्शयति। अहं पार्यात्पारे भवादतिदूरवर्तिनो विघ्नकारिणोऽह्नः पुरा पूर्वं स्तवै। स्तवानि। यत्र यस्यां धिषणायामेव जातायां सत्यां स इन्द्रो नोऽस्मानंहसः पापरूपाद्दारिद्र्याद्यथा पीपरत् यथा पारं नयेत् तथास्मदुभयपार्श्ववर्तिधनार्थिनो जना हवनते। आह्वयन्ति। तत्र दृष्टान्तः। नावेव यान्तम्। यथा नद्यादिषु नौकया यान्तं गच्छन्तं पुरुषमुभय उभयकूलवर्तिनो जना हवन्ते। आह्वयन्ति। तद्वत्। विवेष। विप्लृ व्याप्तावित्यस्य लिटि णलि रूपम्। लित्स्वरः जजान। जन जनन इत्यस्य लिटयुत्तमे णलि रूपम्। वाक्यभेदादनिधातः। अंहसः। अम गत्यादिषु। अमेर्हुक् च (उ० ४-२१२) इत्यसुन्प्रत्ययो हुगागमश्च। नित्स्वरः पीपरत्। पॄ पालनपूरणयोरित्यस्य लुङि चङि ह्रस्वाभ्यासेत्वदीर्घगुणाः। यथायोगादनिघातः। लित्स्वरः। नावेव। नुद प्रेरणे इत्यस्माद्ग्लानुदिभ्यां डौ (उ० २-६४) इति डौप्रत्ययः। नुद्यत इति नौः पूवः। सावेकाच इति तृतीयाया उदात्तत्वम्। इवेन नित्यसमासो विभक्त्यलोप इत्यादि। उभये। उभशब्दात्परस्य तयप उभादुदात्तो नित्यम् (पा० ५-२-४४) इत्ययजादेशः। वचनसामर्थ्यादादेरुदात्तत्वम्। हवन्ते। ह्वयतेर्लटि रूपम्।।

विष् 3., to fill, penetrate; undertake, accomplish.

पीपरत्, subj. aor. caus.; rt. पृ 3., to pass.

धिषणा f., divine will, power, divine inspiration.

पार्य (पार), adj., the furthest, last, decisive.

जजान in the first pāda cannot be 1. sg. pf. par. (Sāy.) but only 3. sg. The subject to जजान may be स्तोत्रं, hymn, which is not expressly given because it is so intimately connected, if not identical, with धिषणा. The situation supposed by the second line is graphically described by Sāy.

धिषणा in the first pāda is by Hillebrandt, Lieder des Ṛgveda, p. 42, taken to mean earth. He translates the pāda:—He accomplished it that the earth brought me forth.

Verse 15.

माध्यंदिने सवन आग्नीध्रीयस्य आपूर्णो अस्येति प्रस्थितयाज्या। सूत्रितं च। आपूर्णो अस्य कलशः स्वाहेति माध्यंदिन्यः (आ० ५-५) इति।।

आऽपूर्णः। अस्य। कलशः। स्वाहा। सेक्ताऽइव। कोशम्। सिसिचे। पिबध्यै। सम्। ऊं इति। प्रियाः। आ। अववृत्रन्। मदाय। प्रऽदक्षिणित्। अभि। सोमासः। इन्द्रम्।।१५।।

हे इन्द्र अस्य तव पानार्थं कलशो द्रोणकलशः सोमेनापूर्णः। स्वाहा स्वाहाकृतो दत्तश्च सोमसहितः कलशः पिबध्यै तव पानार्थम्। सिसिचे। तं सोमं चोदिताधारे सिञ्चामि। तत्र दृष्टान्तः। कोशं सेक्तेव। यथा सेक्तोत्सेचको जलपूर्णात्कोशात् दृतेः सकाशाज्जलं पात्रान्तरे सिञ्चति तद्वत्। प्रियाः स्वादुतमाः सोमासो दत्तास्ते सोमा इन्द्रं त्वामभि अभिलक्ष्यैव मदाय तव हर्षार्थं प्रदक्षिणित् प्रादक्षिण्येन समाववृत्रन्। सम्यगावृत्य वर्तन्ताम्। आपूर्णः। पृ पालनपूरणयो रित्यस्य कर्मणि निष्ठा। रदाभ्यामिति तस्य नत्वम्। गतिरनन्तर इति गतिस्वरः। स्वाहा। निपातत्वादाद्युदात्तः। सेक्तेव कोषम्। न लोकाव्ययेति षष्ठीप्रतिषेधः। सिसिचे। षिच श्ररण इत्यस्य लिटि रूपम्। पिबध्यै। पा पान इत्यस्य तुमर्थे शध्यैन्प्रत्ययः। शित्त्वात्पिबादेशः। नित्त्वादाद्युदात्तः अववृत्रन्।

वृतु वर्तन इत्यस्य लङि शप्। बहुलं छन्दसीति तस्य शपः श्लुः। व्यत्ययेन परस्मैपदम्। बहुलं छन्दसीति झे रुडागमः।।

पिबध्यै, inf. dat. rt. पा 1.

अववृत्रन्, 3., plur. aor. rt. वृत् 1.; (समा) अभि वृत्, to turn towards.

प्रदक्षिणित्, right hand side, side of honour.

Verse 16.

न। त्वा। गभीरः। पुरुऽहूत। सिन्धुः। न। अद्रयः। परि। सन्तः। वरन्त। इत्था। सखिऽभ्यः। इषितः। यत्। इन्द्र। आ। दृळ्हम्। चित्। अरुजः। गव्यम्। ऊर्वम्।।१६।।

हे पुरुहूतेन्द्र गभीरो गम्भीरः सिन्धुः समुद्रस्त्वा त्वां न वारयति। ततः परि परितो वर्तमानाः सन्तोऽद्रयः शैलास्त्वां न वरन्त। न वारयन्ति। किन्तु त्वामनुसृत्य वर्तन्ते। यद्यस्मात् इत्था इत्थमनेन प्रकारेण सखिभ्यः सखिभिर्देवैरिषितः प्रार्थितस्त्वं हळहं चिदतिप्रबलमपि गव्यं गवि भवमवटे वर्तमानमूर्वमूर्वानलमारुजः। सम्यगभाङ्क्षीः। गभीरः। गाधृ प्रतिष्ठालिप्सयोर्ग्रन्थे च। अस्मादीरच् प्रत्ययः। धकारस्य भकार आकारस्य ह्रस्वश्च गम्भीरगम्भीरौ। (उ० ४-३५) इत्यनेन निपात्यते। चित्स्वरः। सिन्धुः। स्यन्दू प्रस्रवणे। स्यन्देः संप्रसारणं धश्चेत्युप्रत्ययः संप्रसारणं दकारस्य धकारः। निदित्यनुवृत्तेराद्युदात्तः। परिषन्तः। सन्तः। अस्तेः शतरि रूपम्। उपसर्गप्रादुर्भ्यामस्तिर्यच्पर इति षत्वम्। केचित्परेः क्रियान्वयमिच्छन्ति। तदा षत्वमनुपपन्नम्। परि। निपातस्वरः। सन्तः। प्रत्ययस्वरः। वरन्त। वृञ् वरणे। भौवादिकः। लङि रूपम्। निघातः। अरुजः। रुजो भङ्गे इत्यस्य लङि रूपम्। गव्यम्। गोर्विकार इत्यर्थे गोपयसोर्यदिति यत्। यतोऽनाव इत्याद्युदात्तत्वम्।।

इत्था, thus, indeed, truly. ऊर्व m., mountain cave.

वरन्त, impf. ātm. stem वर, rt. वृ 5., to keep away.

सखिभ्यः probably refers to the Aṅgiras and is dat. plur.: for the sake of the Aṅgiras; differently Sāy.: सखिभिर्देवैरिति.

Verse 17.

शुनम्। हुवेम। मघऽवानम्। इन्द्रम्। अस्मिन्। भरे। नृऽतमम्। वाजऽसातौ। शृण्वन्तम्। उग्रम्। ऊतये। समत्ऽसु। घन्तम्। वृत्राणि। संऽजितम्। धनानाम्।।१७।।

हे इन्द्र वाजसातौ। वाजस्यान्नस्य सातिर्लाभो यस्मिन् सोऽयं वाजसातिः। अस्मिन्भरे। बिभ्रति जयलक्ष्मीमनेन योद्धार इति भरः संग्रामः। तस्मिन् संग्रामे शुनं शूनमुत्साहेन प्रवृद्धम्। यद्वा शुनमिति सुखनाम। सुखकरं मघवानं धनवन्तमत एवेन्द्रं निरतिशयैश्वर्यसंपन्नं नृतमं सर्वस्य जगतोऽतिशयेन नेतारं त्वां हुवेम। कुशिका वयं यज्ञार्थमाह्वयेम। तथा शृण्वन्तमस्माभिः क्रियमाणां स्तुतिं शृण्वन्तमुग्रं शत्रूणां भयंकरं समत्सु संग्रामेषु वृत्राणि वृत्रोपलक्षितानि सर्वाणि रक्षांसि घ्नन्तं हिंसन्तं धनानां शत्रुसंबन्धिनां संजितं सम्यग्जेतारं त्वामूतये रक्षणाय वयमाह्वयेम। शनम्। टुओश्वि गतिवृद्ध्योरित्यस्य निष्ठायां यस्य विभाषेतीट्प्रतिषेधः। यजादित्वात्संप्रसारणम्। दीर्घाभावश्छान्दसः। प्रत्ययस्वरः। हुवेम। ह्वयतेर्बहुलं छन्दसीति संप्रसारणे कृते शपो लुकि कृते च लङि रूपम्। निघातः। भरे। भृञ् भरणे। घः वृषादित्वादाद्युदात्तः। वाजसातौ। षणु दाने। भावे क्तिन्। जनसनेत्यादिनानुसिकस्यात्वम्। बहुव्रीहौ पूर्वपदस्वरः। समत्सु। अद भक्षणे। संपूर्वात् क्विप्। संभक्षयन्ति योद्धृणामायूंषीति समदः संग्रामाः। कृदुत्तरपदस्वरः। घ्नन्तम्। हन हिंसागत्योरित्यस्य शतरि गमहनेत्यादिनोपधालोपः। हो हन्तेरिति घत्वम्। संजितम्। जि जये। क्विप्।।

शुनम् (शिव) adv., hail!

NO. 12.

MAṆḌALA III. **SŪKTA 33.**

प्रपर्वतानामिति त्रयोदशर्चं चतुर्थं सूक्तम्। अत्रेयमनुक्रमणिका। प्रपर्वतानां सप्तोना संवादो नदीभिर्विश्वामित्रस्योत्तितीर्षोस्तत्र नदीवाक्यं चतुर्थीषष्ठ्यष्टमीदशम्यः षष्ठीसप्तम्योस्त्विन्द्रस्तुतिरन्त्यानुष्टुबिति। अत्र चतुर्थीषष्ठ्यष्टमीदशमीनां नदीवाक्यत्वान्नद्य एव ऋषयः शिष्टानां विश्वामित्रवाक्यत्वात्स एव ऋषिः। अन्त्यानुष्टुप् शिष्टास्त्रिष्टुभः। इन्द्रो देवता। यद्यपि षष्ठ्यां सप्तम्यां च *विश्वामित्रेण

---

* विश्वामित्रो नद्यः इत्यादर्शः।

नद्यः स्तूयन्ते तथापि इन्द्र एव देवता। सूक्तविनियोगो लैङ्गिकः। पुरा किल विश्वामित्रः पैजवनस्य सुदासो राज्ञः पुरोहितो बभूव। स च पौरोहित्येन लब्धधनः सर्वं धनमादाय विपाट्छुतुद्योः संभेदमाययावनुयुरितरे। अथोत्तितीर्षुर्विश्वामित्रोऽगाधजले ते नद्यौ दृष्टोत्तरणार्थमाद्याभिस्तिसृभिस्तुष्टाव।।

The hymn is a dialogue between Viśvāmitra and the twin streams Vipāṭ and Sutudrī. The details are given in Sāy.'s commentary.

Verse 1.

प्र। पर्वतानाम्। उशती इति। उपऽस्थात्। अश्वे इवेत्यश्वेऽइव। विसिते। इति। विऽसिते। हासमाने इति। गावा इव। शुभ्रे इति। मातरा। रिहाणे इति। विऽपाट्। शुतुद्री। पयसा। जवेते इति।।१।।

पर्वतानां गिरीणां शैलानामुपस्थादुत्संगान्निर्गत्योशती समुद्रगमनं कामयमाने। गमने दृष्टान्तः। अश्वे इव। †वडवे यथा विषिते मन्दुरातो विमुक्ते हासमाने अन्योन्यं जवेन स्पर्धमाने। यद्वा हृष्यन्त्यावश्वे इव वडवे इव त्वरया गच्छन्त्यौ परस्परं हृष्यन्त्यौ। तथा गावेव शुभ्रे। यथा द्वौ गावौ शोभमानौ वर्तेते तद्वच्छुभ्रे शोभमाने। किंच मातरा। यथा मातरौ धेनू रिहाणे। अन्तर्णीतसनर्थो लिहिः। वत्सं जिह्वया लेढुमिच्छन्त्यौ शीघ्रं गच्छतस्तद्वत्समुद्रं गन्तुं जवाद्रच्छन्त्यौ पयसा संयुक्ते। विपाट् कूलविपाटनात् विपाशनाद्वा विमोचनाद्वा विपाट्। शुतुद्री। शु क्षिप्रं तु तुन्ना तुन्नेव द्रवति गच्छतीति शुतुद्री। एतन्नामके नद्यौ प्रजवेते। समुद्रं प्रति शीघ्रं गच्छतः। अत्र निरुक्तम्। पर्वतानामुपस्था दुपस्थानादुशत्यौ कामयमाने अश्वे इव विमुक्ते इति वा विषण्णे इति वा हासमाने हासतिः स्पर्धायां हर्षमाणे वा गावाविव शुभ्रे शोभने मातरौ संरिहाणे विपाट्छुतुद्यौ पयसा प्रजवेते (नि० ९-३९) इति। उशती। वश कान्तौ। अस्य शतुर्ङित्त्वाद्ग्रहिज्यावयीत्यादिना संप्रसारणम्। विषिते। षिञ् बन्धन इत्यस्य कर्मणि निष्ठा। संहितायां परिनिविभ्यः सेवसितसयसिवुसहेत्यादिना (पा० ८-३-७०) षत्वम्। गतिरनन्तर इति गतेः प्रकृतिस्वरः। हासमाने। हासतिः स्पर्धाकर्मा हसे हसने वा। शानच्। तस्य लसार्वधातुकस्वरे कृते धातुस्वरः। रिहाणे।

† आदर्शे वडवे इति नास्ति।

लिह् आस्वादने। स्वरितेत्त्वादुभयपदी। शानच्। अदादित्वाच्छपो लुक्। लकारस्य रेफश्छान्दसः। रेफमवलम्ब्य णत्वम्। चित्त्वादन्तोदात्तः। विपाट्। पट गतौ पश बाधनस्पर्शनयोरिति वा ण्यन्तावेतौ विपूर्वौ। शकारस्य व्रश्चादिना षत्वम्। शुतुद्री। छान्दसी रूपसिद्धिः। जवेते। जुङ् गतौ। भौवादिकः। ङित्त्वादात्मनेपदम्। आतो ङित इतीयादेशः। निघातः।।

प्र जू 9., to break forth, rush on.

उ॒श॒ती, f., pt. pres. par. rt. वश् 2., to desire.

वि षि॑त, pt. pf. pass., rt. सो (सि) ४.

हास् 1., ātm., to rival, to race. रिह्=लिह् 2.

The licking of the calves by the cows is the upamāna for the licking of the banks by the waves of the two streams.

Verse 2.

इन्द्रे॑षिते। प्र॒ऽस॒वम्। भिक्ष॑माणे॒ इति॑। अच्छ॑। स॒मु॒द्रम्। र॒थ्या॑ऽइव। या॒थ॒ः। स॒मा॒रा॒णे इति॑ सं॒ऽआ॒रा॒णे। ऊ॒र्मिऽभिः॑। पिन्व॑माने॒ इति॑। अ॒न्या। वा॒म्। अ॒न्याम्। अपि॑। ए॒ति॒। शु॒भ्रे॒ इति॑।।२।।

हे नद्यौ इन्द्रेषिते इन्द्रेण प्रेषिते प्रसवं तस्येन्द्रस्यानुज्ञां भिक्षमाणे प्रार्थयमाने युवां समुद्रमच्छाभिमुख्येन याथः गच्छतः। तत्र दृष्टान्तः। रथ्येवेति। यथा रथिनौ लक्ष्यं देशमभिगच्छतस्तद्वत्। किं कुर्वत्यौ। समाराणे परस्परं संगच्छन्त्यावूर्मिभिस्तरङ्गैः पिन्वमाने परसरप्रदेशं संतर्पयन्त्यौ शुभ्रे शोभमाने। युवां समुद्रं गच्छथ इति पूर्वेणान्वयः। तथा वां युवयेर्मध्येऽन्यैकान्यामपरां नदीमप्येति। अपि गच्छति। परस्परमैक्यमापद्यत इत्यर्थः। इन्द्रेषिते। इष गतावित्यस्य कर्मणि निष्ठायास्तीषसहेत्यादिना इडागमः। तृतीया कर्मणीति पूर्वपदस्वरः। प्रसवम्। षू प्रेरण इत्यस्याप्। थाथादिस्वरः। भिक्षमाणे। भिक्ष याञ्चायाम्। आत्मनेपदी। शानचो लसार्वधातुकस्वरेणानुदात्तत्वे धातुस्वरः। रथ्येव। रथस्येमौ। तस्येदमित्यर्थे रथाद्यदिति यत्प्रत्ययः। तित्स्वरितः। इवेन विभक्त्यलोपः। याथः यातेर्लटि रूपम्। समाराणे। ऋ गतावित्यस्य लिट्। संपूर्वस्यार्तेः समो गमीत्यादिनात्मनेपदंत्वात्तस्य कानजादेशः। ऋच्छत्यृतामिति

गुणः। पिन्वमाने। पिवि सेचने। भूवादिः। लसार्वधातुकस्वरेण शानचोऽनुदात्तत्वे धातुस्वरः।।

आराण, pt. pf. ātm., rt. ऋ to go.

अच्छ, prepos. and postops. with accus., towards, to.

Verse 3.

अच्छ। सिन्धुम्। मातृऽतमाम्। अयासम्। विऽपाशम्। उर्वीम्। सुऽभगाम्। अगन्म। वत्सम्ऽइव। मातरा। संरिहाणे इति संऽरिहाणे। समानम्। योनिम्। अनु। संचरन्ती इति संऽचरन्ती।।३।।

हे नद्यौ मातृतमामतिशयेन मातरं सिन्धुं स्रवन्तीं शुतुद्रीं त्वामच्छाभिमुख्येनायासम् विश्वामित्रोऽहं प्राप्तोऽभूवम्। उर्वीं महतीं सुभगां सौभाग्यवतीं विपाशं त्वामगन्म। वयं प्राप्ताः स्मः। किं कुर्वत्यौ। मातरा मातरौ द्वे धेनू वत्समिव संरिहाणे। अन्तर्णीतसनर्थो लिहिः। जिह्वया लेढुमिच्छन्त्यौ यथा वत्समनुगच्छतस्तद्वत् समानमेकं योनिं स्थानं समुद्रमनु अभिलक्ष्य संचरन्ती सम्यक् चरन्त्यौ। *युवामयासमिति पूर्वेणान्वयः। अयासम् या प्रापण इत्यस्य रूपम्। इडभावश्छान्दसः। अगन्म। गमेर्लङि बहुलं छन्दसीति शपो लुक्। म्वोश्चेति मकारस्य नकारः। निघातः। संचरन्ती। चरतिर्गत्यर्थः। तृतीयायुक्तत्वाभावादात्मनेपदाभावः। शतुर्लसार्वधातुकस्वरेणानुदात्तत्वे कृते धातुस्वरः।।

योनि is consistently, but probably not so correctly, explained by Sāy. as स्थान, समुद्र. It is more likely that the common bed of the twin rivers after they have joined each other is meant.

Verse 4.

एना। वयम्। पयसा। पिन्वमानाः। अनु। योनिम्। देवऽकृतम्। चरन्तीः। न। वर्तवे। प्रऽसवः। सर्गऽतक्तः। किम्ऽयुः। विप्रः। नद्यः। जोहवीति।।४।।

---

* अयासिषमिति इत्यादर्शः।

एवं स्तुते नद्यौ विश्वमित्रं प्रत्यूचतुः। एनैनेन पयसा पिन्वमानाः संतर्पयन्त्यो देवकृतं देवेनेन्द्रेण कृतं संदिष्टं योनिं स्थानं समुद्रमनुलक्षीकृत्य चरन्तीर्गच्छन्त्यो वयमास्हमे। द्वयोर्बहुवचनं पूजार्थम्। तासामस्माकं सर्गतक्तः सर्गे गमने प्रवृत्तः प्रसव उद्योगो न वर्त्तवे। निवर्तनाय न भवति। किंयुः किमिच्छन्नसौ विप्रो ब्राह्मणो नद्यो नदीरस्मान् जोहवीति। भृशमाह्वयति। एना। इदंशब्दस्य तृतीयाया एनादेशः। सुपां सुलुगिति तृतीयाया अजादेशः। ऊडिदमिति विभक्तेरुदात्तत्वम्। पिन्वमानाः। पिवि सेचने। देवकृतम्। तृतीया कर्मणीति पूर्वपदप्रकृतिस्वरः। वर्त्तवे। वृतु वर्तने। तुमर्थे तवेन्प्रत्ययः। नित्स्वरः। सर्गतक्तः। क्ते चेति पूर्वपदप्रकृतिस्वरः। किंयुः। किमिच्छन्। क्यचि मान्ताव्ययप्रतिषेधः (पा० ३१-८-१) इति छान्दसत्वादत्र प्रतिषेधो न भवतीति क्यच्। क्याच्छन्दसीत्युप्रत्ययः। प्रत्ययस्वरः। नद्यः। छान्दसो यणादेशः। जोहवीति। ह्वयो यङ्लुक्यभ्यस्तस्य चेति संप्रसारणे कृते गुणो यङ्लुकोरित्यभ्यासस्य गुणः। यङो वेतीडागमः। गुणः। निघातः।।

एना, instr. sg. अयम्.

वर्तवे, inf. dat. rt. वृ 5. 1., to cover, to check.

सर्गतक्त, hurrying in the current, hurriedly galloping.

किंयु, with what desire?

जोहवीति, intens. rt, हू (ह्वे), to call.

Note the plur. in चरन्तीः which may refer to various branches of the main rivers.

Verse 5.

रमध्वम्। मे। वचसे। सोम्याय। ऋतऽवरीः। उप। मुहूर्तम्। एवैः। प्र। सिन्धुम्। अच्छ। बृहती। मनीषा। अवस्युः। अह्वे। कुशिकस्य। सूनुः।।५।।

विश्वामित्रो नदीः प्रतिब्रूते। ऋतावरीः। ऋतमुदकम्। तद्वत्यो हे नद्यो यूयं मे विश्वामित्रस्य मम सोम्याय। उत्तीर्याहं सोमं संपादयामीत्येवं सोमसंपादिने। वचसे तदर्थमेवैः। पञ्चम्यर्थे तृतीया। शीघ्रगमनेभ्यो मुहूर्तं मुहूर्तमात्रमुपरमध्वम्।

उपपूर्वो रमिरुपसंहारे वर्तते। क्षणमात्रं शीघ्रगमनादुपरता भवत। सामान्येन नदीषूच्यमानासु समीहितं प्रयोजनमकुर्वतीषु पुरोवर्तिनीं शुतुद्रीं प्रति ब्रूते। कुशिकस्य राजर्षेः सूनुविश्वामित्रोऽहं बृहती महत्या मनीषा मनीषया स्तुत्यावस्युरात्मनो रक्षणमिच्छन् सन् सिन्धुं शुतुद्रीं त्वामच्छाभिमुख्येन प्राह्वे। प्रकर्षेणाह्वयामि अत्र निरुक्तम्। उपरमध्वं मे वचसे सोम्याय सोमसंपादिन ऋतमित्युदकनाम प्रत्यृतं भवति मुहूर्तमेवैरयनैखनैर्वा। प्राभिह्वयामि सिन्धुं बृहत्या महत्या मनीषया मनस ईषया स्तुत्या प्रज्ञया वावनाय कुशिकस्य सूनुः। कुशिको राजा बभूव (नि० २-२५) इति । रमध्वम्। रमु उपरमे। उपपूर्वाद्रमतेर्विभाषाकर्मकात् (पा० १-३-८५) इत्यात्मनेपदम्। ऋतावरीः। ऋतशब्दान्मत्वर्थे छन्दसीवनिपाविति वनिप्। वनो र चेति ङीप् रेफश्चान्तादेशः। वा छन्दसीति सवर्णदीर्घः। आमन्त्रितस्य पादादित्वात्षाष्ठिकमाद्युदात्तत्वम्। एवैः। इण् गतौ। इण्शीङ्भ्यां वन्। आर्द्धधातुकलक्षणो गुणः। नित्स्वरः। बृहती मनीषा। उभयत्र तृतीयायाः पूर्वसवर्णदीर्घः। अवस्युः। अवो रक्षणमिच्छन्। सुप आत्मनः क्यच्। नः क्य इति नकारान्तस्य पज्ञाया नियमितत्वादत्र सकारस्य रुर्न भवति। क्याच्छन्दसीत्युप्रत्ययः। अह्वे। ह्वयतेर्लुङिसिच आत्मनेपदेष्वन्यतरस्यां (पा० ३-१-५८) इत्यङादेशः। गुणः। निघातः।।

उप रम् 1., to stop.

एव (rt. इ) m., quick movement, speed.

ऋतावन्, f. ०वरी, ever flowing. प्र अह्वे, aor. rt. हू.

Pāda 3 is elliptic, as एति has to be understood.—Sāy., following Yāska, takes बृहती मनीषा to be instr. sg., बृहत्या मनीषया, and reads the third and fourth pādas together:—With the mighty hymn Kuśika's son, desirous of help, has called out to the river.

Verse 6.

इन्द्रः। अस्मान्। अरदत्। वज्रऽबाहुः। अप। अहन्। वृत्रम्। परिऽधिम्। नदीनाम्। देवः। अनयत्। सविता। सुऽपाणिः। तस्य। वयम्। प्रऽसवे। यामः। उर्वीः।।६।।

नद्यः प्रत्यूचुः। हे विश्वामित्र वज्रबाहुः। वज्रयुक्तो बाहुर्यस्यासौ वज्रबाहुः। तादृशो बलवानिन्द्रो नदीरस्मानरदत्। रदतिः खनतिकर्मा। अखनत्। कथमखनत्। उच्यते। नदीनां शब्दकारिणीनामपां परिधिं परितो निहितमदकमन्तः कृत्वा परितो वर्तमानमित्यर्थः। तादृशं वृत्रम्। वृणोत्याकाशमिति वृत्रो मेघः। तं मेघमपाहन्। जघान। तस्मिन् हत आपः पतिताः। ताभिर्गच्छन्तीभिर्वयं खाताः। एवं मेघहननद्वारेणाखनत्। न केवलमखनत् किं तर्हि सविता सर्वस्य जगतः प्रेरकः सुपाणिः शोभनहस्त उत्पत्तिस्थितिकर्तृत्वात्तादृशो देवो द्योतमान इन्द्रोऽस्माननयत्। मेघभेदनं कृत्वोदकप्रेरणेन समुद्रमपूरयत्। तस्य तादृशसामर्थ्योपेतस्येन्द्रस्य प्रसवेऽभ्यनुज्ञायां वर्तमाना उर्वीरुदकैः प्रभूता वयं यामः। गच्छामः। न तव वचनादुपरमामहे। उक्तार्थं यास्को ब्रवीति। इन्द्रो अस्मानरदद्वज्रबाहू रदतिः खनतिकर्मापाहन्वृत्रं परिधिं नदीनामिति व्याख्यातम्। देवोऽनयत्सविता सुपाणिः कल्याणपाणिः। पाणिः पणायतेः पूजाकर्मणः प्रगृह्य पाणी देवान्पूजयन्ति। तस्य वयं प्रसवे याम उर्वीरुर्व्यः। (नि० २-२६) इति। अरदत्। रदतेर्लङिरूपम्। वज्रबाहुः। बहुव्रीहौ पूर्वपदस्वरः। अहन्। हन्तेर्लङिरूपम्। निघातः। परिधिम्। डुधाञ् धारणपोषणयोरित्यस्मात्कर्मण्युपसर्गे घोः किरिति किप्रत्ययः। आतो लोपः। कृदुत्तरपदस्वरः। अनयत्। नयतेर्लङिरूपम्। सुपाणिः। पण व्यवहारे स्तुतौ च। अशिपणाय्यौ रुडायलुकौ च (उ० ४-१३२) इतीण्। आयलुक्। बहुव्रीहौ नञ्सुभ्यामिति स्वरः। प्रसवे। षू प्रेरणे। ऋदोरबिति भावेऽप्प्रत्ययः। थाथघञ्क्तेत्युत्तरपदान्तोदात्तत्वम्। यामः। या प्रापण इत्यस्य लटि रूपम्। निघातः। उर्वीः। उरुशब्दाद्वोतो गुणवचनादिति ङीप्। वा छन्दसीति सवर्णदीर्घः। प्रत्ययस्वरः।।

With सुपाणि compare Nr. 9.2. Note the uncommon metrical shape of the third pāda.

Verse 7.

प्रऽवाच्यम्। शश्वधा। वीर्यम्। तत्। इन्द्रस्य। कर्म। यत्। अहिम्। विऽवृश्चत्। वि। वज्रेण। परिऽसदः। जघान। आयन्। आपः। अयनम्। इच्छमानाः।।७।।

योऽयमिन्द्रोऽहिं मेघं विवृश्चत् उदकप्रेरणार्थं जघानेति यत्कर्म च्छेदनरूपं

तदिदं तस्येन्द्रस्य वीर्यं सामर्थ्यं शश्वधा सर्वदा प्रवाच्यम्। प्रकर्षेण वचनीयम्। तथा स इन्द्रः परिषदः परितः सीदत आसीनान् प्रतिबन्धकारिणोऽसुरान् वज्रेण विजघान। अथायनं स्थानमिच्छमाना इच्छन्त्य आप आयन्। यान्ति। प्रवाच्यम्। वच परिभाषण इत्यस्माद्दहलोर्ण्यदिति ण्यत्। णित्त्वादुपधावृद्धिः। वचोऽशब्दसंज्ञायाम् (पा० ७-३-६७) इति कुत्वाभावः। व्यत्ययेनेनाद्युदात्तत्वम्। यद्वा वाचयतेरचो यत्। यतोऽनाव इति स्वरः। शश्वधा। शश्वच्छब्दात्स्वार्थे धाप्रत्ययस्तकारलोपश्च द्रष्टव्यः। विवृश्चत्। ओव्रश्चू छेदने। तुदादिः। लङि ग्रहिज्यावयीत्यादिना संप्रसारणम्। सह सुपेत्यत्र सहेति योगविभागात्समासः। समासस्वरः। परिषदः। क्विप्। संहितायां सदिरप्रतेरिति षत्वम्। जघान। हनतेर्लिटि णलि रूपम्। निघातः। आयन्। अय गतावित्यस्य लङि रूपम्। पादादित्वादनिघातः। इच्छमानाः। इषु इच्छायामित्यस्माद्व्यत्ययेन शानच्। तस्य लसार्वधातुकस्वरे कृते प्रत्ययस्वरः॥

वि वृश्चत्, impf. rt. व्रश्च् 6., to cut.

Verse 8.

एतत्। वचः। जरितः। मा। अपि मृष्ठाः। आ। यत्। ते। घोषान्। उत्ऽतरा। युगानि। उक्थेषु। कारो इति। प्रति। नः। जुषस्व। मा। नः। नि। करिति कः। पुरुषऽत्रा। नमः। ते॥८॥

नद्यः प्रसंगादिन्द्रस्तोत्रं कृत्वा विश्वामित्रं प्रत्यूचुः। जरितः स्तोतर्हे विश्वामित्र ते त्वदीयं यत्संवादात्मकं वचरत्वं *मनीषा इत्यादि घोषानुद्घोषयन्वर्तसे तद्वचो मापि मृष्ठाः। मा विस्मार्षीः। किं कारणम्। उत्तरा युगान्युत्तरेषु याज्ञिकेषु युगेष्वहःसूक्थेषु कारो शस्त्राणां कर्तस्त्वं नोऽस्मान्प्रति जुषस्व। संवादात्मकेन तेन वाक्येन प्रतिसेवस्व। इदानीं नोऽस्मान् पुरुषत्रा मा निकः। उक्तिप्रत्युक्तिरूपसंवादवाक्याध्यापनेन नितरां पुंवत् प्रागल्भ्यं मा कार्षीः। ते तुभ्यं नमः। मृष्ठाः। मृजूष् शुद्धावित्यस्य लङि व्यत्ययेनात्मनेपदम्। अदादित्वाच्छपो लुक्। व्रश्चादिना षत्वम्। निघातः। घोषान्। घुषिर् संशब्दन इत्यस्य शतरि सर्वविधीनां छन्दसि विकल्पिततत्वादतो गुण इति पररूपत्वाभावः।

---

* नोऽभीत्या इत्यादर्शः।

सवर्णदीर्घः। शतुर्लसार्वधातुकस्वरे कृते धातुस्वरः। युगानि। युजिर् योगे। उञ्छादिषु घञन्तत्वेन निपातनादगुणत्वम् विशिष्टविषयं च निपातनमिष्यते। कालविशेषे रथाद्युपकरणे चेति तत्र पाठादेवान्तोदात्तत्वम्। कालाध्वनोरत्यन्तसंयोग इति द्वितीया। कारो। करोतेः कृवापाजिमीत्यादिना उण्प्रत्ययः। आमन्त्रितत्वा-न्निघातः। कः। करोतेर्लुङि च्लेर्मन्त्रे घसेत्यादिना लुक्। हल्ङ्यादिना सिपो लोपः। न माङ्योग इत्यडभावः। पुरुषत्रा। देवमनुष्यपुरुषपुरुमर्त्येभ्यो द्वितीयासप्तम्योर्बहुलमिति सप्तम्यर्थे त्राप्रत्ययः। प्रत्ययस्वरः।।

मृष् 6., aor. मृष्ठाः, not to heed, to forget.

आ घुष् 1., subj. घोष्, घोषान्, to listen.

प्रति जुष् 6., to delight in, to praise.

कः 2., sg. inj. aor.; rt. कृ.

Verse 9.

ओ इति। सु। स्वसारः। कारवे। शृणोत। ययौ। वः। दूरात्। अनसा। रथेन। नि। सु। नमध्वम्। भवत। सुऽपाराः। अधःऽअक्षाः। सिन्धवः। स्रोत्याभिः।।९।।

विश्वामित्रो नदीः प्रत्युवाच। स्वसारो भगिन्यः सिन्धवो हे नद्यः कारवे स्तोत्रं कुर्वाणस्य मम वचनं सु सुष्ठु ओ शृणोत। शृणुतैव। अनसा शकटेन रथेन च सह दूराद्विप्रकृष्टाद्देशाद्वो युष्मान्ययौ प्राप्तोऽस्मि। यूयं स सुष्ठु निनमध्वम्। आत्मना स्वयं प्रह्वा भवत। तथा सुपाराः। रथादीनां तीरात्सुखेनावरोहणारोहणे यथा स्यातां तथा शोभनरोधसश्च भवत। किंच यूयं स्रोत्याभिः स्रवणशीलाभिरद्भिरधो अक्षा रथाङ्गस्याक्षस्याधस्ताद्भवत। यदापोऽचस्याधस्ताद्भवन्ति तदा रथादीनि नेतुं शक्यन्ते। तस्मात्तत्परिमाणोदका भवतेत्यर्थाभिप्रायः। ओ इति प्रगृह्यसंज्ञा। शृणोत। श्रु श्रवण इत्यस्य लोटि तप्रत्ययस्य तप्तनप्तनथनाश्चेति तवादेशः। पित्त्वाद्गुणः। निघातः। ययौ। या प्रापणे इत्यस्य भूतमात्रे लिट्युत्तमे णल्यात औ णल इत्यौकारः। एकादेशस्वरः। वः। युष्मच्छब्दस्य द्वितीयाया बहुवचनस्य वस्नसाविति वसादेशः। षू। निपातस्येति संहितायां दीर्घः। नमध्वम्। णमु प्रह्वत्वे शब्दे चेत्यस्य कर्मकर्तरि

न दुहस्नुनमां यक्चिणाविति प्रतिषेधाद्यगभावः। अधो अक्षाः। अधरशब्दस्य पूर्वाधरावराणामसि पुरधवश्चैषामित्यसिप्रत्ययोऽधादेशश्च। अक्षशब्दोऽशू व्याप्तावित्यस्मादशेर्देवने (उ० ३-६५) इति सप्रत्ययान्तः। कृदुत्तरपदप्रकृतिस्वरः। सिन्धवः। आमन्त्रितत्वान्निघातः। स्रोत्याभिः। स्रोतःशब्दात्स्रोतसो विभाषा ड्यड्ड्यौ (पा० ४-४-११३) इति ड्यप्रत्ययः। डित्त्वाट्टिलोपः। प्रत्ययस्वरः॥

आ श्रु 5., (with dat.) listen to.

सुपार adj., fordable, of easy banks.

Verse 10.

आ। ते। कारो इति। शृणवाम। वचांसि। ययाथ। दूरात्। अनसा। रथेन। नि। ते। नंसै। पीप्यानाऽइव। योषा। मर्यायऽइव। कन्या। शश्वचै। ते इति ते॥१०॥

नद्यः पूर्वं विश्वमित्रवाक्यं प्रत्याख्ययानया ऋचा तस्य वाक्यमाशुश्रुवुः। कारो स्तोत्रं कुर्वाण हे विश्वामित्र ते तव वचांसीमानि वाक्यान्याशृणवाम। शृणुमः। तव समीहितं प्रयोजनं कुर्म इत्यर्थः। अनसा शकटेन रथेन च सह ययाथ। यतो दूरादागतोऽसि। वयं च ते त्वदर्थं निनंसै। नीचैर्नमाम। प्रत्येकविवक्षयात्रैकवचनम्। रथेन गन्तुं गाधोदका भवामेत्यर्थः। तत्र दृष्टान्तः। पीप्यानेव योषा। पीप्याना पुत्रं स्तनं पाययन्ती योषा माता यथा प्रह्वीभवति। दृष्टान्तान्तरम्। यथा कन्या युवतिर्मर्यायेव मनुष्याय पित्रे भ्रात्रे वा शश्वचै परिष्वजनाय नम्रा भवति तद्वत्ते त्वदर्थं प्रह्वीभवामः। ते इति पुनरुक्तिरादरार्था। एतामृचं यास्क एवं व्याचष्टे। आशृणवाम ते कारो वचनानि याहि दूरादनसा च रथेन च निनमाम ते पाययमानेव योषा पुत्रं मर्यायेव कन्या परिष्वजनाय निनमा इति वा (नि० २-२७) इति। कारो। संबुद्धौ शाकल्यस्येतौ (पा० १-१-१६) इति प्रगृह्यसंज्ञा। शृणवाम। श्रु श्रवण इत्यस्य लोट्याडुत्तमस्य पिच्चेत्याडागमः। पित्त्वरद्गुणः। निघातः। ययाथ। या प्रापण इत्यस्य भूतमात्रे लिटि थल्येकाच उपदेशेऽनुदात्तादितीट्प्रतिषेधः। लित्स्वरः। अनसा। सहार्थे तृतीया। नंसै। णमु प्रह्वत्व इत्यस्य लेटय्युत्तमे लेटि सिब्बहुलमिति सिप्। वैतोऽन्यत्रेत्यैकारादेशः। निघातः। पीप्यानेव। पीङ् पाने इत्यस्यान्तर्भावितण्यर्थस्य लिटि कानचि रूपम्। चित्स्वरः। योषा। यु मिश्रणे। वृतृ

वदिहनीत्यादिना (उ० ३-६२) सप्रत्ययः। यौतीति योषा। वृषादित्वादाद्युदात्तः। शश्वचै। ष्वञ्जपरिष्वङ्ग इत्यस्मात्संपदादिलक्षणो भावे क्विप्। पृषोदरादि-त्वादिष्टरूपसिद्धिरन्तोदात्तश्च।।

नंसै, 1. sg. aor. subj.; rt. नम् 1.

शश्वचै, 1. sg. aor. subj. caus.; rt. श्वञ्च् 1., to make bend, to yield.

मर्य m., youth, lover.

पीप्यान, pt. pf. ātm.; rt. पि 3. (प्यै), to suck.

Note that in the second line one river alone speaks; but possibly the simile in the third pāda is adduced by one and that in the fourth by the other of the twin streams.

Verse 11.

यत्। अङ्ग। त्वा। भरताः। संऽतरेयुः। गव्यन्। ग्रामः। इषितः। इन्द्रऽजूतः। अर्षात्। अह। प्रऽसवः। सर्गऽतक्तः। आ। वः। वृणे। सुऽमतिम्। यज्ञियानाम्।।११।।

विश्वामित्रो नदीः प्रत्युवाच। अङ्गेत्यामन्त्रणे। हे नद्यो यद्यस्माद्युष्माभिरुत्ति-तीर्षोर्ममोत्तरणमभ्यनुज्ञातं तस्माद्भरता भरतकुलजा मदीयाः सर्वे त्वा परस्पर-मेकतामापन्नां नदीं त्वां संतरेयुः। सम्यगुत्तीर्णा भवेयुः। तदेव विशिनष्टि। गव्यन् गा उदकानि तरीतुमिच्छन्निषितस्त्वयाभ्यनुज्ञात इन्द्रजूतो युष्माकं प्रवर्तकेणेन्द्रेण च प्रेरितो ग्रामो भरतानां संघोऽर्षात्। संतरेत्। यतः सर्गतक्तो गमनाय प्रवृत्तः प्रसवस्तेषामुद्योगेऽह पूर्वं युष्माभिरनुज्ञातः। अहं तु यज्ञियानां यज्ञार्हाणां वो युष्माकं सुमतिं शोभनां स्तुतिमा वृणे। सर्वतः संभजे। भरताः। भरतशब्दादुत्सादित्वादञ्। तस्य यञञोश्चेति लुक्। अतच्प्रत्ययस्वरः। संतरेयुः। तरतेर्लिङि जुसि रूपम्। झेर्लसार्वधातुकस्वरे धातुस्वरः। तिङि चोदात्तवतीति गतेर्निघातः। गव्यन्। गा आत्मन इच्छन्। सुपः क्यच्। एकादेशस्वरः। ग्रामः। ग्रसतेरा च। (उ० १-१४२) इति मन्प्रत्यय आकारादेशश्च। नित्स्वरः। इन्द्रजूतः। जू इति सौत्रो धातुर्गत्यर्थः। श्र्युकः कितीति निष्ठायामिट्प्रतिषेधः।

तृतीया कर्मणीति पूर्वपदप्रकृतिस्वरः। अर्षात्। ऋ गतावित्यस्य लेटि तिपि सिब्बहुलमिति सिप्। लेटोऽडागमः। एकाच इतीट्प्रतिषेधः। गुणः। प्रत्ययस्य पित्त्वादनुदात्तत्वे धातुस्वरः। वृणे। वृङ् संभक्तावित्यस्य लटि रूपम्। यज्ञियानाम्। यज्ञर्त्विग्भ्यां धखञाविति घप्रत्ययः। प्रत्ययस्वरः।।

यद् अ॒ङ्ग, if indeed.

ग॒व्यन्, pt. pres. from गव्य, eager for cows, prey, booty.

अर्षा॑त्, sbj., rt. ऋष् 1., to shoot off, ruch, flow violently.

आ वृ 9., to request. ग्रामं॑ m., village, clan, band.

Verse 12.

अता॑रिषुः। भ॒रताः। ग॒व्यवः॑। सम्। अभ॑क्त। विप्रः॑। सु॒ऽम॒तिम्। न॒दीना॑म्। प्र। पि॒न्व॒ध्व॒म्। इ॒षय॑न्तीः। सुराधाः॑। आ। व॒क्षणाः॑। पृणध्वम्॑ या॒त। शीभ॑म्।।१२।।

गव्यवो गा आत्मन इच्छन्तो भरता भरतकुलजाः सर्वेऽतारिषुः। तां नदीं समतरन्। विप्रो मेधावी विश्वामित्रो नदीनां सुमतिं शोभनां स्तुतिं समभक्त। समभजत। यूयं तु यथापूर्वमिषयन्तीः कुल्यादिद्वारान्नं कुर्वाणा अत एव सुराधाः शोभनधनोपेता यूयं वक्षणाः कृत्रिमसरितः कुल्याः प्र पिन्वध्वम् प्रकर्षेण तर्पयत। आपृणध्वम्। ताः सर्वतः पूरयत च। शीभं शीघ्रं गच्छत च। अतारिषुः। तॄ प्लवनतरणयोरित्यस्य लुङि सिचि वृद्धिः। परस्मैपदेष्विति वृद्धिअडागमस्वरः। गव्यवः। सुपः क्यच्। क्याच्छन्द-सीत्युप्रत्ययः। तस्य स्वरः। अभक्त। भज सेवायामित्यस्य लुङि सिचो झलो झलीति लोपः। पादादित्वादनिघातः। पिन्वध्वम्। पिवि सेचन इत्यस्य लोटि रूपम्। निघातः। इषयन्तीः। इषं कुर्वत्यः। तत्करोतीति णिच्। णाविष्ठवत्प्रातिपदिकस्येतीष्ठवद्भावाट्टेरिति टिलोपः। वा छन्दसीति सवर्णदीर्घः। प्रत्ययस्वरः। पृणध्वम्। पृण प्रीणने। लोटि रूपम्। व्यत्ययेनात्मनेपदम्। वाक्यभेदादनिघातः। यात। या प्रापण इत्यस्य लोटि रूपम्। अत्रापि न निघातः। शीभम्। शीभृ कत्थने। श्लाध्यतेऽनेन तद्वानिति करणे घञ्। ञित्स्वरः।।

इषय (denom. इष्, food), to give food.

व॒क्षणा॑ f., lower part of the body, belly, bed of river.

शीभ॑ (only adv. शीभ॑म्), quick.

Verse 13.

उत्। व॒ः। ऊ॒र्मिः। शम्या॑ः। ह॒न्तु॒। आप॑ः। योक्त्रा॑णि। मु॒ञ्च॒त॒।
मा। अदु॑ःऽकृतौ। विऽए॑नसा। अ॒घ्न्यौ॑। शून॑म्। आ। अ॒र॒ता॒म्।।१३।।

पूर्वमुत्तितीर्षुर्विश्वामित्रो नदीरुक्त्वाधुनोत्तितीर्षुः पुनराह। हे नद्यो वो युष्माकमूर्मिस्तरङ्गः शम्या *युग्यकटपार्श्वादिसंलग्ना रज्जव उदूर्ध्वं यथा भवन्ति तथा हन्तु। गच्छतु। स तरङ्गो रज्जूनामधो गच्छत्विथभिप्रायः। तथा हे आपो यूयं योक्त्राणि ता रज्जूर्मुञ्चत। यथा न स्पृशन्ति तथा यान्त्वित्यभिप्रायः। व्येनसा विगतपापे अत एवादुष्कृतौ कल्याणकर्मकारिण्यौ अघ्न्यावघ्न्ये न केनापि तिरस्करणीये विपाट्छुतुद्यौ शूनं समृद्धिम्। आरतामागच्छताम्। एवं विश्वामित्रो नदीः स्तुत्वा ताभिरनुज्ञातोऽतरदिति। ऊर्मिः। ऋ गतौ। अर्तेरुच्चेति मिप्रत्ययः। ऊरित्ययमादेशो धातोः। ऋच्छतीत्यूर्मिः। प्रत्ययस्वरः। शम्याः। शमु उपशमे। पोरदुपधादिति यत्प्रत्ययः। यतोऽनाव इत्याद्युदात्तत्वम्। हन्तु। हन हिंसागत्योरित्यस्य लोटि रूपम्। निघातः। योक्त्राणि। युजिर् योगे। करणे दाम्नीशसयुयुजेत्यादिना ष्ट्रन्प्रत्ययः। नित्स्वरः। मुञ्चत। मुच्लृ मोक्षणे। निघातः। अदुष्कृतौ। इसुसोः सामर्थ्य इति विसर्जनीयस्य षत्वम्। व्येनसा। बहुव्रीहौ पूर्वपदस्वरः। सुपो डादेशः अघ्न्यौ। हन हिंसागत्योरित्यस्य नञ्-पूर्वस्याघ्न्यादयश्चेति निपातनाद्यक्। कित्त्वादुपधालोपः। हो हन्तेरिति घत्वम्। सर्वविधीनां छन्दसि विकल्पितत्वादत्रौङः शीभावाभावः। एकादेशस्वरः। शूनम्। श्वयतेर्नपुंसके भावे क्त इति क्तः। यजादित्वात्संप्रसारणम्। हल इति दीर्घत्वम्। ओदितश्चेति निष्ठानत्वम्। निष्ठा च द्व्यजनादित्याद्युदात्तः। अरताम्। ऋगतावित्यस्य लुङि च्लेः सर्तिशास्त्यर्तिभ्यश्चेत्यङादेशः। ऋदृशोऽङि गुणः। न माङ्योग इत्यडभावः। निघातः।।

उद् हन् 2., to lift up. शम्या॑ f., pin of the yoke.

योक्त्र॑ n., rope, thongs by which an animal is fastened to the yoke.

---

* शम्या युगकीला इत्यादर्शः।

अ॒घ्न्य m., bull.

शू॒नं (शून्य) n., void, loss; शू॒नम् आ ऋ, to come to grief.

This ṛc gives the purpose of the whole hymn: it is the prayer for fording a river without accident. In order to emphasize the prayer, the whole preceding Ākhyāna of a famous river-crossing—for such is the hymn—has been narrated.

The last ṛc is not organically connected with the rest of the hymn. Ṛc 12 shows the accomplished fact of the crossing, ṛc 13, on the other hand, shows an incident during the crossing. That incident is an unfortunate one which is little in keeping with the mighty, successful prayer of Viśvāmitra. The metre, besides, in the first pāda is of a modern type, and so are the two duals अदु॒ष्कृतौ and अ॒घ्न्यौ in the third and fourth pādas. Finally in Sāṅkhāyana Gṛhyasūtra I. 25.20 the ṛc is mentioned as a protecting formula against deep passages at a river-crossing.

If we adopt Sāy.'s view who considers this ṛc to be a part of the narrative itself, then we would have to suppose that after the crossing of the Bhāratas someone—perhaps a दुष्कृत् in opposition to his अदु॒ष्कृतौ अ॒घ्न्यौ—tries to follow the Bhāratas on the ford they had gone; but the swollen waves rushed on and at the prayer of Viśvāmitra at least the innocent beasts are saved.

Sāy. interprets अ॒घ्न्यौ as the two streams. It seems better to take them as the two animals before the cart.

NO. 13.

MAṆḌALA III. **SŪKTA 42.**

उप नः सुतमिति नवर्चं चतुर्थं सूक्तं वैश्वामित्रं गायत्रमैन्द्रम्। उप न इत्यनुक्रमणिका। पूर्वसूक्तेन सहोक्तो विनियोगः।।

Verse 1.

उप॑। नः। सुतम्। आ। गहि। सोम॑म्। इन्द्र। गोऽआ॑शिरम्। हरि॑ऽभ्याम्। यः। ते। अस्मऽयुः।।१।।

हे इन्द्र नोऽस्मदीयं सुतमभिषुतं गवाशिरं पयसा मिश्रितं सोमं प्रति उपागहि। समीप आगच्छ। यतो हरिभ्यामश्वाभ्यां युक्तस्तव रथोऽस्मयुरस्मान्का-मयमानो वर्तते। गवाशिरम्। आङ्पूर्वस्य श्रीणातेः क्विप्यपस्पृधेथामानृचुरित्यादिना शिरित्यादेशः। बहुव्रीहौ पूर्वस्वरः।।

अस्मयु, favourable to us, friend.

The third pāda, according to Sāy., refers to Indra's car. But the construction is so awkwardly elliptic that Sāy. has to understand the very subject of the sentence and युक्तः along with the हरिभ्याम्. Sāy. would translate thus:— They car (yoked) with the two bay ones is favourable to us.—It seems better to take हरिभ्याम् along with आ गहि, and to interpret (with Oldenberg) अस्मयु as referring to the Soma which is called a friend, अस्मयु, in ṚV. IX. 2. 5; 6. 1; 14. 8; 64. 18; 78. 5.

Verse 2.

तम्। इन्द्र। मद॑त्। आ। गहि। बर्हिःऽस्थाम्। ग्राव॑ऽभिः। सुतम्। कुवित्। नु। अस्य। तृष्णव॑ः।।२।।

हे इन्द्र ग्रावभिः सुतमभिषुतं बर्हिःष्ठां बर्हिषि स्थितं मदम्। मद्यतेऽनेनेति मदः सोमः। तमिमं सोममागहि। आगच्छ। कुवित्प्रभूतं यथा भवति तथास्य सोमस्य पाने नु क्षिप्रं तृष्णवः। तृप्तो भव। मदम्। मदी हर्षे। मदोऽनुपसर्ग इत्यप्प्रत्ययः। तस्य पित्त्वादनुदात्तत्वे धातुस्वरः। बर्हिष्ठाम्। ष्ठा गतिनिवृत्तौ। क्विप्। संहितायां पूर्वपदसकारस्यादेशप्रत्ययोरिति षत्व्। ष्टुत्वम्। कृदुत्तरपदस्वरः। तृष्णवः। तृप प्रीणन इत्यस्य लेट्यडागमः। कुविद्योगादनिघातः। क्षुभ्रादिषु नृनमनतृप्नोतीति पठितम्। तथापि सर्वविधीनां छन्दसि विकल्पित्वदत्र णत्वप्रतिषेधो न भवति। प्रत्ययस्वरः।।

तृप्णवः, sbj. rt. तृप् 5., to enjoy.

कुविद्, pronominal interrog. particle with accentuated subj., taking the place of an elliptical expression of doubt, such as:—I wonder whether—.

Verse 3.

इन्द्रम्। इत्था। गिरः। मम। अच्छ। अगुः। इषिताः। इतः। आऽवृते। सोमऽपीतये।।३।।

हे इन्द्र इषितास्त्वदर्थं प्रेरिता इत्थेत्थमनेन प्रकारेणोच्यमाना मम गिरः स्तुतिलक्षणा वाच इन्द्रं त्वामितोऽस्माद्देवयजनदेशादच्छागुः। आभिमुख्येन गच्छन्तु। किमर्थम्। सोमपीतये सोमपानार्थमावृते त्वामावर्तयितुम्। इत्था। इदंशब्दात्था हेतौ च छन्दसीति व्यत्ययेन थाप्रत्ययः। इदम् एतेतौ रथोरितीदित्यादेशः। प्रत्ययस्वरः। अच्छ। अच्छगत्यर्थवदेष्विति गतिसंज्ञा। अगुः। इण् गतावित्यस्य लुङि रूपम्। निघातः।।

आ वृते, dat. inf. rt. वृत् 3., to turn to.

इत्था, on this wise, properly, rightly.

Verse 4.

इन्द्र। सोमाः। सुताः। इमे। तान्। दधिष्व। शतक्रतो इति शतऽक्रतो। जठरे। वाजिनीवसो इति वाजिनीऽवसो।।५।।

हे शतक्रमो इन्द्र इमे सोमाः सुताः। ग्रावभिस्त्वदर्थमभिषुताः। हे वाजिनीवसो अन्नधन। यद्वा। वाजोऽन्नमासु फलत्वेनास्तीति वाजिन्यः क्रियाः। तासां वासक हे इन्द्र तान्सोमरसान् जठरे दधिष्व। धारय। वाजिनीवसो। वाजशब्दान्मत्वर्थेऽत इनिठनावितीनिप्रत्ययः। ऋन्नेभ्यो ङीबिति ङीप्। तासां वसो। संबुद्धौ चेति गुणः। आमन्त्रितत्वादाष्टमिकमनुदात्तत्वम्।।

Verse 6.

विद्म। हि। त्वा। धनंऽजयम्। वाजेषु। दधृषम्। कवे। अध। ते। सुम्नम्। ईमहे।।६।।

हे कवे क्रान्तदर्शिन्निन्द्र वाजेषु युद्धेषु दधृषं शत्रूणामभिभवितारमत एव धनंजयम्। धनं जयतीति धनंजयः। तादृशं त्वा त्वां विद्म हि। जानीमः खलु। अथानन्तरं ते तव सुम्नं धनमीमहे। याचामहे। विद्म। विदेर्लटि विदो लटो वेति मसो मादेशः। पादादित्वादनिघातः। धनंजयम्। जि जय इत्यस्माद्धन उपपदे संज्ञायां भृतृ वृजिधारिसहितपिदम इति खच्प्रत्ययः। अरुर्द्विषदजन्तस्य मुमिति पूर्वपदस्य मुमागमः। चित्त्वादन्तोदात्तः। दधृषम्। ञिधृषा प्रागल्भ्य इत्यस्य यङ्लुक्यभ्यासस्य रीगागमाभावश्छान्दसः। तदन्तात्पचाद्यचि यङोऽचि चेति यङो लुक्। लघूपदधगुणे प्राप्ते न धातुलोप इति तस्य प्रतिषेधः। चित्त्वादन्तोदात्तः।।

वि॒द्म, pf. rt. विद् 2., to know.

ई 2.4; ātm., to go quick, to ask for, to beg.

अध॑ indecl. particle, hence, then.

Verse 7.

इ॒मम्। इ॒न्द्र॒। गोऽआ॑शिरम्। यव॑ऽआशिरम्। च॒। न॒ः। पि॒ब॒। आ॒ऽगत्य॑। वृष॑ऽभिः। सु॒तम्।।७।।

हे इन्द्र गवाशिरं गव्यमिश्रणोपेतं सोमं तथा यवाशिरं यवमिरणोपेतं वृषभिर्ग्रावभिः। सुतमभिषुतं नोऽस्मदीयमिमं सोमं देवयजनमागत्य पिब। गवाशिरं यवाशिरमित्यत्र आङ्पूर्वस्य श्रीणातेः क्विप्यपस्पृधेथामानृचुरित्यादिना शिरित्यादेशः। बहुव्रीहौ पूर्वपदप्रकृतिस्वरः।।

यवा॑शिर, mixed with barley.

Sāy. connects सु॒तम् with वृष॑भिः and interprets the latter by ग्राव॑भिः, the press-stones. This is neither natural nor necessary, hence not acceptable.

Verse 8.

तुभ्य॑। इत्। इ॒न्द्र॒। स्वे। ओ॒क्ये॑। सोम॑म्। चो॒दा॒मि॒। पी॒तये॑। ए॒षः। र॒र॒न्तु॒। ते॒। हृ॒दि।।८।।

हे इन्द्रतुभ्येत्तुभ्यमेव पीतये पानार्थं स्वे स्वकीय ओक्ये स्थाने जठरेऽभिषुतमिमं सोमं चोदामि। प्रेरयामि। एष पीतः सोमस्ते तव हृदि हृदये ररन्तु। अत्यर्थं रमताम्। तुभ्य। युष्मच्छब्दस्य चतुर्थ्येकवचने तुभ्य मह्याविति तुभ्यादेशः। सुपां सुलुगिति सुपो लुक्। ङयि चेत्याद्युदात्तः। ओक्ये। वस्वादित्वात्स्वार्थिको यत्प्रत्ययः। तित्स्वरितः। चोदामि। चुद प्रेरणे। ण्यन्तस्य लटि रूपम्। बहुलमन्यत्रापीति णेर्लुक्। निघातः। ररन्तु। रमु क्रीडायामित्यस्य यङ्लुकि लोटि सर्वविधीनां छन्दसि विकल्पितत्वादत्राभ्यासस्य नुमभावः। संहितायामन्येषामपीत्यभासस्य दीर्घः। निघातः। हृदि। हृदयशब्दस्य पद्धन्नोमास् हृदित्यादिना हृदादेशः। ऊडिदमिति विभक्तेरुदात्तत्वम्।।

ओक्यं (ओक), homely, home.

ररन्तु, 3. sg. impv.; rt. रन् 1. 4; to be well, to rejoice.

चुद् 1., to impel, to urge on, force upon.

Verse 9.

त्वाम्। सुतस्यं। पीतये। प्रत्नम्। इन्द्र। हवामहे। कुशिकासः। अवस्यवः।।९।।

हे इन्द्र अवस्यवस्त्वतो रक्षणमिच्छन्तः कुशिकासः कुशिकगोत्रोत्पन्ना वयं सुतस्य ग्रावभिरभिषुतस्य सोमस्य पीतये पानार्थं प्रत्नं पुरातनं त्वां हवामहे। स्तुति लक्षणाभिर्गीर्भिराह्वयामः। पीतये। स्थागापापचो भाव इति क्तिन्। हिष्ठवत्सरतिशत्थान्तानाम् (फि० १-७) इत्यन्तोदात्तत्वम्। हवामहे। ह्वयतेर्लटि बहुलं छन्दसीति संप्रसारणे रूपम्। अवस्यवः। अव इच्छन्तीत्यर्थे सुपः क्यच्। क्याच्छन्दसीत्युप्रत्ययः। कुशिकासो अवस्यव इत्यत्र संहितायामव्यादवद्यादित्यादिना (पा० ६-१-११६) एङः प्रकृतिभावः।।

NO. 14.

MAṆḌALA IV. **SŪKTA 30.**

नकिरिन्द्रेति चतुर्विंशत्यृचं नवमं सूक्तं वामदेवस्यार्षं गायत्रम्। अष्टमी चतुर्विंशी च द्वे अनुष्टुभौ। इन्द्रो देवता। दिवश्चिदघेत्ययं तृच उषोदेवताक इन्द्रदेवताकश्च। तथा चानुक्रान्तम्। नकिश्चतुर्विंशतिदि विश्चित्तृच उषस्यश्च

(p. 202) उत्तमावर्जमिदं सूक्तम्। तथाच सूत्रितम् नकिरिन्द्र त्वदुत्तर इत्यदुत्तरइत्युत्तमारेत् (आ० ६-४) इति।।

Verse 1.

नकिः। इन्द्र। त्वत्। उत्ऽतरः। न। ज्यायान्। अस्ति। वृत्रऽहन्। नकिः। एव। यथा। त्वम्।।१।।

हे वृत्रहन्निन्द्र वृत्रस्य नाशकेन्द्र। लोक एकोऽपीति शेषः। त्वत्त्वत्त उत्तर उत्कृष्टतरो नकिरस्ति। न भवति। त्वत्तो ज्यायान् प्रशस्यतर एकोऽपि नास्ति। हे इन्द्र त्वं लोके यथा प्रसिद्धो भवसि तथाविध एकोऽपि नकिरेवास्ति। नैव भवति। कश्चिदपि लोक इन्द्रसदृशो नास्तीत्यर्थः।।

The whole hymn consists of tṛcas.

Verse 2.

सत्रा। ते। अनु। कृष्टयः। विश्वा। चक्राऽइव। वावृतुः। सत्रा। महान्। असि। श्रुतः।।२।।

हे इन्द्र कृष्टयः प्रजास्तेत्वामनुलक्षीकृत्य सत्रा सत्यमेव ववृतुः। वर्तन्ते। तत्र दृष्टान्तः। विश्वा विश्वानि व्याप्तानि चक्रेव चक्राणीव। यथा चक्राणि। शकटमनुवर्तन्ते तद्वत्। हे इन्द्र महांस्त्वं सत्रा सत्यमेव श्रुतो विश्रुतोऽसि। गुणैः प्रख्यातो भवसि।।

सत्रा, all together.

The difficulties in this ṛc arise from ते and विश्वा in the first two pādas. We may with Pischel (ZDMG. XXXV. 714 ff.) take ते to be an accusative, depending on अनु, after. It is true, अनु governs mostly, though not exclusively, the accusative case, exceptions are अनु प्रत्नस्यौकसः I. 30. 9, अनु द्युभिः IX, 86. 42. Or ते may be dative of advantage, for thee, in thy honour. Or ते may depend on a substantive which, like मनस्, क्रतु, महित्वम्, itself is governed by अनु, but omitted. Or does ते belong to विश्वा, meaning: all this is yours?

Is विश्वा, correct? If so, then we may take it with चक्रा, (like) all wheels, every wheel (Sāy.). Or taking it with ते, we have to translate either:— The peoples like wheels follow all (accusative) that is yours;—or (विश्वा nominative):— the peoples, (yea) everything, follow thee like wheels. In the latter translation विश्वा would correspond to चक्रा. Or, finally, is विश्वा to be changed into विश्वाः belonging to कृष्टयो? The idea विश्वाः कृष्टयः is genuinely Ṛgvedic, and the corruption into विश्वा might have been occasioned by चक्रा close by. Thus Grassmam, Geldner, Oldenberg. Our translation is based on the more likely interpretation.

Verse 3.

विश्वे। चन। इत्। अना। त्वा। देवासः। इन्द्र। युयुधुः। यत्। अहा। नक्तम्। आ। अतिरः॥३॥

हे इन्द्र विश्वे चनेत्सर्व एव देवासोऽसुरान्विजिगीषवो देवा अना प्राणरूपेण बलेन त्वा त्वां सहायं लब्ध्वा युयुधः। असुरैः सह युद्धं चक्रुः। यद्यस्मा-त्कारणादहा अहःसु नक्तं रात्रिषु चातरः। आ समन्तात् शत्रूनवधीः। अतः-कारणाद्युयुधुरिति पूर्वेण संबन्धः॥

अना (अनया, अमुया, Lat. enim), for.

चन, च न, neither, not even.

आ तृ, to make to cross, penetrate, to prolong towards, into; the causal meaning of आ तृ has its parallel in प्र तृ आयुः, to prolong life.

Sāy's commentary on ṛcas 3-7 cannot be accepted without reserve. Pādas 1 and 2 of ṛc 3:—विश्वे चनेदना त्वा देवास इन्द्र युयुधुः। contain the general statement:—All the gods together did not fight (vanquish) Indra, though he may have been performing feats to which they were opposed.— Pādas

3 of ṛc 3, and ṛcas 4-6 (which form a tṛca) are the proof and illustration of the general statement. Both the grammatical construction and the accent favour this view. In spite of the apparent correlation of the threefold यत्रे at the beginning of ṛcas 4-6 with अत्रे in अत्राह दानुमातिरः, pāda 3, ṛc 7, the context forbids to take ṛcas 4-6 as "adjectival clauses to verse 7." V.G. Bijāpūrkar, Ṛiksangraha, notes i. 1.). The events alluded to in the passage refer mostly to phenomena of light. Ṛc 3 treats of the staying of Sūrya against the common order; ṛc 4 mentions the hiding of the sun by an eclipse or clouds in favour of Kusta and the "hard pressed ones", probably in a battle against the Dāss Suṣṇa. Ṛc 6 speaks of a favour which is the inversion of the last, viz., the disclosing of the sun, and finally of the help given to Etaśa. In ṚV. V. 29. 10 Indra gives one of the two wheels of the sun to Kutsa to drive on with, whilst in our ṛc Indra hides the wheel, the sun. Thus it seems the old great Indra-myth of the winning of the sun on behalf of mankind is here illustrated by a particular case, the regulating of the sun's course and the sun's effect in favour of some individual friend of Indra. For, Kutsa generally appears in the ṚV. as a hero associated with Indra in the defeat of Suṣṇa and in the winning of the sun.

Whether Etaśa "seems merely to designate the horse of the sun" (Macdonell and Keith, Vedic Index, s.v.) or in certain passages is "a protege whom Indra helped against the sun-god Sūrya" (Roth, Petersburg Dict. s.v.) may remain a matter of controversy. The accent shows that in ṛcas 5 and 6 (against the Padapāṭha) two different events in each are mentioned, in ṛc 5 the fight of the opposing gods and the conquest of the enemies, in ṛc 6 the freeing of the sun for a mere mortal and Indra's support of Etaśa. More exact details about all the events in these ṛcas and about most of the others narrated in this hymn are wanting. Nor are we to expect a smooth epic exposition of events in hymns of this nature and age.

Verse 4.

यत्र॑। उ॒त। बा॒धि॒तेभ्यः॑। च॒क्रम्। कुत्सा॑य। युध्य॑ते। मु॒षा॒यः। इ॒न्द्र॒। सूर्य॑म्।।४।।

यत्र यस्मिन्युद्ध उतापि च हे इन्द्र त्वं बाधितेभ्यः कुत्ससहायेभ्यो युध्यते युद्धं कुर्वते कुत्साय च सूर्यं सूर्यसंबन्धि चक्रं मुषायः। अमुष्णाः। अपहृतवानसीत्यर्थः। तस्मिन्युद्धे प्रावः शचीभिरेतशमिति परेण संबन्धः।।

मुषाय denomin., to steal, rob.

Verse 5.

यत्र॑। दे॒वान्। ऋ॒घा॒य॒तः। विश्वा॑न्। अयु॑ध्यः। एकः॑। इत्। त्वम्। इ॒न्द्र॒। व॒नून्। अह॑न्।।५।।

हे इन्द्र त्वमेक इदसहाय एव यत्र यस्मिन् संग्रामे देवानिन्द्रादीनृघायतो बाधमानान्विश्वान् सर्वान् राक्षसादीनयुध्यः। युद्धमकरोः। तथा वनून् हिंसकानहन्। अवधीः।।

ऋघाय denomin., to shake, tremble (with rage), to be furious.

व॒नु (rt. वन्), eager, desirous, enemy.

Verse 6.

यत्र॑। उ॒त। मर्त्या॑य। कम्। अरि॑णाः। इ॒न्द्र॒। सूर्य॑म्। प्र। आ॒व॒ः। शची॑भिः। एत॑शम्।।६।।

यत्र यस्मिन् संग्राम उतापि च हे इन्द्र त्वं मर्त्याय मनुष्यायैतशाख्याय ऋषये सूर्यमरिणाः। अहिंसीः। कमिति पूरणः। तदानीं शचीभिर्युद्धकर्मभिरेत-शमेतत्संज्ञकमृषिं प्रावः। प्रकर्षेणारक्षः।।

कम् emphasizes the dative.

रि 9., to let loose.

Verse 7.

किम्। आत्। उ॒त। अ॒सि॒। वृ॒त्र॒ऽह॒न्। मघ॑ऽवन्। म॒न्यु॒मत्ऽत॑मः। अत्र॑। अह॑। दानु॑म्। आ। अ॒ति॒रः॥७॥

हे वृत्रहन् वृत्राणामावरकाणां तमसां हन्तर्मघवन्धनवन्निन्द्र त्वमादनन्तरमेव उतापि च। किमिति प्रश्ने। मन्युमत्तमोऽसि। अत्यन्तं क्रोधवान् भवसि। अत्रास्मिन्नन्तरिक्षे अह एव दानुं दनोः पुत्रं वृत्रमातिरः। आ समन्तादहिंसीः॥

Verse 8.

ए॒तत्। घ॒। इत्। उ॒त। वी॒र्य॑म्। इन्द्र॑। च॒कर्थ॑। पौंस्य॑म्। स्त्रिय॑म्। यत्। दु॒ःऽह॒ना॒युव॑म्। वधीः॑। दु॒हि॒तर॑म्। दि॒वः॥८॥

हे इन्द्र उतापि च यत् यस्त्वमेतदुपलक्षितं पौंस्यं बलं वीर्यं सामर्थ्योपेतं चकर्थ। कृतवानसि। घेदिति पूरणौ। किंच दुर्हणायुवं दुष्टं हननमिच्छन्तीं दिवो दुहितरं द्युलोकसकाशादुत्पन्नां स्त्रियमुषसं वधीः। अवधीः॥

दु॒र्ह॒णा॒यु, hard-hearted, ungracious.

Verse 9.

दि॒वः। चि॒त्। घ॒। दु॒हि॒त॒रम्। म॒हान्। म॒ही॒यमा॑नाम्। उ॒षस॑म्। इ॒न्द्र॒। सम्। पि॒ण॒क्॥९॥

हे इन्द्र महांस्त्वं दिवो दुहितरं द्युलोकस्य पुत्रीं महीयमानां पूज्यमानामुषसमुषोदेवीं संपिणक् चिद्ध। संपिष्टवानसि खलु॥

पिणक्, impf. rt. पिष् 7., to crush.

Verse 10.

अप॑। उ॒षाः। अन॑सः। स॒र॒त्। संऽपि॑ष्टात्। अह॑। बि॒भ्युषी॑। नि। यत्। सी॒म्। शि॒श्नथ॑त्। वृषा॑॥१०॥

वृषा कामानां वर्षितेन्द्रो यत् यदा सीमेतदुषः संबन्धि शकटं निशिश्नथत्। न्यवधीत्। तदोषा उषोदेवता बिभ्युषीन्द्रसकाशाद्भीता सती संपिष्टादिन्द्रेण संचूर्णितादनसः शकटादपसरत्। अपासरत् अपजगाम। अहेति पूरणः॥

शिश्नथत्, aor. rt. श्नथ् 2., to pierce, to shatter.

Verse 11.

एतत्। अस्याः। अनः। शये। सुऽसंपिष्टम्। विऽपाशि। आ। ससार। सीम्। पराऽवतः।।११।।

सुसंपिष्टमिन्द्रेण सुष्ठु संचुर्णितमस्या उषसः संबन्ध्येतदनः शकटं विपाशि विपाडाख्या नदी। तस्यां तत्तीर आशये। आ समन्ताच्छेते। अशेत। सीमियमुषोदेवता शकटे भग्ने सति परावतो दूरदेशात्ससार। अपससार।।

शये, 3. sg. pres. ātm. rt. शी 2., to lie.

Sāy's interpretation has to take आ out of its natural connection with विपाशि, has to neglect altogether सीम्, and to take the ablative परावतः as meaning "into the distance": all this is hardly acceptable.

Verse 12.

उत। सिन्धुम्। विऽबाल्यम्। विऽतस्थानाम्। अधि। क्षमि। परि। स्थाः। इन्द्र। मायया।।१२।।

हे इन्द्र उतापि च विबाल्यं विगतबाल्यावस्थां संपूर्णजलां वितस्थानां वितिष्ठमानां सिन्धुं नदीमधिक्षमि क्षमायां मायया प्रज्ञया परिष्ठाः। पर्यस्थाः। सर्वतः। स्थापनं कृतवानसि।।

तस्थान, pt. pt. pass. rt. स्था.

Verse 13.

उत। शुष्णस्य। धृष्णुऽया। प्र। मृक्षः। अभि। वेदनम्। पुरः। यत्। अस्य। संपिणक्।।१३।।

उतापि च हे इन्द्र धृष्णुया धृष्णुः धर्षकस्त्वं शुष्णस्य शुष्णनाम्नोऽसुरस्य संबन्धि वेदनं वित्तमभि अभितः सर्वतः प्र मृक्षः। प्रकर्षेणाबाधथाः। यद्यदास्य शुष्णस्य पुरः पुराणि नगराणि संपिणक्। संपिष्टवानसि। तदा प्र मृक्ष इति संबन्धः।।

धृ॒ष्णु adj., धृ॒ष्णु॒या adv., courageously, boldly.

अ॒भि प्र मृ॒ष् to catch, take hold of, seize; मृक्षः, 2. sg. aor. par.

Verse 14.

उ॒त। दा॒सम्। कौ॒लि॒ऽत॒रम्। बृ॒ह॒तः। पर्व॑तात्। अधि॑। अव॑। अ॒ह॒न्। इ॒न्द्र॒। शम्ब॑रम्॥१४॥

उतापि च हे इन्द्र त्वं दासमुपक्षपयितारं कौलितरं कुलितरनाम्नोऽपत्यं शम्बरमसुरं बृहतो महतः पर्वतादद्रेरध्युपरि अव अवाचीनं कृत्वाहन्। हतवानसि॥

अधि॑ postpos., with ablative, down from.

Verse 15.

उ॒त। दा॒सस्य॑। व॒र्चिनः॑। स॒हस्रा॑णि। श॒ता। अ॒व॒धीः॒। अधि॑। पञ्च॑। प्र॒धीन्ऽइ॑व॥१५॥

उतापि च हे इन्द्र त्वं प्रधीनिव चक्रस्य परितः स्थितान् शङ्कूनिव हिंसकान्पञ्चशता पञ्चशतानि पञ्चशतसंख्याकान् सहस्राणि सहस्रसंख्याकान्दासस्य लोकानामुपक्षपयितुर्वर्चिनो वर्चिनामकस्यासुरस्य संबन्धिनोऽनुचरान्पुरुषानध्यधिकमवधीः। हतवानसि॥

प्र॒धि m., felly.

Sāy. is satisfied with a comparatively small number of destroyed Dāsas. The wording would seem to favour our rendering in the translation. The simile of the wheel, the circumference of which is cut up into the fellies, to illustrate the thorough destruction of men is very appropriate.

Verse 16.

उ॒त। त्यम्। पु॒त्रम्। अ॒ग्रुवः॑। परा॑ऽवृक्तम्। श॒तऽक्र॑तुः। उ॒क्थेषु॑। इन्द्रः॑। आ। अ॒भ॒ज॒त्॥१६॥

उतापि च शतक्रतुः *शतकर्मेन्द्रस्त्यं तं प्रसिद्धमग्रुव एतन्नाम्न्याः पुत्रं

* प्रथमावृत्तौ शतकर्मा इति नास्ति।

परावृक्तमेतन्नामकमुक्थेषु स्तोत्रेष्वभजत्। भागिनं कृतवान्। अयमर्थो वम्रीभिः पुत्रमग्रुवः (ऋ. ४-१९-९) इत्यस्यामृचि प्रतिपादित इति।।

अग्रू f., the unmarried one, the maid.

परा वृज्, 7., to give up, to cast away.

Verse 17.

उत। त्या। तुर्वशायदू इति। अस्नातारा। शचीऽपतिः। इन्द्रः। विद्वान्। अपारयत्।।१७।।

उतापि च अस्नातारास्नातारौ ययातिशापादनभिषिक्तौ त्या त्यौ तौ प्रसिद्धौ तुर्वशायदू तुर्वशनामानं यदुनामकं च राजानौ शचीपतिः कर्मणां पालकः। यद्वा। शचीन्द्रस्य भार्या तस्याः पतिर्भर्ता। विद्वान् सकलमपि जानन्निन्द्रोऽपारयत्। अभिषेकार्हावकरोत्।।

अ स्नातृ, not bathing, not getting wet.

Verse 18.

उत। त्या। सद्यः। आर्या। सरयोः। इन्द्र। पारतः। अर्णाचित्ररथा। अवधीः।।१८।।

उतापि च सद्यः सपदि हे इन्द्र त्वं त्या त्यौ तावार्यावार्यत्वर्याभि मानिनौ सन्तावपि। इन्द्रविषयभक्तिश्रद्धारहितावित्यर्थः। सरयोः सरय्वा नद्याः पारतः पारे तीरे वसन्तार्णचित्ररथा अर्णनामकं चित्ररथनामकं च राजानाववधीः। अहिंसीः।।

Verse 19.

अनु। द्वा। जहिता। नयः। अन्धम्। श्रोणम्। च। वृत्रऽहन्। न। तत्। सुम्नम्। अष्टवे।।१९।।

हे वृत्रहन् वृत्रस्य हिंसकेन्द्र त्वं जहिता जहितौ सर्वैर्बन्धुभिस्त्यक्ताबन्धं चक्षुर्हीनमेकं श्रोणं च पङ्गुमपरं च द्वा एतौ द्वावनुनयः। अन्धपङ्गुत्वपरिहारेणानु-नीतवानसि। हे इन्द्र ते त्वया दत्तं तत्सुम्न सुखमष्टवे व्याप्तुं कोऽपि न प्रभवतीति शेषः।।

अष्टुं, inf. rt. अंश् 5., to attain; अष्टवे, dat.

जुहित, pt. pf. pass. rt. हा 3., to leave.

Verse 20.

शतम्। अश्मन्ऽमयीनाम्। पुराम्। इन्द्रः। वि। आस्यत्। दिवःऽदासाय। दाशुषे।।२०।।

इन्द्रोऽश्मन्मयीनां पाषाणैर्निर्मितानां पुरां शम्बरस्य संबन्धिनां नगराणां शतं शतसंख्याकं दिवोदासायैतन्नामकाय दाशुषे हविर्दत्तवते यजमानाय व्यास्यत्। व्यक्षिपत्।।

Read अश्मन्मयीन+अम्. The ṛc. is apt to throw some light on the military architecture, and possibly on architecture in general, in Vedic times.

Verse 21.

अस्वापयत्। दभीतये। सहस्रा। त्रिंशतम्। हथैः। दासानाम्। इन्द्रः। मायया।।२१।।

इन्द्रो मायया स्वकीयया शक्त्या दासानां लोकानामुपक्षपयितॄणां राक्षसादीनां त्रिंशतं त्रिंशत्संख्याकानि सहस्रा सहस्राणि दभीतये दभीतयनामक-स्यार्थाय हथैर्हननसाधनैरायुधैरस्वापयत्। अवधीत्।।

हथ m., deadly blow.

Verse 22.

सः। घ। इत्। उत। असि। वृत्रऽहन्। समानः। इन्द्र। गोऽपतिः। यः। ता। विश्वानि। चिच्युषे।।२२।।

उतापि च हे इन्द्र यस्त्वं ता तानि विश्वानि समस्तान् शत्रून् चिच्युषे। प्राच्यावयः। हे वृत्रहन् वृत्राणां हिंसकेन्द्र गोपतिर्गवां पालकः स त्वं समानः सर्वेषां यजमानानां समः सन् प्रख्यातोऽसि। घेदिति पूरणौ।।

च्यु 1., to move, shake.

Verse 23.

उत। नूनम्। यत्। इन्द्रियम्। करिष्याः। इन्द्र। पौंस्यम्। अद्य। नकिः। तत्। आ। मिनत्।।२३।।

उतापि च हे इन्द्र यत्पौंस्यं त्वदीयं बलमिन्द्रियं सामर्थ्योपेतं नूनं करिष्याः। कृतवानसि खलु। अद्याद्यतनः कश्चित्तद्बलं नकिरामिनत्। न हिंस्यात्।।

करिष्याः, fut. sbj. rt. कृ.

आ मिनत्, subj. rt. मी 9., to damage, prevent.

Verse 24.

वामंऽवामम्। ते। आऽदुरे। देवः। ददातु। अर्यमा। वामम्। पूषा। वामम्। भगः। वामम्। देवः। करूळती।।२४।।

हे आदुरे शत्रूणामादारयितरिन्द्र ते तव वामं वामं यद्यद्वननीयं संभजनीयं धनमस्ति लोके तद्वामं वस्वर्यमारीणां नियमयितैतन्नामको देवो ददातु। प्रयच्छतु। तथा करूळती कृत्तदन्तः पूषा पोषको देवो वामं धनं ददातु। भगोऽपि धनं ददातु। ननु करूळतीत्येतत्संनिहितत्वाद्भग इत्यनेन संबन्धनीयम्। अथवार्यमादीनां त्रयाणामपि विशेषणत्वेन भाव्यम्। कथं पूष्णो विशेषणं स्यादिति साकाङ्क्षत्वान्नासांनिध्याकाङ्क्षयोः सद्भावेऽपि योग्यतामन्तरेणान्वयायोगात्। तस्मात्पूषा प्रपिष्टभागोऽदन्तक (तै. सं. २-६-८५) इत्यादिश्रुतिषु पूष्ण एवादन्तकत्वेन प्रसिद्धेर्व्यवहितस्यापि तस्यैव विशेषणत्वं युक्तम्। वामं वननीयं भवतीत्यादि निरुक्तम् (६-३१) अत्र द्रष्टव्यम्।।

आदुरि (आ दृ) adj., attentive.

करूळतिन्, with decaying teeth.

करूळती seems, against Sāy., to be an epithet of Pūṣan.

If not the legend itself, some forerunner of it, as it is mentioned is Satapathabrāhmaṇa 1. 7. 4. 7, may have been current when this hymn was written. The fact that Pūṣan is thus twice invoked, once with वामं पूषा between Aryaman and Bhaga, and once with वा॒मं दे॒वः करू॑ळती, may be explained by the desire to rank Pūṣan among other auspicious deities, on the one hand, and by the earnest appeal, on the other, to Pūṣan by means of his most prominent characteristic.

NO. 15.

MAṆḌALA V. **SŪKTA 1.**

आत्रेये पञ्चमे मण्डले षडनुवाकाः। तत्र प्रथमेऽनुवाके चतुर्दश सूक्तानि। तत्राबोध्यग्निरिति द्वादशर्चं प्रथमं सूक्तम्। अत्रेयमनुक्रमणिका। अबोधि द्वादश बुधगविष्ठिराविति। पञ्चमे मण्डलेऽनुक्तगोत्रमात्रेयं विद्यादिति परिभाषितत्वादाम्त्रेयौ बुधगविष्ठिरावृषी। अनादेशपरिभाषया त्रिष्टुप्। मण्डलादिपरिभाषयग्निर्देवता। प्रातरनुवाक आग्नेये क्रतौ त्रैष्टुभे छन्दस्याश्विनशस्त्रे चैतदादिचत्वारि सूक्तानि। तथा च सूत्रितम्। अबोध्यग्निः समिधेति चत्वारि (आ० ४-१३) इति। अध्यायोत्सर्जनोपाकरणयोर्धामं ते विश्वमिति द्यृचत्वेन विनियोग उक्तः।।

Verse 1.

अबो॑धि। अ॒ग्निः। स॒म्ऽइधा॑। जना॑नाम्। प्रति॑। धे॒नुम्ऽइ॑व। आ॒ऽय॒तीम्। उ॒षस॑म्। य॒ह्वाःऽइ॑व। प्र। व॒याम्। उ॒त्ऽजिहा॑नाः। प्र। भा॒नवः॑। सि॒स्र॒ते॒। नाक॑म्। अच्छ॑।।१।।

अयमग्निर्जनानामध्वर्य्वादीनां समिधा समिद्भिरबोधि। प्रबुद्धोऽभूत्। धेनुमिव। अग्निहोत्रार्थधेनुं प्रति यथा प्रातर्बुध्यते तद्वदायतीमागच्छन्तीमुषसं प्रति। उषःकाल इत्यर्थः। अथ प्रबुद्धस्याग्नेर्भानवो ज्वाला यह्वा महान्तो वयां शाखां प्रोज्जिहानाः प्रोद्गमयन्तो वृक्षा इव प्रोज्जिहानाः स्वाधिष्ठानं त्यजन्तो नाकमन्तरिक्षमच्छाभिमुख्येन प्रसिस्रते। प्रसरन्ति।।

The simile यु॒व्हा इ॑व॒ प्र व॒याम्० in the second line was conceived well by the poet, but not quite so consistently carried out. Though birds flying up to a branch is not such an impossibility as Peterson (in the 1st ed. p. 216) thought it to be, yet one would prefer to see the birds flying from the branch towards the sky, rather than towards the branch. But then the upameya would give the *terminus a quo,* the upamāna giving the *terminus ad quem* of the movement in question, which is against the rules of a good comparison in which both the upamāna and the upameya must give either the place wherefrom the movement starts or that whereto it tends, if the term is at all a part of the comparison. जिहा॑न cannot be taken to belong to the root हा 3., par., to leave: thus both grammar and the concinnity of the simile, a taste for which the Vedic poets may very well be credited with, suggest the rendering given in the translation. Sāy.'s interpretation seems to be rather forced; the commentator Mahīdhara, explaining Vājasaneyi-Saṁhitā XV. 24 where this ṛc occurs, misinterprets प्र उ ज्जिहा॑नाः.

य॒व्ह m., quick moving, bird (?).

व॒या (द्रया?) f., branch.

प्र उ॒द् जिहा॑न, pt. pres. ātm; rt. हा 3., ātm; to rise, fly up towards.

सि॒स्र॒ते, 3. plur. pres. ātm; rt. सृ 3.

Verse 2.

अबो॑धि। होता॑। य॒जथा॑य। दे॒वान्। ऊ॒र्ध्वः। अ॒ग्निः। सु॒ऽमनाः॑। प्रा॒तः। अ॒स्था॒त्। सं॒ऽइ॑द्धस्य। रूश॑त्। अ॒द॒र्शि॒। पाज॑ः। म॒हान्। दे॒वः। तम॑सः। निः। अ॒मो॒चि॒॥२॥

अयं होता होमनिष्पादकोऽग्निर्देवान्यष्टव्यान्यजथाय यष्टुमबोधि। बुध्यते। सोऽग्निः प्रातःकाले सुमनाः शोभनमनस्को यजमानानुग्रहबुद्धिः सन् ऊर्ध्वोऽस्थात्। उत्तिष्ठति। समिद्धस्यास्य रुशद्रोचमानं पाजो बलं ज्वालालक्षणमदर्शि। दृश्यते। अथ तथाभूतो महान्देवस्तमसोऽन्धकारान्निरमोचि। निर्मुक्तोऽभूत्॥

रुश् (रूच्), only pt., bright.

पाज॑स् n., glow, light.

Verse 3.

यत्। ईम्। ग॒णस्य॑। र॒श॒नाम्। अजी॑ग॒रिति॑। शुचि॑ः। अ॒ङ्क्ते॒।

शुचिऽभिः। गोभिः। अग्निः। आत्। दक्षिणा। युज्यते। वाजऽयन्ती। उत्तानाम्। ऊर्ध्वः। अधयत्। जुहूभिः।।३।।

यद्यदेमयमग्निर्गणस्य सङ्घात्मकस्य जगतो रशनां *रज्जुमिव व्यापार-प्रतिबन्धकं तमोऽजीगः। गिरति गृह्णाति वा। समिद्धो भवतीत्यर्थः। तदा शुचि दीप्तोऽग्निः शुचिभिर्गोभिर्दीप्तै रश्मिभिरङ्क्ते। व्यनक्ति विश्वं जगत्। आदनन्तरमेव दक्षिणा प्रवृद्धा वाजयन्त्यन्नमिच्छन्त्याज्यधारा युज्यते। युक्ता भवति। अथवा दक्षिणा प्रवृद्धाज्यधारा युज्यते। तां च धारामुत्तानामूर्ध्वतानामुपरि विस्तृतामूर्ध्वं उन्नतः सन् जुहूभिरधयत्। पिबति।।

अजीगर्, aor. rt. गृ, to arouse, wake up.

जुहू f., ladle, tongue.

धा 4., to suck, sip, drink.

रशना is according to Sāy. the darkness. Oldenberg (Textkrit. i. l.) says the रशना, rope, with which the animal Agni is tied and led on, is the prayer, etc. For the leading on of Agni with a rope he fitly refers to ṚV. IV. 1.9. Agni then rouses the prayer of the worshipping गण. The sequel, first, the rope, then the ointing, would correspond with the ritual of the animal sacrifice. Or does रशना mean the तन्ति to which the calves are tied (see Gobhilagṛhyasūtra III.6 and ṚV. VI. 24. 4)? The more usual modern interpretation is to take रशना to mean the line, the row of followers or worshippers, which cannot be said to be quite satisfactory either.

Hillebrandt, Lieder d. ṚV. p. 12, takes रशनां to stand for रशना, the string. He translates:—Since the string of the crowd (of the fingers) roused him.

गोभिः, the cause, stands for घृतेन, the effect; cp. the classical घृतमायुः of the Alaṁkāraśāstra.

---

* आदर्शे रज्जुरिव इति पाठः।

Pischel's view, Ved. Stud. II. 113, that जुहूभिः means "with ladles" and is to be taken with ऊर्ध्वा is not convincing.

उत्तानाम् cannot mean the दक्षिणा; the thing qualified by उत्तानाम् is contained in the second pāda. The cow, i.e. घृत, is raised in the ladle and in a broad stream poured into the fire.

The expression दक्षिणा युज्यते shows that the professional reward of the priest was compared to a car.

Verse 4.

अग्निम्। अच्छ। देवऽयताम्। मनांसि। चक्षूंषिऽइव। सूर्ये। सम्। चरन्ति। यत्। ईम्। सुवाते इति। उषसा। विरूपे इति विऽरूपे। श्वेतः। वाजी। जायते। अग्रे। अह्नाम्।।४।।

अग्निं देवमच्छाभिमुख्येन देवयतां देवानात्मन इच्छतां यजमानानां मनांसि संचरन्ति। देवा यष्टव्यास्तदर्थं कदायं वर्धिष्यतीति ध्यायन्तीत्यर्थः। चक्षूंषीव सर्वेषां प्राणिनां यथा सूर्ये संचरन्ति तद्वत्। यद्यदेमेनमग्निमुषसा सह विरूपे *नानारूपे द्यावापृथव्यौ सुवाते। जनयतः। तदानीं श्वेतः प्रकृष्टवर्णोपेतो वाजी वेजनवानग्निरह्नामग्र उदयकाले जायते। प्रवर्धत इत्यर्थः।।

सुवाते, 3. du. pres. ātm.; rt. सू 2., to bear.

उषसा may be taken as a regular dual, referring to the morning and evening twilights. But the white horse is said to be born by them in the beginning of the day. Besides, the two twilights are not so vastly different in shape or colour from each other that the difference would call for the characteristic epithet विरूपे. Sāy.'s interpretation has the defect of supplementing सह in order to take उषसा as instr. sg. There remains the possibility to regard उषसा as the first member of

---

* प्रथमावृत्तौ नानारूपे इति नास्ति।

an incomplete, but quite Vedic, *dvandva* cpd. Considering the context, the most natural complement would then seem to be रात्री॑, night.

It is not a matter of course that the white horse is Agni in the form of the sun (Peterson, 1st ed.). Cp. first line of the next ṛc.

Verse 5.

जनि॑ष्ट। हि। जेन्यः॑। अग्रे॑। अह्ना॑म्। हि॒तः। हि॒तेषु॑। अ॒रु॒षः। वने॑षु। दमे॑ऽदमे। स॒प्त। रा॒। दधा॑नः। अ॒ग्निः। होता॑। नि। स॒सा॒द॒। यजी॑यान्।।५।।

अयमग्निर्जेन्य उत्पादनीयोऽह्लमग्र उदयकाले जनिष्ट। प्रादुरभूत्। पश्चात् हितेषु वनेषु वनोत्थेषु कोष्ठेष्वरूष आरोचमानः सन् हितः। स्थापितः। पश्चाद्दमे दमे तत्तद्यागगृहे सप्त रत्ना रमणीयाः सप्त ज्वाला दधानो धारयमाणः। अथवा यजमानेभ्यः सप्तविधानि रत्नानि दधानोऽग्निर्होता होमनिष्पादकः सन् यजीयान्यष्टब्यः सन् निषसाद। निषण्णो भवति।।

यजी॑यस्, comparative of the verbal यज्, better (or very) skilled in sacrificing.

जेन्य॑ (जन्), noble, of noble lineage.

Verse 6.

जीवति यजमाने मृत इति शब्दो यदि स्यात्तदानीं सुरभिमतीष्टिः कार्या। तत्रेयमनुवाक्या। सूत्रितं च। अग्निर्होता न्यसीदद्यजीयान्त्साध्वीमकर्देववीतिं नो अद्य (ऐ० ब्रा० ७-९) इति

अ॒ग्निः। होता॑। नि। अ॒सी॒द॒त्। यजी॑यान्। उ॒पऽस्थे॑। मा॒तुः। सु॒र॒भौ। ऊ॒ं इति॑। लो॒के। युवा॑। क॒विः। पु॒रु॒निः॒ऽस्थः। ऋ॒तऽवा॑। ध॒र्ता। कृ॒ष्टी॒नाम्। उ॒त। मध्ये॑। इ॒द्धः।।६।।

अयमग्निर्होता होमनिष्पादकः सन् यजीयान्यष्टव्यश्च सन् न्यसीदत्। निषसाद। कुत्रेति तदुच्यते। मातुः सर्वस्य निर्मातुर्भूम्या उपस्थ उत्सङ्गे

तत्रापि सुरभौ आज्यादिसौरभ्ययुक्ते लोके सर्वैर्द्रष्टव्य स्थाने वेदिलक्षणे। उतापि च युवा नित्यतरुणः सर्वत्र मिश्रितो वा कविर्मेधावी पुरुनिःष्ठो बहुस्थान ऋतावा यत्रवान्धर्ता सर्वस्य धरक एवं भूतः सन् कृष्टीनामृत्विग्यजमानानां मध्य इद्ध *दीप्तः सन् वर्तत इति शेषः।।

उ॒ लो॒क, possibly from उ॒रू लो॒क, originally seems to have been one word, split up by the diaskeuasts of the primitive text.

Verse 7.

प्र। नु। त्यम्। विप्र॑म्। अ॒ध्व॒रेषु॑। सा॒धुम्। अ॒ग्रिम्। होता॑रम्। ई॒ळ॒ते॒। नम॑ःऽभिः। आ। यः। त॒तान॑। रोद॑सी॒। इति॑। ऋ॒तेन॑। नित्य॑म्। मृ॒ज॒न्ति॒। वा॒जिन॑म्। घृ॒तेन॑।।७।।

त्यं तमग्निं नर्मोभः स्तुतिभिर्नु क्षिप्रमीळते। स्तुवन्ति। कीदृशं तम्। विप्रं मेधाविनमध्वरेषु साधुं फलसाधकं होतारं होमनिष्पादकम्। यो देवो रोदसी द्यावापृथिव्यावृतेनोदकेनाततान। विस्तारितवान्। अग्नौ प्रास्ताहुतेरादित्यद्वारा वृष्ट्युत्पादकत्वात्। अथवा ऋतेन सत्यभूतेन हविषा दिवं तथाभूतेन वृष्ट्यादिफलेन भुवं चाततान। वाजिनमन्नवन्तं देवं यजमाना नित्यं घृतेनोदकेनाज्येन वा मृजन्ति। परिचरन्ति।।

ईड् 2., ātm., to praise.

मृज् 2., par., to wipe, polish, make shine.

Verse 8.

मा॒र्जा॒ल्य॑ः। मृ॒ज्य॒ते॒। स्वे। दमू॑नाः। क॒वि॒ऽप्र॒श॒स्तः। अति॑थिः। शि॒वः। न॒ः। स॒हस्र॑ऽशृङ्गः। वृ॒ष॒भः। तत्ऽओ॑जाः। विश्वा॑न्। अ॒ग्ने॒। सह॑सा। प्र। अ॒सि॒। अ॒न्यान्।।८।।

मार्जाल्यः संमार्जनीयोऽयमग्निर्मृज्यते। परिचर्यते। स्वे स्वकीये स्थाने। कीदृशोऽयम्। दमूना दानमना दान्तमना वा कविप्रशस्तः कविभिर्मेधाविभिः प्रशस्तः प्रकर्षेण स्तुत्यो नोऽसमाकमतिथिवत्पूज्यः शिवः सुखकरश्च।

* समिद्धः सन् इत्यादर्शः।

सहस्रशृङ्गोऽपरिमितज्वालो वृषभो वर्षिता फलानां तदोजाः। यत्प्रसिद्धं बलं तेजो वास्ति तदेवौजो यस्य तादृशः। सर्वबलस्वरूप इत्यर्थः। अथ प्रत्यक्षवादः। हे अग्ने विश्वानन्यान् स्वव्यतिरिक्तान् सर्वान् सहसा बलेन प्रासि। प्रेति परेत्यर्थे। पराभवसि। व्याप्तुं वा प्रभवसि।।

मार्जाल्यं (मृज्), one who likes to be cleaned.

दमूनस्, belonging to the house, house-friend.

Verse 9.

प्र। सद्यः। अग्ने। अति। एषि। अन्यान्। आविः। यस्मै। चारुऽतमः। बभूथ। ईळेन्यः। वपुष्यः। विभाऽवा। प्रियः। विशाम्। अतिथिः। मानुषीणाम्।।९।।

हे अग्ने त्वं यज्ञमासाद्य प्र सद्यस्तदानीमेवान्यान् स्वसमानानत्येषि। अतिक्रामसि। यस्मै चारूतमः सन्नाविर्बभूथ। किंच त्वमीळेन्यः स्तुत्यो वपुष्यो वपुष्करो दीप्तिकरो वा विभावा विशिष्टदीप्तिमान् प्रियः प्रियभूतो विशां सर्वेषां प्राणिनां तथातिथिः पूज्यो मानुषीणां प्रजानां भवसि।।

Verse 10.

तुभ्यम्। भरन्ति। क्षितयः। यविष्ठ। बलिम्। अग्ने। अन्तितः। आ। उत। दूरात्। आ। भन्दिष्ठस्य। सुऽमतिम्। चिकिद्धि। बृहत्। ते। अग्ने। महि। शर्म। भद्रम्।।१०।।

हे यविष्ठ युवतमाग्ने तुभ्यं क्षितयो मनुष्या भरन्ति। संपादयन्ति। किम्। बलिं पूजां हविर्लक्षणामन्तितोऽन्तिकादुतापि च दूरात्। आ इति चार्थे। किंच भन्दिष्ठस्यातिशयेन स्तोतुः सुमतिं स्तुतिमाचिकिद्धि। आजानीहि। हे अग्ने ते तव शर्म सुखमस्मभ्यं दातव्यं *बृहन्महत् महि भद्रं महत्स्तुत्यं च।।

चिकिद्धि, impv. par.; rt. चित् 2., to see, perceive; आ चित्, to notice.

भन्दिष्ठ (भन्द्) the best, most shining, brilliant.

---

* आदर्शे बृहन्महद्भद्रं स्तुत्यं च इति पाठः।

In the third pāda आ भन्दिष्ठस्य सुमतिं चिकिद्धि, भन्दिष्ठस्य has been made by Oldenberg (S.B.E. XLVI. pp. 364-65) to refer to Agni. Consequently the whole pāda is to be considered as an address to the यजमान. Sāy. sees in the third as well as in the other three pādas an address to Agni and understands भन्दिष्ठस्य of the best worshipper. His view, as being more consistent, is preferable.

Verse 11.

आ। अद्य। रथम्। भानुऽमः। भानुऽमन्तम्। अग्ने। तिष्ठ। यजतेभिः। संऽअन्तम्। विद्वान्। पथीनाम्। उरू। अन्तरिक्षम्। आ। इह। देवान्। हविःऽअद्याय। वक्षि।।११।।

हे भानुमो दीप्तिमन्नग्ने अद्यास्मिन्यागदिने भानुमन्तं दीप्तिमन्तं समन्तं समीचीनप्रान्तोपेतं रथं जयतेभिर्यष्टव्यैर्देवैः सहा तिष्ठ। आरोह। विद्वान्यष्टव्य-देवपरिज्ञानवांस्त्वं पथीनां देवयजनमार्गान्प्रति। द्वितीयार्थे षष्ठी। उर्वन्तरिक्षं प्रभ्भूतेऽन्तरिक्षे देवानयष्टव्यान्हविरद्याय हविर्भक्षणायेहावक्षि। आवहसि।।

वक्षि, 2. sg. aor. subj.; rt. वह् 1.

समन्त adj., neighbouring, together with.

हविरद्य (अद्) n., the eating of the हविस्, the sacrificial meal. Sāy. takes the accusative उर्व१न्तरिक्षम् to be independent of विद्वान् and to mean प्रभूते अंन्तरिक्षे. Oldenberg, 1. c., thinks that "विद्वान्, which may be construed with the genitive or with the accusative, stands here with both cases." He translates the passage:—knowing the paths, the wide air. Neither of these two interpretations seems to be satisfactory. अन्तरि क्षम् means that which is lying between, the midspace, the distance. Accordingly we might translate:—the distance of the ways. Or we may consider the phrase पथीनामुर्व१नतरिक्षम् to be a primitive *hypallage:*—he knows the midspace of the ways—, instea of:—he knows the ways of the midspace. Or, and better, उ॒र्व१॒॑न्तरि॑क्षम् is considered to be accusative of spacial extension:—through, all along the aerial space.

Verse 12.

अवो॑चाम। क॒वये॑। मेध्या॑य। वचः॑। व॒न्दारु॑। वृ॒ष॒भाय॑। वृष्णे॑। गवि॑ष्ठिरः। नम॑सा। स्तोम॑म्। अ॒ग्नौ। दि॒विऽइ॑व। रु॒क्मम्। उ॒रु॒ऽव्यञ्च॑म्। अ॒श्रे॒त्।।१२।।

वयमात्रेयाः कवये मेधाविने मेध्याय मेधार्हाय वृषभाय वर्षकाय फलानां वृषणे सेक्त्रे यूने वन्दारु वन्दनशीलं वचः स्तोत्रमवोचाम्। अथ ऋषिरात्मानं परोक्षेणैव निर्दिश्यच स्तुतिमुपसंहरति। गविष्ठिरोऽयमृषिर्नमसा नमस्कारेण हविषा वा युक्तं स्तोमं स्तोत्रं अग्नावश्रेत्। श्रयति स्म। दिवि रुक्मं रोचमानं उरुव्यञ्चमुरुगमनमादित्यमिव।।

मेध्य॑, wise, worthy of praise.

व॒न्दारु॑ (rt. वन्द्), praising.

रु॒क्म m., gold, esp. of the sun, considered as the golden ornament of heaven.

उ॒रु॒व्यच् adj., far-reaching, far-spreading.

NO. 16

MAṆḌALA V. **SŪKTA 63.**

ऋतस्य गोपाविति सप्तर्चं सप्तमं सूक्तम्। अत्रेयमनुक्रमणिका। ऋतस्य सप्तार्चनाना जागतमिति। आत्रेयोऽर्चनाना नाम ऋषिः। जगती छन्दः। तुह्यादि-परिभाषया मित्रावरुणौ देवता। विनियोगो लैङ्गिकः।।

Verse 1.

ऋत॑स्य। गो॒पौ॒। अधि॑। ति॒ष्ठ॒थः॒। रथ॑म्। स॒त्य॑ऽधर्माणा। प॒र॒मे। वि॒ऽओ॑मनि। यम्। अत्र॑। मि॒त्रा॒व॒रु॒णा॒। अव॑थः। यु॒वम्। तस्मै॑। वृ॒ष्टिः। मधु॑ऽमत्। पि॒न्व॒ते॒। दि॒वः।।१।।

हे ऋतस्योकदस्य गोपौ रक्षितारौ सत्यधर्माणा सत्यधर्माणौ युवां रथमधितिष्ठथः। आरोहथोऽस्मद्यज्ञमागमनार्थम्। कुत्र। परमे व्योमनि निरतिशय आकाशे। हे मित्रावरुणौ युवं युवामत्रास्मिन्यज्ञे यं यजमानं अवथो रक्षथः तस्मै यजमानाय वृष्टिः पर्जन्यो मधुमदुदकं दिवो द्युलोकात्पिन्वते। सिञ्चति। वर्धयति।।

Ṛcas 1-2 show Mitrā-Varuṇā as rain-giving deities.

मधु॑मत् is adv.

पि॒न्व॒ते॒, rt. पिन्व् 1., to be full, run over, stream amply.

प॒रमे व्यो॑मनि has by Sāy. been connected with अधि॑ तिष्ठ॒तो रथे॑.

Our translation brings out better the साम्राज्य of Varuṇa whose law also the gods obey.

Verse 2.

सं॒ऽराजौ। अ॒स्य। भुव॑नस्य। रा॒ज॒थः। मि॒त्रा॑वरुणा। वि॒दथे॑। स्व॒ःऽ शा॑। वृ॒ष्टिम्। वा॒म्। राध॑ः। अ॒मृ॒त॒ऽत्वम्। ई॒म॒हे॒। द्यावा॒पृथि॒वी इति॑। वि। च॒र॒न्ति॒। त॒न्य॑वः।।२।।

हे मित्रावरुणा *मित्रावरुणौ सम्राजौ सम्यग्राजमानौ युवामस्य भुवनस्य राजथः। ईशाथे। स्वर्दृशा स्वर्गस्रूय द्रष्टारौ युवां विदथेऽस्मद्यज्ञे सम्राजाविति संबन्धः। वां युवां वृष्टिं राधो धनं वृष्ट्याख्यं धनममृतत्वं स्वर्गं चेमहे। प्रार्थयामहे। युवयोस्तन्यवो विस्तृता रश्मयो द्यावापृथिवी वि चरन्ति। विविधं प्राप्नुवन्ति। अथवा वृष्टिं धनममृतत्वं चेमहे।।

वि॒दथ॑ (rt. विद्) n., knowledge, sacred knowledge (both theoretical and practical), divine wisdom, omniscience; the wise ones (in an assembly). On the derivation of वि॒दथ॑ from the rt. विध् see Oldenberg, *Vedaforschung*, p. 28, note 2.

---

* प्रथमावृत्तौ मित्रावरुणा इति नास्ति।

This derivation may lead to the meaning: divine service, cult.

On the two alternatives of interpreting the third pāda वृष्टिं वां राधो अमृतत्वमीमहे see Sāy.'s comm.

राजथो is better taken to govern विदथे than भुवनस्य, as is done by Sāyaṇa.

तन्यु m., thunder, thunderer; adj., thundering, roaring.

Verse 3.

संऽराजौ। उग्रा। वृषभा। दिवः। पती इति। पृथिव्याः। मित्रावरूणा। विचर्षणी इति विऽचर्षणी। चित्रेभिः। अभ्रैः। उप। तिष्ठथः। रवम्। द्याम्। वर्षयथः। असुरस्य। मायया।।३।।

सम्राजौ सम्यग्राजमानावुग्रोद्धूर्णबलौ वृषभा वर्षितारौ दिवो द्युलोकस्य पती स्वामिनौ पृथिव्याश्च पती विचर्षणी सर्वस्य द्रष्टारौ मित्रावरुणौ। एवं महानुभावौ चित्रेभिश्चायनीयैरभ्रैर्मेधैः सह रवं स्तोत्रमुपतिष्ठथः। पश्चात् द्यां च वर्षयथोऽसुरस्योदकनिरसितुः पर्जन्यस्य मायया प्रज्ञया सामर्थ्येन।।

Ṛcas 3-6 describe the rainy season.

विचर्षणि adj., ever-active.

असुरस्य माया, on its meanings see V.K. Rajwade in proceedings of the First Oriental Conference, Poona, 1919. The असुर here may be Parjanya (Sāy.), or Varuṇa himself, as he is repeatedly mentioned in connection with मायाः—in ṛcas 4, 7 of this hymn, in V. 85. 5, 6; IX. 73.9; VIII. 41.3; Varuṇa is called मायिन् in VII. 28.4, etc. Or, finally, असुर may signify the old, nameless, celestial god. माया covers both the abstract (supernatural or preternatural) power and the concrete deed and proof of it.

Verse 4.

माया। वाम्। मित्रावरुणा। दिवि। श्रिता। सूर्यः। ज्योतिः। चरति।

चित्रम्। आयुधम्। तम्। अभ्रेण। वृष्ट्या। गूहथः। दिवि। पर्जन्य। द्रप्साः। मधुऽमन्तः। ईरते।।४।।

हे मित्रावरुणा वां युवयोर्माया दिवि श्रिता। आश्रिता। कैषा युवयोर्माया। उच्यते। सूर्यः सर्वस्य प्रेरको ज्योतिर्दीप्यमानश्चित्रं चायनीयमायुधमुक्तलक्षणा-युधरूपश्चरति। परिभ्रमत्यन्तरिक्षे। शत्रुमारकत्वादायुधमुच्यते। तं सूर्यमभ्रेण मेघेन वृष्ट्या च* दिवि गूहथः। गोपायथः हे पर्जन्य देव त्वया मित्रावरुणाभ्यां वृष्ट्यर्थं प्रेरितेन मधुमन्तो द्रप्सा ईरते। ईर्यन्ते। त्वत्सृष्टा वा गच्छन्ति।।

ईर् 2., ātm., to bring; instrans., to begin, to come.

द्रप्स m., drop. It has been proposed (by Ludwig and Bergaigne) to read पर्जन्यद्रप्सा instead of पर्जन्यद्रप्साः. The change is not necessary, since in course of the hymns often enough new gods are introduced besides those to whom the hymn is actuallty addressed. Thus the appearance of Parjanya besides Mitrā-Varuṇā need not create any critical suspicion. Parjanya, moreover, is mentioned in 6 below. ज्योतिः and चित्रमायुधम् are appositions to सूर्यो.

Verse 5.

रथम्। युञ्जते। मरूतः। शुभे। सुऽखम् शूरः। न। मित्रावरुणा। गोऽइष्टिषु। रजांसि। चित्रा। वि। चरन्ति। तन्यवः। दिवः। संऽराजा। पयसा। नः। उक्षतम्।।५।।

हे मित्रावरुणा युवयोरननुग्रहात् मरूतः शुभ उदकार्थं सुखं शोभनाक्षद्वारं रथं युञ्जते। अश्वैर्योजयन्ति। शूरो न शूर इव। स यथा युद्धार्थं रथं युनक्ति तद्वत्। गविष्टिषु गवामुदकानामेषणेषु निमित्तेषु चित्रा चायनीयानि रजांसि लोकान् तन्यवस्ततास्ते मरूतो विचरन्ति। विविधं चरन्ति। तस्मात्तैः सहितौ हे सम्राजा युवां दिवो द्युलोकात्पयसोदकेन नोऽस्मानुक्षतम्। सिञ्चतम्।।

शुभ् f., splendour, dat. sg.: for display, for a pageant.

* आदर्शे च इति नास्ति।

गविंष्टि f., conquest of cattle, battle, fray.

Verse 6.

वाचम्। सु। मित्रावरुणौ। इराऽवतीम्। पर्जन्यः। चित्राम्। वदति। त्विषिऽमतीम्। अभ्रा। वसत। मरुतः। सु। मायया। द्याम्। वर्षयतम्। अरुणाम्। अरेपसम्॥६॥

हे मित्रावरुणौ युवयोरनुग्रहात् पर्जन्यो मेघः सु सुष्ठिरावतीमन्नवतीमन्न-साधिकां चित्रां चायनीयां त्विषीमतीं दीप्तिमतीं वाचं गर्जनशब्दं वदति। शब्दयति वृष्ट्यर्थम्। मरुतश्चाभ्रा अभ्राणि मेघान् सु सुष्ठु वसत आच्छादयन्ति मायया स्वप्रज्ञया। युवां च पर्जन्येन मरुद्भिश्च सहारुणामरुणवर्णामरेपसमपापां वृष्ट्यविघातिनीं द्यां वर्षयतम्॥

इरावत्, containing refreshment (इरा), refreshing, wet.

वसत, 3. plur. inj. ātm.; rt. वस् 2.

अरेपस्, untainted, stainless, bright. अरेपसम् seems to be a proleptic expression to bring out the brightness of heaven after the thunderstorm.

Verse 7.

धर्मणा। मित्रावरुणा। विपःऽचिता। व्रता। रक्षेथे इति। असुरस्य। मायया। ऋतेन। विश्वम्। भुवनम्। वि। राजथः। सूर्यम्। आ। धत्थः। दिवि। चित्र्यम्। रथम्॥७॥

हे मित्रावरुणा विपश्चिता प्राज्ञौ युवां धर्मणा जगद्धारकेण वृष्ट्यादिलक्षणेन कर्मणा व्रता यज्ञादिकर्माणि रक्षेथे। पालयथः। असुरस्य मेघानां निरसितुः पर्जन्यस्य मायया प्रज्ञया च ऋतेनोदकेन यज्ञेन वा निमित्तेन विश्वं भुवनं सर्वं भूतजातं विराजथः। विदीपयथ इत्यर्थः। सूर्यमा सूर्यं च चित्र्यं पूज्यं रथं रंहणस्वभावं दवि द्युलोके धत्थः। धारयथः जगदुपकारार्थम्॥

This ṛc describes other activities of the twin-gods Mitrā-Varuṇā.

NO. 17.

MAṆḌALA V. **SŪKTA 73.**

षष्ठेऽनुवाके पञ्चदश सूक्तानि। तत्र यदद्य स्थ इति दशर्चं प्रथमं सूक्तमात्रेयस्य पौरनाम्न आर्षमानुष्टुभमाश्विनम्। अनुक्रान्तं च। यदद्य दश पौर आश्विनं तदानुष्टुभं त्विति। तदित्युक्तत्वादिदमादीनि षट् सूक्तान्याश्विनानि। आनुष्टुभं त्विति तुशब्दादिदमुत्तरत च द्वे आनुष्टुभे। प्रातरनुदाक आश्विने क्रतावानुष्टुभे छन्दस्याश्विनशस्त्रे चेदमादिके द्वे सूक्ते। यदद्य स्थ इति सूक्ते (आ० ४-१५) इति सूत्रितम्।।

Verse 1.

यत्। अ॒द्य। स्थः। प॒रा॒ऽवति॑। यत्। अ॒र्वा॒ऽवति॑। अ॒श्वि॒ना॒।
यत्। वा॒। पु॒रू। पु॒रू॒ऽभु॒जा॒। यत्। अ॒न्तरि॑क्षे। आ। ग॒त॒म्।।१।।

हे पुरूभुजा बहुषु यज्ञेषु भोक्तारावधिकं रक्षितारौ वा हे अश्विनो यद्यद्यास्मिन् काले परावत्यत्यन्तं दूरदेशे द्युलोके स्थो भवथः। यद्वा। अर्वावत्यरणवति गन्तुं शक्ये प्रदेशेऽन्तिके स्थः। यद्यदि वा अथवा पुरू बहुप्रदेशेषु स्थः। यद्यद्यन्तरिक्षे स्थः तस्मात्सर्वस्मादद्यागतम्। आगच्छतम्।।

अ॒र्वा॒वत् f., neighbourhood; प॒रा॒वत् f., distance. The two expressions always occus together in a sentence.

पुरू, Sāy. बहुप्रदेशेषु. One feels tempted (with Oldenberg, Textkrit. i. l.) to read पुरौ for पुरू. But the author of the hymn is evidently playing with पुरू in ṛcas 1 and 2, and Sāy.'s interpretation gives a fairly good antithesis to अन्तरिक्षे, creating thus a parallelism between प॒रा॒वति॑ and अ॒र्वा॒वति॑. Because पुरू is one of the members of the antithesis and पुरूभुजा an epithet of the Aśvinā (see above No. 5. 13, 14), Roth's view is not likely that as in पुरू पु॑रूहूतः (VIII.2. 32.) पुरू is merely put in to strengthen the पुरू in the compound पु॒रु॒हू॒तः that follows: so also here पुरू is used to emphasize the पुरू in पु॒रु॒भू॒जा॒. The view may be admitted for VIII. 2. 32, but has to be rejected for our passage, if for no other but for stylistic reasons. Comp. finally पुरूभूतमा in ṛc 2 which implies either a (simultaneous) presencee in a variety of places or frequent appearances to persons.

Verse 2.

इह। त्या। पुरूऽभूतमा। पुरू। दंसांसि। बिभ्रता। वरस्या। यामि। अध्रिगू इत्यध्रिऽगू। हुवे। तुविःऽतमा। भुजे।।२।।

इहास्मिन्यज्ञे त्या तौ पुरूभूतमा पुरूणां बहूनां यजमानानां भावयितृतमौ पुरू पुरूणि दंसांसि कर्माणि बिभ्रता धारयन्तौ वरस्या वरणीयावध्रिगू अन्यैर-धृतगमनकर्माणौ यामि। उपागच्छामि। तुविष्टमा प्रभूततमौ। भुजे भोगाय पालनाय वा हुवे। आह्वयामि।।

अध्रिग, proceeding unchecked.

वरस्या, instr. sg. of वरस्या f., desire after fortune (वरस्).

Verse 3.

ईर्मा। अन्यत्। वपुषे। वपुः। चक्रम्। रथस्य। येमथुः। परि। अन्या। नाहुषा। युगा। मह्ना। रजांसि। दीयथः।।३।।

हे अश्विनौ युवां रथस्य युष्मदीयस्यान्यञ्चक्रमीर्मा। अर्तेरीर्मेति रूपम्। गन्तर्यादित्ये वपुषे तस्य शोभायचै वपुर्वपुष्मत् तेजोवत् चक्रं येमथुः। नियमितवन्तौ स्थः। अन्या अन्येन चक्रेण मह्ना महत्त्वेन स्वसामर्थ्येन नाहुषा युगा। नहुषा मनुष्याः। तेषां युगा युगोपलक्षितान् कालान् प्रातरादिसवनान् अहोरात्रादिकालान्वा रजांसि लोकांश्च परिदीयथः। परिगच्छथः। न्य१न्ध्यस्य मूर्द्धनि चक्रु रथस्य येमथुः (ऋ० १-३०-१९) इत्युक्तम्।।

ईर्मा=इह, Ved. Stud. I. 212, ff. वपुस् n., Sāy.: तेजोवत्,

अन्या=अन्येन. मह्ना, with might, quick.

दी 4., to fly (of birds and gods).

The best interpretation of this ṛc would seem to have

been put forward so far by Pischel, Ved. Stud. I. 212 ff. The car of the Aśvinā is in many ways different from the mythological vehicles mentioned by the ṚV. "It is peculiar in construction, being threefold, having three wheels, three fellies (on the wheels), and some other parts triple. One of the wheels was lost when the Aśvinā came to the wedding of Sūryā" (Macdonell, Vedic Mythology, p. 50). From our passage and I. 30. 19 it follows that one wheel runs along the spaces, the heavens; the other or others then must move in a place which is not heaven; for in this consists according to our passage the wonderful character of the car. In both passages it is said that this wheel is stopped on earth. Griffith (following Sāy.'s lead) translates:—Another beauteous wheel you have fixed there to decorate the car.—But an extra wheel was probably in vedic times and for the Aśvinā's car no more an ornament than a spare wheel on the vehicles of the 20th century.

Verse 4.

तत्। ऊं इति। सु। वाम्। एना। कृतम्। विश्वा। यत्। वाम्। अनु। स्वते। नाना। जातौ। अरेपसा। सम्। अस्मे इति। बन्धुम्। आ। ईयथुः।।४।।

हे विश्वा व्याप्तौ यत् येन स्तोत्रेण वां युवामनु ष्टवे अनु स्तुवे तदु। उ इति पूरणः। एना अनेन पौरेण सु सुष्टु वां युवाभ्यां कृतं संपादितं भवतु। नाना पृथगेव जातौ समृद्धावरेपसाऽपापौ अस्मे अस्मभ्यं बन्धुमन्नं धनं वा समेयथुः। सम्यक् गमयथः। सम्यक् प्रयच्छतमित्यर्थः।।

अनु ष्टवे, 3. sg. pres. ātm.; rt. स्तु 1.

बन्धु m., relative, kinship.

एना is interpreted by Sāy. as पौरेण (the ṛṣi of the hymn?). This is likely neither from the point of grammar nor from that of the context. Grassmann translates एना with "here".

Better seems Ludwig's version:—with that one, viz., the wheel.

Verse 5.

आ। यत्। वाम्। सूर्या। रथम्। तिष्ठत्। रघुऽस्यदम्। सदा। परि। वाम्। अरूषाः। वयः। घृणा। वरन्ते। आऽतपः।।५।।

हे अश्विनौ वां युवयोः सदा सर्वदा रघुष्यदं शीघ्रगं रथं सूर्या युवयोः पत्नी यद्यदातिष्ठत् आस्थितवती तदा वां परिवरन्ते। परितो वृण्वन्ति। के। अरूषा आरोचमाना घृणा दीप्ता आतप आतापनाः शत्रूणां वयोऽश्वाः। अथवा तप इति विशेष्यम्। वयो गन्तार उक्तलक्षणा आतपः सर्वतस्तापयित्र्यो दीप्तयः परिवरनते।।

रघु ष्यद् (ष्यन्द्), quick moving, running.

आतप् f., glow, glowing heat.

घृण=दीपत (Sāy.).

परि वृ 5., to keep away something (accus.) from someone (dat).

Note the different tense in तिष्ठत् and वरन्ते.

For घृणा which is hardly correct we have to read घृणाः. The red birds are the winged horses of the Aśvinā.

Verse 6.

युवोः। अत्रिः। चिकेतति। नरा। सुम्नेन। चेतसा। घर्मम्। यत्। वाम्। अरेपसम्। नासत्या। आस्ना। भुरण्यति।।६।।

हे नरा नेतारावश्विनौ युवोर्युवयोः। युवामित्यर्थः। अत्रिरसमत्पिता ऋषिः सुम्नन सुखेनाग्निदाहोपशमरूपेण हेतुना चेतसादरयुक्तन मनसा। चिकेतति। जानाति। स्तुतवानित्यर्थः। सति दुःखे सुखमुक्ष्यते। दुःखस्य कः प्रसङ्ग इत्यत आह। यद्यस्मात् हे नासत्यौ वां युवयोरास्नास्येन तन्निष्पन्नेन स्तोत्रेण धर्मं दीप्तं दहन्तमग्निमसुरैः स्वदाहाय प्रक्षिप्तमरेपसमपापं सुखकरं भुरण्यति प्राप्तवान्।

भुरण्यतिर्गतिकर्मा। अत्रेरग्नेः सकाशाद्रक्षणं हिमेनाग्निं घ्रसम् (ऋ० १-११६-८) युवमृबीसमुत तप्तमत्रये (ऋ०१०-३९-९) इत्यादिभिः स्पष्टं प्रदर्शितम्।।

चिकेतति, 3. sg. sbj.; rt. चित्, to perceive.

आसन् n., mouth.

भुरण्य (denom. भुरण, भुर्), to be busy, active; to set going, to fan (a flame).

Verse 7.

उग्रः। वाम्। ककुहः। ययिः। शृण्वे। यामेषु। संऽतनिः। यत्। वाम्। दंसःऽभिः। अश्विना। नरा। आऽववर्तति।।७।।

उग्र उद्गूर्णबलो वां युवयोः ककुह उच्छ्रितो महान् ययिर्गन्ता संतनिः सततं गच्छन् रथो यामेषु गामनेषु यज्ञेषु वा शृण्वे। श्रूयते। हे अश्विना हे नरा यद्यस्माद्वां युवां दंसोभिः कर्मभिरत्रिरस्मत्पितावर्तति आवर्तयति।।

शृण्वे, 3. sg. pres. ātjm., used in a passive sense.

आ ववर्तति, 3. sg. sbj.; rt. वृत्, used in a causative sense.

सन्तनि m. f., sound, noise.

Verse 8.

मध्वः। ऊं इति। सु। मधुऽयुवा। रूद्रा। सिसक्ति। पिप्युषी। यत्। समुद्रा। अति। पर्षथः। पक्वाः। पृक्षः। भरन्त। वाम्।।८।।

हे मधूयुवा मधुरस्य सोमादेर्मिश्रयितारौ हे रूद्रा। रूत् स्तुतिः तथा द्रवणीयौ रूद्रपुत्रौ वा। मध्वो मधुररसेन सु पिप्युषी सुष्ठु प्याययन्ती स्तुतिरस्मत्कृता सिषक्ति। सेवते। यद्यदा समुद्रा समुद्रवणसाधनान्यन्तरिक्षाण्यतिपर्षथः अति- पारयथः। यज्ञं प्राप्नुथ इत्यर्थः। पक्वाः। पृक्षोऽन्नानि हविर्लक्षणानि वां भरन्त। भ्रियन्ते यजमानैः।।

सच् 3. (Avestan *hac*), to accompany, follow.

भरन्त, used passively.

पर्षथः, aor. rt. पृ 3., to pass.

मधूयु, loving honey. पृक्ष् f., refreshment, food.

The पि॒प्युषी॑ has been said by Sāy. to be the स्तुति, by Griffith the वाच्. मध्वः॑ which seems to go with पि॒प्युषी॑—though gen. sg.—and म॒धू॒यु॒वा appear to point to the skin, दृतिः m., mentioned in V. 45. 3; the f. gender of पि॒प्यषी॑ is possibly an inconsistency caused by the crossing of the idea of दृतिः m. and of गौः f.

Verse 9.

स॒त्यम्। इत्। वै ऊँ॒ इति॑। अ॒श्विना॑। यु॒वाम्। आ॒हुः। म॒यः॒ऽभुवा॑। ता। याम॑न्। या॒म॒ऽहूत॑मा। याम॑न्। आ। मृ॒ळ॒यत्ऽत॑मा।।९।।

हे अश्विना युवां सत्यमित् सत्यमेव। वा इति पादपूरणः। मयोभुवा सुखस्य भावयितारावाहुः पुराविदः। ता तौ सुखकरत्वेन पसिद्धौ युवां यामन्यज्ञे यामहूतमागमनार्थं भृशमाह्वातव्यौ भवतमिति शेषः। यामन्नस्मद्यज्ञेऽस्मदर्थागमने वा मृळयत्तमा चातिशयेन सुखयितारौ भवतम्। आकारश्चार्थे।।

म॒यो भू, giving refreshment, bringer of good cheer.

Verse 10.

इ॒मा। ब्रह्मा॑णि। वर्ध॑ना। अ॒श्विऽभ्या॑म्। स॒न्तु॒। शंऽत॑मा। या। तक्षा॑म। रथा॑न्ऽइव। अवो॑चाम। बृ॒हत्। नमः॑।।१०।।

अथ स्तुतिं निगमयति। इमेमानीदानीं कृतानि ब्रह्माणि परिवृढानि स्तोत्राण्यश्विभ्यां वर्धना वर्धनानि समर्धकानि शंतमा सुखतमानि सन्तु। या यानि तक्षाम संपादयाम रथानिव शिल्पी तद्वत्तक्षाम तानि सन्तु। वयं बृहत् प्रभूतं प्रभूतफलप्रदं नमो नमस्कारोक्तिमवोचाम।।

शंत॑म, most auspicious.

NO. 18.

MANNḌALA V. **SŪKTA 80.**

द्युतद्यामानमिति षड्चमष्टमं सूक्तम्। तत्रानुक्रमणिका। द्युतद्यामानं षडिति। सत्यश्रवा ऋषिः। अनुक्तत्वचात् त्रिष्टुप्। उषस्यं त्वित्युक्तत्वादुषा देवता।

प्रातरनुवाक उषस्ये ऋतौ त्रैष्टुभे छन्दस्याश्विनशस्त्रे चेदं सूक्तम्। सूत्रितं च। द्युतद्यामानमुषो वाजेन (आ० ४-१४) इति।।

Verse 1.

द्युतत्ऽयामानम्। बृहतीम्। ऋतेन। ऋतऽवरीम्। अरुणऽप्सुम्। विऽभातीम्। देवीम्। उषसम्। स्वः। आऽवहन्तीम्। प्रति। विप्रासः। मतिऽभिः। जरन्ते।।१।।

द्युतद्यामानं दीपतरथां बृहतीं महतीमृतेन सत्येन यज्ञेन वर्तावरीमृतवतीम-रूणप्सुमरूणरूपां विभातीं व्युच्छन्तीं देवीं द्योतमानामुषसं स्वरावहन्तीं सूर्यं गच्छन्तीम्। एवं महानुभावामुषसं विप्रासो मेघाविन ऋत्विजो मतिभिः स्तुतिभिः प्रतिजरन्ते। स्तुवन्ति।।

द्युतद्यामन्, with a brilliant road.

अरूणप्सु, of red appearance.

प्रति जृ 1., to salute, welcome.

Verse 2.

एषा। जनम्। दर्शता। बोधयन्ती। सुऽगान्। पथः। कृण्वती। याति। अग्रे। बृहती। विश्वऽइन्वा। उषाः। ज्योतिः। यच्छति। अग्रे। अह्नाम्।।२।।

दर्शता दर्शनीयैषोषा बोधयन्ती। कम्। जनम्। प्रसुपतमित्यर्थः। पथः सुगान् सुगमनान् कृण्वत्यग्रे सूर्यस्य पुरस्ताद्याति। गच्छति। कीदृश्युषाः। बृहद्रथा प्रभूतरथा बृहती महती विश्वमिन्वा विश्वं व्याप्रवाना विश्वतर्पणा वा। ईदृश्युषा अह्नामग्रे ज्योतिस्तेजो यच्छति।।

दर्शत, visible, conspicuous, beautiful.

विश्वमिन्व, penetrating all, furthering all, all-impelling.

अग्रे in pāda 2, ahead (of the sun).

Verse 3.

एषा। गोभिः। अरुणेभिः। युजाना। अस्रेधन्ती। रयिम्। अप्रऽआयु।

चक्रे। पथः। रदन्ती। सुविताय। देवी। पुरुऽस्तुता। विश्वऽवारा। वि। भाति।।३।।

एषोषा अरुणेभिररूणववैर्गोभिर्बलीवर्दै रथं युजाना योजयन्त्यस्रेधन्त्यशुष्यन्त्यक्षीणा वा। किम्। रयिं धनमप्राय्वप्रगन्तृ अविचलितं चक्रे। करोति। किं कुर्वती। पथो मार्गान् रदन्ती प्रकाशयन्ती। किमर्थम्। सुविताय सुष्ठु गमनाय देवी द्योतमाना पुरूष्टुता बुहुभिः स्तुता विश्ववारा सर्वैर्वरणीया विभाति। प्रकाशं करोति।।

युजान, pt. aor. ātm.; rt. युज् 7., with instr., to yoke one's car with, to drive with.

अस्रेधन्ती (pt. pres. rt. स्रिध् 1., to blunder, hurt), not going wrong.

अप्रायु adv., incessantly.

Verse 4.

एषा। विऽएनी। भवति। द्विऽबर्हाः। आविःऽकृण्वाना। तन्वम्। पुरस्तात्। ऋतस्य। पन्थाम्। अनु। एति। साधु। प्रजानतीऽइव। न। दिशः। मिनाति।।४।।

एषोषा व्येनी भवति विशेषेण श्वेता भवति द्विबर्हा द्वयोः प्रथममध्यमयोः परिवृढोषाः पश्चात्तन्वं स्वीयां तनूमाविष्कृण्वाना प्रकटीकुर्वती। कुत्र। पुरस्तात् पूर्वस्यां दिशि। किंच ऋतस्यादित्यस्य पन्थां पन्थानं साधु सभ्यगन्वेति। किंच प्रजानतीव विश्वं प्रज्ञापयन्ती। इवेति संप्रत्यर्थे। न दिशो मिनाति। न हिनस्ति। प्रत्युत दिशः प्रकाशयति। अथवा प्रजानतीवानुगन्तव्यमिति प्रकर्षेणावगिच्छन्तीी च ऋतस्य पन्थामन्वेति।।

व्येत, f व्येनी variegated, of various, changing colours.

द्विबर्हस्, of double strength, double greatness.

The second line takes up the idea expressed by अस्रेधन्ती in ṛc 3.

Verse 5.

एषा। शुभ्रा। नं तन्वः। विदाना। ऊर्ध्वाऽइव। स्नाती। दृशये। नः। अस्थात्। अपं। द्वेषः। बाधमाना। तमांसि। उषाः। दिवः। दुहिता। ज्योतिषा। आ। अगात्।।५।।

एषोषाः शुभ्रा न शुभ्रवर्णा निर्मला स्वलंकृता योषिदिव तन्वोऽङ्गानि विदाना प्रज्ञापयन्ती स्नाती स्नानं कुर्वाणोर्ध्वेवोन्नतेव स्नानादुत्तिष्ठन्तीव नोऽस्मदर्थ-मस्माकं पुरतो वा दृशये सर्वेषां दर्शनायोदस्थात्। पूर्वस्यां दिश्युत्तिष्ठति। किं कुर्वती। द्वेषो द्वेष्याणि तामंस्यपबाधमाना दिवो दुहितोषा ज्योतिषा तेजसा सहागात्। आगच्छति।।

स्नाती, स्नात्, pt. pres. rt. स्ना.

In the realistic interpretation of the Ved. Stud. I. 308 ff. the translation of pādas 1 and 2 would be:—She there, the daughter of heaven, like a belle (or rather courtezan) in the presence of men displays her body.—This interpretation is mainly based on the view that already in Vedic times immorality was organised. This view, however, has not found general acceptance. See Winternitz, Geschichte der Indischen Litteratur, 2nd ed., vol. I., p.60.

Verse 6.

एषा। प्रतीची। दुहिता। दिवः। नृन्। योषाऽइव। भद्रा। नि। रिणीते। अप्सः। विऽऊर्ण्वती। दाशुषे। वार्याणि। पुनः। ज्योतिः। युवतिः। पूर्वऽथा। अकरित्यकः।।६।।

एषोषा प्रतीच्यभिमुखा सती दिवो दुहिता नृन् सर्वान् प्राणिनः प्रति भद्रा योषेव कल्याणवेषा योषिदिवाप्सो रूपं निरिणीते। प्रेरयति। किंच दाशुषे हविर्दात्रे यजमानाय वार्याणि वरणीयानि धनानि व्यूर्ण्वती प्रयच्छन्ती युवतिर्नित्ययौवना सर्वत्र मिश्रयन्ती वा पुनरद्यद्यपि पूर्वथा पूर्वमिव ज्योतिस्ते जोऽकः। करोति।।

रि 9., to let loose, नि रि, to let fall, bend down.

अप्सस् n., bosom; form (Sāy.).

ऊर्ण्वती, pt. pres. stem ऊर्णु, rt. वृ; वि वृ to uncover, to unfold. Read वि ऊर्ण्वती.

NO. 19.

MAÇḌALA VII. **SŪKTA 61.**

उद्वां चक्षुरिति सप्तर्च षष्ठं सूक्तं वसिष्ठस्यार्षं त्रैष्टुभं मैत्रावरुणम्। उद्वां सप्तेत्यनुक्रमणिका। विनियोगो लैङ्गिकः।।

Verse 1.

उत्। वाम्। चक्षुः। वरुणा। सुऽप्रतीकम्। देवयोः। एति। सूर्यः। ततन्वान्। अभि। यः। विश्वा। भुवनानि। चष्टे। सः। मन्युम्। मर्त्येषु। आ। चिकेत।।१।।

हे वरुणा मित्रावरुणौ देवयोर्द्योतमानयोर्वा युवयोश्चक्षुः प्रकाशकं तेजः सुप्रतीकं शोभनरूपमेवंरूपः सूर्यस्ततन्वांस्तेजो विस्तारयन्नुदेति। उद्गच्छति। अथोदितो यो देवो विश्वा सर्वाणि भुवनानि भूतजातान्यभिचष्टे अभिपश्यति स देवो मर्त्येषु प्रवृत्तं मन्युं स्तोत्रं कर्म वा चिकेत। आजानाति।।

मन्यु m., (religious) eagerness, zeal; Sāy. स्तोत्रं कर्म वा.

Verse 2.

प्र। वाम्। सः। मित्रावरुणौ। ऋतऽवा। विप्रः। मन्मानि। दीर्घऽश्रुत्। इयर्ति। यस्य। ब्रह्माणि। सुक्रतू इति सुऽक्रतू। अवाथः। आ। यत्। क्रत्वा। न। शरदः। पृणैथे इति।।२।।

हे मित्रावरुणौ वां युवयोर्मन्मानि मननीयानि स्तोत्राणि स प्रसिद्धो विप्रो मेधावी ऋतावा यज्ञवान् दीर्घश्रुच्चिरकालं श्रोता एवमुक्तलक्षणो वसिष्ठ इयर्ति। प्रेरयति। यस्यर्षेब्रह्माणि परिवृढानि स्तोत्राणि हे सुक्रतू शोभनकर्माणाववाथो रक्षथः। यत्कर्म शरदो बहून् संवत्सरानापृणैथे आपूरयेथे स उदियर्ति।।

क्रत्वा according to (as is) his will; आ यत्क्रत्वा न शरदः

पृणैथे॑, that you may fill his years as is his desire. See Ved. Stud. I. 276.

Verse 3.

प्र। उ॒रोः। मि॒त्रा॒व॒रु॒णा॒। पृ॒थि॒व्याः। प्र। दि॒वः। ऋ॒ष्वात्। बृ॒ह॒तः। सु॒दा॒नू॒ इति॑ सुऽदानू। स्पशः॑। द॒धा॒थे॒ इति॑। ओष॑धीषु। वि॒क्षु। ऋध॑क्। य॒तः। अनि॑ऽमिषम्। रक्ष॑माणा।।३।।

हे मित्रावरुणा मित्रावरुणौ युवामुरोर्विस्तीर्णायाः पृथिव्या अपि प्र। प्रिरिरिचाथे। अस्येदेव प्ररिरिचे (ऋ० १-६१-९) इत्यादिषु प्रशब्दस्य रिरिच इत्यनेन सह संबन्धदर्शनादत्राप्युचितक्रियाध्याहारेण रिरिच इति योज्यम्। तथर्ष्वाद्गुणैर्महतो बृहतः स्वरूपतोऽतिमहतो दिवो द्युलोकादपि प्ररिरिचाथे हे सुदानू शोभनदानौ। किंचौषधीषु विक्षु प्रजासु निमित्तभूतासु प्रजासु चेति वा स्पशो रूपं दधाथे। धारयेथे। किं कुर्वन्तौ। ऋधग्यत ऋधक् *सत्ये नयतो विवेकात् सत्येन गच्छतो जनाननिमिषमव्यवधानेन सर्वदा रक्षमाणा पालयन्तौ।।

विश्, f., dwelling, house, family, village, clan, community.

ऋध॑क्=पृथक्

This ṛc has (last by Macdonell, Ved. Reader, pp. 120-21, who follows in the main Ludwig and Grassmann in this point) been translated:—From the wide earth, O Mitrā-Varuṇā, from the high lofty sky, O bounteous ones, ye have placed your spies that go separately, in plants and abodes, ye that protect with unwinking eye—Both grammar and contents lend little support to this translation. प्र neither with nor without धा does mean "from". Nor is it likely that Mitrā— Varuṇā withdraw "from the wide earth and from the high lofty sky" their spies in order to keep the handful of Āryas in check, to say nothing of the doubtful compliment contained in this statement. Besides, the "plants and abodes" would seem to

* आदर्शे सत्येन यतो इति पाठः। अनयोः प्रथमावृत्तिस्थः पाठः श्रेयान्।

belong to "the wide earth" too. Sāy., referring to I. 61. 9: अस्येदेव प रिरिचे महित्वं दिवस्पृथिव्याः पर्यन्तरिक्षात् understands रिरिचे after प्र, which gives an interpretation decidedly better than the one adopted by Macdonell. We may doubt whether उरोः is n. and an equivalent to अन्तरिक्षात्; cp. III. 46. 3: प्र मज्मना दिव इन्द्रः पृथिव्याः प्रोरोर्महो अन्तरिक्षादृजीषी. पृथिव्याः would then be depending on उरोः. This would do away with the somewhat unusual m. or n. उरोः for the fem. उर्व्याः, which has to be accepted, if we take उरोः to be adj. to पृथिव्याः. The grammatical anomaly, however, is not an impossibility in the ṚV.

In the first pāda read प्र उरोर्.

The metre shows that in the fourth pāda the Abhinihita Saṁdhi यतोऽनिमिषं is to be restored in the Saṁhitāpāṭha and Padapāṭha.

ऋधग्यतो may be made to depend either on रक्षमाणाः or on दधाते; in the latter case it will probably govern ओषधीषु विक्षु.

"The text of Sāyaṇa is corrupt here. See Max Müller, Varietas Lectionis (Vol. III, p. 9). Müller has not notice that विवेकात् here is the explanation of an immediately preceding नयतः wrongly supposed to be in the text. He prints ऋधक्सत्येन यतो विवेकात्, instead of ऋधक्सत्ये नयतो विवेकात्. ऋधक्सत्ये is the common grammatical explanation of the word ऋधक्. Compare Siddhānta Kaumudī p. 169.* It looks as if Sāyaṇa's note was ऋधग्यतः ऋधक्सत्ये सत्येन गच्छतः, and as if some specially careless and audacious person interpolated नयतो विवेकात् after सत्ये under the mistaken impression that the word in the text was not यतः but नयतः" Peterson, 1st ed.

---

* P. 102, 3rd ed. Siddhānta-Kaumudi, ed. by Gādgil and Pans ikar, N.S. P., Bombay 1904. Editor.

Verse 4.

शंस । मित्रस्य । वरुणस्य । धाम । शुष्मः । रोदसी इति । बद्बधे । महिऽत्वा । अयन् । मासाः । अयज्वनाम् । अवीराः । प्र । यज्ञऽमन्मा । वृजनम् । तिराते ।।४।।

हे ऋषे मित्रस्य वरुणस्य च धाम तेजःस्थानं शंस। स्तुहि। ययोर्देवयोः शुष्मो बलं रोदसी द्यावापृथिव्यौ सह वर्तमाने महित्वा स्वमहत्त्वेन बद्बधे वन्धति पृथक् स्थापयति इयं पृथिवीयं द्यौरिति पृथक्करोति। द्यावापृथिवी सहास्तामिति श्रुतेः। अयज्वनामननुष्ठातॄणां मासाः कालावयवा अवीरा अपुत्रा एवायन्। यन्तु। गच्छन्तु। तद्विपरीतो यज्ञमन्मा यज्ञार्थं मतिमानयज्वा वृजनं बलं प्रतिराते। प्रवर्धयतु। प्रपूर्वस्तिरतिर्वर्धनार्थः।।

शंसा, padapāṭha शंस, 2. sg. impv.; शंसा would then be a direct command of the singer addressed to himself, after having referred to himself already in ṛc 2. But considering that the poet speaks of himself in the first person in the first and second pādas of ṛc 6, it is preferable to take शंसा as 1. sg. sbj. par.

बद्बधे, 3. sg. pres. ātm. intens.; rt. बाध्; (बध्).

अबीराः is used in the predicative sense, as sonless ones.

वृजन n., (वर्ग) party, following, (sacrificial) community.

Verse 5.

अमूरा । विश्वा । वृषणौ । वाम् । न । यासु । चित्रम् । ददृशे । न । यक्षम् । द्रुहः । सचन्ते । अनृता । जनानाम् । न । वाम् । निण्यानि । अचिते । अभूवन् ।।५।।

हे अमूरामूढौ हे विश्वा व्याप्तौ हे वृषणौ वर्षितारौ वां युवाभ्यामिमा इमानि स्तंतिवचांसि क्रियन्ते। यासु स्तुतिषु चित्रमाश्चर्यं न ददृशे न दृश्यते न यक्षं न पूजा दृश्यते। युवाभ्यां महिम्नोऽपि महत्त्वात् प्रयत्नेन क्रियमाणमपि स्तांत्रं न चमत्करोतीत्यर्थः। जनानामनृता स्तुतविषयाणि स्तोत्राणि द्रुहो द्रोग्धारः

सचन्ते। सेवन्ते। न महान्तः। वां युवाभ्यां क्रियमाणानि निण्यान्यन्तर्हितानि रहस्यान्यपि स्तोत्राण्यचितेऽज्ञानय। *नाभूवन्। न भवन्ति।।

अमू॑र Sāy. अमूढ, wise.

विश्वा॑ du., both of you two, in a predicative sense.

वृ॒ष॒णौ॒ voc. du., without accent because separated from अमू॑रा by विश्वा॑ and in the middle of the pāda.

चि॒त्र n. = आश्चर्य, marvel, jugglery, trickery.

य॒क्ष n., magic (both अभिचार and कृत्या).

द्रुह् f., falsehood, deception, misfortune, trap.

अ॒चिते॑, dat. inf. ददृशे, 3. sg. ātm. with pass. meaning.

Verse 6.

सम्। ऊं॒ इति॑। वा॒म्। य॒ज्ञम्। म॒ह॒य॒म्। नमः॑ऽभिः। हु॒वे। वा॒म्। मि॒त्रा॒व॒रु॒णा॒। स॒ऽबाधः॑। प्र। वा॒म्। मन्मा॑नि। ऋ॒चसे॑। नवा॑नि। कृ॒तानि॑। ब्रह्म॑। जु॒जु॒षन्। इ॒मानि॑।।६।।

हे मित्रावरुणौ वां युवयोर्यज्ञं नमोभिर्नमस्कारैः स्तुतिभिः समु महयम। संपूजयाम्यहम्। तदर्थं हे मित्रावरुणा मित्रावरुणौ वां सबाधो बाधायुक्तोऽहं हुवे। आह्वयामि बाधापरिहाराय। वां युवामृचसे सेवितुं नवानि नूतानि स्तुत्यानि वा मन्मानि स्तोत्राणि प्रभवन्त्वित्यध्याहारः। कृतानि मया समूहीकृतानीमानीदानीं क्रियमाणानि ब्रह्म परिवृढानि स्तोत्राणि युवां जुजुषन्। प्रीणयन्तु।।

सम् म॒ह॒यम्, 1. sg. inj. causat.; rt. मह्, सम् मह्, to exalt, glorify, solemnise.

ऋ॒चसे॑, dat. inf. rt. अर्च्. See ZDMG 55. 311, n. 3.

जुजुषन् 3. plur. subj. pf.; rt. जुष् 6.

The originality of the poetic conceptions, मन्मानि etc., and the prayers ब्रह्माणि etc., is often emphasised in the ṚV.

* प्रथमावृत्तौ अभूवन् भवन्ति इति पाठः।

Verse 7.

इयम्। देवा। पुरःऽहितिः। युवऽभ्याम्। यज्ञेषु। मित्रावरुणौ। अकारि। विश्वानि। दुः ऽगा। पितृतम्। तिरः। नः। यूयमै पात। स्वस्तिऽभिः। सदा। नः।।७।।

*अनया स्तुतिमुपसंहरति। हे देवो देवौ मित्रावरुणौ युवभ्यां युवाभ्यां यज्ञेष्वियं पुरोहितिः पुरस्क्रिया पूजा स्तुतिलक्षणाकारि। कृताभूत्। तां सेवित्वा विश्वानि सर्वाणि दुर्गा दुःखेन गन्तव्यान्यापदस्तिरस्तिरस्कुरूतम्। तथा कृत्वा नोस्मान्पिपृतं पारयम्। शिष्टो गतः।।

पिपृतं, 2. du. impv. pres.; rt. पृ 3., to pass; तिरस् पृ, causat, to put beyond, across. देव., voc, du.

यूयं पात स्वस्तिभिः सदा नः is the general refrain addressed to all the gods, not only to Mitrā-Varuṇā. This ṛc lacks the originality claimed for the rest of the hymn, the whole ṛc being only repeated from the preceding hymn, VII. 60. The fourth pāda is the standing conclusion of the Vasiṣṭha hymns.

NO. 20.

MAṆḌALA VII. **SŪKTA 71.**

पञ्चमेऽनुवाक एकोनविंशति सूक्तानि। तत्राप स्वसुरिति पडटचं प्रथमं सूक्तं त्रैष्टुभमाश्विनम्। अनुक्रम्यते च अपस्वसुः षडिति। गतो विनियोगः।।

Verse 1.

अप। स्वसुः। नक्। जिहीते। रिणक्ति। कृष्णीः। अरूषाय। पन्थाम्। अश्वऽमघा। गोऽमघा। वाम्। हुवेम। दिवा। नक्तम्। शरूम्। अस्मत्। युयोतम्।।१।।

* अयं मंत्रे भाव्यकृता (७-६०-१२) इत्यत्र व्याख्याततत्वादादर्शो इयं देवेति सप्तमी गता। एतावानेव निर्देशः। चतुर्थचरणस्तु (७-१-२०) इत्यत्र नोऽस्मान्यूयं त्वत्परिवाराश्च सर्वे स्वस्तिभिरविनाशिभिर्मङ्गलैः। तथा च यास्कः। स्वस्तीत्यविनाशनामास्तिरभिपूजितः स्वस्तीति (नि० ३-२१)। सदा पात। रक्षत। इति व्याख्यातः।।

स्वसुः स्वसृस्थानीयाया उषसः सकाशन्नग्नक्तं रात्रिरपजिहीते। अपगच्छति। तस्या अवकाशं दत्वा स्वयमपगतेत्यर्थः। स्वसा स्वस्त्रे ज्यायस्यै योनि मारैक् (ऋ०१-१२४-८) अत्युक्तम्। कृष्णीः कृष्णवर्णा रात्रिरूषायोरोचमानायाह्ने सूर्याय वा पन्थां पन्थानं मार्गं रिणक्ति। रेचयति। यस्मादेवं तस्माद्युवयोरागमन-समयत्वात् हे अश्वामघाश्वधनौ हे गोमधा गोघनौ। उभयोः। प्रदातारावित्यर्थः। ईदृशौ वां युवां हुवेम। स्तुमः। आह्वयामः। दिवा नक्तं सर्वदा शरूं हिंसक-मस्मदस्मत्तौ युयोतम्। पृथक्कुरूतम्।।

नश्, nom. sg. नक्, night; occurs only here.

जि॒ही॒ते॒, 3. sg. pres. ātm; rt. II. हा 3., to go forth.

शरू f., arrow (of death and disease).

यु॒यो॒त॒म् (यु॒यु॒तम्), 2. du. pres. impv.; rt. यु 3., to separate.

Verse 2.

उ॒प॒ऽआया॑तम्। दा॒शुषे॑। मर्त्या॑य। रथे॑न। वा॒मम्। अ॒श्वि॒ना॒। वह॑न्ता। यु॒यु॒तम्। अ॒स्मत्। अनि॑राम्। अमी॑वाम्। दिवा॑। नक्त॑म्। मा॒ध्वी॒ इति॑। त्रासी॑थाम्। नः॒।।२।।

हे अश्विनौ युवामुपायातम्। उपागच्छतमस्मदाह्वानं प्रति। किमर्थम्। दाशुषु हविषां दात्रे यजमानाय तदर्थं रथेन वामं वननीयं धनं वहन्ता वहन्तौ। अस्मदस्मत्तो युयुतम्। पृथक्कुरूतम्। किम्। अनिराम्। इरान्नम्। *तदभाववद्दा- रिद्यमित्यर्थः। अमीवां रोगं च। हे माध्वी मधुमन्तौ युवां नोऽस्मान् दिवा नक्तं सर्वदा त्रासीथाम्। रक्षतम्।।

त्रासी॑थां, 2. du. aor. opt. ātm.; rt. त्रा, to protect. It is here accented though verb of the principal clause, possibly on account of the stress on it. See ZDMG. 60. 739.

अनि॑रा f., drought, thirst, death of thirst.

अमी॑वा f., sickness.

---

* आदर्शे तदन्नदारिद्र्यमित्यर्थ इति पाठः।

Verse 3.

आ। वाम्। रथम्। अवमस्याम्। विऽउष्टौ। सुम्नऽयवः। वृषणः। वर्तयन्तु। स्यूमऽगभस्तिम्। ऋतयुक्ऽभिः। अश्वैः। आ। अश्विना। वसुमन्तम्। वहेथाम्।।३।।

अवमस्यामासन्नायां व्युष्टौ व्युच्छन उषसि वां युवयो रथं सुम्नायवः सुखेन योजयनतोऽश्वा वृषणो वर्षका युवामा वर्तयन्तु। स्यूमगभस्तिं सुखरश्मिं स्यूतरश्मिं वसुमन्तं प्रदेयधनयुक्तं रथे हे अश्विनाश्विनावृतयुग्भिरूदकयुक्तैरश्वैरु-दकप्रदैरश्वैरावहेथाम्।।

सुम्नायु, favourable, kindly.

अवम, adj. with pronominal loc. sg.

व्युष्टि f., the brightening up, the dawn.

गभस्ति m. shaft. स्यूमन् n., thong.

स्यूम गभस्ति, bahuvr. cpd.: with thoughs for a shaft, drawn with thongs.

Verse 4.

यः। वाम्। रथः। नृपती इति नृऽपती। अस्ति। वोळ्हा। त्रिऽवन्धुरः। वसुऽमान्। उस्रऽयामा। आ। नः। एना। नासत्या। उप। यातम्। अभि। यत्। वाम्। विश्वऽप्स्न्यः। जिगाति।।४।।

हे नृपती नृणां यजमानानां पालकावश्विनौ वां युवयोर्यो रथो वोळ्हा युवयोर्वाहकोऽस्ति सर्वदा संनिहितो वर्तते। कीदृशोऽसौ। त्रिवन्धुरः सारथ्यधि-ष्ठानस्थानत्रयोपेता वसुमान् धनवानुस्त्रयामोस्त्रं दिवसं प्रति गन्ता। एनैतेन रथेन हे नासत्याश्विनौ नोऽस्मानुपायातम्। यद्रथो यश्च रथो वां विश्वप्स्न्यो व्याप्तरूपोऽ-भिजिगाति अभिगच्छति। अथवाह। यद्यस्माद्विश्वप्स्न्यो वसिष्ठो वां जिगाति स्तौति अत उपायातम्।।

त्रिवन्धुर, three-seated.

विश्वप्स्न्य, containing all nourishment, all-nourishing; Sāy.

व्याप्तरूपः, with penetrating form; of many a form, manifold; every.

जिगाति, 3. sg. indic. (or) sbj.; rt. गा 3., to go.

Sāy.'s second interpretation of pāda 4 would seem better than the first, if जिगाति could be taken as a form of गै, to sing, and if it were provd that विश्वप्स्न्यं signifies Vasiṣṭha. Tentatively we may translate:—Since every one praises you, come, O Nāsatyā, with that car which is, O lords of men, your vehicle, three-seated, filled with riches, faring at day-break.

Verse 5.

युवम्। च्यवानम्। जरसः। अमुमुक्तम्। नि। पेदवे। ऊहथुः। अश्वम्। निः। अंहसः। तमसः। स्पर्तम्। अत्रिम्। नि। जाहुषम्। शिथिरे। धतम्। अन्तरिति।।५।।

हे अश्विना युवां युवां च्यवानं जरसो जीर्णाद्रूपादमुमुक्तम्। अमुञ्चतम्। युवं च्यवानमश्विना जरन्तं पुनर्युवानम् (ऋ० १-११७-१३) इति ह्यन्यत्र। तथा पेदव एतन्नामकाय राज्ञ आशुं शीघ्रगामिनमश्वं निरूहथुः। न्यवहतं युद्धे। युवं श्वेतं पेदवे (ऋ० १-११८-९) इति निगमः। तथात्रि महर्षिमंहस ऋबीसादग्नेः सकाशात्तमसश्च गुहान्तः सिथताञ्च। सकाशान्निष्पर्तम् न्यपारयतम्। युवमृबीसमुत तप्तमत्रय ओमन्वन्तं चक्रथुः (ऋ० १०-३९-९) इति निगमः। तथा जाहुषं शिथिरे शिथिले भ्रष्टे स्वराष्ट्रेऽन्तर्मध्ये पुनर्निधातम्। न्यधातम्। परिविष्टं जाहुषं विश्वतः सीम् (ऋ० १-११६-२०) इति ह्युक्तम्।।

अमुमुक्तं, plupf. rt. मुच्.

निस् स्पर्तम्, 2. du. aor.; rt. स्पृ 5., to release.

जरस् f., =जरा, old age.

Verse 6.

इयम्। मनीषा। इयम्। अश्विना। गीः। इमाम्। सुऽवृक्तिम्।

वृषणा। जुषेथाम्। इमा। ब्रह्माणि। युवऽयूनि। अग्मन्। यूयम्। पात। स्वस्तिऽभिः। सदा। नः।।६।।

*हे आश्विनाश्विनावियं मनीषा स्तुतिर्युवयोः कृतेति शेषः। तदेवादरार्थं पुनरूच्यते। इयं गीः स्तुतिः कृता। हे वृषणा कामानां वर्षकाविमामस्मत्कृतां सुवृक्तिं शोभनां स्तुतिं जुषेथाम्। सेवेथाम्। इमेमानि ब्रह्माणि कर्माणि स्तुतिरूपाणि युवयूनि युवां कामयमानानि सन्त्यग्मन्। गच्छन्तु युवाम्। यूयं पातेति सिद्धम्।।

मनीषा इयम्, no saṁdhi, because मनीषा precedes the caesura.

अग्मन् 3. plur. aor.; rt. गम्.

सुवृक्ति f., song of praise, cp. प्र वृञ्जे No. 5.1.

NO. 21.

MAṆḌALA VII. **SŪKTA. 77.**

उपो रूरूच इति षडृचं सप्तमं सूक्तं वसिष्ठस्यार्षमुषस्यम्। तथाचानुक्रान्तम्। उपोरूरूचे षडिति। प्रातरनुवाकाश्विनशस्त्रयोरूक्तो विनियोगः।।

Verse 1.

उपो इति। रूरूचे। युवतिः। न। योषा। विश्वम्। जीवम्। प्रऽसुवन्ती। चरायै। अभूत्। अग्निः। सम्ऽइधे। मानुषाणाम्। अर्कः। ज्योतिः। बाधमाना। तमांसि।।१।।

इयमुषा उपो समीपएव सूर्यस्य रूरूचे। दीप्यते। युवतिर्यौवनोपेता योषा न योषिदिव। सा यथा वस्त्राभरणादिना पत्यः समीपे प्रदीप्यते तद्वत्। किं कुर्वती। विश्वं सर्वं जीवं जीवसंघं चरायै संचाराय प्रसुवन्ती प्रेरयन्ती। किंचाग्निर्मानुषाणां मनुष्याणामर्थाय समिधेऽभूत्। समिन्धनीयोऽभवत्। कृत्यार्थे केन्। समिधः संस्तमांस्यन्धकारान्बाधमाना बाधमानं †वा बाधकं ज्योतिस्तेजः

* इयमृक् आदर्शे ७-७०-७ इत्यत्र व्याख्यातत्वात् केवलं इयं मनीषेति षष्ठी गता इत्येतावान्निदर्शः।

† आदर्शे वा इति नास्ति।

संघमकः। अकार्षीत्। अथवा। औषसं ज्योतिस्तमांसि बाधमाना बाध्यमानान्यकः। अकरोत्।।

चरायै, dat. inf. rt. चर्; see Lanman, Noun-Inflection, p. 554. n. 9. समिध्, fuel, kindling.

मानुषाणाम् may either contain the agent of kindling:—for kindling by men, or may depend on Agni:—Agni of men, Agni for the benefit of men. (Sāy.).

Verse 2.

विश्वम्। प्रतीची। सऽप्रथाः। उत्। अस्थात्। रूशत्। वासः। बिभ्रती। शुक्रम्। अश्वैत्। हिरण्यऽवर्णा। सु शीकऽसं क्। गवाम्। माता। नेत्री। अह्नाम्। अरोचि।।२।।

विश्वं कृत्स्नं जगत्प्रति प्रतीच्यभिमुखी सप्रथाः सर्वतः पृथुतरोदस्थात्। उदगच्छत्। उदिता च रूशद्दीप्तं शुक्रं तेजोमयं वासो वसनीयं तेजःसमूहं बिभ्रती धारयन्त्यश्वैत्। वर्धते। हिरण्यवर्णा हेतरमणीयवर्णोपेता। सुदृशीकसंदृक्। संदर्शयतीति संदृक् तेजः। सुष्ठु दर्शनीयं संदृक् तेजो यस्याः सा तादृशी। गवां वाचां गवामेव वा माता निर्मात्री। उषःकाले हि पक्षिमनुष्यादीनां वाचो निर्गच्छन्ति। गवामपि तस्मिनकाले संचारात्तन्निर्मातृत्वम्। अथवा रश्मीनां निर्मात्री। अरोचि रोचतेऽह्नां नेत्री दिवसानां प्रापयित्री।।

अश्वैत्, impf. (or) aor. rt. श्वित, to be briliant, to shine.

शुक्रम् may best be taken as adv.

अरोचि, 3. sg. aor. ātm; rt. रूच्.

Verse 3.

देवानाम्। चक्षुः। सुऽभगा। वहन्ती। श्वेतम्। नयन्ती। सुऽदृशीकम्। अश्वम्। उषाः। अदर्शि। रश्मिऽभिः। विऽअक्ता। चित्रऽमघा। विश्वम्। अनु। प्रऽभूता।।३।।

देवानां चक्षुश्चक्षुःस्थानीयं तेजो वहन्ती धारयन्ती सुभगा शोभनधना

सुदृशीकं सुदर्शनमश्वं सर्वदा गन्तारमादित्यं नयन्ती प्रापयन्ती। किम्। श्वेतं श्वेतवर्णोपेतं सूर्यम्। प्रकाशयुक्तं कुर्वतीत्यर्थः। कीदृश्युषाः। रश्मिभिः स्वकीयै-र्व्यक्तादर्शि। दृश्यते च। चित्रामघा विचित्रधना विश्वमनु सर्वं जगदनुलक्ष्य प्रभूता प्रवृद्धा। सर्वजगद्व्यवहारायेत्यर्थः।।

Verse 4.

अन्ति॑ऽवामा। दू॒रे। अ॒मित्र॑म्। उ॒च्छ॒। उ॒र्वीम्। गव्यू॑तिम्। अभ॑यम्। कृ॒धि॒। नः॒। य॒वय॑। द्वेषः॑। आ। भ॒र॒। वसू॑नि। चो॒दय॑। राधः॑। गृ॒ण॒ते। म॒घो॒नि॒।।४।।

हे उषः अन्तिवामा। अन्त्यस्मदन्तिके वामं वननीयं धनं यस्याः सान्ति-वामा। त्वममित्रमस्मच्छत्रुं दूरेऽस्मत्तो विप्रकृष्टदेशे वर्तमानं कृत्वा व्युच्छ। विभाहि। यथामित्रो दूरे भवति तथा व्युच्छेत्यर्थः। तथोर्वीं गव्यूतिं भूमिभयं नोऽस्माकं कृधि। कुरु। सिं च द्वेषोऽस्मद्देष्टृ न्यावय। अस्मत्तः पृथक्कुरु। *वसूनि शत्रूणां धनान्याभर। आहर। राधो धनं चोदय प्रेरय गृणते स्तुवते मह्यं हे मघोनि धनवति।।

अन्ति॑ वाम, with wealth near at hand. Note the contrast expressed in अन्ति॑वाम and दू॒रे उच्छ. This contrast, however, is not a sufficient reason to read अन्ति॑ वा॒म.

अभ॑यम् subst. n., or adv.: safely.

Verse 5.

अ॒स्मे इति॑। श्रेष्ठे॑भिः। भा॒नुऽभिः॑। वि। भा॒हि॒। उषः॑। दे॒वि॒। प्र॒ऽति॒रन्ती॑। नः॒। आयुः॑। इष॑म्। च॒। नः॒। दध॑ती। वि॒श्व॒ऽवा॒रे॒। गोऽम॑त्। अश्व॑ऽवत्। रथ॑ऽवत्। च॒। राधः॑।।५।।

हे उषो देवि अस्मे अस्मभ्यं श्रेष्ठेभिः प्रशस्यैर्भानुभी रश्मिभिः प्रकाशैर्वि-भाहि। प्रकाशय। किं कुर्वती। नोऽस्माकमायुरायुष्यं प्रतिरन्ती। वर्धयन्ती।

---

* अयं वसून्याद्याहरांतोंऽशः प्रथमावृत्तौ नास्ति।

वर्धयन्ती। हे विश्ववारे विश्वैः संभजनीये देवि नोऽस्मभ्यमिषं च गोमद्गोभिर्बहुभि-रूपेतमश्वावदश्वैश्चोपेतं *रथवद्रथैरूपेतं राधो धनं च दधती विभाहीति।।

Verse 6.

याम्। त्वा। दिवः। दुहितः। वर्धयन्ति। उषः। सुऽजाते। मतिऽभिः। वसिष्ठाः। सा। अस्मासु। धाः। रयिम्। ऋष्वम्। बृहन्तम्। यूयम्। पात। स्वस्तिऽभिः। सदा। नः।।६।।

हे दिवो दुहितरूषः सुजाते शोभनजनने यां त्वा त्वां मतिभिः स्तोत्रैर्वसिष्ठा वर्धयन्ति सा त्वमस्मासु वसिष्ठेष्वृष्वं प्रदीप्तं बृहन्तं महान्तं रयिं धनं धाः। धेहि।।

धाः, 2. sg. aor. sbj.; rt धा.

NO. 22.

MAṆḌALA VII. **SŪKTA 86.**

धीरा त्वस्येत्यष्टर्चं षोडशं सूक्तं वसिष्ठस्यार्षं त्रैष्टुभं वरुणदेवत्यम्। तथा चानुक्रान्तम्। धीराष्टौ वारूणं हेति। गतो विनियोगः।।

Verse 1.

धीरा। तु। अस्य। महिना। जनूंषि। वि। यः। तस्तम्भ। रोदसी इति। चित्। उर्वी इति। प्र। नाकम्। ऋष्वम्। नुनुदे। बृहन्तम्। द्विता। नक्षत्रम्। पप्रथत्। च। भूम।।१।।

अस्य वरुणस्य जनूंषि जन्मानि महिना महिम्ना तु क्षिप्रं धीरा धीराणि धैर्यवन्ति भवन्ति। यो वरुण उर्वी विस्तीर्णे रोदसी चिद्द्यावापृथिव्यावपि वि तस्तम्भ विविधं स्तब्धे स्वकीये स्थाने स्थिते अकरोत्। यश्च बृहन्तं नाकमादित्यं नक्षत्रं चर्ष्वं दर्शनीयं द्विता द्वैधं प्र नुनुदे प्रेरयति स्म। अहनि सूर्यं दर्शनीयं प्रेरयति रात्रौ रक्षत्रं तथेति द्विप्रकारः। भूम भूमिं च यः पप्रथत् अप्रथयत् विस्तारितवान्। तस्यास्य वरुणस्येत्यन्वयः।।

---

* एतद्विशेषणं प्रथमावृत्तौ न दृश्यते।

जनुस् m. n., birth, being, creature; plur. = जन्मानि, जातानि, generations.

धीरं, firm, stable, immutable, not shaken.

नाकं m., firmament, heaven.

नक्षंत्र n. sg. day-star, sun.

द्विता indecl., double, both, in a double manner or direction, eastwards and westwards, during day and night.

The first pāda contains a statement which is established by pādas 2-4. पप्रथंत्, beginning a new sentence, is accented. This accent of पप्रथंत्, besides the context, speaks against the likelihood, that नक्षंत्रम् might depend on पप्रथंत् as well.

Verse 2.

उत। स्वयां। तन्वां। सम्। वदे। तत्। कदा। नु। अन्तः। वरुणे। भुवानि। किम्। मे। हव्यम्। अहृणानः। जुषेत। कदा। मृळीकम्। सुऽमनाः। अभि। ख्यम्।।२।।

वरुणं शीघ्रं दिदृक्षमाण ऋषिरनया वितर्कयति। उतेति विचिकित्सायाम्। उत किं स्वया तन्वा स्वीयेनात्मीयेन शरीरेण सं वदे। सहवदनं करोमि। आहोस्वित् तत्तेन वरुणेन सह संवदे। कदा नु कदा खलु वरुणे देवेऽन्तर्भुवानि। अन्तर्भूतो भवानि। वरुणस्य चित्ते संलग्नो भवानीत्यर्थः। अपि च मे मदीयं हव्यं स्तोत्रं हविर्वाहृणानोऽक्रुध्यन् वरुणः किं केन हेतुना जुषेत। सेवेत। सुमनाः शोभनमनस्कः सन्नहं कदा कस्मिन्काले मृळीकं सुखयितारे वरुणमभिख्यम्। अभिपश्येयम्।।

स्वयां तन्वां, with one's own body, person, with oneself.

भुवानि, 1. sg. aor. sbj.; rt. भू.

ख्यम्, 1. sg. aor. inj.; rt. ख्या.

किम्, interrog. particle.

Verse 3.

पृच्छे। तत्। एनः। वरुण। दिदृक्षु। उपो इति। एमि। चिकितुषः। विऽपृच्छम्। समानम्। इत्। मे। कवयः। चित्। आहुः। अयम्। ह। तुभ्यम्। वरुणः। हृणीते॥३॥

हे वरुण तदेनः पापं पृच्छे। त्वां पृच्छामि। दिदृक्षु। छान्दसः सुलोपः। द्रष्टुमिच्छन्नहम्। येन पापेन हेतुना त्वदीयैः पाशैर्बद्धोऽस्मि। पृष्टः संस्तत्पापं कथय। अहं विपृच्छं विविधं प्रष्टुं चिकितुषो विदुषो जनानुपो एमि। उपागाम्। ते कवयश्चित् क्रान्तदर्शिनो जनाश्च मे मह्यं समानमित् समानमेवैक*रूपमेवाहुः। अकथयन्। यदाहुसतदाह। हे स्तोतः तुभ्यमयं हायमेव वरुणो हृणीते। क्रुध्यतीति। अतः क्रोधं परित्यज्यासमान्पाशेभ्यो मोचय॥

पृच्छे, 1. sg. pres. ātm.; rt. प्रछ् (प्रच्छ्) 6. वि पृच्छऽम्, acc. inf. उपो=उप उ.

दिदृक्षु has been interpreted in the following ways:—

(1) loc. plur. of दिदृश्, among those who see (Ludwig).

(2) दिदृक्षु n. subst., curiosity, =दिदृक्षा (Geldner).

(3) दिदृक्षूपो m. nom. sg., with wrong accent and saṁdhi, for दिदृक्षुरूषो, desirous to see, to find out (Sāy.).

(4) दिदृक्षु n. adj. desider. rt. दृश्, used adverbially (Lanman, Bergaigne), hence shift of accent from first to second syllable (Oldenberg, Textkrit. i. l., Macdonell, Ved. Reader, p.137).

Verse 4.

किम्। आगः। आस। वरुण। ज्येष्ठम्। यत्। स्तोतारम्। जिघांससि। सखायम्। प्र। तत्। मे। वोचः। दुःऽदभ। स्वधाऽवः। अव। त्वा। अनेनाः। नमसा। तुरः। इयाम्॥४॥

---

* एकरूपम् इति प्रथमावृत्तौ नास्ति।

हे वरुण ज्येष्ठमधिकं किमाग आस। कोऽपराधो मया कृतो बभूव। यद्येनागसा सखायं मित्रभूतं सन्तं स्तोतारं जिघांससि हन्तुमिच्छसि। हे दूळभ दुर्दभ अन्यर्बाधितुमशक्य स्वधावस्तेजस्विन् हे वरुण तदागो मे मह्यं प्रवोचः। प्रब्रूहि। एवं सति तस्य प्रायश्चित्तं कृत्वानेना अपापः सन्नहं तुरस्त्वरमाणः शीघ्रो नमसा नमस्कारेण हविषा वा त्वामवेयाम्। उपगच्छेयम्।।

यद् that, so that.

स्व॒धाव॑त् adj., voc. sg. स्वधावस्, self-dependent.

अव॑ इ, come to. प्र वो॒च॒ः, inj., aor.

तु॒र adj., superior to, quick.

Read ज्य+इष्ठं॑; तुरेयाम्, with double contraction.

Verse 5.

अव॑। द्रु॒ग्धानि॑। पित्र्या॑। सृ॒जं न॒ः। अव॑। या। व॒यम्। च॒कृ॒म। त॒नूभि॑ः। अव॑। रा॒ज॒न्। प॒शु॒ऽतृ॒प॑म्। न। ता॒युम्। सृ॒ज। व॒त्सम्। न। दाम्नः॑। वसि॑म्।।५।।

हे वरुण पित्र्या पितृतः प्राप्तानि नोऽस्मदीयानि द्रुग्धानि द्रोहान् बन्धनहेतुभूतानव९सृज। विमुञ्च। अस्मत्तो विश्लेषय। वयं च या यानि द्रोहजातानि तनूभिः शरीरैश्चकृम कृतवन्तः स्म तानि चाव सृज। हे राजन् राजमान वरुण पशुतृपं न तायुं स्तैन्यप्रायश्चित्तं कृत्वावसाने घासादिभिः पशूनां तर्पयितारं स्तेनमिव दाम्नो रज्जोर्वत्सं न वत्समिव च वसिष्ठं मां बन्धकात्पापादव सृज। विमुञ्च।।

द्रु॒ग्ध, pt. pf. pass. rt. द्रुह; subst. n., misdeed.

प॒शु॒तृप् m., cattle-lifter, cattle-thieef.

अव॑ सृज् in the first pāda is construed with the accus. of the object and dat. of the person, in the third and fourth pādas with the accus. of the person and the dat. of the object.

Pischel, Ved. Stud. I. 106, takes प॒शु॒तृपं॑ न ता॒युं to be

attraction to वसिष्ठम् and stand for the nominative. Consequently he translates:—Release, O king, Vasiṣṭha (from sin) as a cattle-thief (releases) the calf from the rope. But Sāy.'s interpretation, see commentary, is really not quite so nonsensical as Pischel was inclined to think.

Read दामनो.

Verse 6.

न। सः। स्वः। दक्षः। वरुण। ध्रुतिः। सा। सुरा। मन्युः। विऽभीदकः। अचित्तिः। अस्ति। ज्यायान्। कनीयसः। उपऽअरे। स्वप्नः। चन। इत्। अनृतस्य। प्रऽयोता।।६।।

हे वरुण स स्वो दक्षः पुरूषस्य *स्वरूपवद्बलं पापप्रवृत्तौ कारणं न भवति। किं तर्हि ध्रुतिः स्थिरोत्पत्तिसमय एव निर्मिता दैवगतिः कारणम्। ध्रु गतिस्थैर्ययोरिति धातुः। सा च ध्रुतिर्वक्ष्यमाणयपा। सुरा प्रमादकारिणी मन्युः क्रोधश्चगुर्वादिविषयः सन्ननर्थहेतुः। विभीदको द्यूतसाधनोक्षः। स च द्यूतेषु पुरुषं प्रेरयन्ननर्थहेतुर्भवति। अचित्तिरज्ञानमविवेककारणम्। अत ईदृशी दैवक्लप्तिरेव पुरुषस्य पापप्रवृत्तौ कारणम्। अपि च कनीयसोऽल्पस्य हीनस्य पुरूषस्य पाप्रवृत्तावुपार उपागते समीपे नियन्तृत्वेन स्थितो ज्यायानधिक ईश्वरोस्ति। स एव तं पापे प्रवर्तयति। तथा चाम्नातम्। एष ह्येवासाधु कर्म कारयति तं यमधो निनीषति (कौ० उ० ३-८) इति। एवं च सति स्वप्नश्चन स्वप्नोऽप्यनृतस्य पापस्य प्रयोता प्रकर्षेण मिश्रयिता भवति। इदिति पूरकः स्वप्ने कृतैरपि कर्मभिर्बहूनि पापानि जायन्ते किमु वक्तव्यं जागति कृतैः कर्मभिः पापान्युत्पद्यन्त इति। अतो ममापराधो दैवागत इति हे वरुण त्वया क्षन्तव्य इति भावः।।

ध्रुति (ध्रु, ध्वृ) f., trick, trap, seduction.

उपार (ऋ) m., "tresspassing", offence.

प्रयोतृ (यु 3., to separate) m., warder off.

---

* स्वभूतं तद्बलम् इत्यादर्शः।

Verse 7.

अरम्। दासः। न। मीळ्हुषे। कराणि। अहम्। देवाय। भूर्णये। अनागाः। अचेतयत्। अचितः। देवः। अर्यः। गृत्सम्। राये। कविऽतरः। जुनाति।।७।।

मीह्ळुषे सेक्त्रे कामानां वर्षित्रे भूर्णये जगतो भर्त्रे देवाय दानादिगुणयुक्ताय वरुणायानागास्तत्प्रसादादपापः सन्नहमरमलं पर्याप्तं कराणि। परिचरणं करवाणि। दासो न यथा भृत्यः स्वामिने सम्यक् परिचरति तद्वत्। अर्यः स्वामी स च देवोऽचितो *अज्ञानस्मानचेतयत्। प्रज्ञापयतु। चेतयतु। गृत्सं स्तोतारं च। कवितरः प्राज्ञतरो देवो राये धनाय धनप्राप्तयर्थं जुनाति। जुनातु। प्रेरयतु।।

कराणि, 1. sg. sbj. aor.; rt. कृ. अरं कृ, to do service.

गृत्स adj., ripe, sensible, experienced.

भूर्णि (भुर्) adj., hurried, zealous.

अर्य m., gentleman, lord, magnate.

जू 9., to speed.

Verse 8.

एकादशिने वारुणे पशावयमिति पुरोडाशस्यानुवाक्या। सूत्रितं च। अयं सु तुभ्यं वरुण स्वधाव एवा वन्दस्व वरुणं बृहन्तम्। (आ० ३-७)

अयम्। सु। तुभ्यम्। वरुण। स्वधाऽवः। हृदि। स्तोमः। उपऽश्रितः। चित्। अस्तु। शम्। नः। क्षेमे। शम्। ऊं इति। योगे। नः। अस्तु। यूयम्। पात। स्वस्तिऽभिः। सदा। नः।।८।।

हे स्वधावोऽन्नवन्वरुण तुभ्यं त्वदर्थं क्रियमाणोऽयमेतत्सूक्तात्मकं स्तोमः स्तोत्रं हृदि त्वदीये हृदये सु सुष्ठूपरित उपगतः समवेतोऽस्तु। चिदिति पूरकः। अप्राप्तस्य प्रापणं योगः प्राप्तस्य रक्षणं क्षेमः। नोऽसमदीये क्षेमे रक्षणे शमुपद्रवाणां णादयो देवा नोऽसमान्सर्वदा स्वस्तिभिरविनाशैः पात। रक्षत।।

* अजानतो इत्यादर्शः।

क्षेमं m., quiet, comfort, possession.

योगं m., acquisition.

NO. 23.

MAṆḌALA VII. **SŪKTA 95.**

प्रक्षोदसेति षड्टचं षष्ठं सूक्तं वसिष्ठस्यार्ष त्रैष्टुभं सरस्वतीदेवताकम्। तृतीया तु सरस्वद्देवताका। अनुक्रम्यते च। प्रक्षोदसा षट् सारस्वतं तु तृतीया सरस्वत इति। गतः सूक्तविनियोगः। प्रथमे छन्दोमे प्रउगशस्त्रे प्रक्षोदसा धायसा सस्त्रएषेति प्रउगम्। (आ० ८-९) इति। सारस्वते पशौ प्रक्षोदसेति वपाया याज्या। सूत्रितं च। प्रक्षोदसा धायसा सस्त्र एषा पावीरवी कन्या चित्रायुः (आ ३-७) इति।

Verse 1.

प्र। क्षोदंसा। धायंसा। स॒स्रे॒। ए॒षा। सरंस्वती। ध॒रुणंम्। आयंसी। पूः। प्र॒ऽबाबंधाना। र॒थ्याऽइव। या॒ति॒। विश्वाः। अ॒पः। म॒हि॒ना। सिन्धुंः। अ॒न्याः।।१।।

सरस्वत्या एषा नदीवन्निगमा। एषा दृश्यमाना नदीरूपा सरस्वत्यायस्ययसा निर्मिता पूः पुरीव धरूणम्। लिङ्गव्यत्ययः। धरूणा धारयित्री धायसा धारकेण क्षोदसोदकेन प्रसस्त्रे। प्रधावति। शीघ्रं गच्छति। सिन्धुः स्यन्दनशीला नदीरूपा सान्या विश्वाः सर्वा अप आपगा महिना महिमन्ना प्रबाबधाना भृशं बाधमाना रथ्येव प्रतोलीव विस्तीर्णा सती याति। गच्छति। यद्वा। रथ्येव रथिनेव यथा रथी रथेन मार्गस्थं तरूगुल्मादिकं चूर्णीकृत्य गच्छति तद्वत् सवकीयेन वेगेन सव संपिषती गच्छतीत्यर्थः।।

बाबध्, intensit. rt. बाध् 1.; प्र बाध्, to push on, press on, to catch up.

क्षोदंस् (क्षुद्) n., flood, deluge.

धायंस् (धि) subst. n., refreshment; adj., refreshing.

ध॒रुणं (धृ) adj., carrying; subst. n., support, fortress.

र॒थ्या॑ f., road, high road.

सिन॑धु m. f., (in the fourth pāda), river.

Verse 2.

सारस्वत एव पशौ वपाया एकाचेतदित्यनुवाक्या। सूत्रितं च। एकाचेतसरस्वती नदीनामुत स्या नः सरस्वती जुषाणा (आ० ३-८) इति।

एका॑। अ॒चे॒त॒म्। सर॑स्वती। न॒दीना॑म्। शुचि॑ः। य॒ती। गि॒रिऽभ्य॑ः। आ। स॒मु॒द्रात्। रा॒यः। चेत॑न्ती। भुव॑नस्य। भूरे॑ः। घृ॒तम्। पय॑ः। दु॒दु॒हे। नाहु॑षाय॥२॥

सहस्रवत्सरेण क्रतुना यक्ष्यमाणो नाहुषो नाम राजा सरस्वतीं नदीं प्रार्थयामास सा च तस्मै सहस्रसंवत्सरपर्याप्तं पयो घृतं च प्रददौ। अयमर्थोऽत्र प्रतिपाद्यते। नदीनामन्यासां मध्ये शुचिः शुद्धा गिरिभ्यः सकाशादा समुद्रा-त्समुद्रपर्यतं यती गच्छन्त्येका सरस्वती नद्यचेतत्। नाहुषस्य प्रार्थनामज्ञासीत्। तथा भवनस्य भूतजातस्य भूरेर्बहुलस्य रायो धनानि चेतन्ती प्रज्ञापयन्ती प्रयच्छन्ती नाहुषाय राज्ञे धृतं पयश्च सहस्रसंवत्सरक्रतोः पर्याप्तं दुदुहे। दुग्धवती। दत्तवती॥

चित् with genit., to mind, to watch over (in pāda 3); transit., to come into notice, to be famous (in pāda 1).

Verse 3.

सरस्वतद्देवताके पशौ स वावृध इति पुरोडाशस्य याज्या। सूत्रितं च। स वावृधे नर्यो योषणासु यस्य व्रतं पशवो यन्ति सर्वे (आ० ३-८) इति।

सः। व॒वृ॒धे॒। नर्य॑ः। योष॑णासु। वृषा॑। शिशु॑ः। वृ॒ष॒भः। य॒ज्ञिया॑सु। सः। वा॒जिन॑म्। म॒घव॑त्ऽभ्यः। द॒धा॒ति॒। वि। सा॒तये॑। त॒न्व॑म्। म॒मृ॒जी॒त॒॥३॥

मध्यस्थानो वायुः सरस्वान्। नर्यो नृभ्यो हितो वृषा सेचनसमर्थः शिशुरल्पः प्रादुर्भावसमयेऽलपतया दृश्यमानो वृषभो वर्षिता एवंभूतः स सरस्वान् यज्ञियासु यज्ञार्हासु योषित्स्वात्मनः कलत्रभूतासु मध्यमस्थानास्वप्सु-

मध्ये ववृधे। वर्धते। स तादृशः सरस्वान् मधवद्यो हविष्मभ्यो यजमानेभ्यो वाजिनं बलिनं पुत्रं दधाति। ददाति। तथा सातये लाभार्थं संस्करोतीत्यर्थः। यद्यप्येषा सरस्वतः स्तुतिस्तथापि सरस्वत्याः प्रीणनार्थं वत्सवनमिति च्छान्दोमिके सारस्वते तृचेऽस्या उक्तो विनियोगो न विरूध्यते।

नर्य adj., virile, kind or friendly towards men.

मामृजीत 3. sg. pf. opt. ātm.; rt. मृज् 2., to wipe. मामृजत refers either to Sarasvatī or to वाजिनं, which then would be the subject in the fourth pāda; in any case it is not likely that तन्वं signifies the body (bodies) of the sacrificing (worshippers), as Sāy. takes it.

वाजिनं probably refers to the valued horses reared east of the Indus.

Verse 4.

दशरात्रेऽष्टमेऽहनि प्रउग उतस्य न इति सारस्वतः सप्तमस्तृचः। सूत्रितं च। उतस्या नः सरस्वती जुषाणेति प्रउगम् (आ० ८-१०) इति। सारस्वते पशौ पुरोडाशस्योत स्या न इत्यनुवाक्या। सूत्रितं च। उत स्या नः सरस्वती जुषाणा सरस्वत्यभि नो नेषि वस्यः (आ० ३-७) इति।।

उत। स्या। नः। सरस्वती। जुषाणा। उप। श्रवत्। सुऽभगा। यज्ञे। अस्मिन्। मितज्ञुऽभिः। नमस्यैः। इयाना। राया। युजा। चित्। उत्ऽतरा। सखिऽभ्यः।।४।।

उतापि च जुषाणा प्रीयमाणा सुभगा शोभनधना स्या सा सरस्वती नोऽस्माकमस्मिन्यज्ञ उपश्रवत्। अस्मदीयाः स्तुतीरूपशृणोतु। कीदृशी सा। मितज्ञुभिः प्रह्वैर्जानुभिर्नमस्यैर्नमस्कारैर्देवैरियानोपगम्यमाना। चिच्छब्दश्चार्थे। युजा नित्युक्तेन राया धनेन च संगता सखिभ्य उत्तरोत्कृष्टतरा। ईदृश्यस्मदीयाः स्तुतीरूपशृणोत्वित्यन्वयः।।

श्रवत्, subj. aor. rt. श्रु.

मितज्ञु, with a bent knee.

युज् adj., allied, lasting.

स्य, स्या, त्यद्, pronj. demonstrat., he, she, that there, the well known.

राया युजा, either:—on account of her lasting wealth—or we have to understand a verb, संगता, for instance.

Verse 5.

पवित्रेष्ट्यां सारस्वतस्य हविष इमा जुह्वाना युष्मदा नमोभिर्दधिक्राव्णो अकारिषम् (आ० २-१२) इति।

इमा। जुह्वानाः। युष्मत्। आ। नमःऽभिः। प्रति। स्तोमम्। सरस्वति। जुषस्व। तव। शर्मन्। प्रियऽतमे। दधानाः। उप। स्थेयाम। शरणम्। न। वृक्षम्।।५।।

हे सरस्वति इमा इमान्यस्मदीयानि हवींषि जुह्वानास्तुीयं जुह्वतो वयं नमोभिस्त्वद्विषयैर्नमस्कारैर्युष्मत्त्वत्सकाशादा। उपसर्गश्रुतेर्योग्यक्रियाध्याहारः। आददीमहि धनानीति शेषः। स्तोमं चास्मदीयं स्तोत्रं प्रतिजुषस्व। प्रतिसेवस्व। वयं च प्रियतमेऽतिशयेन प्रिये तव त्वदीये शर्मञ्छर्मणि सुखे दधाना निधीयमानाः सन्तः शरणं न वृक्षमारयभूतं वृक्षमिवोपस्थेयाम। वामुपतिष्ठेम। संगच्छेमहि।।

जुह्वाना may be taken either:—

as nom. plur: जुह्वतः (Sāy.); or

as neuter nom. plur., with इमा, the verb to be understood; or

as neuter accus. plur., to be connected withh दधाना. The concinnity of the whole ṛc as well as the parallelism of दधानाः with जुह्वाना seems to favour Sāy.'s view.

युष्मद आ may refer to the यजमानः—from you, on your part, in your name-; or to the rivers, Sarasvatī above all:—in your pressence.

Verse 6.

अयम्। ऊं इति। ते। सरस्वति। वसिष्ठः। द्वारौ। ऋतस्य। सुऽभगे। वि। आवरित्यावः। वर्ध। शुभ्रे। स्तुवते। रासि। वाजान्। यूयम्। पात। स्वस्तिऽभिः। सदा नः।।६।।

हे सुभगे शोभनधने सरस्वति अयं वसिष्ठस्ते त्वां *ऋतस्य यज्ञस्य संबन्धिन्यौ द्वारौ पूर्वापरे व्यावः। विवृणोति। उ इति पूरकः। हे शुभ्रे शुभ्रवर्णे देवि वर्ध। वर्धस्व तथा स्तुवते स्तोत्रं कुर्वते वसिष्ठाय वाजरनन्नानि रासि। प्रदेहि। अन्यद्गतम्।।

रासि, 2. sg. pres.; rt. रा 2., to give, used in the sense of the imperative.

NO. 24.

MAṆḌALA VIII. **SŪKTA 29.**

बभ्रुरेक इति दशर्च नवमं सूक्तम्। मरीचिपुत्रः कश्यपो वैवस्वतो मनुर्वा ऋषिः तथाचानुक्रभ्यते। बभ्रुर्दश कश्यपो वा मारीचो द्वैपदमिति। दशापि द्विपदा विंशत्यक्षरा विराजः। पूर्ववद्विश्वेदेवा देवता। तृतीये छन्दोमे वैश्वदेवसूक्तात्पूर्वमेव द्वैपदं सूक्तं शसनीयम्। सूत्र्यते हि। बभ्रुरेक इति द्विपदासूक्तानि पुरस्ताद्वैश्वदेवसूक्तानाम् (आ० ८-९) इति।

The deity according to tradition (See Sāy.'s introductory remark) are the Viśve Devāḥ. In reality it "is a collection of riddles, in which each stanza describes a deity by his characteristic marks, leaving his name to be guessed. The deities by the successive stanzas are : Soma" (not quite certain), 2. Agni, 3. Tvaṣṭṛ (probably), 4. Indra, 5. Rudra, 6. Pūṣan, 7. Viṣṇu, 8. Aśvinā, 9. Mitrā-Varuṇā, 10. Aṅgirasas or more likely Atris, perhaps even the Maruts. The reason why such prominent deities as Bṛhaspati and Savitṛ should be excluded is not apparent. See Macdonell, Ved. Reder, p.

* यंतुः इत्यादर्शे विशेषः।

148. On the metre see Appendix III. II. Mixed Stanzas, p. LXVII.

Verse 1.

बभ्रुः। एकः। विषुणः। सूनरः। युवा। अञ्जि। अङ्क्ते। हिरण्ययम्।।१।।

अत्र दशानामृचां [1]किंचित्पदलिङ्गात्पृथग्देवताः। अत्र प्रथमायां बभ्रुरित्यनेन सोमोऽभिधीयते। सौम्यं बभ्रुमालभेत (तै० सं० २-१-३३) इत्यादिषु दृष्टत्वात्। बभ्रुर्बभ्रुवर्णः [2]सर्वलतादिषु परिपक्वः। यद्वा। डुभृञ् धारणपोषणयोः कुर्भ्रश्च (उ० १-२३) इति कुप्रत्ययः। सर्वस्य सुधामयैः [3]किरणैस्तावदुदिते चन्द्रमसि [4]सर्वे स्वदुःखोपशमनेन पुष्यन्ति खलु। तादृशो विषुणो विष्वगञ्चनः सूनरः सुष्ठु रात्रीणां नेता। रात्रयश्चन्द्रनेतृकाः खलु। एतादृशो युवा प्रतिदिवस माविर्भूतत्वात्तरूण एको देवः सोमो हिरण्ययं हिरण्मयमञ्जि। अभिव्यज्यते प्रकाश्यतेऽनेनेत्यञ्जि आभरणम्। अभिव्यक्तिसाधनं कुण्डलमुकुटादिकं स्वशरीरमङ्क्ते। अभिव्यञ्जयति।।

बभ्रु, brown, an epithet distinctive of Soma.

विषुण adj., of varied form (better than विश्वगञ्जन, Sāy.).

अञ्जि m.f. n.=अलंकार, आारण, तिलक. It may be the golden ring on the finger which is prescribed at the उपांशुसवन and all the following सवनs of the Agniṣṭoma. See Āpastamaba Srautasūtra, XII. 7. 12, and Hillebrandt, Rituallitteratur, p. 129.

Verse 2.

योनिम्। एकः। आ। ससाद। द्योतनः। अन्तः। देवेषु। मेधिरः।।२।।

1. किंचित्पदं... देवतम् इत्यादर्शः।
2. शबलतादिषु इत्यादर्शः।
3. दुद्रते इत्यादर्शः।
4. दुःखोपशमनानि पुष्टानि खलु इत्यादर्शः।

अत्र योनिमिति लिङ्गादग्निरूच्यते। अग्नये गृहपतये इत्यादिषु दृष्टत्वात्। देवेषु देवानामन्तर्मध्ये द्योतनः स्वतेजसा दीप्यमानो मेधिरो मेधाबी। अथवा मेधाकाङ्क्षिणां स्तोतॄणां मेधादातृत्वेन मेधायुक्तः। एवंविध एकोऽग्निर्योनि स्थानभूतमाहवनीयादिकमा ससाद। हविःस्वीकरणार्थमासीददति।।

योनिम् refers to th sacred fire or fire-place (आहवनीयाधि-कम् Sāy.).

Verse 3.

वाशीम्। एकः। बिभर्ति। हस्ते। आयसीम्। अन्तः। देवेषु। निऽध्रुविः।।३।।

देवेष्वन्तर्देवानां मध्ये द्योतमानो निध्रुविर्निश्चले स्थाने वर्तमानः। यद्वा नितरां गमनमस्यास्तीति निध्रुविः सर्वदा गच्छन्। अथवा संग्रामेषु शत्रूणां पुरतोऽतिशयेन स्थैर्यवान्। एतादृश एकस्त्वष्टनामको देव आयसीमयोमय-धारां वाशीम्। वाशृ शब्दे। शब्दयत्याक्रन्दयति शत्रूननयेति वाशी तक्षण-साधनं कुठारः। तं स्वकीये हस्ते बिभर्ति। धारयति।।

वाशी f., axe.

निध्रुवि, strenuous, persevering, =अपस्तम.

Verse 4.

वज्रम्। एकः। बिभर्ति। हस्ते। आऽहितम्। तेन। वृत्राणि। जिघ्नते।।४।।

अत्र वज्रलिङ्गादिन्द्रो देवता। एक इन्द्र आहितं स्वकीयहस्ते निहितं वज्रमेतन्नामकमायुधं बिभर्ति। धत्ते। स एवेन्द्रस्तेन निहितेन वज्रेण वृत्राण्या-वरकाणि रक्षांसि पापानि वा जिघ्नते। भृशं हन्ति।।

जिघ्नते, 3. sg. pres. stem. जिधन; rt. हन्.

Verse 5.

तिग्मम्। एकः। बिभर्ति। हस्ते। आयुधम्। शुचिः। उग्रः। जलाषऽभेषजः।।५।।

अत्र जलाषभेषज इत्यनेन रूद्रोऽभिधीयते। शुचिः। शुच दीप्तौ। सर्वतः स्वतेजसा दीप्यमानः। यद्वा। शुच लोके। शत्रूणां शोचयिता दुःखयिता। अत एवोग्र उदूर्णबलो जलाषभेजो रोगापनयनेन सुखकरभैषज्यवान्। यद्वा। स्तोतृ णां दुःखरूपसंसारोच्छेदेन सुखकारिभिषग्रूपः। प्रथमो दैब्यो भिषगित्या दिश्रुतिभिरस्य भिषक्त्वं श्रूयते। तादृश एको रूद्रस्तिग्मं तीक्ष्णधारमायुधम्। आयुध्यति संप्रहरति शत्रूननेनेत्यायुधं पिनाकस्तं स्वकीये हस्ते बिभर्ति।।।

जलाष adj., healing, cooling.

If the first pāda ends with आयुधं and the second begins with शुचिर्, the pāda is by two syllables too long. The defect may be removed by deleting either शुचिर् or उग्रो. The आयुध here implies bow and arrow.

Verse 6.

पथः। एकः। पीपाय। तस्करः। यथा। एषः। वेद। निऽधी-नाम्।।६।।

पथ इति लिङ्गेन पूषा निगद्यते। संपूषन्नध्वनस्तिर (ऋ० १-४२-१) इत्यादिषु दृष्टत्वात्। एकः पूषनामको देवः पथो मार्गान् पीपाय। प्यायति-र्वर्धनकर्माप्यत्र रक्षणार्थः। येऽग्निहोत्रादि कर्म कुर्वनित तेषां स्वर्गमार्गं ये दुष्कृतं कर्म कुर्वनित तेषां यातनामार्गं च रक्षति। उभयेषां मार्गविपर्ययो यथा न भवति तथा पालयतीत्यर्थः। एष सोऽयं पूषा निधीनां पृथिव्यां निहितानि धनानि वेद। वेत्ति। ज्ञात्वा स्तोतृ णां तानि ददातीत्यर्थः। तत्र दृष्टान्तः। तस्करो यथा यथा चोरः पथि गच्छतां तानि ददातीत्यर्थः। तत्र दृष्टान्तः। तस्करो यथा। यथा चोरः पथि गच्छतां पुरूषाणां धनहरणार्थं मार्गं रक्षति। [1]तथा च स चोरो गृहे निहितानि ज्ञात्वा तदाहृत्य [2]स्वसहायेभ्यो यथा [3]तानि ददाति तद्वत्।।

---

1. तथा च स चोरो इति प्रथमावृत्तै नास्ति।
2. नापि स्व इति।
3. न च तानि इति।

पी॒पा॒य॒, pf. par. rt. पि, प्या, to swell, transitive meaning.

य॒थाँ॒ unaccented because at the end of pāda, and with anunāsika to avoid hiatus.

वे॒द॒ with genit. नि॒धी॒नाम्. Though Sāy. takes तस्क॑रो य॒था॒ँ with both pādas, it is more likely that it belongs to the second only.

Verse 7.

त्रीणि॑। एक॑ः। उ॒रु॒ऽगा॒यः। वि। च॒क्र॒मे॒। यत्र॑। दे॒वास॑ः। मद॑न्ति।।७।।

उरूगायो विचक्रम इति पदलिङ्गाद्विष्णुरूच्यते। उरूगाथ उरूभिर्बहुभिर्गातव्यः। यद्वा। बहुषु देशेषु गन्ता बहुकीर्तिर्वा। सर्वान् शत्रून् स्वसामर्थ्येन शब्दयत्याक्रन्दयतीति वोरूगायः। एतादृश एकोऽसहायो विष्णुस्त्रीणि पदानि भुवनानि विचक्रमे। साधुपादेन विक्रान्तवान्। वेः पादविहरणे (पा० १-३-४१) इति क्रमतेरात्मनेपदम्। यत्र येषु लोकेषु देवास इन्द्रादयो देवा मदन्ति यजमानदत्तैर्हविर्भिर्माद्यन्ति तानि विचक्रम इत्यन्वयः।।

त्रीणि॑, viz. वि॒क्रम॑णानि.

उ॒रू॒गा॒य is characteristic of Viṣṇu.

यत्र॑ refers only to the place of the last step.

Note that this Gāyatrī shows the more (modern) trochaic cadence.

Verse 8.

विऽभि॑ः। द्वा। च॒र॒तः। एक॑या। स॒ह। प्र। प्र॒वा॒साऽइ॑व। व॒स॒तः।।८।।

एकया सहेति लिङ्गादश्विनावभिधीयेते। द्वा द्वौ द्वित्वसंख्योपेतावश्विनौ विभिः। वी गत्यादिषु। क्विप्। छान्दसो ह्रस्वः। गमनसाधनैरश्वैश्चरतः। संचरेते। किंचेमावश्विनावेकया सूर्याख्यया ताभ्यां स्वयं वृतया स्त्रिया सह प्रवसतः प्रवासं सर्वत्र गमनं कुरूतः। प्रवासे दृष्टान्तः। प्रवासेव। यथा प्रवासिनौ द्वौ पुरुषावेकया स्त्रिया सह प्रवसतस्तद्वत्।।

With the second pāda compare No. 17, 5, above. प्र॒वासे॑व has been by Böhtlingk-Roth (Dict.), Lanman and Hillebrandt taken to be an irregualr contraction of प्र॒वासमि॑व. They consequently translate:—on a journey, as it were. But the dual (Padap. and Sāy.) प्र॒वासा seems preferable.

Verse 9.

सद॑ः। द्वा। च॒क्रा॒ते॒ इति॑। उ॒प॒ऽमा। दि॒वि। स॒म्ऽराजा॑। स॒र्पिरा॑सुती। इति॑ स॒र्पिःऽआ॑सुती।।९।।

सम्राजाविति लिङ्गेन मित्रावरुणावभिधीयेते। उपमा उपमौ परस्परं स्वकान्त्योपमानभूतौ। यद्वोपमीयत आभ्यां सर्वमित्युपमौ सर्वस्य। एतावेव सम्राजा सम्राजौ सम्यग्दीप्यमानौ सर्पिरासुती। सर्पिर्घृतमाभ्यामासूयत इति सर्पिरासुती। घृतहविष्कौ द्वा द्वौ मित्रावरुणौ दिवि द्युलोके सदः। सीदन्त्यत्रेति सदः स्थानम्। तच्चक्राते। अकार्ष्टाम्।।

Sāy.'s grammatical interpretation of उ॒प॒मा (du. nom. in apposition to द्वा) is certainly better than that of Oldenberg who thinks of adverbial instrumental. But Sāy. is hardly correct when he makes उ॒प॒मा to mean simile or upamāna. The idea of "highest" is much more natural, whether उ॒प॒मा is qualified by दि॒वि or not. This interpretation of उ॒प॒मा is borne out by स॒म्राजा॑.

Verse 10.

अर्च॑न्तः। एके॑। महि॑। साम॑। म॒न्व॒त॒। तेन॑। सूर्य॑म्। अ॒रो॒च॒य॒न्।।१०।।

एकेऽत्रयो महि महत्साम त्रिवृत्पञ्चदशादि मन्वत। अमन्वत। तदेवार्चन्तः पूजयन्त एतादृशा अत्रयस्तेनोक्तेन साम्ना सूर्यमरोचयन्। अदीपयन्। त एवात्र देवता।।

Sāy. is of opinion that by the tenth ṛc the Atris are

meant. Macdonell's view (l. c.) that the Aṅgirasas must "undoubtedly be meant here" is even from the passages adduced by him, I. 62. 2; X. 62. 3, not so clearly eastablished as he seems to have convinced himself.

NO. 25.

MAṆḌALA X. **SŪKTA 72.**

तत्र देवानामिति नवर्चमनुवाकापेक्षया चतुर्थं सूक्तम्। आनुष्टुभं देवदेवत्यम्। लोकनाम्नः पुत्रो बृहस्पतिराङ्गिरम एव वा बृहस्पतिर्ऋषिः। अथवा दक्षस्य दुहिता दितिर्ऋषिः। तथा चानुक्रान्तम्। देवानां नव लौक्यो वा बृहस्पति-र्दाक्षायण्यदितिर्वा दैवमानुष्टुभमिति। गतः सूक्तविनियोगः।।

Verse 1.

दे॒वाना॑म्। नु। व॒यम्। जाना॑। प्र। वो॒चा॒म॒। वि॒प॒न्यया॑। उ॒क्थेषु॑। श॒स्यमा॑नेषु। यः। पश्या॑त्। उत्ऽत॑रे। यु॒गे।।१।।

अदितिर्दाक्षायण्यनेन सूक्तेन स्वयं यथादित्यानजनयत्तद्ब्रवीति। बृहस्पत्यृषिपक्षे स ऋषिरदितेः सकाशादादित्योत्पत्तिप्रकारमाह। वयं देवानामा-दित्यानां जाना जन्मानि प्रबोचाम। प्रकथयाम। विपन्यया विस्पष्टया वाचा। बयमिति वोचामेति चोभयत्र पूजार्थं बहुवचनम्। अथैकवदाह। यो देवानां गणः पूर्वे युग उत्पन्नोऽप्युक्थेषु शस्यमानेषु यागे शस्त्रेष्वनुष्ठीयमानेषूत्तरे युगे वर्तमानं स्तुवन्तं स्तोतारं पश्यात् पश्यति। अनेकेष्वपि युगेषु गतेषु कर्मसु स्तूयमानो वर्तत इत्यर्थः।।

पश्या॑त् in an injunctive sense: he shall, may see.

जाना॑ n., birth, origin. It implies the act of birth and its product as well, see ṛc 2.

वि॒प॒न्या, only instrum. in admiration.

Sāy.'s interpretation of the second line उ॒क्थेषु॑ श॒स्यमा॑नेषु यः पश्या॒दुत्त॑रे यु॒गे is not very acceptable. The opinions of the most recent commentators on this passage differ widely. None of them is either very convincing or free from difficulties. The best interpretation seems still to be contained in Ludwig's translation, where he makes यः to refer to a demonstrative pronoun, to be understood in the first line.

Verse 2.

ब्रह्मणः। पतिः। एता। सम्। कर्मारःऽइव। अधमत्। देवानाम्। पूर्व्ये। युगे। असतः। सत्। अजायत॥२॥

ब्रह्मणोऽन्नस्य पतिरदितिरेतैतानि देवानां जन्मानि कर्मार इव स यथा मस्त्रयाग्निमुपधमति प्रज्वलनार्थमेवं समधमत्। उदपादयदित्यर्थः। देवानां पूर्व्ये युगे। आदिसृष्टावित्यर्थः। तेषामुपादानकारणादसतो नामरूपवर्जितत्वेना-सत्समानाद्ब्रह्मणः सकाशात्सन्नामरूपविशिष्टं देवादिकमजायत। प्रादुरभूत्। असद्वा इदमग्र आसीत्ततो वै सदजायत (तै०उ० २-७) इति हि श्रुतिः। न सदात्मकस्य प्रपञ्चस्यासत्कारणत्वं युक्तमिति वाच्यम् छन्दोगैः कथमसतः सज्जायेतेत्यसत्कारणत्वमाक्षिप्य सत्त्वेव सोम्येदमग्र आसीदित्यबधारितत्वात्। (छा०उ० ६-२२) तर्ह्यसत्कारणप्रतिपादकवाक्यानां का गतिरिति चेत् तेषामव्याकृतत्वाभिप्रायत्वात् तद्धेदं तर्ह्यव्याकृतमासीत् (शत० १४-४-२-१५) इति श्रुतेः। यद्येवं तर्ह्यदितेः सकाशात्कथं देवाद्युत्पत्तिः। वायोरग्निरित्यादिवत् *अधिष्ठानात्सकाशात्तदुत्पत्तेः। यद्वा। देवानां कारणभूतं सदसतो ब्रह्मणः सकाशादुत्पन्नमिति योजनादुक्तन्योयोऽस्मिन्पक्षेऽपि समान एव॥

कर्मार m., (कृ, कर्मन्) smith.

सम् ध्मा, to forge together.

The first pāda is metrically defective, being too short by one syllable. It would be tempting to understand (with Ludwig) by एता the भुवनानि, things, creatures, rather than जन्मानि, Sāy. The रशना arrangement, however, of the first five and the last two ṛcas of this hymn speaks against it. In these ṛcas the first pāda of the following ṛc takes up the idea expressed by the

---

* अधिष्ठानसकाशात् इत्यादर्शः।

preceding ṛc. Besides, the creation of the universe (तद्) and of the earth is given in ṛcas 3 and 4.

Verse 3.

देवानाम्। युगे। प्रथमे। असतः। सत्। अजायत। तत्। आशाः। अनु। अजायन्त। तत्। उत्तानऽपदः। परि।।३।।

†पूर्वार्धमुक्तम्। तदन्वाशा दिशोऽजायनत। तत्परि तदन्वित्यर्थः। उत्तानपदः। उत्तानमूर्ध्वतानं पद्यन्त इत्युत्तानपदो वृक्षाः। तेऽजायन्त। प्रादुरभवन्।।

आशा (rt. अंश्?) f., =दिश्.

उत्तानपद् has commonly been translated by "mother of the world". Oldenberg with good reason doubted this interpretation; he thinks of certain ascetical postures. The second तद् should be taken into account; it seems to be the same as in तदनु before. The author is not accurate in his arrangement, as may be seem from verse 4, making in verse 3 the quarters to originate from सत्, but in verse 4 from भूः. It is then not altogether out of the question that in तद् परि he reverts to the previously mentioned सत्, as Oldenberg too thought. In that case उत्तानपद् would refer to असत् itself, which we may take to mean the travailing primitive mother or, as masculine, the primal principle in some ascetical posture. Hillebrandt., Lieder des ṚV., page 129, note 3. उत्तानपद् still baffles interpretation; the etymological meaning "turning (the soles of) the feet upwards" is not very helpful.

Verse 4.

भूः। जज्ञे। उत्तानऽपदः। भुवः। आशाः। अजायन्त। अदितेः। दक्षः। अजायत। दक्षात्। ऊं। इति। अदितिः। परि।।४।।

† पूर्वमत्रार्धरूपेण।

भुरूत्तानपदो वृक्षाज्जज्ञे। तथा भुवः सकाशादाशा अजायन्त। तथादितेर्दक्षोऽजायत। उत्पन्नः। दक्षादु दक्षादप्यदितिः पर्यजायत। न स्वोत्पन्नं कार्यं स्वस्यैव कारणमपि भवतीति विप्रतिषिद्धमिति वाच्क्ष्यम्। यास्काचार्य इदमेव वाक्यमुदाहृत्य विरोधमाशंक्य पर्यहरत्। तथा हि। अदितेर्दक्षो अजायत दक्षाद्वदितिः परीति च तत्कथमुपपद्येत समानजन्मानौ स्यातामित्यपि वा देवधर्मेणेतरेतरजन्मानौ स्यातामितरेतरप्रकृती (नि० ११-२३) इति।।

उ, enclitic particle, but preceding other particles (by the Padapāṭha given as ऊं [इति]; comp. Pāṇini I. 1. 17), and, again, on the other hand, in turn.

The position of आशा in ṛcas 3 and 4 prepares for the playful inversion अदितेर्दक्षो अजायत दक्षाद्वदितिः परि in this ṛc.

Verse 5.

अदितिदेवताके पशावदि तिर्ह्यजनिष्टेत्येषा हविषोऽनुवाक्या। सूत्रितं च। अदितिर्ह्यजनिष्ट सुत्रामाणं पृथिवीं द्यामनेहसम् (आ० ३-८) इति।

अदितिः। हि। अजनिष्ट। दक्ष। या। दुहिता। तव। ताम्। देवाः। अनु। अजायन्त। भद्राः। अमृतऽबन्धवः।।५।।

हे दक्ष तव या दुहिताभूत्सादितिरजनिष्ट हि पुत्रानादित्यान्। तदेवाह। तां देवा अन्वजायन्त भद्राः। स्तुत्या भजनीया अमृतबन्धवोऽमरणबन्धनाः।।

Verse 6.

यत्। देवाः। अदः। सलिले। सुऽसंरब्धाः। अतिष्ठत। अत्र। वः। नृत्यताम्ऽइव। तीव्रः। रेणुः। अप। आयत।।६।।

अनयोत्तरेण चादित्याः स्तूयन्ते। यद्यदा हे देवा अदोऽमुष्मिन्सलिले यूयं सुसंरब्धाः सुष्ठु लब्धात्मानोऽतिष्ठत स्थितवन्तः। आपो वा इदं सर्वम्। (तै० आ० १०-२२) अप एव ससर्जादाविति श्रुतिस्मृती। अत्रास्मिन्सलिले नृत्यतामिव वो युष्माकं संबन्धी तीव्रो दुःसहो रेणुरंशभूत एकोऽपायत। अपागच्छत्। दिवं प्रति गत इति सूर्याभिप्रायम्। परा मार्ताण्डमास्यदिति वक्ष्यति।।

अ॒दः, adv., originally neuter pron., after यद्ः—in a certain place, corresponding to तत्र.

सुसं॑ब्ध, pt. pass., well supported, stuck together.

आ॒य॒त॒, 3. sg. impf. ātm; rt. इ.

Verse 7.

यत्। दे॒वा॒ः। यत॑यः। य॒था॒। भुव॑नानि। अपि॑न्वत। अत्र॑। स॒मु॒द्रे। आ। गू॒ळ्हम्। आ। सूर्य॑म्। अ॒ज॒भ॒र्त॒न।।७।।

यद्यदा हे देवाः यतयो यथा। वृष्ट्या नियमयन्तीति वा वर्षणेन यातयन्तीति वा यतयो मेघाः। ते यथोदकैर्भुवनानि लोकं पूरयन्ति तद्वत्स्वतेजोभिरपिन्वत। पूरितवन्तः। अत्र समुद्रेऽप्स्वागूळ्हं निगूळ्हं सूर्यं प्रातरूदयायाजभर्तन। आहृतवन्तः।।

पिन्व्, to make grow, to fatten.

अ॒ज॒भ॒र्त॒न, 2. plur. plupf. par.; rt. भृ.

यति॑, ruler, workman; Yatis, an ancient clan, in ṚV. VIII. 3. 9; 6. 18, seeming to be real persons, connected with the Bhṛgus. In our passage they appear to be rather mythological figures. Cp. Macdonell and Keith, Index, s. v.

Verse 8.

अ॒ष्टौ। पु॒त्रास॑ः। अदि॑तेः। ये। जा॒ताः। त॒न्व॑ः। परि॑। दे॒वान्। उप॑। प्र। ऐ॒त्। स॒प्तऽभि॑ः। परा॑। मा॒र्ता॒ण्डम्। आ॒स्य॒त्।।८।।

अष्टौ पुत्रासः पुत्रा मित्रादयोऽदितेर्भवन्ति येऽदितेस्तन्वः परि शरीराज्जाता उत्पन्नाः। अदितेरष्टौ पुत्रा अध्वर्युब्राह्मणे परिगणिताः। तथा हि।ताननुक्रमिष्यामो मित्रश्च धाता चार्यमा चांशश्च भगश्च विवस्वानादित्यश्चेति। तथा तत्रैव प्रदेशान्तरेऽदितिं प्रंस्तुत्याम्नातम्। तस्या उच्छेषणमददुस्तत्प्राश्नात् सा रेतोऽधत्त तस्यै चत्वार आदित्या अजायन्त सा द्वितीयमपचदित्यष्टानामादित्यानामुत्पत्तिर्वर्णिता। (तै० सं० ६-५-६-१) सादितिः सप्तभिः पुत्रैर्देवानुपप्रैत्। उपागच्छत्। अष्टमं पुत्रं मार्ताण्डं सूर्यं परास्यत्। उपरि प्राक्षिपदित्यर्थः।।

For an astronomical interpretation of this ṛc. see B.G. Tilak, The Artic Home in the Vedas, pp. 157-59, 282.

Verse 9.

सप्तऽभिः। पुत्रैः। अदितिः। उप। प्र। ऐत्। पूर्व्यम्। युगम्।
प्रऽजायै। मृत्यवे। त्वत्। पुनः। मार्ताण्डम्। आ। अभरत्।।९।।

पूर्वमन्त्रोक्त एवार्थः पुनरत्रोच्यते। सप्तभिर्मार्ताण्डव्यतिरिक्तैर्मित्रादिभिरदितिः पूर्व्यं पुराणं युगमुपप्रैत्। उपगता। अथ प्रजायै प्राणिनामुत्पत्तये मृत्यवे तेषां मरणाय मार्ताण्डं मृताद्यृद्धादण्डाज्जातं मार्ताण्डनामान सूर्यं पुनराभरत्। आहरत्। द्युलोकेऽधारयत्। प्राणिमरणजननादीनां सूर्योदयास्तमययात्तता स्फुटा। तस्यै व्यृद्धमाण्डमजायतेत्यादि ब्राह्मणम्।। (तै० सं० ६-५-६-१)।

त्व, त्वद् partly, on the other hand.

प्रजायै belongs to the sentence in pādas 3 and 4.

त्वद् indicates the opposition between Aditi's seven sons and the ancient generation (the gods; comp. Tilak, The Artic Home, pp. 157-58) on the one hand, and Mārtāṇḍa and the rising and dying (human) generation on the other. पुनर् belongs to आभरत्.

NO. 26.

MAṆḌALA X. **SŪKTA 108.**

किमिच्छन्त्येकादशर्चं नवमं सूक्तं त्रैष्टुभम्। ऐन्द्रपुरोहितस्य बृहस्पतेर्गोषु बलनाम्नोऽसुरस्य भटैः पणिनामकैरसुरैरपहृत्य गुहायां निहितासु सतीषु बृहस्पतिप्रेरितेनेन्द्रेण गवामन्वेषणाय सरमा नाम देवशुनी प्रेषिता। सा च महतीं नदीमुत्तीर्य वलपुरं प्राप्य गुप्तस्थाने *निहितास्ता गा ददर्श। अथ तस्मिन्नन्तरे पणयं इदं वृत्तान्तमवगच्छन्त एनां मित्रीकर्तु संवादमकुर्वन्। तत्र प्रथमातृतीयाद्या अयुजोऽन्त्यावर्जिताः पणीनां वाक्यानि। अत्र त ऋषयः सरमा देवता। द्वितीयाचतुर्थ्याद्या युज एता एकादशी च षट् सरमावाक्यानि।

* नीतास्ता इत्यादर्शः।

अतस्तासु सा ऋषिः पणयो देवता। तथाचानुक्रन्तम्। किमिच्छन्ती पणिभिर- सुरैर्निगूढा गा अन्वेष्टुं सरमां देवशुनीमिन्द्रेण प्रहितामयुग्भिः पणयो मित्रीयन्तः प्रोचुः सा तान् युग्मान्त्याभिरनिच्छन्ती प्रत्याचष्ट इति। गतो विनियोगः।।

Verse 1.

किम्। इच्छन्ती। सरमा। प्र। इदम्। आनट्। दूरे। हि। अध्वा। जगुरिः। पराचैः। का। अस्मेऽहितिः। का। परिऽतक्म्या। आसीत्। कथम्। रसायाः। अतरः। पयांसि।।१।।

अनयागच्छन्तीं सरमां दृष्ट्वा पणयो वदन्ति। सरमा सरणशीलैतन्नामिका देवशुनी किमिच्छन्ती किं प्रार्थयमाना सतीदमस्मदीयं स्थानं प्रानट्। प्राप्नोत्। आङ्पूर्वो नशिर्व्याप्तिकर्मा। तस्य लुङि मन्त्रे घसेत्यादिना च्लेर्लुक्। छन्दस्यपि दृश्यत इत्याडागमः।। पराचैः पराञ्चि पराङमुखान्यावृत्तिवर्जितानि यानि गमनानि तैर्जगुरिरूद्गूर्णः। महता प्रत्नेनापि गन्तुं न शक्यत इत्यर्थः। गृ निगरणे। आदृगमहनेत्यादिना किन्प्रत्ययः। बहुलं छन्दसि (पा. ७-१-१०३) इत्युत्वम्। तादृशेऽयमध्वा दूरे हि। विप्रकृष्टः खलु। यद्वा। पराचैः पराञ्चनैर्जगुरिरत्यर्थं गन्त्री पार्ष्णिागमनालोकमाना सतीदं स्थानं प्राप्नोति। दूरेऽयमध्वा यदृच्छया गन्तुं न शक्यते। अतो वयमेतां पृच्छामः। हे सरमे का कीदृश्यस्मेहितिः। कोऽस्मास्वर्थहितिः। कोऽस्मातु त्वदपेक्षितार्थो निहितः। यद्वा। अस्मासु कोऽर्थो गतः। दधातेर्हिनोतेर्वा क्तिनि रूपम्। आगच्छन्त्यास्तव का कीदृशी परितक्म्या रात्रिरासीत्। यद्वा। तकतिर्गत्यर्थः। परिकनं परितो गमनं भ्रमणं वा कीदृशमासीत्। कथं च रसायाः शब्दायमानाया अन्तरिक्षनद्या योजनशतविस्तीर्णायाः पयांस्युद- कान्यतरः। तीर्णवत्यसि। एतद्वद। अत्र किमीच्छन्ती सरमेदं प्रानडित्या दिकं निरूक्तं द्रष्टव्यम्।। (नि० ११-२५)

आनट्, 2.3. sg. aor. par.; rt. नश्;प्र नश्, to come.

जगुरि, (rt. गृ , to swallow, or intensit. rt. गम्?) disappearing, losing itself; (or rt. जृ , जुर्) wasting (transitive), trying.

अस्मे हिति f., mission, charge to us.

इदम्, here.

Verse 2.

इन्द्रस्य। दूतीः। इषिता। चरामि। महः। इच्छन्ती। पणयः। निऽधीन्। वः। अतिऽस्कदः। भियसा। तत्। नः। आवत्। तथा। रसायाः। अतरम्। पयांसि।।२।।

अनया तान्सरमा प्रत्युवाच। हे पणय एतन्नामका असुराः। इन्द्रस्य दूतीः। सुपां सुलुगिति प्रथमैकवचनस्य सुश्छान्दस्यः। अहमिषिता तेनैव प्रेषिता सती चरामि। युष्मदीयं स्थानमागच्छामि। किमर्थम्। वो युष्मदीयान्युष्मदीये पर्वतेऽधिष्ठापितान्महो महतो निर्धीन्बृहस्पतेर्गोनिधीनिच्छन्ती कामयमाना सती चरामि। किंचातिष्कदः। स्कन्दिर्गतिशोषणयोः। भावे क्विप्। अतिष्कन्दनादति-क्रमणाज्जातेन भियसा भयेन तन्नदीजलं नः। पूजायां बहुवचनम्। मामावत्। अरक्षत्। तथा तेन प्रकारेण रसाया नद्याः पयांसुदकान्यतरम्। तीर्णवत्यसि।।

स्कन्द् 1., to fall; अति स्कन्द् to jump over; स्कदः, abl. inf. Saramā could either jump or swim over the Rasā. If she had jumped over the river, Rasā's prestige of being a large water might have been destroyed, would at least have suffered. Thus Rasā facilitated Saramā's swimmjing across (Geldner, Kommentar i. l.) Oldenberg, Textkrit. i. l., translates:—On account of the fear of jumping over, this (consciousness of being sent by Indra) helped us. The instrumental भियसा does not seem to fit too well into this interpretation. Geldner's view is more concrete. It justifies the emphatic pointing out how the waters were crossed; Oldenberg's translation shows only how Saramā got courage to cross, not how she actually crossed. But against Geldner's view stands this that तत् and तथा in ṛc 2 apparently answer to का and कुथं in ṛc 1; besides, Rasā has to be understood in Geldner's rendering.

Verse 3.

कीदृङ्। इन्द्रः। सरमे। का। दृशीका। यस्य। इदम्। दूतीः। असरः। पराकात्। आ। च। गच्छात्। मित्रम्। एन। दधाम। अथ। गवाम्। गोऽपतिः। नः। भवाति।।३।।

तेषां वाक्यम्। हे सरमे तव स्वामीन्द्रः कीदृक्। कियत्पराक्रमवान्। का दृशीका। तस्य कीदृशी दृष्टिः। दृष्टिरूपा सेना कियती। यस्य दूतीर्दूती त्वमिदमस्मदीयं स्थानं पराकादतिदूरादसरः आगमः। इति तामुक्त्वेदानीं ते परस्परमाहुः। एषा सरमा आगच्छाञ्च आगच्छतु च। गमेर्लेट्याडागमः। स्वामी भवाति। भवतु। न ह्येकस्या गोः किंतु बहूनां गवां स्वामी भवतु। वृत्त्यवृत्तिभ्यां स्वामित्वं बाहुलयं च विवक्ष्यते।।

दृशीका f. =दृष्टि, appearance.

एना instr. अयम्, with him (Indra).

गच्छात्, दधाम, भवति, pres. subj.

Verse 4.

न। अहम्। तम्। वेद। दभ्यम्। दभत्। सः। यस्य। इदम्। दूतीः। असरम्। पराकात्। न। तम्। गूहन्ति। स्रवतः। गभीराः। हताः। इन्द्रेण। पणयः। शयध्वे।।४।।

सरमा वदति। हे पणयः तमिन्द्रं दभ्यं हन्तव्यमिति न वेद। न जानामि। दभेरचो यत्। कथम्। स इन्द्रो दभत्। सर्वाञ्जनान्दभति। हिनस्त्वेव। दभेर्लेटि रूपम्। वाक्यभेदादनिघातः। यस्य दूतीर्दूत्यहमिदं युष्मदीयं स्थानं पराकादति-दूराद्देशादसरं प्राप्ताभूवम्। इन्द्रो हिंससितव्यो न भवतीत्यत्र युक्तिमाह। स्रवतः। स्रवणं स्रवः। तमाचरन्ति। आचारार्थे क्विप्। तुगागमः। जसि रूपम्। स्रवणशीला गभीरा गम्भीरा नद्यस्तमिन्द्रं न गूहन्ति। न संवृण्वन्ति। नाच्छाइत्येनं प्रकटी-कुर्वन्ति। गुह् संवरणे भौवादिकः। तसमाद्धे पणयो यूयमिन्द्रेण तादृशपराक्रमेण हताः सन्तः शयध्वे। शीङ् स्वप्ने। बहुलं छन्दसीति शपो लुगभावः।।

दभत् inj.

स्रवत् f. (स्रु) river.

Verse 5.

इमाः। गावः। सरमे। याः। ऐच्छः। परि। दिवः। अन्तान्। सुऽभगे। पतन्ती। कः। ते। एनाः। अव। सृजात्। अयुध्वी। उत। अस्माकम्। आयुधा। सन्ति। तिग्मा।।५।।

क्रुद्धाः पणयः प्रत्यूचुः। हे सुभगे शोभनसौभाग्यवति हे सरमे दिवो द्युलोकस्यान्तान्पर्यन्तान्परि पतन्ती कुत्र गावस्तिष्ठन्तीति परितो गच्छन्ती त्वमिमाः परिदृश्यमाना या गावः। सुबूव्यत्ययः। गा गेच्छः कामयसे ता एना गास्ते त्वदीयः कोऽयुध्वी अयुद्धवा अवसृजात्। अस्मात्पर्वतादवसृजेत्। विनिर्गमयेत्। सृजेर्लेटि रूपम्। अयुध्वी युधेः क्त्वाप्रत्यये स्नात्व्यादयश्चेति निपातितः। नञ्समासत्वाल्ल्यबादेशाभावः। नञः प्रकृतिस्वरत्वम्। उतापि च। अस्माकं तिग्मा तीक्ष्णान्यायुधा आयुधानि सन्ति। तस्मादस्माभिर्युद्धमकृत्वा को नाम गा आहरति।।

परि॑ पत्, to catch running, to run up to.

आयु॑ध्वी=अयुद्ध्वी, without fighting.

Read आ गच्छः॑, दि॒वोनता॑न्.

Verse 6.

अ॒से॒न्या। वः। प॒ण॒य॒ः। वचां॑सि। अ॒नि॒ष॒व्याः। त॒न्वः॑। स॒न्तु॒। पा॒पीः। अधृ॑ष्टः। व॒ः। ए॒तवै। अ॒स्तु॒। पन्था॑ः। बृह॒स्पति॑ः। व॒ः। उ॒भ॒या। न। मृ॒ळा॒त्।।६।।

सा तान्निराह। हे पणयो वो युष्माकं वचांसि पूर्वोक्तानि वचनान्यसेन्या असेन्यानि। सेनार्हाणि न भवनित। सेनाशब्दात्तदर्हतीत्यथे छन्दसि चेति यत्प्रत्ययः। नञा समासः। ययतोश्चातदर्थे (पा० ६-२-१५६) इत्युत्तरपदान्तो-दात्तत्वम्। तदा तन्वो युष्मदीयानि शरीराण्यनिषव्या इष्वर्हाणि न सन्तु पराक्रमराहित्येन। पूर्ववत्प्रत्ययः। ओर्गुणः (पा० ६-४-१४६) इति गुणः। स्वरश्च तादृक् यतः पापीः पापयुक्तानि खलु। छन्दसीवनिपाविवतीप्रत्ययः। जसः शः। किंच वो युष्मदीयः पन्था मार्ग एतवै गन्तुमधृष्टोऽसमर्थोऽस्तु। इण् गतावित्यस्य तुमर्थे तवैप्रत्ययः तवै चान्तश्च युगपत् (पा० ६-२-५१) इति धातोः प्रत्ययस्य च युगपदुदात्तत्वम्। तत्र हेतुमाह। वो युष्मदीयानुभयो भयविधान्पूर्वोक्तांस्तन्वो देहान्बृहस्पतिरिन्द्रप्रेरितो न मृळात्। न सुखयतु। किंतु बाधेत। मृड सुखने। लेट्यडागमः।।

अ॒नि॒ष॒व्य, arrow-proof.

असेन्य, not martial, not hostile, making no impression.

अधृष्ट (धृष्) not to be conquered, unapproachable, unsurmountable.

उभयाा, instr. sg., either way, anyway.

The ṛc is Saramā's answer to the taunt of the Paṇis in 5. The difficulty is whether we have to understand in the first pāda सन्ति or सन्तु. If सन्ति is supplied, the sentence in the first pāda becomes a general statement to the effect that, though the Paṇis may be invulnerable and the access difficult, yet their challentge will be met by Bṛhaspati, (since) words do not deserve a repartee with weapons. In this interpretation उभया can be taken literally. If we supply सन्तु, as is done in the translation, the first pāda becomes consive and co-ordinated with the sentences in pādas 2 and 3. Besides this concinnity, the word असेन्य in a line with अनिषव्य and अधृष्ट seems to speak for this view, and उभया may be understood in a wider sinse:—so or so, in any case, anyway.

Verse 7.

अयम्। निऽधिः। सरमे। अद्रिऽबुन्धः। गोभिः। अश्वेभिः। वसुऽभिः। निऽऋष्टः। रक्षन्ति। तम्। पणयः। ये। सुऽगोपाः। रेकु। पदम्। अलकम्। आ। जगन्थ।।७।।

ते पुनराहुः। हे सरमे अयं निधिरस्मदीयः कोशोऽद्रिबुध्नः। अन्ध बन्धने। बन्धेर्ब्रधिबुधी च (उ० ३-५) इति नप्रत्ययो बुध इत्यादेशः। अद्रिर्बन्धको यस्य तादृशः। तथा हतैर्गोभिरश्वेभिरश्वैश्च वसुभिरात्मीयैर्धनैश्च न्यृष्टो नितरां प्राप्तो भवति। ऋषी गतौ। क्तप्रत्यये श्वीदितो निष्ठायामितीट्प्रतिषेधः गतिरनन्तर इति गतेः प्रकृतिस्वरत्वम्। सुगोपाः गुपू रक्षणे। आयप्रत्ययान्तता त्क्विप्यातोलो-पयलोपौ। सुष्ठू गोपायितारो ये पणयस्तेऽसुरास्तं निधिं रक्षन्ति। पालयन्ति। रेकु। रेकृ शङ्कायाम्। औणादिक उप्रत्ययः। शङ्कितं गोभिः शब्दायमानं पदमस्माभिः पालितं स्थानमलंकं व्यर्थमेवाजगन्थ। आगतवत्यसि। गमेर्लिटि रूपम्।।

अद्रिं बुध्न, resting on a rock, whose bottom or pavement is a rock.

नि ऋष् 6., to draw down, to fill.

रेकु, where nothing is to be had.

अलकम्, in vain.

Verse 8.

आ। इह। गमन्। ऋषयः। सोमऽशिताः। अयास्यः। अङ्गिरसः। नवऽग्वाः। ते। एतम्। ऊर्वम्। वि। भजन्त। गोनाम्। अथ। एतत्। वचः। पणयः। वमन्। इत्॥८॥

सरमा पुनः प्रत्युवाच। हे पणयः सोमशिताः सोमेन तीक्ष्णीकृताः सोमपानेन मत्ताः। शिञ् निशाने। कर्मणि क्तप्रत्ययः। तृतीया कर्मणीति पूर्वपदप्रकृतिस्वरत्वम्। तादृशा नवग्वा नवगतयः। यद्वा। अङ्गिरसां सत्रमासीनानां मध्ये केचन नवसु माःस्वध्यतिष्ठन् ते नवग्वाः। अनेन दशग्वा अप्यचुपलक्ष्यन्ते। उभयविधास्तेऽङ्गिरस ऋषयः तेषां प्रथमोऽयास्य एतन्नामा च त एत इह युष्मदीये स्थान आगमन्। आगच्छेयुः। गमेश्छन्दसि लुङ्लुङ्लिट इति सार्वकालिको लुङ्। लृदित्त्वाच्च्लेरङ्। आगत्य च ते गोनाम्। गोः पादान्त इति च्छन्दसि नुडागमः। गवामूर्वं तं समूहं वि ाजन्त। विभागं कुर्युः। अत्रापि पूर्ववत्सार्वकालिको लुङ्। अथानन्तरं पणयो यूयमेतद्वचः पूर्वं यद्व्यर्थमागतासीति यद्वाक्यमवोचत तद्वाक्यं तदा वमन्निद्वमन्तः परित्यजन्त एव भवथ। वमु उद्गिरणे। शतरि सुपां सुलुगिति जसो लुक्। नुमागमः। संयोगान्तस्य लोपः। यद्वा। लङि रूपं स्वरश्छान्दसः॥

सोम शित (rt. शा 3., to whet), instigated, inspired, by soma.

ऊर्व m., cave, herd in the cave.

Note गोनाम् for गवाम्.

Verse 9.

एव। च। त्वम्। सरमे। आऽजगन्थ। प्रऽबाधिता। सहसा। दैव्येन।

स्वसासरम्। त्वा। कृणवै। मा। पुनः। गाः। अप। ते। गवाम्। सुऽभगे। भजाम।।९।।

तयैवमुक्ते सति पणयः प्रणयवाक्यमाहुः। हे सरमे त्वं दैव्येन देवसंबन्धिना सहसा बलेन प्रबाधिता यथा तथा वलपुरं प्राप्य तत्र स्थिता गा दृष्ट्वा पुनरागच्छेति तेन प्रपीडिता त्वमेवं चेदाजगन्थ आगतवत्यसि। चशब्दश्चेदर्थे। निपातैर्यद्यदिहन्तेति तिङो निघाताभावः। गमेर्लिटि थलि रूपम्। सह सुपेत्यत्र सहेति योगविभागात्समासः। तिङि चोदात्तवतीति गतेर्निघातः। लित्स्वरः। तर्हि त्वा त्वां स्वसारं भगिनीं कृणवै। करवै। सामूहापेक्षैकवचनम्। त्वं तु पुनर्मा गाः। इन्द्रादीन्मागच्छ। अपि तर्हि हे सुभगे सरमे ते त्वदीयानां गवां समूहं पर्वतादपगमय्य भजाम। त्वं च वयं च विभजाम। विभागं करवामेत्यर्थः।।

कृणवै, 1. sg. subj. ātm.; rt. कृ.

गाः, 2. sg. subj. aor.; rt. गा.

अप भज्, to cede, to let one share in.

Verse 10.

न। अहम्। वेद। भ्रातृऽत्वम्। नो इति। स्वसृऽत्वम्। इन्द्रः। विदुः। अङ्गिरसः। च। घोराः। गोऽकामाः। मे। अच्छदयन्। यत्। आयम्। अप। अतः। इत। पणयः। वरीयः।।१०।।

सा तान्प्रत्याचष्टे। हे पणयः अहं भ्रातृत्वं न वेद। न जानामि। तथा स्वसृत्वं च नो वेद। नैव जानामि। के जानन्ति। तानाह। इन्द्रो घोराः शत्रूणां भयंकरा अङ्गिरसश्च विदुः। जानन्ति। किंच। अस्मात्स्थानादहं यद्यदायम् इन्द्रादीन्प्राप्नवम्। अय पय गतौ। लङि रूपम्। तदा मे मदीया गोकामा युष्माभिरपहृता गाः कामयमाना इन्द्रादयः अच्छदयन्। युष्मदीयं स्थानमाच्छादयनित। छद अपवारणे। अतःकारणाद्धे पणयो वरीय उरूतरं गवां वृन्दं परित्यज्यापेत। अन्यत्स्थानं प्रति गच्छत। यद्वा। वरीयः प्रभूतमतिदूरं देशं गच्छत। इत। इण् गतौ। लोटि रूपम्। वरीयः। उरूशब्दादीयसुनि प्रियस्थिर-त्यादिना वरादेशः।।

छद्, छन्द् 2. 10., to appear as.

Verse 11.

दूरम्। इत। पणयः। वरीयः। उत्। गावः। यन्तु। मिनतीः। ऋतेन। बृहस्पतिः। याः। अविन्दत्। निऽगूळ्हाः। सोमः। ग्रावाणः। ऋषयः। च। विप्राः।।११।।

हे पणयः यूयं वरीय उरूतरं दूरं दूरदेशमित। गच्छत। युष्माभिरपहृता गाव ऋतेन सत्येन मिनतीर्मिनत्यो द्वारस्य पिधायकं पर्वतं हिंसन्त्यो विदारयन्त्य उद्यन्तु। तस्मादुग्दच्छन्तु। यद्वा। मिनतीः। व्यत्ययेन कर्मणि शतृ। मीयमाना युष्माभिर्बाध्यमानास्ता गावः। सुब्व्यत्ययः। गा ऋतेन स्तुतिभिर्गन्तव्येनेन्द्रेण सहायेन बृहस्पत्यादय उद्यन्तु। पर्वतादुग्दमयन्तु। निगूढा नितरां स्थापितरा या गा बृहस्पतिरविन्दत् लप्स्यते तथा सोमस्तदभिषवकारिणो ग्रावाणश्च विप्रा मेधाविन ऋषयोऽङ्गिरसश्च लप्स्यन्ते। विद्लृ लाभे तौदादिकः। तस्माच्छन्दसि लुङ्लङ्लिट इति भविष्यदर्थे लङ्। शेमुचादीनामिति। नुमागमः।।

मी 9., to violate, break out; see Sāy. comm.

Though the Anukramaṇī says that ṛc 11 is spoken by Saramā, it is not improbable that a voice from above spoke these words. The passage मिनतीर्ऋतेन, as it stands, contains a paradox. The rt. मी implies cheating, taking in, which is not compatible with ऋतं. But the cows have a right to break out. Oldenberg (Textkrit. i. l.) proposes मिमतर् from rt. मा 3., to bellow, moo, which would suit very well, since lowing of the cows is essential in the myth of thir liberation. Sāyaṇa too takes ऋतेन together with उद्यन्तु.

NO. 27.

MAṆḌALA X. **SŪKTA 139.**

सूर्यऽरश्मिः। हरिऽकेशः। पुरस्तात्। सविता। ज्योतिः। उत्। अयान्। अजस्रम्। तस्य। पूषा। प्रऽसवे। याति। विद्वान्। संऽपश्यन्। विश्वा। भुवनानि। गोपाः।।१।।

सूर्यरश्मिः। उषसः प्रादुर्भावानन्तरं सूर्यस्योदयात्पूर्वं यः कालस्तस्य कालस्याभिमानी देवः सवितेत्युच्यते। सूर्यरश्मिः सूर्यस्य सर्वस्य प्रेरकस्यादित्यस्य रश्मिरेव रश्मिर्यस्य स तथोक्तः हरिकेशः हरयो हरणशीला हरितवर्णा वा केशाः केशस्थानीयाः प्रकाशमाना वा दीप्तयो यस्येदृशः सविता सर्वस्य प्रेरको देवः पुरस्तात्पूर्वस्यां दिश्यजस्रमनवरतं ज्योतिस्तेज उदयान्। उद्याति। उग्दमयति। यातेरन्तर्भावितण्यर्थाच्छान्दसो लङ्। व्यत्ययेन बहुवचनम्। संहितायां दीर्घादटि समानपाद इति नकारस्य रूत्वम्। आतोऽटि नित्यमिति सानुनासिक आकारः। तस्य सवितुः प्रसवे प्रेरणेऽनुज्ञायां सत्यां विद्वाञ्ज्ञानन्गोपा गोपायिता रक्षिता पूषा पोषको देव आदित्यो याति। नभसि गच्छति। किं कुर्वन्। विश्वा विश्वानि सर्वाणि भुवनानि भूतजातानि संपश्यन् सम्यक् प्रकाशयन्।।

अजस्र not fatigued, indefatiguable, unfailing.

अयान्, 3. sg. aor. par.; rt. यम् 1.

Verse 2.

नृचक्षाः। एषः। दिवः। मध्ये। आस्ते। आपप्रिऽवान्। रोदसी इति। अन्तरिक्षम्। सः। विश्वाचीः। अभि। चष्टे। घृताचीः। अन्तरा। पूर्वम्। अपरम्। च। केतुम्।।२।।

नृचक्षा नृन्मनुष्यान्पश्यन् यद्वा नृभिर्नेतृभी रश्मिभिः प्रकाशमान एष सविता दिवो द्युलोकस्य मध्य आस्ते। निषीदति। किं कुर्वन्। रोदसी द्यावापृथिव्यावन्तरिक्षं चापप्रिवान् स्वतेजसा पूरयन्। प्रा पूरणे। असमाच्छान्दसो लिट् क्वसुरादेशः। वस्वेकाजाद्धसामितीडागमः। स देवो विश्वाचीर्विश्वमञ्चनतीः सर्वव्यापिनीः प्राच्यादिमहादिशोऽभिचष्टे। प्रकाशयति। तथा घृताचीर्घृतं दीप्तं रूपमञ्चन्तीराग्नेय्यादिविदिशश्च प्रकाशयति। अञ्चतेः क्विन्नन्तादञ्चतेश्चोप-संख्यानमिति ङीप्। ततो भसंज्ञायामच इत्याकारलोपे चाविति दीर्घत्वम्। उदात्तनिवृत्तिस्वरेण ङीप उदात्तत्वे प्राप्ते चाविति पूर्वस्याच उदात्तत्वम्। तथा पूर्वं पूर्वभागं केतुं प्रज्ञापनीयमपरं पृष्ठभागं चानतरान्तरालं चाभिचष्टे। प्रकाशयति।।

नृचक्षस्, with the eyes of man, observing men, (Sāy.), overseer.

प॒प्रि॒वांस् pt. pf. par.; rt. प्रा 2., to fill.

घृ॒ताच् (घृत अच् towards the butter), rich in ghee, yielding ghee, fat (दिश्).

वि॒श्वाच् (विश्व अच्, towards all), far-extending, Sāyaṇa: सर्वव्यापिन्.

के॒तु m., brightness, light, sign. The पूर्वं and अपंर के॒तु अ॒न्त॒रा, between.

Verse 3.

रा॒यः। बु॒न्धः। सं॒ऽगमंनः। वसू॑नाम्। विश्वा॑। रू॒पा। अ॒भि। च॒ष्टे॒। शचीभिः। दे॒वःऽइंव। स॒वि॒ता। स॒त्यऽधंर्मा। इन्द्रः। न। त॒स्थौ॒। सं॒ऽअ॒रे। धनंनाम्।।३।।

राधो धनस्य बुध्नो बन्धको मूलभूतो वा। ऊडिदमित्यादिना रैशब्दाद्विभक्तेरूदात्तत्वम्। तथा वसूनां धनानां संगमनः संगमयिता प्रापयिता ईदृशः सविता शचीभिर्दीप्तिभिर्विश्वा रूपा सर्वाणि रूपाणि निरूपणीयानि पदार्थजातान्यभिचष्टे। अभिपश्यति। प्रकाशयति। अपि च देव इवायं सविता सावको देवः सत्यधर्मा सत्यमवितथं धर्म धारणं धारणहेतुभूतं कर्म वा यस्य तादृशो भवति। तथेन्द्रो नेन्द्र इव धनानां समरे संग्रामे सम्यक्प्रापणे तस्थौ। अयं सवितोद्युक्तः संस्तिष्ठति।।

बुध्न m., bottom, foundation.

सं॒गमं॑न m., collector, gatherer.

स॒त्यधंर्मन्, one whose laws are in force, are kept.

The hymn has been by Grassmann, transl., split into two, comprising ṛcas 1-3 and 4-6. Geldner also in Ved Stud. III. pp. 52 ff. thinks ṛcas 4-6 to be a version of the Viśvāvasu myth, hanging with the contents of ṛcas 1-6 to be only one hymn on account of the consistency of the seting and the contents. Pūṣan, according to him, is the main figure in ṛcas

1-3; and because Pūṣan is the god who brings back lost property, the seeking and finding mentioned in 3-6 is adduced, cp. अविन्दत् in 6. Oldenberg, l.c. tentatively offers the following disposition of the hymn:—Savitṛ is mentioned only in the introduction (1 ab) and in the comparision (3 c). Pūṣan, who sees everything, sees consequently the waters wherever they are (2 cd). The waters have fled before Viśvāvasu (4), i. e., the rain-clouds have become invisible. Indra searches for them in the regions of the sun. He has found so many things before (6): thus he will find the waters and, as we have to supply from ṛcas 1-3, Pūṣan will assist him, Viśvāvasu in addition (cp. 5) helping. This view is weakened by the fact that in 1-3 Pūṣan is not the central figure, and by Oldenberg's own statement that the connection between ṛcas 1-3 and 4-6 is rather vague. It supposes, besides, certain interpretation of individual words which appear to be less acceptable than Geldner's. Thus Geldner's interpretation seems better and is followed here.

According to Geldner ṛcas 4-6 contain the Itihāsa of the flight of the soma into the waters, a parallel to Agni's flight into the same element. There are two versions of this itihāsa, one in ṚV. VIII. 96. 13-15, the other here in our passage, also in ṚV. IX. 62. 1 and more explicitly in Tāṇḍya Brāhmaṇa VI. 9. 22:—छन्दांसि वै सोममाहरंस्तं गन्धर्वो विश्वावसुः पर्यमुष्णात्तेनापः प्राविशत्ततं देवता अन्वैच्छंस्तं विष्णुरप्सु पर्यपश्यत् स व्यकाङ्क्षदयन्नू३ना३ इति तं पदा प्रास्फुरत्तस्मात्पृथगिन्दवोऽसृज्यन्त स देवताभ्योऽभितस्तिष्ठन्तीभ्य एते असृग्रमिन्दव इति प्राब्रवीत्। So far the Tāṇḍya Brāhmaṇa.

Verse 4.

विश्वऽवंसुम्। सोम। गन्धर्वम्। आपः। ददृशुषीः। तत्। ऋतेन। वि। आयन्। तत्। अनुऽअवैत्। इन्द्रः। ररहाणः। आसाम्। परि। सूर्यस्य। परिऽधीन्। अपश्यत्।।४।।

हे सोम त्वया सहितं गन्धर्वं गीतरूपां गां शब्दं धारयन्तं विश्वावसुमेतत्संज्ञं

माम्। उत्तरत्र तच्छब्दश्रुतेर्यच्छब्दाध्याहारः। यदापो वसतीवर्याख्या ददृशषी-र्दृष्टवत्यः। दृशेर्लिटः क्वसुः। उगितश्चेति ङीप्। वसोः संप्रसारणमिति संप्रसारणम्। जसि वा छन्दसीति पूर्वसवर्णदीर्घः। तत्तदानीमृतेन यज्ञेन हेतुना व्यायन्। विविधमगच्छन्यष्टजनाः। तग्दमनमासामपां ररहाणो गमयितेन्द्रोऽनववैत्। अन्वबुध्यत। बुद्ध्वा च कुत्र यज्ञः प्रवृत्त इति सूर्यस्य परिधीन्परितो धीयमानान्प्राच्यादिदिग्विभागान्पर्यपश्यत्। परितो दृष्टवान्।।

ददृशुषीः, nom. plur. fem. pt. pf. par.; rt. दृश्.

अन्ववैत्, 3. sg. impf par. अनु अव इ to follow. The compounds with the rt. इ are often used when gods "go after" their lost property. On the accent see Delbrück, AIS. p. 47.

ररहाण pt. pf. ātm. rt. रंह्, to hasten.

Sāyaṇa understands त्वया सहितम् after सोम and explains ऋत as या. ऋत repeatedly in ṚV. is यज्ञ and so is सोम as well. ऋतेन seems to be rather sociative instrumental than हेतु instr. (Sāy.).

परिधि signifies a bar of defence or protection, an obstacle blocking or locking up, see 12. 6. Does now सूर्यस्य परिधीन् refer to the darkened (because obstructed) or imprisoned sun (Geldner, 1. c.)? Or is the गन्धर्व to be identified with the sun-god (Sāy. comm. ṚV. VIII. 1. 11; AV. II. 2. 1; Roth, Grassmann, PW. s.v. गन्धर्व)? The occurrence of this Itihāsa in Savitṛ hymn is in favour of this latter interpretation, which however cannot be said to be certain. Nor is it beyond doubt by whom ṛc 4 is spoken.

तदुन्ववैदिन्द्रो ररहाण आसाम् is not a Jagatī but a Triṣṭubh with one trochee too many. Read इन्दर.

Verse 5.

विश्वऽवसुः। अभि। तत्। नः। गृणातु। दिव्यः। गन्धर्वः। रजसः। विऽमानः। यत्। वा। घ। सत्यम्। उत। यत्। न। विद्म। धियः। हिन्वानः। धियः इत्। नः। अव्याः।।५।।

विश्वावसुर्गन्धर्वो नोऽस्माकं तदभि गृणातु। अभिमुखं ब्रवीतु। गृ शब्दे क्रैयादिकः। प्वादित्वाद्ध्रसवः। कीदृशः। दिव्यो दिवि भवः तथा रजस उदकस्य विमानो निर्माता। किं पुनस्तत्। यद्वा घ यच्च खलु सत्यमवितथं यथार्थफलं कर्मजातम्। उतशब्दश्चार्थे। यच्च न विद्म न जानीमः। तदुभयं ब्रवीत्वित्यर्थः। ऋचि तुनुघेत्यादिना घशब्दस्य सांहितिको दीर्घः। शिष्टः पादः प्रत्यक्षकृतः। हे विश्वावसो धियः कर्माणि हिन्वानः सोमेन प्रवर्धयन्। हि गतौ वृद्धौ च। यद्वा। धियः स्तुतीर्हिन्वानः प्राप्नुवन् नोऽस्माकं धिय इत्कर्माण्येव बुद्धीरेव वाव्याः। रक्ष।।

अव्याः 3. sg. prec. par.; rt. अव्.

This ṛc is probably spoken by Indra. He is not quite sure of the situation and applies to the गन्धर्व for information.

Verse 6.

सस्रिम्। अविन्दत्। चरणे। नदीनाम्। अप। अवृणोत्। दुरः। अश्मऽव्रजानाम्। प्र। आसाम्। गन्धर्वः। अमृतानि। वोचत्। इन्द्रः। दक्षम्। परि। जानात्। अहीनाम्।।६।।

सस्रिम् अद्भिः संस्नातं प्रकर्षेण सर्वस्य जगतः स्नापयितारं मेघम्। ष्णा शौचे। आदृगमहन इति किन्प्रत्ययः। लिडवद्भावाद्द्विर्वचनम्। नदीनां शब्दकारिणी- नामपां चरणे संचरणस्थानेऽन्तरिक्षेऽविन्दत्। इन्द्रोऽलभत। लब्ध चाश्मव्रजानाम्। अश्मा व्याप्तो मेघः। तत्र व्रजन्तीनाम्। यद्वा। मेघो व्रजो गोष्ठं निवासस्थानं यासां तादृशीनामपां दुरो द्वाराणि मेघान्निर्गमनप्रदेशान- पावृणोत्। अपावृतवान्। यद्वा। अश्मसु शिलासु व्रजन्तीनां गच्छन्तीनां व्याप्तगमनानां वा नदीनां गङ्गायमुनादीनां चरणे संचरणे प्रवहणे निमित्तभूते सति तदर्थमिन्द्रः। सस्त्रिं मेघमविन्दत्। अलभत। लब्ध्वा चान्तर्गतानामपां

निर्गमसाधनानि मेघस्य दुरो द्वाराण्यपावृणोत्। अपावृतवान्। तथासां नदीनाममृतान्यमरणसाधकान्युदकानि गन्धर्वो गोर्वज्रस्य धर्ता विश्वावसुरूपेण वर्तमान इन्द्रः प्रवोचत्। प्रब्रवीति। प्रवोढुमनुजानाति। तथा दक्षम्। दक्षत्युदकं प्रयच्छतीति दक्षो वर्षणसमर्थो मेघः। तादृशं मेघमहीनां मेघानां मध्ये परिजानात्। परितः सर्वतो जानाति। ज्ञा अवबोधने। लेट्यडागमः। ज्ञाजनोर्जेति जादेशः।।

सस्रिं (from rt. सन् 8., to gain), winning, robbing; (from rt. स्ना 2., to bathe), immerged.

अश्मंवज्रानाम् bahuvr. cpd.

अ॒ही=स्त्री (Sāy. IX. 77.3). Mādhava, referring to Nirukta I. p. 70, line 8 ff. Calc., Bibl. Indica ed., interprets अ॒ही as rivers. Note that the difference in accent between अ॒ही, woman, and अहिं, dragon, also bars the rendering of अ॒ही in this passage with dragon.

It would seem that the events of the first and second pādas are given in an inverted order. This is suggested by the events themselves and by the Vala myth, ṚV. I. 62. 5, which relates that Indra liberated Soma together with Uṣas, the Sun, and the cows. According to the present version of the Viśvāvasu myth the waters at the moment of their liberation see Viśvāvasu, the real Soma thief, and snatch the Soma from him.

APPENDIX I

MAIN PECULIARITIES OF VEDIC GRAMMAR IN THE SELECTED HYMNS

PHONETICS—*The Alphabet.* ड and ढ between vowels regularly become ळ and ळ्ह:—जि॒ह्री॒ळानस्यं 1.2;मृ॒ळी॒कार्यं 1.3; वो॒ळ्हा 20.4; मी॒ळ्हुषें 22.7; but मी॒ढ्वान्. In the older hymns र stands sometimes for the later ल:—रि॒हा॒णे 12.1,3.

Final vowels are often (under the influence of metre) lengthened:—भवंता 12.9;पिबां 11.2;श्रुघी॒ 1. 19;विद्मा 13.6;एना 012.2,3; ऋतांवस् 8. 6; note अश्रामघा 20. 1;सान्ति 8.1 (s. Ṛg-Prðatisðakhya IX.25.584).

Svarabhakti. When a consonant is in conjunction with र or a nasal, a very short vocalic tends to be developed between them. The length of the vowel is according to the Prātiśākhyas ½, ¼, or 1/8 matras and its sound like अ. But cp.Rg-Prat. I.17.34,36, and Taitt.-Prat. II. 19. The metre often makes the prounciation of a (short) vowel between the consonant and the र or the nasal necessary:— दु॒र॒शत (दु॒र्श॒त), इन्दरं (इन्द्रं), पर(प्र), यु॒जन (यु॒ज्ञ

Resolution. Not unfrequently the आ especially of the gen. plur, ending. आम् has to be read अ+आ :— जनांन+अम् 1. 14; द+अस्वंती 3.1.

SANDHI. *Vowels*. Against the rules of sandhi hiatus is often (according to metrical need) not avoided :—

Within the word itself :—दुआदर्श 1.8; तुअम्1.20;वंसुअ 3.11;साम्राजिआय 1.10;

Within the compound:—सुअस्ति 5. 6,8; अधोअक्ष 12.9; अधिआसते 1.9;

Between the words of a sentence:—पुस्त्यासु आ 1.10.

Initial अ after ए and ओ is only occasionally elided:—सद्यो अपिबो० 11.10; नो अस्थात 18.5;विभीदक अचिति 22.6; नो अस्तु 22.8.

Final आ is shortened or nasalised before ऋ:—शवस ऋतप्रजात 7.15;विधर्तां ऋतं 8.4. The आ of यथा at the end of the pada before ए is nasalised to avoid hiatus in यथा एष 24.6.

Before vowels there remain unchanged :—

The ए of the pronouns त्वे,अस्मे,युष्मे;

The final ओ (अ + उ) of अथो,मो,ना.

On the other hand there is double saṁdhi in तुर इयाम् to be read तुरेयाम् 22.4.

Consonants. Final न् before vowels is changed after a long vowel to anunāsika ँ : if the preceding vowel is आ,to more anunāsika ँ; if the preceding vowel is ई, ऊ, ot ऋ, न् is changed to anunāsika plus र :—चिकित्वाँ अभि 1.11; स्तोमाँ इयर्मि 5.1;अध्वरा उप 3.11; 'प्रधाँरिव 14.15.

Final न् before य,र,व,ह, generally remains unchanged; yet sometimes आन्, ईन् ,ऊन् are changed into आ, ँइर, ऊँर्, before य, र, व, ह,:—पूर्णार्हतम् 6.2.

Sometimes saṁdhi rules which in classical language apply only within the same words hold good in Vedic language between different words:—प्र ण॰ 1.12; नि षसाद 1.10.

The consonant छ after a short vowel (the अ of the augment, e.g.) appears doubled in the form of च्छ (see Ṛg-Part.VI.1.380):—अच्छदयन् 26.10.

Final ङ् and न्, if followed by vowels and preceded by a short vowel, are doubled—कीदृङिङन्द्र 26.3; अहन्नहिम् 2.1.

DECLENSION

A. **Type of declension.**

Certain polysyllabic stems in ई and ऊ, रथी, तनू, fot instance,are inflected like the monosyllabic stems धी and भू, excepting the gen. plur., where they show ॰नाम. Thus acc. sg. मन्वम्, instead of the classial तनूम; रथीः, दूतीः 26.2, 3, 4, nom. sg. masc. fem.(like the classical लक्ष्मीः).

B. Endings.

I. Singular.

1. The Instrumental occasionally adds only ॰आ to the masc. stem in ॰अ and the fem. stem in ॰आ (instead of ॰एन masc.,॰अया fem.) महित्वा 19.4; वरस्या 17.2.Derivative fem.stems frequently show only ॰ई instead of ॰याः—तपनी 7.14; श्रुष्टी 10.8.Stems in ॰मन sometimes do not syncopate the vowel अ of the suffix ॰मन् in the ending ॰मना ; if they do syncopate the vowel, the म् or the न् may be dropped:—महिना 2.8; 23.1.
2. *Locative*. Stems in इ take ॰आ or ॰औरः—सुरभा 15.6; आजा 5.2,15. Stems in ॰अन् usually the drop the ॰इः—यामन् 17.9; परिज्मन् 9.2.

3. *Vocative.* Stems in ०मत, ०वत्, ०वस्, ०यस, from their vocative in ०अस् :—भानुमस् 15.11; स्वधा॒वस 22.4, 8.

II. Dual.

Nouns. The nom., acc., and voc. take ०आ motr usually than ०औ :—नास॑त्या ; एष्टा॑ नरा॒ निचे॑तारा 6.2; वेनन्ता 1. 6. Feminines in derivative ०ई remain unchanged:—देवी.

Pronouns. The personal pronouns of the first and second person distinguish five cases;e.gr. :—nom.युवम्; acc. युवा॑म्; instr. युवाभ्या॑म् or युवभ्या॑म; abl.युवद्; loc. युवो:.

III. Plural.

Nominative. Masculine stems in ०अ often take आस: instead of आ:—जना॑स:, कुशि॒का॑स: 13.9. Fem.stems in ०ई take ०स् only :—कृष्णी: 20.1; दु॒दृशुषी॑: 27.4; thus nom. and acc. are identical in form. Neuters take ०आ,०ई,०ऊ (sometimes shortened to अ,इ,उ) as well as ०आनि, ०ईनि, ०उनि:—वना 10.2; अभ्रिया॑ 5.1;ता 2.15; कर्म॑ 11.8; वसु॑ 7.9.

Instrumental. Stems in अ take ०एभि: nearly as often as ऐ: :—रथै॑भि:3.7; य॒ज॒तेभि॑: 15.11.

Note (1) The ending is dropped in अ॒नर्वन् 5.16.

(2) In 26.8 at the end of the pada occurs the gen. plur. गोना॑म् which is much less common than गवा॑म्.

(3) Adjective in ०वन् form their fem. in वरी:—ऋ॒ताव॑री 18.1; the fem. of युवन् is यु॒वति, nom.sg.युवति: 21.1.

CONJUGATION

1. *The Augment, usually* अ०, may be lengthened, either metrically, or (in the case of 7-8 roots) permanently:—आ

बर् (वृ), आ रैक (रिच्). The augment can without change of meaning always be dropped.

2. *Prefixes* rather often follow the verb to which they belong, instead of preceding it:—मिमिक्ष्वा 3.16. The prefixes may be separated from the verb by particles and other words:—प्र ण आयूंषिता तारिषत् 1.2.

3. *Endings*. The primary ending of the 1. plur. p ar. ०मसि is much commoner than (the classical) म: :—मिनीमसि 1.1. The 2. sg.impv. par.has a not uncommon alternative ending in ०तात,(added to the weak stem), which expresses an injunction to be carried out in the future:—यच्छतात् 3.15. In the 2. plur. ०थन and ०तन often occur beside ०थ and त :—स्थन, जुहोतन. The 3. sg.pres. atm.may be identical in form with the 1:—शये(for शेते)2.9.

4. *The Reduplication syllable* is often lengthened:—वावृधे (वृध्).

5. The (rare) *Pluperfect* is formed from the perfect stem by prefixing the augment and adding the secondary terminations:— अमुमुक्तम् (मुच्) 5.14;अजभर्तन (भृ) 25.7.

6. Besides the Moods of the classical language there are the Subjunctive and Injunctive in the Vedic Sanskrit. The Subjunctive is much more common than the optative. Its meaning, expressing will, is imperative:—भुवानि 22. 2; वोचावहै 1.17; उच्छात् 3. 3; (न) अश्नवत 7.4. If used with an interrogative the subj. expresses a will with doubt, approximating a wish:—कुविन्न्वंस्य तृष्णवं: 13.2. Sometimes its meaning is equivalent with a future indicative:—घाति 9.1; मुचाति 9. 3. Especially in relative clauses the subj. may have a final or conseqential sense:—घोषान् 12.8.

The subj. is formed by adding ०अ to the present, aorist, or perfect stem. In the अ conjugation it therefore ends in आ :—भार्वति 9.11. In the second conjugation ०अ is added to the strong stem which remains throughout:—तृप्णवं 13. 2. The ending are partly primary, partly secondary :—मुचाति 9.3;करत् 1.12.

The fairly common injunctive is identical in form, with a past tense, impf, aor.,plupf.,without the augment:—मा स्थाम् 8.11; (प्र)णक् (नश्), कृम (कृ) 7.12.

The general meaning of the inj. expresses a desire combining the senses of the subj., opt.,. and impv. It appears mostly in principal clauses; in negative sentences it is the only mood with which the negative particle मा can be used:—मा छेदि, मा शारि 8.5.

The three moods, subj., opt.,impv. occur in the pf. and aor. as well as in the present :—Pf.opt.जगम्याम् 5. 25; वृत्याम् 11. 13; pf. impv. सुमुग्धि 1.21; ववृत्स्व 11.5; aor. subj. घाति 9.1; aor. impv. अरताम् 12.13.

7. *Voices.* The forms of the ātmanepadam may be employed in a passive sense, except as a rule in the present and the imperfect. But शृण्वे 17. 7, 3. sg. pres. atm. rt. श्रु, is used in a passive sense.

8. *Participles.* In addition to the participles surviving in the classical language the Veda has an aorist participle both in parasmaip. and ātmanep.:—कन्त,क्राण, rt. कृ.

9. Besides the *Gerund in* ०त्वा there is a commoner one in ०त्वी :—हित्वी 9.6; (अ)युद्ध्वी 26.5. The vowel of the gerunds with prefixes ending in ०य and ०त्य is usually

lengthened :—प्र प्रुथ्यां,वि मुच्यां 11.1; आ गत्यां 13.7.—Note the *Gerundive* कर्त्वां 1.11.

10. In the present selection a good may *Infinitives* are to be found having the form of an acc.; acc.; but mostly forms of dat. occur, rarely gen. and abl. The acc. is formed from the root:—(वि) पृच्छम् 22.3. The dat. is formed from the root or from vedrbal nouns in ०अस्,०तु,or ०धि:—(वि) चक्षे 5.14.16;जीवसे 1.21; पातवे5.22; सर्तवै 2.12;सर्तवै 11.6 (note double accent !) पिबध्यै 11.15; चरायै (?) 21.1. See Lanman, Noun-Inflection, P.554 c. The only gen. and abl. forms that occur are:—निमिषः 8.6: (अति) स्कदः 26.2; both being formed from the root.

PREPOSITIONS (POSTPOSITIONS)

The real prepositions are almost entirely restricted to the use with the acc.,loc. These "prepositions" as a rule follow, but also often precede, their case.

(a) With acc.:—अति beyond; अधि,on to;अनु, after; अन्तर्, between ; अच्छ, अभि, आ,उप,प्रति,towards; परि, round ;तिरस, accross;पुरस,before.

(b) With loc:—अधि, on ; अन्तर्, within; अपि, आ, उप, near; पुरस्, before.

(c) With able:—अधि, from upon ;अन्तर, from within ;आ, away from (or) up to; परि, from(around);पुरस्, before.

ADVERBS

Some (instrumental) case forms of nominal and pronominal stems are used as adverbs:—रघुया 8.4; घृष्णुया 14.13;अमुया 2.8; उभया 26.6.

APPENDIX II

THE ACCENT

Nature of the accent. The Vedic accent is a musical one, depending mainly on pitch. This is indicated by the name of the chief tone, उदात्त, raised. Three degrees of pitch are to be distinguished, the high, properly represented by the उदात्त, raised; the middle, shown by the स्वरित, sounded; and the low, given by the अनुदात्त, not raised. But in the Ṛgveda the उदात्त, the rising accent, has secondarily acquired a middle pitch, lower than the initial pitch of the स्वरित. The अनुदात्त is the low tone of the syllables preceding the उदात्त.

The स्वरित is a falling accent representing the descent from the उदात्त pitch to tonelessness. It rises slightly above उदात्त pitch before descending: here therefore it has something of the nature of a circumflex. The स्वरित is in reality always an enclitic or dependent accent following the उदात्त; but it assumes the appearance of an independent accent in the following cases where the preceding उदात्त is lost by the euphonic change, the fusion or the elision of the vowel which bears the उदात्त —

(a) When the उदात्त, इ, ई, or उ, ऊ is changed into य or व before a dissimilar अनुदात्त vowel:—व्याप्त (वि आ॑प्त). This is known as क्षैप्र स्वरित;

(b) When the same combination lies further back and always

belongs to the word:— स्वं॑र् from सुअर्. The metre often requires the resolved reading सुअ॑र्. This is known as जात्य or नित्य स्वरित ;

(c) When the उदत्त and अनुदात्त vowels are fused into one long vowel or dipthong:—दि॒वी॑व from दि॒वि इ॑व. This is known as प्रश्लिष्ट स्वरित;

(d) When an initial अनुदात्त vowel is absorbed by a final उदात्त ए or ओ.—ते अं॑ऽब्रुवन् from ते अं॑ब्रुवन्. This is known as अभिनिहित स्वरित.

The independent स्वरित, playing the part of the उदात्त and the स्वरित, is never changed into the अनुदात्त.

Method of marking the accent. 1. The system followed by the Ṛ.V. is peculiar in not directly marking the उदात्त, the principal accent, at all. This seems to be due to the fact that in the ṚV. the pitch of the उदात्त is intermediate between the two other tones. Hence the preceding अनुदात्त, as having a low pitch, is indicated below the syllable bearing it by a horizontal stroke, while the following स्वरित, which at first rises to a slightly higher pitch and then falls, is indicated above the syllable bearing it by a vertical stroke; e. gr.:—अ॒भिमा॑तयः 1.14; वक्षणा॑: 2.1 The उदात्त is always preceded by the अनुदात्त, कु॒दा क्ष॒त्रश्रिय॑म् 1.5; except when the उदात्त is on the first syllable of a line (hemistich), मा नौ॑ व॒घाय॑० 1.2; and when it is preceded by another उदात्त, तदित्स॑मानम्० 1.6. Consequently successive उदात्ताः at the beginning of a hemistich are indicated by the absence of all marks till the (enclitic or dependent) स्वरित which follows the last of them, or till the अनुदात्त which (ousting the dependent स्वरित) follows the last of them as a preparation for another उदात्त (or for an independent स्वरित):—न यं दिप्स॑न्ति॰ 1.14.

2. The syllable after the उदात्त is marked with a स्वरित. Hence every स्वरित accent indicates that the syllable preceding has the उदात्त. If however the syllable after the उदात्त precedes another, following, उदात्त the स्वरित becomes (according to rule 1. above) अनुदात्त, to announce the coming उदात्त :—दर्शं॒ नु वि॒श्वद॑र्शतं॒ दर्शं॒ रथ॒मधि॒ क्षमि॑ 1.18.

3. One or more successive unaccented syllables at the beginning of a hemistich are marked with the अनुदात्त, e. gr.:— अ॒ना॒र॒म्भ॒णे 5.5. The अनुदात्त following a स्वरित is not marked at all, except when it precedes another उदात्त:—कु॒दा क्ष॑त्र॒श्रिय॑म् 1.5. More than one अनुदात्तs following aस्वरित are not marked at all, except the last immediately preceding the उदात्त or independent स्वरित :—अजो॑हवीन्नासत्या क॒रा वां॑ 5.13. Hence one or more successive syllables after स्वरित which are not marked are अनुदात्त syllables.

4. A syllable not marked may be either उदात्त, or अनुदात्त. It is उदात्त when preceded by a marked is अनुदात्त, by another उदात्त, or when beginning a line (hemistich). It is अनुदात्त when preceded either mediately or immediately by a स्वरित.

5. If the independent स्वरित immediately precedes the उदात्त it is accompanied by the numeral १, when the syllable with the independent स्वरित is short ; it is accompanied with the numeral ३, when it is (by nature and not only by position) long. The figure bears the sign for both the

स्वरित and the अनुदात्त which precedes the उदात्त. E.gr.:—उक्थ्यं१ बृहस्पते 7.14. See 9.4;9.8;12.7;etc. अभिदिप्स्वो ३ मृधो० 7.13.see 11.11;13.8;22.2. Note that the long vowel before the ३ receives the अनुदात्त sign as well.

Accent of single words. Every Vedic word is, as a rule, accented and has one main accent only. This main accent is either the उदात्त or the independent स्वरित. Exceptions:—

1. **Double accent:—** infinitives in ०तवै, एतवै; देवता-द्वन्द्व cpds., मित्रावरुणा ; simillarly तुर्वशायदु 14.17,अर्णाचित्ररथा 14. 18. Note also the double accent of बृहस्पति and of शचीपति 14.17, which by the Padapāṭhas is dissolved into शचीऽपति.

2. **Want of accent:—** Some words never have an accent; others lose it under certain conditions .

A. Never accented are:—

   a. the following forms of the personal pronoun of the first and second persons: मा, त्वा, मे, ते;नौ,वाम्; नः,वः, and of the demonstrative stems इ and सः—ईम् 15.3, and सीम् 14.10.

   b. the particles च, उ, वा, इव, घ, ह, चिद् स्म, स्विद्.

B. Without accent according to meaning and position are:—

   a. oblique cases of the pronouns अ, if replacing a preceding substantive and not beginning the sentence or pāda, e.gr.:— अस्य जनिमानि, his (Agni's)births; but अस्या उषसः, of that dawn.

   b. यथा almost always when, in the sense of इव, it occurs at the end of a pāda, e. gr.:—तायवो यथा तस्करो यथा 24.6; कम्, always when following नु, सु,हि 8.8.

The accent of individual words has to be seen in the dictionary or the text. The most important rules for the use of the accent in declension and conjugation may easily be learnt from the text.

Accent of compounds. As a rule आम्रेडित compounds (द्यविं-द्यवि), बहुव्रीहि compounds and governing compounds (यातयज्जन) accent the first member; कर्मधारय, तत्पुरुष, and द्वन्द्व compounds accent the last member. Note the accent of याद्राध्यंम्, 9.8. If the simple word is accented in the compound , the accent generally remains on the same syllable as it was outside the compound.

Sentence accent. The vocative retains the accent only at the beginning of a sentence or a pāda, in all other positions the vocative loses its accent. The accent can be on the first syllable of the vocative only, whether it be a single word or a complex expression. E.gr. :— होर्तर्यविष्ठ सुक्रतो दमूंनाः ṚV. IV.4.11.

The finite verb of a principal clause is unaccented unless it begins a sentence :—अहन्नहिमन्वपस्तंतर्द 2.1. Since a vocative does not count in a sentence, a verb following it is accented,e.gr.:—आश्रुंत्कर्ण श्रुधी हवं० ṚV.I.10.9. A sentence being regarded as capable of having only one verb, all verbs syntactically connected with the same subject as the first are accented as beginning a new sentence:—तरणिरिज्जंयति क्षेति पुष्यंति ṚV. VII. 32.9.

In subordinate clauses (introduced by the relative pronoun or its derivatives, and the particles हि, च, चेद्, नेद्, कुविद्) the verb is always accented:—न यं दिप्संन्ति दिप्सवो० 1.14. When two principal clauses are in a relation of antithesis, the first is often treated as subordinate, and its verb accented. Emphasis on a verb may also call for the accent:— इन्द्र सोमं सोमपते पिबेमं० Ṛ.V. III. 32.1; दिवा नक्तं माध्वी त्रासीथां नः 20.2.

In principal clauses the verbal prefix is separated from the verb and accented; in subordinate clauses it is compounded with the verb and loses its accent :— अञ्जः समुद्रामव जग्मुरापः 2.2.; वेदा य उपजायते 1.8.

RULES

For converting the accent of the Saṁhitāpāṭha into that of the Padapāṭha and vice versa

A. Saṁhitāpāṭha > Padapāṭha

1. The rules for accentuation in the ṚV. apply in the Saṁhitāpāṭha to the whole line; in the Padapāṭha to individual words only. Consequently the figures १॒॑ and ३॒॑ are not written in the Padapāṭha. For they show the peculiar relation between the accents of two different words within the Saṁhitāpāṭha. Outside the Samhitāpāṭha these words are accentually independent; the signs १॒॑ and ३॒॑ are therefore not put in the Padapāṭha where this special relation ceases to exist. The syntactical position of nouns and verbs in the sentence influences the accent of the individual word.

   तेजि॑ष्ठया तप॒नी र॒क्षस॑स्तप॒ ये त्वा॑ नि॒दे द॑धि॒रे दृ॒ष्टवी॑र्यम्।
   आ॒विस्तत्कृ॑ष्व॒ यदस॑त्त उ॒क्थ्यं१॒॑बृह॑स्पते॒ वि प॑रि॒रापो॑ अर्दय।।७।१४।।

2. Every Vedic word has, as a rule, one main accent and one main accent only, viz., the उदात्त or independent स्वरित, on which the (ordinary) स्वरित and अनुदात्त depend. Write each word of the ṛc separately without saṁdhi.

   तेजि॑ष्ठया। तप॒नी। र॒क्षस॑ः। त॒प॒। ये। त्वा॑। नि॒दे। द॑धि॒रे। दृ॒ष्टवी॑र्यम्। आ॒विः। तत्। कृ॑ष्व। यत्। अस॑त्। ते। उ॒क्थ्यं१॒॑बृह॑स्पते॒। वि। प॑रि॒राप॑ः। अर्दय।।

3. The main accent, उदात्त or independent स्वरित in the

Saṁhitāpāṭha, is never to be changed or shifted in the Padapāṭha. The other accents, the ordinary स्वरित and the अनुदात्त, are to be put in the Padapāṭha so as to show the position of the उदात्त. If, on syntactical grounds, a word has lost or changed its accent in the Saṁhitāpāṭha, the accent is not restored or changed back in the Padapāṭha.

तेजिष्ठया। तपनी। रक्षसः। तप। ये। त्वा। निदे। दधिरे। दृष्टवीर्यम्। आविः। तत्। कृष्व। यत्। असत्। ते। उक्थ्यम्। बृहस्पते। वि। परिरापः। अर्दय।।७।१४।।

B. Padapāṭha > Saṁhtāpāṭha.

1. General rules see under A.1.2.

भरेषु। हव्यः। नमसा। उपसद्यः। गन्ता। वाजेषु। सनिता। धनंधनम्।। विश्वाः। इत्। अर्यः। अभिदिप्स्वः। मृधः। बृहस्पतिः। वि। ववर्ह। रथान्। इव or रथान्ऽइव।।७।१३।।

2. Restore saṁdhi.

भरेषु हव्यो नमसोपसद्यो गन्ता वाजेषु सनिता धनंधनम्।

विश्वा इदर्यो अभिदिप्स्वो मृधो बृहस्पतिर्वि। ववर्हा। रथाँ इव।।

3. Change secondary accents, viz., स्वरित and अनुदात्त, according to preceding or following उदात्त. Put in the figures १ and ३ where necessary.

भरेषु हव्यो नमसोपसद्यो गन्ता वाजेषु सनिता धनंधनम्।

विश्वा इदर्यो अभिदिप्स्वो३मृधो बृहस्पतिर्वि। ववर्हा। रथाँ इव।।

APPENDIX III

THE METRE

(Adapted from A.A. Macdonell, A Vedic Grammar for Students, Oxford, 1916. pp. 436ff.)

The main principle governing vedic metre is measurement by number of syllables. The metrical unit is the पाद, quarter, in the sense of the verse or line which is a constituent of the stanza. Such verses consist of 8, 11, 12 or (not so common) 5 syllables. The verse is further regulated by a quantitative rhythm (unaffected by the musical accent) in which short and long syllables alternate. Nearly all metres have a general iambic rhythm inasmuch as they show a preference for the even syllables (second, fourth and so on) in a verse being long rather than short. In every metre the latter part of the verse (the last 4 or 5 syllables), called the cadence, is more rigidly regulated than that of the earlier part. Verses of 11 and 12 syllables are characterised not only by their cadence, but by a caesura or metrical pause after the fourth or the fifth syllable, while veses of 5 and 8 syllables have no such pause.

Verses combine to form a stanza or ṛc, the unit of the hymn, which generally consists of not less than 3 or more than 15 such units. The stanzas of common occurence range, by increments of 4 syllables, from 20 (4×5) to 48 (4×12) syllables in length. A stanza may consist of a combination of metrically identical or of metrically different verses and either 2 or 3 stanzas may further be combined to form a strophe.

The following general rules of prosody are to be noted :

1. The end of a verse regularly coincides with the end of a word because each verse in a stanza is independent of the rest in structure.
2. The quality of the first and last syllables of a verse is indifferent : it may be and is considered long or short as the metre requires.
3. A vowel becomes long by position if followed by two consonants. One or both of these consonants may belong to the following word. The palatal aspirate छ and the cerebral aspirate ळह (ढ) count as double consonants.

4 One vowel is shortened before another; the (otherwise long) vowels ए and ओ are also prounounced short before अ.

5 The semi-vowels य and व, both within the word and in saṁdhi, have often to be pronounced as इ and उ.

6. Contracted vowels must often be restored, i.e., आ has to be read as अ अ, ई as इ इ, etc.:—च॒ अ॒ग्नये॑ for चा॒ग्नये॑; वि इन्द्र॑ः for वि॑न्द्रः; also आ ई॑न्द्र for एन्द्र॑.

7 The initial अ when dropped after ए and ओ must nearly always be restored.

8. The long vowel of the gen. plur. ending ०आम्, and of such words as दा॑स, शू॑र—as well as ए (in ज्यइ॑ष्ठ for ज्यें॑ष्ठ) or (in अइ॑च्छस् for ऐ॑च्छस्) must often be pronounced as equivalent to two short syllables.

1. Simple Stanzas.

The Vedic hymns consist chiefly of simple stanzas, that is of such as are formed of verses which are all metrically identical. Different stanzas are formed by combining 3, 4, 5, or 6 identical verses.

1. Verse of 8 syllables. This is a dimeter verse consisting of two equal members of 4 syllables each, the opening and the cadence. In the opening the first and third syllable are idifferent, while the second and fourth are preferably long. When the second is short, the third is almost invariably long. In the cadence the rhythm is typically iambic, the first and third syllables being almost always short, while the second is usually long. Thus the prevailing scheme of the whole verse is:—U - - U - I UU - U - -

a. The गायत्री stanza consists of 3 octosyllabic verses:—

यच्चिद्धि ते विशो यथा	- - U - I U - U - I
प्र देव वरुण व्रतम्।	U - UU I U - U - II
मिनीमसि द्यविद्यवि।। १। १	U - U - I U - U - II

A comparatively rare but definite type shows a decided trochaic rhythm in the cadence ,while the iambic rhythm of the opening is more pronounced than usual.

यग्नं देवासो मदन्ति।।२४। ७। U - - - I - U - U

Only hymns 1 and 13 are written in गायत्रीs.

b. The अनुष्टुभ् stanza, the forerunner of the epic and classical श्लोक stanza consists of 4 octosyllabic verses, divided into 2 hemistiches:—

वयश्चित्ते पतत्रिणो	U - - - I U - U - I
द्विपच्चतुष्पदर्जुनि।	U - U - I U - UU II
उषः प्रारन्नृतूरनु	U - - - I U - UU I
दिवो अन्तेभ्यस्परि।।४।३।	UU - - I U - UU II

2. Verses of 11 syllables differ from those of 8 in consisting of 3 members, the opening, the break, and the cadence. They also contrast with the latter in two other respects: their cadence is trochaic, and they have a caesura which follows either the fourth or the fifth syllable. The rhythm of the syllables preceding the caesura is prevailingly iambic, being or. The rhythm of the break between the caesura and the cadence is regularly or. Thus the structure of the whole regular त्रिष्टुभ् is as follows:—

   प्र वृक्षणा अभिनृत्पर्वतानाम् । २।१। U - U -, UU - I - U - - I

   अञ्जः समुद्रमवं जग्मुरापः।२।२। - - U - U, U U I - U - - I

   The त्रिष्टुभ् stanza, the commonest in the Ṛ.V. and in our selection, consists of 4 verses of 11 syllables divided into 2 hemistiches. Hymns 2, 5, 6, 8, 9, 11, 15, 18-23, 26, 27 are written in त्रिष्टुभ् stanzas.

3. The verse of 12 syllables is probably an extension of the त्रिष्टुभ् verse by one syllable which given the trochaic cadence of the latter an iambic character. The rhythm of the last 5 syllables is therefore:—

   The added syllable being the only point of difference, the scheme of whole verse is:—

   तस्मै वृष्टिर्मधुमत्पिन्वते दिवः।

   ऋतस्य गोपावधि तिष्टतो रथम् ।

   The जगती stanza is the third in order of frequency in the Ṛ.V.; in this selection only hymn 16 is written in it. The stanza consists of 4 verses of 12 syllables divided into 2 hemistichs.

   The त्रिष्टुभ् has been developed into the classical इन्द्रवज्रा and the उपेन्द्रवज्रा ।। etc. ; the जगती verse into the वशंस्थ and the इन्द्रंवंशा etc.

II. Mixed stanzas.

The only different verses normally used in combination to form stanza are the गायत्री and the जगती. The mixed stanzas occurring in this selection are the बृहती, 10,3, consisting of 3 गायत्रीs and 1 जगती :—8, 8, 12, 8—36 syllables in all, the सतोबृहती in Nr.3, consisting of 2 जगतीs :— 12, 8, 12, 8—40 syllables in all. Both stanzas are divided into 2 hemistichs.

In hymn 24 there is the (rather rare) combination of a जगती and a गायत्री verse to be found, forming distichs of 12+8. See Oldenberg, Prolegomena, p. 100 f.

III. Straphic Stanzas.

Two or three stanzas are sometimes found strophically combined, forming couplets or triplets.

Three simple stanzas in the same metre are thus connected in गायत्री triplets, called तृचs, in hymns 1.14.

In the present selection the only mixed stanza in different metres is the बार्हतप्रगाथ, in Nr. 3, being a couplet formed by the combination of a बृहती with a सतोबृहती stanza:—8, 8; 12, 8 +12, 8; 12, 8 (76) syllables.

Stanzas in a different metre are added to hymns or sections of hymns as conclusions, without forming strophes with the preceding stanzas. Thus there are in

No.	7:	stanza	1-14	जगती;	stanza	15	त्रिष्टुभ्.
		"	16-18	"	"	19	"
"	10:	"	1-8	बृहती;	"	9	त्रिष्टुभ्.
"	12:	"	1-12	त्रिष्टुभ्;	"	13	अनुष्टुभ्-
"	14:	"	1-7	गायत्री;	"	8	अनुष्टभ्.
"	9:	"	9-23	"	"	24	"

Note that the गायत्री is not used as a conclusion, a त्रिष्टुभ्

stanza at the end of a जगती hymn being the most common.

APPENDIX IV

VEDIC MYTHOLOGY

A. GENERAL CHARACTERISTICS.

The Ṛ̣V. is important both as a monument of the Indo-Germanic mythology and as a document for the history of language. In both respects the Veda, the Ṛ̣V. especially, is rivalled only by Greek mythology and language. The relics of all the other branches of the Indo-Germanic family are, if not scanty and comparatively late, at least not so complete as the Vedic ones. And though other mythologies may show changes and evolutions, these developments, after all, do not affect the whole pantheon. But it is just the change of individual gods in fall and rise and the evolution of the whole Vedic pantheon that makes this mythology so important. There are not only vital changes to be observed within the mythology itself, but the reader can perceive how the basis of the whole ancient Indian religion gets shifted. The Ṛ̣V. is thus destined to form the link between the Indo-Aryan, or at least Indo-Iranian, religious beliefs and the later specifically Indian phases of religious forms. For, mythology in all its bearings betrays the nature of the religious convictions and practices of a people to a very great extent.

In the Ṛ̣V. gods arise, as it were, under our eyes; we may watch the Vedic theologian-poet how he सं कर्मारं इव (देवान्) अधमत्, 25.2. The general line of literary and mythological evolution is the following :—first, the phenomenon of nature (physical or mental), then the personification of the phenomenon, then (in some cases)separation or abstract conception of some prominent quality, and possibly again personification of that. Of many hymns whose देवता is said to be Uṣas, Sūrya, Pṛthivī, etc., the subject -matter is primarily or even exclusively not that. देवता, but the physical phenomenon, manifesting a superhuman and, in most cases, kindly power. The power supposed to be behind the natural force—an idea which, in a modified form, is found in as late a work as Śaṅkarācārya's Bhāṣya on the Bādarāyaṇasūtrāṇi (I. 2. 18-20)—gradually became personified whereupon both the natural phenomenon and the personification became the subject of an apotheosis; and it is thus that there arose such concrete fitures as Súrya, Agni, Uṣas. Their personality and office are described in so graphic a manner as if the ṛṣi had been an old personal friend of theirs. Not all the figures of the Vedic pantheon are so perspicous in their origin. In fact, the two greatest gods of Vedic India. Indra and Varuna, have served their connection with the underlying fact of nature to such an extent that they have to allow scholars to quarrel about their original meaning.

Prajāpati and other later conceptions excepted, the greatest majority of the Vedic gods trace their genealogy back to some element or event in nature in the wider sense. If the name of the deity remained the same as that of the natural phenomenon, the personification has not become so pronounced; the two co-exit in the mind of the poet and find, as is the case with Uṣas, expression in turns. If on the other hand the name no more signifies the real or the main natural basis, the personification becomes clearer. This personification chiefly led to anthropomorphism of the nature and the office of the gods: they have body and soul as men have, only of greater dimension and, perhaps, a better kind. The Vedic gods and goddesses are deified men and women, quite human, sometimes too human. The personification rarely justly admired in Greek mythology. It is true, Vedic mythology has no Kālī with her horrors—though Rudra is terrible enough—yet a mere comparison between Indra and Ares, the Indian and the Greek war-gods, would bring out the difference which is characteristic of both mythologies. Prajāpati may be mentioned as an example of a deity that was first an abstraction, merely the lord of certain number or class of things, but the abstraction, through the connection with some cosmic act or a prominent natural power, later took up a concrete form. Savitṛ is an instance of the separation which led to the conception of an independent deity.

The want of a real, consistent working out of the gods' figures and offices is responsible for a certain amount of democracy among the Vedic deities. The term pantheon, implying hierarchy of celestial beings with something like a fixed constitution of their own, cannot be applied in the strict sense to the assembly of the gods known from the Veda. For that too many figures are overlapping, and too many offices are held in common by two or more deities. The undeniable communism among the Vedic gods has led M.Muller, it seems, to propound his theory of Henotheism or Kathenotheism, "the belief in individual gods alternately regarded as the highest." But, strictly speaking, this very comunism contains an objection to, as well as a reason for, Henotheism. The theory has an element of truth in its favour, but is not acceptable in its full bearing. There is indeed a certain undercurrent noticeable in Vedic polytheism which considers all the various figures of the pantheon as manifestations of the one supreme principle. This tendency is most clearly expressed in the conception of the Ṛta, from which some deities are said to originate, in which many participate, and according to which nearly all work. This undercurrent is the first phase of the evolution of Vedic beliefs into the pantheistic monotheism, fairly well outline in the tenth maṇḍala and boldly expressed in the latest parts of the Śruti.

It is, however, not safe to say that "Vedic deities are represented (in the ṚV. Saṁhitā) as independent of the rest". On the contrary, the Vedic mythology is remarkable for the interdependence of the individual gods, Indra and Varuṇa not excepted. It may even happen that an abstract conception like that of Savitṛ is said to rule over Indra, (Nr. 9. 9.), who in his turn lords it over Sūrya, I. 101. 3, the concrete basis of Savitṛ. Such and other mutual relationships make the suzerainty of one even for a time impossible. Moreover, there is a group of deities, the Viśve Devāḥ, constituted with the set purpose to praise the minor gods and put them side by side with the bigger ones: a levelling process more favourable to equality among the celestials than to the raising of one even for a short period to the supremacy over the rest. Cp. Nr. 24. May be that this or that deity was held in higher esteem by one ṛṣi or even śākhā than the other, but that does not amount to a generally recognised and practised henotheism. The upper class among the gods very likely always found worshippers enough who could and would keep their favourite deities in the dominatinposition they had inherited. A levelling of the whole mythological assembly by making Indra and other "overlords" climb down in turn could hardly have served the interests of these worshippers. The ṛṣis and theologians were in all likelihood acquainted well enough with the respective position of each god in the ṚV. Saṁhitā, and their laudations, including the accession to a throne which never existed, need not be taken too seriously. These bombastic praises sometimes defeat their own purpose: in II. 1.3-4 Agni is *honoris causa* identified with no less than six deities, among whom there are Indra and Varuṇa. The rise of Agni to the role attributed to him there would mean the fall of Indra and Varuṇa themselves. The frequent bringing together of two deities in dvandva compound and the forming of groups of more than two is also against the raising of one of these above the rest. Besides the professional zeal of the ṛṣi for the god who happens to be the subject matter of his composition, the indefinite shape and office of many Vedic gods as well as the absence of one recognized head, are responsible for the possible, though not real, usurpation of the supremacy. Zeus and Jupiter, in spite of occasional domestic troubles and palace revolutions, were masters of their celestials; Indra or any other Vedic god never attempted to be so. Henotheism or Kathenotheism is out of the question for the simple reason that ancient India did not possess a pantheon in the strict sense of the word with a head acknowledge by all the gods.

Of the proposed classifications of the Vedic deities each is labouring under some defect or other. The traditional division of the gods according to their place (Yāska, Nir. 7.5, following ṚV. I 139 II) into the पृथिवीस्थानाः, terrestrial, the अन्तरिक्षस्थानाः or मध्यमस्थानाः, aerial or intermediate, and the द्युस्थानाः, celestial deities, suppose that the origin, nature and activity of each deity has been fully ascertained. That, however, is not the case; for it is true to an unpleasant extent that "nothing in all mythology is more difficult than the attempt to get a clear view of the gods of Vedic India". An historical division into IndO- European, Iranian and Indian deities would require complete information about the date of every god from the Indo-European down to the Indian period.

But the dates, such as are available, leave doubts about the period of many gods, and in too many cases the information is decidedly defective, especially as far as the Germanic, Slavonic and Celtic mythologies are concerned. The division (proposed by Bloomfield, Religion of the Veda, p. 96) into prehistoric, transparent, translucent, opaque, and abstract or symbolic gods rests on the historical and the exegetical principle, and is likely to suffer from the faults of both these principles. It is not certain which gods have to be relegated to the prehistoric period; and a god may be transparent, translucent or opaque, just as the interpretations offered are accepted or rejected. One or the other etymological explanation proposed by Bloomfield is of a somewhat acrobatic nature, anyhow. After all, it seems best to revert to Yāska's classification. The order of the द्युस्थान gods contains Dyaus, Varuṇa, Mitra, Súrya, Savitṛ,Puṣan, the Asvinā, and the goddesses Uṣas and Rātrī. The अन्तरिक्षस्थान class is made up of Indra, Apāṁ Napāt, Rudra, the Maruts, Vāyu, Parjanya, and Āpas. The पृथिवीस्थान category is represented by Pṛthivī, Agni, and Soma.

B. INDIVIDUAL DEITIES.

VARUṆA.

Both the figure of Varuṇa and his office in the ṚV. are of incommon interest and importance. Though he has all the insignia of high rank in the Vedic pantheon, yet only a comparatively small number of hymns—about ten in all—in the whole ṚV. Saṁhitā are addressed to him. Three out of these, Nrs. 1, 8, 22, are contained in this Selection; two more, Nrs. 16 and 19, being addressed to Mitrā-Varuṇā. The reasons for this small number of Varuṇa hymns in the ṚV. are not far to seek. First, Varuṇa does not represent in an unmistakable manner some magnificent phenomenon of nature, like Uṣas. In fact, it has not been settlled to this day what event, element or force in nature Varuṇa is representing. Second, Varuṇa is intimately connected with man's confession of sin and repentance, a process in the individual that naturally will not claim so much public attention or even individual occupation as, say, Agni's activities or Indra's great, though legendary, deeds. The statement may be generally true or not that the Indogermanic people in their earlier history do not show the same attention to moral and ethics, both practical and theoretical, as say, Agni's activities or Indra's great, legendary, deeds. The statement may be generally true or not that the Indogermanic people in their earlier history do not show the same attention to moral and ethics, both practical and theoretical, as the Semitic nations do. The presumption, anyhow, will be that the Āryas in their literal struggle for life more earnestly and more frequently did turn to buoyant Indra for victory than to the solemn, less noisy Varuṇa, whose rule and rod, in spite of the threat of the ṛṣis, many a clever sinner, at least seemingly, escaped.

But nobody will deny that the few Varuṇa hymns are full of some of the truest and deepest ethical feelings. There is hardly a ṛc, certainly not a whole sūkta, which does not keep the general idea of Varuṇa's character and of man's responsibility to him and to Ṛta view. Some of the verses rank along with the sublimest a repentant heart has felt and poured out in human language. It may be said that the repentance expressed in Varuṇa hymns is servile, proceeding mainly, if not alone, from the fear of punishment. This cannot be denied and centuries had to be added to the life and evolution of the Indian peoples till भक्ति could, at least in part, take the placc of servile fear. But nobody with the evidence of the Varuṇa hymns before him can gainsay that the indelible distinction between right and wrong is testified to hear. The common convictions that wrong has to be repented of, and atoned for, and that punishment will overtake the evil-doer one way or the other, have not often found a more graphic expression in literarure. Again, the repentance of the Vedic sinner was not without some element of piety and filial sentiment towards the offended diety. For, the offender whistfully recalls the time when he was on a friendly footing with his god. Cp. 1.17. Just in these hymns a delightful naïveté peeps through the solemn language which is as direct as that in the song of the bankrupt and repentant dice player, X.34. Taken all in all, the Varuṇa hymns rank with the best religious poetry Indo-Germanic antiquity has produced; for the history of ethics they are most valuable monuments of the Vedic age.

In the Varuṇa hymns of this Selection the figure of the god is fairly well delineated. He is the Man *par excellence*, 1, 5; he is clad in a shining armour, 1. 13, which suggests the earnestness and power of the revenging god. Self-existence and strength are especially attributed to him, 22.4, etc.; 8.8. He, being styled क्ष॒त्रश्रि॑यम्, 1.5, is the glory of the principle of authority and rule, and of the persons that wield these powers. Varuṇa is well qualified for a ruler, for he is addressed as मेधिर, 1.20, praised as क॒वि, 8.1, even क॒वित॑र, 22.7. Varuṇa is an absolute sovereign, स्व॒राज् 8.1; the concrete and abstract attribute of overlord, स॒म्राज्, साम्रा॑ज्य, is often given to him. Naturally he becomes a प्र॒णे॒तृ, 8.3; his sway does not only reach far and wide, ep. उ॒रु॒शंस॑, 8.3, but he governs even in minor matters, न॒हि त्वदा॒रे नि॒मिष॑श्च॒नेशे॑, 8.6. As he is far-seeing उ॒रु॒चक्षस्, 1.5, and omniscient, 1.7, 8, 9, 11, it is quite natural that it becomes hard, if not impossible, to deceive him, 8.8; 22.4. Even those who might usually get the better of men and even gods shrink from the attempt to cheat Varuṇa,

1.14. The more so as the god's vigilance is concretely his स्पशः, posted over the whole extent of Varuṇa's jurisdiction, cp. 1.13. The feeling of confidence prompts the poet to pray that he and his clients may be सुभगासः, 8.2, in Varuṇa's, the पुरुवीर's, shelter, 8.3. and law. In 8.10 the singer asks for help against false friends and true foes.

It may be hard to decide whether in the ṚV. Varuṇa or Ṛta is superior in power; for the connection between Varuṇa and Ṛta is undoubtedly a very intimate one. Varuṇa is ऋतावन्, 8.6; the unchangeable व्रतानि are founded on him as on a rock, 8. 8. The singer means to pay a compliment to Varuṇa himself when he asks:—ऋध्याम ते वरुण खामृतस्य, 8.5. The conception and name of Ṛta, Avestan *Asha,* coneiform (old) Persian *Arta,* appear as early as 1600 B.C in Iranian royal names. At the middle of the second millennium B.C., then this term must have been a familiar one and embodied an ideal of kingship. The Ṛta in the ṚV. signifies the cosmic as well as the ritual order and the norm for the conduct of man. It is therefore, but natural that a personality so closely connected with Ṛta, the order, the Right, should become the guardian of the moral law and the revenger of its infringements. It is true that Varuṇa associated with Ṛta is also the upholder of the cosmic and physical order 1.20;22.1, the विधर्ता, 8. 4, and that the forces of nature are said to work according to this Ṛta, 8. 4; yet Varuṇa's characteristic activity is, above all, the guardianship of the moral world. Hence the attitude of the sinner towards Varuṇa:—he makes a straightforward confession of the wicked deed and shows an earnest will to get out of the clear debt by resorting to all means in his power, such as invocation, sacrifice, even by asking spiritual advice from the "wise". There is really very little pharisaic pride in the sinner who compares himself with a calf, tied by the crime like a rope, 22.5. Only here and there the attempt is made to shift the personal responsibility on to bad habits or outside influence, 22.6. Also vicarious responsibility and atonement is expressed in 22.5. But whoever may finally be in fault, the repentant sinner is prepared to serve Varuṇa as a slave, 22.7. There was some palpable reason for being afraid of Varuṇa's anger; for, the usual punishment inflicted by him was dropsy, naturally enough resorted to by Varuṇa, the स॒मु॒द्रियः॑ 1.7. Considering the terrible effects of this disease the sinner was certainly right earnest when prayed to the god not to cut the thread of the weaver and not to put an untimely end to his work, 8.5.

In Indra the elemental powers of physical nature are embodied, in Agni the cult of the Vedic age has been represented, in Ārya have been revealed.

ADITI and the ĀDITYAS

Opinions are divided on the meaning of Aditi. One view interprets Aditi, according to the etymology of the word, as freedom from (moral) fetters, from limits—bondlessness and boundlessness—liberty, infinity, the infinite in general. Another view takes Aditi to mean the indestructible, celestial light. To judge from data given by Vedic literature, the latter view seems to be more probable. Aditi is called ज्योति॑ष्मति, Uṣas is अदि॑ते॒रनी॑कम्, Aditi resides in the प॒र॒मे व्यो॑मन्. If Aditi were simply infinity all the gods would fittingly have been her offspring; but, as a matter of fact, only a certain, comparatively small group are called her sons. Now all these sons, as far as they are concrete figures and not mere personifications of abstract ideas, are gods connected with light. Āditya in later times is simply the sun-god. None of the wind or storm-gods are in Aditi's family. The Ādityas are several times called अदितेः पुत्राः, 8. 3, analogous to Agni's being the सहसः पुत्र, and Indra's the शवसः पुत्र. In the case of Aditi this may have led to considering the feminine Aditi as the mother of the Ādityas; and the personification was resorted to here, though it did not take place in the case of सहस् and शवस्. A complete analogy to the formation of Aditī may be found in that of Śacī, the wife of Indra. The genesis of Śacī started from शचीपति, lord of strength, an epithet of Indra. Cp. Macdonell, Ved. Myth. p. 122.

The Ādityas, in any case, have to be considered as a group of gods by themselves. They represent the calm majesty of divine rule, not the bold, smashing manner Indra stands for. It is even possible that in the circle of gods headed by Varuṇa, and in that led by Indra, the traces of two civilisations, meeting on Indian soil, are expressed. Vedic mythology would thus confirm the results arrived at by linguistic facts from modern Indian languages. The number of the Ādityas is not fixed: 5, 7, 8, in the Brāhmaṇas even 12, are given. Nowhere does the ṚV. enumerate the seven names; six are given in II. 27. 1. They are:—Mitra, Aryaman, Bhaga, Varuṇa, Dakṣa , Aṁśa. It may be taken as certain that some of the Ādityas are older than Aditi, their mother. Varuṇa, Mitra, Aryaman are inherited from the Indo-Iranian period, either with or without metamorphosis. Aditi, on the other hand, appears clearly as a personified abstract idea, brought into parental relation with these three and the other Ādityas. Some of the Ādityas, however, may be younger than Aditi. Dakṣa, mentioned in 25.4, 5, is nothing but the deified (intellectual) Skill or Dexterity. He there appears as the son and father of Aditi, who thus becomes the mother and the eldest sister of the Ādityas. Aryaman, 9. 9; 14. 24, is rather often mentioned in the ṚV., but he is practically without personal traits. The appellation अर्यमन् frequently means comrade, groomsman. Aryaman as god seems to signify almost the same as Mitra, at least as far as his relation to man is concerned. Bhaga, I.c., repeatedly used as an attribute of other deities, is equivalent to Dispensing. Bhaga, the Āditya, Āditya, means both the Dispenser (of wealth) and Bounty, Fortune. The same word, in Slavonic languages Bogū, has come to signify देव, god. In 25. 8 Mārtāṇḍa is mentioned as eighth Āditya. The sons with whom Aditi there approaches the gods may be the traditional seven Ādityas; the eighth, whom she casts away and takes up again, has with good reason been said to be the son-god, more accurately, the evening sun-god.

Except Varuṇa, Mitra is the most important Āditya. Through the close union with Varuṇa, indicated by the frequent dvandva compound मित्रावरुणा, Mitra has lost so many of his personal features that his concrete figure can hardly be constructed. In 16. 1 Varuṇa and Mitra are addressed together as ऋतस्य गोपा, सत्यधर्मणा, they are सम्राजा स्वर्दृशा, 16.2; उग्रा, 16.3; विपश्चिता, 16.7; अमूरा, 19. 5. Mitra has been compensated for the loss of individuality by participating in Varuṇa's activities and attributes. Mitrā-Varuṇā in our hymns appear in natural co-operation with the Maruts and Parjanya, 16. 4, 6; 5. The two deities have, among other things, माया in common. Māyā has wrongly been interpreted as divine trickery, more cunning than the human one and thereby able to entrap the sinner. On Māyā see Notes, p. 223. In 19.1 the sun is also called the common eye of Mitra and Varuṇa. There, then, the union amounts to identification in one person. Generally, however, Varuṇa and Mitra thoughout the Veda are felt as being in some contast to each other. This contrast is mostly explained as that between the sun or the day on the part of Mitra and the moon or the night on the side of

Varuṇa. This interpretation would explain the fact that in India as well as in Iran Mitra is the god of guardian of the oath and of contracts; he figures as the god of truthfulness and fidelity, a declared enemy of double-dealing in every form. It might, together with Varuṇa's office, give a clue to the question why the majesty of Varuṇa appears somewhat sombre, at any rate solemn.

Even Varuṇa, in spite of his high rank in the ṚV., is a falling god, Mitra indeed playing in India a far less important part than in Iran and the Avesta. A prehistoric deity in Iran, raised in many parts of Western Asia to supreme rank by Mithraism, Mitra is hardly more than a shadow of Varuṇa in the ṚV. Only one hymn, and that not a very personal one, III. 59, is addressed to him alone.

Mitrā-Varuṇā have been identified with the Iranian *Ahura-Mithra;* Varuṇa has been taken to be the equivalent of *Ahuramazda* in the Avesta. The first equation is acceptable; the second is true only in a qualified sense. Varuṇa was the Indian successor, but not the direct lineal descendent of the Indo-European *Dyaus pitar or Dyaus asura.* Ahuramazda in the Avesta is a creation of Zarathustra's reform. The same Ahura that rose in (East) Iran so as to become the highest deity ceded his position and power in the ṚV. to Varuṇa. The phrase असुरस्य माया seems to reflect this evolution. The view that the Avestan *Amesha spentas* are a mythological parallel to the Ādityas is not tenable.

The theory advanced by Oldenberg that Varuṇa and the other Ādityas had been taken over from a Semitic people, the Babylonias (or Accadians ?) rightly has not been accepted. The suppositions of it are as unsafe as the arguments unconvincing. It seems, besides, very unlikely that the greatest, if not the only, ethical deity the Vedic mythology possesses should have been imported from outside. The subsequent history of the religion and philosophy of India does not show the people so devoid of moral conceptions that the Vedic times, in which ethical convictions were at least as alive as in later periods, should have gone a-begging for some concrete form of their ideas. It is strange, however, that Varuṇa is not surrounded by any myths. An indigenous Indian growth would explain this want quite sufficiently, as Zarathustra's figure too is not encumbered by any mothologi-cal tradition.

On the original nature and position of Varuṇa a good many views have been put forward. Considering that Varuṇa in later times is a water-god, he has been said to have been a god of the sea, whose power waned in direct proportion to the distance the migrating Āryas put between themselves and the ocean. This view interprets the Veda and its times too exclusively by the following ages. Another theory brings Varuṇa in connection with वर्ण, which, on the analogy of the old Slavonic *vranu*, is said to mean the black, dark colour. This opinion seems to contain an element of, though not the whole, truth. It is very probable that the name of Varuṇa is derived from the root वृ, to cover, encompass, Varuṇa thus being the "encompasser". The greatest encompasser is the sky, द्यौः, whose aspect must have made a great impression on a people living mostly in the open. And just as the dawn caught the imagination of the Āryas by its beauty and regularity, so must the sky, especially the starry sky, have attracted their attention. The sky at night being rules, as it were, by the moon, it was but natural that that luminary should gradually have become the main basis of Varuṇa. Thus the contrast between Mitra and Varuṇa is explained;

Varuṇa's superior rank in the ṚV. is originally founded on the all-encompassing sky, enveloping even the sun, the physical basis of Mitra. This conception offers a fitting explanation of most of the Vedic data. A few others, such as Varuṇa's riding on a car, either singly, 1.18, or jointly with Mitra, or the sun being the eye of Mitra and Varuṇa are found in a special connection, as in 19.1. or Varuṇa considered as dissociated from the natural basis, is simply put as deity side by side with the sun-god.

The question whether Varuṇa is etymologically the same as the Greek ΟΥΡΑΝΟΣ is old and new at the sasme time, as it is not decided up to now, Authorities of the first rank on linguistics have accepted the equations :

uoru-ṇnos-or Uoruenos = ΟΥΡΑΝΟΣ

uoru-nos = वरुण.

Yet the consent is not universal among scholars. Every body will, however, be prepared to admit that Varuṇa and ΟΥΡΑΝΟΣ are at least two parallel formations of *var* and *varu* respectively, though they may not be phonetically identical. Varuṇa may have been an attribuite of द्यौः. In Greek mythology द्यौः, the appellative, become ΖΕΥΣ, "the dweller in the serene hights of heaven", the supreme ruler and thunderer. In India the attribute developed into Varuṇa with his universal physical and moral jurisdiction.

SAVITṚ

Only one sūkta, Nr.9 (II.38), in this Selection is a Savitṛ hymn. As it describes Savitṛ's activity at sunset alone, it does not give a complete idea of the god and his work, and a fuller treatment based upon the data of the whole ṚV. Saṁhitā, is required.

Savitṛ is so closely related to Sūrya that they are often treated as one and the same divine personality. In the mantras of the same sūkta, sometimes even in the selfsame ṛc., the sun-god is called now Sūrya, now Savitṛ, see IV. 14. 2; X. 158. 1-4; etc. In such cases the wording and context may possibly enable the reader to find out which is meant. Generally, though, Savitṛ stands out as the moving, impelling, enlivening, god. The etymology of Savitṛ, clearly leading to the root सू 6., gives a correct and exhaustive notion of the deity.

With golden arms or hands – the rays of the sun – Savitṛ rises in the skies, setting in motion every creature. In the same way he sets everything at rest, letting the night come on, II 38. Savitṛ thus manifests himself as the lord of the day and the night as well. As lord of the night he is asked to keep away evil dreams. To represent Savitṛ as it lord of the night, and working after Sūrya's setting, seems indeed inconsistent with his unquestionably essential character as a sun-god. But the power so overwhelmingly shown during the day is supposed not to be exhausted even during the darkness. As Uṣas is the glory both of the rising and the setting sun, so is Savitṛ the impelling power of the sun at work and at rest, in sight and out of it.

Savtṛ ascends his road on the firmament on a golden car, drawn by a couple of golden steeds, for golden are nearly all the things connected with Savitṛ. His activity is not restricted to the physical world; for he disples misfortune and oppression as well as darkness. He chases away the demons, giving comfort, contentment and happiness to body and soul of man. Even a moral trait is to be discerned in Savitṛ, nature and doing— he appears as a purifier from sin. This however, seems to be a later attribute, possible borrowed from Varuṇa, but more likely a result of the poet's reasoning that health and happiness all round are incompatibly with sin. Savitṛ's care for the struggling mortals on earth extends to their welfare in the other world. He leads them after death to the abode of bliss. Even the gods owe him as much as their immortality.

In some respects the personification has gone further in the case of Savitṛ than in that of Sūrya. For, there are traits of an individual personality in Savitṛ which cannot be explained on the ground of the basic natural phenomenon. Sūrya merely the sun-god, representing the is luminary, and being himself the sun; in Vedic poetry he lives as a shining, glorious youth, a hero driving in a chariot. Savitṛ, on the other hand, is a divine power, guiding the sun and embodying its impelling force. As both are physically identical, Savitṛ and Sūrya are time and again identified in mythology. There, however, the development of Savitṛ's personality did not stop. He came to stand for the impelling power, physical, intellectual and moral in the universe. This seems to be the reason for the extraordinarily prominent position Savitṛ occupies in the practical life of the orthodox Hindu, whose days are regulated by ideas and rules ultimately and in the main emanating from the Śruti. For there is no deity of the Vedic age that has been so long, so often, and so universally called upon in a prayer as Savitṛ has been in the Sāvitṛī (III. 62. 10) :—

तत्सवितुर्वरेण्यं भर्गो देवस्य धीमहि।
धियो यो नः प्रचोदयात्।।

This Gāyatrī is another testimony for the real object of worship of him who calls upon the deity for light and help.

There are no parallels to the name of Savitṛ in other Indo-Germanic mythologies. The god Janus seems to have occupied a somewhat similar position in Roman mythology, holding an office very much like that of Savitṛ in India. There seems to be, however, at least one Indo-Germanic trait common to the deities representing the sun or being themselves the sun, a trait which is the more surprising as it is only of secondary importance. ṚV. V . 82.9. speaks of Savitṛ's song or sound :—

य इमा विश्वा जातान्याश्रावयति श्लोकेन।
प्र च सुवाति सविता ॥

Heavenly Scholars, with the exception of one, seem to be agreed that the line of evolution of Savitṛ's figure started from the material, astronomical body of the sun. Sūrya, in later Vedic times invariably the sun, "signifies the sunbody , Savitṛ the divine power behind it", cp. I. 35. 9; 1. 124. 1. The प्रसव is the characteristic of Savitṛ, just as the rule over the waters is that of Varuṇa. An abstract force then, has been split off from the concrete physical body; a force, which however in its turn became itself personified. But it remained all along so closely united with the sun itself that Savitṛ is undoubtedly a sun-god throughout. The view that Savitṛ is merely the name for an abstrct "Impeller", an impelling power—has not been accepted.

AŚVINĀ

There are not less than 50 entire Aśvin hymns in the ṚV. Saṁhitā; in others, besides, the Aśvinā are invoked or celebrated. The Aśvinā thus come after Indra, Agni, and Soma, as far as the number of hymns is concerned. Their importance, however, for the common man in his practical life, and consequently their popularity, very likely has been even greater than that of Soma. The number of attributes and names given to them suggests that they were by no means figures petrified by the ritual and stylistic conventions. The Aśvinā are नरा, 5. 7, 11, 12, etc. निचेतारा, 6. 2 ; रुद्रा, 17. 8; मयोभुवा, मृळयत्तमा, 17. 9 ; अरेपसा 17. 4 ; सुदानू, 6. 4; मघवाना,

6, 5 ; एष्टा, 6. 2. Significant for their origin is the epithet दिवो नपाता, 6. 1. The epithet नासत्या, 5. 1' 4, etc., commonly interpreted as the Not-untrue Ones, has become a proper noun. Their strength and irresistibility is emphasized in epithets like तुविष्टमा and अधिगू, 17. 2. In 17.4 they are said to be नाना जातौ, which in the context there expresses their non-human origin and nature, rather than their duality. Their place seems to be anywhere and nowhere exclusively: they are far and near, flying through the middle-space, 17. 1, or working on the ocean, 5. 3, 5. In 6.1 the poet calls on them, कुह चित्सन्तौ. The time of their appearance is said by the old Vedic interpreters to be from midnight to the complete victory of the sunlight over darkness; more accurately, they appear after the darkness-dispelling Agni and Uṣas, but before the sun in its full glory, cp. 6. 6. So the ritual and the Ṛk text itself, on the whole suggest. As far as the Aśvinā depend on victuals at all, their favourite food is honey, see 17. 8. They are माध्वी, 6. 4; 20. 2, and मधुयुवा, 17. 8. The predilection of the Aśvinā for honey has led to attributing them even a goad of honey The मधु, constantly mentioned in connection with these morning-gods, has appropriately been interpreted as the dew in the early morn. The Aśvinā's car is स्यूमगभस्ति, 20. 3; त्रिवन्धुर, 20.4, characteristics which are calculated to enhance the दस्रता of the Aśvinā themselves. About half a dozen members of the animal kingdom in turns are said to be yoked to the car of the Aśvinā; they rank from birds and winged steeds to the humbler ass. For the maritime exploits of the Aśvinā a marvellous craft is ready, 5. 3, 5. The regularity of the gods' appearance is expressed by the adjective ऋतयुज्, 20. 3, given to their horses.

Beyond the partaking of the soma together with Sūrya

(and Uṣas), the relation of the Aśvinā to the other male gods is not one of alliance or great intimacy. Once, 5. 21, in the four Aśvin hymns of this Selection —Nrs. 5, 6, 17, 20—they are called इन्द्रवन्ता. But their friendship with Sūryā, whose attention they seem to have attracted during races, was cemented by not less than a marital union between them and the Sun-Maiden or Daughter of the sun. The relation thus created is crossed by another marriage transaction between the Sun-Maiden and the Moon, the Aśvinā contenting themselves this time with being the groomsmen. The close relation between the Aṣvinā and Sūryā, however, seems to have formed the main legendary strain. In the short selection of riddles, anyhow, in Nr. 24, where the special mark of each deity is given, the riding of the Aśvinā in the company of Sūryā is mentioned as their peculiar characteristic.

The Aśvinā's attitude towards man is that of helping friends; it is even said of them समस्मे बन्धुमेयथुः, 17. 4. Their kind, saving benevolence is, in fact, the most prominent feature of the twin-gods. Their help is less assistance in the turmoil of battle and the dangers of conquest than the healing power, mending the damage inflicted by the struggle of life, by hostile, preternatural powers and, especially, the ill-will of man, one's own relations not excepted. They are the भिषजा among gods , 5. 16. The prayer for a happy old age, 5. 25, shows how individual life was put under their protection. The part the Aśvinā play in the celebration of marriage is illustrated already in the ṚV. (X. 15), where they are asked "to conduct the bride hom on their car, and they (with other gods) are besought to bestow fertility on her".

The wonderful and benevolent deeds ascribed to the Aśvinā are almost completely enumerated in the hymns of this Selection. It may be that one or more of them have their

Indo-Germanic parallels; on the whole these exploits seem to be of Indian origin. The cluster of kindly acts, attributed to these twin-deites, has in the fertile imagination of Vedic Aśvinā worshippers become a jungle growth, which it is impossible to penetrate, and the mythological roots of each of which it is equally impossible to lay bare. Even the fact of nature, underlying the Aśvinā, is not settled with absolute certainty. Already Yāska was at a loss to say what the Aśvinā represented. Besides the fact that he classes them among the द्युस्थाना देवता:, Yāska's own meaning on the point (Nir. XII.1) cannot be said to be clear. Roth, i. 1., thinks Yāska means Indra and the sun, others "that he means the transition from darkness to light, which represents an inseparable duality corresponding to their (the Aśvinā's) twin nature ". In Nir., 1.c., Yāska also states that some of his predecessors regarded the Aśvinā as heaven and earth (cp. Śatap. Br. IV 1,5,16), that others saw in them day and night, others again sun and moon, and that the Aitihāsikas looked on them as two kings, performers of holy deeds. Nearly everyone of these ancient views has been adopted by some modern scholar or other and refuted by the rest. Recent Veda exegesis has not advanced much beyond Yāska and his predecessors, except that the Aśvinā have been identified with the morning and evening star. Of late, views seem to converge to the morning star hypothesis, as it is perhaps best supported by the mythological data in the Ṛ̣V. and, especially, seems strengthened by comparative mythology.

For, a striking similarity exists between the Aśvinā and the Lettic god's sons. The parallel does not include the name Aśvinā itself, but its meaning "possessors of horses", "provided with horses" (not necessarily "riders"), expresses a characteristic also observed in the Lettic gods. The Aśvinā's title दिवो नपाता, however, is almost a translation of the Lettic

Dēwa *Deli* and the Lithuanian *Dēwo Sunelei*. moreover, the name of Sūryā, सूर्यस्य दुहिता, corresponds to the Lettic *Saules Meita,* and so does the Aśvinā's relation as husbands or groomsmen to Sūryā to that of the Lettic gods to Saules Meita. The succouring activity of the Aśvinā, their rescues from dangers of the sea in particular, find a parallel in the feats of the Lettic god's sons.

Another close Indo-Germanic parallel to the Aśvinā is offered by the twin sons of Zeus, the ΔΙΟΣΚΟΨΡΟΙ, a name which again in sense at least is identical with दिवो नपाता, the appellation of the Aśvinā. The Greek Dioscours, Latin *Casto* and *pollux*, are perhaps even more "horsy" than the Aśvinā. They too are helping and rescuing deities on sea as well as on land. In dire distress they appear as quick as thought, like the Aśvinā, whose car is मनोजव. The red-brown, tawny colour of the horses is common on both sides, when the Aśvinā rescue Bhujyu (ṚV. I. 117. 14), and the Dioscours save sailors from shipwreck. Some scholars have been bold enough to see in Helena, the sister of the Dioscours, a phonetic equivalent to सरण्यू, the mother of the Aśvinā. In the marriage of the Dioscours with *phoibe* and *Hilaira,* two goddesses of light, the point of the parallel with the Aśvinā seems twisted.

Of the Lettic god's sons and the Dioscours it can be said with certainty that they are gods of light. Moreover, the former are undoubtedly, the latter very probably, the morning and evening star. There is then a strong presumption for considering the Aśvinā as morning and evening star as well. There are, it is true, some difficulties against this interpretation of the Aśvinā (and their Indo-European brothers and cousins) which have to be met. First. the morning and evening star are not two, but one and the same. This is readily admitted as an astronomical fact, which however is of little force, as the identity was not recognised till the Aśvina had long grown out of their natural basis. A more serious difficulty arises out of the inseparable duality of the Aśvinā who appear, according to the Śruti, both in the morning ; the morning and evening star being just as invariably separated. Now Lettic songs suggest that the sun marries the morning star in the morning, espousing the evening star in the evening. Thus we arrive at the marriage of the one Sūryā with the two Aśvinā. The similarity between the two made them appear as a pair of twins, though naturally they remained नाना जाता, and could not coalesce into one personallty: As the morning star shone at that time which was almost exclusively reserved for the cult—for the evening was not acceptable to the gods—the evening star had to cede its time to the morning star, but kept its existence and character in the pair. Besides, the morning being, more than any other, the time of relief from distress, its morning star monopolised also the attention otherwise given to the evening star. Like the evening star so has the evening appearance of Uṣas been entirely lost sight of; and like the Aśvina so has Varuṇa, in the dvandva compound Mitrā-Varuṇā, been almost entirely severed from the natural phenomenon he represents.

That the Aśvinā are the mythological personification of the constellation of the Gemini must be rejected on astronomical grounds. That they do not stand for any natural phenomenon at all, but are succouring saints of purely Indian Origin does not, after the above exposition, require special refutation. But it may be that the Aśvinā as physicians, as deities brought in connection with the abominable सुरा, 5. 7, and as gods whose chariot was also drawn by the śūdra ass, were the mythological product of another ethnological and social stratum than that which honoured Indra.

UṢAS

From a poetical point of view Uṣas is the most important and attractive figure in Vedic literature. As lyrics the 20 hymns in which Uṣas is addressed rank high, and the fact that she is mentioned altogether about 300 times in the ṚV. shows that both as natural phenomenon and poetical fiction Uṣas was an object of attention and admiration on the part of the poets and the people alike. This fact is not to be overlooked when the question of the literary character and merit of the ṚV. is discussed.

There is one view which maintains that the Vedic hymns are in the main the product of the versifying art of the priests or such as would lay claim to that office and title. If that view be correct, poetry would be not more than a cloak to cover lean or even lifeless theological and mythological notions, and the practical means for bringing home speculations hatched out in sacerdotal circles and more or less directly connected with the vital question of the दक्षिणा. Besides, poetry would serve as a popular background for the often complicated and to the common man unintelligible ritual. For, rites and ceremonies had at early times become so numerous and intricate that they could not be justified on the universal and general ground of sacrificing to the deity. A reason for the embarassing details and technical *minutiæ* had to be furnished and, if possible, an explanation given that was based on the past. Myths and Itihāsas would serve this prupose quite well and they were propounded either as found in the floating mass of ancient tradition or dressed up according to need. This tendency, so conspicuous in the Brāhmaṇas, would then have had its roots already in the composition of the hymns themselves. Poetry in this opinion is the handmaid of sacrificial technique.

The Other view is that the Vedic hymns originally and mainly contain the outpourings of religious and poetical feelings, inspired by the personal need of body and soul as well as by the beauty and grandeur of the surrounding nature; a direct confession and prayer clad in poetical grab. Sometimes the religious, sometimes the poetical element would prevail; but both would be found free from a professional tedency. These inspirations and their utterance would, as a matter of course, generally be confined to families and circles in which tradition and talent made such feelings deeper and their expression more artistic: yet they were not the monopoly of a small caste, shutting themselves off from the rest of the people. The Uṣas hymns as a whole, at any rate, cannot be said to betray a primary tendency of serving a caste interest ; they are too full of the general human element for that. Nor can they be considered as sacrificial poetry in the same way as the Agni hymns. The lyrical element is too preponderating for such an assumption. No fair literary critic would put the Uṣas hymns on a level with samples of ritual poetry, streotyped in the poetical workshops of versifiers, the acme of whose productions was the prayer for not too small a fee. On the contrary, Uṣas, the Dawn, with its right royal splendour, its unbrailing regulatrty, its unbihinds progress, its pleasant physical effects, with the hopes this magnificent phenomenon raised at the begining of each and every new day: all this filled the unsophisticated mind of the ancient Ārya with those feelings which we find expressed in the Usas hymns.

It would be wrong to gauge by the part which Uṣas played in the cult her literary and poetical position, and the popularity she enjoyed above all the goddesses of the Vedic age. To her, together with Agni and the Aśvinā, as the deities ushering in the day, hymns were addressed at the earliest morning of the day of Soma sacrifice, but no libations were offered up. A comparison of an Uṣas hymn with any of those sūktas that were appointed for the accompaniment of the orthodox rite will show the different spirit which animates them and the difference of purpose of either.

The four Uṣas hymns of this Selection (Nrs. 3, 4, 18,21) give a fairly correct idea of the person, position, and work of the deity. Compared with the wealth of poetical ideas, the relations to the sacrificial are indeed few and common. Beyond the request to bring the gods to the sacrifice feast and the mention of the ṛṣi poet who composed a hymn in her honour and belonged to such and such a school, 3 11, 12, 4, Uṣas is hardly brought into intimate connection with the rite. The imagery, on the other hand, by which her person is brought out in full relief, the epithets given to her character, the activities she exercises for the benefit of men, made her appear as a figure that would satisfy the artistic as well as the realistic need of the warring but nature-admiring Ārya. She is expected to meet the material, intellectual and moral wants alike. She comes with splendour, द्युम्नेन, 3. 1, she is विभावरी, 3. 1, विभाती, 18. 1, व्येनी, 18. 4. The रुशन्तो अर्चयः, 3. 1, proclaim her presence, for she is रश्मिभिर्व्यक्ता, 21. 3 As she marches on, she becomes. द्विबर्हा, 18. 4, and finally she is spread all over the world, विश्वमनु प्रभूता, 21. 3. She carries the eye of the gods and leads on the fine, white horse, the sun, 21 3.

Though these attributes describe the natural phenomenon in the first place, yet the Vedic poets have tried to make her appear as a living personality as well, and have described her in terms and comparisons that may have appeared to them as the nearest approach to the ideal of beauty. She is युवतीः, 18. 6, appears युवतिर्न योषा, 21. 1. It is true that in 18.5, 6 the personal charms of Uṣas are set forth in a manner that touches the border line of poetical and moral beauty. But it would not be figure; the poets themselves took care to set attributes like सूनरी, 3.5, भद्रा, 18.6, सुजाता, 21.6, against more sensuous eptithets. Besides, it is significant enough that such a concrete figure with here and there too much flesh and blood has been described in 21. 2 according to an irreprochable standard of morality and beauty. In fact, through her physical charms Uṣas' person is standing out from all the rest of the Vedic gods and goddesses, yet the main stress seems to be laid on her activity for the benefit of the world, see 3.1, etc. Certainly the conclusion from too concrete a description and some sensuous smiles, used in connection with Uṣas the licentiousness of the Vedic age would be a fault against more than one law of logic.

Uṣas' life and work is regulated by ऋत, so much so that she is called ऋतावरी, 18. 1; cp. 18. 3, 4. Her activity is divided between stirring up to active life and bestowing boons on mankind. She is जीरा रथानाम्, 3. 3, and makes the ways passable, 18. 2, 3. Uṣas is nothing less than विश्रमिन्वा, 18. 2; cp. 21. 1. Even brute nature obeys her behest, 4. 3; 3. 8. All life and breath is said to depend on her, 3. 10. It is the very nature of Uṣas to shower graces on mankind, for she is addressed मधोनि 21.4 विश्ववारे, 21.5; 18.3. Her favours range from the nature of ordinary वाम and रै, Wealth, to the prolongation of life, 21.5. But at the same time, by her daily regular appearance at morning and evening time, she makes the number of days full, wasting thus the living being's life, 3. 5. Quite a special feature in the figure of Uṣas is her power of dispelling hatred and enmities together with darkness 3. 8; 18. 5; 21.4. As Uṣas herself is unfailing, so has her kindness been exercised from time immemorial, 18. 6; 3. 14. The dark night makes room for her, 20. 1; every morning she opens the portals of heaven, 3. 15, and is for ever the leader of the days , 21. 2.

Uṣas is riding on a big car, 3. 10; 18. 2; even with a hundred cars she, the सुभगा approaches men, 3. 7, a number apt to give an idea of the quantity of her gifts. The car is drawn by ruddy steeds or kine, 4. 1; 18. 3, most likely the rays of the dawn.

Uṣas is the daughter of heaven, 3. 1, 9, etc. Sometimes she is called the wife or mistress of the sun, सूर्य, as she is followed by him ; sometimes, the mother, since she precedes the sun. The night is Uṣas' sister, not rarely joined with her in the dvandva compound नक्तोषासा or उषासानक्ता. With the Aśvinā and Agni, 21. 1, she is connected in poetry as well as in the ritual.

The Uṣas cult was neither so frequent nor of such a nature with Indo-European peoples outside India as to justify the view that it was at any time an Indo-European worship. On the other hand, the regularity and beauty of dawn throughout the Indian continent make it quite probable that the worship of Uṣas could have developed here more than in any other country inhabited by Indo-Germanic.nations. But as we have clear traces that the young sun, re-aappearing after the winter, was an object of Indo-European cult, and as the Indian Uṣas in ancient times (cp. Śatapatha Br. VI. 1. 3. 8 and Maitr. S. II. 13. 10) was considered as the wife of the year and the mistress of the seasons, or, as in our text, 21. 2, the leader of the days, the original worship of Uṣas may have had for its object not so much the daily dawn as the dawn of the young sun in the beginning of the new year. This would agree very well with the liberation of the cows, the rays of dawn, by Indra from the cave, which is nothing else but the bringing out of the young sun and its dawn from darkness by

Indra, the god of light, associated with Agni and Bṛhaspati. This myth as well as the phrase उषसं उळहाः, ṚV. VI. 60. 2, would refer to climates in which the bringing out of sun and dawn supposes a struggle against adverse powers. It could hardly be applied to the Indian dawn with its almost mathematical regularity and its glorious, unimpeded march onwards. Uṣas is called सूर्या, which by Patañjali, II 20, also is interpreted as सूर्यस्य स्त्री, and is not to be taken to designate a sun-goddess. This, together with the Vedic view that Uṣās is the wife or mistress of the sun, suggests both the close original relationship, physical and mythological, between the sun and dawn and the deities they represent, Sūrya and Uṣ as, on the one hand, and, on the other, the independent development of the Uṣas cult in India.

The etymology of Uṣas is as clear as significant. It leads back to the root.वस्, उष् 6. The same root with the preposition वि, often used in connection with the dawn's appearance and illuminating activity, is to be found in Vivasvat. From the same Indo-Germanic root from which Uṣas ultimately has been derived come the Greek ΗΩΣ and the Latin *Aurora* (for *Ausosa)*. The Germanic goddess *Ostara* (Ostern), the Lithuanian *Auszrine,* and probably the Slavonic *Utro,* morning, and *Yutribog*, the morning-god, are connected with this same root as well.

INDRA

Indra appears in the ṚV. as national god of a warring and conquering people. At the same time he is not the pure creation of the Āryan invasion and progress, but has crossed with the Āryas the threshold of India, coming with them from earlier homes. This is clear from the fact that in the older parts of the ṚV. Indra never appears but as a fully-developed personality, in the main a well-defined figure with a definite task. It is rather in the later hymns that the position and existence of Indra is questioned and thus the earlier clear lines blurred.

Both from his actual position as war-god and his inherited task as the liberator of the water, it follows naturally that Indra's physical side is more developed than his moral character or his intellectual attainments. It would also follow from Indra's history as well as that of his people that the cosmic aspect of his nature is older than the martial one. It should not surprise us either that the liberator of the waters grew less definite in the same measure as the war-god's features became clearer; and finally it seems obvious that both sides of Indra's character changed with the changing nation and its times. Indra's nature and position in general is best described by the negative characteristics given in 14.1:

नकिरिन्द्र त्वदुत्तरो न ज्यायाँ अस्ति वृत्रहन्।
नकिरेव यथा त्वम् ॥

His size is more than gigantic, it is indeed cosmic, and the standard of measure given by the hymns is nothing but the confession of inability to describe him properly, 11. 7, 11. The colour of his skin and hair is tawny; tawny are also his horses, 11. 5. Such then must of the Indra hymns were composed. Indra's sign of suzerainty and outfit for rule and conquest consists mainly in the thunderbolt,. वज्र. More than any other god he is वज्रिन् and वज्रहस्त, in fact the वज्र is Indra's distinctive mark, 24. 4. In battle he appears on a car, as रथेस्थ(ा). The desire to raise Indra to the top of the pantheon attributed him many laudatory but fairly consistent epithets: he is full grown, youthful, huge and over-topping everything else, never ageing, cp. 11. 7. His strength is that of a bull.

The fact that he is said to be *the* bull sheds light both on the theological ideas of the Vedic Āryas and their occupation. Endowed with unconquerable strength, शचीभिः, 14. 6, he, the lord of strenth, शचीपति, 14, 17, performs herculean deeds, worthy of his character and position, वीर्याणि, 2. 1. Nobody would dare to oppose him, 14. 1, 23, 22; for those who attempted to restrict him do not fare well, no matter whether friend or foe, cp. 14. 3 ff., whether powers on high or on earth, 11, 9, 16. His sway, however, does not seem to have been always undisputed: see 2. 14, where he is flying before the revenger of Vṛtra. That the Paṇis should feign contempt of Indra, 26. 3, is but natural. To the Vedic ṛṣi he is the god on whom not only the cosmic, but also the social order and the animal kingdom depended, 2.15; 14.2.

Indra's exuberant strength occasionally oversteps the limits of moderation in eating and, especially, drinking. Apart from evidently poetical exaggeration, making Indra empty whole lakes of soma, and a good number of them too, he is the सोमपा *par excellence* and the सोमपति, 11. 1: the whole hymn 13 is very little besides a drinking song. In other hymns soma is described in such terms that the poet seems to think Indra could not resist an invitation couched in them. It should be remembered, however, that soma-drinking was very early drawn within the ritual and made part of the worship, 11. 10; moreover, that at these early times we would look in vain for well-balanced measures and proportions in graphical descriptions; finally it was thought that Indra's grace and goodwill was not altogether independent of the convenient quantity of soma offered to him in sacrifice and myth. Yet the god's inborn drinking habits, 11. 9, 10, as well as the gross irregularities in his family life, seem to point to a time far removed from that of even the oldest Upaniṣads. The vast differences in ethical and intellectual notions and valuations between the earliest and latest Vedic epochs will have to be taken into account, not less than the linguistic and literagy discrepancies, when the age of the ṚV. has to be treated of. A parricide as the highest deity would be hardly possible in the Upaniṣad.

Compared with the overwhelming physical character Indra's intellectual and moral attributes are few and not imposing. They are just such as his rough and ready general appearance would admit and his position require. He is अद्रोघ, 11. 9; he is bountiful, मघवन् so much so that this is a distinctive epithet of his; he is धनंजय for his worshippers, 13. 6; cp. 11.17. Not too often he is called कवि, 13. 6, the wise one. The lack of purely moral attributes is in a way made up by Indra's qualities of a hero in war and battle. He is, especially considering the soma oblations, expected to side with the Āryas, and to get the invoking and offering party out of difficulty, if there should be a competition of claimants on his help, 11. 14. There are, however, traces of events (and times?) when Indra turned against Āryas, 14. 18.

Indra has been born, 11. 9, 10. As we should expect from an Indo-Germanic point of view, his father seems according to some statements to be Dyaus. Following other passages Indra's progenitor is Tvaṣṭṛ, who also fashioned Indra's वज्रं, 2. 2, and eventually had his head cut off by his own son. As Indra's brothers appear Agni and Pūṣan. Indrāṇī, his wife, looks very much like a literary construction, without a real mythological background. Indra is most naturally and most frequently joined with Agni; his being together with Vāyu and Varuṇa is both less frequent and less natural. The war-gods unswerving allies are the Maruts, already his faithful companions in the Vṛtra duel. They supplement both courage and strength when Indra himself is on the point of failing. At the psychological moment he is sent by them into the fray with Vṛtra, finds out the foe's weak spot, 11. 4, and conquers, foiling tricks and magic, माया, 2. 4; cp. 14. 12, 21; 26.4.

All the commentators are agreed that Indra is connected with the release of the waters. Whether he is the god of the thunderstorm and monsoon rain, or the god who broke the fetters of frost and winter and, melting the snow on the mountains, sent down the rivers into the plains, depends on the nature of his opponent Vṛtra. Vṛtra's removal is Indra's greatest deed; because he is Vṛtrahan, the ritual recognizes him as the Mahendra. The indigenous ancient and medieval interpreters of the ṚV. as well as a good many, if not the majority of, Western scholars, take Vṛtra to be demon of drought who shut up the waters in the clouds; the minority of scholars sees in Vṛtra a frost and winter demon. It should be possible with the help of the Ṛk text itself, the parallels in other mythologies, and the figure which Indra plays in the Vedic ritual, to arrive at a satisfactory solution of the problem.

The question is to be approached from a wide range of view and has to be considered in all bearings. What appears natural and is acknowledged by everybody, as far as linguistic and philosophical data are concerned, has with unfortunate results been neglected where one should least expect it. It would be idle to deny all geographical and climatic influences on the tradition of the Indra-Vṛtra myth. Undoubtedly these influence helped to remodel to certain extent the original myth, and may have given rise to the interpretation of the mythological figure of Indra as the god of the thunderstorm.

It will be admitted that the greater part of the Indra hymns were composed in, or not too far from, the Punjab, and at times at which its climatic conditions had made an impression on the mind of the poets, which probably would mingle with recollections of earlier times and places. Though rivers in the Punjab have changed here and there their course and thereby the features of the landscape, there is no evidence that this has been either cause or effect of substanial climate changes. Nor do we know of other proofs for such changes of climate and weather. Now the statistics of the present day show that the sky is generally less clouded, that the thunderstorms are less frightening, that the monsoon rain is weaker in the Punjab than in other parts of India. Exceptionally heavy rainfalls are neither above the average quantity of water, nor more frequent than in the rest of India. In fact, they are so rare that they could hardly form the basis for a popular dragon-slaying myth. Thus arises a strong presumption that the poets of the Vedic Indra hymns had one phenomenon of nature in view and their interpreters in far distant places in India another. For it is clear that the Vedic singers describe as a heroic feat of their favourite god that fact in nature which was of supreme importance to their lives and welfare. Just as they hoped from him victory over their enemies, so was he to them the source of bodily sustenance in the struggle for life against nature. No doubt, rain formed an essential condition of vegetable and animal life in the home of the Vedic Āryas; and consequently it had an influence on their idea of Indra, the highest god and his arch-enemy Vṛtra, whose conquest was Indra's proudest title to sovereignty. But as there are other factors in the origin and formation of the myth to be considered, and as thunderstorm and rain were not of such a nature as to be necessarily or primarily the basis of the Indra-Vṛtra duel, it would hardly be correct to take thunderstorm and rain as the only natural basis of the Vṛtra myth.

The chronological sequel of the Vedic terms for "year" is हिमा॑, श॒रद्, व॒र्ष, indicating the onward march of the ancient immigrants from their Indo-Āryan homes, across the mountain barrier through the Punjab into the Gaṅgā-Yamunā Doab, East and South down to "Hindostān". This way then, we should presume, the Indra Vṛtra myth travelled, and its origin is to be sought at the starting point of the migration. For, as has been pointed out, Indra appears in the ṚV. as a well-known. defined deity, whose deed is extolled to such an extent and with such indefatigable persitency that the poets, not to become stale and trite, had to vary the narrative in details, or could rest satisfied when they had described the unique feat more by hints and references than actual delineation. If Indra in the ṚV. is not a growing but a full-grown deity, it follows that Vṛtra and the myth on which Indra's greatness rests are also of the same age and origin as Indra, that they are at least pre-Indian. Will now the Ṛk text bear out this assumption that the Vṛtra, myth is not a purely Indian growth and vṛtra, consequently, not the cloud demon but rather the frost demon from whose grasp the waters have been wrenched and, as a matter of fact, have to be wrenched every year anew?

Hymn Nr. 2 of this selection may be called representative of the heroic Indra hymns in so far as nothintg in it is contradicted by more than a negligeable number of passages in the whole ṚV. Saṁhita, and statements of this hymn are confirmed by the bulk of the Indra songs. The following is the myth in a nutshell :—A god is fighting with a snake-shaped demon and opens the interior of the mountains from which the waters of rivers of flow, rushing to the sea. There is really no question or mention either of thunderstorm or rain; the clouds play quite an inferior part in the whole myth. The waters released by Indra are आपः, 2. 2; they are (seven) streams.(सुप्त) सिन्धवः, 2. 12; and अर्णा, 11. 5. They run like horses at a race, अत्याँ इव प्रासृजः सर्तवाजौ, 11. 6. cp.

12. 2, 6, 7. Did rain in those times flow horizontally, or were there vertical races held, or were the Vedic poets such poor observers of nature? Vṛtra on his part is प्रथमजा, 2. 3, 4, which may, or may not, be equivalent to pre-Indian. He is पर्वते शिश्रियाण, reclining on the mountain, 2. 2. Since that combat, i. e., from time immemorial nobody tried again to challenge Indra, 2. 4. The adjective शयान, 11. 6, is somewhat hard to conceive, if clouds and the air were the support of the dragon. Nowhere is the crashing fall of Vṛtra from the clouds mentioned, yet there he lies like trunks of trees, smashed with an axe, scattered over the earth, 2.6 crushed to atoms Vṛtra lies all over the place, 2. 7. The waters pass by him (अति), he is lying at their feet, 2. 8 ; cp. 2.9, 10. All this seems to fit well enough for a demon, lying mangled on the ground, in this case the slope of the mountain, where he had been sprawling. But the description would be of little credit to Vedic ṛṣis and poets, if they wanted to picture a demon floating on the clouds. The latter are invariably calleld पर्वत, a fairly good, but not always correct rūpaka, which besides would be considerably in advance of the strage at which we find alaṁkāras employed in the ṚV. That the Nirukta and the Nighaṇṭuka give the equation पर्वत=मेघ only proves that at their times the old, real meaning of Vṛtra had been superseded by a modern one. That hail falls when the monsoon rain is being introduced by thunderstorms is not so common as to warrant its insertion in the Vṛtra fight , 2, 13, but it is a common occurrence in the places where the myth originated and in adjacent regious, at the time when frost is thawing and the rivers set free. Thus the Ṛk text itself supports the view that Vṛtra is a demon of frost, succumbing yearly to Indra, the god of light and warmth.

But Indra's weapon is the वज्र, thunderbolt. "Thunder&

bolt" is a misleading translation which proves very little. The वज्र, is some sort of a club or an axe, made of ore (iron?), it is आयस. The "thunderbolt" is in some places called as rock, and it is not certain whether the Vedic ṛṣis under-stood by वज्र the flash of lightning. Besides the वज्र Indra possesses an arsenal of primitive weapons, stones, axes, jaws, wheels, bows and arrows. It should not be overlooked either that the Vedic Bṛhaspati, the Iranian Mithra, the Greeks Zeus wield the "thunderbolt " as well as Indra. Nobody says they are all or primarily gods of the thunderstorm. when the Vedic poets were actually out to praise a deity as the god of the thunderstorm, they were lacking neither correct observation of facts, nor imaginative power, nor force of expression. Cp. the hymn V. 83 in honour of Parjanya, a god who, it is to be feared, will be ousted from position and employment, if Indra is to be recognised as the god of the thunderstorm. Readers of classical Sanskrit literature will easily discover the difference not only of style between the magnificent picture of a thunderstorm there and this supposed description of it in the Indra-Vṛtra myth.

Further proofs for the true nature of Indra and Vṛtra are to be found in parallels of other Indo-Germanic mythologies, which employ more or less the same imagery for the same underlying fact. "The poets of northern countries where winter is the inclement, hostile season,chaining up the rivers, furnish us with parallels (to the Vṛtra fight) not to be found in descriptions of the thunderstorm in classical Sanskrit. Comparing the wording in the texts of the north Germanic and other poets with the Vedic pharaseology, we can little doubt that the Vedic similes have not arisen in India but in a country where the 'hideous winter' lies on land and water, where ice giants overcome streams and lakes, and nature is sleeping its winter sleep. The freeing of nature from the fetters of winter is to be compared to Vṛtra roused from his sleep by Indra's thunderbolt. The myth of the Vṛtra fight came with the Indians from Kashmir or the North-Western countries to their new home, carrying along a certain number of ideas and similes that looked like erratic drift. In the ṚV. this myth and its basis was still recognised, as the Vedic hymns were composed on, and in the vicinity of, the large rivers whose volume of water is smallest in winter. But when the climate of the Gangetic plain offered new impressions, the old tradition became obliterated and thus changed both Indra and his opponent Vṛtra ... The enemy of the ice and winter giant cannot be anybody else but Indra, the god of spring and summer, the sun-god, simultaneously with whose rising course in the sky the setting free of the waters begins. Hillobrandt, Ved. Myth., Kl. Ausg., pp. 87f.

The Vedic ritual points the same way. There is a difference of opinion, it is true, as to what gods are taking part in the morning and evening libations; but all the hymns without exception give Indra either by himself or accompanied by the Maruts the midday oblation, cp. 11. 1. 3. Thus Indra is here made the mythological representative of the sun at the zenith. Moreover in Ait. Br. II. 44 the soma day is compared with the sun, whose course is followed in the recitation, and according to the same Brāhmaṇa, III. 43. 6 the Agniṣṭoma corresponds to the year. The Agniṣṭoma-ekāha is thus the symbol of the whole year, and Indra's natural basis is the sun at the zenith not only of the day but of the whole year. For, the Brāhmaṇas are unanimous in saying that the summer is Indra's season and the Agniṣṭoma is a celebration at the beginning of the spring, or the year, i.e., at the time when the power of the sun begins to assert itself again. Two further important soma sacrifices, besides others, the Mahāvrata and the Atirātra, also centre round Indra. Both of them are feasts of the solstices. Indra thus is confirmed as a sun-god by the ritual which, though in course of time often lost in technicalities and details, has independently preserved in the underlying idea of the sacrifice the original Indo-Iranian conception of Indra.

Thus the meteorological conditions both of the Indo-Iranian and the Vedic home, the Ṛk text itself, Indo-European parallels, as well as the partly contemporary, partly subsequent ritual, favour the view that Vṛtra is originally a frost and winter demon and Indra, consequently, a god of light. It is not without importance that there are passages in the ṚV. "where the thunderstorm is divested of mythological imagery".

Independent of the Vṛtra myth is the liberation of the cows from वल, the cave. This signifies the bringing forth of the sun's rays at dawn, 11. 16. Indra seems to have been as impetuous in this as in his other doings. Uṣas once tarried too long, whereupon Indra killed her and smashed her car, 14. 8, 9. Other opponents of Indra are Śuṣṇa, Śambara, Varcin 14. 13, 14. 15. who, with the possible exception of Śuṣṇa, do not lend themselves to a mythological explanation. Probably they are historical names, whose bearers obstructed the march of the Āryas. They, either directly called Dāsas or thought to be in connection with them, appear in the ṚV. mostly as hostile to the migrating Indians. But on behalf of the liberal and pious Divodāsa Indra's power is enlisted, and he helps Divodāsa—which hardly means the Dāsa from heaven—not less than the Āryas, 14. 20. Dāsa generally means enemy, and the Dāsas are identical with the Dāhas of the Avesta, a tribe dwelling in regions N.W of India. The paṇis are not the miserly offerers, stigmatised by the Brāhmaṇas, but a atribe which seems to have caused great damage to cattle and other property of the wandering Indians. They were occupying the banks of the Rasā, the *Rañhā* of the Avesta, a river of the earlier common homes. It is probable that the myths in which Etaśa figures signify astronomical facts. In the ṚV. Etaśa appears as a horse, especially of the sun, and as a charioteer of the sun. Hence the opinion of some scholars that the central idea of the Indra-Etaśa events is a race in the skies.

Indra's characteristic Vedic epithet is Vṛtrahan. It has its parallel in the Avestan *Verethragna*, though the latter means simply god of victory, without exclusive reference to Indra. The Armenian *Vahagn* (Vṛtra-death) may come from Iran. A coin of Kanerki bears the inscription *Ordagno*, whose origin is unmistakable. Thus both Vṛtra and the Indra-Vṛtra myth are of pre-Indian, and at least Indo-Iranian origin. Indra's only parallel, on the other hand, is *Andra* in the Avesta, Indra being there like so many of his compeers a demon. The etymology of Indra is doubtful since the days of Yāska, cp. Nirukta, 10. 8. The derivation from इन्दु, drop, has not much to recommend it. Better seems to be the etymology going back to the root इन्, इन्व् 8., to have power over, to rule.

The sovereign position of Indra in Vedic India is brought out by the great number of hymns in his honour: one fourth of the sūktas of the whole ṚV. Saṁhitā is praising or invoking solely Indra. In this Selection hymns 2, 11, 13,14 are addressed to Indra exclusively; in 12, 24,26 he is merely mentioned.

AGNI

Weather and warfare determined Indra's mythological figure; the household life of the ancient Ārya was instrumental in fixing the conception and personalaity of Agni. Agni and Indra have this in common that they are connected with two of the most necessary conditions of human existence: Indra is the giver of water, Agni not only gives, but is, fire. This accounts for the great number of Agni hymns in the Ṛ.V. Saṁhitā, over 200 in all, a figure second only to that of the Indra hymns. In this Selection only hymns 10 and 15 are addressed to Agni. The natural basis for the mythological Agni is clear; it is the element of fire, kindled and kept up in the house, and visible and active in nature. The character of the natural phenomenon did not lend itself to a very clear personification; in additiion, the fire was too near to allow a fiction of the imagination to take the place of the concrete fact. Barring some good similes, the imagery round about Agni is chiefly connected with the sacrifice and its ritual. Thus it is said that he shaves the earth as the barber a beard, but much oftener he is represented as eating the oblation with his tongues.

Naturally Agni is addressed as brilliant, भानुमस्, 15. 11; called विभावा, 15. 9; with thousand horns, सहस्रशृङ्गः,15. 8; as he, lit every day, he is युवा, 15. 6 even यविष्ठ्यः, 10. 6. But being kept up and worshipped since time immemorial, and having officiated at the first sacrifice of the gods, he is also प्रत्नः, 10. 8. The attribute यविष्ठ्य (यविष्ठ) refers of course as well to the fact that Agni's godhead is of comparatively young date. All the attributes given to him show Agni as a kind, helpful deity, see 10. 1; 15. 5 and *Passim*. His knowledge is beyond the common measure, cp. मेध्याय, 15. 12; विप्रम्, 15. 7. Being wise himself, he is praised by the wise, कविप्रशस्तः, 15. 8. He is noble —born, जेन्यः, 15. 5. The physical nearness of the fire as well as its constant company during the whole life, and even beyond, let Agni appear as the personal, devoted friend of man, almost one of his own, मानुष, 10. 6, certainly a frequent and welcome guest, अतिथिः, nay, an intimate house-friend, दमूनाः, 15. 8. Agni's powerful benevolence impresses itself upon the simple-minded; even the beasts feel well and safe in his keeping, 10. 7. The principle "So much for so much", otherwise applied in the relation between man and Vedic gods, is to a certain extent replaced here by a higher of friendship, cp. 10. 1, 3. Not only the individual is committed to his care, the clans as a whole also depend on him, 15. 6, 8, 9. With his mental power, क्रत्वा, he is able to protect all the sacrifices, 10. 6. Like Indra he is called a bull, 15. 8, 12, in 10, 4 he is likened to a lion. No obstacles or dangers will keep Agni back from his purpose, 10. 4; as Indra is said to possess माया, so does Agni enjoy दंसना, 10. 7. In fact, especially on behalf of a favourite, Agni ssurpasses "all the others", 15. 9. But he is not so often credited with creative or other cosmic powers or their exercise, it seems to be a kind of henotheistic tendency and a borrowing from Indra, if in 15.7 and other passages he is said to have spread out heaven and earth, etc. Agni 's outfit , suiting his position, is not much more than a shining car, 15. 11, utilized and mentioned in particular in connection with his priestly functions.

Of greater mythological importance than the personal traits of Agni are the data about his origins, forms and dwelling places. As the daily, kindling of the fire for profane and sacred use was much more common than other modes of his manifestation,. This birth of Agni is oftenest mentioned and most clearly described. Being produced from the two kindling sticks the अरणी, these become Agni's parents, to be devoured, however, by their offspring forthwith. The ten fingers wielding the sticks are compared to ten virgins; as the production of fire by friction requires considerable physical effort, Agni is called सहसः सूनः. Because Agni is produced from wood, the wood and the plants in general are said to be his hiding place.

The second birth of Agni is from the waters. This birth

has impressed the poets and theologians of the Indo-Iranian times so much that Agni produced in this way has not only got a special name in अपां नपात्, Avestan *Apām Napō,* but has actually been split off into a new personality, a separate deity from Agni. Apāṁ Napāt is not only the Son of the waters, but their lord and giver as well. See ṚV. II. 35; X. 30; VII. 47; IV. 48 (?). The more common view is that Apāṁ Napāt stands for lightning, produced from the clouds. This is hardly correct for the Vedic age. May be that the lightning contributed to the idea that Agni dwelt in the aerial waters, just as well as a firebrand extinguished by being thrown into water contributed to the nation of Agni's hiding in the terrestrial waters. For, Agni is supposed to have his hiding place in the lakes, rivers, and the water rising from the earth into the plants. But it is rather the cloud as it drops the water and fertilizes the earth, that is the aerial-water abode of Agni; the water on the earth and in the plants forms a terrestrial parallel to it. It is then not so much the form of lightning that is the physical basis for Apāṁ Napāt, but it is rather the fire as it resides in the aerial waters. The view that Apāṁ Napāt is Agni in form of lightning, and was worshipped as such, cannot be said to have been proved, and it is perfectly idle to discuss what form of lightning enjoyed this worship. The "blinding flash", a destructive, momentary force and, for the matter of that, a firly rare one too, is not apt to enter into the calm, benevolent role which Agni in his other mmanifestations plays. It might be objected that Apāṁ Napāt has been declared to be "a new personality, a separate deity from Agni". The objection remains the same whether lightning or fire in the cloud water is the physical basis of Apāṁ Napāt. Nor should it be forgotten that Agni's threefold origin, existence, and place "represents the earliest Indian trinity". In a triune being we should expect that sometimes the unity, sometimes the triplicity of it is being brought out. The proof has been attempted that Apāṁ Napāt is identical with the moon. The view has not found general acceptance. All the scholars, however, are agreed that Apāṁ Napāt goes back to the Indo-Iranian period. The idea of Agni born from the waters may have led to a "contamination" of him with an older, originally really different figure, to whom Agni lent his other characteristics as they were of similar origin.

The third of Agni's births is in the heavens, from whence he is brought down to the earth by Mātariśvan, the Indian pendant of the Greek *Prometheus*. He conferred the boon of the fire on man; the Bhṛgus introduced it among their kind. It has been said that "hardly anaything but lightning can be his (Mātariśvan's) basis". Some, though not all, older Ṛk texts seem to favour this view by the identification of Mātariśvan with Agni. But in III 5. 9, 10 we are able to see how the separation of Agni and Mātariśvan became recognized so that they remained two distinct and essentially different figures, though connected as cause and effect, or discovered and discover. It must be admitted that in some of the older and generally in the younger passages of the ṚV., in the Atharva Veda "and other Saṁhitās, the Brāhmaṇas and all the subsequent (sacred as well as classical) literature, the name is a designation of wind." Agni brought from heaven by Mātariśvan might be the jungle fire, kindled by the friction of branches moved in the wind. It is but natural that in the ṚV. the sun is one form in which Agni appears; but it is not quite correct to say that in the Vedic hymns the sun is identical with Agni. Because the sun is one of the many forms of Agni and himself such a prominent phenomenon and power, so to speak an independent physical and mythological personality, and because sun and fire are rather compared, then identified, with each other, the conclusion is legitimate that the sun and Agni are not identical.

Owing to this threefold birth and existence Agni and

things connected with him appear often threefold. Thus he is said to have three heads, three bodies, three stations, etc.

Agni the fire-god or his name is found with Indians, Iranians, Greeks, Romans, Lithuanians, Letts. We may then assume that the personification and deification of the fire is of Indo-European or primitive Āryan origin. The custom of offering gifts to the gods in fire also is an Indo-European institution. Round Agni in his sacred character as sacrifical fire centred the poetical and theological intuition of the Vedic ṛṣis, and they would try to create a figure worthy of the high rank the fire occupied in the worship of the deity. Their imagination was indefatigable in clothing the bare fact of sacred fire, lit and kept up, with an imagery more original and richer than there is round any other mythological figure in the Veda.

In the early morn, at the approach of dawn, the sacrificial fires are kindled; as birds fly up, so the flames rise heavenwards. The upright one, whose red glow shines far and wide, has been brought out of the darkness. Agni's ointment is ghee, and with his tongues he drinks the sacrificial liberation. In fuller day-light he appears as a white horse. He is going to be placed at the mother's bosom, the (वेदिं). There he officiates as a well experienced (यजीयान्), and fully qualified होतृं, stroked continually with ghee and groomed like a horse. (Cp. hymn 15). The consumption of the sacrificial gifts by Agni completed the idea of his being a god; the upward direction of his flame suggested that he was carrying the offerings to the other gods. Thus he was looked upon as a regular messenger, दूत, 10. 8, and even mediator between the deity and man. Because he has been born in the highest heaven, himself a god, and knowing the ways all along, he is to bring the gods to the sacrifice: he is not only a हव्यवाहंन, but a देववाहंन as well. The very first ṛc of the ṚV. Saṁhitā salutes him as a ऋत्विज्, पुरोहिंत, and होतृ. Agni Agni, as a matter of fact, is the priest par excellence, and as, Indra among Maruts as other ware like deities is the great soldiere and commanden so appears. Agni as the high-priest among gods and men, 10. 3. Though he is the youngest, his priesthood is acknowledged by all the clans; from far and near they bring offerings to him, 15. 9. Throughout the ṚV. one may read, mostly between the lines but unmistakingly, the idea that Agni is or was a demon-dispelling, Rakṣas-killing power. This reputation of his, together with the positive benefits bestowed by him on everybody, and the sacred character with which, as the divine होतृ, he was bound to be invested, could not but make Agni the most popular deity of the whole Vedic pantheon.

In 10. 2 there is the mention of Agni having, at the sight of the wood, gone into the waters. This may refer to the time of the year when sacrifices are in abeyance, the पितृयाण, when the पितरौ देवशंत्रव: rule : that the period during which the sun is in the southern, the moon in the northern zodiac. When sun and moon have changed their position then is the देवयान, when the gods reign and sacrifices are offered up to them. (cp. Hillebrandt, Ved. Myth. Kl. Ausg., pp. 50f.) This explanation appears to be astronomically not quite accurate and suffers from the difficulty that the Agni's flight into the waters seems to be referred to as the object of an ancient myth; thus it would have to be shown that the fact underlying the myth and the arrangement of the ritual during the देवयान and the पितृयाण are fairly contemporary. A similar difficulty from chronology might be raised against that interpretation of the same myth which sees in the आपं:, Agni's refuge, the monsoon rain and its conditions and consequences. It is more likely that the waters. It is oftener said, the तमस्, darkness, refers to the short days of the damp, foggy months during which in the earlier homes of the Āryas the sun-Agni was hidden. Considering the close alliance between Indra and

Agni there may be a meteoro-logical connection between the flight of Agni into the waters and the Indra-Vṛtra fight.

In addition to the form of Apāṁ Napāt Agni appears as *Agni Vaiśvānara* and *Agni Narāśaṁsa, the* Avestan *Nairyō-sañha*. It seems that Agni Vaiśvānara stands in the ṚV. for the Āhavanīya, and Agni Narāśaṁsa for the Dakṣiṇa, fire. The original meaning of Tanūnapāt, a rather rare name for Agni, may be taken to be Son of (his own) body, a conception opposed to that by which Agni is represented as having been born from the अरणी, his parents. Agni may be said to be the son of his own body either because his origin from the wood is unique, sudden and due to himself, or because there is always at least part of the fire's self in the wood as long as the wood lasts.

The etymology of Agni seems to lead back to the root अज् 1, Latin ago Greek αγω which would convey the idea of Agni=the Nimble, Agile. The name of Agni has its Indogermanic parallels in the Latin *ignis,* Slavonic *ogni;* the god Agni finds a parallel besides the Lithuanian *Ugnis szventa* and the Lettish *Ugguns māta*.

BṚHASPATI.

In eleven hymns of the ṚV. Saṁhitā Bṛhaspati is addressed; by either of his two most common names he is mentioned altogether about 170 times. The nature of this god is not homogeneous like that of Indra or Uṣas, but appears as a mixture of the martial element, smashing, fighting, and conquering, chiefly represented by Indra, and the priestly element, which finds expression not so much in sacrificial functions as in the power inherent in prayer and hymn. Perhaps Bṛhaspati means a compromise between Kṣatriya and Brāhmaṇa ideal. The heterogeneous character of Bṛhaspati is evident from his names and attributes. Bṛhaspati and Brahmaṇaspati, double accented aluk compounds, are rather mechanical names, like Prajāpati, which nevertheless show the sphere over which this god is set to rule. From the professional activity and his realm we may conclude to the character of Bṛhaspati. Even his vehicle is a ऋतस्य रथं, a designation next to impossible for Indra's car. That the same car of Bṛhaspati is भीम, ज्योतिष्मत्, and the like, 7. 3, is due partly to his participation in warlike exploits, partly to a complimentary description with stereotyped epithets. In war and strife Bṛhaspati as companion of Indra seems to exhibit more coolness and tenacity, amounting to irresistibility, than the greater war-god who, once roused, makes a thunderstorm-like onslaught, but has to be cheered into action by the Maruts. Bṛhaspati is also called वज्रिन्; in the fray he rent with fiery gleams the fences of Vala. Yet he is accompanied by a singing hosts, ऋक्वंन् गण, whence his title गणपंति, and, more becoming his brahmanical character, he splits Vala with a roar, not with the वज्रं, and shouting he drives out the lowing cows, cp. ṚV. IV. 50, 5. According to Nr. 7. 18, the mountain yields to Bṛhaspati's beauty and majesty. His martial character seems to be due more to his close union with Indra than to spring from his own nature. It appears safer to assume that the original conception of Bṛhaspati was sacerdotal, and that the remaining characteristics and epithets were pegged on him somehow. The Brāmaṇa, the priest of the orthodox ritual, and Brahmā, the creative principle in the later Trimūrti, appear as the embodiments of a developed idea, the first conception of which is personified and deified in the Vedic Brahmaṇaspati. Nor is there another deity that would serve as forerunner of the (masculine) Brahmā of the Trimūrti and the (neuter) Brahma of the Upaniṣads. The priestly character of Bṛhaspati is expressed in the hymns of the family books of the ṚV. Saṁhitā as well as in the younger maṇḍalas I and X: he appears in the ṚV. as the heavenly पुरोहित, who rouses the gods by the sacrifice. He is made to play the part of a mediator between gods and men when it is said of him that he gave the sacrifice to men, who had become destitute of religion. Bṛhaspati's mediatory activity is also hinted at in the phrase अधिवक्तारमस्मयुम्. Without him the sacrifice does not proceed: in this there is a reflex of the monopoly of the sacrifice in the hands of the priestly class.

The etymology of Bṛhaspati, and more perhaps that of Brahmaṇaspati, would suggest that this god was considered to be the presiding or ruling and administering deity of the brahman, which itself is an older conception than either Bṛhaspati or Brahmaṇaspati. Prayer is at least as old as sacrifice, and it is not all necessary to consider Bṛhaspati as a special form the root बृह, बृंह, has well been brought in connection with the Irish *bricht,* Northern *bragr.* But the statement is very doubtful :—"As brahman has arisen from the depth of magic to the most sublime conception of Indian philosophy, so has 'the lord of prayer' his root in a god of the magical fire,.... his protector." In the same line moves the interpretation of brahman with *Zauberfluidum,* magical fluid, essence. Now, in the first place, magic fluid, or essence does not seem to be very illuminating. Then, this interpretatioin as well as the statement quoted above leaves out of sight the important distinction between downright magic—whether while or black, does not matter much—and the real, genuine, religious devotion, practiced and expressed in prayer, both fixcd and official and improviscd and individual. It is really not necessary to believe that for the explanation of every concept in religion and philosophy we have to descend into "the lowest bathos of savage folk belief." This view, still fairly common, loses credibility and accept-ability in direct ratio to the progress of research. Brahman, of which Bṛhaspati is said to be the lord, is from the point of the deity the spirit that moves to, and helps and accomplishes, the devotion; from the point of man it is lifting up of one's mind and will and feeling to the deity. Both the later Philosophical and rilgious development in India and the parallel evolution in Iran favour this view, to say nothing of a good many Ṛk texts with very clear meaning concerning Bṛhaspati and what he stands for. The place for magic spell is the Atharva Veda, and just there Bṛhaspati does not figure largely at all.

A slightly different side of Bṛhaspati's nature is brought out by the epithet ऋतप्रजात in 7.15 and by ऋतस्य धर्तरि, 7. 17. The rest of the attributes, like असुर्य, 7. 2; कवि, 1; प्रचेतस्, 2; विचक्षण, 6, are taken from the common stock of descriptive qualities granted to the Vedic gods. Bṛhaspati's relation to the gods is not quite uniformly represented: in mantra 17 of No. 7—the only Bṛhaspati hymn of this Selection— Tvaṣṭṛ figure as his parent; but in 25. 2 he forges all the gods, Tvaṣ-ṭṛ included, like a blacksmith, देवानां जाना ब्रह्मणस्पतिः सं कर्मारे इवाधमत्. This contradictory statement agrees well with Brahmaṇaspati's heterogeneous nature, half mythological figure, half philosophical,speculative conception. It is also said that the gods got their share of sacrifice through him, 7. 2. That Bṛhaspati is an enemy of the Rakṣasas, 7. 14, is but natural; and so is the request to ruin and punish the impious, the godless, and the scoffer of the gods.

The favourable, kind disposition of Bṛhaspati towards men is clearly stated: for them he is a गोपाः, 7. 6, सुगोपाः, 5; leading, protecting by सुनीतिभिः, 4; furthering welfare as a

पथिकृत्, 6, सुवृध्, 9, and सस्निं 10. He grants उत्तमं वयः, 10 ; and uncommon fortune, 15. A frequent object of the prayer to Bṛhaspati is the foiling of the enemy and his wiles, of the double-dealing, the backbiter. He is asked to undo the cheat as war-chariots are smashed, 13; for he is the द्रुहो हन्ता, 17. The haughty, disregarding all bounds and laws, is to be put down by Bṛhaspati, 7.12. The whole activity of Bṛhaspati, his attitude towards द्रुह् in particular, makes him most of all the gods in the Ṛ.V. resemble Ahuramazda of the Avesta. Quite in keeping with Bṛhaspati's other attributes are ऋणया, 11, 17 and ऋणच्चित्, 17. Evidently the poet wants to lay stress on the moral side of Brahmaṇaspati's office when he asserts: तवं व्रतायं मतिभिर्जरामहे, 7. 6.

Bṛhaspati has quite a province of his own in the ब्रह्मन् and the cognate conceptions and actions. He is the जनिता ब्रह्मणाम्, 7. 2; the सूक्तस्य यन्ता, 19. From the phrase प्र सुशंसा मतिभिंस्तारिषीमहि, 10, it becomes clear that the right frame of mind will win the god's favour. Ṛk 16 implies that Bṛhaspati knows the सामन्; 17 may even be interpreted to mean that he himself has been fashioned "out of every Sāman". This might lend some contenance to the view that Bṛhaspati is in essential connection with the much practiced and much abhorred magic, ostracized by Āpastambīya Dharmasūtra I. 3 10. 19 (17). This law-book enumerates the voice productions of dogs, donkeys, wolves, shakals, and owls, the sound of musical instruments, weeping, and the sound of Sāmans, as noises at which the Veda study has to be interrupted. But in the first place, the author of the Āpastambīya Sūtra and others are not so much horrified at the contents of the Sāman, which is mostly borrowed fromthe Ṛ.V., as at its melody, which at least partly owed its origin to popular songs of the rank of lower magic. Second, it should not be overlooked that the Sāmaveda in ancient literature sometimes was even put above the ṚV.—compare Bhagavadgītā, X. 22, and the Mahābhārata *passim*. This high estimation of the Sāmaveda is not likely to be a sudden innovation, seeing that even the etymology of Sāman, which implies calming, quieting, seems to point rather to the power of prayer and devotion to win the favour of the deity. Sāman, then, would be closely akin to brahman. This brahman, originally something like the धिषणा, in later times became principle in Vedānta philosophy.

A Vedic instance of a sententious saying is to be found in 7. 19 :—विश्वं तद्भद्रं यदवन्ति देवाः.

SARAMĀ

Besides the various animals that are privileged to serve as vehicle of the gods, the animal kingdom is represented in Vedic mythology also by Saramā, according to Yāska, Nir. 11. 25, the देवशुनी, the bitch of the gods. She has become known in connection with Indra's attempt at releasing the cows from the clutches of the Paṇis, a feat in which Saramā did reconnoitring and messenger service. From hymn No. 26, which gives the account of her journey from afar and across the Rasā. and of her parleying with the paṇis, it is clear that she fulfilled her errand with prudence and fixity of purpose, The two flat-nosed, four- eyed, brindled dogs of Yama, the Sārameyas, are the offspring of Saramā. Their main duties are to track out those among mortals that are to die and to keep guard over them on their path to Yama's realm.

THE RIVERS

The Vipāś, Śutudrī, and Sarasvatī are mentioned in this Selection. The twin-streams Vipāś and Śutudrī are celebrated in No. 12; the Sarasvatī forms the subject of hymn 23. Their main characteristics are easily gathered from the sūktas themselves; naturally they are in both descriptions very much the same. It is, in particular,noteworthy that in the case of none does the description amount to a clear deification; the personification is more expressed in the case of Sarasvatī than that of Vipāś and Śutudrī. The naturaly phenomenon of the flow of the water and its surroundings has impressed the poet far more than the idea of goddess. The Sarasvatī, however, all along assumes more flesh and blood of a female deity than the others do. Her concrete shape and fullness of life has, it would seem, led to the creation of a corresponding male deity, Sarasvat, who is somewhat abruptly introduced into Vedic mythology. Sarasvat is hardly more than an "extension" of the female deity, as Indrāī is one of the male god. Cp. ṚV. VII. 96 .6, where breasts are attributed to Sarasvat. Sarasvatī's abundance of vitality is also shown by her long life in Indian literature. The Vājasaneyī Saṁhitā, XIX. 12, says that when the gods by means of a sacrifice performed a heavenly cure, the Aśvinā as physicians gave vigour to Indra, Sarasvatī doing her share by Vāc. Not unlikely this was the starting point for the evolution of the Vedic river-goddess into the Sarasvatī, the classical muse, especially the goddess of wisdom and eloquence. The identification between the two has, as a matter of fact, been carried out to the full extent already by the (Śatap. and Aitar.) Brāhmaṇas.

The Nirukta, 9. 26, is the authority for the statement that the earlier name of the Vipāś had been *Uruñjira.* Vipāś is the Greek *Hyphasis, Hypanis* or *Bipasis,* the modern *Beas* in the Punjab. The Sutlej is the modern equivalent for the Vedic Śutudtī, which is said to mean flowing in a hundred channels; the Greeks knew the river as *zaradros.* Great difference of opinion prevails about the identity of the

Sarasvatī. The name at least is "identical with that of the Avestan river *Haraqaiti* in Afghanistan, and it may have been the latter river which was first lauded as the Sarasvatī (Hopkins, Religions of India, p. 31). But Roth (Petersburger Wörterbuch, s.v.), Grassmann (Wörterbuch, s.v.), and Zimmer (Altindisches Leben, p. 10) are of opinion, that in the ṚV. Sarasvati usually and originally meant a mighty stream, probably the Indus (Sarasvatī being the sacred and Sindhu the secular name). but that it occasionally designates the small stream in Madhyadeśa to which both this name and its sacred character were in later times transferred. Max Müller believes it to be identical with this small river Sarasvatī, which with the Dṛṣ-advatī formed the boundaries of the sacred region Brahmāvarta, and which loses itself in the sands of the desert, but in Vedic times reached the sea. (Vedic Hymns, Sacred Books of the East, Vol. XXXII. p. 60). According to Oldham (Journal, Royal As. Soc. 25. pp. 49-76) a survey of ancient river-beds affords evidence that the Sarasvatī was originally a tributary of the Śutudrī (the modern Sutlej; Muir, Original Sanskrit Texts, II. 345), and that when the latter left its old bed and joined the Vipāś, the Sarasvatī continued to flow in the old bed of the Śutudrī. See Macdonell, Ved. Myth. pp. 87 f.

APPENDIX V

THE AGE OF THE ṚGVEDA

Of great consequence as the age of the ṚV. may be for the literary history of India and beyond, yet even today it seems impossible to fix it. An absolute chronology, intersected by settled limits of characteristic periods, is out of the question, as the dates required are obtainable neither from the ṚV. itself, nor from outside. The only safe statement at present seems to be that the ṚV. hymns, possibly together with a certain number of AV. hymns, are the oldest stratum of Indian literature. The ṚV. thus being the *terminus a quo*, the upper limit of the whole Śruti, the date of the rest of the Vedic literature will be uncertain as long as the age of the ṚV. cannot be fixed definitely.

The most comfortable theory on the age of the Veda is expressed by the round statement which declares that the ṚV., such as it is now, is eternal. This, however, probably goes beyond the meaning of the अनादित्वम् of the ṚV., as upheld by orthodox tradition. Strictly speaking, this traditional view would assert that the Mantras, eternal in themselves and their existence in Īśvara, were "seen" by the ṛṣis at a certain time and then promulgated by them in the present form and with the present contents. It is the time of "seeing" and "publication" of the hymns that is in question. To say that the Veda is simply eternal is but another form of the honest though painful: "we don't know".

The problem of the age of the ṚV. is as old as the Vedic studies. It has occupied the scholars especially since the revival of Sanskrit learning in this country and the introduction of Sanskrit philology in Europe. As criticism progressed, the claims raised in the beginning if not for tthe अनादित्वम्, at least for an age that would surpass that of all other literary documents, have decreased. As the beginning of the 19th centuary F. Schlgel, one of the founders of Sanskrit learning and research in Europe, wrote that he expected nothing less from India but ample information on the history of the primitive world, shrouded hitherto in utter darkness. In 1852 A. Weber perhaps voiced the then still fairly common view when he stated that the Indian literature passed for the oldest literature of which there were written documents extant, and justly so. But in 1876 he expressed himself more guardedly, qualifying the former statement by the clause:— "In so far as this claim may not now be disputed by the Egyptian monumental records and papyrus rolls, or even by the Assyrian literature which has but recently been brought to light". Weber became a confirmed skeptic about this problem: he did not only not try a more accurate determi-nation and circumscription of the Vedic age, but declared all efforts in that direction as hopeless.

In 1859 Max Müller claimed 1000-1200 B.C. as the lower limit for the beginning of Vedic poetry. With regard to the upper limit Max Müller never pretended to lay down a fixed date. In fact, with all his remarkable gift of intuition and combination, he declared that no power on earth would ever be able to say whether the Vedic hymns were composed in the second, third or fourth millennium B.C. The problem was in 1885 approached by Ludwig from the astronomical side and, about twenty years leter, simultaneously but independently, also by Jacobi and Tilak (1893). The net result of all these theories is that dates differing by not less than 2000 years have been stated for the age of the Veda, and that

Whitney's remark, that all the data given in the history of Indian literature are but ninepins put up, as it were, only to be thrown down again, appears as true today as ever.

Max Müller based his statements on the undeniable fact that Buddhism, a reaction against Brahmanism, supposes for its existence the whole Śruti. That Śruti, therefore, must have existed before 500 B.C. Now the origin of the Sūtras and Vedāṅgas is, on the one hand, contemporary with the rise of Buddhism, on the other they follow closely upon the Brāhmaṇa period. The Brāhmaṇa period is preceded by the Saṁhitā period, before which the hymns were composed.For each of these periods, Max Müller assumed 200 years, a calculation that, starting from 400 B.C., would take him up to 1000-1200 B.C., the so-called Mantra period in which the Vedic hymns were composed. The theory, either as put forth by its author, and repeated faithfully or made worse by followers, has been reiterated so long and persistently till it finally became something like a shibboleth of orthodoxy in chronological questions of the Veda. Müller's theory has even in an accentuated form been accepted quite of late by one of the foremost authors on the ṚV. who, after adducing a new argument, says :—"We must thus rest content with the moderate estimate of the thirteenth century B.C. as the approimate date for the beginning of the Rigvedic period." (Macdonell, Vedic Reader, p. XII).

Max Müller's theory, however, has more than one weak spot. First, the assumption of 200 years for each of the periods is quite arbitrary. In particular, it does not seem to take sufficiently into account the difference of conditions for the evolution of language between then and now. In the second place, it seems fairly certain that linguistic, literary and historical reasons necessitate a more remote upper limit for the age of the Veda than Max Müller was inclined to acknowledge. The statement which would take the thirteenth century as the approximate date of even the beginning of the Ṛgvedic period rests mainly on the relation between the ṚV. and the oldest parts of the Avesta, and the date of Zarathustra. The oldest parts of the Avesta are said hardly to date earlier than from about 800 B.C. The relationship between Avesta and Veda "is so close that the language of the Avesta, if it were known at a stage some five centuries earlier could scarcely have differed at all from that of the Ṛgveda. Hence the Indians could not have separated from the Iranians much sooner than 1300 B.C." We have to admit that the Indo-Iranian language, the parent of the languages of the Avesta and the ṚV. than Pāli does. For, the means of expression are in the oldest portions of the Avesta surpri-singly similar to those of the ṚV., which proves that both the languages cannot differ so very much from their common origin. The changes, mostly of a phonetic nature, are more on the side of Iran than of India. It is also suggested that the difference between Indo-European and Indo-Iranian is greater than between the latter and the Vedic language.

But to a certrain extent this new argumen mentioned above for a younger date of the Veda suffers from the same defect as Müller's original hypothesis-for such is Müller's view and not more. It would seem somewhat arbitrary to prescribe to a language the rate at which it may change or must have changed. Such an imperative becomes more fatal when it is applied to a literary, and more awkward still when applied to a sacred language. According to Müller's hypothesis the Mantra period extents over circa 200 years, from 1000-1200, within which time fairly considerable changes of language are supposed to have taken place. One or more hymns, therefore, of the present collection must have been composed about 1200 B.C., one or more about 1000 B.C.

But do the hymns of the ṚV. really show such differences of language as the theory requires? Can it, in particular, be shown from the ṚV. hymns that during the Mantra period such a gradual and steady change of language took place as is necessary, if the argument from the change of the idiom is to have any force at all?

To judge from external circumstances, has not the language of the ṚV. as well as that of the Avesta to be considered as a sacred language, at least to a certain extent? On the outside the assumption does not seem to be altogether beyond the range of possibility, if not probability, that in Vedic times the "crowd", talking their own language, watched the functions of the ritual and listened to the chanting of the mantras with as much attention and devotion and as little grasp of their meaning as they do now, say, at a marriage feast. Moreover the authors of the Vedic hymns may have had some interest in showing as little change as possible in their language as compared with that of their predecessors. An internal proof, however, for the assumption that the Vedic idiom was a literary and sacred language is to be found in the ṚV. Saṁhitā itself. It may be admitted that within sacerdotal circles a language was spoken which phonetically coincided with that of the hymns. This (more professional) language may have differed from that of the hymns in so far as it was prose and avoided archaic expressions in cases where younger and more practical forms were avilable. But there was, at least in certain strata of the populace, a language current which was developed far beyond the sacred language of the hymns and showed the main characteristics of the oldest phase of "Middle Indian", of the so-called Pāli stage. The conclusion, then, seems legitimate that the living speech of the bulk of the Āryan "clan" was essentially different from the sacred one. Thus the argument from the development of language to establish the length of the Mantra period becomes inapplicable. There is more to be said for, than against, the statement that the contents of the present ṚV. Saṁhitā required centuries to come into existence. And other centuries may have been necessary for the origin of older, lost pieces.

It is well known that on account of linguistic differences chronological ones have been stated in the ṚV. Saṁhitā. The tenth maṇḍala, especially, has since the days of Roth been recognized to be of younger date. The language of this maṇḍala differs in many ways from that of the other nine maṇḍalas to such an extent that it has been said to represent in those respects the transition between the Vedic language strictly speaking and that of the other (younger) Saṁhitās. But barring the tenth maṇḍala and certain portions of the first, there is from a linguistic point of view the same idiom to be observed in the whole ṚV. Saṁhitā.

It might be, however that the uniformity of language in the first nine maṇḍalas and their difference from the tenth is due to the present Saṁhitā, based on such principles of arrangement as would relegate all the hymns written in a younger language to the tenth maṇḍala. Before this artificial arangement the same hymns, composed at different times, might have been found between those written in the older language, and were thus scattered over the whole number of Vedic sūktas. In this way the Vedic hymns might, after all, according to their date prove a steady, natural development of language. But, in the first place, this supposes a double and parallel linguistic tendency in the literary activity of the Vedic age: a consciously archaic one, represented by the hymns of the first nine maṇḍalas, and a progressive one, keeping more or less abreast with the non-liturgical, non-sacred literary activity, appearing sporadically, and represented by the sūktas of the tenth maṇḍala. Secondly, it is "as clear as well known " that maṇḍala II-VII, contain the hymns of one particular family of author-ṛṣis, and that all hymns addressed to सोम पवमान are brought together in the ninth maṇḍala. For maṇḍalas II-VII, then, it is the authorship, and not a linguisic consideration such as archaic language, that is the principle of arrangement. There are no proofs whatsoever that hymns written in a younger language might have been subtracted from any of the family books and been put together in some other collection, the tenth maṇḍala Say maṇḍala X is outside the principle according to which the sūktas have been assigned to books II-VII. In fact, it is a unit by itself, collected and arranged according to a consistent principle. This principle is of a chronological nature: the tenth book is the maṇḍala which contains the younger hymns, either isolated or aranged in groups. Thirdly, "at the time when the tenth maṇḍala came into existence, the first nine maṇḍalas formed a large body of hymns, acquainted with which the poets of the tenth maṇḍala must have grown up, the knowledge of which they show in their own songs again and again": a body of hymns of which apparently not only the present contents but even the present arrangement was known to some of the authors of the tenth maṇḍala. Finally, it should not be forgotten that the reason why the hymns of the tenth maṇḍala stand out against those of the other nine maṇḍalas is to be found not only in their form, comprising metre and vocabulary besides grammar, but in their contents as well, if not more.

If there were a section at least in the ṚV. Saṁhitā that could and should prove the gradual and steady development of the Vedic language, it would be the ninth maṇḍala, the Soma book. For "this maṇḍala cannot have existed independently before maṇḍalas II-VII, but is rather their product. The Pavamāna hymns have to be attributed to the same Gṛtsamadas, Vasiṣṭhas, etc., who composed the bulk of books

II-VII. Consequently, the various ṛṣi families shared in the authorship of the Pavamāna hymns and a collection of such hymns in the form of the ninth maṇḍala could only have been made when the hymns composed in various circles of poets were brought together and the specific Soma hymns separated from the rest. The ninth maṇḍala, therefore, covering a wide range of time, should, if any, show the marks of development of language. But this is in no way the case. The linguistic change noticeable in the whole ṚV. was not so gradual and steady as Müller's hypothesis damands, and the conclusion drawn from a change of language that does not exist, consequently, cannot be accepted.

Something might be learnt from Latin, quite a good parallel, as far as the evolution of a literary and sacred language is concerned, to the language of the Vedic hymns. Latin has been a literarey at least a learned and sacred language for almost 1900 years. Yet, some violent changes in pronunciation excepted, which can be traced and explained, this language is practically the same today as it was shortly after the time of Caesar. How little may be gathered from mere language is shown by the Maitrāyaṇīya Upaniṣad: some critics take it to be an old, others a young work. To measure the change of language both of the Veda and the Avesta by a standard approximating that of modern living languages, would show a want of method equalled by the application of the same rate of evolution in ideas and conditions prevalent in Europe now to the Indo-Iranians some 3000 years back.

Taking all the necessary circumstances into consideration, it should be not quite so impossible to "assume that the Iranian and India language (of the Avesta and the Veda!) remained practically unchanged for the truly immense period(?) of over 3000 years", if it could be proved that the Vedic hymns go back to the third millennium B.C. The astronomical arguments used by Tilak and Jacobi make an attempt to show this. Already in the Vedic age the necessity was felt to combine the lunar with the solar year. For this purpose certain full-moon *nakṣatras* were brought into special relation to the beginning of the seasons and of the year. Now with the help of astronomical calculations it was thought possible to find out certain fixed data, provided the observations, in Vedic times had been made correctly, and the beginning of the seasons and of the year could be ascertained. It appears that at the time of the Brāhmaṇas the Kṛttikās (Pleiades), which then were at the beginning of the nakṣatras, coincided with the spring equinox. On the other hand, there were indications in the Vedic texts which suggested that in older times the spring equinox coincided with Mṛgaśiras (Orion). The precession implied in this distance (from the Kṛttikās, to Mṛgaśiras) requires a period of about 2000 years, as about 2500 B,C.the precession was in the Kṛttikās, in about 4500 B.C. in Mṛgaśiras. Tilak puts the Vedic hymns as far back as 6000 B.C.; Jacobi is content with dating the beginning of Vedic civilisation at about 4500 and considers the ṚV. hymns as the ripe, perhaps even late, fruit of that age. They may belong to the second half of the period, extending, as it does from 4500-2500 B.C.

The attributing of the ṚV. hymns to this period was, in Jacobi's opinion, confirmed by the following observation. In the marriage ceremonial of the Gṛhyasūtras Dhruva, the polar star, is pointed out to the bride as an ideal of steadiness and faithfulness. The polar star—in consequence of the precession—is changing in course of time. The present polar star on the northern hemisphere is Alpha in the Little Bear. But already 2000 years ago this star was so far distant from the celestial pole that in Vedic antiquity it could not possibly have been considered as the polar star. Its place was at that time, more accurately in 2870 B.C., occupied by Alpha Dracins, this being the only maṇḍalastar bright enough to serve the purpose of the polar star. Since in the ṚV. hymns themselves this custom of pointing out the polar star is not (yet) mentioned, the Vedic civilization has, according to this theory, to be put at the period antecedent to the third millenium. The argument based on the polar star appears to be more convincing than that founded on the nakṣatras and the equinoxes. It has been urged against the latter that the early Indians were not well known, not even likely, to have possessed such astronomical knowledge as the proof credited them with. This objection has no more force than any other argument taken *ex silentio;* nor does it seem to touch upon the real difficulty. The main crux, lies rather in the certain and fixed beginning of the year. The Śatapathabrāhmaṇa, XII. 8. 2. 35, for instance, avowedly admits that all the seasons may start the year. Suffice to say that nothing in Indian history forbids to date the ṚV. as far back as the third millennium and to put the Vedic civilization at the fourth millennium. For, "the ṚV. is pretty nearly the final expression of its own type of composition; it presupposes a long period of antecedent activity, obviously going back to the common Indo-Persian or Aryan time." The ṚV. repetitions "mark the entire Mantra literature as, in a sense, epigonal..."

The problem of the age of the Veda, the farthest reaching of all question in Indian literary history, has gained fresh interest by the discoveries of Hugo Winckler at Boghazköi in Asia Minor. There clay tablets were found, coming from the capital of the Chetites, and dated at from 1400-1200 B.C. Among the tablets there were documents of contracts concluded between the king of the Chetites and the king of Mitani at the beginning of the 14th century. The contracts contain invocations of the tutelary deities of the two kingdoms to protect the agreements. Babylonian and local gods are mentioned, and there appear among those Mitani the following names (ilāni) mi-it-ra-as-si-il (ilāni) u-ru-w-na-as-si-el [varient: a-ru-na-as-si-il] (ilu) in-dar [variant: in-da-ra] (ilāni) na-sa-a (t-ti-ia-a) n-na [variant: na-s [a]-at-ti-ia-an-na].

This question now arises, What deities do these tablets signify. It should not be left out of sight that the reading is by no means certain throughout, and that the explanation and identification of the names is not above suspicion. It will also be useful to remember that the (Mitannian) suffixes assil or assiel and anna of the above names bear a rather striking resemblance with the Tokharian case ending assal (comitative) and aññä (nom. plur.) The names of the gods mentioned in the tablets have in succession been declared to be Āryan (Ed. Meyer), Indo-Iranian (Oldenberg., Keith, Macdonell) and finally Vedic or purely Indian (Jacobi, Konow), more or less according to the age which some of these scholars previously had fixed for the Veda. The "Āryan" and "Indo-Āryan" hypotheses seem to labour from the logical defect that they make *the* Āryans and *the* Indo-Iranians dwell in (and around) the country of Boghazköi, instead of a smaller or greater part of them. The form of the names may Indo - Iranian or may not. The changes which foreign names both of celestials and men may undergo when they are used in a foreign country and have to be written or engraved by native masons are well illustrated by Aśoka's Rock edict XIII and Heliodor's inscription at Besnagar. Winternitz seems unfortunately to be right in declaring that the only thing certain in this question is this that everything is uncertain. Probable, as it may be, that Mitra, Varuṇa, Indra, and the Nāsatyas of the tablets are Vedic gods, it is also certain that the suffixes, in which the names found at Boghazköi end, appear to be anything but Vedic. But are we quite so sure that these names cannot be anything but Vedic? If all the documents necessary for a verdict in this matter ever existed, they have unfortunately not come down to us.

The data for building up a solid argumentation are indeed much too scanty, and the possibilities of miscalculation much too numerous to allow a conclusion from the finds at Boghazköi, to the age of the Veda. The fact alone seems established that in the 15th century B.C. some gods whose names we meet in the Vedic hymns were, in the region round Boghazköi, popular enough to figure as heavenly witnesses in a state treaty. Indra indeed plays here the role of Saul among the prophets, among whom he is not ranked in the ṚV. ; but that is a minor detail. It is, moreover, probable that about the same time or earlier there were hymns composed in honour of these and other gods in north-western India. The contemporary appearance may be due to parallel but independent tradition or, less likely, to import from India. There seems, however, no visible logical connection between this and the assertion that these names prove for the Vedic hymns an age rising to the third millennium.

The discussions on the Boghazköi tablets inspired Sir R.G.Bhandarkar to point out an altogether new line of unravelling the old problem of the Vedic age. He suggested that "the inquiry should take its start from the word *Asura*. Assyria", the Nestor of Indian Sanskrit learning thinks, "corresponds to *Asuryāḥ* as applied to *Lokāḥ* in the Īśāvāsyopaniṣad (Verse 3) and may be regarded as meaning the country of the Asuras. Thus then it is not unlikely that just as in India the progress of the Aryans was contested by the Dasyus, so was it contested by the Asuras of Assyria and they were thus compared with the Dasyus... In later times especially when the Aryans settled in the region of the five rivers, and afterwards when their religious system was developed in Brahmāvarta, the reminiscences of the human Asuras and the fight of the Aryans with them, and their civilization led to the whole subject having transformed itself into a myth of the determined enmity between the *devas* and the Asuras". Inspite of the resistence, Bhandarkar thinks, some Āryan tribes at least made their way from North Mesopotamia to India and developed their religion at such a date that "by the middle of the 15th century B. C. the Indian Aryans had progressed so far in the development of their religion as to conceive of five deities, one single and four aranged into groups of two each. These groups along with the grammatical forms(?) of the names are exactly as they exist in the Ṛg Veda. A great deal of hymnal literature must have gathered round those names by that time; and its origin may... be pushed back to about 2500 B. C."

Bhandarkar only claims to "have thus simply indicated a new line of research". The new line in any case has the merit of showing the complexity of the problem, as so many issues are bound up with it. It involves among others the question of the original home of the Āryas and their migrations, also their relation to the Iranians, who evidently had got another impression of the "Asuras". Besides the more ethnographical difficulties, some linguistic puzzles would have to be solved. But if the hypothesis proves correct, it will point more in the direction than Max Müller's statements.

The final result of the preceding discussions on the age of the (Ṛg) veda is the following:—The Vedic literature (not Vedic age!) has its lower chronological limit lying at 500, or perhaps better at 800 B.C. The upper limit is an unknown x, which, however may not safely be pushed lower down than 1200, and is more probably to be sought in the third millennium B. C. than in the second.

BIBLIOGRAPHY

I. Texts.

The śruti texts and commentaries, as far as helpful in the interpretation, in particular:—Rig-Veda Samhita. The Sacred Hymns of the Brāhmaṇs together with the Commentary of Sāyanācārya Ed. by Max Müller. Second ed. Vols I-IV. London, 1890-92. A separate Vol. with Indices.

Āpastambīyadharmasūtram. Ed. G. Bühler. B. S. S. XLIV. Bombay, 1892.

The Mahābhārata, Bombay and Calcutta ed.

II. Grammar, etc.

Arnold, Edward Varnon. Historical Vedic Grammar. New Haven, Conn., 1897 (reprint from the JAOS. XVIII, 1897).

Arnold E. Vernon. Vedic Metre in its Historical Development, Cambridge, 1905.

Delbrück, B. Altindische Syntax. Halle, 1888. Abbreviated AIS.

Lanman, Charles R. A Statistical Account of Noun-Inflection in the Veda (Reprint from JAOS. X. 1878).

Macdonell, Arthur A. A Vedic Grammar. Encyclopedia of Indo-Aryan Research, 1. 4. Strassburg, 1910.

Macdonell, Arthur A. A Sanskrit Grammar for Beginners. 2nd ed. London, 1911.

Macdonell, Arthur Anthony. A Vedic Grammar for Students, Oxford, 1916

Pāṇini, अष्टाध्यायी.

Rig-Veda-Pratiśākhya. Das älteste Lehrbuch der vedischen Phonetik, Ed. Max Müller, Leipzig, 1869.

Wackernagel, Jakob. Altindische Grammatik. Vols. I. II. Göttingen, 1896, 1905

Whitney, William Dwight. A Sanskrit Grammar. Leipzig, Ist ed. 1879.

Whitney, William Dwight. The Roots, Verb-Forms, and Primary Derivations of the Sanskrit Language, Leipzig. 1885.

III Dictionaries, Concordances, etc.

Bloomfield Maurice. A Vedic Concordance. Cambridge, Mass., 1906. Harvard Oriental Series X.

Bloomfield, Maurice. Rig-Veda Repetition. Parts 1-3. Cambridge Mass., 1916. Harv. or. Ser. XX. XXIV.

Böhtlingk, Otto, und Roth, Rudolf, Sanskrit-Wörterbuch. St.Petersburg, 1855-75. Abbr. PW.

Geldner. Karl, F.Der Rigveda in Auswahl. Erster Teil: Glossar Stuttgart, 1907.

Grassmann, Hermann, Wörterbuch zum Rig-Veda. Leipzig, 1873.

Macdonell, Arthur Anthony, and Keith, Arthur Berriedale. Vedic Index of Names and Subjects. London, 1912.

Vishweshwaranand, Swami, and Nityanand, Swami. A Complete Alphabetical Index of all the Words in the

Atharvaveda, Bombay, 1907.

Ṛgveda, Bombay, 1908.

Yajurveda, Bombay, 1908.

Samaveda, Bombay, 1908.

IV. Interpretation of the Ṛgveda.

Bijāpūrkar, Vishnu Govind. Ṛiksangraha or A University selection of Vedic Hymns with the Commentary of Sāyaṇācārya with Notes, 2nd. ed. Bombay, 1907.

Geldner, Karl F. Der Rigveda in Auswahl. Zweiter Teil: Kommentar. Stuttgart. 1909.

Kaegi, Adolf. The Rigveda. The oldest Literature of the Indians. Translated (from the German) by R. Arrowsmith. Boston and Kātyāyana's Sarvānukramaṇī of the *Rigveda*. With Extracts from Shadguruśishya's Commentary, entitled Vedārthadīpikā. Ed. with Critical Notes and Appendices by A. A. Macdonell. Oxford., 1886.

Macdonell, Arthur Anthony. A Vedic Reader for Students. Oxford 1917.

Oldenberg, Hermann. Die Hymnen des Rigveda. Vol. I. Metrische und textgeschichtliche Prolegomena. Berlin, 1888.

Oldenberg, Hermann. Ṛgveda. Textkritische and exegetische Noten. Erstes bis sechstes Buch, Berlin, 1909. Siebentes bis zehntes Buch, Berlin, 1919.

Oldenberg Hermann, Vedaforschung. Berlin and stattgart, 1905.

Rajwade, V. K. असुरस्य माया in Ṛgveda. Proceedings of the First Oriental Conference, Poona, 1919.

Śaunaka, The Bṛhaddevatā attributed to. Critically edited.... by Arthur Anthony Macdonell. Part I. Introduction and Text and Appendics. Part II. Translation and Notes. Cambridge, ass., 1904. Harv. Or, Ser. Vols. V. VI.

श्रीयुतयास्कमहर्षिप्रकाशितं निघण्टुभाष्यरूपं निरुक्तम्। निघण्टुपाठसमुपेतम्।

पण्डितशिवदत्तशर्माकृतटिप्पण्यादिभिश्च समलङ्कृतम्। मुम्बयां संवत् 1969

V. Translations of the Ṛgveda.

Geldner, Karl, und Kaegi, Adolf. Siebenzig Lieder des Rigveda übersetzt. Mit Beiträgen von R. Roth. Tübingen, 1875.

Grassmann, Hermann. Rigveda. übersetzt und mit kritischen und erläuternden Anmerkungen versehen. Part I. II. Leipzig, 1876, 1877.

Griffith, Ralph T. H. The Hymns of the Rigveda, translated with a popular Commentary. Vols. I. II. Benares, 1896, 1897.

Hillebrandt, Alfred. Lieder des Ṛgveda, übersetzt. Göttingen und Leipzig, 1913.

Ludwig, Alfred. Der Rigveda zum ersten Male vollständig ins Deutsche übersetzt. Mit Commentar und Einleitung. Vols. I-VI. Prag, 1876-88.

Sacred Books of the East :

Vol. XXXII. Müller, F. Max. Vedic Hymns, translated. Part I. Oxford, 1891.

Vol. XLVI. Oldenberg, Hermann. Vedic Hymns, translated. Part II. Oxford 1897.

VI. History, Customs and Manners, Mythology, Philosophy, Religion, etc.

Bergaigne, Abel. La Religion Vedique dapres les hymns du Rig-Veda. Vols. I-III. Paris, 1878-1882. Index,1897.

Blanford, Henry F. A Practical Guide to the Climates and Weather of India, Ceylon and Burmah, and the storms of Indian Seas. London, 1889.

Bloomfield Maurice. The Religion of the Veda. The ancient Religion of India. (From Rig-Veda to Upanishads). New York and London, 1908.

Brunnhofer, Hermann, Urgeshchichteder Arier, Vols. 1-III Leipzig, 1893.

Dutt. Romesh Chunder, A History of Civilisation in Ancient India. Revised ed. Vols. I. II. London, 1893. (Trübner's Oriental Series).

Hillebrandt, Alfred. Vedische mythologie. Vol. I-III. Breslau. 1891-1902.

Hillebrandt, Alfred. Vedische Mythologie. Kleine Ausgabe. Breslau, 1910.

Hillebrandt, Alfred. Rituallitteratur. Vedische Opfer und Zauber. Encyclopedia of Indo-Aryan Research, III. 2. Strassburg, 1897.

Lassen, Christian. Indische Altertumskunde. Leipzig, London; Vol. I. 2nd ed. 1867; Vol. II. 2nd ed. 1874; Vol. III. 1868; Vol. IV. 1861.

Macdonell Arthur A. A History of Sanskrit Literature. London, 1909.

Macdonell, A. A. Vedic Mythology. Encyclopedia of Indo-Aryan Research, III. 4, Strassburg, 1897.

Oldenberg, Hermann. Religion des Veda. 2nd ed. Berlin, 1917.

Pischel, Richard, und Geldner, Karl F. Vedische Studien. Vols. I-II. Stuttgart, 1889-1901.

v. Schroeder, Leopold. Indiens Literature und Culture in historischer Entwicklung. Leipzig, 1887.

v. Schroeder, Leopold. Mysterium und Mimus im Rigveda. Leipzig, 1908.

v. Schroeder, Leopold. Rede und Aufsätze, vornehmlich über Indiens Literature und Kulture Lripzig, 1913.

v. Schroeder, Leopold. Arische Religion. Vols. 1914, 1916.

Sieg, Emil. Sagenstoffie des Ṛgveda. Stuttgart, 1902.

Tilak, Bāl Gangādhar. Orion or Researches into the Vedas. Bombay, 1893.

Tilak, Bāl Gangādhar. The Arctic Home in the Vedas. and Bombay, 1903.

Weber, Albrecht. The History of Indian Literature. Translated from the Second German Edition by Mann and Zachariae. London, 1904 (Trübner's Or. Ser.)

Winterniz. M. Geschichte der indischen Litteratur. Vol. I. 2nd ed. Leipzig. 1909.

Zimmer, Heinrich. Altindisches Leben. Die Culture der vedischen Arier. Nach den Samhita zusammengestellt. Berlin, 1879.

VII. Studies and Eassay published in honour of prominent Vedic Scholers.

Festgruss an Otto von Boehtlingk. Stuttgart, 1888.

Festgruss an Rudolf v. Roth. Stuttgart, 1893.

Gurupūjākaumudī (in honour of Weber). Leipzig, 1896.

Album Kern. Leiden, 1903.

Festschrift für Ernst Windiṣch. Leipzig, 1914.

Festschrift für Carl Andreas. Leipzig, *Notes* 9192 *Hymns from the Ṛgveda Notes* 9394 *Hymns from the Ṛgveda*1916.

Aufsätze Ernst Kuhn gewidmet. Breslan,1916.

Commemorative Essays presented to Sir Ramkrishna Gopal Bhandarkar (Bhandarkar Commemoration Volume). Poona,1917.

Festgabe on Adolf Kaegi. Frauenfield. 1919.

Studies in honour of Maurice Bloomfield. New Haven, 1920.

VIII. Journals.

Annals of the Bhandarkar Oriental Research Institute, Poona.

Göttingische Gelehrte Anzeign. Göttingen. Abbrev. GGA.

American Oriental Society. New Haven, Conn. JAOS

Journal of the Royal Asiatic Society of Great Britain and Ireland, JRAS

Journal of the Bombay Branch of the R.A.S. Bombay, JBoBrRAS,

Oriental Journal. Vienna.

der Deutschen Morgenländischen Gesellschaft. Leipzig, ZDMG.

INDEX

R

S

T

U

V

✤✤✤